The Nineties in America

The Nineties in America

Volume II

Gephardt, Dick—*Rules, The*

Editor

Milton Berman, Ph.D.

University of Rochester

Managing Editor

Tracy Irons-Georges

SALEM PRESS, INC.
Pasadena, California
Hackensack, New Jersey

Editorial Director: Christina J. Moose

Managing Editor: Tracy Irons-Georges
Copy Editors: Timothy M. Tiernan, Rebecca Kuzins
Editorial Assistant: Dana Garey
Photo Editor: Cynthia Breslin Beres
Production Editor: Joyce I. Buchea

Acquisitions Editor: Mark Rehn
Research Supervisor: Jeffry Jensen
Research Assistant: Keli Trousdale
Graphics and Design: James Hutson
Layout: Frank Montano

Title page photo: *Kurt Cobain leads the popular grunge band Nirvana.* (AP/Wide World Photos)

Cover images (pictured clockwise, from top left): President Bill Clinton and Vice President Al Gore, 1993. (AP/Wide World Photos); General H. Norman Schwarzkopf, 1991. (AP/Wide World Photos); Brandi Chastain, Women's World Cup Final, 1999. (AP/Wide World Photos); Keyboard. (©Kts/Dreamstime.com)

∞ The paper used in these volumes conforms to the American National Standard for Permanence of Paper for Printed Library Materials, Z39.48-1992 (R1997).

Library of Congress Cataloging-in-Publication Data

The nineties in America / editor, Milton Berman.
p. cm.
Includes bibliographical references and indexes.
ISBN 978-1-58765-500-5 (set : alk. paper) — ISBN 978-1-58765-501-2 (v. 1: alk. paper) — ISBN 978-1-58765-502-9 (v. 2 : alk. paper) — ISBN 978-1-58765-503-6 (v. 3 : alk. paper)
1. United States—History—1969—Encyclopedias. 2. United States—Social conditions—1980—Encyclopedias. 3. United States—Politics and government—1989-1993—Encyclopedias. 4. United States—Politics and government—1993-2001—Encyclopedias. 5. United States—Intellectual life—20th century—Encyclopedias. 6. Popular culture—United States—History—20th century—Encyclopedias. 7. Nineteen nineties—Encyclopedias. I. Berman, Milton.
E839.N56 2009
973.92—dc22

2008049939

First Printing

PRINTED IN THE UNITED STATES OF AMERICA

Table of Contents

Complete List of Contents

Volume I

Volume II

Volume III

The Nineties in America

■ Gephardt, Dick

Identification Prominent Democratic politician
Born January 31, 1941; St. Louis, Missouri

Gephardt served as a U.S. representative from Missouri for twenty-eight years, was the minority leader in the House of Representatives from 1995 to 2003, and twice ran for president of the United States.

Starting out as a young child in a traditional working-class family, Richard Andrew "Dick" Gephardt graduated from Northwestern University in 1962. He then attended the University of Michigan Law School, where he graduated in 1965 and was admitted to the Missouri bar that same year. From 1965 to 1972, Gephardt served in the Missouri Air National Guard. During this time, he received his start in Missouri politics. Between 1968 and 1971, he served as the Democratic committeeman for the Fourteenth Ward in St. Louis. He became an alderman in 1971 and served in that position until 1976. On January 3, 1977, Gephardt replaced Leonor Sullivan as the representative for Missouri's third district.

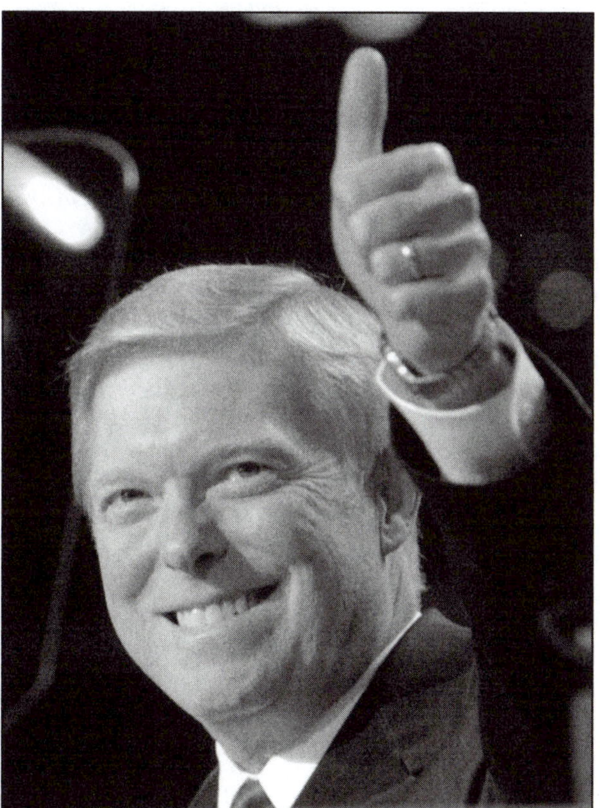

House minority leader Dick Gephardt. (AP/Wide World Photos)

In June, 1989, Gephardt became the majority leader of the House of Representatives. When the Democrats lost control of the House in 1994, Gephardt became the minority leader, serving from 1995 to 2003. During this time, he advocated the expansion of national health care, supported progressive taxation, arms control, and encouraged fair trade practices by trying to penalize nations that would restrict the importation of U.S.-made goods. Although at the beginning of the decade Gephardt was in favor of a pro-life amendment to the Constitution, by the end of the 1990's and perhaps influenced by his decision to run for president, he had abandoned his support of such legislation.

In 1987-1988, Gephardt sought the Democratic nomination for president. He started off strong with victory in Iowa but dropped out due to lack of finances and a poor showing on Super Tuesday. He was briefly considered as a vice presidential candidate when Al Gore won the party nomination in 2000, but Gore selected Joe Lieberman of Connecticut instead. In 2004, Gephardt again ran for president but was viewed as too old-fashioned, and he slowly faded out of the political spotlight.

Impact Despite two failed bids for the presidency, Gephardt served his district and his party well. A strong Democratic partisan, he voted along party lines 85 to 94 percent of the time between the 102nd and 108th Congresses.

Further Reading

Gephardt, Richard, with Michael Wessel. *An Even Better Place: America in the Twenty-first Century.* New York: PublicAffairs, 1999.

Gottlieb, Alan M., and Dave Workman. *Double Trouble: Daschle and Gephardt, Capital Hill Bullies.* Bellevue, Wash.: Merril Press, 2001.

Kathryn A. Cochran

See also Bush, George H. W.; Clinton, Bill; Gore, Al; Health care reform; Liberalism in U.S. politics.

■ Gifford, Kathie Lee

Identification American television host, actress, and singer

Born August 16, 1953; Paris, France

Gifford was one of the most popular daytime television personalities of the 1990's.

On June 24, 1985, Kathie Lee Gifford, then known as Kathie Lee Johnson, joined Regis Philbin as the cohost of the WABC-TV New York morning talk show, *The Morning Show.* On October 18, 1986, the aspiring talk-show host married former New York Giants football player and sports broadcaster Frank Gifford. In September, 1988, the popular hour-long morning show had its name changed to *Live with Regis and Kathie Lee.* That same year, Buena Vista Television began the national syndication of the show. By the early 1990's, the show had become one of the most popular morning talk shows on television, and Gifford had become a television celebrity.

The show's success was due in part to the fact that *Live with Regis and Kathie Lee* was aired live and unrehearsed. On a daily basis, both Philbin and Gifford shared their personal lives with the viewing audience. Gifford's sense of humor, charisma, and openness about her life, both good and bad, made her popular with fans. Throughout the decade, she shared untold numbers of stories about her marriage and two children and also shared her personal struggles, including her husband's infidelity.

Utilizing her celebrity, Gifford also pursued numerous business ventures during the 1990's. She published eight books, including several cookbooks and children's books as well as an autobiography. She appeared in television advertisements for Carnival Cruise Lines and Ultra Slim Fast and supported children's charities and the Special Olympics. From 1991 through 1995, she and Philbin cohosted the Miss America Pageant. In 1995, she introduced a profitable clothing line at Wal-Mart stores. Controversy followed in 1996, when it was disclosed that some of the clothing merchandise had been manufactured in Honduran sweatshops that employed children. Gifford denied any knowledge of the exploitation and later vowed to fight such practice, supporting antisweatshop legislation.

Throughout the decade, Gifford guest-starred on dozens of sitcoms and prime-time television shows. She also continued to pursue her singing career by performing at several New York City nightclubs. In 1993, she released two albums, *Sentimental Journey* and *It's Christmas Time.* On July 28, 2000, Gifford cohosted her last morning show with Philbin.

Kathie Lee Gifford with cohost Regis Philbin in 1992. (AP/Wide World Photos)

Impact One of the most popular talk-show hosts of the 1990's, Kathie Lee Gifford endeared herself to television audiences with her natural sense of humor, positive energy, and openness about her personal life.

Further Reading

Gifford, Kathie Lee, with Jim Jerome. *I Can't Believe I Said That! An Autobiography.* New York: Pocket Books, 1992.

Hill, E. D. *Going Places: How America's Best and Brightest Got Started Down the Road of Life.* New York: ReganBooks, 2005.

King, Norman. *Regis and Kathie Lee: Their Lives Together and Apart.* Secaucus, N.J.: Carol, 1995.

Bernadette Zbicki Heiney

See also Fashions and clothing; Music; Television; Wal-Mart.

■ Gingrich, Newt

Identification Speaker of U.S. House of Representatives, 1995-1999

Born June 17, 1943; Harrisburg, Pennsylvania

A colorful and outspoken former professor of history who was elected to the U.S. House of Representatives in 1978, Gingrich proved instrumental in allowing the Republican Party to achieve its first majority in the House after forty years of Democratic Party dominance.

It is ironic that the man who would become the face of the "Republican Revolution" barely won reelection to his own seat in the House of Representatives during the midterm elections of 1990. Less than a year before, the boisterous congressman from Georgia had been named the House minority whip, after a decade of using every means at his disposal to revive the fortunes of his party in the House of Representatives.

Contract with America and House Speaker In his position as minority whip, Gingrich was responsible along with a number of other Republican congressmen for creating the Contract with America. This document, introduced shortly before the midterm elections of 1994, was a list of ten legislative initiatives focusing on the principles of limited government and fiscal responsibility that Republicans promised to pass if they became the majority party. A few months later, when they won control of the House of Representatives through the addition of fifty-four seats, Republicans named Gingrich the first Republican Speaker of the House in four decades.

When Gingrich became Speaker, he initiated a number of measures that increased his power. He had wanted to remake the position of Speaker from one of powerful symbolism into one that had the ability to dictate a political agenda. The House had been organized under a seniority system for decades. Gingrich realized that the only way his agenda could be successful was if the system was changed, and he installed his own loyalists as chairs of many of those key committees that dictated how the House's business was done. By the end of the first one hundred days in the majority, Gingrich and his "revolutionaries" had passed all but one of the initiatives of the Contract with America. However, most of the bills failed to pass both chambers of Congress and be signed into law by President Bill Clinton.

Gingrich had a substantial amount of support in the House of Representatives, having been partially responsible for the victory of many House newcomers in 1994. Those men and women owed him their loyalty; therefore, early in his reign as Speaker, Gingrich and his lieutenants were in control of much of the legislation that moved through the institution. However, despite achieving his goals of becoming Speaker and attaining political power, at times Gingrich behaved like the combative rabble-rouser who had first arrived in Congress in the late 1970's. His vitriolic comments about the Democrats as "enemies of normal Americans" caused *The Washington Post* to name the Speaker "the most hated man in Congress."

Government Shutdown and 1996 Elections An example of the pugnacious behavior Gingrich often displayed was his comment to *Time* magazine regarding his intention to shut the government down if President Clinton did not accept the Republicans' demand to cut Medicare. "He can run the parts of government that are left [after the cuts], or he can run no government," Gingrich boasted in May, 1995. Arguments between Gingrich and the president over that program, along with a number of other pieces of fiscal legislation, culminated with the government shutdown in November, 1995, followed by the government again coming to a halt in early 1996. While many of Gingrich's colleagues agreed that the legislation was fiscally irresponsible, the reasoning was overshadowed following the Speaker's negative comments toward Clinton over poor treatment he received by the president's staff following a trip on Air Force One. Many considered the budget battle and Gingrich's negative media portrayals as responsible for Clinton's resounding reelection in November of 1996.

Attempt at Removal Despite these defeats at the hands of Clinton, Gingrich continued to try to use the Republican majority to control the national legislative agenda. In June, 1997, the Republicans submitted a bill to the White House focusing on disaster relief for flood victims. Besides the major legislation, the bill also contained a number of conservative amendments that Gingrich believed the president would not dare to veto. When Clinton chose to veto the bill, Republicans were outraged as they were criticized by the media and the public for utilizing obstructionist tactics. Following the legislative defeat, a number of House Republicans sought to remove Gingrich from his position as Speaker. However, Gingrich still had a great deal of support within the House, and no overwhelming alternative to fill the position existed.

1998 Elections and Loss of Power When newspapers revealed in late 1997 that Clinton had engaged in an affair with former White House intern Monica Lewinsky, Gingrich utilized the incident as a means of rallying public opinion against the president. Still, many conservatives were cautious, warning Gingrich not to focus all his energies in the hopes of chasing the president from office. The animosity of the Republicans' attack on the president did not match that of the public. In the end, Gingrich's choice to ignore outside counsel served him poorly. The Republicans' refusal to put the president's indiscretion behind them caused a public backlash that hurt their party during the 1998 elections.

In the summer of 1998, the public became even more angry with the Republican leadership when Clinton painted them as a "do-nothing Congress" for their failure to come to an agreement on education legislation, forcing them to remain in session until both sides could come to a compromise. The battle lasted well into October and contributed to the Republicans losing five seats in the House of Representatives when the votes were tallied that November. It was the worst loss for the congressional majority in a midterm election in more than half a century. As the public face of the Republican Party, Gingrich was held responsible for his party's loss. Shortly after the election, he not only stepped down as Speaker but also resigned his position in Congress, despite having been elected by his district to a tenth term. Following his departure from government, Gingrich became a commentator with Fox News and joined a number of institutes that focus on various areas of public policy.

Impact Newt Gingrich was a rare politician who not only had the vision of a national Republican realignment but also possessed the knowledge and skill to bring that goal to fruition. Despite being punished for a number of ethics violations during his congressional tenure, Gingrich brought his party back to the majority in the House of Representatives after forty years. His Contract with America ignited the passions of a new generation of Republican legislators who, despite his absence, held that mandate of leadership until the Democrats regained the majority following the midterm elections of 2006.

Further Reading

Gibbs, Nancy, and Michael Duffy. "Fall of the House of Newt." *Time,* November 16, 1998, 46-55. Report on Gingrich and his party's fall from power.

Gingrich, Newt. *To Renew America.* New York: HarperCollins, 1995. Gingrich outlines his political philosophy and his policy goals.

Sheehy, Gail. "The Inner Quest of Newt Gingrich." *Vanity Fair,* September, 1995, 149-151. A look at Gingrich from the perspectives of his family, friends, associates, and himself.

Laurence R. Jurdem

See also Christian Coalition; Clinton, Bill; Clinton's impeachment; Clinton's scandals; Conservatism in U.S. politics; Contract with America; Elections in the United States, midterm; Elections in the United States, 1996; Lewinsky scandal; Republican Revolution; Term limits.

■ Ginsburg, Ruth Bader

Identification Associate justice of the United States since 1993

Born March 15, 1933; Brooklyn, New York

In 1993, Ginsburg became the second woman to sit on the U.S. Supreme Court.

Prior to joining the U.S. Supreme Court, Ruth Bader Ginsburg was best known for her work as the first director of the Women's Rights Project of the American Civil Liberties Union (ACLU). She was the victorious counsel of record in numerous equal protection lawsuits that came before the Supreme Court in the 1970's. These cases constituted much of the significant sex equity litigation of the twentieth century and had great constitutional and societal significance. Between 1980 and 1993, Ginsburg sat on the U.S. Court of Appeals for the District of Columbia Circuit.

On June 14, 1993, when President Bill Clinton nominated Ginsburg to succeed Justice Byron White on the U.S. Supreme Court, he spoke of her "pioneering" work on behalf of women. Her nomination sailed through the Senate Judiciary Committee by an

18 to 0 vote. The full Senate confirmed her appointment on August 3, 1993, by a vote of 96 to 3. Ginsburg became the 107th justice, the second woman to sit on the Court (joining Sandra Day O'Connor), and the first Jewish justice since Abe Fortas's departure in 1969.

Ruth Bader Ginsburg accepts her nomination to the U.S. Supreme Court in 1993. (NARA)

Through the October, 1999, term of the Court, Ginsburg authored 146 opinions: sixty-one majority opinions, forty concurring opinions, thirty-eight dissenting opinions, and seven opinions in part concurring and in part dissenting. More than one-third of her opinions for the Court were unanimous. A liberal associate justice, she most often agreed with Justices John Paul Stevens, David Souter, and Stephen G. Breyer. She most often disagreed with Chief Justice William H. Rehnquist and Justices Antonin Scalia and Clarence Thomas.

The subject matter on which Ginsburg has written the most opinions is civil procedure, a topic she taught while a law school professor during the 1960's and 1970's. She has exhibited a strong opposition to state-sanctioned religious exercises, and she has consistently voted to uphold affirmative action programs and minority-majority districts. She authored the majority opinion in *Chandler v. Miller* (1997), in which the Court struck down Georgia's 1990 law requiring candidates for public office to submit to drug testing to certify that they were drug-free.

Ginsburg has continued to interpret the equal protection clause of the Fourteenth Amendment to prohibit artificial barriers to equal opportunity. Most notably, she authored the majority opinion in *United States v. Virginia* (1996), in which the Court struck down Virginia's exclusion of capable women from educational opportunities at the Virginia Military Institute.

Impact Ginsburg's contribution to women's rights in the United States was secure long before she joined the Supreme Court in 1993. As a justice, she emerged as among the most liberal members of the Court.

Further Reading

Glenn, Richard A. "Ruth Bader Ginsburg." In *Great American Lawyers*, edited by John R. Vile. Santa Barbara, Calif.: ABC-Clio, 2001.

Perry, Barbara A. *"The Supremes": Essays on the Current Justices of the Supreme Court of the United States*. New York: Peter Lang, 2001.

Richard A. Glenn

See also Clinton, Bill; Jewish Americans; Supreme Court decisions; Thomas, Clarence; Women's rights.

■ Giuliani, Rudolph

Identification Mayor of New York City, 1994-2001
Born May 28, 1944; Brooklyn, New York

Giuliani reduced citywide crime and corruption, brought conservative values to New York City, and was mayor during the September 11, 2001, terrorist attacks.

Rudolph Giuliani graduated magna cum laude from New York University Law School in 1968. He began his career as assistant U.S. attorney prosecuting bank robbers, kidnappers, and corrupt officials. In 1972, he was appointed federal prosecutor for the Knapp Commission, investigating police corruption. Starting in 1975, he served as associate deputy attorney general in Washington, D.C., where he changed political party affiliation from Democrat to Republican. In 1983, he was appointed U.S. attorney for the Southern District of New York. In this position, he earned a reputation for prosecuting organized crime leaders. In 1986, he prosecuted "The Commission" case, jailing Genovese, Colombo, and Lucchese gangsters. Giuliani began giving press conferences and appeared on talk shows. In 1987, he prosecuted Wall Street financiers Ivan Boesky and Dennis Levine for insider trading, and the "Pizza Connection" drug case, which centered on a scheme to use a number of pizza parlors as fronts for a heroin and cocaine smuggling ring. In 1989, Giuliani ran for mayor against Democratic Manhattan Borough president David Dinkins, an African American. Dinkins was popular with blacks and whites, who saw him as a remedy for race relations, crack, and street crime. Dinkins defeated Giuliani by 42,000 votes but was an ineffectual leader.

In 1993, Giuliani ran against Dinkins as a liberal Republican and won by 2 percent of the vote. Mayor Giuliani announced a "quality of life" campaign: Police swept problem areas, arresting even small-time criminals. Graffiti vandals, prostitutes, and squeegee men were removed by police. The campaign drew criticism from civil libertarians.

When Giuliani took office in 1994, the city's deficit was $2 billion. Giuliani cut the city's budget to the bone, eliminating offices, committees, and social

New York mayor-elect Rudolph Giuliani hugs his wife, Donna, as they celebrate with supporters on November 3, 1993. Giuliani, a Republican, defeated Democratic mayor David Dinkins. (AP/Wide World Photos)

programs. He also eliminated fifteen thousand municipal jobs and called for increases in worker productivity. He sold the city-owned television station, its two radio stations, and a city-owned hotel; he privatized building maintenance, garbage collection, and road resurfacing. His struggle with the Board of Education to cut jobs was especially bitter, and he gained a reputation as an autocratic bully. In 1994, for example, lawyers from the city's Legal Aid Department went on strike, and its managers voted for pay raises. Giuliani cut the department's budget by 16 percent and offered a new contract with a no-strike clause and mandated reorganization.

By 1995, crime had dropped by 33 percent. By 1996, with a booming economy, the city had a $450 million surplus revenue. Giuliani's mayoral opponent in 1997 was Democrat Ruth Messinger, who lost by a significant margin. In his second term, police cameras were installed in Washington Square Park, and smoking was banned in city restaurants. Giuliani ordered a controversial crackdown on jaywalkers and the homeless, and his plan for a gambling casino on Governor's Island collapsed.

Impact A 1997 Federal Bureau of Investigation (FBI) report stated that people were more likely to be victims of serious or violent crimes in Anchorage, Alaska, than in New York City. Crime continued to decline in 1999, while the city announced a $2.6 billion surplus. New Yorkers appreciated the restored order, but Giuliani was criticized as abrasive and seeking power by gutting departments and services. In the aftermath of the terrorist attacks on September 11, 2001, he received world praise for his firm control of emergency services and liaisons with federal agencies.

Further Reading

Giuliani, Rudolph. *Leadership.* New York: Hyperion, 2002.

Kirtzman, Andrew. *The Emperor of the City.* New York: William Morrow, 2000.

Jim Pauff

See also Conservatism in U.S. politics; Crime; Crown Heights riot; Dinkins, David; Lee, Spike; Liberalism in U.S. politics; Mafia; Police brutality; Recession of 1990-1991; Republican Revolution; Sharpton, Al; Terrorism; World Trade Center bombing.

■ Glenn, John

Identification U.S. politician and astronaut
Born July 18, 1921; Cambridge, Ohio

A notable career in the U.S. military and his fame as the first American to orbit Earth continued with Glenn's election to four terms in the U.S. Senate and a return to space in 1998 as the world's oldest astronaut.

Following his election to the Senate in 1974 as a Democrat, John Glenn was reelected in 1980, 1986, and 1992. His committee assignments included Armed Services, Foreign Relations, and the Special Committee on Aging. He chaired the Governmental Affairs Committee (1987-1995).

Glenn's record in the U.S. Senate was unblemished until, along with four other senators, he became involved in a financial scandal involving a failed savings and loan company that sought their assistance in dealing with its problems. The Senate Ethics Committee began hearings in November of 1990 to investigate allegations of improper efforts to assist Charles Keating, the company head. The com-

John Glenn in 1998. (NASA)

mittee eventually exonerated Glenn in August, 1991. Known for his honesty and ethical standards, he later referred to this controversy as the lowest point in his life. In the aftermath of the "Keating affair," Glenn defeated his Republican opponent in the 1992 Senate election by a wide margin. He considered running for a fifth term but announced in February, 1997, that he would retire from the Senate at the end of his fourth term, an unprecedented record for a U.S. senator representing Ohio.

During the 1990's, Glenn supported America's space program as the United States joined other nations to create an International Space Station (ISS) for joint scientific research. He expressed a strong desire to participate as a crew member of one of the space shuttles flying to the ISS. Then in his seventies, he believed that the experience of an older person in space might assist the study of aging and possible effects on the body. Few took him seriously at first, but he continued his determined efforts to gain approval. Finally, the National Aeronautics and Space Administration (NASA) announced in early 1998 that he would return to space. Glenn became a payload specialist assigned to undertake physiological tasks and other experiments on the STS-95 space shuttle *Discovery* (launched on October 29 and returned to Earth on November 7, 1998).

Another focus was Glenn's involvement in establishing the John Glenn Institute for Public Service and Public Policy at the Ohio State University in 1998. The institute encouraged students to academically train in preparation for public-service careers.

Impact John Glenn's career in public service reveals a deep appreciation for his country. This continued during the 1990's as a member of the U.S. Senate. His 1998 shuttle flight reaffirmed his long interest in space technology. His support for the John Glenn Institute for Public Service and Public Policy also showed his commitment to utilize his talents and experience to expand opportunities for others who seek to serve their nation. Glenn has been an inspiration to many Americans.

Further Reading

Glenn, John, and Nick Taylor. *John Glenn: A Memoir.* New York: Bantam Books, 1999.

Green, Robert. *John Glenn: Astronaut and U.S. Senator.* Chicago: Ferguson, 2001.

Montgomery, Scott, and Timothy R. Gaffney. *Back in Orbit: John Glenn's Return to Space.* Atlanta: Longstreet Press, 1998.

Taylor Stults

See also Bondar, Roberta; Elections in the United States, 1992; Lucid, Shannon; Space exploration; Space shuttle program.

■ Global warming debate

Definition Controversy about a worldwide environmental problem

Human-induced warming of the Earth's climate emerged as a major scientific, social, political, and economic issue during the 1990's, as the effects of climate change became evident in everyday life in locations as varied as small island nations of the Pacific Ocean and the shores of the Arctic Ocean.

For the past two and a half centuries, at an accelerating rate, the basic composition of Earth's atmosphere has been materially altered by the fossil-fuel emissions of human industry. Industry and transport have been emitting increasing amounts of greenhouse gases, including carbon dioxide and methane, which, along with various other synthetic chemicals, retain heat near the surface, contributing to significant warming.

Changes in the Atmosphere The proportion of carbon dioxide, the most important of these gases, rose from 280 parts per million (ppm) in about 1880 to roughly 365 ppm in 1999 (and 383 ppm in 2007). Methane's preindustrial range in the atmosphere was 320 to 780 parts per billion (ppb); by 1999, that level had risen to about 1,700 ppb, a steeper rise, in proportional terms, than carbon dioxide. Carbon dioxide is two hundred times more plentiful in the atmosphere than methane, but a molecule of methane can retain twenty-five times as much heat as one of carbon dioxide.

Global temperatures spiked in the late 1980's and 1990's, repeatedly breaking records set only a year or two earlier. The warmest year in recorded history to that time was 1998, breaking the record set in 1996, which exceeded 1995's new benchmark. According to the National Aeronautics and Space Administration (NASA) Goddard Institute for Space Studies, the ten warmest years since reliable records have been kept on a global scale (roughly 1890) by 1999 had occurred after 1980. Temperatures continued to rise steadily after the 1990's.

Scientific Consensus and Dissent Though lively debates in political circles and the news media have sometimes raised questions about whether human activity is significantly warming the Earth, scientific evidence in support of global warming accumulated steadily during the 1990's. With the exception of a minority of contrarians, the human role in a rapid warming of the Earth has become nearly incontrovertible.

At the same time that scientific consensus on the seriousness of global warming formed during the 1990's, however, so did resistance to the idea by a much smaller number of dissenters, some of them funded in part by major fossil-fuel companies. Generally, the skeptics believe that warming will be a balm for humanity. A skeptics' journal, the *World Climate Report*, replied to an editorial in the prominent British medical journal *The Lancet* that asserted that malaria and other mosquito-borne diseases will spread into the temperate zones as global temperatures rise. According to the contrarians, malaria's spread has very little to do with temperature or humidity and more to do with medical technology and air conditioning. The contrarians assert that epidemics of malaria were common in most of the United States before the 1950's. In 1878, 100,000 Americans were infected and one-quarter of them died.

Impact At stake in the global warming debate is the way in which humans will produce and use energy for the foreseeable future. Many scientists believe that the Earth's entire energy infrastructure will have to be changed to avoid a crisis. Scientists who study the future potential of human-induced warming also point to several other natural mechanisms that could cause the pace of climate change to accelerate, releasing carbon dioxide and methane from permafrost. Melting Arctic ice also creates a darker ocean surface, changing albedo (reflectivity), causing more heat to be absorbed. The possibility of a "runaway" greenhouse effect by the year 2050 has been raised, often with a palatable sense of urgency.

Across Alaska, northern Canada, and Siberia, scientists are finding telltale signs that permafrost is melting at an accelerated rate. As permafrost melts, additional carbon dioxide and methane convert from solid form, stored in the earth, to gas, in the atmosphere, retaining more heat. Human contributions of greenhouse gases are provoking natural processes at an alarming rate. The Arctic ice cap melted steadily during the 1990's, a trend that continued in the subsequent decade. Inuit hunters have reported that enough methane is bubbling out of the Canadian north to light fires. Yellow jacket wasps have been sighted on the far northern Canadian Arctic, where the Inuit have no words in their own language to describe them. In 2006, a manatee, a subtropical marine animal, was observed swimming in the Hudson River near Manhattan Island.

Subsequent Events Using a complex set of feedbacks ("thermal inertia"), scientists conclude that humans will feel today's emissions as heat roughly half a century from now. In the oceans, the feedback loop is longer, probably a century and a half, maybe two. The real debate is not over how much the oceans may rise from melting ice by the end of this century (one to three feet, perhaps) but how much melting will be "in the pipeline" by that time. James E. Hansen, director of the NASA Goddard Institute for Space Studies, estimates that thermal inertia by the year 2100 may guarantee a 25-meter (82-foot) sea-level rise within two centuries. Such a rise could put millions of people out of their homes.

Further Reading

Gelbspan, Ross. *The Heat Is On: The High Stakes Battle over Earth's Threatened Climate.* Reading, Mass.: Addison-Wesley, 1997. A guide to the political battle over global warming during the 1990's.

Houghton, John. *Global Warming: The Complete Briefing.* New York: Cambridge University Press, 1997. A concise but expert outline of the issue as it stood in the 1990's.

Johansen, Bruce E. *The Global Warming Desk Reference.* Westport, Conn.: Greenwood Press, 2001. A summary of the field as it stood at the end of the decade.

Lynas, Mark. *High Tide: The Truth About Our Climate Crisis.* New York: Picador, 2004. A travelogue that illustrates everyday impacts of a changing climate.

Bruce E. Johansen

See also Agriculture in the United States; Air pollution; Airline industry; Architecture; Biosphere 2;

Clean Air Act of 1990; Clinton, Bill; Earth Day 1990; *Earth in the Balance*; Gore, Al; Kyoto Protocol; Nunavut Territory; Science and technology.

■ *GoodFellas*

Identification American gangster film
Director Martin Scorsese (1942-)
Date Released on September 19, 1990

Widely lauded for its skillful directing, Oscar-caliber performances, and references to real-life events, GoodFellas *is one of the most critically acclaimed gangster movies of all time and has earned its place in the American film canon.*

The script for *GoodFellas* is derived from the Nicholas Pileggi book *Wiseguy* (1986), which draws heavily from the real-life experiences of Henry Hill, an American gangster and confederate of the Lucchese crime family. The movie follows Henry from childhood as he starts out performing menial tasks for the local mob, run by Paul Cicero (played by Paul Sorvino and based on real-life Lucchese crime figure Paul Vario). Henry's crime activities increase as he matures into a full-blown "wiseguy," earning the respect of his cohorts, including Tommy DeVito (Joe Pesci), based on Tommy DeSimone, and Jimmy Conway (Robert De Niro), based on Jimmy Burke.

One of the compelling aspects of *GoodFellas* is the surface appeal of Henry's life as the story starts out. The audience is introduced to extremely charismatic characters who are treated with respect and living above the standards of average people. They are shown to have a life of freedom and little responsibility to the establishment. As Henry Hill states, "If we wanted something, we just took it."

However, as the story unfolds, the underlying violence and accountability of Henry's world increasingly surface. In a pivotal scene, Tommy shoots a waiter named "Spider" in the foot. Later, as the bandaged Spider defends himself against Tommy's belittlements, Tommy murders him in cold blood. This psychopathic action, one of the many shocking scenes in the film, exemplifies how the seemingly fun and prosperous life of the gangster can flip into brutality at any moment. As the narrative progresses, Henry's life increasingly disintegrates as the negative forces play themselves out. In the end, after Henry is busted by the police, he is reduced to becoming one of the most despised personas in the mob world: an informant. Henry's world has crumbled, and, as he says at the end, "I get to live the rest of my life like a schnook."

Impact *GoodFellas* not only resonated with audiences worldwide but also established a template for many future gangster films and television series. Martin Scorsese grew up in the Bronx, and throughout his film career his understanding of street nuance set a new standard in the entertainment industry. For example, the Home Box Office (HBO) series *The Sopranos* drew influence from *GoodFellas* and Scorsese's work, and many of the actors from the film itself crossed over to the show. In addition to artistic influence, *GoodFellas* brought renewed attention to gangster life. Henry Hill has become somewhat of a celebrity, being expelled from the witness protection program and appearing on various talk shows.

Further Reading

Friedman, Lawrence S. *The Cinema of Martin Scorsese.* New York: Continuum, 1997.

Scorsese, Martin. *Scorsese on Scorsese.* Rev. ed. London: Faber & Faber, 2003.

Wood, C. J. *Nicholas Pileggi and Martin Scorsese: "Wiseguy" and "GoodFellas"—Mob Rules.* http://www.spikemagazine.com/1003nicholaspileggi.php, 2003.

Jarod P. Kearney

See also Academy Awards; Crime; Film in the United States; Mafia.

■ Gordon, Jeff

Identification American race car driver
Born August 4, 1971; Vallejo, California

As four-time NASCAR Winston Cup champion, three-time winner of the Daytona 500, and four-time winner of the Brickyard 400, Gordon has earned a permanent spot in the history of auto racing.

As early as age four, Jeff Gordon was racing BMX bikes locally, often competing against older children. At age five, his father purchased two quarter-midget racers for Gordon and his older sister. He raced quarter-midget cars and go-karts successfully before growing tired of the sport and temporarily taking up water skiing. At the age of thirteen, Gordon's life changed forever. For the first time, he raced a 700-horsepower sprint car at the All Star Florida Speedweeks competition. His interest in sprint-car racing was the major reason the Gordon family moved to Pittsboro, Indiana, where there were more opportunities available for a young auto racer.

It was suggested that Gordon try driving stock cars, so he went to the Buck Baker Racing School at Rockingham Speedway in North Carolina. Gordon's enthusiasm and natural talent caught the attention of Hugh Connerty, who found funding for Gordon to race at the Busch Grand National race in 1990. In 1991, Gordon raced for Bill Davis and won the title Rookie of the Year in both the Busch Series and the Winston Cup. In 1992, Gordon won his first career win at the Winston Cup race at the Atlanta Motor Speedway and was noticed by Rick Hendrick. Gordon joined the Hendrick Motorsports team.

In 1993, Gordon became the first rookie in history to win the 125-mile qualifying race during Speedweek at the Daytona International Speedway. In 1994, he continued his list of successes with victories at the inaugural Brickyard 400 in Indianapolis and the Coca-Cola 600 in Charlotte. In 1995, Gordon won the Winston Cup championship to become the youngest driver in the modern era to win the crown championship. The next year, he led in Winston Cup Series victories (ten) and laps led (2,313). The year 1997 brought Gordon another Winston Cup championship, with ten victories and one pole. He became the youngest driver ever to win the Daytona 500 and the second driver in history to win the Winston Million—a million-dollar award granted to the winner of three of the four top races on the Winston Cup circuit. That year, he broke the all-time single-season earnings record by winning over $4 million. In 1998, Gordon again won the Winston Cup championship, with thirteen victories, and became the first driver to win the Brickyard 400 twice.

Success continued to follow Gordon throughout the following years. He founded the Gordon/Evernham Motorsports team with his crew chief and, in 1999, established the Jeff Gordon Foundation, which helps chronically ill children. He won his fourth Winston Cup in 2001.

Impact Throughout the 1990's, Gordon proved that one does not necessarily have to win every race in order to be in contention for the championship title. From his rookie year in 1993 through 1999, he never finished out of the top ten in points, and he managed to win three Winston Cup championships. His consistency, drive, and dedication to the sport of auto racing alone are admired by many fans.

Further Reading

Cothren, Larry. *Jeff Gordon: The NASCAR Superstar's Story.* St. Paul, Minn.: Motorbooks International, 2005.

Gordon, Jeff, and Steve Eubanks. *Jeff Gordon: Racing Back to the Front—My Memoir.* New York: Atria Books, 2003.

Kathryn A. Cochran

See also Auto racing; Sports.

■ Gore, Al

Identification U.S. senator from Tennessee, presidential candidate, U.S. vice president, environmentalist, and author

Born March 31, 1948; Washington, D.C.

Gore was a notable force in the proliferation of Internet usage both nationally and internationally. His focus on environmental issues, such as global warning, helped popularize and make mainstream a topic that had previously been a subject discussed primarily among scientists.

Al Gore, Jr., began the decade of the 1990's adjusting to the many changes in his professional and personal life. Having lost a campaign to become the Democratic nominee for president in 1988, Senator Gore was reassessing his political talents and pondering his future in politics. He was also coming to terms with nearly losing his only son, Albert Gore III, who had been seriously injured when hit by a car in 1989. Gore's wife, Tipper, was suffering from a bout of severe depression caused by her son's critical illness and the sometimes oppressive responsibilities of being a political wife. All of this caused Gore to reconsider his priorities. He struggled to balance his political life with a desire to make his own mark beyond politics and to honor his deep commitment to his wife and children.

Gore entered a period of self-examination and exploration. He spent more time with his family and wrote a book on a subject about which he felt very strongly: *Earth in the Balance: Ecology and the Human Spirit,* which focuses on an environmental crisis of global proportions. Gore claimed that human-caused changes have resulted in catastrophe for the earth's environment, citing the greenhouse effect of global warming and damage to the ozone as extremely dangerous to the survival of humans, animals, and plant life. Still a senator, Gore spent three years writing the book. In it, he laid out environmental crises and potential solutions. His proposals included nature preservation, population control, environmentally friendly technologies, an international exchange of solutions and policies, and enforceable international agreements aimed at preserving, protecting, and improving planet health. *Earth in the Balance* was published in 1992 and became a best seller, eventually being translated into more than thirty languages.

Gore also had a tremendous interest in the potential for global communication achieved through the use of computer and telephone technologies. He focused on a means to transfer economic information on an international basis and was very influential in popularizing and streamlining use of the Internet. Once fully mainstreamed, such technology made possible a merging of individual nation economies toward a world economy, which some economists criticized as having a dangerous leveling or flattening economic effect. In 1991, Congress passed the High Performance Computing and Communication Act, which had been introduced years earlier as the Gore Bill. This bill led to the creation of the "information superhighway"—an early term for the Internet.

Al Gore. (U.S. Department of Defense)

Joining Forces with Bill Clinton Republican president George H. W. Bush was up for reelection in 1992. Gore decided not to seek the Democratic nomination to oppose Bush. Troubled by memories of his failed 1988 attempt, and acknowledging his wife's resistance to enduring another presidential campaign, he let slide an opportunity to pursue the top spot. Arkansas governor Bill Clinton won the battle to become the Democratic presidential candidate for 1992. Gore was asked to be on Clinton's list of vice presidential running mates, and he answered in the affirmative. It was not lost on Gore that the vice presidency was a position that his father, Albert Gore, Sr., had coveted but never attained. Clinton liked Gore's traits of a solid, broad intellect, rigid discipline, firm grasp of even obscure policies, and, perhaps most presciently, his reputation for loyalty.

Both Clinton and Gore were from southern states. Generally, presidential candidates choose a vice president from a geographic location different from their own. Clinton, however, felt that Gore brought so many other positives to the ticket that he did not worry about regional balance. Gore's studiousness and reputation for details nicely contrasted and balanced the perception of Clinton as perhaps a little too laid-back and impetuous. Gore's image as a rock-solid family man and upright citizen also appealed to Clinton, who faced constant criticism for questionable morals and dubious personal economic investments. The pair won the 1992 election, and President Clinton made good on his promise that Gore would be the most influential vice president in American history. Clinton gave Gore broad influence, especially in matters of the environment and telecommunications. Gore was instrumental in helping Clinton design a successful plan to cut the federal deficit, which had skyrocketed under previous Republican administrations.

Clinton and Gore were reelected in 1996. Clinton's sexual involvement with a young female aide, Monica Lewinsky, however, cast a dark shadow over the rest of Clinton's presidency and resulted in his impeachment. Though Clinton remained in office and enjoyed Gore's loyal support, the scandal damaged Gore's chances of winning the presidency in 2000.

Impact Although Al Gore's dream of becoming president of the United States was not realized, his achievements as vice president, environmentalist, and technology proponent made significant contributions to the United States and the world.

Further Reading

Gore, Albert. *Earth in the Balance: Ecology and the Human Spirit.* Boston: Houghton Mifflin, 1992. A scientific treatise, combined with sometimes emotional narrative, on ecological problems. Gore won the Nobel Peace Prize with the Intergovernmental Panel on Climate Change in 2007 in part for the content and impact of this book.

Maraniss, David, and Ellen Nakashima. *The Prince of Tennessee: The Rise of Al Gore.* New York: Simon & Schuster, 2000. Political biography spanning Al Gore's rise to national prominence. In-depth discussion of the impact of Gore's family, especially his father, Senator Albert Gore, Sr.

Turque, Bill. *Inventing Al Gore.* Boston: Houghton Mifflin, 2000. Biography by a Washington, D.C., political correspondent for *Newsweek* magazine. Explores Gore's personal and political history, as well as his inner workings.

Twyla R. Wells

See also Balanced Budget Act of 1997; Campaign finance scandal; Clinton, Bill; Clinton, Hillary Rodham; Clinton's impeachment; Clinton's scandals; *Earth in the Balance*; Educate America Act of 1994; Elections in the United States, 1992; Elections in the United States, 1996; Global warming debate; Internet; Lewinsky scandal; World Wide Web.

■ Grafton, Sue

Identification American author of crime fiction
Born April 24, 1940; Louisville, Kentucky

Grafton became known primarily for her "alphabet series" of detective novels featuring female private investigator Kinsey Millhone, which began in the 1980's and achieved wide success during the 1990's.

Sue Grafton's Kinsey Millhone is often cited as one of the first "tough" female private investigators, and the series adheres to many conventions of hard-boiled detective fiction, which was popularized in the first half of the century in the works of writers such as Dashiell Hammett, Raymond Chandler, and Ross Macdonald.

Grafton's detective, like those of her predecessors, is unmarried and somewhat cynical. She does not conduct her investigations from the sitting-room setting of the classical sleuth (such as Sherlock Holmes) but goes wherever her investigations take her, often finding herself in violent confrontation with criminals on the brink of being exposed. Possessing less of a dark side than some of her hard-boiled predecessors (she does not, like Hammett's Continental Op, threaten to go "blood simple"), Kinsey retains the tradition's emphasis on wisecracking persistence, an alternately friendly and contentious relationship with law enforcement, and a frankness with regard to "the job." Kinsey is not an upper-class sleuth conducting investigations primarily for intellectual pleasure. She is, like Chandler's Marlowe, a working detective with bills to pay. Also like Marlowe, Kinsey is characterized as someone who lands in the detective profession in part because she possesses an independent streak that makes her a poor fit for occupations requiring obedience to superiors and cooperation with colleagues. Kinsey's solitude is mitigated somewhat by the presence of kindly friends and neighbors such as the affable landlord Henry and brusquely maternal Rosie, proprietor of Rosie's Café. Entries in the series during the 1990's increased Kinsey's social interconnectedness even further, with story lines focusing more on Kinsey's personal life, and with the introduction of Kinsey's estranged extended family.

The series began in 1982 with *A Is for Alibi* and has continued through the alphabet with a new entry being added every one or two years. The chronology of the story itself, however, progresses more slowly.

Thus, even late entries in the series remain set in the 1980's. For example, in *S Is for Silence* (2005), Kinsey goes to a strip mall (not a "big box," or warehouse, center) in search of a pay phone (there are no cell phones yet), and Henry goes to the theater to see the 1987 film *No Way Out* starring Kevin Costner. Grafton's stories do, however, implicitly reference events beyond Kinsey's time frame. For example, a subplot in *P Is for Peril* (2001) seems to have been inspired by the widely publicized Menendez brothers murder trial of the 1990's.

Impact Sue Grafton's success helped pave the way for many female-authored detective series with tough female protagonists, including Patricia Cornwell's Kay Scarpetta series, Nevada Barr's Anne Pigeon series, and Linda Barnes's Carlotta Carlyle series, all of which enjoyed widespread popularity in the 1990's.

Further Reading

Kaufman, Natalie Hevener, and Carol McGinnis Kay. *"G" Is for Grafton: The World of Kinsey Millhone.* New York: Henry Holt, 1997.

Mizejewski, Linda. *Hardboiled and High Heeled: The Woman Detective in Popular Culture.* New York: Routledge, 2004.

Christine Photinos

See also Crime; Literature in Canada; Literature in the United States; Menendez brothers murder case; Publishing.

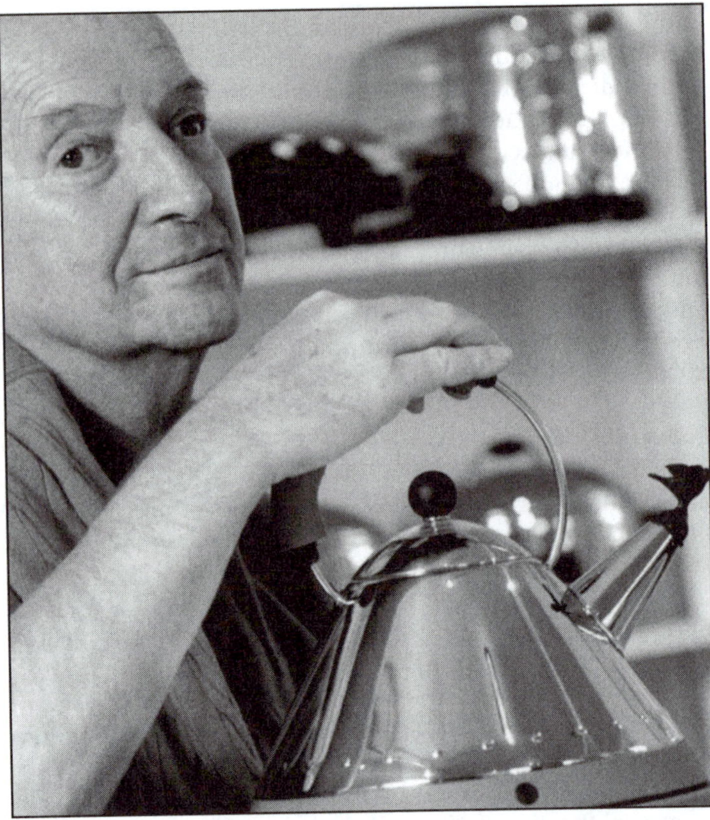

Michael Graves poses with a teapot he designed. His partnership with Target stores made him a household name. (AP/Wide World Photos)

■ Graves, Michael

Identification American architect and designer
Born July 9, 1934; Indianapolis, Indiana

During the 1990's, Graves revolutionized the design of everyday objects and the way they are marketed.

By the 1990's, Michael Graves had already established himself as an important thinker and teacher of architecture, with many well-known building commissions. His inclusion as one of the New York Five (with Peter Eisenman, Richard Meier, Charles Gwathmey, and John Hejduk), an unofficial group of modernist architects who had made their reputations during the 1970's in reaction to the designs and issues of the 1960's, guaranteed his place in cultural history. Graves's architectural assignments have included museums, college buildings, business towers, arts centers, libraries, hotels, and residences. Commissions during the 1990's included the Team Disney Building in Burbank, California, and two resort hotels for Disney World in Orlando, Florida.

Graves, however, was interested in more than buildings by the 1990's. With his two firms, Michael Graves & Associates (specializing in architecture and interior design) and Michael Graves Design Group (product and graphic design), he had found new media for his interests. He designed the workspaces and chairs for his seventy employees and formed partnerships to explore applications of his aesthetic to fabrics, dinnerware, jewelry, lighting fixtures, and housewares. His signature touch involves

a whimsical twist on the classical designs that he had learned to love during his early studies in Italy.

In 1998, Target stores announced an exclusive Michael Graves line of home products, including closet organizers, teakettles, and laundry baskets. Graves proclaimed that good design should be accessible to everyone. The line proved immensely successful with Target shoppers, paving the way for other "class" designers to partner with stores that served the masses. Graves's products made him a household name as well as a presence in peoples' kitchens, and he raised Target's prestige and stock price.

Graves owns a special etching machine to autograph his more expensive products, which appreciate in value. He has designed china and silverware for Italian manufacturer Alessi, packaging for a new corporate image for Lenox china, a coffeemaker for a third company, and blankets and throws with another partner. He was awarded the National Medal of Arts in 1999 and the Gold Medal of the American Institute of Architects in 2001. He maintains his design firms and store in Princeton, New Jersey.

Impact Michael Graves filled a major niche in modern architecture and high-quality design. Graves and his contemporaries, who have been criticized for their celebrity client lists and popular appeal, have informed the work of some younger architects.

Further Reading

Eisenman, Peter, et al. *Five Architects: Eisenman, Graves, Gwathmey, Hejduk, Meier.* New York: Oxford University Press, 1975.

Frampton, Kenneth. *Modern Architecture: A Critical History.* London: Thames and Hudson, 1992.

Patton, Phil. *Michael Graves Designs: The Art of the Everyday Object.* New York: Melcher Media, 2004.

Jan Hall

See also Architecture; Art movements; Fashions and clothing; Gehry, Frank; Stewart, Martha.

■ Greenspan, Alan

Identification American economist and chairman of the Board of Governors of the Federal Reserve system, 1987-2006

Born March 6, 1926; New York, New York

Greenspan was the longest-serving chairman of the Federal Reserve, serving throughout the decade of the 1990's and steering the economy through one of the longest bull markets in living history into what became the dot-com bubble.

Alan Greenspan began the 1990's in his third year as chairman of the Federal Reserve, which made him arguably the single most influential force on the U.S. financial markets. The Federal Reserve sets the federal fund rate, which affects the rate at which banks can borrow from each other, which in turn influences the prime rate (typically 3 percent higher than the federal rate).

In 1991, Greenspan was faced with a scandal at Salomon Brothers, whose bond-trading division under the leadership of the notorious John Meriwether was caught submitting false bids to the U.S. Trea-

Alan Greenspan. (AP/Wide World Photos)

sury. As a consequence, the federal government was about to withdraw Salomon's trading privileges, which would have led to bankruptcy. However, after a direct appeal from Warren Buffett, Salomon's largest investor, Greenspan spared the bank this fate. In 1992, Greenspan was elected to his second term as chairman of the Federal Reserve after being nominated by George H. W. Bush. Despite his Republican background, Greenspan was reelected in 1996 and 2000 by the Bill Clinton administration.

Greenspan is renowned for his goal of zero inflation. In 1994, when he was engineering a series of interest-rate increases, he was subjected to much criticism for being willing to sacrifice economic growth in pursuit of this unobtainable goal. However, in 1998 inflation hit an eleven-year low, unemployment was at a twenty-four-year low, and consumer confidence was higher than any other period in the past three decades.

The following year, he crossed paths with John Meriwether again, who at this time was running Long-Term Capital Management. The hedge fund was facing a liquidity crisis, having lost $4.6 billion in less than four months. The fund was one of the largest of its kind, and it was feared that its collapse could have triggered a stock market crash. Greenspan intervened and brokered a deal with the creditors. Subsequently, the stock market continued to climb and culminated in the stock market crash in 2000, bursting the dot-com bubble. Many have come to blame Greenspan for his intervention, believing that a stock market correction in 1998 would have prevented the crash of 2000.

Greenspan also served on the boards of many companies, including Alcoa, Automatic Data Processing, Capital Cities/ABC, General Foods, J. P. Morgan, Morgan Guaranty Trust Company of New York, Mobil Corporation, and the Pittston Company.

Impact Greenspan was often cited as being the second most powerful man in the United States during the 1990's after the president. His monetary policy led to the longest sustained bull market in recent history and a housing boom across North America.

Further Reading

Greenspan, Alan. *The Age of Turbulence: Adventures in a New World.* New York: Penguin Books, 2007.

Hartcher, Peter. *Bubble Man: Alan Greenspan and the Missing Seven Trillion Dollars.* New York: W. W. Norton, 2006.

Martin, Justin. *Greenspan: The Man Behind Money.* Cambridge, Mass.: Perseus Books, 2001.

Rikard Bandebo

See also Buffett, Warren; Bush, George H. W.; Business and the economy in the United States; Dotcoms; Recession of 1990-1991; Stock market.

■ Griffey, Ken, Jr.

Identification Professional baseball player
Born November 21, 1969; Donora, Pennsylvania

Griffey won four American League home run titles and ten straight Gold Glove Awards (1990-1999) in the 1990's.

Ken Griffey, Jr., son of former major-league outfielder Ken Griffey, Sr., was drafted first overall by the Seattle Mariners in 1987. He hit a double in his major-league debut on April 3, 1989, and hit a home run off his first pitch at the Seattle Kingdome. The six-foot, three-inch, 205-pound Griffey, who bats and throws left-handed, became in 1990 the first Mariner ever selected to the starting lineup of the All-Star Game. His father joined Seattle that August, the first time a father-son duo played simultaneously on the same major-league team.

The younger Griffey, often compared with his idol Willie Mays, showed exceptional ability to hit with power, run, field, and throw. In 1991, he batted a career-high .327 with 100 runs batted in (RBIs). Two years later, Griffey led the American League (AL) with 359 total bases and became the fourth major leaguer under age twenty-four to record three consecutive seasons with at least 100 RBIs. His 45 home runs in 1993 ranked second in the AL. In July, Griffey tied a major-league record by homering in eight consecutive games. In 1994, he won his first AL home run crown with 40 and finished second in slugging percentage.

Griffey peaked in the late 1990's, becoming the fourth major leaguer to belt 40 home runs in five straight seasons and leading the AL in home runs for three consecutive seasons. He hit 56 home runs in 1997 and 1998 and clouted 48 home runs in 1999. Griffey captured the AL Most Valuable Player (MVP) honors in 1997, pacing the AL with a career-high 147 RBI and recording a career-best 185 hits. He finished third in the AL with 146 RBIs in 1998 and

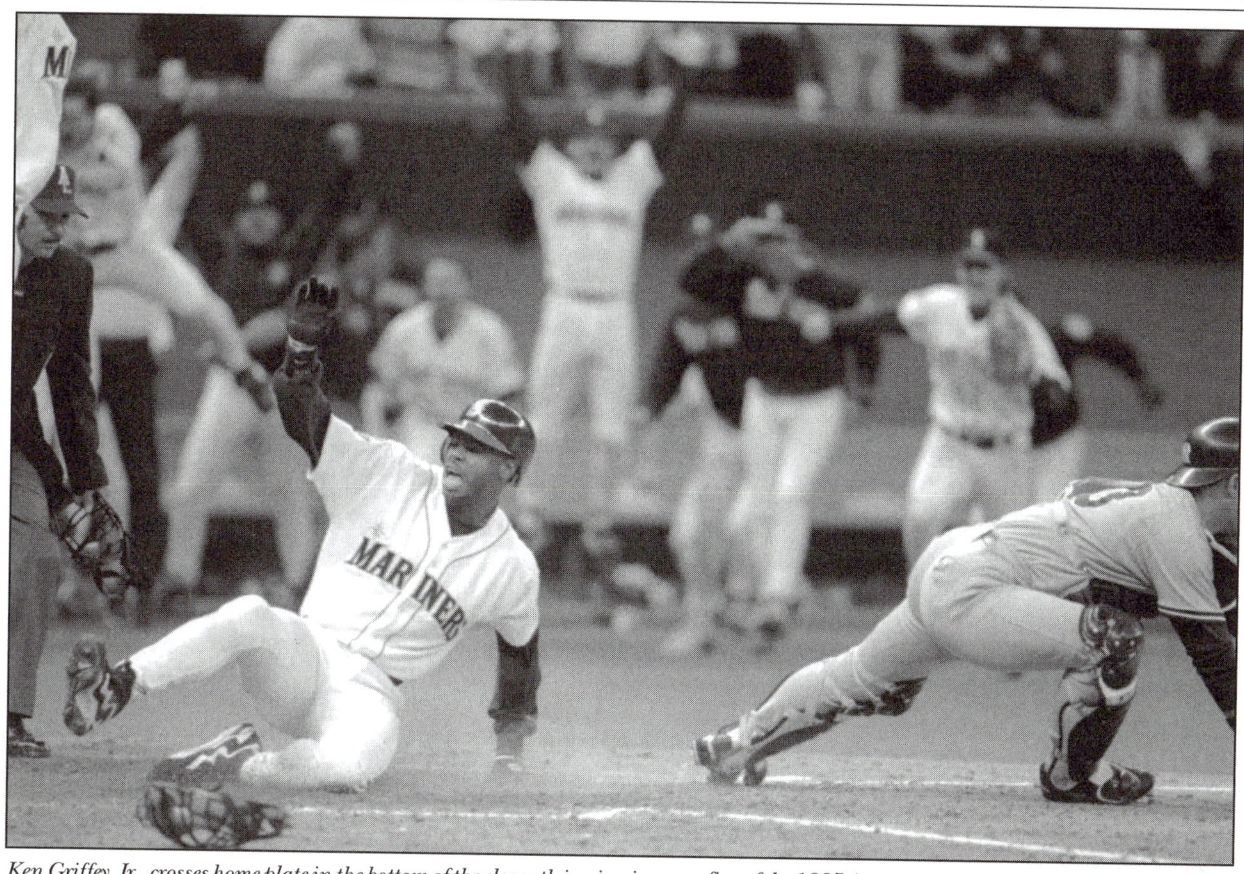
Ken Griffey, Jr., crosses home plate in the bottom of the eleventh inning in game five of the 1995 American League Division Series. The Seattle Mariners defeated the New York Yankees 6-5. (AP/Wide World Photos)

shared third with 134 RBIs in 1999. The fleet-footed Griffey excelled defensively, diving for sinking liners and making numerous leaping catches to rob opponents of home runs. His arm ranked among the best center fielders.

Griffey led Seattle to postseason appearances in 1995 and 1997. He tallied one of the most important runs in Mariner history, scoring from first base on Edgar Martinez's double in the eleventh inning of game five of the 1995 AL Division Series to eliminate the New York Yankees. He batted .391 with 7 RBIs and tied a single-series record with 5 home runs. He holds Mariner records for most runs (1,063), hits (1,742), home runs (398), and RBIs (1,152). In February, 2000, Seattle traded Griffey to the Cincinnati Reds.

Impact During the 1990's, Griffey earned seven *Sporting News* Silver Slugger Awards and was named to the AL All-Star Team each year (1990-1999). In 1999, he made Major League Baseball's All-Century Team. Griffey ranks sixth in career home runs, trailing only Barry Bonds, Hank Aaron, Babe Ruth, Willie Mays, and Sammy Sosa.

Further Reading

Griffey, Ken, Jr. *Junior: Griffey on Griffey*. New York: HarperCollins, 1997.

Jackson, Reggie, ed. *Ken Griffey, Jr.* Dallas: Beckett, 1999.

Thornley, Stew. *Super Sports Star: Ken Griffey, Jr.* Berkeley Heights, N.J.: Enslow, 2004.

David L. Porter

See also African Americans; Baseball; Baseball realignment; Baseball strike of 1994; Home run race; McGwire, Mark; Ripken, Cal, Jr.; Sosa, Sammy; Sports.

■ Grisham, John

Identification American novelist
Born February 8, 1955; Jonesboro, Arkansas

A master of the legal thriller, Grisham was the best-selling novelist of the 1990's.

John Grisham was an avid reader as a boy and discovered John Steinbeck's novels while attending high school. Although he never planned to become a writer, Grisham began keeping a journal while he was an undergraduate at Mississippi State University. He graduated with a degree in accounting in 1977 and earned a law degree from the University of Mississippi in 1981. He then practiced criminal and personal injury law in Southaven, Mississippi, a suburb of Memphis, Tennessee, and was elected to the Mississippi House of Representatives in 1983. He served in the state's legislature until 1990.

Grisham's first book, *A Time to Kill*, was turned down by over twenty-five publishers until 1988, when Wynwood Press paid him an advance of $15,000 and brought it out with an initial print run of five thousand copies. (Grisham bought one thousand copies for himself.) The novel was inspired by the testimony of a twelve-year-old rape victim that Grisham heard in 1984, and it took him three years to write the book. From 1984 to 1989, he got up at 5:00 A.M. every day and wrote for at least two hours. His second novel, *The Firm*, came out in 1991. It was the number-one best seller of that year and was on *The New York Times* best seller list for forty-seven weeks. He was able to become a full-time writer after selling the film rights. He wrote eight more novels during the decade, and each one reached the top of *The New York Times* best-seller list.

John Grisham. (AP/Wide World Photos)

Grisham reached an even wider audience when six of his novels were made into films during the 1990's. He also wrote the original screenplay for the film *The Gingerbread Man* (1998), although he was very unhappy with director Robert Altman's rewrites. The television series *The Client* (1995-1996) was based on Grisham's 1993 book by that title.

Impact The legal thriller dates back to at least the 1896 short story "The Corpus Delicti" by Melville Davisson Post. Attorney turned author Scott Turow (*Presumed Innocent*, 1987) is the novelist usually credited with reviving the genre in the late twentieth century, and Grisham became its most commercially successful practitioner. Other lawyers turned authors during the decade included Mimi Lavenda Latt (*Powers of Attorney*, 1993), Richard North Patterson (*Degree of Guilt*, 1993), Lisa Scottoline (*Everywhere That Mary Went*, 1993), and Steve Martini (*Undue Influence*, 1995).

Grisham's books sold over sixty million copies during the 1990's. They have sold more than 235 million copies worldwide and have been translated into twenty-nine languages. *The Pelican Brief* (1992) alone sold over eleven million copies in the United States. Along with Tom Clancy and J. K. Rowling, he has sold more than two million copies in a first printing.

Further Reading

Pringle, Mary Beth. *John Grisham: A Critical Companion.* Westport, Conn.: Greenwood Press, 1997.

Weaver, Robyn M. *John Grisham.* San Diego, Calif.: Lucent Books, 1999.

Thomas R. Feller

See also Book clubs; Literature in the United States; Publishing.

■ Grunge fashion

Definition Fashion trend

Grunge fashion ironically arose from a complete rejection of fashion. The look created by muted colors and lumberjack plaid flannel, long hair, goatees, and clunky boots embodied the new no-frills ideal of the grunge rock movement that contradicted the previously popular all-frills bombast of hair metal. Grunge appeal influenced not only varied genres of the music scene nationwide but also saturated American culture, the effects of which can still be seen today in the popular casual wear of a long-sleeve T-shirt beneath a polo shirt, for example.

Grunge has been hailed by the fashion-forward and myriad magazines as antistyle since its inception. Born of the Seattle music scene of the early 1990's, which produced bands such as Nirvana and Pearl Jam, the grunge movement evolved out of a widespread refusal among these bands and their fan bases to participate in trendy styles of clothing and hair. Instead, these bands wore onstage that which they might wear each day, and being the Pacific Northwest, this included flannel, long-sleeve T-shirts, jeans, and boots. Much of the look established by this musical movement originally meant to symbolize the working-class spirit that focused on music rather than image, but ultimately the image became inseparable from the music. As with many other previous music and fashion trends, "grunge" came to symbolize an entire subculture that would be a defining element of the 1990's.

Aesthetically, the minimalist approach reflected the collective apathy expressed by those at the latter end of Generation X; the appeal of thrift store fare paired with expensive Doc Martens footwear popularized by grunge swept the United States, moving grunge from an alternative movement out of Seattle to a cross-genre popular fashion trend.

Impact Effects of grunge permeated American culture in the larger sense, and one does not have to look far to note the 1990's emphasis on olive and slate colors in home and office decor. Fashion designers such as Calvin Klein exploited grunge themes and incorporated them into clothing lines. More recently, Marc Jacobs's 2004 fall line was touted as "grunge inspired" by many fashion magazines.

Other key influences in this fashion fad include the rebirth of the coffeehouse culture, also established largely in Seattle in the early 1990's. Before Starbucks became ubiquitous, the dark coffeehouse with mismatched chairs and tableware, full of smoking bookworms and hip young professionals, was a staple of Seattle life. The link between the coffeehouse and the grunge music scene culminates in a film such as Cameron Crowe's *Singles* (1992), which chronicles the lives of a group of twentysomethings through the ennui of this cultural moment.

Further Reading

Anderson, Kyle. *Accidental Revolution: The Story of Grunge.* New York: St. Martin's Griffin, 2007.

Lieberman, Rhonda. "Springtime for Grunge." *Artforum International* 31, no. 8 (April, 1993): 8.

Lomas, Clare. *The 80's and 90's: Power Dressing to Sportswear.* Milwaukee, Wis.: Gareth Stevens, 2000.

Christina C. Angel

See also Alternative rock; Coffeehouses; Fads; Fashions and clothing; Grunge music; Heroin chic; Lollapalooza; Nirvana.

■ Grunge music

Definition Alternative rock subgenre inspired by a combination of sounds from heavy metal and punk rock

Grunge music, which originated in the Seattle area, became commercially successful in the early 1990's and quickly became the most popular alternative music of the time. In addition, grunge became the defining music of Generation X, who came of age during this decade.

The term "grunge" was coined by a British journalist to describe the style of music played by a group of bands in the Seattle area in the late 1980's. At the time, the most well-known grunge band was a group called Green River, whose popularity was limited to the Seattle area. Despite the fact that Green River was together for only a few short years, the band released three albums on the record label Sup Pop, a company that would become famous for signing some of the most prominent grunge bands. Green River's style greatly influenced the grunge movement, and, after the band broke up, four of Green River's former members went on to form two other

Selected 1990's Grunge Rock Albums

Year	Album	Band
1990	*Facelift*	Alice in Chains
	Louder than Live	Soundgarden
	Apple	Mother Love Bone
1991	*Badmotorfinger*	Soundgarden
	Every Good Boy Deserves Fudge	Mudhoney
	Nevermind	Nirvana
	Pretty on the Inside	Hole
	Ten	Pearl Jam
	Uncle Anesthesia	Screaming Trees
1992	*Dirt*	Alice in Chains
	Piece of Cake	Mudhoney
	Sweet Oblivion	Screaming Trees
1993	*In Utero*	Nirvana
	Painkillers	Babes in Toyland
	Vs.	Pearl Jam
	World of Noise	Everclear
1994	*Dystopia*	Babes in Toyland
	Jar of Flies	Alice in Chains
	Live Through This	Hole
	MTV Unplugged in New York	Nirvana
	Sixteen Stone	Bush
	Superunknown	Soundgarden
	Vitalogy	Pearl Jam
1995	*Foo Fighters*	Foo Fighters
	My Brother the Cow	Mudhoney
	Sparkle and Fade	Everclear
1996	*Down on the Upside*	Soundgarden
	Dust	Screaming Trees
	No Code	Pearl Jam
	Razorblade Suitcase	Bush
1997	*The Colour and the Shape*	Foo Fighters
	Deconstructed	Bush
	So Much for the Afterglow	Bush
1998	*Celebrity Skin*	Hole
	Yield	Pearl Jam
1999	*There Is Nothing Left to Lose*	Foo Fighters

well-known grunge bands. Stone Gossard and Jeff Ament, after a stint in the short-lived but immensely popular Seattle band Mother Love Bone, made up the core of the band Pearl Jam; Steve Turner and Mark Arm formed a group called Mudhoney.

Grunge Goes Mainstream By the early 1990's, the grunge movement had grown beyond its original geographic boundaries and, seemingly overnight, permeated the popular culture. The band that was largely responsible for propelling grunge music to the forefront of mainstream rock was a group called Nirvana. Led by singer Kurt Cobain, the band formed in 1988 and released its first album, the critically acclaimed *Bleach*, on Sub Pop a year later. It was the album *Nevermind*, however, released in 1991, that would enjoy wide commercial success.

Nevermind's first single, "Smells Like Teen Spirit," peaked at number six on the *Billboard* charts in early 1992 and can be credited with giving grunge music both national and worldwide popularity. More significant than its chart success was the fact that the song and, subsequently, the album, proved to be an anthem to scores of teenagers and young adults, further strengthening grunge music's popularity.

Other Seattle bands would also enjoy mainstream success in the early 1990's. Pearl Jam released its first album, *Ten*, in 1991. By 1992, the album had reached number two on the *Billboard* charts. Pearl Jam had three hit singles from *Ten*: "Alive," "Even Flow," and "Jeremy." Another prominent grunge band was Alice in Chains, whose first album, *Facelift*, was released in 1990. Other Seattle grunge bands that achieved mainstream success in the early 1990's include longtime Seattle mainstays Soundgarden, Temple of the Dog (consisting of members of Soundgarden and Pearl Jam), and the Screaming Trees.

Grunge music was not limited by one particular sound or convention. While the musical style of most grunge musicians was

Eddie Vedder of Pearl Jam performs in 1994 in Chicago. (Hulton Archive/Getty Images)

a combination of punk and heavy metal, there was much variation among bands. For example, Alice in Chains was noted for its driving, distortion-laded heavy metal paired with drug-influenced lyrics, whereas Pearl Jam became famous for its melodic rock and catchy yet cryptic lyrics.

Grunge Culture Grunge musicians rejected expensive, highly staged performances; most would not use pyrotechnics or other complicated lighting and visual effects during their shows. Grunge music eventually became so popular that it even influenced the fashion of the time. Many grunge musicians were known for their unkempt appearance, wearing thrift store clothing and most notably flannel shirts, a look copied by grunge followers and marketed by the fashion industry. Grunge seeped further into the mainstream by providing a backdrop for the Seattle-based movie *Singles* (1992), which featured guest appearances by Soundgarden's Chris Cornell and members of Pearl Jam as bandmates of star Matt Dillon's group Citizen Dick. Consequently, the movie's sound track read like a who's who of the prominent grunge musicians of the day.

Despite their huge success, many grunge musicians were uncomfortable with their mainstream popularity. Accustomed to recording for small, independent record labels and playing to relatively small crowds, they were not used to dealing with the national recording industry or performing in stadium-like atmospheres. Nirvana's front man Kurt Cobain provides the most notable example of the difficulties grunge musicians had with their success. Cobain suffered from serious drug addiction and, as a result of this and complications from the pressures he felt from his status as an icon of the grunge movement, eventually committed suicide. His death on April 5, 1994, is often cited as the end of the grunge era.

Impact While the popularity of grunge music was primarily limited to the early 1990's, its influence would continue through the rest of the decade and into the next. Bands like Pearl Jam had long been experimenting with different musical styles that moved them beyond the constraints of the subgenre. In addition, Nirvana's drummer, Dave Grohl, following Cobain's death and the subsequent dissolution of the band, formed a group called the Foo Fighters, whose sound, while markedly different from Nirvana's, was significantly influenced by grunge. Other post-grunge bands included Bush and Candlebox.

Further Reading

Anderson, Kyle. *Accidental Revolution: The Story of Grunge.* New York: St. Martin's Griffin, 2007. Provides a history of grunge music in the 1990's, from its origins in Seattle to its mainstream popularity.

True, Everett. *Live Through This: American Rock Music in the Nineties.* London: Virgin Books, 2001. Presents a history of grunge music in the 1990's based on interviews from some of the movement's most prominent bands such as Soundgarden, Hole, and Nirvana.

_______. *Nirvana: The Biography.* Cambridge, Mass.: Da Capo Press, 2007. Describes the history of the band Nirvana while concentrating on the life of Cobain.

Lindsay Schmitz

See also Alternative rock; Grunge fashion; Lollapalooza; Love, Courtney; Music; Nirvana.

■ Gulf War

The Event After Iraq invades and occupies Kuwait, a thirty-four-nation coalition of military forces responds by attacking the Iraqi army, driving it out of Kuwait

Date January 17-February 28, 1991

Place The Persian Gulf, the waterway linking Iraq, Iran, Kuwait, and several other countries with the Arabian Sea

Iraqi aggression against Kuwait and Saudi Arabia was stopped, thereby preventing Iraqi president Saddam Hussein from controlling most of the world's known oil reserves.

When the modern Iraqi state was established after World War I, Kuwait was created as a separate state, although historically the two countries had been governed together from the capital in Baghdad. During the spring of 1990, Iraq presented demands on Kuwait and opened negotiations with the country, while massing troops along the southern border with Kuwait, presumably poised for an offensive to settle such disputes as the location of the border between the two countries.

As Iraqi troops were moving south toward Kuwait, American ambassador April Glaspie was summoned by Iraqi president Saddam Hussein on July 25, 1990, to inform her of Iraq's grievances with Kuwait and of his promise to resolve the issues peacefully. After expressing concern over the threat posed by the troop movements, she indicated that the United States was neutral toward disputes between Arab-speaking countries.

Subsequently, during a congressional hearing, an assistant secretary of state reported that there were no contingency plans to repel an attack by Iraq on Kuwait, as the United States had no military alliance with either country. Baghdad interpreted American disinterest as a green light for Iraq to annex Kuwait.

Iraq's Attack and the Immediate Response On August 2, a full-scale Iraqi attack was launched on Kuwait, whereupon Washington summoned the U.N. Security Council for an emergency meeting that resulted in a resolution calling on Iraq to withdraw. Four days later, as Iraq took control of Kuwait, the Security Council authorized economic sanctions. On

Members of the U.S. Army's 101st Airborne Division take position in Iraq on February 25, 1991. (AP/Wide World Photos)

August 7, the United States dispatched two aircraft carriers and two battleship groups to the Persian Gulf and, on the pretext that Iraq might also invade Saudi Arabia, airlifted troops to the latter country.

With American backing, the Security Council on November 29 demanded that Iraq withdraw from Kuwait by January 15, 1991. To enforce the resolution, the Security Council authorized the use of force. U.S. president George H. W. Bush and Secretary of State James Baker then persuaded thirty-four other countries to form a coalition to drive Iraqi forces from Kuwait. Although all were aware that Iraq had violated the U.N. Charter by waging aggressive war, some countries were attracted to join the coalition by American promises of aid or debt forgiveness.

Differing peace proposals were offered. Whereas the United States demanded that Iraq unconditionally withdraw from Kuwait, Baghdad offered to pull out of Kuwait only if Syrian troops pulled out of Lebanon and Israeli troops abandoned the Gaza Strip, the Golan Heights, and the Palestinian West Bank. Iraq's terms were rejected. On January 12, 1991, Congress authorized Bush to wage war on Iraq despite sizeable votes against the operation.

The War Code-named Operation Desert Storm, some 660,000 troops were ultimately mobilized to attack Iraq on January 17, 1991; the American portion was about 74 percent. The initial offensive consisted of aerial attacks on Iraq's border with Saudi Arabia and in western Iraq, followed by a bombardment of Baghdad. The initial aim was to destroy the Iraqi air force; next, bombing sought to disrupt command communications. Later, the remaining military targets and relevant infrastructure were bombed.

Iraq responded with ineffective antiaircraft fire, attempted to send airplanes and naval forces to Iran, dumped oil into the Persian Gulf, attacked a town inside Saudi Arabia and was easily repelled, and launched missiles at Israel, which shot them down but otherwise refrained from involvement in the war. Thanks to American air supremacy, coalition ground forces decisively entered Kuwait in late January. The war was extensively covered around the clock on the Cable News Network (CNN), including live reporting of flashes of light from bombardments and the launching of artillery.

On February 2, Iraq accepted a cease-fire agreement proposed by Russia. The terms involved a withdrawal of Iraqi troops to preinvasion positions within three weeks, followed by a total cease-fire and U.N. Security Council monitoring of the cease-fire and withdrawal. The United States rejected the proposal, demanding that Iraq exit from Kuwait within twenty-four hours, during which time the coalition would not attack Iraqi troops.

Since negotiations were deadlocked, American, British, and French forces attacked inside Iraq, exposing the vulnerability of Hussein's military defenses. On February 26, Iraqi troops began to leave Kuwait, setting fire to oil fields as they exited, but coalition forces bombed the retreating columns up to 150 miles south of Baghdad. On February 27, President Bush declared that the war was over, that Kuwait had been liberated.

After Iraq surrendered, Baghdad was allowed to use armed helicopters to assist in rebuilding damaged transportation infrastructure that was being used by retreating forces. From March 10, coalition troops began to withdraw from Iraq, some staying in Kuwait and in Saudi Arabia to ensure security against future Iraq aggression.

Aftermath On February 2, a radio station in Saudi Arabia operated by the Central Intelligence Agency (CIA) called on Shiites to rebel inside Iraq. Similar statements encouraged Kurds in the north to try to topple Hussein. However, when the rebellions occurred after Hussein surrendered, Iraq's helicopters gunned down the rebels, and American forces did nothing in support.

The Security Council responded to massacres of Kurds and Shiites by establishing no-fly zones over northern and southern Iraq, respectively, to be enforced by American, British, and French military aircraft. Nevertheless, Hussein's antiaircraft and surface-to-air missiles challenged the enforcement, resulting in frequent sorties thereafter to bomb both types of installations. In a sense, the Gulf War did not end in 1991 but continued right up to 2003.

Iraq's remaining air force was also used to suppress rebellions between the two no-fly zones. Although some Saudi officials urged that the no-fly zone be extended over the entire country in order to facilitate those seeking to overthrow Hussein, their suggestion was ignored during the rest of the 1990's.

A U.N. Special Commission (UNSCOM) was assigned to inspect Iraq's compliance with a Security Council order to dismantle all weapons of mass destruction. In 1999, UNSCOM left Iraq, which claimed

Gulf War Cease-Fire Is Announced

On February 27, 1991, President George H. W. Bush announced the end of the Gulf War. The address was broadcast live on nationwide radio and television:

Kuwait is liberated. Iraq's army is defeated. Our military objectives are met. Kuwait is once more in the hands of Kuwaitis, in control of their own destiny. We share in their joy, a joy tempered only by our compassion for their ordeal. . . .

Seven months ago, America and the world drew a line in the sand. We declared that the aggression against Kuwait would not stand. And tonight, America and the world have kept their word.

This is not a time of euphoria, certainly not a time to gloat. But it is a time of pride: pride in our troops; pride in the friends who stood with us in the crisis; pride in our nation and the people whose strength and resolve made victory quick, decisive, and just. And soon we will open wide our arms to welcome back home to America our magnificent fighting forces.

No one country can claim this victory as its own. It was not only a victory for Kuwait but a victory for all the coalition partners. This is a victory for the United Nations, for all mankind, for the rule of law, and for what is right.

After consulting with Secretary of Defense [Dick] Cheney, the Chairman of the Joint Chiefs of Staff, General [Colin] Powell, and our coalition partners, I am pleased to announce that at midnight tonight eastern standard time, exactly 100 hours since ground operations commenced and 6 weeks since the start of Desert Storm, all United States and coalition forces will suspend offensive combat operations. It is up to Iraq whether this suspension on the part of the coalition becomes a permanent cease-fire. . . .

This suspension of offensive combat operations is contingent upon Iraq's not firing upon any coalition forces and not launching Scud missiles against any other country. If Iraq violates these terms, coalition forces will be free to resume military operations.

At every opportunity, I have said to the people of Iraq that our quarrel was not with them but instead with their leadership and, above all, with Saddam Hussein. This remains the case. You, the people of Iraq, are not our enemy. We do not seek your destruction. We have treated your POW's with kindness. Coalition forces fought this war only as a last resort and look forward to the day when Iraq is led by people prepared to live in peace with their neighbors. . . .

This war is now behind us. Ahead of us is the difficult task of securing a potentially historic peace. Tonight though, let us be proud of what we have accomplished. Let us give thanks to those who risked their lives. Let us never forget those who gave their lives. May God bless our valiant military forces and their families, and let us all remember them in our prayers.

that all such programs had been dismantled. The Security Council then authorized the replacement of UNSCOM with the U.N. Monitoring, Verification and Inspection Commission (UNMOVIC), which did not begin work in Iraq until 2002, when the United States claimed that weapons of mass destruction remaining in the country constituted a serious threat.

When casualty numbers for the war were assessed, some 146 Americans had died in battle, and 467 had been wounded. Other members of the coalition had lost 65 soldiers, and 319 had been wounded. However, more than 25 percent of the ground troops were declared permanently disabled by the Department of Veterans Affairs, suffering from unknown causes that have been characterized as the Gulf War syndrome. Estimates of Iraq casualties differ; there were at least 24,000 deaths, including 4,000 civilians.

The conduct of the war, including the use of cluster bombs and daisy cutters as well as the number of civilian deaths, prompted some observers to accuse the United States of committing war crimes. In 2003, a war crimes case based on the Gulf War was filed in a Belgian court against former president Bush, former secretary of defense Dick Cheney, former Joint

Chiefs of Staff chair Colin Powell, and former commander in chief Norman Schwarzkopf. Later in the year, after the United States threatened to move headquarters of the North Atlantic Treaty Organization (NATO) from Belgium to protest the case and similar pending lawsuits, the case was dismissed.

Impact Constrained by economic sanctions and two no-fly zones, living conditions in Iraq nosedived while Kuwait enjoyed increasing prosperity. Economic sanctions remained on Iraq despite the devastation of its infrastructure. Insufficient food and medicine were available for ordinary people, so the United Nations agreed to establish an oil-for-food program, which ultimately involved kickbacks to Hussein. United Nations corruption, as later reviewed, led to calls for reform of the organization, especially by officials in the administration of President George W. Bush.

Meanwhile, the presence of American troops remaining in Saudi Arabia after the war rankled some in the region. One in particular, Osama Bin Laden, began to build support for his organization, al-Qaeda, which was dedicated to the removal of the American military presence in the Middle East and to the toppling of Western-backed governments in Arab-speaking countries that he characterized as "apostate" regimes. Al-Qaeda's policies and program were subsequently revealed by bombings of American embassies in Kenya and Tanzania in 1998, the assault on the USS *Cole* in the Yemen harbor in 2000, and the terrorist attacks on American soil on September 11, 2001.

Some American observers, who regretted the failure to topple Hussein in 1991, urged a second war with Iraq, especially after the terrorist attacks on September 11, 2001. The second war against Iraq began on March 20, 2003.

Further Reading

Blum, William. *Killing Hope: U.S. Military and CIA Interventions Since World War II.* Monroe, Maine: Common Courage Press, 2005. Written by a former employee of the U.S. Department of State, the book condemns American foreign adventures, often kept secret, on a country-by-country basis, including those involving Iraq.

Brune, Lester H. *America and the Iraqi Crisis, 1990-1992.* Claremont, Calif.: Regina Books, 1993. A historical account that examines the policy choices, including criticisms of Bush's concept of a "new world order" in which the United States might play a dominant world role as the world's only superpower.

Bush, George H. W., and Brent Scowcroft. *A World Transformed.* New York: Random House, 1998. The former president and his national security adviser present an account of the foreign policy of the United States under their leadership, including a detailed justification for their decision not to topple Hussein in 1991, when American troops were only hours away from Baghdad. The authors argue that most countries in the Gulf War coalition would have refused to go along and that the economic and human cost of extending the war would have been excessive.

Hilsman, Roger. *George Bush vs. Saddam Hussein: Military Success! Political Failure?* Novato, Calif.: Presidio, 1992. A former Department of State official analyzes whether the Gulf War achieved the political objective of stabilizing the Middle East.

Munro, Alan. *Arab Storm: Politics and Diplomacy Behind the Gulf War.* New York: I. B. Tauris, 2006. The British ambassador to Saudi Arabia before and during the Gulf War, Munro provides an account of the various diplomatic efforts to organize the military coalition that evicted Iraq from Kuwait.

Nye, Joseph S., Jr., and Roger K. Smith, eds. *After the Storm: Lessons from the Gulf War.* Lanham, Md.: Madison Books, 1992. A collection of ten essays commenting on the successes and failures of the war in the context of diplomatic, economic, political, regional, and strategic international affairs.

Renshon, Stanley A., ed. *The Political Psychology of the Gulf War: Leaders, Publics, and the Process of Conflict.* Pittsburgh: University of Pittsburgh Press, 1993. Covers psychological aspects of the decision to go to war, focusing on Bush's punitive attitudes while Hussein was seeking to appear as a stronger leader in the Middle East than his rivals, groupthink driving decision makers to go to war, and the public's willingness to trust their president's judgment despite serious misgivings in Congress.

Sifry, Micah L., and Christopher Cerf, eds. *The Gulf War Reader: History, Documents, Opinion.* New York: Times Books, 1991. A balanced compilation of relevant essays, official publications, and editorials about the Gulf War.

Smith, Jean Edward. *George Bush's War.* New York: Henry Holt, 1992. Argues why Hussein was a hero in the Middle East and how Bush rallied support for the war.

Michael Haas

See also Baker, James; Bush, George H. W.; Cheney, Dick; CNN coverage of the Gulf War; Foreign policy of Canada; Foreign policy of the United States; Gulf War syndrome; Middle East and North America; Patriot missile; Powell, Colin; Schwarzkopf, Norman; Speicher, Michael Scott; United Nations; Wolfowitz, Paul.

■ Gulf War syndrome

Definition A cluster of illnesses associated with military service in the Gulf War of 1991

A group of physical and mental disorders among Gulf War veterans created a political furor in the 1990's. Despite numerous studies, no common cause has been identified, and a majority of experts deny that Gulf War syndrome is a distinct illness.

The Gulf War of 1991 was unusual among wars in its short duration and the small percentage of the 660,000 deployed American military personnel who experienced actual combat. About a year after the war ended, veterans' clinics began reporting demobilized soldiers with a cluster of chronic debilitating physical symptoms including fatigue, headache, muscle and joint pain, skin rashes, chest pain, and diarrhea, plus psychological symptoms including sleeplessness and depression. There were also reports of elevated birth defects among demobilized military and their spouses. A series of articles in *The Washington Post* in July, 1994, called public attention to the problem and spurred Congress to pass a law providing special compensation for Gulf War veterans disabled by unexplained illnesses.

Various causes have been postulated for Gulf War syndrome, including Iraqi biological warfare agents, pesticides, American depleted-uranium weapons, chemical agents released when Iraqi stores were bombed, endemic infectious diseases, pollution from oil well fires, exposure to petroleum products, vaccines for anthrax and botulism, and pyrostigmine bromide, used to counteract nerve gas. Numerous studies by government and independent investigators have concluded that none of these can alone account for more than a small fraction of the reported health problems. However, pyrostigmine and pesticides have synergistic effects, and multiple simultaneously administered vaccines, some experimental, could well cause problems. Actual exposures to pesticides, chemical weapons, and depleted-uranium residues may have been higher than the levels the studies found harmless. Since effects of carcinogens can take decades to manifest themselves, the true scope of Gulf War-associated illnesses may still be unknown.

Some of the reported symptoms resemble stress-related combat fatigue or post-traumatic stress disorder (PTSD), but this is an unlikely primary cause in view of the short duration of the war and the small percentage of soldiers directly exposed to combat.

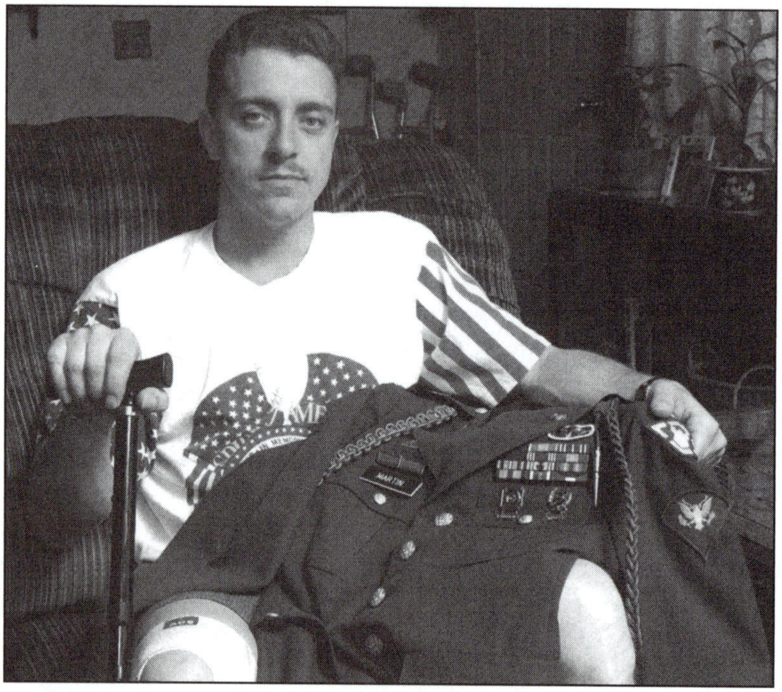

Gulf War veteran Brian Martin suffered from a number of maladies that he attributed to exposure to toxic substances during the war. (AP/Wide World Photos)

Impact Comparison of deployed American soldiers with those who stayed home indicated no statistical difference in incidence of Gulf War syndrome, whereas illness rates were much lower among British soldiers who served in Iraq. Some people view Gulf War syndrome as a political creation designed to discredit Republicans. However, most of the affected veterans have genuine physical illnesses not common in previous wars or among civilians, suggesting that one or more of the health hazards enumerated above, or one not yet identified, is indeed responsible.

Further Reading

Fulco, Carolyn E., Catharyn T. Liverman, and Harold C. Sox, eds. Institute of Medicine. Committee on Health Effects Associated with Exposures During the Gulf War. *Gulf War and Health.* 5 vols. Washington, D.C.: National Academy Press, 2000-2005.

Hyams, Kenneth C., Stephen Wignall, and Robert Roswell. "War Syndromes and Their Evaluation: From the U.S. Civil War to the Persian Gulf War." *Annals of Internal Medicine* 125, no. 5 (1996): 398-405.

Rosof, Bernard M., and Lyla M. Hernandez, eds. *Gulf War Veterans: Treating Symptoms and Syndromes.* Washington, D.C.: National Academy Press, 2001.

Martha Sherwood

See also Gulf War; Health care.

■ Gun control

Definition Regulation of the selling, possession, and use of firearms

President Bill Clinton's administration sought to enact tough federal gun control legislation, but a powerful pro-gun lobby proved a formidable opponent during Clinton's tenure.

Although Republican presidential candidate George H. W. Bush had run on a strongly pro-Second Amendment platform in 1988, with an endorsement from the National Rifle Association (NRA), President Bush in early 1989 had become a gun control advocate. He banned the importation of "assault weapons" (military-style self-loading rifles, shotguns, and pistols). In 1991, he said he would support the Brady bill, which included a waiting period provision for handgun purchases, but only if it was accompanied by a law allowing courtroom use of gun-related evidence that had been seized in violation of the Fourth Amendment. The bill was named for James S. Brady, press secretary to President Ronald Reagan who was shot and subsequently paralyzed during an assassination attempt on the president by John Hinckley, Jr., in 1981. In 1990-1992, all but a few states rejected efforts to pass assault weapons bans or handgun waiting periods; state inaction hindered the push for federal laws.

The Early Clinton Administration While Bush's support for gun control had been sporadic, gun control was a priority under Bill Clinton's administration. The Bureau of Alcohol, Tobacco, and Firearms (ATF) aggressively used regulatory and enforcement powers on a broad front. By the end of the decade, the ATF had reduced the number of federally licensed firearms dealers by approximately 70 percent.

In 1993, Congress passed the Brady bill, signed into law as the Brady Handgun Violence Prevention Act, which went into effect the next February. The act established a waiting period of five government working days for handgun sales, during which local police would conduct a background check of handgun buyers. The law applied to the twenty-eight states that did not already have a background-check provision.

Thanks to NRA efforts, the act's handgun waiting period provision would be replaced in 1998 by the National Instant Check System (NICS). Under NICS, retail purchasers of handguns or long guns in all fifty states must undergo a computerized "instant check" of criminal and other records. The check is conducted by a state agency or by the Federal Bureau of Investigation (FBI), depending on the state. In practice, the background check sometimes takes minutes but can often take hours.

In August, 1994, after intense struggle, Congress passed the Violent Crime Control and Law Enforcement Act, a comprehensive anticrime law that included many gun control provisions, most notably one about which congressional Democratic leaders had privately warned President Clinton: a ban on the possession or sale of new assault weapons and of magazines holding more than ten rounds. Also in 1994, eleven states enacted restrictions or bans on juvenile gun or handgun possession, joining the eighteen states that already had such laws.

The midterm elections of that year resulted in the greatest Republican sweep in decades. In December, President Clinton blamed the Republicans' success on the assault weapons issue, declaring that "the NRA is the reason the Republicans control the House."

Mid-decade The Republican landslide also affected the states. The next year saw state after state enacting a cornucopia of pro-gun laws. State "preemption" laws eliminated municipal or county gun controls. "Instant check" laws exempted states from the Brady Handgun Violence Prevention Act and sometimes eliminated waiting periods that had previously existed in state law.

Most significant, state "shall-issue" laws required that permits to carry defensive handguns in public places be issued to all adult applicants who passed a background check and a safety class. During the 1990's, shall-issue laws went from being the exception to being the norm. On the federal level, the progun majorities in Congress knew that they could not overcome a presidential veto, so there was little congressional action. President Clinton continued to use the executive branch to push for gun control, such as an administrative order banning the import of scores of types of firearms.

In 1997, a 5-4 Supreme Court decision in *Printz v. United States* declared part of the Brady Act unconstitutional, holding that Congress could not order state and local officials to carry out background checks.

In 1998, nearly five years after the Brady Handgun Violence Prevention Act was signed into law, President Bill Clinton (adjusting microphone) and James Brady call on Congress to extend the law. (AP/Wide World Photos)

The Final Clinton Years Stymied in Congress and in all but a few state legislatures, the nation's leading gun control organization, Handgun Control, Inc. (HCI), convinced several big-city mayors to sue handgun manufacturers, under the theory that the manufacturers were legally responsible for handgun crimes. Chicago and New Orleans sued in November, 1998, and within a few months several dozen cities had filed similar cases, with the support of the Department of Housing and Urban Development, headed by Andrew Cuomo.

The Columbine High School massacre on April 20, 1999, near Littleton, Colorado, seemed to provide antigun forces with their greatest opportunity yet, but relatively little gun control legislation resulted. However, the tragedy did cause many schools to abolish shooting sports programs; it also led to more restrictions on gun possession by young people and to enactment of California's purchase limit of one handgun per month.

Impact During the 1990's, the gun control debate became more prominent in American politics than at any previous time in U.S. history. In only a few states (most notably California, New Jersey, and Maryland) were gun control laws significantly stricter at the end of the decade than before. In most of the rest of the country, gun purchasers were now subject to NICS, but some other restrictions had been removed. Reversing a gun control trend of several decades, the shall-issue laws of the 1990's reestablished the social and legal legitimacy of carrying concealed handguns in public.

Subsequent Events President Clinton credited the NRA with providing the crucial margin in George W. Bush's victory over Al Gore in the 2000 presidential election. The gun issue appeared to have accounted for Bush's narrow wins in Missouri, Arkansas, Tennessee, West Virginia, and Florida. The federal assault weapons ban expired in September, 2004. The large majority of states, as well as Congress, enacted legislation to prohibit municipal antigun lawsuits.

Further Reading

Bijlefeld, Marjolijn. *People For and Against Gun Control: A Biographical Reference.* Westport, Conn.: Greenwood Press, 1999. Fair and sympathetic biographies of leaders in the gun debate.

Kleck, Gary. *Targeting Guns: Firearms and Their Control.* New York: Aldine, 1997. Superb analysis of the subject by a renowned criminologist.

LaPierre, Wayne. *Guns, Crime, and Freedom.* Washington, D.C.: Regnery, 1995. The author, who has served as executive vice president and chief executive officer of the NRA, makes the pro-gun case in the first gun policy book ever to make the best seller lists.

Simkin, Jay, Aaron S. Zelman, and Alan M. Rice. *Lethal Laws: "Gun Control" Is the Key to Genocide.* Milwaukee: Jews for the Preservation of Firearms Ownership, 1994. Influential analysis of twentieth century genocides. Cited by former House Speaker Newt Gingrich.

Utter, Glenn H. *Encyclopedia of Gun Control and Gun Rights.* Phoenix, Ariz.: Oryx Press, 1999. A competent survey of the subject as it existed in the late 1990's.

Weir, William. *A Well Regulated Militia: The Battle over Gun Control.* North Haven, Conn.: Archon Books, 1997. The constitutional theories of the gun control lobby.

David B. Kopel

See also Bush, George H. W.; Carjacking; Clinton, Bill; Clinton, Hillary Rodham; Columbine massacre; Crime; Drive-by shootings; Elections in the United States, midterm; Ferguson, Colin; Gore, Al; Militia movement; Oklahoma City bombing; Reno, Janet; Republican Revolution; Waco siege.

Hackers

Definition People who use programming skills to gain unauthorized access into computer systems, usually for malicious purposes

The introduction of personal computers and computer networks in the 1980's invited attacks by a number of hackers. By the 1990's, these attacks had alarmed those in government, law enforcement, and the general public to such an extent that some of the hackers were prosecuted and incarcerated.

Humankind devised ways of misusing or damaging the resources of others long before the invention of computers and networks. One of the earliest misuses of technology was the phreaking attacks by John Draper, nicknamed "Captain Crunch," and others in the 1970's. They devised methods of simulating a long-distance telephone signal and were able to make free long-distance phone calls. In 1972, Draper was one of the first technology abusers to be successfully prosecuted. In 1980, a group called the 414s, who took their name from the Milwaukee area code, executed one of the earliest attacks on a computer. They used personal computers with modems to break into a number of mainframes. The attacks were simple, including guessing passwords, but were among the first computer break-ins.

Viruses and Worms A virus is a self-replicating code that spreads by inserting copies of itself into programs or other files. A worm is a self-replicating program that spreads by sending copies of itself to other computers on a network. In addition to replication, viruses and worms damage the computers they are stored on by deleting files, slowing computation, or other actions. In the late 1980's and early 1990's, a number of viruses and worms were introduced. The Morris worm flooded ARPANET (the precursor to the Internet) in 1988, becoming one of the first denial-of-service attacks. In 1991, the Michelangelo virus was discovered on a computer in New Zealand. It was a boot sector virus aimed at MS-DOS and designed to attack computers on the Renaissance artist's birthday. Many predicted that the Michelangelo virus would do great damage, but effective countermeasures were developed that limited its effect.

In 1995, the first macro virus, called WM.Concept, was developed. While it was not a serious threat, the Melissa macro virus that appeared in 1999 was. When a user opened an infected file, Melissa attempted to e-mail a copy of the virus to fifty other people using the Microsoft Outlook address book. In May, 2000, the ILOVEYOU worm appeared and began spreading around the world. It infected graphics files on a computer and spread by causing copies of itself to be sent to everyone in an infected computer's address book. While Melissa and ILOVEYOU created havoc for computer users in the late 1990's, antivirus vendors developed effective countermeasures to these and other viruses and worms that appeared during this period.

The Two Kevins While there were many hackers at work during the 1990's, the most famous were Kevin Mitnick and Kevin Poulsen. In 1989, Kevin Mitnick (who had earlier been arrested for phreaking) was convicted and placed on probation for monitoring the e-mails of workers at Digital Equipment Corporation (DEC). He continued to hack computers and by 1992 was on the run after his probation was revoked. In 1994, he attacked the computer of Tsutomu Shimomura. Shimomura, a very capable computer security expert, helped the Federal Bureau of Investigation (FBI) find Mitnick in North Carolina in 1995. Mitnick pleaded guilty to hacking and served almost five years in prison. He was released in 2000 and has become a computer security expert, specializing in preventing social-engineering attacks.

Poulsen, nicknamed "Dark Dante," specialized in hacking government and military systems. In 1989, he was charged with a number of attacks and went into hiding. He continued to hack computers, often

Birth of a Social Engineer

In his 2002 book The Art of Deception: Controlling the Human Element of Security *(coauthored with William L. Simon), Kevin Mitnick describes how he got his start on the road to computer hacking:*

My first encounter with what I would eventually learn to call *social engineering* came about during my high school years when I met another student who was caught up in a hobby called *phone phreaking.* Phone phreaking is a type of hacking that allows you to explore the telephone network by exploiting the phone systems and phone company employees. He showed me neat tricks he could do with a telephone, like obtaining any information the phone company had on any customer, and using a secret test number to make long-distance calls for free. (Actually it was free only to us. I found out much later that it wasn't a secret test number at all. The calls were, in fact, being billed to some poor company's MCI account.)

That was my introduction to social engineering—my kindergarten, so to speak. My friend and another phone phreaker I met shortly thereafter let me listen in as they each made *pretext* calls to the phone company. I heard the things they said that made them sound believable; I learned about different phone company offices, lingo, and procedures. But that "training" didn't last long; it didn't have to. Soon I was doing it all on my own, learning as I went, doing it even better than my first teachers.

The course my life would follow for the next fifteen years had been set.

using phone technology. In 1994, he was caught and pleaded guilty to a number of computer crimes. He served almost four years in prison and was barred from using computers for three years after his release. He later became a journalist, writing about computer security, among other things.

Social Engineering and Trojan Horses In social engineering, a hacker uses deception to gain information that can be used to compromise the security of a computer or network. A Trojan horse is a program designed to appear to be doing one thing (such as searching the Internet for information) but that actually does something else (such as searching a computer's cookies for a credit card number). A Trojan horse is often introduced into a system by social engineering. For example, a Trojan horse can be installed by requesting a user to click a link in an e-mail or Web page. It is interesting that some of the earliest attacks by Mitnick and Poulsen were through social engineering, and that many of today's worst attacks are perpetrated by Trojan horses, installed by social engineering.

There were numerous Trojan horses in the 1990's. Some of the most interesting Trojans were programs that appeared to be remote administration tools for Microsoft Windows 98. The same technology that could be used for remote administration of Windows was perfect for a Trojan horse that could take information from a user's computer, while being controlled remotely. ProRAT (Professional Remote Administration Tool) and Back Orifice (developed by Josh Buchbinder, better known as Sir Dystic of the Cult of the Dead Cow) were two remote administration tools that had Trojan horse versions.

Impact During the 1990's, hackers attacked a number of important computer systems. As a result of their success, government, industry, and individual computer users realized that securing their computers and computer networks was extremely important. Society ceased thinking of hackers as misguided enthusiasts and began to treat them as criminals.

Further Reading

Baase, Sara. *A Gift of Fire: Social, Legal, and Ethical Issues for Computing and the Internet.* 3d ed. Upper Saddle River, N.J.: Prentice Hall, 2007. A well-written book that covers cyber security, privacy, and law.

Mitnick, Kevin D., and William L. Simon. *The Art of Intrusion: The Real Stories Behind the Exploits of Hackers, Intruders, and Deceivers.* New York: John Wiley & Sons, 2005. Another book by Mitnick describing hacking from the viewpoint of a real hacker.

Mitnick, Kevin D., William L. Simon, and Steve

Wozniak. *The Art of Deception: Controlling the Human Element of Security.* New York: John Wiley & Sons, 2002. A book whose primary author, Mitnick, is one of the most famous hackers of all time.

Ralston, Anthony, Edwin D. Reilly, and David Hemmendinger, eds. *Encyclopedia of Computer Science.* New York: John Wiley & Sons, 2003. This text is one of the standard reference works in its field. The fourth edition has very accurate articles covering all areas in and related to computers, including many articles on computers security.

George M. Whitson III

See also Apple Computer; CGI; Computers; DVDs; E-mail; Instant messaging; Internet; Michelangelo computer virus; Microsoft; MP3 format; PDAs; Silicon Valley; Spam; World Wide Web; Y2K problem.

■ Hairstyles

Definition Popular styles or manners of arranging the hair

The 1990's saw a return to natural and low-maintenance hairstyles for both men and women.

During the 1990's, African American women wore popular 1960's hairstyles, like the bob and the beehive; Caucasian women cut their Farrah Fawcett styles into shorter styles; and African American and Caucasian men cropped, spiked, or flat-topped theirs. In the early 1990's, the "Kimberly crop," named for the actress Kimberly Foster of the prime-time soap opera *Dallas,* was trendy among white women. The early 1990's also witnessed a popular resurgence of hard rollers, the kind that do not use electricity; their rise in popularity accompanied the return to natural hair, not processed by harsh chemicals and heat. Cornrows, offered in the Caribbean to tourists, saw a revival during those first years of the decade.

African American women, who had long struggled with "nappy" hairstyles that required hours of preparation and treatment, dismissed texturizers, Jheri curls, and perms in favor of close crops, natural waves, and braids. Beehives, Afros, and French twists were also popular natural alternatives. The year 1992 also witnessed the rise of the grunge subculture, with its accompanying dyed-black, long, stringy hairstyle for both girls and boys. The grunge and goth styles were generally popular for white people, particularly those under age twenty-five.

1993-1995 As the decade progressed, many women of all ethnicities refused to cut their long hair short, a trend that one reporter called "Rapunzel worship," or the popular belief that a woman's hair is her crown of glory. In 1993, computers helped men and women "try on" a hairstyle before a cut: Software programs used pictures of clients' faces to display images of trendy cuts. Newspapers across the country kept tabs on First Lady Hillary Rodham Clinton's hairstyles. By 1994, stylists and their clients were ready to express imagination with their hairstyles, such as creative updos. For black women's hair, one new style dictated short or shaved, like black recording artist Me'Shell Ndegeocello's buzz cut.

By mid-decade, men's unorthodox hairstyles began to draw more media attention, particularly when the hairstyle was long or of an unnatural color. As men's hair lengthened, young women, inspired by the actresses on the hit television show *Beverly Hills, 90210,* cut their long locks shorter. Young women and girls began coloring pieces of their hair, known as "chunks" or "streaks," in primary or neon colors or wearing similar hair pieces, spawning a ripple of middle and high school rules against such behaviors. Because hairstyles received coverage on television, African Americans such as talk-show host Oprah Winfrey were able to dispel many long-standing myths about black hair, including why black men and women do not wash their hair daily, which relates to hair health, not hygiene.

1996-1999 In 1996, with long hair for men and short hair for women in vogue, high-profile men and women began to wear their hair however they wanted, inspiring the nation to do the same. There were, as usual, hair trends, but for the most part Americans felt free to do what they wanted. The previous decades witnessed job instability and public scrutiny concerning extraordinary hairstyles, but as the public's knowledge about different hairstyles and textures increased, so did acceptance. "The Rachel," a hairstyle popularized by Jennifer Aniston's character Rachel Green on the television show *Friends,* encouraged women to grow their hair and layer it. Other celebrities who influenced hairstyles of the late 1990's include Halle Berry, George

Clooney, Michael Jordan, Joan Lunden, Madonna, Sinéad O'Connor, and David Schwimmer. Sports figures such as Mac Cozier and Cobi Jones sported dreadlocks; the style was popular mostly for black hair, but "dreads" also found their way into white men's and women's tresses.

When Michael Jordan went bald in 1997, he started a hairstyle trend for men unlike any America had ever seen. Perhaps the low-maintenance bald look for men encouraged renewed interest in the messy updo for women, who could simply collect their hair into a scrunchie, a cloth-covered rubber band, letting wisps of it dangle around their faces. The messy updo was also partly political: Appearing to spend less time on hair implied that these women spent time on more important things. Just after President Bill Clinton's impeachment trial, Hillary sported a new, chic hairstyle, which a watching nation attributed to her need for refinement after the Monica Lewinsky scandal.

Impact The "Less is more" attitude of the 1990's held true for the decade's hairstyles. The big hairstyles of the 1980's were no longer in vogue, and there was a return to natural hair. Celebrity-influenced hair trends continued, the most notable of which was "the Rachel."

Further Reading

Jones, Lisa. *Bulletproof Diva: Tales of Race, Sex, and Hair.* New York: Doubleday, 1994. Anthology of essays that explore the 1990's multicultural woman and her politicized fashion messages.

McCracken, Grant. *Big Hair: A Journey into the Transformation of Self.* Woodstock, N.Y.: Overlook Press, 1996. Traces hairstyles, mostly women's, through history, offers scientific information about hair, and connects the biology of hair to hair's pop culture prestige.

Mancuso, Kevin. *The Mane Thing.* Boston: Little, Brown, 1999. Composed of illustrations of hairstyle trends of the 1990's, as well as hair-care tips mostly for women, this collection surveys hairstyles across American culture.

Sherrow, Victoria. *Encyclopedia of Hair: A Cultural History.* Westport, Conn.: Greenwood Press, 2006. Anthology offering myriad essays detailing American hairstyles' history, trends, and cultural meanings.

Ami R. Blue

See also African Americans; *Beverly Hills, 90210*; Boy bands; Clinton, Hillary Rodham; Clooney, George; Fads; Fashions and clothing; *Friends*; Generation Y; Grunge fashion; Jordan, Michael; Madonna.

■ Haiti intervention

The Event The United States intervenes in Haiti in order to remove the military junta and restore democratic institutions

Date U.S. troops arrived September 19, 1994

The military intervention led by the United States in Haiti was a response to the ongoing terror regime established by General Raoul Cédras and his military junta, which ousted democratically elected Jean-Bertrand Aristide in September, 1991.

Between 1991 and 1994, General Raoul Cédras's military junta conducted a campaign of killing and torture of people who were believed to be opposed to the government, leading to an exodus by Haitians seeking asylum in the United States. The overwhelming influx of Haitians into the United States, along with other strategic reasons, led U.S. president Bill Clinton to push for a forced military intervention in Haiti in 1994.

Haiti's history is one of political instability and conflicts. The country was the second nation in the Americas to become independent, in 1804, and the only nation to be established by a successful slave rebellion. Since the country's independence, the political struggles have led to a number of autocratic regimes, including the rule of François "Papa Doc" Duvalier (1957-1971) and his son Jean-Claude "Baby Doc" Duvalier (1971-1986). In 1990, Jean-Bertrand Aristide was elected in Haiti's first democratic elections, but his government lasted less than eight months. On September 30, 1991, a military junta overthrew Aristide, mainly because of his reform policies, which included the demilitarization of the country as well as a comprehensive redistribution of wealth plan. After the coup, Cédras's junta started to persecute Aristide's supporters, leading to the raping, torturing, and killing of thousands of Haitian citizens.

Haiti's Problem Is a U.S. Problem During the Cédras regime, thousands of Haitians fled their terror-ridden country in makeshift boats in an attempt to reach the United States. In his final months in office, President George H. W. Bush ordered the U.S. Coast Guard to turn all fleeing Haitians back to their country, claiming that the United States was not prepared to receive this great influx of refugees. Though then presidential candidate Bill Clinton had promised to allow fleeing Haitians asylum in the United States, his policy changed when he took office in 1993. Clinton tried to resolve the crisis through diplomacy with the Haitian military junta, with no success. Finally, after running out of options, Clinton concluded that the only solution to this problem would be a U.S. military intervention in Haiti.

While the military intervention was not popular with Congress and voters, Clinton saw the intervention as imminent. The military operation was planned as a forced intervention, but in a last attempt to convince Cédras's government to leave office peacefully, Clinton sent former president Jimmy Carter in a high-level mission to negotiate with the Haitian government. Carter's offer was accepted by Cédras and his military junta, but they decided to step down from office mainly because U.S. troops were en route to Haiti.

Because Cédras and his government had accepted to step down from power, the military campaign changed from a forced invasion into a semipermissive occupation in which twenty thousand U.S. troops attempted to restore stability in the country. The military intervention, called Operation Uphold Democracy, evolved into a humanitarian effort led by the United States and was later joined by other countries. The reinstatement of Aristide and the consequent democratic elections generated hope that Haiti was moving in the right direction toward political, social, and economic development. Unfortunately, the Haitian government

Haitians cheer as U.S. helicopters escort Army Humvees through Port-au-Prince on September 20, 1994. Supporters of exiled Haitian president Jean-Bertrand Aristide welcomed the intervention. (AP/Wide World Photos)

proved ineffective at tackling the country's most important issues—namely, unemployment and the lack of foreign investment.

Impact The 1994 intervention was a last resort by the Clinton administration to curb Haitian immigration into the United States as well as an attempt to reestablish democratic rule in the country. This intervention had a great impact on the politics of Haiti and subsequently led to the development of a U.N. humanitarian mission in the country. The intervention and the policies enacted before the intervention also set the tone of American foreign policy in Latin America in the 1990's and generated heated debates regarding immigration from Latin American countries into the United States.

Further Reading

Ballard, John R. *Upholding Democracy: The United States Military Campaign in Haiti, 1994-1997.* Westport, Conn.: Praeger, 1998. Focuses on the other agencies responsible for the planning and implementation of the intervention, including nongovernmental organizations, intergovernmental agencies, private volunteer organizations, and other actors.

Girard, Philippe R. *Clinton in Haiti: The 1994 U.S. Invasion of Haiti.* New York: Palgrave MacMillan, 2004. Focuses on the political career of Aristide and the foreign policy dynamics between Haiti and the United States.

Perusse, Roland I. *Haitian Democracy Restored, 1991-1995.* Lanham, Md.: University Press of America, 1995. Focuses on Aristide and his presidency before the military junta overthrow. Also looks at the role of the United States, the United Nations, and other organizations in the intervention.

Pezzullo, Ralph. *Plunging into Haiti: Clinton, Aristide, and the Defeat of Diplomacy.* Jackson: University Press of Mississippi, 2006. Provides an insider's look at the negotiations between the United States and Haiti before, during, and after the intervention.

Pedro dos Santos

See also Bush, George H. W.; Christopher, Warren; Clinton, Bill; Foreign policy of the United States; Illegal immigration; Immigration to the United States; Latin America.

■ Hale-Bopp comet

The Event The appearance of a magnificent naked-eye comet

Date July 22, 1995-fall, 1997

The discovery and later naked-eye appearance of Comet Hale-Bopp galvanized the world's interest in astronomy.

People often feel that the professional scientist who uses the largest telescope and very sophisticated technology makes the greatest discoveries in astronomy. While this is often true, there is still room for the amateur sky watcher to make important discoveries. This is what happened to Alan Hale and Thomas Bopp on the night of July 22-23, 1995. Hale was viewing in the region of the constellation Sagittarius when he noticed a fuzzy object in his telescope's field of view. Thinking that this might be a possible comet, he made sure he was not looking at a similar known object. Once convinced it was a comet, Hale sent an e-mail message to Brian Marsden at the Central Bureau for Astronomical Telegrams in Cambridge, Massachusetts, informing him of his find. Unknown to Hale, in Stanfield, Arizona, Bopp was also observing in the same region of sky. He too found the fuzzy object and observed its motion against the background stars. He also knew that it was a comet and sent his discovery to the Central Bureau for Astronomical Telegrams via telegram, but Hale's message had arrived first. In science, when two individuals independently make the same discovery at almost the same time, both are given equal credit.

In 1994, people watched images of Comet Shoemaker-Levy collide with Jupiter, and in 1996 the brilliant Comet Hyakutake dominated the evening sky. With predictions that Comet Hale-Bopp would even outshine Hyakutake, people around the world anxiously awaited its arrival. In March, 1997, Comet Hale-Bopp stretched halfway across the evening sky and was easily seen by millions of people.

Impact Many people enjoyed their view of Comet Hale-Bopp, but some viewed its appearance very differently. A religious group called Heaven's Gate believed that the appearance of the comet had special meaning for them. The group's founder, Marshall Applewhite, told thirty-eight of his followers that Earth was about to be "cleansed" by a cosmic event and that they had to immediately leave the planet.

He convinced them that a spaceship carrying Jesus Christ was hiding behind the comet and was coming for them; the only way they could leave was by committing suicide, allowing their souls to join the spaceship as it neared Earth. On March 26, 1997, Applewhite and his followers were found dead, victims of a mass suicide.

Further Reading

Burnham, Robert. *Great Comets.* New York: Cambridge University Press, 2000.

Newcott, William R. "The Age of Comets." *National Geographic Magazine* 192, no. 6 (December, 1997): 94-109.

Sagan, Carl, and Ann Druyan. *Comet.* New York: Random House, 1985.

Paul P. Sipiera

See also Astronomy; Heaven's Gate mass suicide; Science and technology; Shoemaker-Levy 9 comet.

■ Hamm, Mia

Identification American soccer player
Born March 17, 1972; Selma, Alabama

Hamm was the most prolific scorer in soccer history, with 158 international goals. A member of the U.S. women's national soccer team from 1987 to 2004, she excelled throughout the 1990's as the U.S. team won the Women's World Cup (1991, 1999) and an Olympic gold medal (1996).

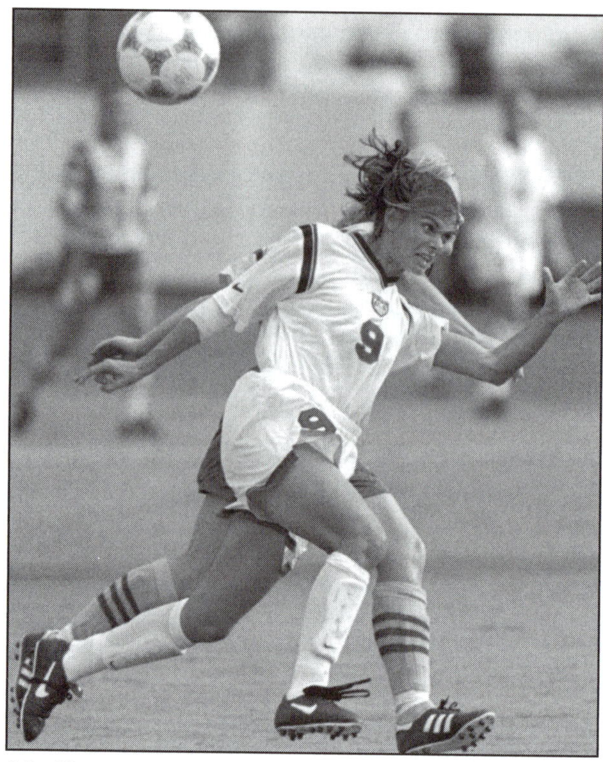

Mia Hamm runs alongside a defender from Sweden during the 1996 Olympic Games. The U.S. women's soccer team went on to win the gold. (AP/Wide World Photos)

Mariel Margaret "Mia" Hamm began her international soccer career while still a teenager, and she bookended an exemplary academic and athletic career at the University of North Carolina at Chapel Hill (UNC) around her participation as a member on the U.S. women's national soccer team in 1991, the first of two such U.S. World Cup champion teams in the 1990's. UNC was 95-1 during Hamm's undergraduate career there, winning the National Collegiate Athletic Association (NCAA) national championship in all four of her years (1989, 1990, 1992, 1993). In each of her last three years, Hamm was both an All-American and Atlantic Coast Conference (ACC) Player of the Year. Although only of average size (five feet, four inches; 125 pounds), she used breakaway speed, unselfish attitude ("there is no 'me' in 'Mia,'" she was fond of saying), and a competitive sense of shared leadership and team spirit that helped to establish and maintain the U.S. women's national soccer team among the elite teams in international competition for nearly two decades.

From her position as a starting forward, Hamm was expected to spearhead the U.S. offensive attack, and she nearly always exceeded expectations, whether through goals, assists, tenacious defense, or her passionate leadership style. In the decade during which the term "soccer mom" became a household word, Hamm became perhaps the most identifiable personification of the female soccer player, presenting an image of female agency that projected an attractive, healthy young female actively competing on the playing field rather than cheering from the sidelines or transporting part of the team from the ubiquitous minivan. Although her UNC teammates fondly nicknamed her "Jordan" (referencing the UNC basketball star Michael Jordan, who rewrote many NBA records during his professional career), her role in the history of women's sports may more accurately be understood with reference to

Jackie Robinson in baseball or Marion Motley in football: She created a new template in terms of excellence and leadership for women in sports.

Impact In addition to providing credibility to U.S. women's soccer as a powerhouse in FIFA (soccer's international governing body) and Olympic competition, Hamm's impact went beyond the sports world to influence the ways in which mass and popular culture both regarded women and used women to market products and attitudes. In 1999, she started the Mia Hamm Foundation, which is dedicated to supporting bone marrow transplant patients and families and providing opportunities for young women in sports. Married in 2003 to professional baseball player Nomar Garciaparra, Hamm seems destined to continue to remain a celebrity role model well beyond her retirement from international competition.

Further Reading

Hamm, Mia, and Aaron Heifetz. *Go for the Goal: A Champion's Guide to Winning in Soccer and Life.* News York: HarperCollins, 1999.

Latimer, Clay. *Mia Hamm.* Mankato, Minn.: Capstone Books, 2001.

Weber, Chloe. *Mia Hamm Rocks!* New York: Welcome Rain, 1999.

Richard Sax

See also Olympic Games of 1996; Soccer; Sports.

■ Hanks, Tom

Identification Award-winning actor
Born July 9, 1956; Concord, California

Hanks, one of the most prolific actors of the modern era, demonstrated an ability to play a variety of dramatic roles addressing a range of social issues.

In the 1990's, comedies such as *Joe Versus the Volcano* (1990); romantic films such as *Sleepless in Seattle* (1993) and *You've Got Mail* (1998); historical dramas such as *A League of Their Own* (1992), *Apollo 13* (1995), and *Saving Private Ryan* (1998); and children's films such as *Toy Story* (1995) and *Toy Story 2* (1999) all demonstrated Tom Hanks's talent for understanding his characters and realistically portraying their motivations and emotions. In the late 1980's and early 1990's, Hanks was known mostly for his roles in comedies such as *Splash* (1984), *The Money Pit* (1986), and *Big* (1988).

Although *Splash* and *Big* were both commercial successes—*Splash* grossed almost $70 million at the box office and *Big* not only grossed more than $150 million but also earned Hanks an Academy Award nomination—they were still regarded as lightweight, family-friendly comedies. It was not until the 1990's that Hanks began to delve more deeply into issue-based dramas where he could challenge his abilities as an actor. Two Awards for Best Actor, for *Philadelphia* (1993) and *Forrest Gump* (1994), as well as two additional nominations for Best Actor, for *Saving Private Ryan* (1998) and *Cast Away* (2000), proved that his change in focus was a wise decision.

With this goal in mind, Hanks began his career as a dramatic actor. *Philadelphia,* a semihistorical examination of one of the earliest AIDS discrimination cases; *Forrest Gump,* a film based on a 1986 novel by Winston Groom that chronicles the social upheaval of the 1960's; *Apollo 13,* which portrays the terrifying events leading up to a near-fatal NASA mission failure; and *Saving Private Ryan,* a panoramic film depicting the lives and missions of World War II-era soldiers, are all examples of films that addressed a variety of social issues, from homophobia to the plight of deployed soldiers. In particular, *Forrest Gump* and *Saving Private Ryan* caused Hanks, and filmgoers, to consider more deeply the sacrifices that previous generations of soldiers have made in the name of American ideals.

Impact Tom Hanks appeared in over a dozen films during the 1990's, putting his acting range to the test by the sheer variety of genres. His talent as an actor notwithstanding, Hanks's increasing popularity in the mind of mainstream America can be attributed partly to his increasing level of social consciousness, as demonstrated by his selection of roles.

Further Reading

Gardner, David. *The Tom Hanks Enigma: The Biography of the World's Most Intriguing Movie Star.* London: John Blake, 2006.

Pfeiffer, Lee, and Michael Lewis. *The Films of Tom Hanks.* Secaucus, N.J.: Citadel Press, 1996.

Julia M. Meyers

See also Academy Awards; Film in the United States; *Forrest Gump*; *Philadelphia*; *Saving Private Ryan.*

■ Happy Land fire

The Event A deliberately set fire in a dance hall kills eighty-seven people

Date March 25, 1990

Place Happy Land social club, Bronx, New York

An unemployed factory worker, whose girlfriend worked at a second floor social club that catered to New York City's Honduran immigrant population, set fire to the club's single exit, trapping scores of patrons.

Lydia Feliciano worked the coat check at Happy Land, one of dozens of so-called social clubs in New York City, neighborhood ethnic clubs that sold large quantities of untaxed liquor in facilities that often did not meet minimum safety codes. Happy Land had operated under the radar for years (although it had been investigated in 1988 and its operators told to shut down as it had no sprinklers or fire alarms and insufficient fire exits). Early on the morning of March 25, 1990, club patrons—no one knows exactly how many—crowded the tiny (sixty-by-twenty-foot) hall to celebrate Carnivale, a festival akin to Mardi Gras. Feliciano's on-again, off-again boyfriend of six years, Julio González, a Cuban army deserter and ex-con who had just lost his job at a Queens lamp factory, argued with her about her working at the club.

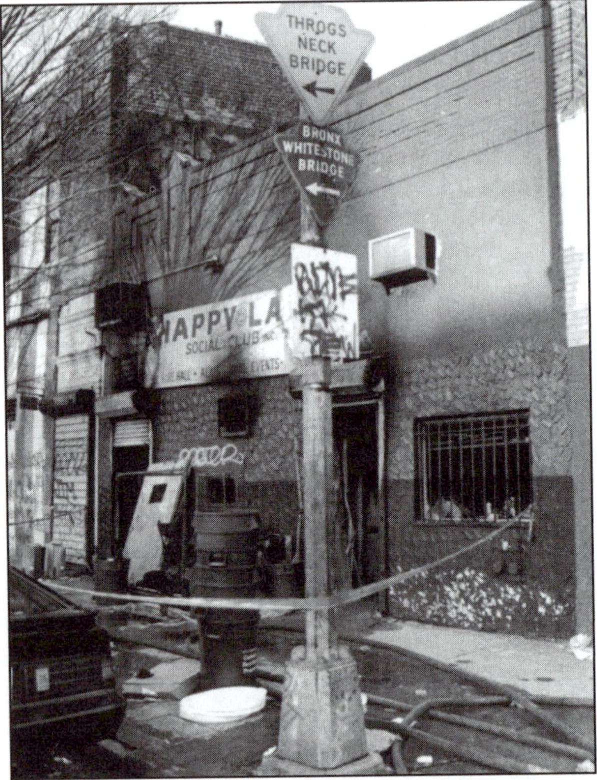

The Happy Land social club, where Julio González committed an act of arson that killed eighty-seven people on the night of March 25, 1990. (AP/Wide World Photos)

After a drunken González was ejected from the club at about 2:30 A.M., he roamed the streets around the club for nearly an hour until he purchased a dollar's worth of gasoline at an Amoco station three blocks away (he told the attendant his car had broken down). Returning to the club, he poured the gas into the hall's only open stairwell, tossed several matches into the puddle, and then crossed the street to watch. The fire exploded up the wooden stairwell; patrons immediately panicked, as the only other exit had been locked to prevent customers from dodging the cover charge. Within three minutes, the hall was engulfed. Thick toxic smoke from the building's insulation and the bar's plastic supplies was trapped in the windowless hall. Firefighters later determined that most of the eighty-seven fatalities were from asphyxiation.

González returned to his apartment and passed out, his gas-soaked clothing next to his bed when he was arrested hours later. He admitted setting the fire and was eventually sentenced to 174 concurrent twenty-five-year sentences (eighty-seven counts of arson, eighty-seven counts of murder)—at the time the most severe prison sentence in New York judicial history.

Impact Although the fire initially created a bond within the city's Honduran community, efforts to forge a permanent ethnic organization lost steam amid allegations of illegal immigrants patronizing the club. Although the number of casualties stirred outrage over the operation of unlicensed clubs, the building's owners argued that such clubs were an integral (and inevitable) part of neighborhood societies and that the heinous nature of this arson was such that it could have affected virtually any facility. A record $5 billion class-action lawsuit brought against the building owners and the city by survivors and victims' families was unsuccessful, as the city had theoretically closed the club two years earlier.

Further Reading

Bukowski, R. W., and R. C. Spetzler. "Analysis of the Happyland Social Club Fire with Hazard I."

Fire and Arson Investigator 42, no. 2 (March, 1992): 36-47.

Corbett, Glenn P., and Donald J. Cannon. *Historic Fires of New York City.* Mount Pleasant, S.C.: Arcadia, 2006.

Hashagen, Paul. *Fire Department, City of New York: The Bravest—An Illustrated History, 1865 to 2002.* Paducah, Ky.: Turner, 2002.

Joseph Dewey

See also Crime; Illegal immigration; Immigration to the United States; Oakland Hills fire; Texas A&M bonfire collapse.

■ Harry Potter books

Identification Best-selling children's fantasy series

Author J. K. Rowling (1965-)

Date Published from 1997 to 2007

These titles became the best-selling children's books of all time, rekindling interest in reading among grade-school children while sparking protest from some Christians.

The idea for the Harry Potter books came to J. K. Rowling in the summer of 1990 while she was riding a train from Manchester to London. That year, she outlined the plots of the first two books, developed the background details, and wrote what eventually became the last book's epilogue. In 1991, she moved to Oporto, Portugal, to teach English. There she wrote the first three chapters of the first book, was married, gave birth to a daughter, and was divorced. Rowling and her daughter moved to Edinburgh, Scotland, in December, 1993. Rowling finished the first book in 1994 while living on welfare. In 1996, it was purchased by Bloomsbury for a small advance, and Rowling also received a grant from the Scottish Arts Council to complete the second book.

Harry Potter and the Philosopher's Stone was published in the United Kingdom in July, 1997, *Harry Potter and the Chamber of Secrets* in July, 1998, and *Harry Potter and the Prisoner of Azkaban* in July, 1999. They all won awards, including the Nestlé Smarties Book Prize, received mostly positive reviews, and became best sellers. Although it did not win, *Harry Potter and the Prisoner of Azkaban* was nominated for the prestigious Whitbread Award. In February, 2000, Rowling was named Author of the Year at the British Book Awards.

With some minor revisions and a new title, the first book, renamed *Harry Potter and the Sorcerer's Stone,* was published in the United States by Scholastic Press in September, 1998. The second book was published in the United States in June, 1999, and the third in September, 1999. On September 26, 1999, the three books occupied the top three spots on *The New York Times* best-seller list. They were the first children's books listed there since E. B. White's *Charlotte's Web* in 1952. The American editions also won awards, such as a Grammy for the audio version of the fourth book, *Harry Potter and the Goblet of Fire* (2000), as read by Jim Dale, and have been the subject of mostly favorable reviews.

Impact Many librarians and teachers have testified that the Harry Potter books are responsible for

J. K. Rowling at a New York bookstore in 1998. (AP/Wide World Photos)

getting many children to read. In addition, many words coined or used by Rowling, called "potter-isms," have entered the English language. Examples are "muggles" and "dementors."

Some conservative Christian groups protested against the books on the grounds that they glorify sorcery and the occult and promote the practice of witchcraft, which is forbidden by the Bible. As a result, the Harry Potter books were consistently the most censored children's books in the United States. Other Christians defended the books as harmless or as having the potential for teaching Christian lessons to children.

The other books in the series are *Harry Potter and the Order of the Phoenix* (2003), *Harry Potter and the Half-Blood Prince* (2005), and *Harry Potter and the Deathly Hallows* (2007).

Further Reading

Heilman, Elizabeth E., ed. *Critical Perspectives on Harry Potter.* New York: Falmer Press, 2002.

Neal, Connie. *What's a Christian to Do with Harry Potter?* Colorado Springs, Colo.: Waterbrook Press, 2001.

Nel, Philip. *J. K. Rowling's Harry Potter Novels: A Reader's Guide.* New York: Continuum, 2001.

Thomas R. Feller

See also Children's literature; Culture wars; Literature in Canada; Literature in the United States; Publishing.

■ Hate crimes

Definition Crimes targeting victims because of prejudice based on race, religion, ethnicity, gender, disability, or sexual orientation

Responding to national outrage at the large number of violent acts motivated by extreme prejudice, both the U.S. Congress and the state legislatures enacted laws designed specifically to punish such acts. Some jurists argued that these laws were inconsistent with the freedom of expression guaranteed by the First Amendment, but the Supreme Court rejected this argument in an important ruling of 1993.

Hate crimes (also called bias-motivated crimes) differ from conventional crimes in that they are not simply motivated by the desire to harm another person or acquire property but are directed at a person because of his or her membership in a particular social group, often with the intention of threatening or subordinating members of that group. Before 1990, twenty states either criminalized or provided enhanced punishment for illegal acts motivated by prejudice, and twenty more states enacted such legislation by 1999. Defenders of the legislation argued that heightened punishment was appropriate because hate crimes increase social conflict and threaten entire groups of people.

Congress enacted four major hate crime statutes during the decade. The Hate Crime Statistics Act (HCSA) of 1990 requires the Federal Bureau of Investigation (FBI) to acquire and publish data on the crimes motivated by "manifest prejudice." The Hate Crimes Sentencing Enhancement Act (HCSEA) of 1994 provided additional penalties for an offender committing a federal crime while motivated by prejudice against the victim's social category. The Church Arsons Prevention Act of 1996 provided for enhanced criminal prosecution for attacks against houses of worship. The Violence Against Women Act of 1994, which provided federal remedies for most gender-based crimes, was ruled unconstitutional on principles of federalism in 2000.

Constitutionality of Hate Crime Laws The U.S. Supreme Court upheld the constitutionality of hate crime legislation in the case of *Wisconsin v. Mitchell* (1993). Todd Mitchell and his codefendants were African Americans who had been sentenced to enhanced punishments under the state's hate crime statute. The state's high court held that the statute was unconstitutional because it punished offenders on the basis of their ideas, thereby having a chilling effect on freedom of expression. The U.S. Supreme Court, however, unanimously disagreed and found the law to be constitutional. Chief Justice William H. Rehnquist wrote that the law simply punished overt conduct and that motive played the same role as in antidiscrimination laws. Only those persons contemplating criminal acts, moreover, would have to worry about whether their speech might be used as evidence under the statute.

The Supreme Court, however, has consistently held that the First Amendment prohibits criminal prosecutions for hate speech that is simply deemed to be offensive or insulting. The case of *R. A. V. v. City of St. Paul* (1992) dealt with a city ordinance that was used to prosecute teenagers for burning a cross on an African American family's lawn. Striking down the ordinance, the Court declared that the First Amendment prohibited "viewpoint discrimination" or punishment for the expression of offensive ideas. The decision left a number of questions unanswered; in particular, it did not clearly distinguish between offensive speech and threatening speech. A decade later, in *Virginia v. Black*, the Court would clarify that government has the authority to punish persons for speech that is intended to intimidate or threaten to harm other persons.

Instances of Hate Crimes Although hate crimes represented less than half of one percent of the reported crimes of the 1990's, their aggregate numbers were nevertheless large. In 1996, the FBI reported a total of 8,759 instances of hate crimes, including 4,600 attacks against black victims, compared with 1,445 attacks against whites. Among the known offenders, 5,891 (or 66 percent) were white, and 1,826 (or 20 percent) were black. The FBI also reported 907 antigay crimes, including 757 crimes against gay men and 150 crimes against lesbians.

The 1990's saw many sensational hate crimes targeted at blacks, including the 1991 beating of Rodney King by police officers in Los Angeles. In 1997, two New York officers pleaded guilty to beating and using a police stick to sodomize Haitian immigrant Abner Louima. The most highly publicized incident was the 1998 murder of James Byrd, Jr., in Jasper, Texas, in which three white men chained Byrd to their pickup truck and then dragged him about three miles. As a result, Byrd was decapitated and his limbs were scattered along the road. Although Texas had no hate crime legislation, two of the offenders were given the death penalty, while the driver of the truck, who did not have any proven racist connections, was sentenced to life imprisonment.

Although minorities were victims in a majority of hate crimes, whites were also victims. For three days in 1991, the Crown Heights neighborhood of Brooklyn, New York, was the scene of anti-Jewish violence after the driver of a Jewish leader accidentally struck and killed a young African American boy. One group of about twenty young black men attacked and brutally murdered a Jewish university student, Yankel Rosenbaum. The Los Angeles riots of 1992 erupted after a jury acquitted the police officers who had beaten Rodney King. For the next two days, many rioters targeted Korean businesses as well as whites like Reginald Denny, a truck driver who was beaten over the head with a fire extinguisher. More than fifty persons died in the riots. The following year, Jamaican immigrant Colin Ferguson boarded a Long Island commuter train and opened fire, killing six people and wounding nineteen. Police discovered that Ferguson possessed antiwhite literature and had written an explanatory note expressing hostility toward whites, Asians, and "Uncle Tom blacks."

Impact During the 1990's, fewer instances of prejudice-motivated violence against minorities occurred than in earlier periods of American history. Some critics believe that a fixation on hate crimes promoted alarmist and pessimistic perceptions about social fragmentation, even resulting in a self-fulfilling prophesy. Deciding whether a particular incident should be classified as a hate crime is a complex matter of interpretation. Many crimes of rape, for example, are thought to be motivated by animosity toward women, but cases of rape are rarely classified as hate crime. Criminologists and jurists disagree about whether the prosecution of hate crimes resulted in a decrease in such incidents. Without hate crimes laws, of course, almost all bias-motivated offenses would still be criminally prosecuted, and juries would usually have the option of considering motivation as one of the aggravating or mitigating factors for deciding the appropriate sentence.

Further Reading

Altschiller, Donald. *Hate Crimes: A Reference Handbook.* Santa Barbara: ABC-Clio, 1999. A useful guide to the relevant legislation, chronology, and statistics, with annotated references to published and Internet sources.

Jacobs, James, and Kimberly Potter. *Hate Crimes: Criminal Law and Identity Politics.* New York: Oxford University Press, 1998. A balanced analysis emphasizing that the notion of hate crimes emerged because of the desire to give symbolic support to historically disadvantaged groups.

Jenness, Valerie, and Ryken Grattet. *Making Hate a Crime: From Social Movement to Law Enforcement.* New York: Russell Sage, 2004. An insightful sociological study with historical information about the social forces that led to the criminalization of hate crimes.

Levin, Jack, and Jack McDevitt. *Hate Crimes: the Rising Tide of Bigotry and Bloodshed.* New York: Plenum Press, 1993. Pioneering study of hate-motivated violence, advocating organized community response as an effective deterrence.

Perry, Barbara. *In the Name of Hate: Understanding Hate Crimes.* New York: Routledge, 2001. Argues the controversial thesis that hate crimes are embedded in continuing patterns of white racism and prejudice against subordinate minorities.

Thomas Tandy Lewis

See also African Americans; Byrd murder case; Crime; Crown Heights riot; Diallo shooting; Ferguson, Colin; Homosexuality and gay rights; Jewish Americans; King, Rodney; Los Angeles riots; Louima torture case; Police brutality; Race relations; Shepard, Matthew; Supreme Court decisions.

■ Health care

Definition Production and consumption of medical services, as well as health outcomes

Although most measures of health improved for the United States and Canada during the 1990's, medical costs increased greatly and health care organization and financing remained highly controversial.

Good health and long life are among the many benefits enjoyed by countries with a high level of income and economic development. The same process that generated technology to augment production brought repeated major discoveries and inventions that have revolutionized the medical care available to most people. Health, however, is not primarily determined by medical care. It also reflects genetic inheritance and lifestyle choices such as diet, exercise, avoiding risk factors such as smoking, excessive alcohol consumption, addictive drugs, obesity, recreational violence, and irresponsible sexual activity. Education has a large influence on health. Better-educated people take better care of themselves, both in and out of the medical system. Persons with less than a high school education have death rates at least double those with education beyond high school. Public health and sanitation programs—including a clean water supply, sewage disposal, pollution control, pure food, and drug surveillance—are also important. While the United States and Canada are very similar in regard to most of these factors, the two countries differ significantly in regard to public policies toward the financing of medical services.

Health indicators for the United States and Canada were already good in 1990 and became significantly better over the decade. In 1990, a female baby could expect to outlive her male counterpart by seven years. For women of age fifty, the gap was about five years, and for women of sixty-five it was slightly under four years. Life expectancy at birth is heavily influenced by nonmedical factors such as murders, automobile accidents, and smoking, all of which affected men much more than women.

Over the course of the 1990's, life expectancy for men increased to a much greater extent than for women, lowering the gap substantially and equalizing the ratio of men to women surviving into advanced age. Both medical and nonmedical influences were important. Deaths from automobile accidents declined in absolute numbers, from 47,000 in 1990 (17.9 per 100,000 population) to 43,000 in 2000 (14.9 per 100,000). Greater use of seat belts, often mandated by law, helped. Murders declined strikingly, from 23,000 in 1990 to 16,000 in 2000. The proportion of cigarette smokers among persons eighteen years and older fell from 25.5 percent in 1990 to 23.2 percent in 2000. Suicides decreased from 12.4 per 100,000 in 1990 to 10.4 per 100,000 in 2000. The proportion of older people receiving flu vaccinations increased markedly, from about one-third in 1989 to nearly two-thirds in 2000.

The U.S. Department of Health and Human Services publication *Health United States 2002* presents comparative data estimating life expectancy for individuals in high- and middle-income countries. Esti-

Life Expectancy in the United States, 1990 and 2000

Age	*Gender*	*1990*	*2000*	*% Change*
At birth	Male	71.8	74.3	3.5
	Female	78.8	79.7	1.1
At age 50	Male	26.4	27.9	5.7
	Female	31.3	32.0	2.2
At age 65	Male	15.1	16.2	7.3
	Female	18.9	19.3	2.1

Source: Statistical Abstract of the United States, 2008, p. 75.

mates for age sixty-five are generally the most relevant for evaluating medical care conditions. From 1992 to 1997, it reported that the life expectancy for males at age sixty-five in the United States rose from 15.4 to 15.9, while the number of remaining years held steady at 19.2 for females at that age. In Canada during this same period, the life expectancy for males at age sixty-five rose from 16.0 to 16.3 and the figure for females at age sixty-five increased slightly, from 20.0 to 21.1.

Infant mortality in 1990 in the United States was almost 1 percent, or 9.2 per thousand live births. By 2000, it had declined to 6.9 per thousand. Much of this improvement reflected better self-care by expectant mothers, particularly nutrition and the avoidance of risk factors. The proportion of pregnant women who smoked dropped from 18 percent in 1990 to 12 percent in 2000.

The four principal causes of death in the United States during the 1990's were heart disease, cancer, stroke, and respiratory conditions, all of which primarily affect older people. The incidence of heart-related deaths declined significantly, however, reflecting both lifestyle changes and improvements in medications, newer surgical techniques, and the wider use of pacemakers and defibrillators. While the overall incidence of deaths per year declined only slightly, it is known from the improvements in survival rates that the deaths occurred later in life. Improved cancer treatments, for instance, were generally able to slow the advance of the disease.

The human immunodeficiency virus (HIV), which causes acquired immunodeficiency syndrome (AIDS), caused much alarm as it spread in the 1980's. Between 1987 and 1994, HIV mortality increased by 16 percent per year. From that point, however, the incidence declined significantly. In 1990, HIV deaths averaged about 10 per 100,000 people, and by 2000 the incidence was only half as large. Much of this improvement occurred as high-risk populations such as male homosexuals and intravenous drug users adapted their behavior to lower the risk of transmission.

Life Expectancy at Age 65, 1992 and 1997

Country	*Gender*	*1992*	*1997*
United States	Male	15.4	15.9
	Female	19.2	19.2
Canada	Male	16.0	16.3
	Female	20.0	20.1
Median of 27 other countries	Male	14.7	15.4
	Female	18.1	19.1

Source: U.S. Department of Health and Human Services, *Health, United States, 2002,* p. 115.

Paying for Medical Services Medical goods and services are provided by private market suppliers in both the United States and Canada, but the financing systems differ substantially. In the United States, the government provides three types of financial support: Medicare, Medicaid, and the programs for federal prisoners, military personnel, and veterans.

Medicare, established in 1965, provided extensive reimbursement of medical expenses for qualifying persons aged sixty-five and older in the 1990's. Most people qualified by paying a Medicare tax, at a rate of 1.45 percent, as part of their Social Security payroll tax. This amount provided hospitalization coverage. For doctor reimbursement, a monthly premium was required. The number of Medicare beneficiaries increased from 34 million in 1990 to 40 million in 2000, and the program's expenditures rose from $111 billion in 1990 to $222 billion in 2000. This rapid growth in expenditures caused alarm among many experts on government finance. As life expectancy increased, the proportion of population on Medicare increased.

Medicaid is a means-tested program that covers medical expenses for low-income persons of any age. Each state creates its own program, but there are federal guidelines and federal financial support. Medicaid coverage of persons under age sixty-five generally averaged around 10 percent in the 1990's, with no clear trend. Only about half the people below the federal poverty line qualified for Medicaid. Medicaid was supplemented by the creation in 1997 of the State Children's Health Insurance Program (SCHIP). By 2000, 3.4 million children were enrolled.

During the decade, most persons under age sixty-five relied on private medical insurance, most of it arranged by employers. Private insurance coverage declined from 76 percent in 1989 to 72 percent in 2000, while the proportion of uninsured people rose from 15 to 17 percent over the same period.

Medical costs in the United States increased rapidly during the 1990's. While consumer prices in general rose about 32 percent from 1990 to 2000, the price index of medical goods and services increased 60 percent. Medical expenditures as a percentage of gross domestic product (GDP) increased from 11.9 percent in 1990 to 13.3 percent in 2000—a higher percentage than any other country. For Canada, the proportion was relatively constant at around 9 percent. In economic jargon, the demand for medical care was price-inelastic. Because most medical expenditures were made through insurance, consumers were relatively indifferent to price. Only about one-fifth of medical expenditures were out-of-pocket.

The supply of medical services was also quite price-inelastic. Medical education remained lengthy, stressful, and incredibly expensive. Many new doctors began their professional careers with student loan debts of $100,000 or more. Between 1990 and 2000, the number of physicians in the United States increased from 615,000 to 814,000, with the ratio of physicians to population increasing from 0.25 percent (or 2.5 per thousand) to 0.29 percent. In Canada, the ratio was slightly higher in 1990 but failed to increase over the decade. Most other high-income countries had more physicians per capita. In 2000, for instance, comparative data on twenty-seven other countries showed that eighteen had more than the United States and twenty-two had more than Canada.

One of the many deterrents to entering medical practice was the high premiums for malpractice insurance—often $100,000 a year. Whereas in many professions, retired people can continue working part-time or as volunteers, insurance considerations largely ruled out this option for doctors.

The high earnings of U.S. physicians attracted many doctors from other countries. Among the roughly 200,000 additional physicians in the United States over the decade, roughly one-third were foreign-educated physicians. By 2000, this group constituted about one-fourth of all physicians in the United States.

The rapid rise in medical costs meant that insurance premiums also increased. The proportion of employers offering medical insurance benefits declined, and the proportion of people without insurance increased. The predicament of the uninsured or underinsured became a major focus of political attention. During Bill Clinton's first term as president, his wife Hillary headed a team that attempted to put together a program to expand federal government medical insurance. No such program was adopted, however.

Medicare and Medicaid did not simply pay patients' medical bills. They pressured suppliers to accept far less than list price—that is, the nominal billed amounts. As a result, suppliers looked for ways to increase list price. This meant that patients not covered by insurance were hit by bills that were far greater than those paid by insurance programs. Increasingly, uninsured patients came to rely on hospital emergency rooms, which were obligated under law to treat all persons. This in turn created financial difficulties for many hospitals.

How Canada Pays Like that of the United States, Canada's medical system has relied on doctors and hospitals that are independent parts of the market economy. However, there has long been a national health program (also called Medicare). Each province determines its own program, but the national government has set major guidelines and provides half the financing. Basic physician and hospital treatments have been provided to patients without direct charge.

During the 1990's, because coverage did not extend to such areas as pharmaceuticals and dental and optical care, about one-third of medical expenditures were privately paid, and the majority of Canadians had some form of private health insurance.

Deaths per 100,000 Persons Aged 65 and Older in the U.S., 1990 and 1999

Year	*Heart*	*Cancer*	*Stroke*	*Respiratory Conditions*	*All Causes**
1990	2,109	1,149	45	508	5,396
1999	1,772	1,133	434	482	5,238

* Includes items not enumerated.
Source: U.S. Department of Health and Human Services, *Health, United States, 2002,* p. 69.

Physicians' incomes were much more dominated by government policy than those in the United States, and their incomes were significantly below those in the United States. As a result, a substantial number of Canadian doctors migrated south for better pay.

Canada's system proved very popular with the general public. A major criticism involved long waiting times for treatment. Canadian hospitals invested far less in expensive high-tech equipment than did U.S. hospitals. However, such equipment was criticized by U.S. observers who believed that patients were being pressured into high-cost diagnostic procedures that may have little benefit. Abundant anecdotal evidence existed of Canadians seeking treatment in the United States either to bypass long waiting times or to secure top-of-the-line specialist treatment for difficult conditions.

Impact By 2000, Americans and Canadians were living longer and healthier lives. Many people adopted healthier lifestyles, although a rise in obesity rates threatened to increase problems such as diabetes. Overall, both the quantity and the quality of medical resources improved. Canadians were generally satisfied with their government-financed medical care system. Americans were not satisfied with the U.S. system—though most had good feelings about their personal medical situation.

The United States was the world leader in medical research and innovation. It spent a much higher percentage of the GDP on medical goods and services than other countries and a far lower proportion of government-financed medical care than most other high-income countries. The rapid rise in medical costs during the decade generated pressures for cost control in the Medicare and Medicaid programs, and some of these controls impaired incentives to provide adequate supply.

For those in the upper half of the population by income, those with more education, and the elderly in general, U.S. medical facilities were probably better than those in other countries. African Americans, Latinos, and the low-income population, however, fared less well. There was chronic agitation for a more comprehensive system of medical insurance, one more nearly comparable to those in Canada and in Europe, but opponents feared that the attending cost controls would damage supply and innovation.

Further Reading

Henderson, James W. *Health Economics and Policy.* 2d ed. Mason, Ohio: Thomson/South-Western, 2002. This college text is designed for noneconomists. Gives an excellent balance of facts and theory.

Rejda, George. *Social Insurance and Economic Security.* 6th ed. Upper Saddle River, N.J.: Prentice-Hall, 1999. A text for college undergraduates. Health problems and policies are emphasized in chapters 7 and 8.

Zweifel, Peter, and Friedrich Breyer. *Health Economics.* New York: Oxford University Press, 1997. A comprehensive analytical survey with an international perspective.

Paul B. Trescott

See also Abortion; AIDS epidemic; Alzheimer's disease; Antidepressants; Cancer research; Drug advertising; Health care reform; LASIK surgery; Medicine; Pharmaceutical industry; Science and technology; Stem cell research; Tobacco industry settlement; Viagra.

■ Health care reform

Definition Legislative initiatives proposed to moderate health care expenditures and to increase coverage of uninsured persons

During this decade, increasing health care costs placed undue burdens on individuals, employers, and governments. Reining in costs and expanding coverage were main aims of the unsuccessful national health care reform initiatives.

Per capita health care expenditures rose from $1,101 in 1980 to $2,813 in 1990. The average annual growth rate of health care expenditures had exceeded that of gross domestic product (GDP) throughout the 1980's, 10.8 percent compared to 7.8 percent. Total health care expenditures rose more modestly throughout the 1990's. By 1999, per capita health care expenditures rose to $4,522, stabilizing at 13.7 percent of GDP. The average annual growth rate of health care expenditures exceeded that of GDP throughout the 1990's, 6.6 percent vis-à-vis 5.3 percent. Total U.S. spending on health care exceeded $1.1 trillion by 1997 and reached nearly $1.3 trillion in 1999. As health care costs rose, so did the number of uninsured persons, roughly 35 million in 1990, to about 45 million in the mid- to late 1990's before declining to about 38.4 million, or 13.7 percent of the population, by 2000.

Major Efforts and Initiatives Bill Clinton incorporated health care reform into the 1992 presidential campaign, dozens of health reform proposals were introduced in Congress, and President George H. W. Bush unveiled his plan. Market-oriented reforms sought incremental modifications of private health insurance markets, single-payer tax-financed plans covered all citizens such as that provided by the Canadian government, and a hybrid to universal coverage called "play or pay" plans mandated employers who did not provide health insurance coverage for their workers to contribute to a fund for uninsured workers.

On January 25, 1993, President Clinton named First Lady Hillary Rodham Clinton chair of the President's Task Force on National Health Care Reform to design a universal health care plan. In a nationally televised address on September 22, President Clinton outlined principles of his Health Security Plan meant to provide health insurance to everyone while containing costs. To achieve universal coverage, most employers would be required to fund health care for their employees, with subsidies to small businesses. The federal government would fund the purchase of private health insurance policies for unemployed persons or part-time workers. To contain costs, regional health care alliances would be developed to publicize competing health insurance policies so that consumers could choose, and the government would develop controls over prices charged by pharmaceutical companies for drugs.

Questions about costs and complexity plagued President Clinton's 1,342-page reform initiative from the start. Many feared they would pay more for health insurance under the plan, and private insurance companies augmented these fears by financing a televised campaign featuring the fictitious middle-class couple Harry and Louise voicing their concerns. The proposed legislation languished in congressional committees. Liberal Democrats such as Minnesota senator Paul Wellstone and Washington representative Jim McDermott favored a single-payer plan similar to Canada's. Others, like Tennessee Democratic representative Jim Cooper, railed against cost-control provisions and the funding necessary to obtain universal coverage. Conservatives of both parties preferred to minimize the role of government involvement in health care, portraying the Health Security Plan as a bureaucratic, big-government scheme. By August, 1993, no reform plan commanded a majority of legislators.

Congressional elections in 1994 returned control of Congress to the Republican Party, signaling a loss of public confidence in government capacity. Balancing the budget, reliance on market-based mechanisms to address social problems, and shrinking the scope of the federal government were evidenced in the Republican's Contract with America, released on September 27, 1994, and promoted by Republican representative Newt Gingrich, its main architect who became House Speaker.

Impact After 1994, cost containment remained the main impetus of incremental market-based health care initiatives. The Health Insurance Portability and Accountability Act of 1996 (HIPAA) included portability provisions to prevent loss of health insurance due to job changes, health insurance access and renewability guarantees, and, on an experimental basis, medical savings accounts (MSA).

The Balanced Budget Act of 1997 expanded the range of managed care options available to Medicare enrollees. Options included provider-sponsored organizations (hospitals or physicians developed plans) and preferred provider organizations (insurance providers developed plans whose enrollees had to obtain treatment from a roster of physicians and hospitals that agreed to charge discounted fees and to secure central approval for treatments). The act also permitted states to implement mandatory Medicaid managed care programs without a waiver from federal authorities. The State Children's Health Insurance Program (SCHIP) was created as Title XXI of the Social Security Act to help states insure uninsured low-income children who were ineligible for Medicaid.

Subsequent Events On December 8, 2003, President George W. Bush signed the Medicare Prescription Drug, Improvement, and Modernization Act of 2003, adding prescription drug benefits to Medicare on a voluntary basis. Health care expenditures rose two to three times faster than GDP after 2000 before tapering off but still exceeded GDP growth between 2004 and 2006. The number of uninsured persons increased again after 2000, reaching a high of nearly

47 million persons (15.8 percent of the population) in 2006. While the percentage of uninsured children declined steadily between 1998 and 2004 from a high of 15.4 percent to a low of 10.4 percent, it rose to 11.2 percent in 2006; between 2001 and 2004, the percentage of insured persons in employer-sponsored health plans declined from 62.7 percent to 59.5 percent. Health care reform to reduce costs and shrink if not eliminate uninsured rates was part of the presidential debates throughout 2008.

Further Reading

Clinton, William J. "Address to a Joint Session of the Congress on Health Care Reform, September 22, 1993." *Weekly Compilation of Presidential Documents* 29, no. 38 (September 27, 1993): 1836-1846. The president announces and outlines the Health Security Plan.

Feldman, Roger D., ed. *American Health Care: Government, Market Processes, and the Public Interest.* New Brunswick, N.J.: Transaction, 2000. This collection of essays examines changes in health care delivery in the 1990's in light of related legislation.

Hacker, Jacob S. *The Road to Nowhere: The Genesis of President Clinton's Plan for Health Security.* Princeton, N.J.: Princeton University Press, 1997. Details how the complex idea of managed competition came to occupy a prominent place in the Clinton administration's health security plan.

Skocpol, Theda. *Boomerang: Clinton's Health Security Effort and the Turn Against Government in U.S. Politics.* New York: W. W. Norton, 1996. Describes the mobilization of antistatist political forces that defeated the Health Security bill between 1992 and 1994.

Smith, David G. *Entitlement Politics: Medicare and Medicaid, 1995-2001.* New York: Aldine de Gruyter, 2002. Examines the politics behind legislative initiatives targeting Medicare and Medicaid spending between 1995 and 2001.

Richard K. Caputo

See also Armey, Dick; Balanced Budget Act of 1997; Canada and the United States; Clinton, Bill; Clinton, Hillary Rodham; Conservatism in U.S. politics; Contract with America; Elections in the United States, midterm; Family and Medical Leave Act of 1993; Gingrich, Newt; Health care; Medicine; Pharmaceutical industry; Poverty; Social Security reform; Welfare reform.

■ Heaven's Gate mass suicide

The Event Thirty-nine members of the Heaven's Gate cult commit suicide
Date March 23-25, 1997
Place Rancho Santa Fe, California

As Comet Hale-Bopp approached Earth, thirty-nine members of the Heaven's Gate cult, led by Marshall Applewhite, committed suicide, believing that they would be transported into the cosmos to reunite with a spaceship from the "level beyond human" traveling behind the comet.

Marshall Applewhite and Bonnie Nettles met in 1972 at a hospital in Houston, Texas, where Nettles worked as a nurse. Applewhite had recently lost his position as the music director at the University of St. Thomas, and his wife had earlier left him because of several homosexual affairs. The loss of his job and ambivalence over his sexuality made him depressed. Nettles was active in New Age thought, including spiritualism and astrology. When she met Applewhite, her marriage was also dissolving. The two became inseparable, although their relationship was described as strictly platonic.

Ti and Do Begin Their Mission Both of them had been hearing voices from unidentified flying objects (UFOs), which persuaded them that they had a des-

Heaven's Gate on Suicide

In 2008, the Heaven's Gate Web site was still accessible and included a statement, excerpted here, regarding the religious group's view of suicide:

The true meaning of "suicide" is *to turn against the Next Level when it is being offered.* In these last days, we are focused on two primary tasks: one—of making a last attempt at telling the truth about how the Next Level may be entered (our last effort at offering to individuals of this civilization the way to avoid "suicide"); and two—taking advantage of the rare opportunity we have each day—to work individually on our personal overcoming and change, in preparation for entering the Kingdom of Heaven.

tiny that required them to leave behind their ordinary lives. "Ti" (Nettles) and "Do" (Applewhite), as they called themselves (referring to notes in the musical scale), headed westward in 1973 on a "trip into the wilderness" to find their calling. On the West Coast, they learned from alien voices that they would be martyred and taken to another planet. Those who wished to join them in that journey would have to undergo a metamorphosis, which required giving up property and human attachments and being celibate, since sex took energy away from "the Process," as they called that metamorphosis. Their followers were told that they could transform their human bodies into eternal, extraterrestrial beings, at which time UFOs would come to take them "home." Little is known about them over the next years except that they dashed from place to place expecting to board a UFO. In 1985, Ti died from cancer. Do declared that she had come from another planet to teach him the Process and that she was returning to the "level beyond human."

Marshall Applewhite. (AP/Wide World Photos)

Do and his followers reappeared in public in 1993, making a video, advertising in magazines, and creating a Web site to gain followers. The site was titled "Heaven's Gate," and became the popular name for the group. They also formed a business for creating Web sites. The members took new names, which ended in *ody*, indicating that they were children in a class learning the Process. Their time was tightly regulated; when they left the group to conduct business, which they always did as male and female pairs, they had to phone in regularly. After two members were arrested for vagrancy because they had no money, members carried five-dollar bills and quarters for the telephone calls. When the group ate out, they ordered the same menu items, and they were described as dressing identically and having the same hair cuts, making it difficult to tell apart the women from the men. Also in 1993, Do and seven other men were castrated to remove their sexual drive, and others were taking chemicals to reduce it.

By then, Do was suffering from coronary arteriosclerosis, and his message became more urgent. In 1996, the group rented a mansion in Rancho Santa Fe, an affluent community near San Diego, with money they made from their Web site business. They rose before dawn every morning to scan the sky for a sign that they would soon be taken from Earth. When Comet Hale-Bopp appeared in 1997, rumors that a UFO had been sighted behind it led the Heaven's Gate members to conclude that Ti was coming to take them home. They bought a powerful telescope to observe the comet.

The Suicides Because they believed that it was necessary to leave their "earthly containers" behind, Do and thirty-eight followers (twenty-one women and seventeen men) committed suicide in a meticulous fashion over a three-day period beginning on March 23. Initially the dead were identified as men, since the police found them dressed alike in black clothing and black athletic shoes with close-cropped hair, making it difficult to determine their gender at first glance. Their faces and chests were covered with purple shrouds. The dead had five-dollar bills and quarters in their pockets, and their bags had been packed neatly in the dormitory-style rooms. They had taken phenobarbital mixed in pudding and had drunk vodka before lying down in bed. The last two had cleaned up the house and sent farewell videos and a letter to a former member before committing suicide themselves. That former member went to the mansion on March 26 and then alerted police.

Charles Humphrey, "Rkkody," a member since 1975, was not present at the mass suicide. He served as a spokesman for the "Away Team" in the months following the incident. Following a botched suicide attempt in May, 1997, that left another member dead, he killed himself in February, 1998, dressed identically to the thirty-nine members who had died the previous year.

Impact News of the mass suicide and the castrations of some cult members astounded the nation. Two sociologists, Robert Balch and David Taylor, studied the cult in the 1970's and the 1980's; their research provided important insights into the process of creating the sort of group coherence that could lead to mass suicide.

The belief system promulgated by Heaven's Gate has baffled civil authorities and ordinary people, seeming poignant to some and ridiculous to many. Such beliefs, however, hold a strong appeal to those who have difficulty in finding meaning in their lives. One message of the suicides at Rancho Santa Fe, therefore, is the degree to which such personalities may be willing to subject themselves to the visions and wills of others.

Further Reading

Balch, Robert. "The Evolution of a New Age Cult: From Total Overcomers Anonymous to Death at Heaven's Gate." In *Sects, Cults, and Spiritual Communities*, edited by William Zellner. Westport, Conn.: Praeger, 1998. A sociologist who studies charismatic leadership, Balch joined Heaven's Gate as an observer-participant for two months in 1975. His work follows the cult from 1975 to 1997.

Lalich, Janja. *Bounded Choice: True Believers and Charismatic Cults.* Berkeley: University of California Press, 2004. A sociologist specializing in cults uses Heaven's Gate as a major example of how cult leaders bind their members to them, even to the point of committing suicide.

Wessinger, Catherine. *How the Millennium Comes Violently: From Jonestown to Heaven's Gate.* New York: Seven Bridges Press, 2000. Contains a lengthy section on Heaven's Gate with details about Applewhite's and Nettles's lives and the founding of their cult. Offers insights into how a group can be motivated into committing mass suicide.

Frederic J. Baumgartner

See also Hale-Bopp comet; Religion and spirituality in Canada; Religion and spirituality in the United States.

■ Heroin chic

Definition Drug-glamorizing fashion style

In the mid-1990's, the look of pale, sickeningly thin fashion models became popular in the fashion industry. Heroin overdoses among fashion photographers and criticism from the public and politicians ended the craze.

Before the 1990's, heroin chic was promoted by photographers like Nan Goldin and Larry Clark (writer-director of *Kids*, 1995). The look was reinvented by New York fashion photographers Mario and Davide Sorrenti, whose work glamorized the fashion trend more than their predecessors had. Their photographs first appeared in British tabloids and later in American high fashion magazines. Connected with Seattle's grunge music scene, the Sorrenti brothers believed their work visually documented the counterculture that thrived on Western consumerism. The models had exhausted facial expressions and unnaturally thin figures and sometimes wore torn stockings. Major designers, most notably Calvin Klein, regularly featured waiflike models in their clothing advertisements. Fashion models Kate Moss and, in the late 1970's and early 1980's, Gia Carangi (the tragic precursor to heroin chic who became addicted to heroin and died of AIDS in 1986) were the most prominent models to portray the heroin chic look. Kurt Cobain, lead singer for the grunge band Nirvana, was the most closely linked entertainer to heroin chic counterculture.

Impact Davide Sorrenti died of a heroin overdose in February, 1997. His death had a strong impact on the New York fashion industry. In May, *The New York Times* published a series of articles on the heroin chic trend. President Bill Clinton criticized the fashion industry for claiming that the advertisements were a form of artistic expression. Some Republicans claimed they were another method used by the liberal media to corrupt American morals. Films such as *Pulp Fiction* (1994) and *Trainspotting* (1996), which dealt with heroin addiction, also drew criticism for allegedly glamorizing the drug. Within weeks of politicians' speeches shunning such advertising, heroin chic had all but disappeared. Its largest promoter, Calvin Klein, began featuring healthier models in advertisements.

Further Reading

Nash, Alanna. "The Model Who Invented Heroin Chic." *The New York Times*, September 7, 1997, p. H90.

Summer, Christine C., and Peter Doskoch. "Tracking the Junkie Chic Look." *Psychology Today* 29, no. 5 (September/October, 1996): 14.

Wren, Christopher S. "Clinton Calls Fashion Ads' 'Heroin Chic' Deplorable." *The New York Times*, May 22, 1997, p. A22.

Dwight Vick

See also Advertising; Drug use; Fads; Fashions and clothing; Grunge fashion; Grunge music; Nirvana; *Pulp Fiction*.

■ Hill, Anita

Identification Law professor who accused Supreme Court justice nominee Clarence Thomas of sexual harassment

Born July 30, 1956; Lone Tree, Oklahoma

Hill is credited for putting a face on sexual harassment in the 1990's and for galvanizing women to vote an unprecedented twenty-eight new women into Congress in 1992, the "Year of the Woman."

On October 11, 1991, Anita Hill testified before Congress in televised hearings that Clarence Thomas had sexually harassed her while she was in his employ. Both Hill and Thomas are African American. Hill's testimony came days before Congress was scheduled to vote on his Supreme Court nomination. Her allegations against Thomas were made public when information from a Federal Bureau of Investigation (FBI) interview regarding these issues was revealed. Thomas was Hill's supervisor from 1981 to 1983, when they both worked for the Equal Employment Opportunity Commission (EEOC). Hill was vilified by several white male senators who claimed she had romantic designs on Thomas, while she was lauded as a hero by many women for exposing sexual harassment in the workplace. Hill appeared poised and professional as she recounted her experiences of being sexually harassed by Thomas. Thomas vehemently denied her allegations. Thomas went on to be confirmed as the next Supreme Court justice by a narrow vote of fifty-two to forty-eight.

Hill details her experiences in her 1997 autobiography *Speaking Truth to Power*. Over the course of her law career, she has served as counsel to the assistant secretary of the Department of Education's Office for Civil Rights (1981), assistant to the chairman of the Equal Employment Opportunity Commission (1982-1983), law professor at the University of Oklahoma (1986), held a position at the Institute for the Study of Social Change at the University of California, Berkeley (1997), and became a professor of the Heller School for Social Policy and Management at Brandeis University (1997), where she remains.

Hill has taught and written about international commercial law, bankruptcy, civil rights, and women's issues. In 1995, she coedited *Race, Gender, and Power in America* with Emma Coleman Jordan. She is a sought-after public speaker.

Anita Hill testifies before the Senate on the nomination of Clarence Thomas to the Supreme Court on October 11, 1991. (AP/Wide World Photos)

Judge Thomas Responds

At the evening session of the hearing of the Senate Judiciary Committee on the nomination of Clarence Thomas to the U.S. Supreme Court on October 11, 1991, Thomas lashed out after testimony was presented against him by Anita Hill, a former employee:

Senator, I would like to start by saying unequivocally, uncategorically, that I deny each and every single allegation against me today that suggested in any way that I had conversations of a sexual nature or about pornographic material with Anita Hill, that I ever attempted to date her, that I ever had any personal sexual interest in her, or that I in any way ever harassed her.

A second, and I think more important point, I think that this today is a travesty. I think that it is disgusting. I think that this hearing should never occur in America. This is a case in which this sleaze, this dirt, was searched for by staffers of members of this committee, was then leaked to the media, and this committee and this body validated it and displayed it at prime time over our entire nation. How would any member on this committee, any person in this room, or any person in this country, would like sleaze said about him or her in this fashion? Or this dirt dredged up and this gossip and these lies displayed in this manner? How would any person like it?

The Supreme Court is not worth it. No job is worth it. I'm not here for that. I'm here for my name, my family, my life and my integrity. I think something is dreadfully wrong with this country when any person, any person in this free country would be subjected to this.

This is not a closed room. There was an FBI investigation. This is not an opportunity to talk about difficult matters privately or in a closed environment. This is a circus. It's a national disgrace. And from my standpoint as a black American, as far as I'm concerned, it is a high-tech lynching for uppity blacks who in any way deign to think for themselves, to do for themselves, to have different ideas, and it is a message that unless you kowtow to an old order, this is what will happen to you. You will be lynched, destroyed, caricatured by a committee of the U.S. Senate rather than hung from a tree.

Impact The Hill-Thomas hearings affected the political landscape of the 1990's because it was the first time that confounding issues of race and gender were concurrently exposed on a national scale.

Subsequent Events In 2007, Clarence Thomas's autobiography, *My Grandfather's Son*, once again highlighted his dealings with Anita Hill. She responded to his declarations that she was a liar by stating in *The New York Times* on October 2, 2007, that his claims were "unsubstantiated representations and outright smears" and that his accounts were dominated by "blatant inconsistencies."

Further Reading

Garment, Suzanne. *Scandal: The Culture of Mistrust in American Politics—Afterword, On Anita Hill and Clarence Thomas.* New York: Times Books, 1992.

Hill, Anita. *Speaking Truth to Power.* New York: Doubleday, 1997.

Morrison, Toni, ed. *Race-ing Justice, En-Gendering Power: Essays on Anita Hill, Clarence Thomas, and the Construction of Social Reality.* New York: Pantheon Books, 1992.

U.S. Congress. Senate. Committee on the Judiciary. *The Complete Transcripts of the Clarence Thomas-Anita Hill Hearings.* Chicago: Academy Chicago, 1994.

Katherine M. Helm

See also African Americans; Civil Rights Act of 1991; Elections in the United States, 1992; Morrison, Toni; Race relations; Supreme Court decisions; Thomas, Clarence; Women in the workforce; Women's rights; Year of the Woman.

■ Hip-hop and rap music

Definition Interconnected styles of music that emphasize rhythmic spoken words set to beats

If critics call the 1980's and early 1990's "the golden age of hip-hop," the later 1990's deserve the label "the rise of rap rivalry."

Rap and hip-hop musicians in the 1990's wrote complex metaphors and multilayered beats, a nod to advancing technology and keen attention to social injustice. Previously unknown rapper Ice Cube released his immediately classic debut *AmeriKKKa's Most Wanted* (1990) and songs such as "The Humpty Dance" by Digital Underground and "Let's Talk About Sex" by Salt-n-Pepa captivated worldwide audiences with new beats and honest topics, while lip-synching Milli Vanilli and rapper MC Hammer—despite the latter's two Grammys and his own cartoon—fell from public grace.

On March 3, 1991, four Caucasian Los Angeles police officers used nightsticks to beat an African American man named Rodney King. A bystander recorded the beating, which immediately aired worldwide, enraging more than just the African American community. When a trial in 1992 acquitted the officers, the worst intercity rioting that the United States had ever seen erupted in Los Angeles. Hip-hop and rap musicians responded with angry, cop-slandering lyrics, which led Vice President Dan Quayle to call for a ban of Tupac Shakur's controversial album *2Pacalypse Now* (1991). Ice-T's rap-metal band's song "Cop Killer" elicited similar responses from the public and caused national law-enforcement protests. The year was not all bad, however, as both Ice Cube and Tupac Shakur (also called 2Pac) made films—*Trespass* and *Juice*, repectively—and the Beastie Boys released *Check Your Head.* In addition, Dr. Dre and Suge Knight created Death Row Records and released Dre's album *The Chronic.* Dre's signature style, G-funk, along with another of his partnerships to then-unknown rapper Snoop Doggy Dogg, propelled West Coast rap back to the top of the charts. Hip-hop artist Jodeci won *Billboard*'s hottest album and song.

In 1993, Snoop Doggy Dogg's *Doggystyle* entered the *Billboard* charts at number one while police charged him with second-degree murder. Meanwhile, the East Coast's Wu-Tang Clan released *Enter the Wu-Tang (36 Chambers)*, Shakur's second album, *Strictly 4 My N.I.G.G.A.Z.*, appeared just before police arrested him on charges of assault and battery, and Sean "Puffy" Combs created Bad Boy Records and signed to his new label Christopher Wallace, known as the Notorious B.I.G. or Biggie Smalls. Female rapper MC Lyte's single "Ruffneck" went gold and received a Grammy nomination, Queen Latifah won a Grammy, and Salt-n-Pepa's *Very Necessary* became the best-selling rap album of all time by a female artist.

New rappers emerged in 1994, including Southern rap duo OutKast and Bone Thugs-N-Harmony, and the East Coast, after a two-year hiatus, recaptured the number one spot with the Notorious B.I.G.'s remix "One More Chance." Queens native Nas released *Illmatic* to critical acclaim, and Snoop Doggy Dogg created the short film *Murder Was the Case.*

Second Half of the Decade The East versus West Coast rivalry exploded in 1995 when, throughout the year, artists and producers from both sides taunted one another with accusations. First, Shakur accused former friend Smalls and Combs of hiring someone to shoot him. Then, Knight insulted Combs, increasing tensions between Death Row and Bad Boy artists. Finally, from prison, Shakur released the critically acclaimed *Me Against the World,* and when Knight paid his bail and hired him to Death Row Records, coastal tensions increased. Jay-Z and Da Brat debuted albums, Mary J. Blige and TLC topped the charts, and Eazy-E died of acquired immunodeficiency syndrome (AIDS).

On September 7, 1996, gunfire injured Knight and Shakur in Las Vegas after Shakur's double album *All Eyez on Me* and B-side single "Hit 'Em Up" slandered Smalls and Death Row Records, a label that Dre soon left to start Aftermath Entertainment. Shakur died in gunfire almost a week later. Bone Thugs-N-Harmony, OutKast, Lil' Kim, Foxy Brown, and the Fugees—who also captured the *Billboard* number one album—delivered powerful records in 1996 that propelled them into the national spotlight.

Only six months after Shakur's murder, Smalls was murdered on March 9, 1997, further shocking the rap and hip-hop community. Days later, his final album, *Life After Death,* became the best-selling rap record of all time. Combs memorialized Smalls and produced *No Way Out* on his own label. That year, several rappers released solo debuts, including Will Smith, Missy "Misdemeanor" Elliot, Master P, and Mase. The Fugees broke up, and several well-known rappers reappeared, including Rakim, Foxy Brown, and Shakur, via an unreleased collection posthumously produced by his mother.

In 1998, Jay-Z, Lauryn Hill, and OutKast produced impressive albums; DMX delivered two; and two new hybrid genres—rap rock and Southern hiphop—brought new talent to the fore, trumping defunct West Coast rap in early 1999. The Hard Knock Life Tour became the first successful rap tour of the decade, and south of the border, Puerto Rican rapper Big Punisher's *Capital Punishment* went platinum. *The Miseducation of Lauryn Hill* won five Grammys, and Eminem, Mos Def and Talib Kweli (as Blackstar), Eve, and Dr. Dre generated powerful hiphop albums.

Impact The decade ended on a positive note and had lasting effects. Gangsta rap and Southern hiphop continue to flourish, and both genres—independently and collaboratively—have gained worldwide recognition and validity. The 1990's brought complexity to the lyrics and beats, but the years also complicated the relationships among rivaling groups: East, West, and South.

Further Reading

Hip-Hop: Beyond Beats and Rhymes—About Hip-Hop. http://www.pbs.org/independentlens/hiphop. This Web site accompanies a PBS documentary by Byron Hurt on hip-hop and masculinity, sexism, violence, and homophobia.

Light, Alan, ed. *The Vibe History of Hip Hop.* New York: Three Rivers Press, 1999. Provides comprehensive, chronological coverage of the genre.

Smiley, Tavis. *Examining Hip-Hop Culture.* http://www.pbs.org/kcet/tavissmiley/special/hiphop. A PBS special highlighting African American perspectives on hip-hop culture; includes numerous comments with possible ideas for argumentative essays on this topic.

Watkins, S. Craig. *Hip Hop Matters: Politics, Pop Culture, and the Struggle for the Soul of a Movement.* Boston: Beacon Press, 2005. Topically organized by essays examining hip-hop culture. Includes an index to help locate information quickly.

Ami R. Blue

See also African Americans; Death Row Records; Drive-by shootings; Fads; King, Rodney; Los Angeles riots; Milli Vanilli; MP3 format; Music; Police brutality; Race relations; Shakur, Tupac; Smith, Will.

■ Hobbies and recreation

Definition Leisure-time pursuits and activities

How Americans used their leisure time changed significantly during the 1990's, in part because of a baby-boomer generation nostalgia craze, prompting growth in collecting hobbies of all kinds, and also because of the growing popularity of Internet-based activities.

Having been brought up during decades when childhood hobbies were strongly encouraged, the baby boomers once again embraced hobbies as they neared retirement. Economic gains made during the 1990's made the collecting hobbies especially attractive, with these accumulations taking almost any form possible. While antiques continued to hold a place of importance among collectors, the pursuit of items from one's own childhood, especially toys, became a passion for many. Traditional collecting categories with a strong nostalgic aspect—such as dolls, automobiles, advertising signs, or candy containers—enjoyed substantial popularity.

This surge in collecting created a greatly increased market for reproduction items, or collectibles, produced specifically for these collectors. Hallmark was a typical company in catering to the nostalgia-minded, while long-established toy retailer F.A.O. Schwarz showed its adaptability to the times in issuing F.A.O. Collectibles catalogs rather than only toy catalogs. Collection-minded adults became the target buyers for many toy companies, with reissues of classic toys from the 1950's and 1960's, collector editions of current-run toys, and expensive special productions related to licensed movie and pop culture characters. Collecting such lines as Hot Wheels, Barbie, and *Star Wars* became more the norm than playing with them.

This intense interest in collecting affected other recreational activities, as the widespread success of Magic: The Gathering demonstrated. Released in 1993, this role-playing/strategy game introduced the modern concept of the collectible card game and prompted a flood of collectible card games in the mid-1990's.

Nostalgia also played a part in the continuing interest in crafts, although some of the traditional arts, such as quilting, fell from the spotlight. Newer crafting hobbies, such as rubber stamping, expanded in popularity. Even if not originating in the 1990's, interest in scrapbooking became so widespread as to make it characteristic of this decade. A hobby that incorporated such other popular crafts as collage-making and papermaking, scrapbooking rose to such a level of mass acceptance that individual scrapbooking retail stores opened across the country. Even if most would soon close due to inadequate business acumen, the presence of such hobby-oriented retail outlets was characteristic of the late years of the decade.

Effect of the Internet As an activity enhanced by the company of friends, scrapbooking was attractive partly for its social aspect. A similar attraction helped generate interest in the new online communities, or digital communities, that resulted from the development of the World Wide Web. New Internet forum software and other developments helped news groups and bulletin boards proliferate and attract sizeable readers and participants. Blogging began gaining in popularity by the end of the decade.

These online communities turned out to be central developments to hobbyists of every stripe, especially during the latter part of the 1990's. Whether the interest was winemaking, reading science fiction, or collecting stoneware, the online world offered ease of communication among hobbyists scattered nationally or even globally. Newsgroups replaced newsletters as means of disseminating information, and many online communities were coterminous with enthusiast, hobby, and craft communities.

The burgeoning online communities also turned a minor sports-oriented diversion of previous decades, fantasy football, into one of the most popular pastimes of the late 1990's. These online activities occupied hours previously given to other hobbies and recreations. The single event that most changed the recreational life of computer-owning Americans, however, was the founding in 1995 of AuctionWeb, renamed eBay in 1997. This online auction house had a bit of the flea market in its makeup—but a flea market with the sky as its limit. With eBay's national and soon global scope, and with offerings that changed from minute to minute, hobbyists found a perfect outlet for their often obsessive interests.

Home entertainment continued its growth in other, more well-established directions as well, with 99 percent of U.S. homes now owning television sets, cable companies thriving, and home film rental businesses enjoying a boom period.

Impact The changes during the 1990's reflected diametrically opposing trends. On one hand, the desire to find a like-minded community spurred people to spend hours at such diverse activities as scrapbooking and newsgroup reading. On the other hand, the bulletin boards, instant communications, and auction sites made it easier to spend more recreational time than ever before alone inside the home.

The ease of Internet trading also eroded some of the institutions that had helped hobbyist and recreational groups gain a sense of community in previous decades. Newsletters, collector magazines, and hobbyist conventions began losing readers and attendees. For similar reasons, business at the flea markets and antique malls that flourished in the 1980's saw the beginnings of decline. By the end of the decade, almost no hobby or recreational pursuit was left unaffected, for better or worse, by the Internet.

Further Reading

Cohen, Adam. *The Perfect Store: Inside eBay.* Boston: Little, Brown, 2003. A fact-filled chronicle of the unconventional online business that changed the face of nearly every hobby.

Haglund, Jill. *Complete Guide to Scrapbooking.* 5th ed. Sarasota, Fla.: TweetyJill, 2000. This best-selling guide describes the techniques, practices, and ideas that helped make scrapbooking one of the most popular hobbies of the 1990's.

Kennedy, Angus J. *The Internet and World Wide Web: The Rough Guide.* London: Rough Guides, 1997. This handbook for both novices and experts covers all aspects of the Internet experience in its earlier days, with accurate description of its recreational and hobby aspects.

Prince, Dennis. *Online Auctions at eBay: Bid with Confidence, Sell with Success.* Rocklin, Calif.: Prima, 1999. Accurate depiction of techniques and practices typical in the 1990's, at this central meeting spot for most of America's collecting communities.

Turlington, Shannon R. *Walking the World Wide Web: Your Personal Guide to the Best of the Web.* Chapel Hill, N.C.: Ventana Press, 1995. A window upon the online world in its earlier days, with focus on its recreational aspects.

Mark Rich

See also Amazon.com; Audiobooks; Blogs; Book clubs; Cable television; Coffeehouses; Digital divide; Fads; Film in the United States; Internet; Music; Television; Toys and games; World Wide Web.

■ Hockey

Definition Team sport

An increase in the popularity of the sport led to an expansion in the number of teams in the National Hockey League (NHL). Especially notable was the location of many of the new franchises, as they were often placed in the Sun Belt of the United States.

Hockey was noteworthy in the 1990's for several reasons. At the professional level, numerous changes occurred. The NHL, the most prestigious professional hockey league in the world, expanded from twenty-one to twenty-eight teams. In addition, several players came from Eastern Europe following the collapse of communism and the disintegration of the Soviet Union. The latter also had an impact on Olympic hockey, as previous decades had been dominated by Soviet teams.

Expansion South and West Entering the 1990's, the NHL had plans for a significant expansion of its number of teams. The league wanted to have thirty franchises by the end of the decade. It was not just the growth in the number of teams that was important; the location of these franchises marked a new approach, as most of the new teams were placed outside of where the sport had long been popular. Two of the franchises were awarded to cities in California: In 1991, the San Jose Sharks entered the league, and in 1993, the Mighty Ducks of Anaheim made their debut. As with California, the American South was not a location with large numbers of hockey enthusiasts, yet the region was awarded many new NHL teams. Florida received two teams, as the Tampa Bay Lightning entered the league in 1992 and the Florida Panthers began playing in Miami in 1993. Two other franchises placed in the South during the decade were the Nashville Predators and the Atlanta Thrashers, making their debuts in 1998 and 1999, respectively. The only new team located in the geographical areas traditional for hockey was the Ottawa Senators, who started playing in 1992.

Not only did the NHL expand its number of teams, but four franchises moved as well. In two cases, teams moved from Canada to the United States. Three of the four relocated franchises moved from cold climates, where hockey was popular, to the Sun Belt, where the sport was less so. In 1993, the Minnesota North Stars became the Dallas Stars. Perhaps the most controversial relocation was made by the Quebec Nordiques, who moved to Denver and became the Colorado Avalanche prior to the 1995-1996 season. In its last year as the Quebec Nordiques, the team finished the regular season with the best record in the Eastern Conference. At the end of the following season, the franchise's first as the Colorado Avalanche, it won the Stanley Cup. The Winnipeg Jets also relocated to an American city, becoming the Phoenix Coyotes before the 1996-1997 season. In 1997, the Hartford Whalers relocated to Raleigh, North Carolina, and became the Carolina Hurricanes.

Realignment Entering the 1993-1994 season, the league rearranged divisions, conferences, and the playoff format. Geography became the primary determinant of the composition of divisions and conferences. Instead of the Wales and Campbell Conferences, there were Eastern and Western Conferences.

The format of the playoffs also changed. Prior to the 1993-1994 season, the top four teams from each of the four divisions qualified for the playoffs. The first two rounds were the divisional semifinals and the divisional finals. Beginning with the 1993-1994 season, the divisional winners along with the six teams with the next best records qualified for the playoffs from each conference. The first two rounds were now the conference quarterfinals and the conference semifinals.

Notable Champions The Edmonton Oilers' dynasty ended in 1990 after the team won its fifth Stanley Cup in seven years. Unlike previous decades, the 1990's did not experience such dynasties in the NHL. The most Stanley Cups won by a single team during the decade was two, achieved by both the Pittsburgh Penguins and the Detroit Red Wings. The Penguins won their championships in the 1990-1991 and 1991-1992 seasons. The Red Wings also won the Stanley Cup in consecutive seasons, in the 1996-1997 and 1997-1998 seasons.

Professional hockey also experienced some significant individual achievements during the 1990's.

The Red Wings' championship in 1997 marked a milestone in coaching. Scotty Bowman became the first coach in the history of the four major professional sports in the United States to win championships with three different teams. In addition, many winners of the Hart Trophy, awarded to the NHL's most outstanding player in a season, demonstrated the increasing importance of players from Europe, especially the arrival of players from the former communist countries of Eastern Europe: Sergei Federov in 1994, Dominik Hasek in 1997 and 1998, and Jaromir Jagr in 1999. Finally, Wayne Gretzky, considered by many to be the greatest hockey player ever, retired in 1999.

Olympic Changes Major changes in international politics had an impact on the Olympics, especially hockey. With the collapse of the Soviet Union just two months before the Winter Olympics of 1992, the fifteen newly independent countries did not have enough time to organize separate teams. Thus, they agreed to play together under the name Unified Team. The team won another gold medal in hockey, but it would be the end of that region's dominance of the sport. With the division of the former Soviet players in subsequent Olympics, other countries began to have more success in hockey. In 1994, Sweden won its first gold medal in the sport after defeating Canada in a shootout; it was considered to be one of the best games ever played in the Olympics.

In the Winter Olympics of 1998, hockey reached three more milestones. The Czech Republic won its first gold medal by defeating Russia. It was also the first time that NHL players were permitted to participate in Olympic hockey. The third achievement was the introduction of women's hockey to the Olympics, as the United States defeated Canada to win the sport's inaugural gold medal.

Impact During the 1990's, the NHL perceived the sport's increase in popularity as a reason to locate new franchises outside its traditional geographical base of fan support. By doing so, league officials hoped to further increase its popularity by attracting new fans in growing areas of the United States. The collapse of communism allowed great hockey players from Eastern Europe to play professionally in the NHL, and the subsequent disintegration of the Soviet Union leveled the competition in Olympic hockey.

Further Reading

Boyd, Bill. *All Roads Lead to Hockey: Reports from Northern Canada to the Mexican Border.* Lincoln: University of Nebraska Press, 2006. Case studies about hockey in selected towns across the United States and Canada.

Danielson, Michael N. *Home Team: Professional Sports and the American Metropolis.* Princeton, N.J.: Princeton University Press, 2001. Analyzes the role of government in attracting and keeping sports franchises to their respective areas.

Wallechinsky, David. *The Complete Book of the Winter Olympics.* Woodstock, N.Y.: Overlook Press, 1998. A brief overview and order of finish for all sports in the Winter Olympics in the modern era.

Kevin L. Brennan

See also Olympic Games of 1992; Olympic Games of 1994; Olympic Games of 1998; Sports.

■ Hogue, James

Identification Ivy League impostor
Born October 22, 1959; Kansas City, Kansas

This petty thief turned fraud gained entrance into Princeton University posing as a self-taught Utah rancher.

James Hogue was born and raised in rural Kansas, where he excelled in both academics and sports, in particular track and cross-country running. He graduated from high school in 1977 and attempted college at both the University of Wyoming and University of Texas but dropped out of both. In 1986, Hogue, then twenty-six years old, decided that he wanted to attempt to gain entrance to Stanford University as an intercollegiate runner. In order to gain an athletic scholarship as a high school runner, he enrolled at Palo Alto High School under the name Jay Huntsman, a sixteen-year-old orphan from Nevada. The real Jay Huntsman was the identity of a deceased infant. A local reporter eventually uncovered Hogue's true identity, and he was arrested. Once released, he moved to Colorado, where he posed as a Stanford professor hired to teach young runners at a cross-country camp, until he was discovered again to be a fraud. He then moved to California, where he was hired as a custom bicycle mechanic. Within months, he stole over $20,000 worth of bicycle parts from his employer and moved to

Utah, where he was eventually arrested and jailed.

While in prison, Hogue applied to various Ivy League schools and eventually gained admission to Princeton University. His application stated that he was eighteen-year-old Alexi Indris-Santana, a self-educated Utah rancher with no formal schooling. Based on his high Scholastic Aptitude Test (SAT) scores, along with his impressive yet fraudulent running career at Palo Alto High School, Princeton offered Hogue a large scholarship for the fall of 1988; however, he was still in a Utah prison. In order to receive a deferment, Hogue lied to Princeton officials, stating that his mother was dying of leukemia in Switzerland and that he had to go back home to be with her until she passed. In the summer of 1989, Hogue was placed on parole but decided to leave Utah in order to pursue his new scheme as a young scholar-athlete at Princeton.

Hogue, now a fugitive from justice, officially became a member of the Princeton class of 1993, and he immediately began to impress his professors, coaches, and peers with his stellar performances both in the classroom and on the track. Hogue lived as Santana until 1991, when a former classmate from Palo Alto High School recognized him at an intercollegiate track meet. She immediately reported his identity to her coach, who in turn spoke to a local journalist who broke the story. Hogue was arrested for defrauding Princeton of nearly $30,000. After pleading guilty to theft by deception in 1992, he was sentenced to three years in jail and five years probation.

Impact James Hogue will be remembered as the con man who pulled off the ultimate scheme—entry into an Ivy League school using made-up school records. Hogue was a master con artist who tricked Princeton into not only allowing him to enter their prestigious school but also giving him a scholarship and arranging for him to receive financial aid.

Hogue was essentially a career criminal whose crimes escalated from petty thefts to higher-level frauds like the Princeton scheme. Although many believed that Hogue had the intellect to do great things the conventional way, he opted for some reason to take the darker road of crime and deception. Since the Princeton fraud, he has been arrested numerous times for other frauds and petty thefts.

Further Reading

Samuels, David. "The Runner." *The New Yorker,* September 3, 2001, 72-85.

_______. *The Runner: A True Account of the Amazing Lies and Fantastical Adventures of the Ivy League Impostor James Hogue.* New York: New Press, 2008.

Paul M. Klenowski

See also Crime; Scandals.

■ Holocaust Memorial Museum

Identification A museum dedicated to the documentation, interpretation, and study of the Holocaust

Date Opened to the public on April 26, 1993

Place Located on the National Mall in Washington, D.C.

The United States Holocaust Memorial Museum serves as the official memorial dedicated to preserving the memory of the millions of European Jews and others killed during the Holocaust during World War II.

Planning for the Holocaust Memorial Museum began with a presidential commission established by Jimmy Carter in 1978; in 1980, the U.S. Congress passed legislation to establish a council charged with planning the memorial. The land for the museum was donated by the federal government, and the funding was secured through the private donations of more than 200,000 individuals. After years of planning by main architect James Ingo Freed, construction of the museum began in July, 1989. After nearly four years of construction, the building was completed in the spring of 1993.

The architectural design of the building is intended to symbolize several aspects of the Holocaust. For example, four towers are located on the north side of the building to represent the watch towers located at many of the death camps. In addition, triangular shapes are located throughout the building to symbolize the triangles that were used to mark the Jewish prisoners. The main part of the museum comprises the permanent exhibition, which details a chronological history of the Holocaust. Included in this exhibition is the Tower of Faces, a three-story-tall tower containing over one thousand photographs of Jewish life in Europe before the Holocaust. In addition to the permanent exhibition, the museum displayed several special exhibitions throughout the 1990's, including "Faces of Sorrow: Agony in the Former Yugoslavia" and "The Nazi

Olympics: Berlin 1936." The museum is also home to the Committee on Conscience, a privately and publicly funded think tank that conducts research on genocide throughout the world.

During the construction phase of the museum in the early 1990's, a controversy developed over how the Holocaust should be remembered in the exhibitions. Many of the museum's planners did not want to use photographs and other artifacts that would depict the Jewish people only as victims. Others, however, argued that displaying such artifacts, while horribly graphic, was the only way to ensure an accurate depiction of the Holocaust. Still other critics believed that a museum that did not commemorate the American experience of the Holocaust should not be built on the National Mall. This controversy had no clear resolution, with some exhibits seemingly satisfying different parties.

Impact Despite the criticisms and controversy, the museum has been visited by millions of visitors from all over the world, including many foreign leaders and dignitaries, since its opening.

Further Reading

Berenbaum, Michael. *The World Must Know: The History of the Holocaust as Told in the United States Holocaust Memorial Museum.* Boston: Little, Brown, 1993.

Linenthal, Edward. *Preserving Memory: The Struggle to Create America's Holocaust Museum.* New York: Viking Press, 1995.

Lindsay Schmitz

See also Architecture; Israel and the United States; Jewish Americans; *Schindler's List.*

■ Holy Virgin Mary, The

Identification Controversial painting
Date Created in 1996; displayed at the Brooklyn Museum of Art, New York City, from October 2, 1999, to January 9, 2000

Defended by many art critics, this painting prompted debate on the use of public money to support a museum displaying a painting that many cultural conservatives considered repulsively sacrilegious.

Nigerian in ancestry, Chris Ofili was born in 1968 in Manchester, England, and raised Catholic. He received formal training in art in London. In 1992, while in Zimbabwe on a scholarship, he decided to use elephant dung in his paintings and soon gained public attention.

Created in 1996, *The Holy Virgin Mary* consists mainly of oil paint, paper collage, polyester resin, and glitter on an eight-by-six-foot sheet of linen whose frame is supported by two clumps of elephant dung, one bearing the word "Virgin" and the other the word "Mary." The painting depicts a black-skinned, cartoonlike woman with mismatched irises, a bulbous nose, and big red lips. Through her leaflike gown her right breast, formed from elephant dung and map pins, protrudes. On the gold-colored background are what at a distance appear to be tiny angels but up close turn out to be women's buttocks and genitals cut from pictures in pornographic magazines.

One of five paintings by Ofili in the exhibition *Sensation: Young British Artists from the Saatchi Collection, The Holy Virgin Mary* provoked less outrage during its initial exhibition, in London, than did another artist's portrait of a murderer. After the run in London and another in Berlin, *Sensation* arrived in New York City, where it was to be presented at the Brooklyn Museum of Art, an institution funded in part by the city and housed on city property.

Even before the opening, scheduled for October 2, 1999, *The Holy Virgin Mary* proved to be the center of American outrage at *Sensation.* The president of the Catholic League, Bill Donohue, called for a boycott and the end of city funding for the museum. Saying that the First Amendment did not require the public to allow its taxes to support offensive art, New York mayor Rudolph Giuliani tried to end city funding for the museum and to evict it from city property. In turn, the Brooklyn Museum of Art sued to keep its city money and building and received not only support from arts-oriented groups and the American Civil Liberties Union but also national publicity. On November 1, while *The Holy Virgin Mary,* specially shielded, continued to draw enormous attention, a federal judge ruled in favor of the museum. *Sensation* stayed there until its scheduled closing on January 9, 2000.

Impact For the defenders of Ofili's *The Holy Virgin Mary,* the eventual settlement in the museum's favor in an appeals court during March, 2000, was a victory for artistic freedom over censorship and, according to some, over white racism. For those who found the painting blasphemous, the case marked a victory for adolescent rebellion supported by taxes.

Further Reading

Adams, Brooks, et al. *Sensation: Young British Artists from the Saatchi Collection.* London: Thames and Hudson, 1998.

Kimball, Roger. "The Elephant in the Gallery, or the Lessons of 'Sensation.'" *New Criterion* 18, no. 3 (November, 1999): 4-8.

Victor Lindsey

See also Art movements; Censorship; Culture wars; Giuliani, Rudolph; Mapplethorpe obscenity trial; National Endowment for the Arts (NEA); Race relations; Religion and spirituality in the United States.

■ Holyfield, Evander

Identification World heavyweight boxing champion

Born October 19, 1962; Atmore, Alabama

Holyfield, known as "The Real Deal," replaced Mike Tyson as the most prominent heavyweight boxer of the 1990's. He engaged in numerous high-profile fights and held several different versions of the heavyweight title during the decade.

After winning a silver metal in the 1984 Summer Olympics, Evander Holyfield turned professional later the same year. By 1988, he had won all three versions of the world cruiserweight title: World Boxing Association (WBA), International Boxing Federation (IBF), and World Boxing Council (WBC). In July of 1988, he gave up these titles to campaign as a heavyweight, and on October 25, 1990, he knocked out James "Buster" Douglas in the third round to win the undisputed heavyweight title, which Douglas had won in a stunning upset over Mike Tyson eight months earlier.

Following three successful title defenses, including victories over former champions George Foreman and Larry Holmes, Holyfield lost the title to Riddick Bowe in November of 1992. A year later, he regained the IBF and WBA titles from Bowe (who had given up the WBC version of the title), but then lost the titles to Michael Moorer by a twelve-round decision in April of 1994. Holyfield suffered a dislocated shoulder in the bout against Moorer and, while at the hospital after the fight, was diagnosed with a heart condition that temporarily forced his retirement from the ring.

After passing the necessary medical exams, Holyfield returned to the ring in May of 1995. He fought for the next year and a half for a chance to fight for a third heavyweight title. His opportunity came on November 9, 1996, when he challenged Tyson for the WBA title. In a dramatic upset, Holyfield defeated Tyson by a technical knockout (TKO) in the eleventh round. Holyfield defended his title in a 1997 rematch with Tyson (which Holyfield won by disqualification when Tyson persisted in biting his ears during the bout) and then added the IBF heavyweight title to his WBA title with a decision win over Moorer in November, 1997. After a controversial draw with WBC heavyweight titleholder Lennox Lewis in March, 1999, Holyfield lost his WBA and IBF titles in a rematch with Lewis the following November.

Mike Tyson, left, and Evander Holyfield battle at the MGM Grand Garden in Las Vegas, Nevada, on November 9, 1996. Holyfield won by technical knockout in the eleventh round. (AP/Wide World Photos)

Impact Small for a modern heavyweight at an average fighting weight of 210 pounds, Holyfield, as his record indicates, was a fierce competitor, making up by conditioning and determination what he lacked in physical size. In addition to his large number of high-profile fights during the decade, he was also involved in some of the more bizarre occurrences in the ring during the period, including the ear-biting incident in the 1997 bout with Tyson and the appearance of a man in a flying parachute that forced a twenty-minute interruption of Holyfield's second fight with Bowe in 1993. Holyfield received numerous boxing awards, including being named *The Ring* magazine's Fighter of the Year twice, in 1996 and 1997. With Tyson in decline and Lewis still in the process of attaining full prominence in the 1990's, Holyfield stands as the decade's dominant heavyweight.

Further Reading

McIlvanney, Hugh. *The Hardest Game: McIlvanney on Boxing*. Rev. ed. Chicago: Contemporary Books, 2001.

Thomas, James J., II. *The Holyfield Way: What I Learned About Courage, Perseverance, and the Bizarre World of Boxing*. Champaign, Ill.: Sports, 2005.

Scott Wright

See also African Americans; Boxing; Sports; Tyson, Mike.

Home Alone *star Macaulay Culkin in 1991.* (AP/Wide World Photos)

■ Home Alone

Identification Comedy film
Director Chris Columbus (1958-)
Date Released on November 16, 1990

An instant hit with the public, this film combined a holiday theme with a child-stranded-at-home story line and broad slapstick humor. The sometimes crude but ultimately sweet movie became one of the biggest movies of 1990 and 1991.

The impeccable casting and solid direction of *Home Alone* overcame a plot with a number of gaping holes. Beyond Macaulay Culkin's star-making turn as Kevin McCallister, Joe Pesci and Daniel Stern played perfect foils as two stooges, Harry and Marv, intent on breaking into every home in the near-deserted neighborhood during the holidays. Kevin's parents, Peter (John Heard) and Kate (Catherine O'Hara), realize too late that they have left their eight-year-old son at home while the rest of the family is in-flight to France. While their attempts to get home to their son provide the heart of the film, it is Kevin's self-reliance and elaborate booby traps that make the film enjoyable to watch.

At the end of its run in 1991, *Home Alone* sat at the top of the box office from its release on November 16, 1990, through February 3, 1991, and held a top-ten spot until April 26, 1991. The total 1990-1991 domestic ($285,761,243) and worldwide gross ($533,800,000) earned the film the distinction of being, at the time, the third-highest-grossing motion picture of all time.

While a box-office success, the film received a lukewarm reception from critics. John Hughes's penchant for writing and producing movies that focus on the experiences of young protagonists (*Sixteen Candles*, 1984; *The Breakfast Club*, 1985; *Ferris*

Bueller's Day Off, 1986) continued with *Home Alone,* but crude jokes and comic violence undermined what was promoted as "a family comedy without the family." While the film did spawn three sequels (1992's *Home Alone 2: Lost in New York,* also starring Culkin, directed by Chris Columbus, and written and produced by Hughes; 1997's *Home Alone 3,* written and produced by Hughes; and the direct-to-video *Home Alone 4,* released in 2002) and a slew of other slapstick-inspired comedies, *Home Alone* was the box-office high point (and turning point) in a long line of incredibly successful films by Hughes.

On the awards front, *Home Alone* was modestly successful. John Williams was nominated for two Academy Awards: for Best Original Score and (with lyricist Leslie Bricusse) Best Original Song, "Somewhere in My Memory." Culkin won an American Comedy Award for Funniest Actor in a Motion Picture (Leading Role), and the film was nominated for two Golden Globe Awards: Best Comedy/Musical and Best Performance by an Actor in a Motion Picture—Comedy/Musical (Culkin). The film, cast, and crew received several other minor awards and nominations.

Impact *Home Alone* set the stage for many subsequent broad comedies of the 1990's and launched the careers of Macaulay Culkin and Chris Columbus. The film remains one of the highest grossing of all time.

Further Reading

Maltin, Leonard, Luke Sader, and Spencer Green. *Leonard Maltin's Movie Encyclopedia: Career Profiles of More than Two Thousand Actors and Filmmakers, Past and Present.* New York: Plume Books, 1995.

Peske, Nancy, and Beverly West. *Advanced Cinematherapy: The Girl's Guide to Finding Happiness One Movie at a Time.* New York: Dell, 2002.

Christopher Strobel

See also Academy Awards; DVDs; Film in the United States.

■ Home run race

The Event Major League Baseball attendance booms as sluggers chase the single-season home run record

Date 1998

The Major League Baseball renaissance of the latter half of the 1990's was inextricably connected to the league-wide surge in home run production. Two players in particular, Mark McGwire and Sammy Sosa, typified the trend with their dramatic pursuit of Roger Maris's home run record.

As the middle of the 1990's approached, a series of circumstances threatened baseball's popularity. Two other American sports leagues, the National Basketball Association (NBA) and the National Football League (NFL)—through innovative marketing and game paces that reflected the increasingly ambulatory American culture—jeopardized baseball's position as the national pastime. Furthermore, the 1994 Major League Baseball players' strike depleted attendance figures and disenfranchised most baseball fans. The home run race of 1998 rescued baseball from its slide in popularity and was the culmination of the decade's unprecedented power display.

On opening day of the 1998 season, Mark McGwire of the St. Louis Cardinals hit his first home run—a grand slam—commencing the historic race. McGwire was the primary candidate to break Roger

Top Single-Season Home Run Hitters (through 2001)

Rank	*Player*	*Home Runs*	*Year*
1	Barry Bonds	73	2001
2	Mark McGwire	70	1998
3	Sammy Sosa	66	1998
4	Mark McGwire	65	1999
5	Sammy Sosa	64	2001
6	Sammy Sosa	63	1999
7	Roger Maris	61	1961
8	Babe Ruth	60	1927
9	Babe Ruth	59	1921
10	Jimmie Foxx	58	1932

Maris's thirty-seven-year-old record of sixty-one home runs. McGwire hit forty-nine home runs in his rookie season (1987), fifty-two in 1996, and fifty-eight in 1997, falling three short of Maris's magical number. Unlike Babe Ruth, who was the first to reach the sixty-home-run plateau, McGwire had competition in his quest to establish a new home run record. The most obvious rival was Ken Griffey, Jr., who hit fifty-six home runs in 1997. Other sluggers such as Manny Ramirez, Greg Vaughn, Barry Bonds, José Canseco, and Albert Belle were legitimate challengers to McGwire's supremacy.

Two months into the 1998 season, McGwire had twenty-seven home runs and a degree of distance between his challengers. Suddenly, Sammy Sosa of the Chicago Cubs emerged as McGwire's primary competitor, hitting twenty home runs in June, a record for one calendar month. The juxtaposition of the two hitters—representing traditional and geographical baseball rivals—framed the already intriguing story line. The relationship between McGwire, a humble, often serious American, and Sosa, an affable, gregarious Dominican, developed into a genuine friendship that advanced the popularity of both players. As the likelihood of a new home run record increased, McGwire mused, "Wouldn't it be great if we just ended up tied?"

On August 19, the Cubs played the Cardinals. In the fifth inning, Sosa hit his forty-eighth home run, passing McGwire for the first time. In the eighth inning, McGwire answered with his forty-eighth and reclaimed the home run lead with a game-winner in the tenth inning. On September 1, McGwire hit his fifty-seventh and broke Hack Wilson's National League record. On September 8, the Cubs and Cardinals reconvened. In the fourth inning, McGwire sent a line drive over the left-field wall to break Maris's record. As he touched home plate, he lifted his son Matt into the air in celebration. Next, he embraced Sosa—the two were compatriots in an exclusive club. In the same week, Sosa hit his sixty-second.

Obscured by the media attention surrounding McGwire and Sosa was the fact that, on Labor Day, Griffey hit his fiftieth home run, signifying the first time three players had hit fifty or more home runs in a year. On the final day of the season, Vaughn joined the fifty-home-run club. The home run race did not end once McGwire and Sosa passed Ruth and Maris. The new home run kings emboldened each other to extend the new all-time mark. On August 25, when Sosa hit his sixty-sixth, he had hit the most single-season home runs in history. His record lasted forty-five minutes before McGwire tied it. Over the last weekend of the season, McGwire hit four more home runs, establishing the record at seventy. The home run record, long thought to be the most elusive of all baseball feats, was broken again in 2001, when Bonds hit seventy-three.

Impact The inflation of home run production in the 1990's—climaxing with the record-breaking 1998 season—was indicative of an era that associated grandiosity with superiority. The home run, a symbol of pomp and potency, reconnected a generation seemingly apathetic toward the game. Given subsequent accusations of a pervasive use of performance-enhancing drugs during the era, speculation clouds the legitimacy of the decade's batting records. Regardless, the home run race of 1998 reminded the American public of both the relevance and necessity of its national game.

Further Reading

McNeil, William. *The Single-Season Home Run Kings: Ruth, Maris, McGwire, Sosa, and Bonds.* Jefferson, N.C.: McFarland, 2003.

Paisner, Daniel. *The Ball: Mark McGwire's Seventieth Home Run Ball and the Marketing of the American Dream.* New York: Viking Press, 1999.

Schreiber, Lee R. *Race for the Record: The Great Home Run Chase of 1998.* New York: HarperCollins, 1998.

Christopher Rager

See also Baseball; Baseball realignment; Baseball strike of 1994; Griffey, Ken, Jr.; McGwire, Mark; Ripken, Cal, Jr.; Sosa, Sammy; Sports.

■ Homeschooling

Definition Education of children at home rather than in a school

Homeschooling is a viable educational option for parents who, for various reasons, wish to be involved in their children's education under conditions involving reduced stress. In the spring of 1999, approximately 850,000 children across the United States were being homeschooled.

An alternative to traditional school, homeschooling is a flexible and diverse educational option for fami-

Ten Most Common Reasons for Homeschooling and the Percentage of Homeschooled Students Whose Parents Gave Each Reason

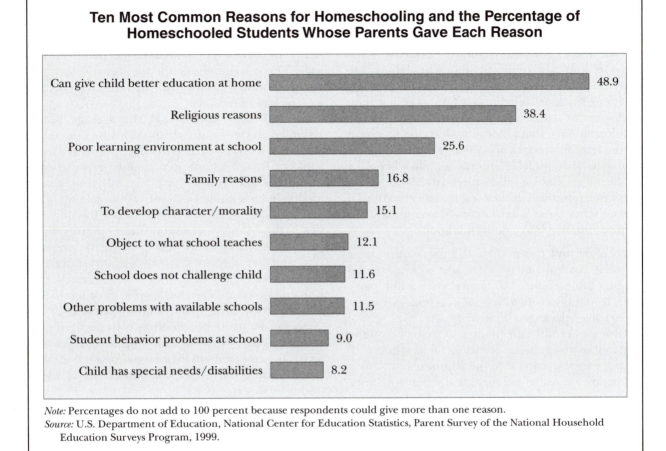

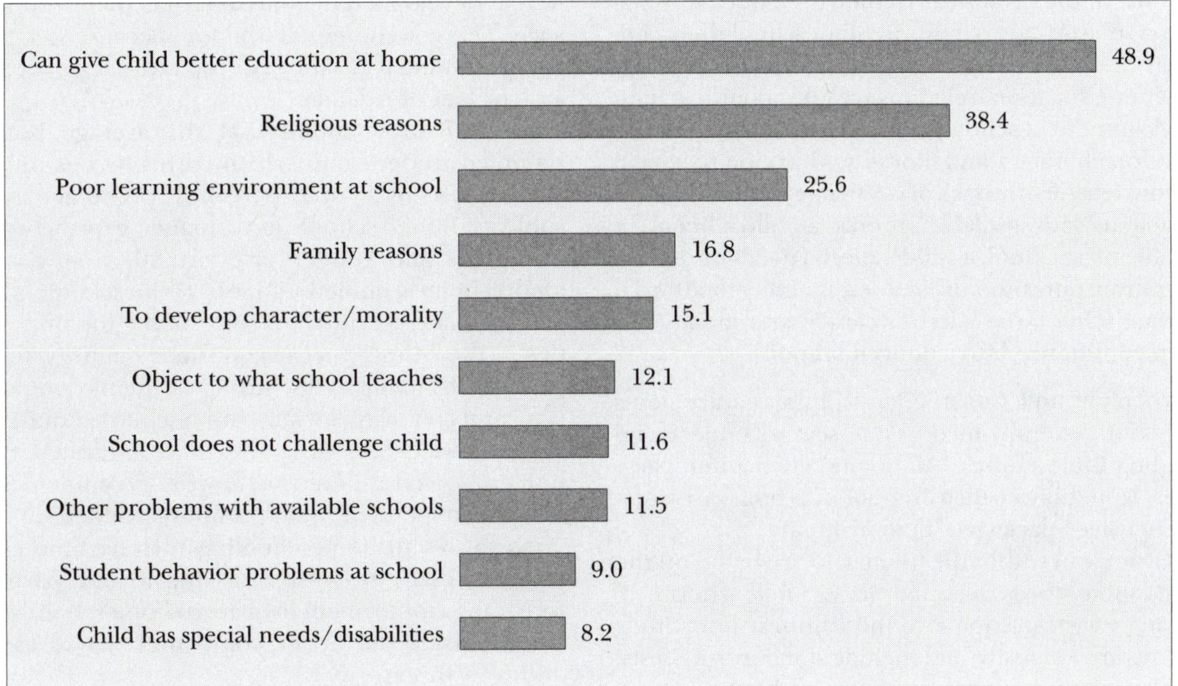

Note: Percentages do not add to 100 percent because respondents could give more than one reason.
Source: U.S. Department of Education, National Center for Education Statistics, Parent Survey of the National Household Education Surveys Program, 1999.

lies. A homeschool can be organized as a traditional school or through an unstructured approach determined by a child's readiness and interests.

The state may compel all children to attend a school, public or private, and home instruction will not suffice as an exemption from compulsory school attendance unless a state statute so indicates. Several states disallowed home instruction because it was believed that sequestration of students from other classmates would inhibit their social development and prevent the children from living normal lives. In states that permitted homeschooling, the key elements in determining the validity and value of homeschooling involved the educational level of the parents and the regularity and time of instruction. Those states prescribed minimal standards for instruction. Courts have upheld such criteria, provided they are reasonable. In challenging homeschooling as an alternative to compulsory attendance, the state has the burden of proving that the parent is not providing adequate instruction. As of the early twenty-first century, homeschooling was legal in all fifty states and throughout Canada. It also became popular in Australia, New Zealand, England, and Japan.

Demographics and Reasons Homeschooling families of the 1990's varied politically and religiously, though the typical homeschooling parents were white married couples who homeschooled their children primarily for religious (Christian) or moral reasons. They had three or more children, and it was usually the mother who remained at home. Single parents also homeschooled. In 1999, 20.6 percent of homeschools in the United States were led by single parents. While the number of students being homeschooled increased in the 1990's and into the early twenty-first century, race and ethnicity rates remained consistent; the homeschooling rate for white students was higher than those for black and Hispanic students.

According to a 1999 survey by the Department of Education's National Center for Education Statistics, reasons for parents to homeschool their children (in descending order) included the following: a better education, religious reasons, poor learning environment at school, family reasons, the desire to develop character and morality, objection to what a school teaches, the lack of challenge at school, other problems with available schools, a child's behavior problems at school, a child's special needs or disabilities, transportation difficulties, inability to afford a private school, the parent's career, and inability to gain admittance into a desired school.

Curriculum and Costs Curriculum requirements vary but generally incorporate several subjects, including Bible studies. "All-in-one" curriculum packages, sometimes called "school in a box," are comprehensive packages that re-create the school environment within the home and are based on the same subject area expectations as public schools, allowing easy transition into the school system. Study guides are extensive and include standardized tests, remote examinations, and an accredited diploma. Learner-paced curricula allow students to progress at their own speed. Regulations regarding homeschooling vary from state to state. Certain states require the completion of paperwork; others simply require notification to the local school district. During the 1990's, homeschoolers were among those taking advantage of educational opportunities at museums and other community forums and often meeting other homeschoolers to form cooperatives, pooling talent and resources to broaden the scope of children's education.

In addition to purchasing supplies and curriculum materials, there was sometimes a financial impact on families because one parent (generally the mother) usually stayed at home to supervise the child's education. In 1998, expenses associated with homeschooling ranged from less than $200 to more than $2,000 per student. The national average expenditure for public school students in 1998 was $6,200 to $6,500 per student.

Pros and Cons The greatest benefit of homeschooling appears to be in strengthening family bonds. Homeschoolers have great flexibility in what and how they learn and receive an education geared specifically to their own needs, personalities, and interests. There is physical and educational freedom, and the family is free to plan off-season vacations as well as develop a timetable that suits their own lifestyle. There is emotional freedom because students can dress and act as they choose without peer pressure or fear of ridicule.

A 1997 study found that the average homeschooled student outperformed his or her public school peers by 30 to 37 percentile points across all subjects. Public school performance gaps between minorities and genders are virtually nonexistent among homeschooled students. Homeschoolers are accepted and recruited by some of the top universities in the country because of their maturity, independent thinking skills, strong academic preparation, and creativity. Socially, homeschooled students excel as well. Several studies have indicated that homeschooled children are more self-confident and less peer-dependent than traditional students.

Negatives to homeschooling include time constraints, financial constraints due to one partner foregoing employment in order to homeschool, and living outside the norm, sometimes viewed as an oddity or threat.

Impact During the 1990's, homeschooling became more common and more widely accepted. Families from diverse backgrounds resorted to homeschooling because they disagreed with the philosophy of American schools and were dissatisfied with the content and quality of the education provided.

Subsequent Events A 2003 survey of seventy-three hundred adults, most of whom had been homeschooled for more than seven years, indicated that they were living more active lives within their communities and were more involved in civic affairs than their non-homeschooled peers. The majority (58.9 percent) reported that they were "very happy" with life, compared with 27.6 percent for the general population.

Further Reading

Guterson, David. *Family Matters: Why Homeschooling Makes Sense.* New York: Harcourt Brace Jovanovich, 1992. Written by a high school educator whose children are homeschooled, the book discusses the benefits and drawbacks of homeschooling and public schooling.

Linsenbach, Sherri. *Essential Homeschooling: Every-*

thing You Need to Know to Educate Your Child at Home. Avon, Mass.: Adams Media, 2006. A basic how-to book for homeschoolers.

Mur, Cindy, ed. *Home Schooling.* San Diego, Calif.: Greenhaven Press, 2003. Presents discussions by scholars on the issues surrounding homeschooling.

Marcia J. Weiss

See also Educate America Act of 1994; Education in Canada; Education in the United States; Mozart effect; Religion and spirituality in the United States; School violence; Year-round schools.

■ Homosexuality and gay rights

Definition Same-sex relationships and the struggle for legal and cultural acceptance of gay, lesbian, bisexual, and transgender people

The gay, lesbian, bisexual, and transgender (GLBT) community suffered from hate crimes in the 1990's, even as the debate over gay rights developed an intense focus on the military and same-sex marriage.

The 1990's saw a move toward greater civil rights activism in the GLBT community. Where the 1970's were considered an era of coming out, and the 1980's were taken up largely by the response to acquired immunodeficiency syndrome (AIDS), the 1990's brought both opportunities and tragedies to draw homosexual civil rights into the forefront of national attention. In the military, the United States adopted the disastrous "don't ask, don't tell" policy, while Canada allowed homosexuals to openly join its military. Canada extended its Human Rights Act to include homosexuals, while three hate crimes against gays in the United States served to draw attention to the need for more inclusive hate crime laws. Also, same-sex couples in both countries began pushing for the right to marry.

The Military Throughout his presidential campaign, Bill Clinton promised gay rights groups that, if elected, he would help improve the status of gays in the military. However, once he was in office, he immediately encountered pressure and had to develop a compromise policy that would be accepted by both Democrats and Republicans. The plan he unveiled in 1992 was labeled "don't ask, don't tell." Essentially, it stated that a person's sexual orientation was private business, forbade anyone in the military from asking another's sexual orientation, and instructed people in the armed forces not to reveal their sexual orientation. The rationalization behind the campaign was that gays could not be persecuted or evicted from the military if nobody knew they were gay. However, in practice, the policy served to push gays in the armed forces even further into the closet. Complaining to a superior officer about being harassed about one's sexual orientation was tantamount to admitting homosexuality, which invited the military ban. Two gay men were murdered in the military before the new policy's consequences became obvious to politicians.

In the same year that Clinton unveiled "don't ask, don't tell" in the United States, Canada lifted its military ban, allowing homosexuals to serve openly in the Canadian Forces. The move did not precipitate any morale loss or other problems for the country, heavily undermining some key arguments by the U.S. military. Indeed, the quiet success served as a spearhead for gay rights groups in the United States.

Hate Crimes and Civil Rights The 1990's also saw hate crimes committed against gays. Three very public cases highlight the issues raised. In 1992, U.S. Navy airman apprentice Terry Helvey beat his colleague Allen Schindler to death because Schindler was gay. Barry Winchell, a private in the Army, was murdered in 1999 by fellow recruit Calvin Glover following harassment about his sexual orientation that Winchell feared to report to his superior officers. Both military cases had similar components. Schindler and Winchell had both been harassed for their sexual orientation, and both feared repercussions if they reported the problems to superior officers. Winchell's death was a spearhead for Clinton to ask Congress to review "don't ask, don't tell," but the policy remains in place.

The third situation involved the murder of college student Matthew Shepard in 1998. Two strangers, Russell Henderson and Aaron McKinney, murdered Shepard for being gay. Shepard met his killers at the Fireside Lounge in Laramie, Wyoming, then drove away with them because he needed a ride, unaware that they were targeting a gay man and intending to rob him. They pistol-whipped Shepard and left him tied to a fence. A cyclist found Shepard by chance, after first mistaking him for a scarecrow, but Shepard later died from his wounds without regaining consciousness. Neither killer could be prosecuted for hate crimes under federal or Wyoming statutes. Though one of Shepard's killers could have faced the death penalty, Shepard's mother interceded, asking that the hatred stop, so both Henderson and McKinney received two concurrent life sentences. Shepard's death spurred action groups to demand legislative action leading to more inclusive hate crime laws, as the Hate Crime Statistics Act that President George H. W. Bush had signed in 1990 stipulated only studying hate crimes against gays, not sanctions against their killers.

Not all civil rights victories in the era stemmed from tragedy. Some successes originated in the work of activists throughout North America. For instance, Nova Scotia added sexual orientation to its Human Rights Act as early as 1991. New Brunswick and British Columbia followed suit in the following year, and Saskatchewan in 1993. That year also marked comic strip artist Lynn Johnston's addition of a coming out theme to her popular strip *For Better or For Worse.* Finally, in 1996, sexual orientation was added to the Canadian Human Rights Act.

In the United States, numerous corporate entities introduced domestic partner health benefits, including those for same-sex domestic partners. In 1996, the Southern Baptist Convention boycotted Disney after it extended benefits to same-sex domestic partners, but the boycott failed to affect the company financially or otherwise. Disney's move encouraged other corporations to follow its lead. Throughout the decade, states ratified constitutional amendments prohibiting employment and housing discrimination against homosexuals. Also, the Supreme Court ruled against a Colorado law that would have prohibited gays and lesbians from legal protections in *Romer v. Evans* (1996).

In the religious sector, some religions began accepting openly gay clergy, including Reform Judaism, which in 1990 agreed to allow gay and lesbian rabbis. Throughout the decade, celebrities came out of the closet, including actress and comedian Ellen DeGeneres and singers K. D. Lang and Melissa Etheridge. Finally, some victories came in the health arena: The 1994 discovery of protease inhibitors led to a decrease of approximately 50 percent in AIDS deaths.

Same-Sex Marriage The battle for gay and lesbian rights in the 1990's, in both Canada and the United States, focused on the struggle to gain equal marriage rights. Starting in 1990, Hawaii became the center of the gay marriage controversy in the United States. Ninia Baehr, her partner Genora Dancel, and two other same-sex couples wished to marry, and they had to go against a state law prohibiting same-sex marriage. Their 1991 lawsuit, *Baehr vs. Lewin* (later renamed *Baehr vs. Miike*), argued that the state constitution's due process and equal protection clauses made the law prohibiting same-sex marriage unconstitutional. The Hawaii Supreme Court supported the couples, and they issued a legal challenge against the law.

In 1996, Judge Kevin Chang ruled that the couples could marry. However, the historic decision did not precipitate a tide of same-sex weddings. Indeed, Hawaiian public opinion was fairly antigay, and state voters amended the constitution in 1998 to prohibit same-sex marriage. The state had already issued an appeal against Chang's 1996 ruling, so when the constitution changed, the Supreme Court had to overturn the decision and prohibit the weddings.

Nationally, antigay backlash reigned as well. When Chang's ruling made gay marriage possible in Hawaii, if only for a short while, conservative House Speaker Newt Gingrich introduced the Defense of Marriage Act (DOMA), defining marriage as between one man and one woman. The bill passed the House of Representatives by a vote of 346 to 67 and the Senate by 85 to 14. Moreover, President Clinton agreed to sign it. The act was aimed at discouraging other states from legalizing gay marriage. While it did not prohibit states from doing so, it announced that other states were not required to recognize such unions. The Religious Right controlled the national discussion, with Gingrich and other majority leaders proclaiming same-sex marriages a threat to "traditional" family values.

However, same-sex couples challenged this position. In 1998, Alaskan courts ruled that the state's constitution did not prohibit gay marriage, but the legislature quickly added a constitutional amendment prohibiting same-sex unions. By 1999, the backlash was decreasing, and some states began accepting the notion of gay legal unions. In 1999, the Vermont Supreme Court determined that the state's constitution ensured same-sex and opposite-sex couples the same protections. The following year,

Vermont became the first state to recognize same-sex civil unions. While not marriages, these unions still carried the same legal rights and responsibilities for couples. More states followed in the early twenty-first century, even as other states enacted gay marriage bans in the 1990's and 2000's.

Impact Attention to gay rights fluctuated throughout the decade, with both those for and those against scoring significant victories. Canada's military moved to allow homosexuals to serve, and the debate over their status in the U.S. armed forces intensified. Canada added homosexuality to its Human Rights Act, while in the United States the hate crimes committed against Allen Schindler, Matthew Shepard, and Barry Winchell (particularly Shepard) served to raise public awareness. Finally, the battle for gay marriage continued into the early twenty-first century, with the country of Canada and some U.S. states ultimately legalizing gay marriage or gay civil unions.

Further Reading

Gallagher, John, and Chris Bull. *Perfect Enemies: The Religious Right, the Gay Movement, and the Politics of the 1990's.* New York: Crown, 1996. Argues that because the Religious Right and gay rights movement exist on the fringes of society, they are ideal opponents, each spurring the other forward. Includes "don't ask, don't tell" and gay marriage debates.

Herman, Didi. *Rights of Passage: Struggles for Lesbian and Gay Legal Equality.* Buffalo, N.Y.: University of Toronto Press, 1994. Discusses the growing gay rights movement in Canada in the late 1980's and early 1990's. Offers perspective on the Canadian scene before the Canadian Human Rights Act was amended in the early 1990's.

Nava, Michael, and Robert Dawidoff. *Created Equal: Why Gay Rights Matter to America.* New York: St. Martin's Press, 1994. Argues that homosexuals are denied constitutional rights in the United States and encourages gay rights activism from readers.

Pierceson, Jason. *Courts, Liberalism, and Rights: Gay Law and Politics in the United States and Canada.* Philadelphia: Temple University Press, 2005. Focuses on the relationship between legal and social justice in the gay community, with discussions of sexual privacy and gay marriage.

Rayside, David Morton. *On the Fringe: Gays and Lesbians in Politics.* Ithaca, N.Y.: Cornell University Press, 1998. Summarizes some key 1990's gay rights debates. Canadian section includes a discussion of the Canadian Human Rights Act. U.S. section discusses the military ban on homosexuals.

Warner, Tom. *Never Going Back: A History of Queer Activism in Canada.* Buffalo, N.Y.: University of Toronto Press, 2002. In-depth research into the Canadian gay rights movement, including the 1990's and the modification of the Canadian Human Rights Act as well as the move toward legalizing gay marriages.

Jessie Bishop Powell

See also AIDS epidemic; *Baker v. Vermont*; Defense of Marriage Act of 1996; DeGeneres, Ellen; Domestic partnerships; Don't ask, don't tell; *Egan v. Canada*; Etheridge, Melissa; Gingrich, Newt; Hate crimes; Lang, K. D.; Marriage and divorce; Queer Nation; Shepard, Matthew; Transgender community.

■ Hubble Space Telescope

Identification An orbiting astronomical telescope
Manufacturer The National Aeronautics and Space Administration and the European Space Agency
Date Launched April 24, 1990, from the Kennedy Space Center in Cape Canaveral, Florida

The first large telescope to take advantage of the clear and undisturbed environment in outer space, the Hubble Space Telescope revolutionized astronomy. After it was repaired in 1993, the telescope produced images of unprecedented clarity.

The Hubble Space Telescope (HST) consists of a single large tubular enclosure, 13.2 meters (about 43.5 feet) long and 4.2 meters (about 14 feet) wide, and weighs about 12 tons. Inside it is the primary mirror, 2.4 meters (about 7.8 feet) in diameter, and other optics, together with several instruments for detecting and analyzing the images formed by the optics. Initially, there were two cameras with charge-coupled device (CCD) detectors and two spectrographs for both high-resolution and faint-object spectroscopy. The optical design is what is called a Ritchie-Chretien Cassegrain, which involves a series of curved mirrors: the large primary mirror, which brings the light to a focus; a smaller secondary mirror, which bounces the light back toward the primary, where it passes through a central hole; and a set of 45-degree mirrors that can reflect the image to a choice of cameras and spectrographs.

A thin aluminum shell covers the entire telescope to protect it from solar radiation, and many layers of insulation help to keep temperatures low, as the instruments must be very cold to operate most efficiently. Inside there are four heavy flywheels that are used to orient the telescope toward the place in the sky that is to be observed. The HST is remarkably accurate at pointing at celestial targets: It can hold on a star or galaxy for a few thousandths of an arc second.

The telescope is powered by two 8-foot-long solar panels, which are mounted to the sides of the telescope and rotate to face the Sun for maximum power. Batteries provide backup power during the times when Earth eclipses the Sun. Since the telescope's launch in 1990, the panels have been replaced twice by newer models, which can generate about 5,700 watts of electrical power.

The HST remains in a low orbit, about 610 kilometers (380 miles) above Earth, so that it can be serviced by astronauts, but the result is that the planet blocks about half of the sky during the 180-minute orbit. Therefore, exposures are limited to less than half that time, and targets are usually visited many times. Very long exposures can be built up in this way to allow Hubble scientists to detect extremely faint objects, a hundred times fainter than those objects detectable from ground-based telescopes.

The telescope was designed to be upgraded as needed, and provisions were made for the easy removal and exchange of various instruments by astronauts visiting the space telescope. This feature resulted in keeping the telescope up-to-date with the most recent technological advances throughout the 1990's and in the early twenty-first century. There were three such shuttle missions in the 1990's.

Disaster, Recovery, and Triumph Shortly after the launch of the Hubble Space Telescope, the worldwide astronomy community, which had waited forty years to have access to the wonders expected to be revealed by the HST, was dismayed to learn that a colossal error had been made by one of the National Aeronautics and Space Administration (NASA) contractors who produced the primary mirror. Instead of sharp images, stars appeared fuzzy and indistinct. The mirror suffered from a defect called spherical aberration: It had the wrong shape.

NASA and the European Space Agency (ESA) immediately appointed a panel of astronomers, engineers, and technicians to design a solution to the problem. It took three years to produce a complicated instrument, the Corrective Optics Space Telescope Axial Replacement (COSTAR), and to have astronauts install it in the HST's interior. This occurred in December, 1993, and the COSTAR worked perfectly. The telescope produced images that were basically as good as the original specifications.

Throughout the rest of the decade, the HST made an astounding number of dramatic discoveries in virtually all fields of astronomy, ranging from

A long view of the Hubble Space Telescope over Shark Bay, Australia. The photo was taken from the space shuttle Discovery. (NASA)

the planets and comets of the solar system to remote galaxies. An especially spectacular achievement occurred in December, 1995, when the telescope was pointed to a particular small area of sky over a period of ten days, resulting in 342 exposures. Called the Hubble Deep Field, this penetration into the universe recorded galaxies 10 to 12 billion light-years away, during the universe's infancy. The HST showed a different universe, one made up of fragments of galaxies that had not yet coalesced to form giant spiral galaxies like the Milky Way.

Cosmology was advanced through the 1990's by these and similar HST discoveries, including the demonstration that the quasars are actually galaxies undergoing collisions that have led to the formation of black holes in their centers. Black holes in the nuclei of nearby galaxies were also discovered using HST velocity measurements, showing that black holes are the explanation for a variety of puzzlingly active galaxies, known but not understood for decades.

Impact The Hubble Space Telescope has had an important impact on the world's understanding of the universe. The heyday of its discoveries occurred in the years 1993-1999, when it revolutionized concepts of cosmology and dramatically expanded knowledge of the physics of stars, as well as the solar system and other planetary systems.

Further Reading

Christensen, Lars Lindberg, and Bob Fosbury. *Hubble: Fifteen Years of Discovery*. New York: Springer, 2006. A richly illustrated look at space through the HST.

Petersen, Carolyn Collins, and John C. Brandt. *Hubble Vision: Further Adventures with the Hubble Space Telescope*. 2d ed. New York: Cambridge University Press, 1998. Offers a comprehensive discussion of the astronomical discoveries made possible by the HST. Includes attractive illustrations, glossary, bibliography, and index.

Smith, Robert W. *The Space Telescope: A Study of NASA, Science, Technology, and Politics*. New York: Cambridge University Press, 1993. Provides a detailed chronological account of the construction of the HST from its inception to launch preparation.

Voit, Mark. *Hubble Space Telescope: New Views of the Universe*. New York: Harry N. Abrams, 2000. A clearly written book on the HST. Concise, but not comprehensive.

Paul Hodge

See also Astronomy; Hale-Bopp comet; Inventions; Mars exploration; Science and technology; Shoemaker-Levy 9 comet; Space exploration; Space shuttle program.

■ Human Genome Project

Identification International research project to sequence the base pairs of DNA in the human genome

Date Officially launched October 1, 1990

Knowledge of the sequence of all 3 billion base pairs of the human genome will allow for a better understanding of the function of genes in healthy human beings, the role genes play in disease, the extent of genetic variation within the human population, and the evolutionary relationship humans have with each other and with other organisms.

The Human Genome Project (HGP) had its origins in a 1984 Department of Energy (DOE) meeting, when sequencing of the human genome was first discussed as a way for the DOE to meet its congressional mandate to monitor and assess environmentally induced genetic damage. In 1985, sequencing of the human genome was seriously proposed by molecular biologist Robert Sinsheimer, then chancellor of the University of California, Santa Cruz. In 1986, Sydney Brenner, a molecular biologist at the Medical Research Council in Great Britain, and Renato Dulbecco, a viral molecular biologist at the Salk Institute in La Jolla, California, independently suggested sequencing the human genome. All of these suggestions came to fruition later in 1986 at the Cold Spring Harbor Laboratory in New York, when a serious proposal to sequence the human genome in a multinational effort was developed. The National Research Council (NRC) and Congress's Office of Technology Assessment soon became interested and sponsored feasibility studies. A committee of the NRC concluded in 1988 that sequencing the human genome was both feasible and desirable.

Technological Developments Several technological inventions and developments made the Human Genome Project possible. These include the invention of the polymerase chain reaction (1985), the invention and subsequent development of automatic deoxyribonucleic acid (DNA) sequencers (1986) and their commercialization by Applied Biosystems,

The Working Draft of the Human "Book of Life"

On June 26, 2000, following remarks by President Bill Clinton and British prime minister Tony Blair, the director of the National Human Genome Research Institute, Dr. Francis Collins, announced that a "first draft" of the human genome had been completed:

Science is a voyage of exploration into the unknown. We are here today to celebrate a milestone along a truly unprecedented voyage, this one into ourselves. Alexander Pope wrote, "Know then thyself. Presume not God to scan. The proper study of mankind is man." What more powerful form of study of mankind could there be than to read our own instruction book?

I've been privileged over the last seven years to lead an international team of more than a thousand of some of the best and brightest scientists of our current generation, some of them here in this room, who have been truly dedicated to this goal. Today, we celebrate the revelation of the first draft of the human book of life. . . .

Today, we deliver . . . the most visible and spectacular milestone of all. Most of the sequencing of the human genome by this international consortium has been done in just the last 15 months. During that time, this consortium has developed the capacity to sequence 1,000 letters of the DNA code per second, seven days a week, 24 hours a day. We have developed a map of overlapping fragments that includes 97 percent of the human genome, and we have sequenced 85 percent of this.

The sequence data is of higher quality than expected with half of it in finished or near-finished form. And all of this information has been placed in public databases every 24 hours, where any scientist with an Internet connection can use it to help unravel the mysteries of human biology. Already, more than a dozen genes, responsible for diseases from deafness to kidney disease to cancer, have been identified using this resource just in the last year. . . .

I think I speak for all of us in this room, and for the millions of others who have come to believe in the remarkable promise of biomedical research, that we must redouble our efforts to speed the application of these profound and fundamental observations about the human genome to the cure of disease. That most desirable of all outcomes will only come about with a continued powerful and dedicated partnership between basic science investigators and academia, and their colleagues in the biotechnology and pharmaceutical industries.

Inc. (1987), the development of yeast artificial chromosomes (1987) and bacterial artificial chromosomes (1992) for cloning large segments of DNA, the invention of fluorescent chain termination sequencing (1987), the development of capillary electrophoresis (1987) and the subsequent development of a capillary sequencing apparatus (1997), the development of the basic local alignment search tool (BLAST, 1990), and the development of computer programs that interpret and assemble DNA sequences (1998).

Origins and Start In 1988, the DOE was the first to expend funds on sequencing the human genome. That year, the National Institutes of Health (NIH) decided to get involved with human genome sequencing and established the Office for Human Genome Research. The National Center for Human Genome Research (NCHGR) was established a year later (and renamed the National Human Genome Research Institute in 1997); James D. Watson, codiscoverer (with Francis Crick) of the structure of DNA, was named as associate director (and later director) for human genomic research. The DOE and NIH agreed to collaborate on sequencing the human genome, launching the HGP late in 1988. The NCHGR officially set the start of the HGP as October 1, 1990.

In 1990, the NCHGR decided to construct a genetic map of the human genome using markers that was later to be followed by sequencing small regions of the genome and then assembling the sequences using the markers as a guide. This strategy would reveal not only the sequence coding for polypeptides but also the control/regulatory regions.

In the summer of 1991, at a congressional briefing on the HGP, J. Craig Venter, a molecular biologist at the NIH, indicated that he had been sequencing parts (about three hundred base pairs) of DNA that were expressed as messenger ribonucleic acid (mRNA) and coded for polypeptides. Venter and many other scientists thought that these polypeptide coding regions, the so-called expressed regions, of the genome were the most interesting and important and should be sequenced first. Venter referred to his short, three hundred base-pair pieces as expressed sequence tags (ESTs). This approach would yield most of the information sought after by the HGP, and the cost would be substantially less. Furthermore, Venter announced that the NIH planned to file patent applications on the sequences. Watson, who opposed patenting, resigned as head of the NCHGR in 1992 in a dispute with Bernadine Healy, director of the NIH. He was eventually replaced by Francis Collins.

In 1996, the NCHGR funded a consortium of six DNA sequencing centers that included the Whitehead Institute at the Massachusetts Institute of Technology, Washington University, Baylor College of Medicine, the University of Washington, Stanford University, and The Institute for Genomic Research (TIGR), a nonprofit sequencing effort established in 1992 by Venter. The Sanger Sequencing Centre in the United Kingdom later joined the HGP, allowing for the establishment of the publicly funded International Human Genome Sequencing Consortium (IHGSC).

Completion of the Project In 1998, Venter announced the establishment of Celera Genomics, a private company devoted to DNA sequencing. Venter claimed that he could sequence the human genome by 2001. With Venter's claim, a sequencing race began between his company and the IHGSC, which intensified its efforts. Each group claimed that it could publish a draft of the sequence earlier than the other. In a June, 2000, meeting at the White House, the IHGSC and Celera jointly announced a working draft of the human genome. The draft of the consortium's project was published in *Nature* on February 15, 2001, while Celera's draft was published in *Science* on February 16. The completion of the project was announced on April 14, 2003, the fiftieth anniversary of the publication of the discovery of the structure of DNA, by the IHGSC. The consortium continues to search for variation within human genomes and the functions of the genes discovered by the project.

Impact The sequencing of the human genome has led to an increased understanding of gene function, the mechanisms and causations of human genetic diseases, the extent of variation within the population, and humans' evolutionary relationship with other organisms.

Further Reading

Davies, Kevin. *Cracking the Genome: Inside the Race to Unlock Human DNA*. New York: Free Press, 2001. Using interviews with Collins and Venter, among many other scientists, Davies presents a rich story of the race to sequence the human genome.

"The Human Genome." *Nature* 409 (February 15, 2001): 745-964. A special issue publishing the working draft announced in 2000, with a collection of relevant papers.

"The Human Genome." *Science* 291 (February 16, 2001): 1145-1434. While the parallel special issue of *Nature* concentrated on the HGP's contribution, this issue concentrated on Celera's.

Richards, Julia E., and R. Scott Hawley. *The Human Genome: A User's Guide*. 2d ed. Burlington, Mass.: Elsevier, 2005. A good general overview of genetics written for the layperson.

Ridley, Matt. *Genome: The Autobiography of a Species in Twenty-three Chapters*. New York: HarperCollins, 1999. The author examines one gene from each chromosome (one per chapter) and writes the history of its role in human development.

Shreeve, James. *The Genome War: How Craig Venter Tried to Capture the Code of Life and Save the World*. New York: Alfred A. Knopf, 2004. An engaging narrative about the personalities and politics behind the Human Genome Project.

Charles L. Vigue

See also Alzheimer's disease; Cancer research; Genetic engineering; Genetics research; Medicine; Pharmaceutical industry; Science and technology.

■ Hurricane Andrew

Identification The most destructive natural disaster to strike the United States in the twentieth century

Date August 24, 1992

The destruction caused by Hurricane Andrew awakened people in coastal areas to the dangers hurricanes pose and resulted in a revision of building codes and preventive tactics in hurricane-prone areas.

Andrew, the first named hurricane of the 1992 hurricane season, began on August 14 as a tropical wave off Africa's west coast. It moved west at about twenty-five miles per hour and on the seventeenth was declared the first tropical storm of the season. By August 22, Andrew, having gained energy as it passed over warm ocean waters, erupted as a hurricane whose wind gusts exceeded 170 miles per hour. The following day it became a category 5 hurricane, the highest category ascribed to such storms, with storm surges of almost twenty feet.

By August 22, forecasters realized that a killer storm was headed for South Florida, which, remarkably, had not experienced a hurricane for the past twenty-five years, a quarter century in which its population more than doubled. Andrew reached the Bahamas late on August 23 and, in passing over land, lost some of its intensity, its winds dropping to 145 miles per hour. As it proceeded west, however, it passed over the warm waters of the Gulf of Mexico, which increased its intensity to over 170 miles per hour.

Before sunrise on August 24, the storm made a direct hit on Homestead, Florida, with sustained winds estimated at 165 miles per hour. On that day, Hurricane Andrew wrought more destruction than any natural disaster in U.S. history to date, and it was not through yet, continuing its course northwest to hit the Louisiana coast.

The Human Toll Hurricane Andrew was directly responsible for fifteen deaths in South Florida, with twenty-five additional deaths related to the hurricane occurring after the storm's initial assault. It is difficult to estimate the psychological trauma that ensues after one lives through a storm as violent and terrifying as this one. Even years after the disaster, many people who lived through the storm in Florida and in coastal Louisiana suffered from severe post-traumatic stress. As the storm raged, people hunkered down in their houses, usually in small, confined areas like bathrooms, hallways, or closets. They were completely at the mercy of the winds and rising waters caused by the storm. This feeling of helplessness left many traumatized for years after the disaster.

So great was the fear engendered in those who survived the storm that over 100,000 of them did not return to the places where they had lived prior to the hurricane. Whole families were virtually wiped out financially by the storm's destruction. Over 250,000 residents of South Florida were homeless after Hurricane Andrew.

The Economic Toll The overall estimated cost of the damage Hurricane Andrew caused exceeded $30 billion in South Florida and another $1 billion in Louisiana. In 2007 dollars, this would come to

Hurricane Andrew approaches Florida and the Bahamas to the west. (National Oceanic and Atmospheric Administration)

over twice the stated amounts. No previous disaster had cost the United States more in damage.

In south Dade County, over 82,000 businesses were wiped out or damaged so severely that they had to suspend operations for long periods after the storm. Insurance adjusters could not keep up with the flood of claims that resulted from the hurricane, and considerable controversy developed over whether the damage done to residences and businesses was the result of water damage and flooding or wind damage. Many insurance policies did not cover flooding, and it was difficult to prove whether wind or water had caused the damage on which policyholders sought settlements. Nine major insurers became insolvent following the storm.

In Dade County, 63,000 of the county's 528,000 residences were completely destroyed, and another 110,000 were severely damaged. Nine of the county's public schools were completely destroyed and another twenty-three were so heavily damaged that they could not immediately resume operation. In an area with many mobile home parks, only one percent of the mobile homes survived the storm.

The hurricane wiped out much of the agricultural production in the areas affected. The tourist industry on which much of South Florida is dependent was also greatly diminished. The storm's ecological damage was notable. Century-old coral reefs off the Florida coast were wholly destroyed.

Impact Hurricane Andrew was a wake-up call for residents of South Florida and coastal Louisiana, the areas in the United States most affected by the hurricane's destruction. Serious deficiencies in construction were discovered as whole neighborhoods were swept away in the wake of the storm.

As a result, many reputable builders drastically improved their construction practices even before they were called upon legally to bring about such improvements. It was not until a decade after the hurricane struck that Florida lawmakers enacted legislation imposing stringent statewide building codes upon builders. Also, considerable attention was given to developing early warning systems and establishing escape routes for those in the path of impending storms.

Further Reading

Emanuel, Kerry. *Divine Wind: The History of and Science of Hurricanes.* New York: Oxford University Press, 2005. A fine, well-illustrated study of hurricanes, with special attention given to Hurricane Andrew in chapter 31.

Lovelace, John K. *Storm-Tide Elevations Produced by Hurricane Andrew Along the Louisiana Coast, August 25-27, 1992.* Baton Rouge, La.: U.S. Geological Survey, 1994. An account of how Hurricane Andrew continued to grow as it crossed South Florida and struck the Louisiana coast, leaving considerable devastation.

Mann, Philip H., ed. *Lessons Learned from Hurricane Andrew: A Conference Sponsored by Florida International University.* Miami: Florida International University Press, 1993. Valuable for the suggestions its contributors make for coping with future hurricanes.

Provenzo, Eugene F., Jr., and Asterie Baker Provenzo. *In the Eye of Hurricane Andrew.* Gainesville: University Press of Florida, 2002. A firsthand account of what it was like to live through Hurricane Andrew, including information about survival and rebuilding after the storm.

Sheets, Bob, and Jack Williams. *Hurricane Watch: Forecasting the Deadliest Storms on Earth.* New York: Penguin Books, 2001. Sound overall coverage with valuable information about how to forecast hurricanes.

R. Baird Shuman

See also Global warming debate; Natural disasters; Oklahoma tornado outbreak; Perfect Storm, the; Storm of the Century.

I

■ Illegal immigration

Definition Entry of persons in violation of U.S. immigration laws

During the decade, approximately half a million persons entered the United States illegally each year, with many experts arguing that the country needed their labor, in contrast to others who asserted that their presence promoted crime and depressed the wages of working citizens.

The Census Bureau estimated that there were about 3.5 million illegal immigrants residing in the United States in 1990 and that the number grew to about 8 million by 2000. For this increase to have occurred, it was necessary for the net increase to have been between 450,000 and 500,000 each year. About 80 percent of the illegal immigrants were from Latin America, including 57 percent from Mexico. Another 10 percent came from Asia, 6 percent were from Europe or Canada, and fewer than 4 percent arrived from Africa. The number of illegal immigrants was only about half as large as the number of permanent residents who had entered legally.

Although illegal immigration resulted from a number of push and pull factors, the overwhelming majority of immigrants entered the United States for one reason: to find gainful employment. More than two-thirds of the illegal workers were holding low-wage jobs, including cleaning, restaurant labor, child care, packaging, and the harvesting of food. A Commission on Immigration Reform presented a 1994 report emphasizing that the only way to reduce their numbers would be to "turn off the jobs magnet that attracts them."

Economists and sociologists disagreed about the effects of the illegal immigrants. Defenders of illegal immigrants argued that they generally performed jobs that citizens were either unwilling or unable to do. Many farmers and other employers insisted that migrant labor was essential in order to compete with imported goods from Mexico and other low-wage countries. Opponents, however, answered that undocumented workers were also replacing U.S. citizens in areas like construction and that their willingness to accept lower wages forced citizens to do the same. Opponents also maintained that illegal immigrants were disproportionately involved in the trafficking of illicit drugs, prostitution, and other crimes. An additional argument was that it was imperative that the country be able to control its borders and enforce its laws.

Attempts at Reform At the beginning of the decade, the major law relating to illegal immigration was the Immigration Reform and Control Act of 1986. This act had granted temporary residency and amnesty to illegal immigrants who had lived in the United States since 1982. The act made it illegal to employ undocumented workers and imposed criminal penalties on employers who knowingly employed illegal immigrants. It also increased funding for the difficult task of attempting to control the U.S.-Mexican border. Despite the law, however, the number of illegal immigrants continued to grow.

By the early 1990's, taxpayers in the border states were increasingly angry and demanding new legislation. On November 8, 1994, almost 60 percent of California voters endorsed Proposition 187, stating that illegal immigrants were ineligible for public education and nonessential health services. Most Latinos, however, bitterly opposed the measure, and their anger helped the Democratic Party prevail in the California elections of 1998 and 2000. Federal courts eventually struck down the proposition's major provisions as unconstitutional. The referendum, nevertheless, alerted politicians to the intensity of concern about the issue.

In 1996, the Republican-controlled Congress responded with the Illegal Immigration Reform and Immigrant Responsibility Act. In an attempt to gain some control over the Mexican border, the statute nearly doubled the size of the Border Patrol and provided funding for motion sensors and other sophisticated technology. It included stiffer penalties for smuggling illegal immigrants into the country and for producing or using fraudulent documents. The new law also limited the ability of noncitizens to challenge Immigration and Naturalization Service (INS) decisions in court.

The 1996 law, however, did not provide the INS with any effective means for cracking down on employers who hired illegal immigrants. Although employers were required to ask for documentation, they had no effective ways to determine whether documents were counterfeit or authentic. By 1999, the INS had stopped raiding companies and farms to round up immigrants working without proper documentation. *Time* magazine reported in 2004 that the number of fines imposed on employers actually decreased by 99 percent during the 1990's. Moreover, when persons were arrested for attempting to cross the Mexican border illegally, they were simply sent back to Mexico, without any effective way to keep them from trying again.

Impact While illegal immigrants made up less than 5 percent of the U.S. workforce, they had a significant impact on the economy in many parts of the country. Although experts disagreed about whether this impact was primarily beneficial or pernicious, the majority of Americans agreed that it was important for the country to enforce its immigration laws. However, all attempts during the 1990's to stem the inflow of illegal immigrants were manifestly unsuccessful. Thus, their numbers would continue to grow, reaching an estimated 10 million by 2006.

Further Reading

Borjas, George J. *Heaven's Door: Immigration Policy and the American Economy.* Princeton, N.J.: Princeton University Press, 2000. A Harvard economist's argument in favor of encouraging additional immigrants with high skills while discouraging the entry of low-skilled workers.

Dow, Mark. *American Gulag: Inside U.S. Immigration Prisons.* Berkeley: University of California Press, 2004. An examination of immigrant detention, arguing that prisoners suffered from widespread abuses and the denial of legal rights.

Haerens, Margaret. *Illegal Immigration.* Detroit: Greenhaven Press, 2006. Clearly written chapters with opposing perspectives on topics like immigration law, border patrol, the guest-worker proposal, and racism.

Huntington, Samuel P. *Who Are We: The Challenges to America's National Identity.* New York: Simon & Schuster, 2004. A Harvard professor's argument that large mass immigration, especially from Latin America, has significant disadvantages.

Jacoby, Tamar, ed. *Reinventing the Melting Pot: The New Immigration and What It Means to Be an American.* New York: Basic Books, 2004. Essays with strongly different views on the ways in which recent waves of immigration have changed the country.

Katel, Peter, Patrick Marshall, and Alan Greenblatt. "Illegal Immigration." In *Issues for Debate in American Public Policy: Selections from the CQ Researcher,* edited by CQ Press. 8th ed. Washington D.C.: CQ Press, 2008. A good summary of statistics and arguments on the various sides of the issue.

Lin, Ann, and Nicole Green, eds. *Immigration.* Washington, D.C.: CQ Press, 2002. A useful collection of essays about the immigration policies of the United States and other countries.

Thomas Tandy Lewis

See also Demographics of Canada; Demographics of the United States; Immigration to Canada; Immigration to the United States; Latinos; Mexico and the United States.

■ Immigration Act of 1990

Identification Immigration law that significantly altered U.S. immigration policy

Date Enacted November 11, 1990; went into effect October 1, 1991

The Immigration Act of 1990 made important changes in U.S. immigration law that resulted in major changes in the size and composition of immigrant flows to the United States.

The Immigration and Naturalization Act of 1965 ended the racial/ethnic quota system for issuing immigration visas that heavily favored Northern and Western European countries. The Immigration Act of 1990, while retaining the focus on reducing racial/ethnic bias, initiated comprehensive changes in U.S. immigration law. The 1965 law had limited annual visas to 290,000 worldwide; the 1990 act raised the number to 700,000 for the first three years, and 675,000 thereafter. Three categories of visas were distinguished—employment-based, family-sponsored, and a new category called "diversity visas"—and each had numerical restrictions. The maximum number of the first two categories was raised to 26,620 per country compared to 20,000 annually under the 1965 law.

The total number of annual visas based on specified occupational categories was increased from 54,000 to 140,000 under the 1990 act, and a larger proportion were allocated for skilled workers. Family-sponsored visas were limited to 480,000 for relatives of both U.S. citizens and "legal permanent resident aliens." Parents, spouses, and minor children of U.S. citizens were included in that number, and, since there was no numerical restriction for these immediate relatives, a minimum of 226,000 visas was established for other family members. Therefore, if more than 254,000 immediate family members of U.S. citizens applied for visas, the total number would be increased.

Diversity visas were created to provide additional visas to countries that had received relatively few in the past. The 1965 law was designed to address racial/ethnic discrimination, but its "family reunification" provisions still favored countries that had received the most visas in the past. The 1990 act provided for 55,000 visas to be issued to countries that had received fewer than 50,000 visas during the previous five years. Each of these countries was limited to 7 percent of the total, or 3,850 diversity visas. Lotteries were to be held to determine which applicants would receive the visas. Qualified applicants had to have worked at a skilled occupation for two years or more and have at least a high school education.

Impact Since October, 1991, both family-based and employment-based annual immigration has increased significantly, the latter showing the greater increases, with a larger proportion of professional and technical workers. Immigrant flows have become more racially/ethnically diverse because of the increase of per-country visa allocations, diversity visas, and an important change regarding family-sponsored visas. Under the 1990 act, visas for the family members of legal permanent resident aliens were given a high priority, the number of visas for their spouses and minor children was significantly increased, and three-fourths of these visas were exempted from countries' total limits. Research has shown that changes in the number and diversity of immigrants since 1990 would have been much less pronounced if the 1965 law had remained in effect.

Further Reading

DeLaet, Debra L. *U.S. Immigration Policy in an Age of Rights.* Westport, Conn.: Praeger, 2000.

Tichenor, Daniel J. *Dividing Lines: The Politics of Immigration Control in America.* Princeton, N.J.: Princeton University Press, 2002.

Jack Carter

See also Canada and the United States; China and the United States; Employment in the United States; Foreign policy of the United States; Illegal immigration; Immigration to the United States; Income and wages in the United States; Mexico and the United States; Race relations.

■ Immigration to Canada

Definition Migration into Canada by people who are citizens of other countries

In the 1990's, Canada had the highest per capita immigration rate in the world, and immigration was the primary dynamic in the growth of Canada's population and labor force. Immigration rates climbed during the decade, so that immigration accounted for about 60 percent of total population growth by the end of the decade.

During the 1990's, the largest immigrant streams came to Canada from the developing countries, especially those in Asia—namely, China, India, Pakistan, Hong Kong, and the Philippines. Throughout Canada's history, its immigration policy has been tied closely to economic conditions, ethnic background, and humanitarian concerns. Beginning in the early twentieth century, Canada's immigration was adjusted each year according to the country's short-term economic indicators—in other words, calculated by the absorptive capacity model. In the late 1980's, that model was replaced with a "fixed-target" policy, which meant the Canadian government could set immigration levels independent of economic conditions, ignoring labor conditions and economic growth rates. Immigration declined in the 1980's in response to a sagging economy but increased through the 1990's as a result of the new target policy. Immigration averaged 190,000 annually in the mid-1990's, declined to 150,000 per year in the late 1990's, and climbed to 200,000 annually by the new century. Between 1981 and 2001, about 3.6 million immigrants found homes in Canada, elevating its population to more than 30 million.

Immigrants in the 1990's concentrated heavily in Canada's cities, especially Toronto, Canada's most racially and culturally diverse city. Immigrants comprised almost 40 percent of Toronto's population in 1991, while the figures were 30 percent for Vancouver, 24 percent for Hamilton, 21 percent for Windsor, 20 percent each for Calgary and Victoria, and 17 percent for Montreal. Canada's three largest cities, Toronto, Vancouver, and Montreal, received about 80 percent of the immigrants during the decade, shouldering high initial costs as well as the ongoing costs of the immigrants' integration. Ethnic networks and neighborhoods exerted a powerful influence on the initial location and integration of these newcomers. For example, Chinatowns grew and thrived in Toronto and Vancouver. The inflow to smaller places and rural areas was very light, with the Maritime provinces and northern territories the least affected.

Policy Changes The decade witnessed a number of significant changes to Canada's immigration and settlement policies. Policy makers increased the requirements for skilled workers, imposed tighter controls on family sponsorship, implemented changes to language-training programs, introduced the landing fee, and put more emphasis on individual economic responsibility and self-sufficiency. Three broad classes of immigrants were admitted: family-class immigrants or those admitted for family reunification; independent or economic-class immigrants selected on the basis of points for occupational skills, education, and suitability to the Canadian environment; and the refugee class, whose admission was based on refugee laws and individual suitability. The independent or economic class typically constitutes about 60 percent of the annual total number of immigrants.

Immigration Problems An economic slowdown in the early 1990's, coupled with continued high immigration, created a complex of problems related to immigrant adjustment such as unemployment and financial crises. The national data indicate a widening of the income gap during the decade with new immigrants doing worse economically than previous immigrants. More than one-third of the immigrants who arrived during the decade lived below the poverty line in 2000, with figures of 47 percent in Montreal and 40 percent in Vancouver. Immigrant incomes in 2000 were 80 percent of the national average after ten years of residence in the country.

The widening gap can be attributed to immigrant origins and educational levels as well as a sagging demand for labor during economic downturns. In the early 1990's, only 13 percent of the immigrants came with university degrees; the change in immigration policy helped to boost that number to 45 percent after 2000. Policy makers worked on ways to better coordinate education, housing, and social services for new arrivals between the various levels of government.

The Canadian government continued to grapple with serious demographic issues related to Canada's aging population, dependency, and the loss of skilled laborers to its American neighbor. The United States exerts a strong pull for skilled immigrants, and even during the best of times, Canada is a way station for many immigrants headed for the bigger economy to the south. The inflow of economic versus political refugees remained an area of discourse, and security issues took on new urgency after the terrorist attacks of September 11, 2001, in New York and Washington, D.C.

Impact The debate continues among Canadian policy makers as to the optimum annual target for the admission of immigrants. Canadian policy today permits a targeted flow of 1 percent of the Canadian population or about 300,000 annually. The selection process remains biased toward young skilled workers who can fill important niches in Canada's modern economy.

Further Reading

Cameron, Elspeth, ed. *Multiculturalism and Immigration in Canada: An Introductory Reader.* Toronto: Canadian Scholars' Press, 2004. Examines the evolution of the multicultural policy in Canada and how that policy changed public thinking; includes contributions by many recent immigrants.

Campbell, Charles M. *Betrayal and Deceit: The Politics of Canadian Immigration.* West Vancouver, B.C.: Jasmine Books, 2000. A critical look at the ideas, attitudes, institutions, and rhetoric tied to the immigration debates in Canada.

Driedger, Leo, ed. *Multi-Ethnic Canada: Identities and*

Inequalities. Toronto: Oxford University Press, 1996. An examination of the impact of the multicultural policy on group status and public thinking and perception.

Knowles, Valerie. *Stranger at Our Gates: Canadian Immigration and Immigration Policy, 1540-2007.* Rev. ed. Toronto: Dundurn Press, 2007. Describes the ethnic and demographic character of immigrant streams into Canada, including the role of the economy and racism in policy making.

Trebilcock, Michael J., and Ninette Kelley. *The Making of the Mosaic: A History of Canadian Immigration Policy.* Toronto: University of Toronto Press, 1998. An examination of the key issues, interests, and attitudes that defined Canadian immigration policy and patterns from the preconfederation period to the late twentieth century.

Ann M. Legreid

See also Asian Americans; Canada and the United States; Demographics of Canada; Employment in Canada; Illegal immigration; Immigration to the United States; Minorities in Canada; Religion and spirituality in Canada.

■ Immigration to the United States

Definition Migration into the United States by people who are citizens of other countries

The influx of millions of legal and illegal immigrants from Mexico and Latin America reshaped the profile of the U.S. population in the 1990's and made immigration a central issue on the country's political agenda.

Growth in the U.S. population as a result of immigration has been a persistent part of the country's history. Even more so than the other "settler societies" of the former British Empire—Canada, New Zealand, and Australia—the United States opened its borders in the mid-nineteenth century, and to no small degree it was the influx of those peoples from foreign lands that enabled the country to expand from coast to coast and emerge as one of the world's great powers. On the other hand, except for the Africans who were forced into the Americas as slaves, before World War II the overwhelming majority of those entering the United States were Europeans. That profile of the country's population changed slightly during the late 1940's and 1950's as U.S. military personnel returned to their homeland with Japanese and Korean war brides. While the Civil Rights movement of the 1960's led to a firm commitment to multiculturalism as a part of the country's ethos by the 1970's, as a result of immigration quotas favoring those with relatives already in the United States, as late as the 1980's most immigrants still came from European points of origin. Then, in the twentieth century's final decade, that profile of the typical immigrant to the United States changed abruptly.

A Shift in the 1990's It is mildly ironic, in the light of the degree to which immigration soon became a divisive issue in U.S. politics, that the 1990's began with legislation designed to depart from the Eurocentric bias of previous immigration laws. Under the Immigration Act of 1990, legal admissions were to be increased by 200,000 per year (to 700,000 per year), and 50,000 of these admissions were reserved for areas from which few had previously immigrated to the United States. Temporary work visas were also made available in expanded numbers—a provision with built-in favoritism toward workers close at hand. Unfortunately, an unintended consequence of a more important policy enacted shortly thereafter resulted in a flood of immigrants from Mexico that quickly dwarfed these allowances. That policy was the North American Free Trade Agreement (NAFTA), whose creation in 1994 forced Mexican farmers to compete with the United States' vastly more efficient agricultural system. Between 1993 and 2002, at least two million Mexican farmers had to abandon their land for want of markets for their produce, and many came north.

Given the fact that at approximately the same time globalization was producing an outsourcing of American jobs to countries with cheaper labor, the arrival of even the allotted number of legal immigrants from Latin America might have produced a minor political backlash. When the numbers entering the country illegally, principally across its southern border with Mexico, came to exceed the total number legally entitled to enter the United States, immigration instead became a major political issue at all levels of government.

Signaling that fact, in 1994 California voters approved, by a 59 to 41 percent margin, a statewide referendum that denied public services to illegal immigrants and public education to their children. Other states with large numbers of illegal immigrants soon followed California's lead. In 1996, the U.S. Senate not only voted overwhelmingly (97-3) to tighten U.S. borders but also voted to broaden the criteria under which legal aliens could be deported and to limit federally funded benefits to legal immigrants. Meanwhile, rumors of a pending "Mexicanization" of the country's Southwest circulated widely, and critics such as Pat Buchanan found receptive audiences for their dire warnings of the pending end of Western civilization.

The immigration issue remained salient entering into the new millennium. By 2000, a thousand illegal immigrants per day were entering the country, and the number of illegal aliens in the United States was estimated to be at least twelve million—more than 5 percent of the population. Of these, two-thirds were Latinos and half were from Mexico. Most startling to the country's political scene, the 2000 census revealed that the Latino community had already surpassed African Americans to become the country's largest minority and that it was also the most rapidly growing segment of the U.S. population.

Impact The daily arrival of more legal and illegal Latino immigrants has created a new set of political challenges and reshaped U.S. politics in the early years of the twenty-first century. The welfare and school systems of state and local governments, for example, have been stretched to accommodate new demands. Meanwhile, political parties have walked the thin line between responding to the widespread demand to halt illegal immigration and a desire to court this rapidly expanding segment of the American electorate. Above all, even as national political leaders have sidestepped the sensitive issue of what to do with the millions of Latinos illegally living in the country, local leaders have had to consider how to assimilate a new, non-English-speaking minority so large and, in the Southwest, so territorially concentrated that many of its members can enjoy a middle-class lifestyle without ever leaving their linguistic community.

Further Reading

Buchanan, Patrick J. *State of Emergency: The Third World Invasion and Conquest of America.* New York: Thomas Dunne Books, 2006. Contains a thorough statement of the extreme Right's uncompromising opposition to admitting further immigrants to the West from the non-European world.

Guerette, Rob T. *Migrant Death: Border Safety and Situational Crime Prevention on the U.S.-Mexico Divide.* New York: LFB Scholarly, 2007. Perhaps the best available work on the growing violence and crime in the zone surrounding the border between the United States and Mexico and on the risks run by those crossing it illegally.

Swain, Carol M., ed. *Debating Immigration.* New York: Cambridge University Press, 2007. An immensely valuable paperback whose well-balanced essays cover economic, social, and political dimensions of the immigrant issue in the contemporary United States.

Joseph R. Rudolph, Jr.

See also Buchanan, Pat; Business and the economy in the United States; Demographics of the United States; Employment in the United States; Illegal immigration; Immigration Act of 1990; Latin America; Latinos; Mexico and the United States; North American Free Trade Agreement (NAFTA).

■ *In Living Color*

Identification Comedy variety television series
Producer Keenen Ivory Wayans (1958-)
Date Aired from April 15, 1990, to August 25, 1994

Later regarded as a springboard for its cast members' careers, this variety show was the first in television history to feature a predominantly African American cast and to be conceived, directed, and produced by an African American family.

In Living Color began airing on the Fox television network in 1990, at a time when the urban entertainment climate was increasingly influenced by hip-hop culture and music. The show's theme song was performed by Heavy D & the Boyz, and the series earned a reputation for showcasing popular hip-hop and R&B artists as its musical guests, including Public Enemy, En Vogue, Tupac Shakur. Sketch comedy segments focused on African American subject matter, and the show had a decidedly urban feel.

The comedy series was created and produced by Keenen Ivory Wayans, and the cast included Wayans's siblings, Damon, Kim, Shawn, and Marlon. Several comedic actors received their start on the show, including Chris Rock, Jamie Foxx, Jim Carrey, David

Alan Grier, and Tommy Davidson. The show's hip-hop dance troupe, the Fly Girls, included Jennifer Lopez, who became a popular singer and actress in the late 1990's.

In Living Color set itself apart from other variety shows of previous decades by putting African American concerns at the forefront and by using African American communication styles to express those concerns, without sacrificing comedy. One of the strengths of the show, aside from its phenomenal cast, was its writing. The show took on white American icons and placed them in an African American context, thereby creating social satire. Often, the show would poke fun at America's conformist culture of the 1950's and 1960's by taking a situation comedy or drama from the era and placing it in a 1990's urban context. In one skit, *Lassie* is set in an inner-city housing project, and the title canine is a pit bull. With titles such as "The Wrath of Farrakhan," "The Making of a Tracy Chapman Song," "Ray Charles in Charge," "Jesse Jackson Children's Books," and "Barbara Bush Visits the Illiterates," the sketches were edgy, witty, and sometimes controversial.

The Wayans and others created memorable recurring characters and sketches, including Homey D. Clown (Damon Wayans), a frustrated ex-convict working as a children's clown; Fire Marshal Bill (Jim Carrey), a deranged officer who teaches fire safety by demonstrating on himself; and the "Homeboy Shopping Network" (Damon and Keenen Ivory Wayans), a parody of the Home Shopping Network that features two black men who sell stolen goods usually from the back of their truck.

By the end of the fourth season, many of the show's most memorable actors had left to pursue other interests, usually film roles. Keenen Ivory Wayans had left because of disputes with Fox over its censorship and syndication of the series.

Impact Offering cutting-edge comedy skits and musical performances, *In Living Color* was a model for future comedy variety shows such as *Chappelle's Show,* starring Dave Chappelle.

From left: Kim Wayans, David Alan Grier, and Jim Carrey at a script rehearsal for In Living Color *in 1991. Keenen Ivory Wayans is on the far right.* (©Neal Preston/ Corbis)

Further Reading

Samuels, Allison. "The Color of Funny." *Newsweek,* August, 2000, 54-56.

Tucker, Ken. "In Living Color." *Entertainment Weekly,* April 27, 1990.

Dodie Marie Miller

See also African Americans; Carrey, Jim; Censorship; Comedians; Hip-hop and rap music; Latinos; Race relations; Rock, Chris; Shakur, Tupac; Television.

■ Income and wages in Canada

Definition Earning and payment of money deriving from capital or labor in Canada

In the 1990's, disparity in income and wages sharply divided Canadian society into economically based classes.

In the 1990's, the income of Canadians often varied significantly depending upon the region of the country in which they lived and worked. The link between income and region was not a phenomenon particular to the decade but rather one dating back to the beginning of the twentieth century. Ontario and British Columbia had the highest per capita incomes, which were one-third higher than those of Newfoundland and New Brunswick. Quebec's per capita income was below the national average but slightly higher than that of the Atlantic coast provinces.

Upper-class families had a significantly higher concentration of the national income. The income of these families came from investments and property ownership (land or companies) as well as from salaries. In general, this was a period in which the majority of Canadian wage and salary earners suffered from low incomes as a result of the increase in part-time and temporary or contract jobs. In the middle of the decade, one in four workers was employed in a part-time position and one in twelve in a temporary or contract job. The majority of these workers were involuntarily working part time and were unable to secure full-time employment. By 1998, part-time jobs had increased by almost 25 percent while full-time positions had only increased by 8 percent.

A major factor affecting wages was the increasing number of women in the workforce. In 1992, almost two-thirds of Canadian families were two-income households. Segregation of the workforce into women's jobs and men's jobs continued to control hiring, as women continued to be employed in lower-paying service, retail, and clerical jobs. Although Canadian women were demanding equal pay and their income had risen from previous years, they earned on average about two-thirds of what male workers received.

In 1993, more than half of elderly widows and almost two-thirds of families headed by single mothers were below the low-income cutoff point, spending more than one-half of their income for food, shelter, and clothing.

Impact The 1990's witnessed considerable disparity in income and wages based on region, sex, age and type of employment. The proliferation of part-time, temporary, and contract jobs resulted in a greater number of women in the workforce and a greater number of individuals holding multiple jobs. Government transfer payments also became a significant part of many household incomes.

Further Reading

Allahar, Anton, and James E. Coté. *Richer and Poorer: The Structure of Inequality in Canada.* Toronto: James Lorimer, 1998.

Blais, François. *Ending Poverty: A Basic Income for All Canadians.* Toronto: James Lorimer, 2002

Shawncey Webb

See also Business and the economy in Canada; Employment in Canada; Income and wages in the United States; Minimum wage increases.

■ Income and wages in the United States

Definition Wages (including salaries) represent compensation in money paid to hired labor while real wages measure the amount of goods and services represented by the money wage; other types of income include property income and government transfer payments

Wages and incomes in the United States rose through most of the decade.

In 1990, the American economy generated $4.9 trillion in personal income. By 1999, this total had grown to $7.8 trillion. The burden of personal taxes rose from 12 to 14 percent. Much of the rise in income reflected the general upward movement of the price level, so real incomes did not rise nearly so much as money incomes. In addition, population increased. After adjusting for all these variables, one

Average Weekly Earnings by Industry, 1990 and 2000

Sector	*1990*	*2000*
Natural resources and mining	$603	$735
Construction	$513	$686
Manufacturing	$436	$591
Trade, transport, and utilities	$332	$450
Information	$480	$701
Finance	$355	$537
Professional and business services	$381	$535
Education and health	$319	$449
Leisure and hospitality	$156	$217
Other services	$298	$413

Source: Statistical Abstract of the United States, 2008, p. 412.

Major Components of Personal Income, 1990 and 1999 (billions of dollars)

Year	*Employee Compensation*	*Proprietors' Income*	*Property Income*	*Government Transfers*	*Total**
1990	$3,338	$381	$975	$573	$4,879
1999	$5,352	$678	$1,411	$988	$7,802
% Change	6	78	45	72	60

*Some minor components are omitted, so total is larger than sum of items listed.
Source: Economic Report of the President, 2008, pp. 260-261.

finds that disposable personal income per capita in 2000 prices averaged $21,281 in 1990 and rose to $24,564 in 1999, an increase of about 15 percent. Employee compensation (wages, salaries, and fringe benefits) represented about two-thirds of the total and increased by 60 percent, as did the total. The income of proprietors (owners of unincorporated businesses and farms) rose more, as did government transfer payments such as Social Security. Property income (rents, interest, and dividends) increased less than did the other income categories.

Wages Average hourly earnings in private employment rose from $10.20 in 1990 to $13.49 in 1999. Much of this increase, however, was offset by the rise in the price level. When adjusted for inflation (expressed in 1982 dollars), the real wage rose only from $7.66 in 1990 to $8.01 in 1999—an increase of about 5 percent. Average weekly earnings rose from $350 in 1990 to $463 in 1999. After adjustment for inflation, however, the increase went from $263 in 1990 to $275 in 1999, again a 5 percent rise.

Considering that labor productivity increased nearly 20 percent over the decade, the foregoing data on real wages (calculated by the Bureau of Labor Statistics) need further inspection. In addition to the wage payout directly received by workers, an additional one-fifth of labor costs involved employer contributions to worker pensions, insurance, and Social Security. Adjusted for inflation and converted to an average per worker, these data show compensation per worker of $21,462 (in 1982-1984 prices) in 1990 and $24,150 in 1999, an increase of about 13 percent.

There were wide differences in wages from one industry to another. An examination of average weekly pay for major sectors shows notable extremes, with very high rewards in natural resource and mining activities and very low rewards in the leisure and hospitality sectors.

The 1990's saw a small shift in the share of income going to families at different levels of income distribution. The top one-fifth of income recipients increased their share of total income over the decade, so that by 1999 they received nearly half of the total. Their increase came at the expense of the other four quintiles.

Hourly Wages for Different Worker Categories, 1990 and 1999

Worker Category	*1990*	*1999*
Union members	$13.16	$17.31
Male	$13.94	$18.08
White	$14.24	$18.56
Black	$12.00	$15.16
Female	$11.81	$16.14
White	$11.92	$16.40
Black	$11.07	$15.16
Nonunion workers	$10.55	$14.44
Male	$12.17	$16.44
White	$12.52	$16.85
Black	$8.87	$12.59
Female	$8.88	$12.38
White	$9.00	$12.58
Black	$7.73	$12.59

Source: Historical Statistics of the United States: Millennial Edition, vol. 2, 2006, p. 351.

Despite these results, the number and percent of persons in poverty declined over the decade. In 1990, 13.5 percent of people were classified as poor; by 1999, this number had declined to 11.9 percent. The percentage reductions were particularly noteworthy for African Americans (from 31.9 to 23.6 percent) and Hispanics (from 28.1 to 22.7 percent).

Share of Income Going to Each Quintile, 1990 and 1999

Quintile	*1990*	*1999*
Lowest fifth	3.8%	3.6%
Second fifth	9.6%	8.9%
Third fifth	15.9%	14.9%
Fourth fifth	24.0%	23.2%
Highest fifth	46.6%	49.4%

Source: Statistical Abstract of the United States, 2008, p. 450.

Membership in labor unions was an important element in wage and employment conditions. In 1990, 16.7 million workers were union members; by 2000, this number had declined slightly to 16.3 million. Union membership in government employment rose from 6.5 million to 7.1 million. An increase in the number of schoolteachers was an important contributor. Union membership declined in private-sector employment, from 10.3 million to 9.1 million, decreasing the unionized percentage from 11 to 9 percent in the private sector. An important factor in this decline was the decrease in employment in manufacturing, a location of traditionally strong unions. Unionized employment, however, fell more than nonunionized employment, as industries such as automobile production became more heavily located in traditional nonunion areas.

Many of the differentials in wage levels comparing union and nonunion workers, male and female workers, and black and white workers arise because the different categories of workers differ in their occupations and sector employment. On average, however, union members earned about 25 percent more than nonunion workers in 1990, declining to 20 percent in 1999. Among union members, men's wage rates exceeded those of women by 12 percent, certainly reflecting different jobs and not different rates for the same job. For nonunion workers, men's wage rates exceeded those of women by 37 percent in 1990, declining to 33 percent in 1999.

Impact During the 1990's, the demand for labor was strong and employment grew sufficiently to absorb the rising population. The top fifth of income recipients increased their share of total income, but this group did not necessarily comprise the same people in 1999 as in 1990. Poverty declined over the decade.

Further Reading

Ehrenberg, Ronald G., and Robert S. Smith. *Modern Labor Economics.* 8th ed. New York: Pearson/Addison Wesley, 2003. This college-level text puts wages and employment into historical and analytical perspective. Includes chapters on pay and productivity, discrimination, and the influence of unions.

Hirsch, Barry T. "Sluggish Institutions in a Dynamic World: Can Unions and Industrial Competition Coexist?" *Journal of Economic Perspectives* 22, no. 1 (Winter, 2008): 153-176. The author's short answer to the question posed by the title is not very well. A good historical review of the extent and influence of unionization.

"Symposium on Discrimination in Product, Credit and Labor Markets." *Journal of Economic Perspectives* 12, no. 2 (Spring, 1998): 63-126. William Darity and Patrick Mason present evidence of persisting discrimination, while James Heckman takes a skeptical view.

Paul B. Trescott

See also Business and the economy in the United States; Employment in the United States; General Motors strike of 1998; Immigration to the United States; Income and wages in Canada; Minimum wage increases.

■ Independent films

Definition Films made outside the Hollywood system

The great popularity of independent films in the 1990's established them as an alternative to Hollywood films.

In the 1990's, independent films escalated into a cinema of diversity that included a great variety of voices and perspectives. In the 1980's and earlier, films were privately made and financed as underground, eccentric, or experimental works. In the 1990's, there was a proliferation of personal films by directors who were denied expression in profits-driven Hollywood. Because of the large number of film school graduates and the popularity of independent films, it became easier to secure financing outside the Hollywood system.

Independent films catered to more mature audiences than the age twelve-to-twenty viewers targeted by Hollywood films, and in view of the wide experiences of the filmmakers themselves, created niche audiences outside the mainstream. Also, during the 1990's, indie films fared well at the Academy Awards, winning Oscars for directing, writing, and editing.

Major Genres The most prominent form of film in the 1990's was noir, a genre that has fascinated the American public since the 1940's with its dark perspectives on lust, greed, and death. Having experienced a comeback in the 1980's in the films of David Lynch, the Coen brothers, and Martin Scorsese, noir continued into the 1990's through the works of these filmmakers as well as of Quentin Tarantino and his imitators. Perhaps reflecting America's moral chaos, noir films became the film of choice for numerous fledgling filmmakers, who counted on the genre's popularity and its relative ease in filming. Classic noir, with its extremes in lighting and character depiction, merges with comedy or coming-of-age elements to depict broad ranges of experience, whereas neo-noir tends to flatten the character excesses so that no characters are as virtuous or evil as in conventional noir. Also, many noir films provided an opportunity to shock the audience with their brutally violent situations and language, as if to leave no taboo unexplored.

Despite the success of serious drama in the hands of some directors, especially John Sayles, the second most prevalent genre in the 1990's was satiric comedy. Following the lead of Robert Altman, many filmmakers attempted character-driven, experimental narratives with cynical political themes. Tim Robbins, one of Altman's protégés, followed similarly in *Bob Roberts* (1992). Other filmmakers created youth-oriented films in which characters confronted anxieties about race, sexual preferences, coming of age, suicide, pedophilia, dysfunctional families, and other extreme subjects that were not usually present in Hollywood films.

Impact The primary venue for showing American independent films, the Sundance Film Festival, located in Park City, Utah, and cofounded by Robert Redford, was established for the purpose of displaying the works of new filmmakers. The festival has been known for its presentation of diverse works by regional artists, women, and ethnic minorities. Beginning as a small showcase for independent films, the annual event has become so enormous that it has moved toward an institutional and mainstream independent cinema festival. Sundance helped to bring attention to such indie films as *Clerks* (1994) and *The Blair Witch Project* (1999).

Films containing social or ethical issues traditionally ignored by Hollywood studios were taken on by independent filmmakers during the 1990's. Talented, creative artists who could not work in the Hollywood system had an opportunity for cinematic self-expression within independent films. Viewers who tired of the traditional viewpoints (white, middle-class, heterosexual, male) yearned for stories that, if not closer to their own lives, at least represented an enjoyable diversity.

Further Reading

Biskind, Peter. *Down and Dirty Pictures: Miramax, Sundance, and the Rise of the Independent Film.* New York: Simon & Schuster, 2004. Biskind devotes much of the book to discussions of Sundance Film Festival cofounder Robert Redford and Miramax cofounder Harvey Weinstein, both of whom are viewed by Biskin as fostering, yet ultimately ruining the "purity" of independent film.

Chion, Michel. *David Lynch.* Rev. ed. London: British Film Institute, 2006. Companion to Lynch's body of work, focusing on themes and motifs behind his surreal films.

Keyssar, Helene. *Robert Altman's America.* New York: Oxford University Press, 1991. Examines the films of Altman, America's premier independent filmmaker, who consistently fuses myths with history to comment on the American Dream.

Rowell, Erica. *The Brothers Grim: The Films of Ethan and Joel Coen.* Lanham, Md.: Scarecrow Press, 2007. Interesting study of the Coen brothers, their beginnings, and their films, including the use of black humor and violence in their films.

Scorsese, Martin. *Scorsese on Scorsese.* Rev. ed. London: Faber & Faber, 2003. Book of interviews with Scorsese, who tells of his love of films; his obsession with New York's Little Italy, the setting of many of his films; and his intense style of filmmaking.

Waxman, Sharon. *Rebels on the Back Lot: Six Maverick Directors and How They Conquered the Hollywood Studio System.* New York: HarperCollins, 2005. Chronicles the rise of Quentin Tarantino, Paul Thomas Anderson, David Fincher, Steven Soderbergh, David O. Russell, and Spike Jonze in their struggle to make films according to their own personal visions. Recounts ego-driven battles that are not always funny.

Mary Hurd

See also Academy Awards; *Blair Witch Project, The*; Coen brothers; Film in the United States; *GoodFellas*; Lee, Spike; *Pulp Fiction*; Sundance Film Festival; Tarantino, Quentin.

■ Instant messaging

Definition A communications mode that allows two or more persons to use digitally based information (generally text) to communicate synchronously over a network of computers

Instant messaging (IM) swept the United States in the 1990's, changing communication styles and expectations of online contact with friends, families, and even strangers.

With the development of the Internet and the World Wide Web, communicating between computers was accomplished through e-mail and bulletin boards. E-mails necessitated a time lag between a sent message and the recipient's reply and required an e-mail address to locate the intended recipient of the message. Bulletin boards operated by dialing into a system and using downloadable software to gain access to an online board. Users, whose identities could remain anonymous, posted messages that all users could read. However, postings appeared in random order, so communication did not lend itself to back-and-forth conversation.

Instant messaging united the best of e-mail and bulletin boards, offering a more instant exchange than e-mail and a more private exchange than a bulletin board. Instant messaging allowed users to chat synchronously through text typing and provided a means to limit the circle of contacts for an online exchange. A user downloaded software to connect to a Web server. From a small window on the screen, the user could add and delete contacts, determine which contacts were online, and click on a contact with whom he or she wished to converse. The user typed a message and clicked a send button. If the recipient was online, the user saw the message scroll across the screen letter by letter with deletions and all other typing actions the sender performed. Although computers connected to the Web server could be located anywhere, users reported that during instant messaging, they felt the "presence" of the other person(s), much like having a phone conversation.

Early versions of IM software were developed by UNIX, America Online (AOL), Prodigy, and CompuServe and connected individual computers to a Web server. Messages from senders and recipients traveled through the Web server, then out to the computer. The popularity of instant messaging soared toward the late 1990's with the introduction of ICQ ("I seek you"), developed by Mirabilis. ICQ was a free instant messaging utility a step beyond other messaging applications. When a user logged into the system, ICQ connected together the computers on the user's contact list. Messages no longer traveled through the Web server and out, but traveled directly between the linked computers. The result for the user was a faster response time between messages, allowing an almost real-time exchange and opening up an increased ability to multitask while online.

Impact Instant messaging laid the foundation for a completely connected world of real-time interchange in the era of multitasking.

Further Reading

Bell, Mary Ann, Mary Ann Berry, and James L. Van Roekel. *Internet and Personal Computing Fads.* New York: Haworth Press, 2004.

Lewis, Michael M. *Next: The Future Just Happened.* New York: W. W. Norton, 2001.

Rheingold, Howard. *The Virtual Community: Homesteading on the Electronic Frontier.* Reading, Mass.: Addison-Wesley, 1993.

Taylor Shaw

See also America Online; Apple Computer; Computers; Dot-coms; E-mail; Internet; Inventions; Microsoft; Science and technology; World Wide Web.

■ Intelligent design movement

Definition Neocreationist campaign to convince educators and others of a purposeful universe

Instigated by a Supreme Court ruling that "creation science" is religion, not science, a group of dedicated Christians argued that natural evidence exists that the universe and all life within it bear witness to a wise designer and that this theory should play a role in public school science classes, a proposal that was successfully challenged by the scientific community.

Although the argument for God's existence from the well-ordered world He created has a long history, the modern intelligent design movement began after the Supreme Court decided, in *Edwards v. Aguillard* (1987), that "creation science," which proposed that scientific facts and theories supported the biblical view of God's creative power, was religion and not science, and that teaching this doctrine in public schools violated the separation of church and state. However, the ruling left open the possibility of teaching a variety of scientific theories about the ways in which the universe, life, and humankind developed. Several Christian scholars realized that they would now have to devise a new strategy to attack what they viewed as the materialistic evolutionary theory originated by Charles Darwin. In the late 1980's, a supplementary high school textbook, *Of Pandas and People* (1989), contained several arguments that supposedly proved that life on Earth was intelligently, not randomly, designed. Christian groups were able to get this book accepted in several school districts, a campaign that continued throughout the 1990's.

The Controversy over Intelligent Design According to several Christian scholars, the intelligent design movement's most influential proponent was Phillip E. Johnson, a Berkeley law professor. In 1991, Johnson published *Darwin on Trial,* which emphasized that Darwinism was nothing but applied materialism and that evidence exists for an intelligent agent's hand in forging the highly organized complexities of various life-forms. Johnson continued to refine his case in his later books, *Reason in the Balance* (1995) and *Defeating Darwinism* (1997). Johnson has been called "the father of the intelligent design movement," but he also had several important followers, including William A. Dembski, a mathematician, philosopher, and theologian, and Michael J. Behe, a biochemist.

Dembski, a convert from Catholicism to Evangelical Christianity, developed, in his books and articles, mathematical arguments to distinguish intelligently designed phenomena from those resulting from random natural causation. Several mathematicians and scientists challenged Dembski's contention that law, chance, and design are mutually exclusive. They also argued that natural laws are able to explain the complexities of life-forms without needing to appeal to an intelligent designer. Michael Behe, a Roman Catholic who contributed to *Of Pandas and People*'s second edition, maintained, in *Darwin's Black Box* (1996), that random causes are unable to explain the development of "irreducibly complex" cellular structures—that is, those unable to function when a single part is missing. For example, flagella, cellular devices used for locomotion and composed of several different proteins, could not have originated via the accidental, incremental additions required by natural selection. However, Kenneth R. Miller, a Roman Catholic biology professor at Brown University, showed that flagella are not irreducibly complex since a small group of proteins from a flagellum can be used by bacteria for activities different from self-propulsion.

Impact Through their books and articles and through such organizations as the Discovery Institute, which created the Center for the Renewal of Science and Culture in 1996 to manage the intelligent design campaign, the neocreationists were able to influence many American communities to adopt intelligent design in their secondary school science curricula. Many members of the scientific community attacked these adoptions. For example, the National Academy of Sciences issued documents stating that intelligent design is not science because its claims cannot be tested by experiment. The American Association for the Advancement of Science argued in its publications that intelligent design is pseudoscience. Throughout the 1990's, the consensus of most members of the scientific community remained that intelligent design is covert religion and that Darwinism, in one form or another, was unscathed by neocreationist attacks.

Subsequent Events The controversy over intelligent design continued into the twenty-first century. In 2002, the Ohio State Board of Education held a public debate between prominent Darwinian evolutionists and neocreationists. In 2005, several people in this debate were called as expert witnesses in the *Kitzmiller v. Dover Area School District* case. A group of parents of high school students had challenged the Dover district's requirement for biology teachers to present intelligent design arguments as an alternative to Darwinian evolution. In a well-documented decision, Judge John E. Jones III ruled in favor of the parents, concluding that intelligent design was unable to uncouple itself from its religious roots. Therefore, the school district's promotion of intelligent design violated the establishment clause of the First Amendment of the U.S. Constitution. Despite these and other defeats suffered by the intelligent design movement, it continued to garner support and advocacy by many members of the conservative Christian community. Consequently, the intelligent design controversy has not yet reached closure.

Further Reading

Behe, Michael J. *The Edge of Evolution: The Search for the Limits of Darwinism.* New York: Free Press, 2007. This successor to Behe's *Darwin's Black Box: The Biochemical Challenge to Evolution* (1996) extends his arguments from cell structures that are "beyond random mutation and natural selection" to the "edge of evolution," where Darwinian explanations are inadequate. Extensive notes, four appendixes, and an index.

Davis, Percival, and Dean H. Kenyon. *Of Pandas and People: The Central Question of Biological Origins.* Dallas: Haughton, 1993. This revised edition edited by Charles B. Thaxton was, in this and other versions, at the center of the controversy over an intelligent design textbook in high school science courses. Glossary and index.

Johnson, Phillip E. *Darwin on Trial.* Washington, D.C.: Regnery Gateway, 1991. This book has been called the "founding document" of the intelligent design movement. Research notes and an index.

Pennock, Robert T. *Tower of Babel: The Evidence Against the New Creationism.* Cambridge, Mass.: MIT Press, 1999. The author, a philosopher of science, has written "the most detailed and comprehensive" critique of the intelligent design movement while elucidating the context within which it originated and developed. Notes, references, and an index.

Scott, Eugenie C. *Evolution vs. Creationism: An Introduction.* Berkeley: University of California Press, 2004. Written by a committed evolutionist, this book provides an accessible primer to the debate over the teaching of evolution in the United States. "References for Further Exploration," name index, and subject index.

Robert J. Paradowski

See also Education in the United States; Homeschooling; Religion and spirituality in the United States; Science and technology; Supreme Court decisions.

■ Internet

Definition A worldwide network of computer networks

In the 1990's, the Internet grew from about 100,000 hosts—connected by the new, and largely untested, transmission control protocol/Internet protocol (TCP/IP) networking protocol—to over one and a half million hosts, connected by a robust TCP/IP internetworking infrastructure. The 1990's also marked the rapid development of the World Wide Web as an important way of distributing information and doing business.

Computers were first used in the 1950's, and from their inception scientists tried to connect them so that they could share printers and data. In 1962, J. C. R. Licklider of Massachusetts Institute of Technology (MIT) gave the first description of an internet as a network of networks. The technology of the 1960's used dedicated circuits to connect computers, and this technique did not support large internets. In 1964, Leonard Kleinrock of MIT described a new technology, packet switching, which sent messages from one computer to another by breaking a message into packets and sending the packets one at a time rather than the entire message all at once.

During the 1970's and 1980's, packet-switched networking developed at a fast pace and demonstrated that it was capable of supporting large internetworks. The TCP/IP network protocol was a packet-switched internetwork protocol, defined in a paper by Robert Kahn and Vinton Cerf in 1974. TCP was a transport protocol to connect individual computers, and IP was a protocol that facilitated the movement of data over the network using routers. Several successful implementations of TCP/IP networks were produced during the 1980's. In 1983, the government required all computers connected to its Advanced Research Projects Agency Network (ARPANET) to implement TCP/IP, and in 1995 Microsoft implemented TCP/IP as its default networking protocol. These two actions effectively made TCP/IP the standard internetworking protocol after 1995.

By the late 1980's, many computer networks were connected by TCP/IP, and there was considerable transfer of data among these computers. However, the data was transferred as files, and it was not particularly attractive when it arrived at a destination computer. From 1989 to 1992, Tim Berners-Lee of the European Council for Nuclear Research (later renamed the European Organization for Nuclear Research), known as CERN, in Switzerland developed the first version of a Web browser and server using the hypertext markup language (HTML) and hypertext transfer protocol (HTTP). Using the Web to disseminate information over TCP/IP internetworks greatly increased its popularity. Many improvements were made to Web servers and browsers over the 1990's, and by 2000 the Internet had become one of the major vehicles for the exchange of information. The first real e-business was a CERN telephone directory created by Berners-Lee in 1992. During the remainder of the 1990's, e-commerce developed at breakneck speed, with many large companies like Amazon.com appearing. While there was a downturn for e-commerce in 2000, the industry recovered shortly after and has since expanded rapidly.

A new version of IP, called IPv6 (version 6), was proposed in 1991. This upgraded IP provides better security and enhanced routing capability. Because the current version of IP is widely used, IPv6 has been making slow but steady progress in being deployed. In 1996, the Internet2 project was announced as the next version of the Internet. A high-speed (100 gigabytes per second) state-of-the-art internetwork, Internet2 will support a variety of media transfers and innovative applications. It is anticipated that Internet2 will use IPv6.

Creation of the Internet In 1969, ARPANET was created under the leadership of the Defense Advanced Research Projects Agency (DARPA) of the Department of Defense. Initially, ARPANET consisted of a small number of government and university computers connected with the network control program (NCP) protocol. In 1983, ARPANET made TCP/IP its core protocol. Over the next few years, TCP/IP matured as an internetworking protocol. By 1990, ARPANET had become difficult to operate, and it was officially retired. ARPANET was replaced by several internetworks (including the National Science Foundation Network, or NSFNet) and a group of organizations (including the Internet Society, or ISOC). By 1991, these internets and organizations were regularly referred to as the Internet.

In 1991, NSFNet decided to allow use of its network by commercial entities as well as the government and universities. This effectively opened the Internet to everyone and resulted in a dramatic increase in the size of the Internet. The Internet Society was chartered in January, 1992. It is a large organization, made up of individuals, companies, universities, and organizations. ISOC determines the policies and standards for the Internet. ISOC has several important boards, including the Internet Architecture Board (IAB), the Internet Engineering Task Force (IETF), and the Internet Research Task Force (IRTF). The IAB provides technical advice to ISOC, the IETF works on specific standards, and the IRTF does long-range planning. In 1995, the Federal Networking Council (FNC), a coordinating group of representatives from the federal agencies involved in networking, officially defined the Internet as the totality of networks that were interconnected by TCP/IP. This is the definition of the Internet used today.

Advances in Networking During the 1990's, there were many advances in TCP/IP software that helped the Internet to grow. When TCP/IP was selected as the internet protocol of ARPANET, it included a number of important features, including Telnet for remote terminal access, file transfer protocol (FTP) for remote file transfer, transmission control protocol (TCP) for reliable connections, IP for routing, and simple mail transfer protocol (SMTP) for e-mail support. In 1990, the simple network management protocol (SNMP) made its debut by remotely operating an Internet toaster. During the 1990's, SNMP continued to add features and applications until a single workstation could manage all the computers on a network.

The most important addition to the TCP/IP protocol suite made during the 1990's was HTTP, proposed by Berners-Lee in 1989 and implemented by him at CERN in 1992. This simple protocol allowed the Internet to support the World Wide Web (WWW), and the WWW became the most important application running on the Internet by the end of the 1990's. The IP gives all computers on the Internet a 32-bit numeric address, such as 121.10.45.255. For a variety of reasons, the Internet community wanted to have a symbolic name for each computer rather than the 32-bit numeric address. In the early days of ARPANET, the symbolic-to-numeric name conversion was handed locally by a hosts file, located on each computer. The domain name system (DNS) was proposed as a better solution for the conversion about 1983, and by 1985 a DNS with several zone servers had been created. In 1993, the NSF started privatizing the DNS by assigning its major administrative functions to private corporations. Since that time, DNS Internet address registration and maintenance of the Internet address database has been handled by a number of companies who jointly maintain thirteen root servers.

A major area of improvement in networking that led to the explosive growth of the Internet in the 1990's was the development of high-speed networks that used fiber-optic cables. Especially important were the backbone internetworks that provided support for transfers of data from one part of the country to another. The increased bandwidth of the communications networks supporting the Internet has resulted in a number of innovative applications, including music and video downloads, rich graphical pages sent over the Web, and telephone service introduced in 1996 that used voice-over IP (VoIP).

The improvements in general computer and communications hardware during the 1990's provided a great deal of support for the Internet. Microchip manufacturers increased their chip density during the 1990's, and this improved the computers sending and receiving data, as well as the communications equipment connecting these computers. Typical of the companies that experienced dynamic growth in the 1990's is Cisco Systems. Founded in 1984, Cisco went public in 1990 with assets of $190 million. In 2000, Cisco was estimated to be worth more than $500 billion. Cisco originally produced simple routers and gateways but later marketed a full range of communications products.

Universal Access The 1990's marked a time of greatly improved access to the Internet from home and the workplace. Microsoft led the way when it included a TCP/IP stack as part of the Windows 95 operating system, but all personal computers and workstations provided TCP/IP support by the end of the 1990's. The introduction of the Mosaic Web browser for the Macintosh and personal computer (PC) in 1993 and Internet Explorer as part of the Windows 95 operating system in 1995 made access to the Web simple. Improvements in hardware used to access the Internet were even greater than those for software. For the home user, the 1990's marked a time of greatly improved choices for high-speed access to the Internet. The 28.8-kilobit modem was introduced in 1994, the 56-kilobit modem in 1996, and the 1- to 2-megabit asymmetric digital subscriber line (ADSL) modem in 1998. These provided home Internet users with a standard telephone line fast access to the Internet. For those with cable television, the cable modem, introduced about 1997, and standardized with the data over cable service interface specification (DOCSIS) protocol in 1999, provided 2- to 10-megabit service that was very reliable. During the same time, cell phone users could communicate with their offices either by 56-kilobit modem or by proprietary cell phone modem. As early as 1995, some were using satellites to access the Internet, although it was expensive.

In the workplace, high-speed access became commonplace in the 1990's. The 10Base-T standard was adopted in 1990, and this allowed companies to provide inexpensive access for their employees, using large switch-based networks. The first wireless local area networks (LANs) appeared about 1997, and in 1999 the IEEE 802.11 wireless LAN standards process began. Wireless access allowed employees to access the Internet without having to plug into an Ethernet connector. At home, inexpensive wireless kits containing access points and connector cards were in wide use by 2000 and allowed multiple home computers access to the Internet.

Internet Applications A number of important Internet applications were developed during the 1990's, the most important of which was the World Wide Web. Berners-Lee implemented a working WWW system at CERN in 1992. Many improvements were made to the basic ideas of Berners-Lee during the decade, including the development of the Mosaic browser by Marc Andreessen and Eric Bina in 1993, the development of Netscape Navigator in 1994 by Andreessen and Jim Clark, and the development of Internet Explorer by Microsoft in 1995. These later browsers added improved graphics and multimedia support. Berners-Lee founded the World Wide Web Consortium (W3C) in 1994, and this organization (replacing the ISOC) became the main standards body for Web-specific activities.

The most-used application of the Internet today is e-mail. The first e-mail system was developed by Ray Tomlinson in 1971. In 1991, Philip Zimmerman introduced a way to send e-mail securely with his Pretty Good Privacy technology. The original e-mail format, defined by the request for comments (RFC) 822, was quite limited, and in 1992 it was enhanced by the multipurpose Internet mail extensions (MIME) to support sending pictures and sound in e-mail. As HTML became a popular format for messages, e-mail clients like Outlook Express and Eudora developed a technique of displaying e-mail as an HTML document, while encoding it in the RFC 822 format using MIME. The addition of the post office protocol (POP) in 1999 greatly enhanced reliable e-mail delivery.

The secure socket layer (SSL) protocol was originally developed by Netscape in 1994 and has been improved by many others since then. It provides a secure communications path for browsers and e-mail programs, and this has made e-commerce over the Internet much safer.

Impact Over the 1990's, the Internet grew exponentially. The number of Web servers, e-businesses, and users greatly increased. Transmission speeds improved throughout the world and changed the way people communicate. In 1990, few used, or even knew of, the Internet; by 2000, the Internet had become an essential tool for most in the United States.

Further Reading

Baase, Sara. *A Gift of Fire: Social, Legal, and Ethical Issues for Computers and the Internet.* Upper Saddle River, N.J.: Prentice Hall, 2002. Interesting coverage of the social and legal issues surrounding the Internet.

Hofstetter, Fred. *Internet Literacy.* New York: McGraw-Hill, 2005. Provides a comprehensive introduction to the Internet and the World Wide Web.

Salus, Peter H. *Casting the Net: From ARPANET to Internet and Beyond.* Reading, Mass.: Addison-Wesley, 1995. A good introduction to the development of ARPANET and the early days of the Internet.

George M. Whitson III

See also Amazon.com; Apple Computer; CGI; Computers; Dot-coms; DVDs; E-mail; Hackers; Instant messaging; Inventions; Microsoft; MP3 format; PDAs; Silicon Valley; World Wide Web; Y2K problem.

■ Inventions

Definition Newly created or improved devices, objects, substances, techniques, or processes

During the 1990's, legal, political, and economic factors affected how patent officials determined which inventions merited patent protection and how legislators and judges perceived laws regulating patents. Rapid developments in genetic and computer engineering intensified competition to secure lucrative patents, and invention underwent a transition in which corporations and industry dominated.

By 1990, the U.S. Patent and Trademark Office (USPTO) had approved five million patents since it was established in 1790. Entrepreneurs realized innovation was essential in the 1990's for businesses to compete in the global market, which thrived on electronics, biotechnology, and telecommunications inventions, filing significantly more patent applications compared to prior decades. Those fields often incorporated complex, emerging technology and scientific ideas unfamiliar to many legal and patent personnel, who, although sometimes lacking sufficient scientific expertise, were in the position to evaluate inventions and rule on disputes regarding which inventions were patentable and ownership of rights. These were crucial issues in the escalating infringement litigation initiated by inventors and businesses guarding their innovations and income those inventions generated. Advocates and critics of patent reform discussed laws relevant to inventions in the United States and internationally and how modifications might affect invention practices and influence trade and economic conditions.

Patent Facts When the 1990's began, U.S. patent law recognized that rights to an invention belonged to whoever initially envisioned it, but most countries' patent laws stated that rights were assured to inventors who first filed applications, complicating legal disputes regarding inventions. Corporations and universities hired researchers and usually owned any inventions those employees created at work. In 1990, inventors filed 163,575 patent applications. The USPTO, staffed by approximately 1,500 examiners, processed most applications within eighteen months, compared to a two-year wait in the 1980's. Annually, the number of applications significantly increased, and review times also grew during the 1990's, reaching twenty-five months by the end of the decade.

In the 1990's, USPTO examiners evaluated invention applications submitted by U.S. and international inventors. Canadian inventors secured patents though their nation's patent office and often also filed for U.S. or foreign patents. Approximately 55 percent of the 109,728 U.S. patents approved in 1992 were issued to U.S. inventors, with 22 percent of the patents being granted to Japanese inventors and 7 percent to Germans. Many U.S. inventors also sought patents in other countries, especially Japan, where technological competition from industries necessitated patent protection. Political changes in Europe, particularly German reunification and socioeconomic reform efforts in the former Soviet Union, impacted 1990's markets for inventions.

The USPTO received less federal funding in the 1990's and relied on increased patent fees approved by the U.S. Congress, collecting several hundred million dollars annually. Costs to maintain a patent for the standard seventeen-year protection period were approximately $6,700, which hindered many individual and small business inventors. By the mid-1990's, inventions enhanced the USPTO's operations when that office permitted inventors to fax applications and considered security and encrypting concerns for future electronic filing online. In 1998, the USPTO added text of post-1976 patents to its online database (www.uspto.gov).

Time Line of Select 1990's Inventions

1990
Hubble Space Telescope
World Wide Web

1991
Digital answering machine
V-chip (television blocking receiver)

1992
Smart pill (computer-controlled medication delivery)

1993
Blue LED (light-emitting diode)
Global positioning system (GPS)
Pentium processor

1994
HIV protease inhibitor

1995
DVD technology
Java computer language

1996
Web TV

1997
Gas-powered fuel cell
Nonmechanical digital audio player
Wi-Fi wireless networking

1998
Viagra (erectile dysfunction drug)

1999
Tekno Bubbles (blacklight bubbles)

Innovations Early 1990's computer-related inventions inspired other inventors whose creations expanded consumers' options for communication and entertainment. In 1990, Tim Berners-Lee, a European Organization for Nuclear Research (CERN) physicist, created a program to transmit text messages, connecting CERN scientists' computers internationally. This World Wide Web became publicly available. Within three years, Marc Andreessen invented a graphical browser, known as Mosaic, which showed images to supplement text. The rapidly evolving Internet attracted several hundred million new users yearly during the 1990's. Online services, particularly shopping and banking, appealed to many people, including hackers and identity thieves who took advantage of security vulnerabilities. Some computer scientists created software, such as Invention Machine Lab, to assist aspiring inventors.

Inventions enhanced medical knowledge and applications, particularly surgical, pharmaceutical, and equipment innovations. In the early 1990's, W. French Anderson utilized gene therapy for treatment. Genetics researcher J. Craig Venter used expressed sequence tags (ESTs) to detect genes in DNA and started the Human Genome Project. By the end of the decade, Venter established Celera Genomics with laboratory equipment maker PE Corporation to use computers to establish a genetic database. Genetic researchers attempted cloning animals in the 1990's. In July, 1996, Keith Campbell and Ian Wilmut of Roslin Institute cloned a sheep named Dolly. Other researchers created genetically engineered flowers and food. While many people supported those achievements, others expressed ethical concerns and protested genetic manipulation.

Other 1990's inventions contributed to transportation and defense needs by improving materials used to construct automobiles, aircraft, and satellites. For example, Peter Searson and Theodore Poehler used their polymer expertise to invent plastic batteries. The Hubble Space Telescope and other aerospace inventions provided researchers with more precise tools to conduct astronomical investigations. Communications inventions permeated daily activities, ranging from personal to industrial and governmental usage. During the decade, inventors designed smaller digital and satellite phones with more functions. Wireless Application Protocol enabled cellular phone connections with the Internet. Introduced in 1992, Sony's MiniDisc enabled users to record and play audio on a device they could easily carry while exercising or pursuing other activities. By 1998, engineers developed MP3 compression methods to store large amounts of digital files.

Patenting Biotechnology Some 1990's inventions were controversial because they presented concerns patent laws did not address. Computer software and biotechnology provoked the most debate about what inventions were patentable. The 1980 U.S. Supreme Court decision supporting Ananda Chakrabarty's patent for a genetically engineered organism had intensified research to identify and secure rights to genetic material. Pharmaceutical and medical investors recognized the financial potential of genetic patents by selling licenses to drug manufacturers. A 1991 trial in San Francisco, California, resulted in a ruling protecting patents the Cetus Corporation had acquired when its researcher, Kary B. Mullis, determined how a polymerase chain reaction produced copies from a genetic sample, impeding other researchers from using that technique without purchasing rights.

In 1992, the National Institutes of Health (NIH) filed for several thousand patents for DNA fragments with unknown genes. Although the USPTO rejected the NIH applications, biotechnology work escalated. Researchers utilized automated sequencers to identify EST. Worldwide, approximately 1,175 patents were issued specifying human DNA sequences by 1995. The USPTO stated that researchers could submit EST patent applications even when associated genes and functions were unknown. This decision upset some researchers because EST patent owners could claim rights to any genes in patented EST, keeping other researchers from investigating those genes.

Overwhelmed by EST applications, the USPTO held public hearings to seek ways to manage biotechnology applications so they would not interfere with review of nongenetic applicants. By spring 1999, the USPTO increased its examiner staff to 3,000 to review approximately 240,000 applications. Some examiners lacked sufficient expertise and experience to review complex biotechnology patent applications, rejecting or accepting applications without being aware of precedents or other crucial information. They occasionally asked applicants to present proof that EST had medical applications. Several scientific groups requested more competent evaluations, and the USPTO provided some biotechnology training to examiners.

Computer Patents Inconsistent evaluation of software during the 1990's also distressed inventors. The USPTO did not routinely patent software until 1994. That year the U.S. Court of Appeals for the Federal Circuit, which had been established in the 1980's specifically for judges experienced in intellectual property law to hear patent cases, stated that software included in hard drives or other storage media such as floppy disks was patentable. While industry leaders, especially the Microsoft Corporation, sought patents to protect their inventions, other software producers, including Oracle Corporation, considered patents detrimental to the creation of future software.

Inventors and executives identified a December, 1993, patent to Compton's New Media as a threat to their multimedia pursuits, especially when Compton's stated it expected royalties from any company using technological aspects of its patent. Some critics suggested that broad software patents gave owners monopolies over intrinsic functions necessary to other companies' services. Commissioner of Patents and Trademarks Bruce A. Lehman, a copyright expert, scheduled meetings at Silicon Valley in California to discuss software patents. Critics complained that examiners lacked computer educational credentials and did not recognize public domain software applications. Lehman and USPTO officials terminated Compton's patent and sought examiners who had experience programming computers or advanced degrees.

Software patents in the 1990's shaped legal precedents for later inventions. When the USPTO denied a software patent to Mary Ellen Zurko, she appealed that decision to the U.S. Court of Appeals for the Federal Circuit. In May, 1998, that court stated the USPTO should not have rejected Zurko's application. Commissioner Lehman responded that the appeals court should not counter the authority of the USPTO's examiners, noting several hundred examiners held doctorates and were competent engineers and scientists. The U.S. Supreme Court heard *Lehman v. Zurko* in November, 1998. On June 10, 1999, the U.S. Supreme Court ruled 6-3 against Zurko, with Justice Stephen Breyer stating that the appeals court had ignored an earlier law requiring judges to respect governmental experts unless they had performed maliciously or negligently. Inventors worried the USPTO might be victorious in all application appeals. Other 1990's court cases considered how inventions such as Amazon.com's one-click ordering function impacted e-commerce competition.

Infringement Lawsuits Inventions' financial success triggered patent infringement, resulting in economic losses for patent owners who often initiated legal action against people and corporations they accused of stealing their patented devices or processes. Patent infringers frequently targeted electronics and pharmaceuticals. Approximately 50 percent more infringement lawsuits were filed in 1990 compared to 1980 statistics. Many of those lawsuits resulted in large monetary reimbursements for royalties inventors had been denied.

During the early 1990's, Robert Kearns, of Detroit, Michigan, received multimillion-dollar settlements from U.S. and international automobile manufacturers who had installed intermittent windshield wipers identical to those he had patented in the early 1960's and shown to Ford Motor Company engineers in Detroit. At that time, Kearns thought Ford would purchase rights to use his invention, but he later realized that manufacturer and others had incorporated his invention in vehicles without his permission and sued.

Other notable 1990's patent infringement cases included the October, 1990, ruling that Eastman Kodak Company pay Polaroid Corporation $909.4 million, the greatest infringement award at that time, because it had infringed on Polaroid's instant photography patents. Two years later, a court ordered Minolta Camera Company to pay Honeywell Incorporated $127 million for using aspects of Honeywell's auto-focus lens patents. In 1997, Raymond Damadian of Fonar Corporation received $103 million from General Electric for using his magnetic resonance imaging. Gilbert Hyatt's 1990 microprocessor patent, based on a 1970 application, upset the computer industry when Hyatt demanded royalties, claiming he was the first inventor to develop a microprocessor.

In the early 1990's, U.S. patent and copyright owners filed over one hundred lawsuits to protest Japanese manufacturers who they claimed had infringed on their intellectual property. For example, in 1993, Eastman Kodak Company began legal proceedings stating Sony Corporation had copied information from Kodak's patent describing video recording technology. Many of the Japanese defendants filed countersuits, resulting in tensions that threatened trade between those countries. U.S. officials discussed how to control infringement with Japanese and other foreign leaders. Trade incentives proved effective to convince other nations to monitor patent infringement.

Jerome Lemelson's 1990's infringement lawsuits were among the most controversial. He received several hundred million dollars from Japanese, European, and U.S. automobile companies and parts companies that had appropriated the bar-coding technology he invented in the 1950's. His critics referred to Lemelson's patents as submarine patents, because information in his applications remained unknown for decades. They insinuated Lemelson had delayed patent approval to claim infringement after manufacturers used similar inventions, an argument which stimulated patent reform. Lemelson dismissed that criticism as absurd.

Patent Reform During the early 1990's, USPTO Commissioner Harry F. Manbeck, Jr., encouraged patent reform to improve the U.S. patent system and make it more compatible with international patenting procedures. Commissioner Manbeck served as chair of the Advisory Commission on Patent Law Reform to consider U.S. and foreign patenting differences which were detrimental to marketing U.S. inventions.

After he became USPTO commissioner in 1993, Lehman emphasized the corporate benefits of invention and the need for U.S. patenting strategies that aided U.S. technology and scientific knowledge to be competitive internationally. Under his leadership, U.S. patent protection extended twenty years from the time inventors applied, replacing the previous seventeen-year period starting when patents were approved. In January, 1994, Lehman and Japan Patent Commissioner Wataru Aso negotiated an agreement stating that U.S. inventors' English-language applications could be filed in Japan before being translated so that U.S. inventors would not be delayed in claiming rights.

In 1996, federal legislators considered an omnibus bill that outlined such reforms as publishing patent applications eighteen months after they were filed. Commissioner Lehman and the bill's supporters emphasized that publication prevented manufacturers from possible infringement charges because they would be aware of inventors' ideas instead of them remaining secret. Opponents included the Small Entity Patent Owners Association, Alliance for American Innovation, and invention groups supporting noncorporate inventors who feared their ideas might be vulnerable to infringement prior to patent approval.

During 1997, U.S. representatives and senators continued to debate the omnibus bill (H.R. 400) in the U.S. House of Representatives, where sponsor Representative Howard Coble (Republican, North Carolina), speaking on behalf of corporate interests, defended the bill against Representative Dana Rohrabacher (Republican, California), voicing independent inventors' concerns. Representative Marcy Kaptur (Democrat, Ohio) secured an amendment that stated university, individual, and small company patent applicants were not required to publish application information. U.S. senators considered the legislation (S. 507) in their proceedings.

When Commissioner Lehman resigned in October, 1998, legislators still disagreed on reforms. His successor, patent attorney Q. Todd Dickinson, supported USPTO Office of Independent Inventor Programs, which sought those inventors' input. Legislators and groups, such as the 21st Century Patent Coalition, continued to seek acceptable patent reforms regarding application publication, patent reevaluation, trade secret provisions, and transforming the USPTO into a corporate organization.

History, Events, and Awards Celebrations and activities held in the United States during the 1990's honored inventions and inventors. That decade began with events commemorating the bicentennial of the 1790 Patent Act. During May, 1990, the Foundation for a Creative America oversaw patent bicentennial festivities that included museum exhibits featuring female and minority inventors. In 1990, the National Inventors Hall of Fame, which had been established in 1973, relocated from the USPTO to the Inventure Place in Akron, Ohio. During the patent bicentennial, the National Inventors Hall of Fame hosted an induction that included the first African American inductees, Percy Julian and George Washington Carver. The next year's induction ceremony admitted Gertrude Elion as the initial female inventor inducted. By 1995, National Inventors Hall of Fame officials chose Stephanie Kwolek, the Kevlar inventor, for induction. In 1998, computer engineer Mark Dean became the next African American inductee, followed the next year by the fourth African American inducted, James West, an acoustical engineer.

The USPTO sponsored the yearly National Inventors Expo in the 1990's. Organizations and periodicals sponsored invention workshops and competitions for children and adults during the decade. In December, 1992, *Successful Farming* magazine held the initial National Farmer Inventors Congress at Des Moines, Iowa, because readers had requested help to patent and market inventions they had innovated for practical agricultural uses. Farmers competed in the affiliated Edisons of Agriculture contest throughout the 1990's, winning farm equipment prizes for their inventiveness.

In 1995, the Massachusetts Institute of Technology first presented the annual invention award, the Lemelson-MIT Prize ($500,000), funded by Jerome Lemelson. Winners during the 1990's included William Bolander, Herbert Boyer, Stanley

Cohen, Douglas Engelbart, Robert Langer, and Carver Mead. Lemelson and his wife gave the Smithsonian Institution money to build the Jerome and Dorothy Lemelson Center for the Study of Invention and Innovation, which was founded in 1995 at the Smithsonian's National Museum of American History.

American Heritage and other mainstream magazines printed articles about the history of invention in the United States. The October, 1991, issue of the scholarly journal *Technology and Culture* focused on invention and patent themes. *Popular Science, Newsweek,* and *Time* profiled the decade's most significant inventions in special issues listing the century's invention achievements. The digital answering machine, Pentium processor, and Java were among the periodicals' choices representing the 1990's.

Impact Inventions developed in the 1990's offered consumers increased technological and scientific choices but limited many inventors' options to create, patent, and market their ideas autonomously. That decade, although honoring historical precedents, marked notable transitions in inventive culture that sought reform and change from patenting methods in prior decades, adjusting to international economic demands and benefits. Corporate interests transformed the invention process from innovation often envisioned by individuals working alone to groups of researchers hired by industries or universities to develop technology capable of generating millions, sometimes billions, of dollars in licensing fees and royalties.

As the USPTO assumed a corporate structure during the 1990's, its rigid bureaucracy and expensive fees became prohibitive to many independent inventors who received less government support in their endeavors. Of the 250,000 applications filed in 1998, only 15 percent were submitted by noncorporate inventors. Affiliated professionals, notably patent attorneys, profited from legal work involved in filing patents and associated litigation.

Subsequent Events Biotechnology and electronic inventions from the 1990's inspired more refined, quicker, or miniature versions that were patented in the early twenty-first century. Inventors filed approximately 312,000 patent applications in 2000, submitting more each year as new materials and economic opportunities spurred invention. The USPTO devised its Genetic Sequence Database, USGENE. As profits motivated both inventors and patent thieves, U.S. legislators continued to debate patent reforms, particularly controlling infringement.

Further Reading

Brown, David E. *Inventing Modern America: From the Microwave to the Mouse.* Foreword by Lester C. Thurow. Introductions by James Burke. Cambridge, Mass.: MIT Press, 2002. Discusses contributions of several 1990's genetics, physics, and computer innovators, including Tim Berners-Lee and Marc Andreessen.

Carey, John. "Patent Reform Pending: A New Bill Has Small Inventors on the Defensive." *Business Week,* November 22, 1999, pp. 74, 78-79. Outlines the status of patent legislation by the end of the 1990's and possible compromises. Notes how Jerome Lemelson's patent settlements provoked demands for reforms.

Carlisle, Rodney P. *Scientific American Inventions and Discoveries: All the Milestones in Ingenuity—From the Discovery of Fire to the Invention of the Microwave Oven.* Hoboken, N.J.: John Wiley & Sons, 2004. Examines such 1990's inventions as carbon composite materials, digital cameras, and computer products, specifying industrial financial losses due to faulty Pentium II chips.

Evans, Harold, with Gail Buckland and David Lefer. *They Made America: From the Steam Engine to the Search Engine: Two Centuries of Innovators.* New York: Little, Brown, 2004. Comprehensive history of U.S. inventions, with a digital age section profiling such significant 1990's inventors as Raymond Damadian.

Giscard d'Estaing, Valérie-Anne, and Mark Young, eds. *Inventions and Discoveries 1993: What's Happened, What's Coming, What's That?* New York: Facts On File, 1993. Features inventions from the early 1990's, placing each invention, sometimes accompanied by an illustration, in appropriate categories identifying its function. Giscard d'Estaing published several other invention almanacs in the 1990's.

Seabrook, John. "The Flash of Genius." *The New Yorker* 68 (January 11, 1993): 38-40, 42-52. Account of how Robert Kearns invented the intermittent windshield wiper and reacted when he discovered his patent had been infringed, including quotes from Kearns and automotive manufacturing representatives regarding Kearns's litigation.

Van Dulken, Stephen. *Inventing the Twentieth Century: One Hundred Inventions That Shaped the World—From the Airplane to the Zipper.* Introduction by Andrew Phillips. Washington Square, N.Y.: New York University Press, 2000. Chapter focusing on the 1990's describes ten inventions, including images or text from patent applications and details relevant to each invention's creation.

Elizabeth D. Schafer

See also Automobile industry; Business and the economy in the United States; Cloning; Computers; Genetics research; Hackers; Human Genome Project; Internet; MP3 format; Nanotechnology; Pharmaceutical industry; Science and technology; Silicon Valley; World Wide Web.

■ *Iron John*

Identification Mythopoetic men's movement book
Author Robert Bly (1926-)
Date Published in 1990

Bly's book, an international best seller that has been translated into many languages, is credited with starting the mythopoetic (pertaining to myths) men's movement in the United States, including workshops and retreats for men led by Bly, Michael J. Meade, James Hillman, and others, as well as hundreds of other men's support groups nationwide.

The title *Iron John* is derived from a legend set down by the Brothers Grimm in Germany in 1820, but which American poet Robert Bly believes could be many thousands of years old. It is a story of a hairy wild man found in a deep pool in a forest, captured and imprisoned in an iron cage in the courtyard of a king's house and liberated by the king's eight-year-old son, whom the wild man takes into the forest, tests in three trials (which the boy fails), and sends out into the world. The king's son endures reverses and rises in his fortune, finally ending up in true fairy-tale fashion recognized as a royal and married to a king's daughter. Through his triumph, he liberates from an enchantment the wild man, who turns out to be a rich and powerful king himself.

The term "wild man," according to Bly, carries with it an enormous amount of historical information, which he details through mythology, theology, psychology, and literature from many cultures through ancient and modern times, all of which add to and explain each other. Bly uses progressive portions of the tale of the wild man/Iron John as a metaphor for different stages of masculine development necessary if modern males are to regain their true direction and their lost vitality.

The book was an immediate success, topping the charts for ten weeks and remaining on the best seller list for a year. It is credited with sparking the men's movement, in which Bly, Michael J. Meade, James Hillman, and others conducted their own weekend retreats, using poems, fairy tales, and myths to teach men to get in touch with themselves and replace passivity with power. In the preface of his book and in interviews, Bly emphasizes his support of the women's movement and denies encouraging subjugation of women. Nevertheless, feminists charged that the movement was misogynist, the media made fun of it, and some critics felt it was based on and designed for a small and select group of white well-to-do men.

Bly is characterized as a poet, author, translator,

Robert Bly. (AP/Wide World Photos)

and storyteller. He is credited with more than eighteen books of poetry, seven anthologies, eleven translations, and seven books of nonfiction, of which *Iron John: A Book About Men* is one.

Impact *Iron John* has become synonymous with the men's movement, including New Warrior Network and Promise Keepers, although their methods and aims may be different. The book and Bly were prominent in the news in the 1990's, reaping both praise and criticism.

Further Reading

Bly, Robert. *Iron John: A Book About Men.* Reading, Mass.: Addison-Wesley, 1990.

Gilmore, David D. *Manhood in the Making: Cultural Concepts of Masculinity.* New Haven, Conn.: Yale University Press, 1990.

Keen, Sam. *Fire in the Belly: On Being a Man.* New York: Bantam Books, 1992.

Erika E. Pilver

See also Culture wars; Life coaching; Marriage and divorce; *Men Are from Mars, Women Are from Venus*; Million Man March; Native Americans; Promise Keepers; Psychology; Religion and spirituality in the United States; *Saving Private Ryan.*

■ Israel and the United States

Definition Diplomatic and strategic relations between Israel and the United States

In the 1990's, two U.S. administrations undertook repeated diplomatic efforts to shepherd peace agreements between Israel and its Arab neighbors. Despite vigorous U.S. diplomacy and numerous formal agreements, final peace between Israel and the Palestinian Arabs could not be attained.

Though not formal allies under any treaty, traditionally friendly bilateral relations between Israel and the United States grew more intimate through intelligence cooperation under U.S. president Ronald Reagan (1981-1989). Under his successor, George H. W. Bush (1989-1993), however, strains emerged over the Gulf War of 1991 that raised questions concerning the strategic value of U.S. ties to Israel. Though many other nations were persuaded to join a military coalition to assist this U.S.-led project to expel Iraq from Kuwait, no Israeli participation was deemed by the United States to be politically feasible. Coalition members supporting the United States included the Arab states of Egypt and Syria, and both were unwilling to fight on the same side as the Jewish state, Israel. During the Gulf War, Iraq repeatedly struck targets in Israel with Scud missiles, expecting that Israeli retaliation would shatter the U.S.-led coalition. To provide Israel incentive not to retaliate, U.S. Patriot antimissile batteries were rushed to Israel on an emergency basis, and senior U.S. diplomat Lawrence Eagleburger was dispatched to Jerusalem to ensure Israeli restraint for the duration of the Gulf War.

Advancing Peace with the Arab World The Bush administration, especially Secretary of State James Baker, approached the post-Gulf War Middle East with the view that opportunities were ripe for new initiatives to maximize U.S. influence. A key obstacle was perceived to be the persistence of hostility between Israel and its Arab neighbors. In this context, the continuing reluctance of many Arab states to cooperate fully with U.S. initiatives led Baker to place new pressures on Israel. Together with the Soviet Union, a peace conference was convened at Madrid, Spain, on October 30, 1991. President Bush opened the conference by declaring the goal of U.S. policy to be "a just, lasting, and comprehensive settlement." This was the first face-to-face public meeting of Israeli officials with representatives of Jordan, Lebanon, Syria, and the Palestinians. The conference resumed in Washington in December, 1991, and in Moscow in January, 1992. Parallel to this high-profile public diplomacy, U.S. officials continued secret contacts with leaders of Palestinian armed groups that had been begun in the 1980's.

Diplomatic breakthroughs followed, with all subsequent steps completed during Bill Clinton's administration (1993-2001). A Declaration of Principles (Oslo Accords) pointing to an ultimate peace agreement (to be negotiated later) was signed between Israel and the leadership of the Palestine Liberation Organization at the White House in Washington on September 13, 1993. On May 4, 1994, agreements were reached founding the Palestinian National Authority (PNA); a formal peace and diplomatic relations were initiated between Israel and Jordan on October 26, 1994. A further interim agreement also was consented to by the PNA and Israel, in Washington on September 28, 1995. These several steps toward ending hostilities advanced U.S. objectives by conveying that the United States was indispensable if regional problems were to be effectively addressed.

Extremists Derail Progress Hard-line nationalists in each community, however, failed to embrace the peace initiatives and undertook to undermine the fragile steps toward peace. On the Jewish holiday of Purim in February, 1994, an American-born Israeli, Baruch Goldstein, massacred twenty-nine Arab Muslims praying at a disputed holy site in Hebron, the Tomb of the Patriarchs, which is known to Muslims as the Ibrahimi Mosque. Extremist Palestinians, chiefly of the Islamist organization Hamas, also accelerated their attacks on Israelis after the signing of the 1993 peace accords: Four suicide bombings in 1994 killed thirty-nine Israelis. The next year, the leading Israeli peacemaker, Prime Minister Yitzhak Rabin, was assassinated by a fellow Israeli on November 4, 1995. After the 1995 interim accord was signed, Hamas bombers killed nearly sixty Israelis in four 1996 attacks.

Repeated sessions led by U.S. negotiator Dennis Ross and vigorous U.S. efforts at mediation could not overcome Israeli suspicions that the PNA was not living up to its obligations to rein in Palestinian terrorists, as it had agreed to do under the peace agreements. Palestinian attitudes also hardened when a new Israeli prime minister, Benjamin Netanyahu, approved expansion of Israeli housing units in disputed suburban areas adjacent to Jerusalem in 1998. The United States expressed its displeasure with Israel's settlement activities in the occupied territories by reducing somewhat its generous loan guarantees to the Jewish state, but these guarantees still amounted to $10 billion (1993-1997). This was in addition to the annual $3 billion in U.S. military and economic aid to Israel given each year in the 1990's.

President Clinton poured much personal energy into trying to stop the unraveling of the Israeli-Palestinian peace agreements in his final years in office. At Wye River, Maryland, in 1998, and at Camp David, Maryland, in 2000, Clinton hosted Palestinian chairman Yasir Arafat and Israeli Prime Ministers Netanyahu (1998) and Ehud Barak (2000). Significant Israeli territorial concessions were offered at the Wye River talks, granting Arafat's Palestinian National Authority practical control over 98 percent of the Palestinian population on the West Bank. At Wye River, Netanyahu also strained Israeli relations with Clinton and with U.S. intelligence agencies by attempting to win release of Jonathan Pollard, a U.S. citizen convicted in 1985 of spying for Israel. Clinton refused this request after Director of Central Intelligence George Tenet threatened to resign. Negotiations on implementing the peace agreements continued under U.S. auspices through the end of the decade, but broad differences remained between the parties over the final status of Jerusalem, exact borders, and the Palestinians' insistence on their "right of return" to homes abandoned in 1948-1949 inside Israel.

Impact Though strained at times, U.S. ties to Israel deepened overall in the 1990's. However, the failure of U.S. mediation efforts regarding the Palestinian element in the Arab-Israeli conflict reinforced skeptical attitudes toward the United States across the Muslim world.

Subsequent Events At Camp David in December, 2000, Clinton persuaded Israel to propose further concessions beyond those offered at Wye River, amounting to 91 percent of the lands in the West Bank and 100 percent of Gaza to be composed as a Palestinian state. Chief U.S. negotiator Ross later blamed Arafat for rejecting what Barak, Clinton, and Ross believed to be generous terms for a final settlement. The lingering pace of U.S.-led peace negotiations in the 1990's had frustrated hopes among many Palestinians, and this reinforced a preference for armed struggle among other Palestinians, chiefly militant Islamists. Widespread civil unrest and violence erupted: The Palestinian second intifada began in September, 2000. The perception that the Palestinian leaders endorsed this renewal of violence undermined Israelis' support for Barak and for his initiatives to offer further territorial concessions. With forward movement toward peace stalled, a new U.S. administration in 2001 substantially disengaged from further attempts at peacemaking, especially after Muslim extremists launched devastating suicide attacks on the United States on September 11, 2001.

Further Reading

Bentsur, Eytan. *Making Peace: A First-Hand Account of the Arab-Israeli Peace Process*. New York: Praeger, 2001. Useful companion when read with Ross and Qurie. Israeli participant finds Madrid Conference and Baker as keys to 1990's peace process.

Druks, Herbert. *The Uncertain Alliance: The U.S. and Israel from Kennedy to the Peace Process.* Westport, Conn.: Greenwood Press, 2001. Carefully evaluates tensions between Israel and U.S. national security interests in the Gulf War and beyond.

Foxman, Abraham. *The Deadliest Lies: The Israel Lobby and the Myth of Jewish Control.* New York: Palgrave Macmillan, 2007. Analyzes the making of U.S. policy toward Israel from the 1970's to the 2000's.

Qurie, Ahmed. *From Oslo to Jerusalem: The Palestinian Story of the Secret Negotiations.* London: I. B. Tauris, 2006. Less focused on U.S. roles, a Palestinian negotiator covers the course of peace negotiations that Ross details from the U.S. perspective.

Ross, Dennis. *The Missing Peace: The Inside Story of the Fight for Middle East Peace.* New York: Farrar, Straus and Giroux, 2004. Chief U.S. Middle East peace negotiator, 1988-2001, chronicles U.S. efforts, analyzing key personalities, issues, and lessons learned.

Gordon L. Bowen

See also Clinton, Bill; Foreign policy of the United States; Gulf War; Jewish Americans; Middle East and North America; Patriot missile; Terrorism.

J

■ *Jenny Jones Show* murder

The Event Scott Amedure confesses his love for his friend Jonathan Schmitz on the air during a taping of the *Jenny Jones Show;* three days later, a humiliated Schmitz shoots Amedure twice in the chest, killing him

Date March 9, 1995

Place Detroit, Michigan

This murder and subsequent trials served to curtail the "ambush-style" talk-show episode of the early 1990's. In addition, the trials brought attention to the use of the "gay panic" defense in the courtroom.

On March 6, 1995, Jonathan Schmitz, a guest with a history of mental illness and substance abuse, was invited to a "secret admirer" episode without the knowledge that the admirer was a man, a friend by the name of Scott Amedure. Though Schmitz was seen to be amicable and joking during the show, he became disturbed after leaving the studio. Three days later, he bought a shotgun, drove to Amedure's trailer home, and shot him twice in the chest.

Schmitz was found guilty of second-degree murder in 1996, but his conviction was overturned on appeal because of a technicality. He was retried and convicted in 1999 and sentenced to twenty-five to fifty years in prison. Schmitz's lawyers had attempted to use the so-called gay panic defense—which tries to characterize the victim as a homosexual predator (according to trial testimony in 1996, Amedure left suggestive notes at Schmitz's home before the latter purchased the murder weapon) whose advances resulted in the defendant's violent action. The argument, which essentially claims that the crime was committed in self-defense, has been criticized as "blaming the victim."

In addition, Amedure's family filed a civil suit against the *Jenny Jones Show* asserting that the show's producers ought to have discovered Schmitz's history of mental illness. The family won the ruling in 1999, and the show was ordered to pay them $25 million. On October 23, 2003, the Michigan Court of Appeals reversed the 1999 decision of the Oakland County jury, ruling that the show's owner, Warner Bros., and its distributor, Telepictures, were not liable for the death of Scott Amedure.

Impact Amedure's murder shook the ground beneath the so-called ambush-style talk shows of Jerry Springer, Geraldo Rivera, and Maury Povich. After the 1996 verdict, ratings for the *Jenny Jones Show* and

Jenny Jones answers questions during testimony in the wrongful death lawsuit brought by the family of Scott Amedure against the Jenny Jones Show. *The show was ordered to pay the family $25 million.* (AP/Wide World Photos)

similar talk shows declined. The *Jenny Jones Show* was subsequently canceled in 2003. Schmitz's trials became the first in a series of cases probing the degree to which a party can be found culpable when someone else pulls the trigger. In addition, talk-show producers became leery of using gay, lesbian, bisexual, and transgender (GLBT) themes in their repertoire, especially "secret crush" episodes. More important, the trials brought to public attention the gay panic defense, which was thrown out by a judge during the 1999 trial for the murder of gay college student Matthew Shepard. Following the *Jenny Jones Show* murder, talk shows became less salacious in dealing with the GLBT community, and the gay panic defense became less popular.

Further Reading

"Can Media Kill?" *The Economist* 351 (May 15, 1999): 26-27.

Dahir, Mubarak. "Homosexual Panicking." *The Advocate*, June 22, 1999, 27-28.

"An Unhappy Rerun." *The Advocate*, October 13, 1998, 14.

Daniel-Raymond Nadon

See also Hate crimes; Homosexuality and gay rights; Shepard, Matthew; Television; Transgender community.

■ Jewish Americans

Definition Americans who are Jews by birth or formal conversion

At the end of the 1990's there were about 4.5 million people who considered themselves Jews in the United States, making it one of the largest Jewish populations in the world. This group constituted close to 2.5 percent of the U.S. population.

During the decade, Jews tended to live in urban centers, with the most significant populations in New York City, Boston, Washington, D.C., South Florida, Los Angeles, San Francisco, and Chicago. These Jews were primarily people who emigrated from Central and Eastern Europe and their American descendants, called Ashkenazi Jews, and people of Western European and North African descent, called Sephardi Jews. There were also small numbers of Jews from Central Asia, called Mizrahi Jews, as well as small populations from Ethiopia, India, and Greece.

Many different cultural traditions are found among the Jewish population in the United States, as well as different religious practices, from Orthodox to Reform. Many who consider themselves "cultural Jews" are entirely secular and run the gamut from agnosticism to atheism.

Jews in Government The 1990's was a period of extraordinary growth of the participation of American Jews in government and politics. More Jews won election to the Senate and the House of Representatives than during any other era in U.S. history. In the early years of the 1950's, only one Jew served in the Senate; in the 1990's, eleven Jews served as senators.

Bill Clinton, president of the United States from 1993 to 2001, made history by appointing two Jews to the U.S. Supreme Court: Ruth Bader Ginsburg in 1993 and Stephen G. Breyer in 1994. During the Clinton presidency, Jews received many cabinet posts and ambassadorial appointments, including the appointment of the first Orthodox Jew to an Arab country, Egypt. Shortly after Ambassador Daniel Kurtzer assumed his duties in Cairo, a kosher kitchen was established in the Cairo embassy. The door had been opened for Senator Joe Lieberman to become the first Orthodox Jewish candidate for vice president of the United States in August, 2000.

Another distinctive legacy of the Clinton administration was the large number of Jews that he appointed to significant policy-making and advisory positions in the federal government's executive branch, more than any other president. American Jews had unprecedented influence in political and public life during the 1990's, influence that would have been impossible in previous decades.

Assimilation In the 1990's, the rate at which Jews intermarried was approximately 52 percent, which was both a cause and an effect of assimilation. Financial pressures are another reason that some American Jews chose to become less affiliated or completely unaffiliated with their Jewish traditions. It is estimated that the during the decade it required between $10,000 to $15,000 per year in discretionary income to provide intensive Jewish experiences for a family of four. Intensive Jewish experiences include synagogue membership, day camp or residential camp, Jewish day school, membership in a Jewish community center, and a federation donation. A survey of Jewish education in the 1990's by Jack Wertheimer found that out of approximately 1.1 million Jewish children in the United States, only about 180,000 attended Jewish day schools. For some American Jews, finding a home in a neighborhood where there was a synagogue added to the cost of living as a practicing Jew.

Another factor in assimilation was that while for almost fifty years American Jews considered Israel the rock that held them steady against the powerful attractions of assimilation, in 1997 the Israeli parliament considered legislation that would legalize Orthodox control over religious conversions in Israel and bar non-Orthodox representatives from local religious councils. The controversy caused American Jews, of whom roughly 80 percent considered themselves Reform or Conservative, to withhold about $20 million in donations to Israel that year, partly to protest the religious policies of Israel's conservative government. Two-thirds of Jewish donations of large amounts that would have gone to Jewish causes in the 1990's went instead to museums, colleges, libraries, and other nonsectarian U.S. institutions.

Impact The rapidly growing numbers of Jews in government who were accepted according to their abilities, the high rate of intermarriage, and the increasing investments diverted from Israel to the United States in the 1990's all were indications that Jews increasingly felt safe, comfortable, and permanent in the United States. Their contributions to society and enrichment of public discourse were far greater than their tiny percentage of the population would suggest. As comfortable as the Jews felt in the United States, their increasing assimilation was seen by Jewish leaders and clergy as detrimental to Jewish identity, continuity, and the worldwide community.

Further Reading

Freedman, Samuel G. *Jew vs. Jew: The Struggle for the Soul of American Jewry.* New York: Simon & Schuster, 2000. Argues that the Jewish community has become fragmented. At a time when the Jewish community should feel secure and cohesive, congregations, neighborhoods, and even families are taking sides about Jewish identity and authenticity.

Heilman, Samuel C. *Portrait of American Jews: The Last Half of the Twentieth Century.* The Samuel and Althea Stroum Lectures in Jewish Studies. Seattle: University of Washington Press, 1995. A look at the situation of American Jews in the last five decades of the twentieth century. Covers the divisions of the 1980's and 1990's between a small core of committed Jews and a large periphery of Jews who do not participate in Jewish traditions.

Meisel, L. Sandy, and Ira N. Forman, eds. *Jews in American Politics: Essays.* Lanham, Md.: Rowman & Littlefield, 2001. An interesting and informative volume that presents a vast array of information while including many general essays on Jews in politics. Opinions across the political spectrum are included. Includes an introduction by Senator Lieberman.

Sheila Golburgh Johnson

See also Allen, Woody; Clinton, Bill; Coen brothers; Ginsburg, Ruth Bader; Hate crimes; Holocaust Memorial Museum; Israel and the United States; Perlman, Itzhak; Religion and spirituality in the United States; Roth, Philip; *Schindler's List.*

■ Jobs, Steve

Identification Cofounder of Apple Computer
Born February 24, 1955; San Francisco, California

His return revitalized Apple Computer, which had been in danger of closing its doors altogether.

The beginning of the 1990's found Steve Jobs in eclipse. Exiled from Apple, he had founded a second computer company, NeXT, to build high-end graphics workstations. However, it was foundering because of erratic management and weak marketing. Jobs found more success with Pixar Studios, in which he applied his computer know-how to the creation of sophisticated graphics and animation for the motion-picture industry. After a close call when Disney rejected the first version of *Toy Story,* released in 1995, Pixar won the executives over with a rewritten version and soon became a leader in computer animation.

In the mid-1990's, Jobs got NeXT out of the hardware business, and the sophisticated NEXTSTEP operating system (OS) became a serious rival for Windows NT in the high-end workstation market. This success paved the way for his return to the company he had originally created. By 1997, Apple had lost its way after a series of uninspiring chief executive officers (CEOs). There was serious speculation it would close its doors. Finally, the board approached Jobs and worked out a complex deal to acquire the NEXTSTEP OS, which would form the core of the new Macintosh OS. Jobs returned to the company and immediately simplified Apple's confusing product line to desktop and laptop machines for professional and consumer use. He also worked out a cooperative deal with Microsoft that provided Apple with vital working capital and ostensibly protected Microsoft CEO Bill Gates from antitrust investigations. When the audience booed his public announcement of the deal, Jobs chided them for ingratitude.

In 1998, Jobs caused a firestorm of controversy when he introduced the iMac, which abandoned several major pieces of Macintosh technology as obsolete in order to introduce new interfaces. His decision proved right, and the iMac was key in reversing Apple's slide to oblivion.

Impact Steve Jobs rebounded from his initial reverses of fortune and reemerged as an innovator in several areas of technology. The success of *Toy Story* proved the capability of computer animation to create lifelike renderings of figures in motion. Jobs's return to Apple and his bold decisions with the iMac not only revitalized the company but also pushed the entire computer industry to adopt the universal serial bus (USB) and FireWire standards, and to move away from floppy disks in favor of recordable and rewritable CDs and DVDs.

Further Reading

Linzmayer, Owen W. *Apple Confidential 2.0: The Definitive History of the World's Most Colorful Company.* 2d ed. San Francisco: No Starch Press, 2004.

Stross, Randall E. *Steve Jobs and the NeXT Big Thing.* New York: Atheneum, 1993.

Young, Jeffrey S., and William L. Simon. *iCon: Steve Jobs—The Greatest Second Act in the History of Business.* Hoboken, N.J.: John Wiley & Sons, 2005.

Leigh Husband Kimmel

See also Apple Computer; Business and the economy in the United States; CGI; Computers; Gates, Bill; Microsoft; Pixar; Science and technology.

■ Joe Camel campaign

Identification Controversial advertising campaign
Date 1987-1997

The mascot for R. J. Reynolds Tobacco Company's Camel brand of cigarettes was retired after claims that it was a ploy to entice children to smoke.

In an effort to revive its sagging cigarette sales, R. J. Reynolds Tobacco Company (RJR) transformed its traditional camel mascot into Joe Camel, a brightly drawn cartoon camel with a cigarette dangling from his mouth. This ultramasculine, "smooth" cartoon character was pictured smoking in a variety of social settings, drinking in bars, shooting pool, or playing his saxophone at a nightclub. Joe Camel appeared nationwide on billboards and posters and quickly became an American pop culture icon. Joe Camel merchandise, such as mugs, jackets, caps, T-shirts, and beach blankets, could be purchased using "Camel cash"—also with the Joe Camel image. Joe Camel sponsored events, such as music concerts and soccer tournaments. Nationwide, RJR's "smooth character" campaign boosted its Camel cigarette sales to an estimated $476 million per year, and Joe Camel quickly became one of the most successful—and controversial—marketing campaigns in U.S. advertising history.

Packs of Camel cigarettes and "Camel cash" on display. (AP/Wide World Photos)

While RJR insisted that it was using Joe Camel only to entice young adult smokers to switch brands, antismoking advocates accused the tobacco company of targeting children. Criticism against Joe Camel was bolstered by a 1991 research study published in the *Journal of the American Medical Association* that revealed children between five and six years old were more likely to recognize Joe Camel than children's cartoon characters such as Fred Flintstone and Mickey Mouse.

In 1991, San Francisco activist Janet Mangini sued RJR, accusing the company of violating California law by unfairly marketing to minors with its Joe Camel cigarette ads, and other cities and counties filed similar suits. In 1997, the Federal Trade Commission filed an unfair-advertising complaint against RJR after its investigation revealed that after the launching of the Joe Camel campaign, the percentage of smokers under the age of eighteen who smoked Camel cigarettes became larger than the percentage of all adult smokers aged eighteen and older who smoked Camel cigarettes. In an out-of-court settlement with Mangini, RJR agree to stop its Joe Camel campaign and to pay $10 million, $9 million of which went to fund educational and advertising programs to dissuade youth smoking.

Impact In July, 1997, RJR retired Joe Camel, replacing him with an updated version of the brand's traditional Old Joe image. In 1998, the tobacco industry and the attorneys general of forty-six states agreed to ban the use of cartoon characters in tobacco advertising, a practice that many were convinced encouraged young people to start smoking.

Further Reading

DeSmith, David. *A Camel Named Joe: The Illustrated Story of an American Pop Icon.* Boston: Ducap Books, 1998.

Fischer, P. M., et al. "Brand Logo Recognition by Children Aged Three to Six Years: Mickey Mouse and Old Joe the Camel." *Journal of the American Medical Association* 266, no. 22 (1991): 3145-3148.

Garfield, Bob. "Camel Gets Adult, Hip—But It's Still Too Late." *Advertising Age* 68, no. 28 (July 14, 1997): 37.

Eddith A. Dashiell

See also Advertising; Tobacco industry settlement.

■ Johnson, Magic

Identification Professional basketball player and HIV/AIDS advocate

Born August 14, 1959; Lansing, Michigan

Johnson announced in 1991 that he had contracted human immunodeficiency virus (HIV) and would retire from basketball. He later resumed his basketball career and became an HIV/AIDS advocate.

Earvin "Magic" Johnson, Jr., was the fourth of seven children born to Earvin Johnson, Sr., and Christine Johnson. He led Michigan State to a national championship in his one year in college, then began a legendary National Basketball Association (NBA) career with the Los Angeles Lakers in 1979.

Much of the media attention focused on Johnson in the 1990's had little to do with sports. In September, 1991, he married his longtime girlfriend. In November, 1991, a blood test showed that he was HIV-positive. A few days later, Johnson shocked sports fans and the general public when he announced that he was retiring from basketball because of the diagnosis. At the time he made his announcement, many Americans still assumed that HIV/AIDS was restricted to homosexuals or drug addicts. The case of Johnson did not fit either of those categories.

Once his wife and baby tested negative, Magic Johnson dedicated his efforts to HIV/AIDS education, a role bolstered by his celebrity status. However, his basketball career was not completely over. He was voted in by fans to play in the 1992 All-Star Game, in which he scored twenty-five points. He played despite objections from some players, namely Karl Malone of the Utah Jazz, who feared on-court contact with Johnson could jeopardize their health. Johnson also played in the 1992 Summer Olympics as part of the formidable "Dream Team," which won the gold medal.

To promote HIV/AIDS education, Johnson authored a book for youth titled *What You Can Do to Avoid AIDS* (1992), undertook numerous speaking engagements, and filmed a television special that was broadcast by the Nickelodeon network. In the spring of 1992, he was invited by President George H. W. Bush to join the National Commission on AIDS. Controversy erupted when critics speculated that Johnson was being appointed to capitalize on his celebrity status and placate African American AIDS activists. Johnson responded that he did not intend to be a token, that he planned to play an active role. He urged President Bush to increase federal support of HIV/AIDS programs, and when no additional support was forthcoming, he used a public letter to resign in September, 1992.

Johnson spent time as an announcer for NBC Sports and served as interim coach of the Lakers in 1994. In 1996, he announced his comeback as a player with the Lakers. This time, players such as Malone voiced their support, and other players such as Charles Barkley and Dennis Rodman indicated the fact that Johnson was HIV-positive made no difference in how they felt about playing against him. Once on the court, the comeback proved to be anticlimactic. Johnson had gained weight, he was thirty-six years old, and he was playing against individuals far more athletic than his opponents had been during his best years. Nevertheless, the fact that an HIV-positive player could endure the physical demands of NBA competition was an important contribution.

Impact Life after basketball was good for Magic Johnson. He operated numerous thriving businesses, including a chain of movie theaters. His Magic Johnson Foundation supported efforts in HIV/AIDS education and set up "empowerment centers" to narrow the digital divide for inner-city youth. Johnson became a role model in business and philanthropy after a legendary basketball career.

Further Reading

Gottfried, Ted. *Earvin "Magic" Johnson: Champion and Crusader.* New York: Franklin Watts, 2001.

Springer, Steve. *Los Angeles Times Encyclopedia of the Lakers.* Los Angeles: Los Angeles Times, 1998.

Michael Polley

See also African Americans; Barkley, Charles; Basketball; Dream Team; Jordan, Michael; Malone, Karl; Olympic Games of 1992; O'Neal, Shaquille; Sports.

■ Jordan, Michael

Identification Professional basketball player
Born February 17, 1963; Brooklyn, New York

Jordan compiled the highest scoring average (30.12 points) in National Basketball Association (NBA) history and won an unprecedented ten NBA scoring titles, leading the Chicago Bulls to six NBA championships in the 1990's.

Michael Jordan starred in basketball at the University of North Carolina at Chapel Hill under legendary coach Dean Smith from 1981 to 1984. In the 1982 National Collegiate Athletic Association (NCAA) championship game, Jordan sank a fifteen-foot jump shot in the closing seconds to give the Tar Heels a dramatic 63-62 victory over Georgetown University. The two-time consensus All-American guard topped the Atlantic Coast Conference (ACC) in scoring as a sophomore and led North Carolina to an ACC title as a junior. In 1984, he won the Naismith and Wooden Awards and led the U.S. Olympic team in scoring en route to a gold medal.

Reviving the Chicago Bulls The struggling Chicago Bulls selected the six-foot, six-inch, 216-pound Jordan as the third overall pick in the 1984 National Basketball Association (NBA) draft. Jordan earned NBA Rookie of the Year honors in 1985, mesmerizing crowds with his blinding speed, physical artistry, and balletic slam dunks. In 1986, he set an NBA Playoffs record with 63 points in a double overtime loss to the Boston Celtics. Jordan won the first of seven consecutive NBA scoring titles in 1987, becoming the second NBA player to score 3,000 points in a season, and led the NBA in steals. He was selected NBA Most Valuable Player (MVP) and Defensive Player of the Year in 1988 and became the second-fastest player in NBA history to reach 10,000 career points.

Jordan and the Bulls captured six NBA championships under coach Phil Jackson in the 1990's. Jordan won his second NBA MVP Award in 1991, leading the NBA in scoring with a 31.5-point average. Chicago swept the Detroit Pistons in the Eastern Conference Finals and defeated the Los Angeles Lakers in the five-game NBA Finals. Jordan, who changed hands in midair while completing a spectacular layup in game two against the Lakers, averaged 31.1 points in the playoffs.

Jordan earned his third NBA MVP Award in 1992, pacing the NBA in scoring with a 30-point average. His dominating performance enabled Chicago to defend its crown in six games over the Portland Trail Blazers. Jordan's six three-point shots during the first half highlighted game one. The "Dream Team," a collection of NBA superstars including Jordan, breezed to a gold medal at the 1992 Olympic Games.

In 1993, Jordan helped the Bulls become the first team since the 1960's to win three consecutive NBA titles, topping the NBA in scoring (32.6-point average) and steals (1.83 average). Chicago overcame the New York Knicks in the Eastern Conference Finals and bested the Phoenix Suns in the NBA Finals. Jordan set an NBA Finals record by averaging 41 points, becoming the first recipient of three straight NBA Finals MVP Awards.

Jordan retired from basketball in October, 1993, citing a diminishing desire to play the game. His physical exhaustion, ever-growing celebrity, and gambling episodes, as well as the murder of his father, James, may have prompted his departure. In 1994, Jordan played minor-league baseball for the Birmingham Barons of the Southern League. His batting struggles and the prolonged strike hastened his return to the Bulls in March, 1995. The Bulls erected a twelve-foot bronze statue of Jordan at their new United Center (replacing Chicago Stadium). They made the playoffs but were ousted by the Orlando Magic in the Eastern Conference Semifinals.

Restoring the Bulls' Dominance The Bulls in 1996 dominated the NBA with a record seventy-two victories. Jordan became the first player since 1970 to capture the NBA regular-season, All-Star Game, and Finals MVP Awards in the same season and took his eighth NBA scoring title, averaging 30.4 points. Chicago regained the NBA championship by defeating the Seattle SuperSonics in the six-game NBA Finals, as Jordan averaged 30.7 points in the postseason.

In 1997, Jordan led the Bulls to sixty-nine wins and a fifth NBA championship in seven years. He garnered another NBA scoring title with a 29.6-point average and tallied his 25,000th career point. Jordan averaged 32.3 points in the NBA Finals, helping Chicago conquer the Utah Jazz in six games. His buzzer-beating shot won game one. Despite being feverish and dehydrated from a stomach virus, Jordan tallied 38 points and converted the game-deciding three-point shot in the final minute to give the Bulls a dramatic 90-88 victory in game five.

In 1998, Chicago finished 62-20 and accomplished a second three-peat. Jordan was chosen the NBA All-Star Game MVP for the third time and led the NBA in scoring for a record tenth time with a 28.7-point average, securing his fifth regular-season NBA MVP Award. Chicago vanquished Utah in the six-game NBA Finals. In the series finale, Jordan enjoyed one of the greatest clutch performances in NBA Finals history. He stole the ball from Karl

Michael Jordan. (AP/Wide World Photos)

Malone and sunk a dramatic shot with less than ten seconds left, giving Chicago an 87-86 victory and its sixth NBA championship. Jordan registered 45 points in that historic game, earning his unprecedented sixth NBA Finals MVP Award.

After leaving the Bulls in January, 1999, Jordan became part owner and president of basketball operations for the Washington Wizards in January, 2000. He played for Washington from 2001 to 2003, becoming the fourth NBA player to attain 30,000 career points, but could not elevate the Wizards to the playoffs.

Jordan, third on the NBA all-time scoring list, recorded 32,292 career points (30.1-point average), 6,672 rebounds, 5,633 assists, and 2,514 steals in 1,072 regular-season games, and 5,987 points (33.4-point average), 1,152 rebounds, 1,022 assists, and 376 steals in 179 playoff games. The fourteen-time NBA All-Star made the All-NBA First Team ten times (1987-1993, 1996-1998) and NBA All-Defensive First Team nine times (1988-1993, 1996-1998), won the NBA regular-season MVP five times (1988, 1991,

1992, 1996, 1998) and NBA Finals MVP six times (1991-1993, 1996-1998), and led the NBA in steals three times (1988, 1990, 1993).

Jordan's extraordinary basketball skills translated into very lucrative product endorsements. Jordan endorsed numerous commercial products for big-name brands, including Nike, Hanes, Wheaties, Coca-Cola, Chevrolet, and McDonald's. The Air Jordan shoe line revived Nike's sneaker sales. These products netted millions annually in sales and made Jordan a global advertising figure. He also starred in the combination live action/animated film *Space Jam* (1996) as himself.

Jordan left the Washington Wizards in May, 2003, and became co-owner of the Charlotte Bobcats NBA team in June, 2006. Owner Robert Johnson granted him final authority on player personnel decisions.

Impact Jordan, whose athletic leaps and dunks influenced a generation of NBA players, won four ESPY Awards for Athlete of the Century, Male Athlete of the 1990's, Pro Basketball Player of the 1990's, and Player of the Decade.

Further Reading

Greene, Bob. *Hang Time: Days and Dreams with Michael Jordan.* New York: Doubleday, 1992. Adeptly captures Jordan's daily life and innermost thoughts.

Halberstam, David. *Playing for Keeps: Michael Jordan and the World He Made.* New York: Random House, 1999. Excellent biographical account of Jordan's epic life.

Jordan, Michael. *Driven from Within.* New York: Atria Books, 2005.

_______. *For the Love of the Game: My Story.* New York: Crown, 1998.

_______. *I'm Back! More Rare Air.* New York: HarperCollins, 1995.

_______. *Rare Air: Michael on Michael.* New York: HarperCollins, 1993. These four autobiographies provide colorful anecdotes and photographs from Jordan's illustrious career.

LaFeber, Walter. *Michael Jordan and the New Global Capitalism.* New York: W. W. Norton, 1999. Shows how Jordan's numerous commercial endorsements changed the global marketplace.

Naughton, Jim. *Taking to the Air: The Rise of Michael Jordan.* New York: Warner Books, 1992. An excellent account of Jordan's early career.

Porter, David L. *Michael Jordan: A Biography.* Westport, Conn.: Greenwood Press, 2007. An up-to-date overview of Jordan's life.

Smith, Sam. *The Jordan Rules.* New York: Simon & Schuster, 1992. A behind-the-scenes critical analysis.

David L. Porter

See also Advertising; African Americans; Barkley, Charles; Basketball; Dream Team; Johnson, Magic; Malone, Karl; Olympic Games of 1992; O'Neal, Shaquille; Sports.

■ Journalism

Definition The gathering and disseminating of news and information via print, radio, television, and the Internet

During the 1990's, the boundaries separating radio, network television, and newspapers began to blur as traditional journalism began to merge with new technologies such as cable television and the Internet.

By the 1990's, consumers of news were no longer content to passively wait for the evening network news programs in order to get updated information. They wanted current news on demand, and that need was met through the growing popularity of twenty-four-hour, real-time news coverage on cable television and the Internet, both of which provided foreign and national stories hours ahead of the evening network news programs that originated in New York. The national news networks faced stiff competition from a number of news-and-information cable networks such as the Cable News Network (CNN), the Cable Satellite Public Affairs Network (C-SPAN), Fox News (owned by Rupert Murdoch's News Corporation), and MSNBC, a joint venture by the National Broadcasting Company (NBC) and Microsoft. People also began to get their information from the Internet, which had become a strong competitor to traditional news organizations and transformed not only how news was gathered but also who reported it.

News on the Internet In order to compete effectively with the rapidly growing, interactive communication technology, the news media rapidly became involved with the Internet by developing their own Web sites. In 1994, there were twenty newspapers online. By mid-1999, there were more than four thousand online newspapers worldwide, the majority of them in the United States. In 1995, the subscription news service the Associated Press (AP) began distributing its news articles and photographs over the Internet. In late 1999, the most popular Web sites for news included sites such as msnbc.com, cnn.com, abcnews.com, usatoday.com, and nytimes.com. Other tools for online journalism included Internet forums, discussion boards, and chat rooms. Internet radio also emerged as an independent media source.

Many people who were not considered professional journalists now had the technology to report and respond to news events. People began to write and post their own stories—known as Web logs or blogs—on the Internet. One of the more popular news-based blogs was the Drudge Report, a conservative, U.S.-based news Web site created by Matt Drudge around 1994. The Drudge Report received worldwide attention on January 17, 1998, when it was the first news source to break the story of White House intern Monica Lewinsky's affair with President Bill Clinton after the mainstream media reportedly had decided not to publish the story.

Media critics warned that Internet news blogs were chipping away at the credibility of the mainstream media and negatively influencing the way in which news was being reported. Mainstream journalists often did not consider bloggers to be professionals because bloggers were not bound by journalistic standards and ethical practices. Online journalists argued, however, that news reported via the Internet was often less biased and more informative than that reported by official media because online journalists were volunteer or freelance reporters and their reporting was free from economic or political influence.

After a slow start, blogging rapidly gained in popularity. Some independent Internet forums and discussion boards began to achieve a level of popularity comparable to mainstream news agencies such as television stations and newspapers. Blog usage spread during 1999, and with the development of blog software programs and services, any individual could become a publisher on a global scale. By the end of the decade, the Internet blogs had evolved from being online diaries, where people would keep running accounts of their personal lives or post links to their favorite Web sites, into a distinct class of online publishing and Web journalism.

Media Convergence Media mergers and technological innovations gave birth to convergence journalism. Print, broadcast, and online news staffs began to forge partnerships in which journalists often worked and distributed news content across several platforms such as newspaper, radio, television, and the Internet. For example, one reporter could be assigned to cover and produce several versions of the same story—one version for newspaper, another version for television, and a third version for the Internet (online journalism). Supporters of media convergence believed that it would deliver stronger local journalism by sharing news gathering and reporting resources.

Throughout the history of journalism, it was common for journalists to study one medium, such as traditional print or television broadcasting, and to work only in their chosen field. By the end of the 1990's, however, journalists were expected to have the skills to write and deliver news content in a variety of formats. To meet this expectation, more and more journalism programs began offering majors in online or convergence journalism.

Impact The Internet and media convergence were significant developments in journalism during the 1990's. By the end of the decade, the merger of traditional media with the rapidly developing Internet and its blogs had transformed the way in which news organizations operated and had blurred the distinctions between advertising, news, entertainment, and editorial content.

Further Reading

Barkin, Steve M. *American Television News: The Media Marketplace and the Public Interest.* Armonk, N.Y.: M. E. Sharpe, 2003. A social and cultural history of television news during the 1980's and 1990's.

Conboy, Martin. *Journalism: A Critical History.* Thousand Oaks, Calif.: Sage Publications, 2004. A history of the development of newspapers, periodicals, and broadcast journalism in which the author demonstrates that concerns about political and economic influence, the impact of advertising, and sensational news coverage are themes that have emerged repeatedly throughout the history of journalism.

Hachten, William A. *The Troubles of Journalism: A Critical Look at What's Right and Wrong with the Press.* 2d ed. Mahwah, N.J.: Lawrence Erlbaum Associates, 2001. A historical critique of journalism and mass communication, including the influence of the Internet on news coverage.

Koldozy, Janet. *Convergence Journalism: Writing and Reporting Across the News Media.* Lanham, Md.: Rowman & Littlefield, 2006. An introductory text on how to think, report, write, and present news across various media such as newspapers, television, and the Internet to prepare journalism students for the future of news reporting.

Sterling, Christopher H., and John Michael Kittross. *Stay Tuned: A History of American Broadcasting.* 3d ed. Mahwah, N.J.: Lawrence Erlbaum Associates, 2001. A thorough review of broadcasting history in the United States from radio to cable television and the Internet.

Eddith A. Dashiell

See also Albert, Marv; Arnett, Peter; Blogs; Cable television; CNN coverage of the Gulf War; Drudge, Matt; Internet; Limbaugh, Rush; O'Reilly, Bill; Talk radio; Telecommunications Act of 1996; Television; World Wide Web.

■ *Jurassic Park*

Identification Science-fiction film
Director Steven Spielberg (1946-)
Date Released on June 11, 1993

This award-winning film introduced unprecedented visual effects, presenting full-motion dinosaurs on the big screen.

Stories about prehistoric beasts that live in modern times date back at least to 1912, when Sir Arthur Conan Doyle published *The Lost World.* His story of a remote plateau where beasts from the Jurassic period dwelled was made into a silent film in 1925, with stop-motion special effects by Willis O'Brien, who also supervised the effects for *King Kong* (1933). Stop-motion is a painstaking procedure in which realistic models are moved one frame at a time and integrated into live-action scenes. It remained the preferred way to animate until director Steven Spielberg abandoned it in favor of computer-generated imagery (CGI) for *Jurassic Park.*

Based on the 1990 novel by Michael Crichton, the film centers on an amusement park that holds cloned dinosaurs, which were re-created from DNA found in Jurassic mosquitoes that sucked dinosaur blood and were later preserved in amber. The park's founder, John Hammond (Richard Attenborough), invites a group of scientists—Dr. Alan Grant (Sam Neill), Dr. Ian Malcolm (Jeff Goldblum), and Dr. Ellie Sattler (Laura Dern)—to reassure his investors, before the park opens, that nothing can go wrong. Things do, of course, and the story follows the group as they try to survive the chaos.

Universal Studios bought the rights to Crichton's novel even before it was published. Spielberg used realistic, computer-generated dinosaurs, a quantum leap from the stop-motion work of O'Brien and his successor, Ray Harryhausen. At the time, *Jurassic Park* broke the record as the highest-grossing film ever. The film earned three Academy Awards: Best Sound Effects Editing, Best Visual Effects, and Best Sound.

In 1995, Crichton published a sequel, *The Lost World,* in tribute to Conan Doyle's 1912 dinosaur novel. Crichton's novel was adapted to film in 1997, and Spielberg directed.

Impact The film sparked interest in dinosaurs and in educational programs as well as films. Computer-generated imagery became the preferred choice for creature special effects and was used in such films as the American version of *Godzilla* (1998), a remake of *King Kong* (2005), and *Jurassic Park III* (2001).

Further Reading

Crichton, Michael. *Jurassic Park.* New York: Alfred A. Knopf, 1990.

DeSalle, Rob, and David Lindley. *The Science of "Jurassic Park" and "The Lost World": Or, How to Build a Dinosaur.* New York: Basic Books, 1997.

Shay, Don. *The Making of Jurassic Park.* New York: Ballantine, 1993.

Paul Dellinger

See also CGI; Cloning; Film in the United States; Genetic engineering; Genetics research; Science and technology.

Kelley, Kitty

Identification American biographer
Born April 4, 1942; Spokane, Washington

Kelley first made her reputation in the 1970's and 1980's as the author of unauthorized, sensationalistic, and best-selling biographies of Jacqueline Kennedy Onassis, Elizabeth Taylor, and Frank Sinatra but perhaps became the most famous biographer of the 1990's with her controversial books on Nancy Reagan and the British royal family.

Kitty Kelley is often cited as one of the factors in the growth of books about famous people and celebrities in the 1990's. A former reporter for *The Washington Post,* Kelley made a major impact on how biographies are written with the publication of *Nancy Reagan: The Unauthorized Biography* (1991), an account that purported to reveal intimate new details about the couple's private life. President Ronald Reagan repudiated Kelley's biography of his wife, disputing her reports that the couple smoked marijuana and that Nancy had had an affair with Frank Sinatra, but many of Kelley's discoveries were later confirmed, including the fact that Nancy had relied on astrologers.

Unusual for a biographer, Kelley became a public figure in her own right, making news and appearing in numerous shows on television and radio. So iconic was she that she was spoofed on *Saturday Night Live* and then became the subject of a biography attempting to expose her lies and half-truths. However, the biographer hardly dented Kelley's reputation—in part because even though she has often been attacked for publishing unsubstantiated stories, she has never lost a lawsuit or had to retract what she has published. Although most reviews of Kelley's work in the 1990's were negative, many journalists nevertheless admired her tenacity in researching her subjects' lives and bringing to biography a new level of candor.

In 1997, Kelley turned her attention to the British royal family in *The Royals,* a book that could not be published in Great Britain because of libel laws, which put the onus on the writer and publisher to prove they have not libeled the subject. In the United States, the law is just the opposite, so that the burden of proof is placed on the plaintiff. *The Royals* became the fourth best-selling nonfiction title of the year in the United States, according to *Publishers Weekly.* Essentially a history of the Windsors, a German family who sought to obscure their roots on the European continent, Kelley's biography portrayed the royals as self-indulgent, scandal-ridden, and in-

Author Kitty Kelley poses next to a poster advertising her book Nancy Reagan: The Unauthorized Biography, *which portrays the former First Lady in an unflattering light.* (AP/Wide World Photos)

competent. Attacked by historians of the British royal family, Kelley's book nevertheless typified much of the negative press surrounding the royal family in the 1990's.

Impact Although Kelley's brand of biography was frequently deplored in the 1990's, a minority of critics—chiefly journalists—admired her tenacity and campaigns to reveal in more candid form the lives of public figures.

Further Reading

Carpozi, George. *Poison Pen: The Unauthorized Biography of Kitty Kelley.* Fort Lee, N.J.: Barricade Books, 1991.

Rollyson, Carl. *A Higher Form of Cannibalism? Adventures in the Art and Politics of Biography.* Chicago: Ivan R. Dee, 2005.

Carl Rollyson

See also Journalism; Literature in the United States; Publishing; Scandals.

■ Kemp, Jack

Identification U.S. secretary of housing and urban development, 1989-1993, and vice presidential candidate, 1996

Born July 13, 1935; Los Angeles, California

Kemp's passion and insight for economic growth through tax relief and balanced budgets, as well as his compassion for the poor, appealed to moderates and centrist Republicans during the 1990's.

Jack Kemp was born to a middle-class family headed by a father who owned his own trucking company. Kemp received his undergraduate degree from Occidental College in 1957 and did postgraduate work at Long Beach State and California Western Universities. In 1958, he married Joanne Main, and together they had four children: Jeffrey, Jennifer, Judith, and James. From 1958 to 1962, Kemp served in the U.S. Army Reserve. Kemp simultaneously began an eleven-year career as a National Football League (NFL) quarterback in 1958, first for the Chargers in Los Angeles and San Diego, then for the Buffalo Bills in New York. Kemp retired from football in 1969.

During the latter years of his NFL career, Kemp became involved in Republican politics. After his retirement from football, he ran for office and, in 1970, was elected to serve as a representative from New York. He remained a congressman from 1971 to 1989. While in Congress, Kemp urged party colleagues to reach out to minorities and to bring them into the Republican fold.

Kemp was truly concerned about the plight of the poor in the United States. This concern suited him well for his work in urban improvement during the early 1990's: Under President George H. W. Bush, Kemp served as the secretary of housing and urban development from 1989 to 1993. Kemp was a Republican, not a conservative ideologue; his positions often sprang from his heart rather than a mind constrained by a conservative tenacity. Thus, in 1994, while weighing options as to whether he should seek the Republican nomination for the presidency in 1996, Kemp opposed Proposition 187, which denied various government benefits to illegal immigrants in California and was supported by 80 percent of that state's Republicans.

Kemp ran as Bob Dole's vice presidential candidate in the 1996 election. Consequently, the Dole-Kemp ticket proposed tax relief and government rebate plans, which were exclusively directed toward the lower and middle classes. While these proposed policies were not symbolic of conservatism, they accurately portrayed Kemp's centrism.

Impact Kemp authored *An American Renaissance: A Strategy for the 1980's* (1979), in which he expounded his theory of economics. This work is an enduring part of the free market and tax-reduction policies that marked the 1994 "Republican Revolution." In 1993, he cofounded Empower America, a private organization devoted to free market economics and the promotion of individual freedoms and personal responsibility.

Further Reading

Dole, Bob, and Jack Kemp. *Trusting the People: The Dole-Kemp Plan to Free the Economy and Create a Better America.* New York: HarperCollins, 1996.

Kemp, Jack F. *An American Renaissance: A Strategy for the 1980's.* New York: Harper & Row, 1979.

AWR Hawkins III

See also Bush, George H. W.; Business and the economy in the United States; Dole, Bob; Elections in the United States, midterm; Elections in the United States, 1996; Illegal immigration; Immigration to the United States; Republican Revolution.

■ Kennedy, John F., Jr.

Identification American lawyer, publisher, and celebrity

Born November 25, 1960; Washington, D.C.

Died July 16, 1999; Atlantic Ocean, eight miles off Martha's Vineyard

Heir to America's leading political dynasty, charismatic, and adventurous, Kennedy was closely watched for his celebrity status, publishing venture, and growing political aspirations.

The only surviving son of the late president John F. Kennedy and Jacqueline Kennedy Onassis, John F. Kennedy, Jr., had been accorded celebrity status for his entire life. When he passed the New York bar exam on his third attempt on July 24, 1990, it was national news, allowing Kennedy to retain his appointment as an assistant district attorney in Manhattan. Over the next few years, the media followed Kennedy closely: both for his romances as *People* magazine's "Sexiest Man Alive," most notably with well-known actors Sarah Jessica Parker and Daryl Hannah, and for possible political aspirations as the leading heir of the Kennedy political dynasty.

When his stint as a prosecutor ended in 1993, Kennedy combined his media and political status by starting the unique magazine *George*. The novel approach of the magazine was indicated by its motto, "Not just politics as usual." The first issue was published in September, 1995, to great publicity, with supermodel Cindy Crawford posing as George Washington on the cover. With numerous successful issues of *George* over the succeeding years, Kennedy could point to a signal achievement. He was no longer famous merely for his name but had become publisher and editor in chief of a national magazine with a fresh and breezy approach to politics, which mirrored the perspective of many in his generation. A further sign of his maturation came on September 21, 1996, when he married the glamorous Calvin Klein publicist Carolyn Bessette.

Kennedy was considering a possible run for the

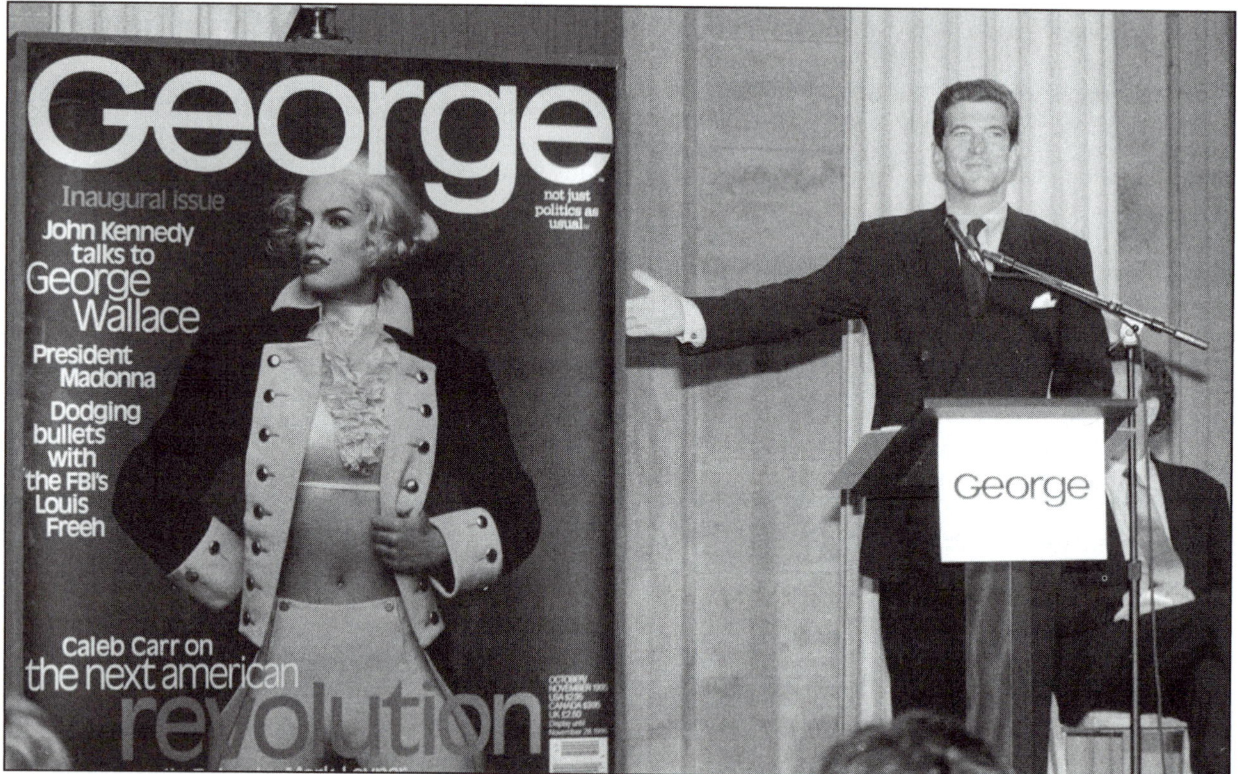

John F. Kennedy, Jr., announces the launch of his political magazine, George, *on September 7, 1995.* (AP/Wide World Photos)

U.S. Senate in 2000 or for New York governor in 2002. Famously married, nationally celebrated, professionally accomplished, Kennedy seemed poised for a dramatic entrance into political life, one that perhaps could have ended in the White House. Tragedy struck, however, on July 16, 1999, when the small airplane that Kennedy was flying crashed into the Atlantic Ocean, several miles off Martha's Vineyard, Massachusetts. Kennedy, an amateur pilot, was flying at night from New York to Massachusetts with his wife Carolyn and her sister Lauren to attend a wedding. President Bill Clinton ordered an extensive maritime search and rescue operation. The remains of the bodies were found five days later and were cremated and scattered into the ocean.

Impact John F. Kennedy, Jr., represented the intersection of two cultural trends of the 1990's: the increasing popularization of politics and the fascination with media celebrities. He fruitfully cultivated this union in his magazine *George*, which strove for serious political commentary with a lively people-centered perspective. However, Kennedy's greatest impact was more one of loss than of accomplishment, as his life was tragically ended just as he seemed poised to realize his full potential.

Further Reading

Blow, Richard. *American Son: A Portrait of John F. Kennedy, Jr.* New York: Henry Holt, 2002.

Heymann, C. David. *American Legacy: The Story of John and Caroline Kennedy*. New York: Atria Books, 2007.

Leamer, Laurence. *Sons of Camelot: The Fate of an American Dynasty*. New York: HarperCollins, 2004.

Howard Bromberg

See also Journalism; Publishing.

■ Kennedy rape case

The Event A member of a prominent political family is tried and acquitted on a charge of rape

Date December 2-23, 1991

This high-profile criminal trial involved William Kennedy Smith, nephew of the late U.S. president John F. Kennedy and Massachusetts senator Ted Kennedy and the son of former U.S. ambassador to Ireland Jean Kennedy Smith.

On the evening of March 30, 1991, William Kennedy Smith met Patricia Bowman at a Palm Beach, Florida, bar he was visiting with his uncle Senator Ted Kennedy and cousin Rhode Island representative Patrick Kennedy. Bowman and a friend went back to the Kennedy estate with Smith and his relatives. Smith and Bowman went for a walk on the beach, and it was there that Bowman alleged that he raped her. After the alleged assault, Bowman returned to the Kennedy home, where she called a friend to pick her up and take her to the police station. After giving a statement to the Palm Beach Police Department, she was taken to Humana Hospital to be examined and treated for injuries.

Upon questioning, Smith denied the rape allegation, stating that they had engaged in consensual sex. Bowman was subjected to two polygraph tests and a voice stress analysis—all of which suggested that she was telling the truth. Additionally, forensic evidence collected at the hospital, including documentation of the bruises on Bowman's body, supported her claim of sexual assault. Smith was eventually arrested and charged with rape, but not before the Kennedy family was publicly accused of stonewalling the authorities and attempting to obfuscate the investigation. Several allegations of preferential treatment were leveled at the police, with critics noting that it took weeks after the alleged assault before Smith was questioned or the property searched for evidence.

Before the trial, three women came forward to the prosecution and alleged that Smith had also raped them. None of the three women had pressed charges at the time of their alleged attack, noting that they did not think they would be believed because of Smith's family connections. The prosecution sought to include their testimony in order to establish a pattern of behavior on the part of the defendant; the judge disallowed their testimony for use as evidence at trial.

On December 2, 1991, the case went to trial and was televised around the world. Bowman's face was electronically blurred during her testimony to protect her identity. The case ended with an acquittal on December 23—a verdict reached after seventy-seven minutes of deliberation.

Impact This trial is considered to be one of the most highly publicized and televised rape trials in U.S. history. After the trial, Bowman allowed reporters to use her photograph and her name in an effort to help rape victims to feel more comfortable talking about their victimization.

Further Reading

Matoesian, Gregory M. *Law and the Language of Identity: Discourse in the William Kennedy Smith Rape Trial.* New York: Oxford University Press, 2001.

Sanday, Peggy Reeves. *A Woman Scorned: Acquaintance Rape on Trial.* New York: Doubleday, 1996.

Rachel Bandy

See also Crime; Scandals.

■ Kerrigan, Nancy

Identification Two-time American Olympic figure skating medal winner

Born October 13, 1969; Stoneham, Massachusetts

Kerrigan's struggle to achieve an Olympic gold medal in 1992 and then in 1994 after becoming the 1993 United States champion was both a sports story and a dramatic sensation.

Nancy Kerrigan grew up in suburban Boston, Massachusetts, where she often played ice hockey with her family of two brothers. She showed talent on skates and was competing in figure skating by the age of nine. She was coached by the well known team of Evy and Mary Scotvald, and she placed third in 1991 at the World Figure Skating Championships. As part of a United States team, which swept the medals at that championship, she was one of the favorites for a medal at the 1992 Winter Olympics, where she won a bronze medal. Her subsequent career was marked by a number of high and low points. She earned a silver medal at the 1992 World Championships. In the following year, she became the United States Champion but fell short of her medal hopes in the long program after a strong beginning at the World Championships in 1993.

Known primarily as an elegant, athletic skater, Nancy Kerrigan gained wider attention in the news media after an incident in Detroit, Michigan, at the Olympic trials in January, 1994. She was clubbed in the knee after a practice session by a man who was hired by the husband of one of her primary competitors, Tonya Harding. After the attack, Kerrigan was filmed holding her knee in pain and screaming "Why?" This clip became famous, appearing in many collections of important sports moments of the twentieth century. Even though she was unable to finish the competition, the United States Olympic Committee gave her a spot on the 1994 U.S. Olympic team, for the Winter Games in Lillehammer, Norway. She won a silver medal and later earned multimillion-dollar endorsements from corporations such as Disney.

After the 1994 Olympics, Kerrigan retired from competition and married her agent, Jerry Solomon, in 1995. They settled in Massachusetts and raised three children. Kerrigan appears in ice skating shows, and she is active with the Nancy Kerrigan Foundation, which she formed to raise awareness for the vision-impaired in honor of her mother, Brenda.

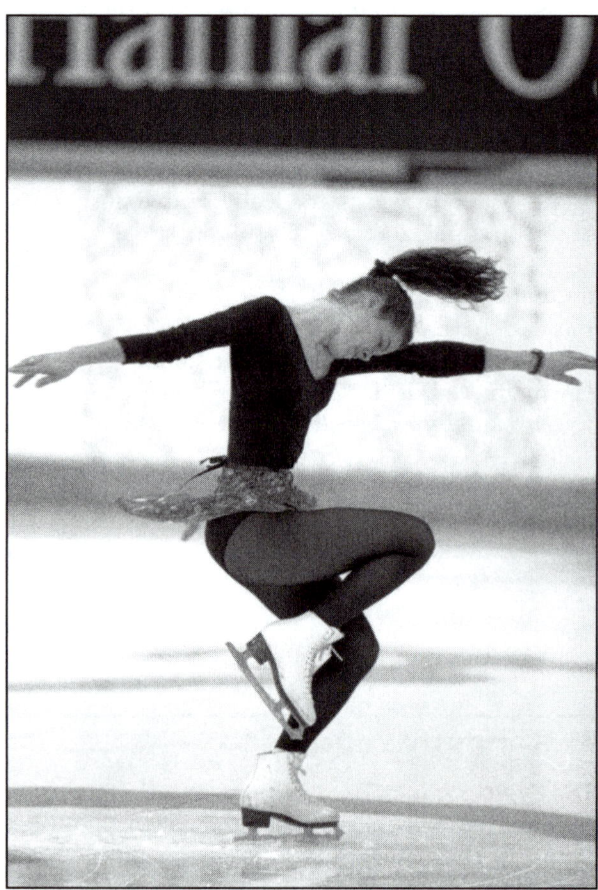

Nancy Kerrigan practices on February 11, 1994, in Norway, one day before the opening ceremony of the Olympics and one month after she was clubbed in the knee by a man linked to competitor Tonya Harding. (AP/Wide World Photos)

Impact Nancy Kerrigan demonstrated the grace and athleticism of figure skating, but her experiences also showed the dark side of the fiercely competitive world of these athletes. Her story contrasts the lofty ideals of the Olympics with the harsh realities of competitive sports.

Further Reading

Baughman, Cynthia. *Women on Ice: Feminist Essays on the Tonya Harding/Nancy Kerrigan Spectacle.* New York: Routledge, 1995.

Kerrigan, Nancy, and Mary Spencer. *Artistry on Ice: Figure Skating Skills and Style.* Champaign, Ill.: Human Kinetics, 2002.

Dolores A. D'Angelo

See also Yamaguchi, Kristi; Olympic Games of 1992; Olympic Games of 1994.

■ Kevorkian, Jack

Identification American pathologist and right-to-die activist

Born May 26, 1928; Pontiac, Michigan

Kevorkian's controversial right-to-die activism revealed how strongly Americans on both sides of the assisted suicide issue felt about their positions and spurred milestone judicial, legislative, and societal responses.

In 1990, Jack Kevorkian became a key figure in a movement that sought to allow physicians to legally assist terminally ill patients in committing suicide. On June 4, 1990, Kevorkian initiated a dramatic strategy for confronting the legal and medical establishments. On that date, he used a machine that he had constructed to help Janet Adkins, a fifty-four-year-old woman with Alzheimer's disease, kill herself. When the patient pushed a button, the machine, which Kevorkian called the Thanatron (Greek for "death machine"), administered a coma-

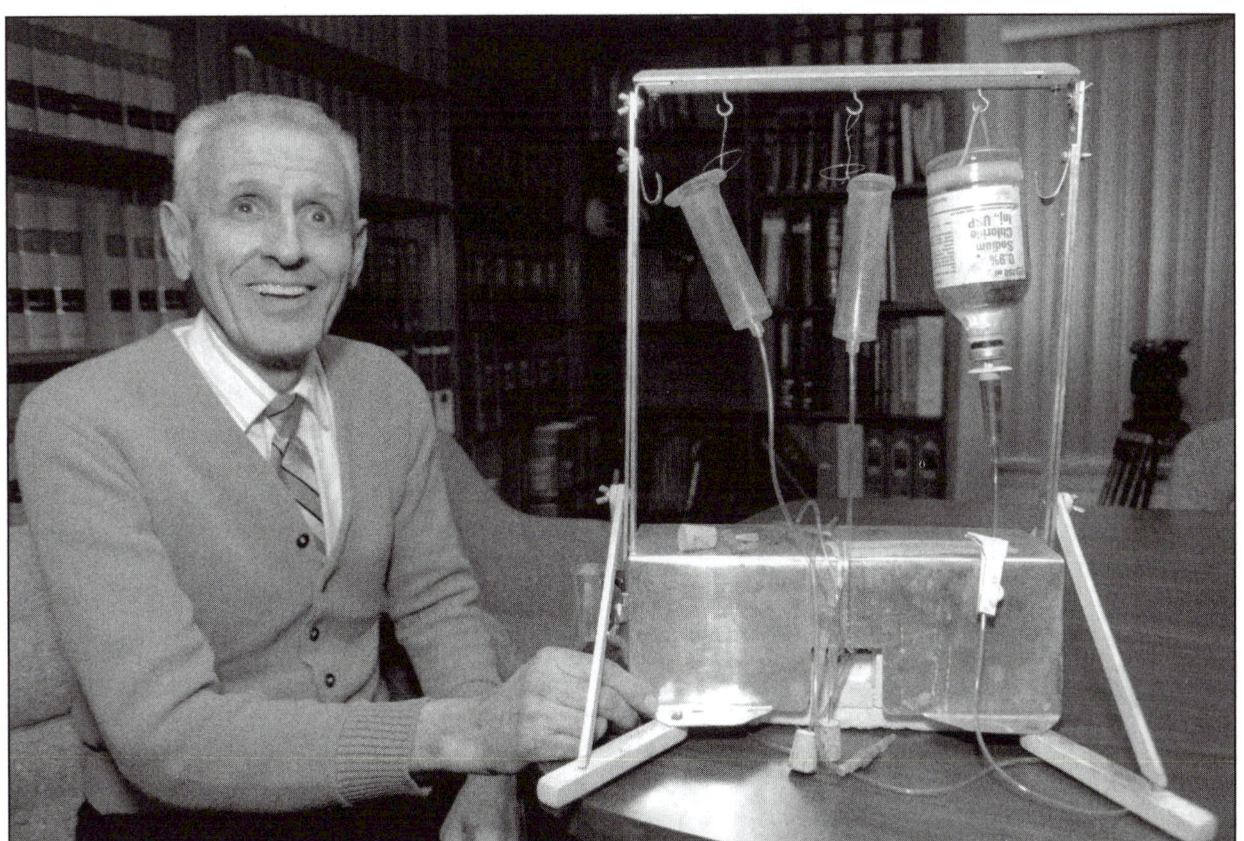

Jack Kevorkian displays his Thanatron, or "death machine," in 1991. (AP/Wide World Photos)

inducing drug intravenously and then released a dose of potassium chloride that caused a fatal heart attack. Kevorkian sought publicity for his cause and the suicide, which had taken place in his 1968 Volkswagen van, and proudly publicly displayed his machine (once on *The Phil Donahue Show*).

This first assisted suicide, which took place in Michigan, where Kevorkian lived most of his life, began a nine-year odyssey that included many assisted suicides (more than 130 by Kevorkian's account) and numerous legal entanglements for Kevorkian. He was charged with murder in Adkins's death, but a judge dismissed the charge. During court appearances, the man now called "Dr. Death" in the media defiantly sought publicity for his cause. Until his March, 1999, trial, the charges were always dismissed, or he was acquitted by a jury.

Kevorkian's medical license was revoked on November 20, 1991, so he could no longer legally obtain or possess the drugs for the Thanatron. He then invented a new machine he called the Mercitron ("mercy machine"), which used a container of carbon monoxide attached to a gas mask to assist patients' suicides. On November 23, 1998, the television program *60 Minutes* broadcast a videotape provided by Kevorkian showing him personally administering a lethal injection to terminally ill Thomas Youk and daring the authorities to arrest and convict him. Kevorkian was charged with second-degree homicide and delivery of a controlled substance, convicted, and, on April 13, 1999, sentenced to ten to twenty-five years in prison. He was paroled on June 1, 2007, because of his failing health, on condition that he not assist with suicides.

Impact Kevorkian's highly publicized activism made the right-to-die issue a high-profile public debate that raised Americans' consciousness regarding the suffering of the terminally ill. While his crusade to legalize physician-assisted suicide helped to initiate referenda in several states that asked voters to approve legalizing active euthanasia, only Oregon actually enacted such a law. The U.S. Supreme Court upheld states' rights to outlaw the practice. However, studies done in the 1990's showed growing support, by doctors and the public in general, for medically assisted termination of life.

Further Reading

Atwood-Gailey, Elizabeth. *Write to Death: News Framing of the Right to Die Conflict, from Quinlan's Coma to Kevorkian's Conviction.* Westport, Conn.: Praeger, 2003.

Kevorkian, Jack. *Prescription: Medicide—The Goodness of Planned Death.* Buffalo, N.Y.: Prometheus Books, 1991.

Jack Carter

See also Health care; Health care reform; Medicine; Physician-assisted suicide; Supreme Court decisions.

■ Khobar Towers bombing

The Event A truck bombing of the Khobar Towers housing complex in Khobar, Saudi Arabia, kills nineteen Americans

Date June 25, 1996

The bombing of the Khobar housing compound was the worst terrorist attack against United States personnel since the 1983 Beirut barracks bombing. It brought pressure on officials in Washington to address the security and intelligence vulnerabilities exposed by the incident, and it heightened awareness of the widening gulf between radical Islam and the West.

The Khobar Towers, located on the Persian Gulf near the city of Dhahran, Saudi Arabia, had been occupied by coalition forces from the United States, Saudi Arabia, France, and the United Kingdom since the start of the 1990 Gulf War. Building 131 was an eight-story high-rise located at the northeastern corner of the complex and occupied by members of the U.S. Air Force's 4,404th Wing.

On June 25, 1996, members of the Fifty-eighth Fighter Squadron housed in building 131 were making preparations to turn over their duties to the Twenty-seventh Fighter Squadron the following day. That same evening, two men drove a Datsun into the parking lot located just north of the complex and adjacent to building 131. At 9:43 P.M., they blinked their car lights as a signal, and the driver of a sewage truck drove into the parking lot. The truck, called a "honey pot" by U.S. troops, had been made into a bomb containing what was later estimated to be more than five thousand pounds of plastic explosives. After backing the truck against a chain-link fence approximately ninety feet from building 131, the driver and a passenger exited the truck and climbed into the back seat of a waiting Chevrolet Caprice. The Chevrolet and the Datsun then drove away.

After observing the activity in the parking lot from his station on the roof of building 131, Staff Sergeant Alfredo Guerrero became concerned and immediately began an evacuation of the building. Guerrero's vigilance was the only source of warning the occupants of the building had, and his actions were credited with saving many lives. He was later awarded the Airman's Medal.

At approximately 9:50 P.M., the truck exploded with a blast felt as far as the Persian Gulf state of Bahrain, some twenty miles away. It killed nineteen Americans and one Saudi. Almost four hundred people of various nationalities were wounded. The blast devastated building 131 and left a crater in the parking lot eighty-five feet wide and thirty-five feet deep. Six other buildings in the complex were heavily damaged or destroyed, and windows were shattered as much as a mile away.

Intelligence Failures and Suspects In Washington, President Bill Clinton vowed that those responsible would not go unpunished. Secretary of Defense William Perry immediately appointed retired general Wayne A. Downing to do a quick review of the facts. The House National Security Committee had a fact-finding team in Saudi Arabia within two weeks. Following their respective investigations, the House report cited intelligence failures, while the Downing report declared that those responsible for force protection had failed to do their jobs satisfactorily. According to the Downing report, intelligence had provided sufficient warning of the terrorist threat to U.S. forces in Saudi Arabia, and there had been both opportunity and motivation to reduce vulnerabilities.

The perpetrators were alleged to be thirteen members of the Saudi Hezbollah (party of God) and one unidentified member of the Lebanese Hezbollah. The Saudi Hezbollah members included the leader of the organization and the head of their military wing. The Saudi group was alleged to have acted, at least in part, on behalf of unnamed Iranian government officials who were said to have supported and directed their activities. The unidentified Lebanese Hezbollah member was said to be the supplier of the explosives that the Saudis were believed to have smuggled into the country by car. Investigators said the bombing was part of a campaign begun by the Saudi Hezbollah in 1993 with the aim of driving the United States from the Persian Gulf.

Immediately after the bombing, all but two of the thirteen Saudis left the country using fake passports. One of those fleeing, Hani Al-Sayegh, was arrested in 1997 in Canada, where he denied any involvement in the bombing. He was later removed to the United States based on a promise to cooperate. He promptly broke that promise and in October, 1999, he was deported to Saudi Arabia to face charges connected to the bombing.

By the end of the 1990's, none of the perpetrators had been brought to trial, and the investigations had still produced insufficient evidence for any indictments. Improvements in relations between Saudi Arabia and Iran had made investigation of the latter country's involvement more difficult. In June, 2001, fourteen men were indicted for the bombing. No Iranian officials were named in the indictment.

Impact Secretary of Defense William S. Cohen, who succeeded Perry in January, 1997, held the commander of the 4,404th Wing, Brigadier General Terryl J. Schwalier, responsible for failure to adequately protect his forces. For that reason, Cohen denied his promotion to major general, even though the promotion had already been announced. In disagreement with Cohen's decision to deny the promotion, the Air Force chief of staff, General Ronald R. Fogleman, retired before the end of his tour of duty.

As a result of the Khobar attack, the Air Force developed its antiterrorism course, increased standoff distances, and improved communication. Comprehensive protection for military members or "force protection" is now an overriding concern in every operational military mission. Since the bombing, force protection often dictates where personnel live, how they behave on and off duty, and even how their mission is performed.

Iran angrily rejected U.S. allegations that elements of the Iranian government were involved in the bombing, and the incident significantly heightened tensions between the two countries. The bombing itself emphasized the growing threat to U.S. and Western interests from radical Islam.

Further Reading

Copeland, Thomas. *Fool Me Twice: Intelligence Failure and Mass Casualty Terrorism.* Boston: Martinus Nijhoff, 2007. Evaluation of intelligence failures in terrorist incidents. Examines five case studies, including the World Trade Center bombing of 1993, the Khobar Towers bombing, and the attacks of September 11, 2001.

Gantzel, Klaus Jurgen, and Torsten Schwinghammer. *Warfare Since the Second World War.* New Brunswick, N.J.: Transaction, 2000. Analysis of the changing nature of war, from interstate to internal conflicts.

Lesser, Ian O. *Countering the New Terrorism.* Santa Monica, Calif.: RAND, 1999. In-depth analysis of trends in terrorism.

Wayne Shirey

See also Clinton, Bill; Cohen, William S.; Defense budget cuts; Foreign policy of the United States; Gulf War; Middle East and North America; Oklahoma City bombing; Olympic Park bombing; Terrorism; Unabomber capture; U.S. embassy bombings in Africa; World Trade Center bombing.

■ Killer bees

Definition Africanized honeybees

Place Texas, Arizona, New Mexico, California, and Nevada

Africanized honeybees—dubbed "killer bees" because of their aggressive nature—spread into the southwestern United States, frightening people and disrupting beekeepers' activities.

An Africanized honeybee. (U.S. Department of Agriculture)

Honeybees were introduced into the New World from Europe in the seventeenth century, but because European bees produce poorly in the tropics, Brazilian scientists began crossing them with more productive (but also more aggressive) African bees in the 1940's. During the following decade, however, African queen bees escaped into the wild. By 1989, swarms of hybrid, or Africanized honeybees, which had inherited the aggressive nature of the African strain, reached northern Mexico. They had now established a pattern of interbreeding with and displacing ordinary honeybees.

Anticipating the bees' arrival, American officials distributed baited traps along the border, and they caught the first specimens near Hidalgo, Texas, in October, 1990. By the end of the year, the bees had been identified in eight of the state's southernmost counties. They attacked a man the following year in Brownsville, Texas, and a fatality—the first in the nation—was reported near Harlingen, Texas, in August, 1993. The victim was eighty-two-year-old Lino Lopez, who had been attempting to remove a swarm from the wall of a building on his ranch.

Within a few years, killer bees entered the other states sharing a border with Mexico. They were first identified in Arizona and New Mexico in 1993, although scientists suspect that the insects may have entered the former state in 1992. The bees reached California in 1994 but did not claim a human victim there until 1999.

Although the news media carried sensational stories about the invading insects, scientists generally rejected the term "killer bees," pointing out that the insects' stings are no more venomous than those of ordinary honeybees. Because the bees are more aggressive, attack in larger swarms, pursue their victims further, and remain agitated longer, scientists did warn that they pose a greater threat. Domestic animals such as dogs and horses that might disturb the bees' colonies were also identified as being in danger.

By the mid-1990's, killer bees appeared to be spreading more slowly and did not reach southern Nevada until 1998. During the following decade, however, they were reported in Louisiana and Florida, having possibly entered as swarms aboard ships, as well as in Arkansas and Virginia.

Impact Killer bees were a media sensation during the early 1990's, but by the end of the decade, only a handful of people had died from their stings in the United States. Experts voiced greater concern about the bees' impact on the honey industry and particularly on the pollination of fields and orchards, as the bees' aggressiveness disrupts beekeepers' standard methods of transporting them and extracting their honey.

Further Reading

Flakus, Greg. *Living with Killer Bees: The Story of the Africanized Bee Invasion.* Oakland, Calif.: Quick Trading Company, 1993.

Tennesen, Michael. "Going Head-to-Head with Killer Bees." *National Wildlife* 39, no. 2 (February/March, 2001): 16-17.

Winston, Mark L. *Killer Bees: The Africanized Honey Bee in the Americas.* Cambridge, Mass.: Harvard University Press, 1992.

Grove Koger

See also Agriculture in the United States; Journalism; Latin America; Mexico and the United States; Natural disasters.

■ King, Rodney

Identification Victim of a highly publicized beating by members of the Los Angeles Police Department

Born April 2, 1965; Sacramento, California

Events following King's beating led to one of the worst riots in modern American history. It also raised troubling questions about the relations between ethnic minorities and large city police departments.

Rodney Glen King was born in Sacramento, California. He struggled in school, was athletic, and enjoyed fishing. At age nine, he was helping his father clean commercial buildings at night and until the early hours of the morning. This lack of sleep did not help his school work. King started drinking at an early age, with most of his adult difficulties stemming from his alcoholism. He eventually dropped out of high school, got married, and held various construction jobs. Before his famous arrest on 1991, he had been convicted of beating his wife (1987) and of assault and robbery at a convenience store (1989), for which he was imprisoned for two years and was out on parole by the end of 1990.

Early in the morning of March 3, 1991, after a high speed chase of nearly eight miles involving officers from a number of jurisdictions, Rodney King was finally stopped. King exited the car, but did not lie face down as ordered by members of the Los Angeles Police Department (LAPD). Instead, he crouched in what some of the officers thought was a menacing position. Though he was then "tasered" twice, King (a large, well-built man) still did not comply with orders and was able to throw off a number of officers who had tried to subdue him. Some of them then proceeded to beat him with nightsticks, hitting him more than fifty times. King was subsequently hospitalized, having suffered a number of broken bones and serious bruises. Much of this episode was videotaped by a civilian who had been awakened by the noise. This citizen eventually gave the tape to a

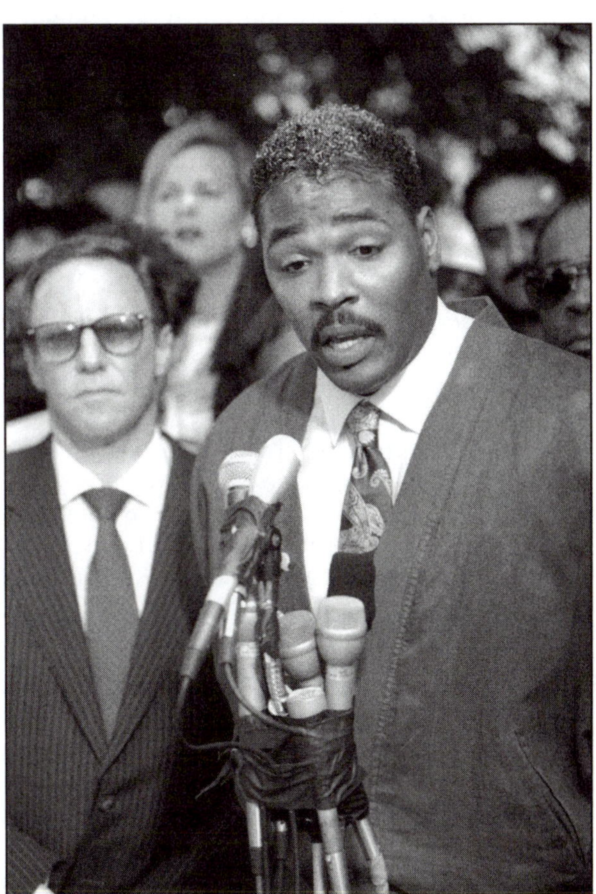

Rodney King pleads for peace in South Central Los Angeles on the third day of the rioting, May 1, 1992. His televised appearance became famous for his appeal, "Can we all get along?" (AP/Wide World Photos)

local television station, which edited it slightly before putting in on the air. Soon, it was picked up by the Cable News Network (CNN) and shown nationally many times. The reaction to the televised tape was very strong. It was followed by a criminal investigation of the officers' behavior as well as a "blue ribbon" commission headed by Warren Christopher. Its report was highly critical of the LAPD. Four of the officers were indicted for their actions.

Although the trial of the officers would normally have taken place in Los Angeles, their attorneys asked for, and received, a change of venue. Consequently, the trial was held in the largely white suburb of Simi Valley. There were no blacks on the jury, which acquitted all of the officers of all charges. After the verdict was announced, riots broke out in South Central Los Angeles. The officers were subsequently indicted under federal law. That trial, which did take place in the city and which did contain a multiethnic jury, led to the conviction of two of them.

Impact The riots that followed the acquittal in the state case lasted about four days and were the worst in modern American history. They resulted in the deaths of more than fifty individuals, more than two thousand injuries that needed hospital attention, and the destruction of nearly one thousand structures. Property losses added up to more than $900 million. One of King's best moments came during the riots, when in a televised interview he pleaded with the public for calm, asking "Can we all get along?" The reputation of the LAPD, which had been high in many quarters, was severely shaken. King eventually received an award of $3.8 million after he filed a civil suit against the city of Los Angeles. He used the money to start Alta-Pazz Recording, a rap record label.

Further Reading

Cannon, Lou. *Official Negligence: How Rodney King and the Riots Changed Los Angeles and the LAPD.* New York: Random House, 1997.

Skolnick, Jerome, and James J. Fyfe. *Above the Law: Police and the Excessive Use of Force.* New York: Free Press, 1993.

David M. Jones

See also African Americans; Christopher, Warren; Los Angeles riots; Louima torture case; Police brutality; Race relations.

■ King, Stephen

Identification American author
Born September 21, 1947; Portland, Maine

Long a prolific best-selling horror and suspense author, King branched out with new forms of publishing in the 1990's.

During the 1990's, Stephen King experimented with selling novels in serial format, as with *The Green Mile* (1996), as well as with genre. He wrote novels from a female perspective—*Gerald's Game* (1992), *Dolores Claiborne* (1992), *Rose Madder* (1995), and *The Girl Who Loved Tom Gordon* (1999)—and the screenplay for the television miniseries *Storm of the Century* (1999). King also spent the decade as a key member of the Rock Bottom Remainders, a charity rock group consisting of published authors. In 1999, King was seriously injured when he was struck by a minivan.

Early in the decade, King worked on two novels that had their genesis as a single novel: *Dolores Claiborne* and *Gerald's Game.* The two works reference each other at a key point in their respective narratives, and both novels deal with physically and sexu-

Stephen King. (Tabitha King)

ally abused women. *Dolores Claiborne* lacks chapter breaks and thus presents itself as one long monologue. Both novels received good reviews and left some wondering if King would abandon the horror genre altogether.

In 1996, King experimented with serial publication. *The Green Mile* was published in six volumes, each released a month apart. King found that this style of writing led to new challenges in maintaining readers' interest with each new installment while still attracting readers who may have missed an earlier segment.

During the decade, King joined the Rock Bottom Remainders, a rock group consisting of King and authors Dave Barry, Ridley Pearson, Barbara Kingsolver, Robert Fulghum, and Amy Tan, among others. He also received critical recognition, winning a 1996 O. Henry Award for the short story "The Man in the Black Suit."

On June 19, 1999, while walking along a road in Maine, King was hit by a man driving a minivan. King later described the driver as "a character out of one of my own novels." King nearly died in the accident but, after five weeks, was back to writing again, completing the nonfiction book *On Writing* (2000).

Impact Stephen King continued his hectic publishing schedule during the 1990's and continued to explore new methods of publication in the next decade. In 2000, *Riding the Bullet,* a sixty-six-page electronic book, or e-book, was downloaded over 500,000 times. Later that year, he tried a serialized e-book experiment, *The Plant,* which was less successful.

Further Reading

King, Stephen. *On Writing: A Memoir of the Craft.* New York: Scribner, 2000.

Russell, Sharon A. *Revisiting Stephen King: A Critical Companion.* Westport, Conn.: Greenwood Press, 2002.

Julie Elliott

See also Literature in the United States; Publishing; Rock Bottom Remainders, The.

■ Kingsolver, Barbara

Identification American author
Born April 8, 1955; Annapolis, Maryland

Kingsolver writes about economic injustice and cultural differences in many of her fictional works. She combines a thoughtful and sensitive view of life with an insightful approach to issues of culture through her novels, stories, and poetry.

Barbara Kingsolver has written novels, short stories, poetry, and essays about topics as wide ranging as missionary life in Africa and community rights in Native American tribal culture. She was born in Maryland but grew up in Kentucky. She left her rural home for college in Indiana, where she majored in biology at DePauw University. With this background of study, Kingsolver often adds vivid description to the settings of her stories. She creates intensely personal tales for each of her characters, which are often set against the larger backdrop of political and economic issues of the time period. Because of her wide range of experience as a scientist, researcher, archaeological worker, and translator, she brings a variety of perspectives to her works. Throughout all of them she remains committed to honesty and social justice. In support of those issues, she established the Bellwether Prize in 1997, which is awarded every other year to a first novel which shows the highest literary quality and the author who shows dedication to creating literature for social impact and change.

Kingsolver uses her characters, such as Leah in *The Poisonwood Bible* (1998), to examine not only the role of missionaries in Africa but also the larger issues of the influence of outside political powers, such as the United States on rural and emerging African nations. She spent time in Africa as a young child with her family. In that setting, she started writing in a journal which she credits as an early influence on her style as a storyteller. Many of her main characters are female and fiercely independent. In *Animal Dreams* (1990) and *Pigs in Heaven* (1993), her major characters face life-changing events within the conflict between Native American culture and mainstream America. Despite these trials, her characters always acknowledge the community in which they live and in this way remind the reader that no one exists separately; we are all part of a greater canvas.

Barbara Kingsolver. (©Seth Kanter/Courtesy, Harper-Perennial)

Impact Kingsolver's writing reinforces the idea that there is a storyteller in every person. She is able to create rich characters and experiences from both her imagination and her varied experiences. Because many of her main characters are female, she underscores the struggles of being a woman set against a backdrop of social issues and change.

Further Reading

A Reader's Guide to the Fiction of Barbara Kingsolver. New York: HarperCollins, 2004.

Snodgrass, Mary Ellen. *Barbara Kingsolver: A Literary Companion.* McFarland Literary Companion 2. Jefferson, N.C.: McFarland, 2004.

Wagner-Martin, Linda. *Barbara Kingsolver.* New York: Chelsea House, 2004.

Dolores A. D'Angelo

See also Literature in the United States.

■ Klaas kidnapping and murder case

The Event Kidnapping and murder of a twelve-year-old girl by a habitual violent offender
Date October 1, 1993
Place Petaluma, California

The kidnapping and murder of Polly Klaas by Richard Allen Davis sparked intense discussion about appropriate sentencing for repeat offenders and measures to ensure the safety of young people.

A lifelong criminal, Richard Allen Davis was first arrested at the age of twelve. By 1993, he had been arrested for forgery, burglary, automobile theft, armed robbery, multiple kidnappings, and sexual assaults. He had served the better part of twenty-six years in prison. In late June, 1993, after serving only half of a sixteen-year sentence for assaulting, kidnapping, and robbing a woman, Davis was paroled from prison, still at war with the world. By October 1 of that year, he was wandering through Petaluma when he noticed a house with windows open. In the house, a group of twelve-year-old girls were having a slumber party. Davis decided to break into the house. Threatening the girls with a knife, he tied them up, put pillowcases over their heads, and abducted Polly Klaas. Davis drove through Petaluma aimlessly, trying to decide how best to dispose of the terrified young girl.

Klaas's disappearance set off a nationwide, two-month search for the girl. Despite encounters with various police officers, Davis brutalized Klaas and murdered her. He was eventually arrested for parole violation and, after confessing to the crime, led investigators to the body. His trial was short, although not uneventful. During his trial, Davis demonstrated callous disregard for his victim as well as for her family and society in general. In June, 1996, he was found guilty of kidnapping and murder. He was sentenced to death in September.

Impact In the short term, the abduction of Polly Klaas terrorized families throughout California, complicating the ordinary tasks of daily living. Ultimately, however, the murder of Klaas spotlighted the shortcomings of the American criminal justice system in appropriately separating habitual violent criminals from potential victims. Several critics at the time and since have questioned how a career criminal like Davis, with his record of violence and callousness, could have merited parole.

As a result of such questions, a wave of laws were passed by various states in the 1990's requiring the imposition of lengthy jail terms on offenders who had been previously convicted of multiple violent crimes. These were known as the three strikes laws, borrowing a term from baseball, indicating that convicts would be given a limited number of chances before facing mandatory lengthy prison sentences.

Further Reading

Bortnick, Barry. *Polly Klaas: The Murder of America's Child.* New York: Pinnacle Books, 1995.

Domanick, Joe. *Cruel Justice: Three Strikes and the Politics of Crime in America's Golden State.* Berkeley: University of California Press, 2004.

Michael R. Meyers

See also Crime; Ramsey murder case; Three strikes laws.

■ Knox pornography case

The Event A series of court reviews that tested definitions of child pornography
Date October 11, 1991-June 9, 1994

The federal court system, amid the heated political atmosphere of the midterm elections of 1994, revisited the legal definition of child pornography as it applied specifically to photography.

In 1991, during a warrant-search of the apartment of Stephen Knox, a history graduate student at Penn State who had been twice convicted of possessing child pornography, agents recovered commercially made videotapes of female teenage models ostensibly in fashion poses. Although the girls, ages ten to seventeen, were not nude (they wore bathing suits, leotards, and underwear), were not posed, and were not engaging in sexual acts, Knox was arrested and subsequently, on October 11, 1991, convicted of possessing child pornography, the court citing that the images frequently lingered on the genital area. However, given the definition of child pornography upheld by courts since the mid-1980's as the "lascivious exhibition" of the genitals of anyone under eighteen, Knox appealed his conviction. The United States Court of Pennsylvania upheld the lower court's ruling (they cited photos in which upper thighs were exposed), and Knox received a five-year prison sentence. His subsequent appeal, to the Third Circuit United States Court of Appeals, was as well denied in October, 1992.

When Knox took his case to the Supreme Court in the fall of 1993, however, U.S. solicitor general Drew Days argued that the genitalia needed to be exposed to qualify as "lascivious exhibition." When the Supreme Court agreed on November 1, 1993, and remanded the decision to the Third Circuit Court, a political firestorm was ignited as the narrowed interpretation would exclude much child pornography from prosecution. Challenged by a vociferous right-wing coalition, the Senate, within three days, voted 100-0 on a nonbinding censure against the Clinton Justice Department (later, in April, the House voted a similar censure). An embattled President Bill Clinton—feeling the first resolve of the political revolution in which conservatives would claim both houses of Congress in an historic midterm election later that year and seeing the political hazards of his administration being viewed as soft on child porn—sent a reprimand to his attorney general, Janet Reno, calling for a tougher definition of child pornography. On June 9, 1994, under considerable media scrutiny and public pressure, the Third District Court rejected Days's argument. Later, after the midterm elections, the Clinton Justice Department reversed its position on Knox, although there was speculation on the level of disagreement within the department over that reversal.

Impact The contentious response over the Knox ruling ignited a national debate over the definition of child pornography, raising thorny questions about what constitutes legitimate commercial modeling and what constitutes exploitative material targeted for pedophiles. Amid a polarized political environment, the courts concluded essentially that photographs were actions not representations protected by First Amendment free speech and consequently could be restricted.

Further Reading

Hixson, Richard F. *Pornography and the Justices: The Supreme Court and the Intractable Obscenity Problem.* Carbondale: Southern Illinois University Press, 1996.

Nathan, Debbie. *Pornography.* Toronto: Groundwood Books, 2007.

Joseph Dewey

See also Censorship; Child pornography; Clinton, Bill; Conservatism in U.S. politics; Contract with America; Culture wars; Elections in the United States, midterm; Mapplethorpe obscenity trial; Photography; Reno, Janet.

■ Komunyakaa, Yusef

Identification African American poet
Born April 29, 1947; Bogalusa, Louisiana

After receiving the Pulitzer Prize in poetry in 1994, Komunyakaa achieved even greater attention, noted as one of the most lauded African American poets.

One of the foremost African American poets of his time, Yusef Komunyakaa wrote and edited a variety of poetry collections during the 1990's. Komunyakaa's poetry collection *Magic City*, published in 1992, explores themes from the author's childhood in the rural American South. His poems illustrate a child's growing awareness of civil rights issues, racial identity, and his place in a rapidly changing community and world. *Magic City* continues the themes found in his earlier volumes *Copacetic* (1984) and *I Apologize for the Eyes in My Head* (1986).

It was his next volume of poetry, *Neon Vernacular: New and Selected Poems*, however, that received the most critical attention. A compilation of his best work from previous poetry collections, along with strong new poetry, this book explores several themes that recur in Komunyakaa's work: the African American experience, the Vietnam War, and jazz and blues music. It was this volume of poetry that won Komunyakaa the 1994 Pulitzer Prize in poetry. That same year, he also received the Kingsley Tufts Poetry Award and the William Faulkner Prize from the Université de Rennes, also for *Neon Vernacular.*

In 1998, Komunyakaa published *Thieves of Paradise*, a finalist for the National Book Critics Circle Award. This collection was influenced by the poet's experience in Australia and reflects his interest in the culture of the Aborigines. Other accolades and awards Komunyakaa received in the 1990's include the Thomas Forcade Award (1991), the Hanes Poetry Prize (1997), and the Morton Dauwen Zabel Award from the American Academy of Arts and Letters (1998). In 1999, he was named a chancellor of the Academy of American Poets.

In addition to publishing his volumes of poetry,

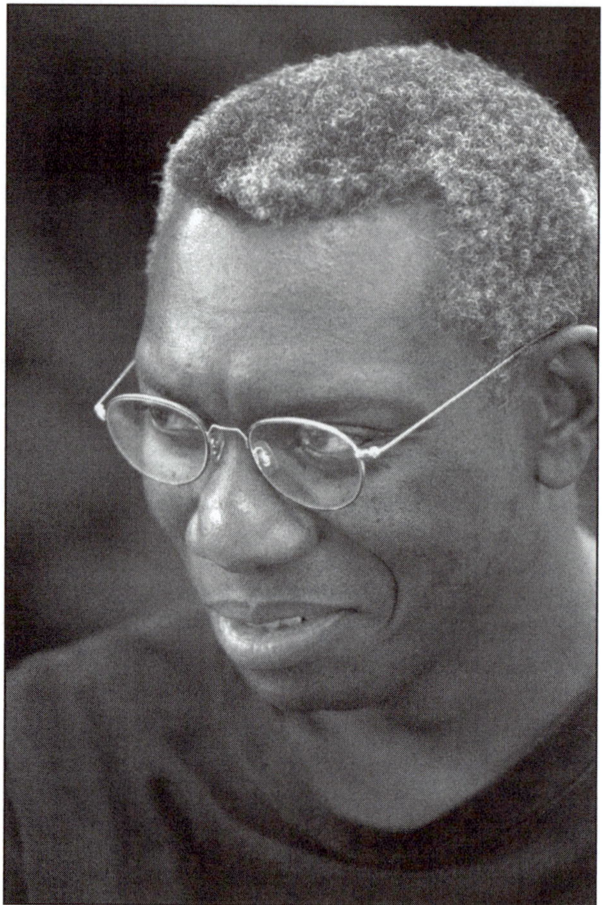

Pulitzer Prize-winning poet Yusef Komunyakaa in 1996. (AP/ Wide World Photos)

Komunyakaa coedited two poetry collections, *The Jazz Poetry Anthology* (1991) and *The Second Set: The Jazz Poetry Anthology* (1996), with poet and jazz musician Sascha Feinstein. These collections feature the work of many major American poets. Komunyakaa also worked with scholar Martha Collins in translating Nguyen Quang Thieu's poetry collection, *The Insomnia of Fire*, published in 1995.

Impact Yusef Komunyakaa's impact on American poetry during the 1990's was significant. His Pulitzer Prize-winning work, *Neon Vernacular,* directed attention to important political and social issues, including the aftermath of the Civil Rights movement, the Vietnam War, and their effects on several generations of Americans. His work with other writers also expanded awareness of jazz poetry and the poetry of Vietnamese writer Nguyen Quang Thieu. Komunyakaa's poetry, which features a spare, image-rich style and a melodic, rhythmic cadence, blended formal poetry with musical forms of jazz and blues, adding to the repertoire of American poetry.

Further Reading

Conley, Susan. "About Yusef Komunyakaa: A Profile." *Ploughshares* 23, no. 1 (Spring, 1997): 202-207.

Gordon, Fran. "Yusef Komunyakaa: Blue Note in a Lyrical Landscape." *Poets & Writers* 28, no. 6 (November/December, 2000): 26-33.

Ringnalda, Don. *Fighting and Writing the Vietnam War.* Jackson: University Press of Mississippi, 1994.

Kris Bigalk

See also African Americans; Alvarez, Julia; Angelou, Maya; Literature in the United States; Poetry; Strand, Mark.

■ Koons, Jeff

Identification American artist
Born January 21, 1955; York, Pennsylvania

Koons gained fame in the United States as a major conceptual/pop artist noted especially for his deployment of kitsch for the purposes of high art.

A hot young artist in the "Reagan years" of the previous decade, in the 1990's Jeff Koons built on his already controversial reputation and reached new levels of both commercial success and artistic recognition. Koons was especially known for transforming simple objects into large and mysteriously empowered sculptures that could be read as either ironic commentary on a shallow and meaningless contemporary consumerism or as a deeper, more ambiguous investigation of pop culture, especially popular imagery associated with childhood. In 1992, for instance, Koons created a major piece called *Puppy*, a monumental forty-three-foot-tall, eighty-eight-ton sculpture of a terrier composed of sixty thousand flowers on a stainless steel armature. The fascinating puppy was displayed for a time in Rockefeller Center in New York City. In 1997, the Solomon R. Guggenheim Foundation installed it permanently outside the Guggenheim Museum in Bilbao, Spain.

Less successful was Koons's 1991 marriage to Ilona Staller, the Italian pornography star. Before their marriage, Koons created and posed with Staller in perhaps his most controversial art pieces—a surreal and sexually explicit series of paintings, photographs, and sculptures called Made in Heaven. The divorce of Staller and Koons later in the decade, followed by a bitter child custody dispute, created yet more publicity for the increasingly notorious artist.

In 1993, Koons began a series of paintings and sculptures titled Celebration, which consisted of works based on childhood toys and trinkets. Of special note were pieces that recalled the entertaining art of twisting balloons into animal shapes, conceptualized by Koons into big balloon dogs rendered in candy-colored chrome. Koons's failed child custody battle and the cost of the ongoing Celebration series led to considerable financial reversals, but he recovered in 1999, when his sculpture based on the cartoon character the Pink Panther sold for just under $2 million.

Koons was often derided for his self-promotion; similarly, his work was dismissed as pandering to the desires of the marketplace. Although his art has been denounced as crass and cynical, many per-

Jeff Koons's Puppy *in Bilbao, Spain.*

ceived mysterious hidden depths beneath his decorative surfaces.

Impact Koons was perceived as a phenomenon both in terms of his commercial success and his controversial art work. Disdained by some critics as decadent, tacky, cheap, and sensationalistic, his pieces nevertheless won a great deal of contemporary institutional acceptance, including an exhibition at London's Royal Academy. Of consistently high market value, his work fetched millions at auction, making him one of the highest-earning artists of his time. He also exerted a major influence on younger artists and found acceptance as an original and important figure within the very high art tradition, whose premises he appeared to subvert.

Further Reading

Sylvester, David. "Jeff Koons." In *Interviews with American Artists.* New Haven, Conn.: Yale University Press, 2001.

Tomkins, Calvin. "The Turnaround Artist: Jeff Koons Up from Banality." *The New Yorker,* vol. 83, no. 9 (April 23, 2007): 58-67.

Margaret Boe Birns

See also Art movements; Christo; National Endowment for the Arts (NEA).

■ Kosovo conflict

The Event Ethnic conflict between Serbs and Albanians in Kosovo
Date 1996-1999
Place Kosovo, Serbia

The war in Kosovo was one of several in the breakup of Yugoslavia that led to North American diplomatic and military involvement.

Kosovo, particularly Kosovo field, is historically sacred ground for the Serbs, the site of a legendary battle against the Ottoman Turks in 1389. Over the centuries, however, the area became the homeland for Albanian Muslims. After World War II, the communist leader Tito (Josip Broz) reconstructed Yugoslavia along national lines into a federation of six republics, with the Serbian republic containing two autonomous regions—the Hungarian Banat and the Albanian Kosovo. The authorities treated the Albanians as second-class citizens, and the region was one of the poorest in the federation. In the 1980's, after the death of Tito, Yugoslavia fractured as nationalism grew stronger among its various constituents. In the 1990's, with the fall of communist governments throughout Eastern Europe, Yugoslavia separated into its constituent republics, and wars erupted between ethnic groups. In the middle of the decade, North Atlantic Treaty Organization (NATO) forces led by the United States intervened in Bosnia, where Serbs, Croats, and Bosniaks (Slavic Muslims) fought among themselves.

Living in an autonomous region rather than a constituent republic, the Albanians in Kosovo were in a special category. Furthermore, there was an independent Albania next to Kosovo to which they could look for support. As ethnic tensions between the Serbs and Albanians increased, many Serbs fled under threat of Albanian terror raids, and rumors that radical Islamic fundamentalists were aiding the Albanians circulated. In 1987, Serbian nationalist Slobodan Milošević visited the region promising to defend Serbian interests. Two years later as president of the republic, he orchestrated changes in Serbia's constitution limiting Kosovo's autonomy and adopted measures causing Albanian unemployment and curtailing cultural activities. In 1991, Albanian nationalists proclaimed the Republic of Kosovo and elected Ibrahim Rugova, an Albanian writer and professor, as president of a shadow government in unsanctioned elections.

In 1996, the Albanians formed an army of its own, the Kosovo Liberation Army (KLA), which received arms from Albania and was able to launch attacks against Serbian police and army units in Kosovo. As they did in Bosnia, NATO countries once again attempted to mediate the crisis.

The United States Intervenes Throughout the decade, U.S. president Bill Clinton sent warnings to Milošević to stop aggression against the Albanian Kosovars. In March, 1998, U.S. secretary of state Madeleine Albright condemned the Serb attacks. In the meantime, the so-called Contact Group (United States, Great Britain, France, Germany, Italy, and Russia) met in London to discuss the Kosovo crisis. The U.N. Security Council condemned Belgrade, imposed economic sanctions, and banned arms sales to Serbia. In May, Milošević and Rugova met without results. Rugova then traveled to the United States, where he met with Clinton, Albright, and

U.N. secretary-general Kofi Annan and requested U.N. and NATO intervention.

Rambouillet Meeting and Air Raids On February 6, 1999, the Contact Group established peace talks between the warring parties in Rambouillet, France. Both Albanian and Serbian diplomats objected to the proposed accords, but the Albanians finally agreed to sign. Milošević agreed to diplomatic observers in the region. However, in the summer, his army began a new offensive, and thousands more Albanian refugees fled into the mountains. Russian president Boris Yeltsin and Clinton then met in Moscow and issued a joint statement calling for negotiations and for Serbia to end its attack, but on American initiative and over Russian objections NATO began a new bombing campaign in Serbia. Clinton ruled out American use of ground forces but indicated that four thousand American peacekeepers would go to Kosovo after the armistice.

NATO objectives in the air raids were to stop all military action, end violence and repression, withdraw the military and police as well as paramilitary forces from the region, establish an international military force and the return of refugees, and force Belgrade to adhere to the Rambouillet Accords. NATO troops including 31,600 Americans and 1,300 Canadians entered into neighboring Albania and Macedonia for protection. About 10,000 Albanian refugees came into the United States and 5,000 to Canada.

Finally, Milošević and NATO reached an agreement in June before a possible ground invasion, and NATO and Russian troops came to the province to supervise the area that was divided between the Albanian and Serb populations. About 600,000 Albanians returned to Kosovo, and 200,000 Serbs and Roma left Albanian areas. Twenty thousand Russian and NATO troops moved into Kosovo as peacekeepers, while the Serbian forces left the area and the KLA demilitarized.

Impact The Kosovo conflict, along with the other wars in the Balkans, established U.S. leadership in dealing with changes in the Balkans, especially Yugoslavia, in the 1990's. Although Washington operated principally through NATO, tensions between the United States and the various European countries led to a number of rifts. The conflict also demonstrated that Washington was willing to use armed force to ensure its policies.

Further Reading

Brune, Lester H. *The United States and the Balkan Crisis, 1990-2005: Conflict in Bosnia and Kosovo.* Claremont, Calif.: Regina, 2005. A discussion of American involvement in the conflict by an author who has written many books on American foreign policy.

King, Iain, and Whit Mason. *Peace at Any Price: How the World Failed Kosovo.* Ithaca, N.Y.: Cornell University Press, 2006. An analysis by authors who have written about the ethics of world crises. They believe that NATO was unprepared to deal with the crisis.

Norris, John. *Collision Course: NATO, Russia, and Kosovo.* Westport, Conn.: Praeger, 2005. An outstanding summary of the conflict.

Ramet, Sabrina P. *Thinking About Yugoslavia: Scholarly Debates About the Yugoslavia Breakup and the Wars in Bosnia and Kosovo.* New York: Cambridge University Press, 2005. A distinguished author surveys and analyzes the literature and debates about the Yugoslavia crises but with a Croatian bias.

Frederick B. Chary

See also Albright, Madeleine; Bosnia conflict; Clinton, Bill; Cold War, end of; Dayton Accords; Europe and North America; Foreign policy of Canada; Foreign policy of the United States; United Nations.

■ Kwanzaa

Definition African American holiday celebrated from December 26 to January 1

In the 1990's, Kwanzaa gained widespread popularity, and its commercialization became evident in this decade.

The term "Kwanzaa" comes from the Swahili phrase *matunda ya kwanzaa,* meaning "first fruits of the harvest." The holiday was created by Maulana "Ron" Karenga in 1966 as an attempt to affirm and celebrate African American culture and values. There are seven principles that focus on community-building, strengthening family relationships, education about black culture, and African American unity and pride. The principles are *umoja* (unity), *kujichagulia* (self-determination), *ujima* (collective work and responsibility), *ujamaa* (cooperative economics), *nia* (purpose), *kuumba* (creativity), and *imani* (faith). Kwanzaa supplies include a mat, seven candles, a kinara to display the candles, a unity cup, and ears of corn. A candle is lit each night, representing a specific Kwanzaa principle.

The 1990's saw a huge rise in the number of African American families celebrating Kwanzaa. Annual Kwanzaa celebrations were evident at black churches, local and national organizations, schools, college campuses, and homes. The commercialization of Kwanzaa became evident when retailers such as J. C. Penney, Bed Bath & Beyond, Wal-Mart, and Kmart began carrying Kwanzaa supplies. Hallmark began mass-producing Kwanzaa greeting cards. It is estimated that over five million African Americans celebrate Kwanzaa, and it is a more than $700-million industry. Kwanzaa expos became popular in U.S. cities. In 1997, the first Kwanzaa stamp was issued by the U.S. Postal Service on October 22. In the late 1990's, President Bill Clinton discussed Kwanzaa in a White House speech affirming its principles and celebration of African American culture.

It is believed that the rise of the African American middle class and the acceptance of multiculturalism contributed to the popularization of Kwanzaa as corporate America recognized the buying power of black consumers. It is mostly celebrated by African American middle-class families.The commercialization of Kwanzaa has led some critics to state that today's Kwanzaa has drifted away from some of its original ideals. One criticism is that Kwanzaa supplies are not often bought from black-owned businesses. However, African American and commercial Kwanzaa suppliers have benefited from Kwanzaa's increased popularity. The Kwanzaa holiday is a popular subject in children's books, cookbooks, and African American magazines.

Impact The popularization of Kwanzaa celebrations by African Americans in the 1990's represented corporate America's long-overdue recognition of the buying power of African American consumers.

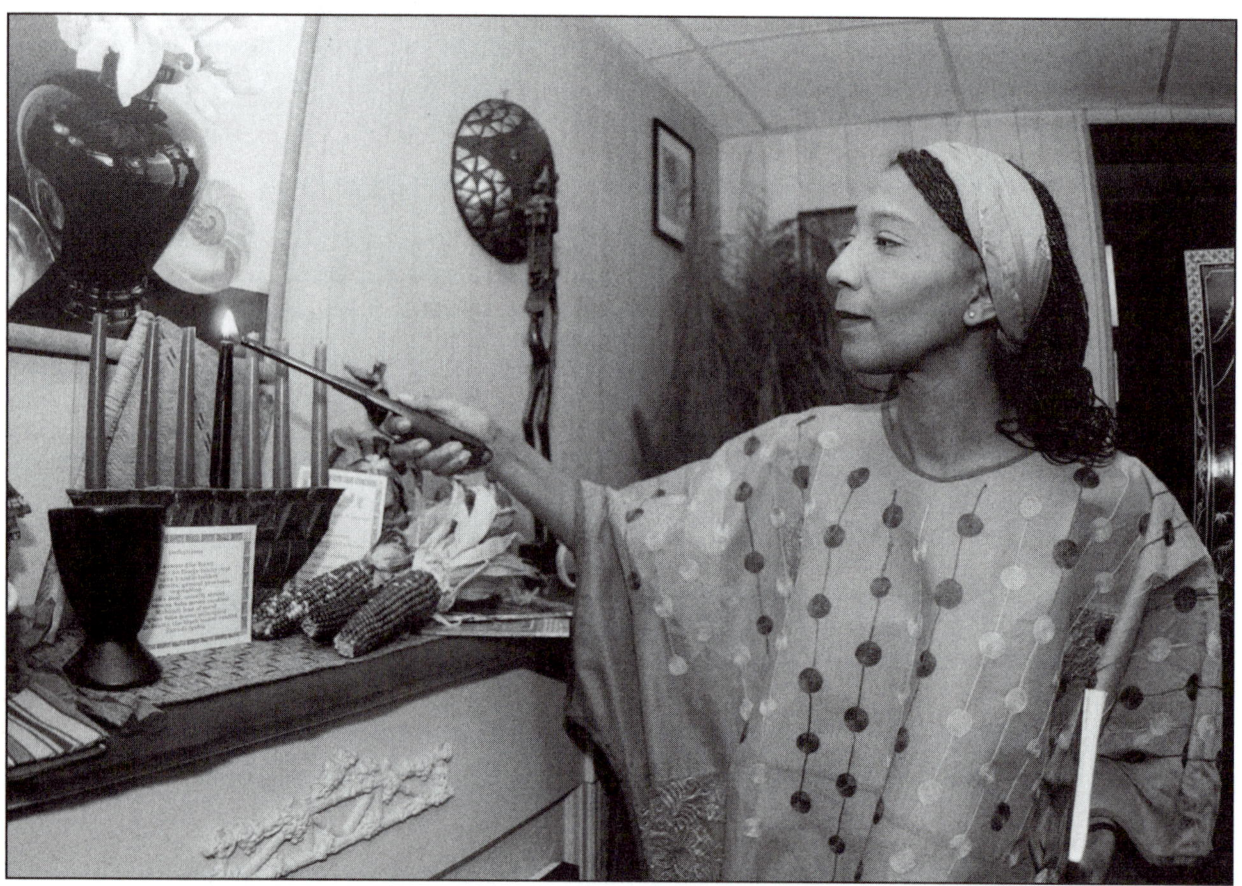

A woman lights a candle in her home to mark the start of the celebration of Kwanzaa. (AP/Wide World Photos)

Further Reading

Karenga, Maulana. *Kwanzaa: A Celebration of Family, Community and Culture.* Los Angeles: University of Sankore Press, 1998.

Winbush Riley, Dorothy. *The Complete Kwanzaa.* New York: HarperCollins, 1995.

Katherine M. Helm

See also African Americans; Amazon.com; Angelou, Maya; Clinton, Bill; Race relations; Wal-Mart; WB television network.

■ Kyoto Protocol

Identification An international agreement to control global warming by curtailing the production of greenhouse gases

Date Negotiated December 1-11, 1997

Building on the voluntary reduction targets of the Framework Convention on Climate Change, negotiated at the Rio de Janeiro summit in 1992, the Kyoto Protocol provided that the industrial nations plus the former Soviet Union and Eastern European countries would reduce the emission of greenhouse gases an average of five percent in the period from 2008 to 2012. The treaty entered into force in 2004 when Russia was the final industrial nation save one to ratify the agreement. The United States has not ratified the Kyoto Protocol and is not expected to do so.

The 1992 Rio Declaration was based on the recognition that the production of carbon dioxide and five other greenhouse gases was helping to cause global warming. The declaration provided for only voluntary reductions. By 1995, it had become evident that governments must agree to mandatory reductions. In the spring of 1997, representatives from industrialized and developing nations met in Kyoto, Japan, to negotiate reduction targets. During the talks, it was agreed that developing nations would be omitted from the first-round obligatory reductions, as such reductions would impose too great a burden on these nations. Although developing nations' output of greenhouse gases was increasing rapidly, it was still less than industrialized nations' emissions.

The U.S. delegation, responding in part to criticism at home, tried to include the less-industrialized nations in the requirements of the treaty but failed to win support. Even though the U.S. Senate indicated its disapproval of what appeared to be the treaty stipulations, the U.S. delegation signed the agreement. Aware of the opposition in Congress, President Bill Clinton chose not to submit it to the Senate for ratification. President George W. Bush would indicate opposition to the treaty after he assumed office in 2001.

In order to enter into force, the protocol required ratification by fifty-five nations, including countries that had been responsible for 55 percent of the emissions produced in 1990. Because of U.S. opposition, it was necessary for all other industrialized nations to ratify the treaty for it to enter into force. Russia's ratification of the treaty in November, 2004, led it to enter into force in February, 2005.

The Kyoto Protocol specified targets for reducing carbon dioxide and five other greenhouse gases in the period from 2008 to 2012. The United States was to reduce emissions by 7 percent from 1990 levels, the European Union and some other European nations were to reduce emissions by 8 percent, Canada and Japan were to reduce emissions by 6 percent, and Russia and Ukraine were to hold emissions constant. The less-developed nations were expected to try to hold down emissions voluntarily, but no targets were mandated. The delegates at Kyoto were aware that less-industrialized nations such as China would have to reduce the growth in emissions in the long run if global warming was to be curtailed. A 5.2 percent reduction in emissions below 1990 levels was expected if all nations met their targets. The primary target of emission reduction was industry, especially coal-fired power plants, but agriculture was also a major source of some greenhouse gases.

Opposition in the United States Opposition to the Kyoto Protocol came from two related groups in the United States. The first, particularly the representatives of some oil companies and their political friends, indicated that global warming was not influenced by human action or that its impact was severely overstated; therefore, there was no need for a reduction in greenhouse gases. By the late 1990's, this perspective was becoming increasingly discredited, as most scientists agreed that global warming was human-caused.

The second group of opponents agreed that global warming was a problem and that actions should be taken to reduce greenhouse gas emissions. They argued that the Kyoto Protocol was a badly flawed agreement, one that would reduce the competitive position of the United States in the world marketplace. These critics pointed to the rapid growth in greenhouse gases by countries such as China. China's path to industrialization was being supported by the extensive burning of coal, a major source of carbon dioxide as well as other polluting gases. Failing to regulate the emissions of nations such as China or India would give them an economic advantage because of their low costs of production. These critics also pointed out that some of the less-industrialized nations would soon be major contributors to the level of carbon dioxide in the atmosphere, so failing to regulate them would make a reduction of greenhouse gases in the atmosphere harder to achieve.

The second group of opponents made strong points against U.S. ratification of the agreement as written. Efforts would be made at a conference held in Berlin in 2002 to try to address some of these criticisms, but no agreement was reached. Supporters of ratification in the United States and abroad made the point that the reduction of greenhouse gases had to start somewhere. The industrialized nations both were the major contributors to emissions and were better able to withstand potential economic costs of reductions.

Impact The failure of the United States to ratify the Kyoto Protocol cast the country in somewhat of a bad light internationally. Some foreign nations see the United States as more concerned with its own short-term self interest than in dealing with a major international problem. Even though the United States has not ratified the agreement, it is making some efforts at reducing greenhouse gas emissions.

Further Reading

Dessler, Andrew E., and Edward Parson. *The Science and Politics of Global Climate Change: A Guide to the Debate.* New York: Cambridge University Press, 2006. Excellent brief analysis of Kyoto in a broader context.

Nordhaus, William D., and Joseph Boyer. *Warming the World: Economics Models of Global Warming.* Cambridge, Mass.: MIT Press, 2000. Economic analysis of the impact of Kyoto by two critics.

Schneider, Stephen H., Armin Rosencranz, and John O. Niles, eds. *Climate Change Policy: A Survey.* Washington, D.C.: Island Press, 2002. Good discussion of Kyoto in the broad context of climate change.

John M. Theilmann

See also Air pollution; Clean Air Act of 1990; Clinton, Bill; Earth Day 1990; *Earth in the Balance*; Global warming debate; Gore, Al.

L

Lagasse, Emeril

Identification World-renowned chef, author, and television personality
Born October 15, 1959; Fall River, Massachusetts

During the 1990's, Lagasse owned and operated several high-end, extremely popular restaurants, and he also became a television star. His enthusiasm for good food inspired a legion of fans to tackle dishes never attempted in their home kitchens.

Growing up in Massachusetts as the son of a French Canadian father and a Portuguese mother, Emeril Lagasse was introduced to ethnic cooking at an early age. As a child, Lagasse embraced his mother's love of cooking, making kale soup and Portuguese stuffing for family gatherings. In 1978, Lagasse completed the culinary program at Johnson and Wales University. After graduation, he studied cooking in France. Returning to the United States, he worked in a variety of restaurants. His big break came in 1982 when Ella Brennan, owner of the prestigious Commander's Palace in New Orleans, was looking for a replacement for legendary chef Paul Prudomme. After a five-day, on-site interview, Lagasse was hired.

In New Orleans, Lagasse learned to incorporate

Late night television host Jay Leno, left, cooks with chef Emeril Lagasse on Leno's show on September 30, 1998. (AP/Wide World Photos)

his Portuguese cooking style with the spices and flavors of creole and Cajun cuisine. Lagasse fell in love with New Orleans and, in 1990, opened his first restaurant, Emeril's, which was named Restaurant of the Year by *Esquire* magazine. He opened NOLA, a second restaurant, in 1992, followed by openings in Las Vegas in 1995 and Orlando in 1999.

Lagasse's fame came through television. When his restaurant successes caught the attention of executives at the newly established Food Network, he was invited to New York and featured in *How to Boil Water* in 1993. Lagasse was encouraged to host his own show, but *Emeril & Friends* was not successful. His next show, *The Essence of Emeril*, drew a larger television audience, and in 1997 the hour-long, unscripted *Emeril Live* became the most successful cooking show on television. Filmed before a live studio audience, Lagasse's show demonstrated a range of cooking, from creole to "jazzed up" meat and potatoes. His opening monologue, lively sense of humor, and down-to-earth approach had audiences responding with whistles, shouts, and applause. The show also featured Cajun musicians and guest stars.

In addition to operating his restaurants and starring on his television show, Lagasse has written best-selling cookbooks, beginning with *Emeril's New New Orleans Cooking* (1993). Lagasse produces a number of products bearing his name; particularly popular are the Essence blends. He has won various awards, both as a chef and as a television personality. In 1999, he was named to *People* magazine's "25 Most Intriguing People of the Year."

Impact With his signature word "Bam!" and expressions such as "Kick it up a notch" and "Pork fat rules," Lagasse not only became part of popular culture but also helped create a fascination with cooking for a wide audience. He recast the image of a premier chef from an elitist trained in Europe to a blue-collar, American-oriented food enthusiast, who demonstrated that cooking haute cuisine "ain't rocket science, it's just cooking."

Further Reading

Hessler, Amanda. "Under the Toque." *The New York Times*, November 4, 1998, p. F1.

Vigue, Doreen. "Kicking It Up a Notch." *The Boston Globe*, April 26, 1998, p. 12.

Marcia B. Dinneen

See also Cable television; Food trends; Television.

■ Lang, K. D.

Identification Canadian pop and country singer
Born November 2, 1961; Edmonton, Alberta, Canada

The singer-songwriter came out as a lesbian in the 1990's, even as she shifted her musical style.

Canadian singer K. D. (Kathryn Dawn) Lang, who styles her name in all-lowercase letters as k.d. lang, has developed a unique style based as much in pop and jazz as in her original love, country music. Most of her 1980's albums bore out her country background, but with Nashville only offering moderate respect to her talent, Lang began to focus on her other interests in the 1990's. Lang became vocal about vegetarianism and animal rights. Then, in 1991, she marked her film debut as the star of *Salmonberries.* Her 1992 album *Ingénue* showed no country influence, and her regular country backup group, the Reclines, was not credited. The single "Constant Craving" from that album won a Grammy Award and critical acclaim.

That year also marked a dramatic change in Lang's public profile. In an article published in the gay magazine *The Advocate*, Lang came out of the closet about her lesbian identity. She had always been popular with lesbian audiences, who welcomed the news, and she maintained a straight audience as well. The following year, she appeared on the cover of *Vanity Fair* dressed as a man. She introduced her friend Melissa Etheridge to the audience at a gay, lesbian, bisexual, and transgender (GLBT) inaugural event for U.S. president Bill Clinton, also in 1993, and Etheridge spontaneously outed herself. Always held to the fringes of country music, Lang was now completely removed from it. A genre associated with conservatism, country was not able to welcome such a radical into its most popular circles. However, Lang's style had always embraced more than country alone, and her move only increased her success in the 1990's.

In 1993, she wrote and performed the sound track for *Even Cowgirls Get the Blues*. In 1995, Lang released *All You Can Eat*, and followed in 1997 with *Drag*. She made two guest appearances in that year on the sitcom *Ellen*, when Ellen DeGeneres's character came out of the closet. As Lang's style shifted, her core audience moved with her, even while she attracted new fans. She took a three-year sabbatical between 1997 and 2000 but returned to music in 2000 with the album *Invincible Summer.*

Impact By refusing to accept the pigeonholes that often come with celebrity, K. D. Lang has made a lasting impact on the music world. Though she does not consider being a lesbian the center of her public persona, and feels frustrated when fans expect her to be emblematic of all lesbians' struggles, she also regularly expresses support for GLBT causes. Her popular and mainstream success in the 1990's came alongside her coming out, and her fan base increased dramatically throughout the decade.

Further Reading

Allen, Louise. *The Lesbian Idol: Martina, kd, and the Consumption of Lesbian Masculinity.* Washington, D.C.: Cassell, 1997.

Starr, Victoria. *K. D. Lang: All You Get Is Me.* New York: St. Martin's Press, 1994.

Jessie Bishop Powell

See also Country music; DeGeneres, Ellen; Etheridge, Melissa; Homosexuality and gay rights; Music.

■ Laparoscopic surgery

Identification Medical procedure
Date Introduced to wide use in 1990

Laparoscopic surgery provided a minimally invasive way to perform a variety of medical procedures, allowing for smaller incisions, less pain, and faster recovery time for the patient.

Laparoscopic surgery, also known as keyhole, pinhole, band-aid, or minimally invasive surgery, is a method of surgery used for many procedures. First developed in the early part of the 1900's for gynecological procedures, laparoscopic surgery became widespread as a medical procedure in 1990 with the development of a clip advancer that allowed surgeons to easily clamp vessels without having to pull out the clip applier, reload, and then reintroduce the applier into the patient's body. This reduced the infection risks associated with laparoscopic surgery.

Uses Laparoscopic surgery is most commonly used for cholecystectomies (removal of the gallbladder). This procedure is accomplished by introducing the surgeon's tools through small incisions in the abdomen. The surgeon uses a camera, scissors, clip advancer, and graspers in four small incisions; space for these instruments is created by pumping a small amount of carbon dioxide into the body to inflate the surgical area. These primary instruments are introduced through a hollow tube known as a trocar, which is also sealed at one end to keep the carbon dioxide from escaping the abdominal cavity. Bile is suctioned from the gallbladder, and the organ is removed through an incision in the navel. Appendectomies are performed in a similar manner.

Laparoscopic surgery is also used for gynecological procedures, the use for which the method was originally devised. Laparoscopy is used to correct intra-Fallopian tube pregnancies, thus preventing serious damage to the patient's reproductive system. It has also been used as a fertility treatment, whereby surgeons introduce both eggs and sperm into the Fallopian tubes. This procedure has largely been discontinued because of the successes with in vitro fertilization, which can be accomplished in a noninvasive fashion.

Laparoscopy is also used to remove parts of the kidneys and colon, though larger incisions are required for these procedures because of the larger size of the organs. This surgical method is also used to correct hernias and for bariatric procedures in obese patients.

Benefits and Risks Laparoscopic surgery has several benefits over more traditional surgical methods, including reduced bleeding, smaller incisions, less pain, and shorter hospital stays. Laparoscopic patients also do not require as much pain medication as traditional surgical patients, reducing the risk of other pulmonary problems associated with some narcotic usage; the reduced bleeding also reduces the possible need for a transfusion. Since small incisions are used, the patient's internal organs are not as exposed to outside contaminants, reducing the risk of infection. Many laparoscopic procedures can now be performed as outpatient surgeries, allowing patients with no complications to go home the same day of the procedure.

Like all surgery, laparoscopic surgery has risks associated with it. Previous scar tissue can prevent surgeons from performing a successful procedure. Some patients with previous pulmonary issues are not able to tolerate the carbon dioxide inflation of the abdominal cavity, forcing surgeons to transition from a laparoscopic procedure to a more traditional procedure. Damage to blood vessels is the most common risk in laparoscopic surgery.

Patient Recovery Patients who receive laparoscopic surgery are generally able to return home on the same day as the procedure. They can experience some pain, both from the actual incisions and manipulation of internal organs as well as from the carbon dioxide remaining in the abdominal cavity. Both sources of pain dissipate after a few days.

Patients may also experience difficulty walking and transitioning from a supine to upright position after the surgery. This also eases after a few days. Full recovery from the procedure can be expected within two to three weeks.

Impact Now a common surgical technique, laparoscopy has changed the field of surgery for both surgeons and patients. Surgeons are able to perform surgeries more quickly and with less risk. Patients experience less pain and recover faster; since laparoscopy is typically an outpatient surgery, this medical development has made many procedures routine and allowed patients to feel more comfortable when faced with the prospect of surgery.

Subsequent Events In 2007, surgeons at Drexel University used a newly developed form of laparoscopic surgery to remove a patient's gallbladder. This method used only one incision, rather than the multiple incisions typically needed. Referred to as single port access surgery, this method is accomplished through an incision in the naval with high-dexterity surgical implements, resulting in a lack of scarring on the torso. Studies indicate that this method may also result in less pain than more traditional laparoscopic surgeries and reduce recovery time even more.

Further Reading

Adler, Robert E. *Medical Firsts: From Hippocrates to the Human Genome.* Hoboken, N.J.: John Wiley & Sons, 2004. Offers a look at the genesis of laparoscopy in the gynecological field.

Kennedy, Michael. *A Brief History of Disease, Science, and Medicine: From the Ice Age to the Genome Project.* Cranston, R.I.: The Writers' Collective, 2004. Like Porter's history, Kennedy's book offers an overview of medical history but adds more detail to developing technologies.

Porter, Roy. *Blood and Guts: A Short History of Medicine.* New York: W. W. Norton, 2004. Porter's short history offers an overview of medical history, including a section devoted to evolving surgical technology that addresses laparoscopic surgery.

Ruggieri, Paul. *The Surgery Handbook.* Omaha, Nebr.: Addicus Books, 1999. Designed for patients approaching surgery, Ruggieri's book offers an overview of different types of surgery and the benefits and drawbacks of each procedure.

Singer, Sanford S. "Laparoscopy." In *Magill's Medical Guide.* 4th rev. ed. Pasadena, Calif.: Salem Press, 2008. A four-column introductory article on the procedure, noting is uses, complications, and a brief history.

Emily Carroll Shearer

See also Health care; LASIK surgery; Medicine; Science and technology.

■ Larry Sanders Show, The

Identification Television comedy series
Date Aired from 1992 to 1998

As a satirical look at network television, this series presented the medium in a way it had not been seen before.

Comedian Garry Shandling had already poked fun at the television business with his first series, *It's Garry Shandling's Show* (1986-1990). Still, the neurotic, self-obsessed character he created for that Showtime series was merely a warm-up for the hugely egotistical yet profoundly insecure antihero of HBO's *The Larry Sanders Show,* created by Shandling and Dennis Klein. Featuring Shandling as Larry Sanders, the Johnny Carson-like host of a late-night television talk show, the program shifted between Sanders's on-air interactions with guest stars, his backstage squabbling with writers and network executives, and his very messy personal life, including a wife (Megan Gallagher) who left him after the first season, a former wife (Kathryn Harrold) almost as neurotic as he, and several girlfriends.

Striving to hold both the show-within-the-show and his star together was producer Artie (Rip Torn), who tried to smooth talk his way through various dilemmas. Other regulars included Sanders's clueless sidekick, Hank Kingsley (Jeffrey Tambor), his

7/2010

unfazed assistant (Penny Johnson), the show's talent booker (Janeane Garofalo), the head writer (Wallace Langham), and Hank's sexy assistant (Linda Doucett).

The broadcast networks had offered comedies about television workplaces, such as *The Mary Tyler Moore Show* and *Murphy Brown*, but without the irreverent edge of *The Larry Sanders Show*. Guests such as Carol Burnett and Robin Williams adopted one persona while on the air and another when the camera was turned off, as the famous dropped their friendly facades. Sanders even had affairs with such guests as Sharon Stone, while Alec Baldwin discussed on the air his relationship with Larry's former wife and David Duchovny seemed to have a crush on the host. In an era filled with entertainment news programs, *The Larry Sanders Show* made fun of the carefully controlled images of celebrities by showing behavior that would horrify their publicists.

The program dealt not only with show business but also with such topics as homosexuality, racism, religion, and sexual peccadilloes. While broadcast network shows had been doing this since the 1970's, they usually treated these subjects didactically. Working under the assumption that 1990's audiences had a greater awareness of irony, *The Larry Sanders Show* simply saw issues as a source of provocative humor.

Impact While earlier HBO series *Dream On* (1990-1996) titillated with nudity and sexual situations, *The Larry Sanders Show* illustrated that the greater freedoms given premium cable programs could result in quality equaling or surpassing that of broadcast network shows. Despite modest ratings, it helped pave the way for such rules-breaking series as *Sex in the City*, *The Sopranos*, and, especially *Curb Your Enthusiasm*.

Further Reading

Friend, Tad. "Garry Shandling's Alter Ego Trip." *Esquire* 120, no. 1 (July, 1993): 35-40.

Shandling, Garry, and David Rensin. *Confessions of a Late Night Talk Show Host: The Autobiography of Larry Sanders as Told to Garry Shandling*. New York: Simon & Schuster, 1998.

Steinberg, Jacques. "Hey Now: It's Garry Shandling's Obsession." *The New York Times*, January 28, 2007, p. 1.

Michael Adams

See also Cable television; Comedians; Late night television; *Murphy Brown*; *Seinfeld*; *Sex and the City*; Television.

■ Las Vegas megaresorts

Definition Lavish, large casino resorts with spectacular side attractions

Place Clark County, Nevada

As approximately a dozen huge new complexes joined or replaced already-famous casino-hotels in the 1990's, the city's image was transformed, shedding the last vestiges of its reputation as a place of gangsters and Hollywood hipsters and becoming an international tourist destination and major convention locale. The resulting economic and population growth exceeded that of most other Sun Belt cities.

After a sixteen-year period in which no new hotel-casinos were built in Las Vegas, the city's tourist industry was in a slump in the late 1980's. New gambling venues had opened in Atlantic City, New Jersey, and were on the verge of opening on many Indian reservations. The downward trends were soon to be reversed in Las Vegas's future, however.

Early Megaresorts The reversal was both foreshadowed and partly inspired by casino financier Steve Wynn's trailblazing Mirage megaresort, which opened in November, 1989. It was expected to be a failure. Its cost ($700 million), its over 3,000 hotel rooms, and its "surround scenes" of tropical foliage, an erupting volcano, and a giant glass-enclosed tropical fish habitat behind the reservation desk all added up to a venture that would take one million dollars a day to operate. One year after its opening, the Mirage was showing a more than $200 million profit and inspired an unprecedented wave of further megaresort construction.

Next to open was the medieval castle-like Excalibur in June, 1990, a project of the publicity-shy Circus Circus owner William Bennett. Designed to pull in visitors with children as well as history buffs, Excalibur set the stage for a decade-long push of Las Vegas as a "Disney World-plus" vacation spot for families. Despite its mock jousting tournaments and pageantry, like other casinos the Excalibur never lost view of the adult traveler and gambler as its primary audience.

October of 1993 saw the advent of Treasure Is-

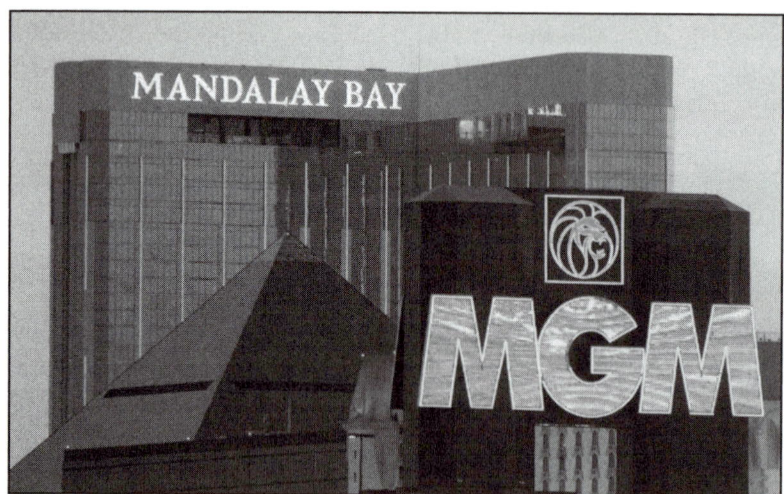

Mandalay Bay, the Luxor, and the marquee of MGM Grand in Las Vegas. (AP/ Wide World Photos)

land, built by Wynn as a destination for the middle-income tourist. Fronting the sidewalk was an elaborate enactment of a pirate battle staged nightly. The new MGM Grand opened on December 18 as the largest hotel in the world. Its chief entrepreneur was Wynn's rival Kirk Kerkorian. Following its predecessor casino's lead, it incorporated movie themes, with the golden MGM lion guarding the main entrance. The Luxor, built as an astonishing black glass pyramid with adjacent sphinx, was another 1993 addition. Its ancient Egyptian theme and high-intensity beacon made it immediately famous, even as its guiding financier, Bennett, remained out of the spotlight.

Later Megaresorts The next wave of megaresorts included the European-themed Monte Carlo (June, 1996), the Stratosphere (April, 1996), and New York-New York (January, 1997). The Stratosphere was an outlier, built at the relatively neglected north end of the Las Vegas Strip by flamboyant promoter Bob Stupak. Its landmark observation tower became the second-tallest freestanding structure west of the Mississippi.

Finally, in the late 1990's came projects that stirred the travel world's imagination once again. Paris Las Vegas opened in September, 1999, a project of Park Place Entertainment's mogul Arthur Goldberg, who backed it to invigorate his new diversified combine of properties. Nearby was the Venetian, a reincarnation of Renaissance Venice complete with canals and a doge's tower. Built by staunchly conservative billionaire Sheldon Adelson, it opened in May, 1999, before its completion, with many legal problems remaining from construction disputes. Despite the difficult beginning, its control of the former Sands convention space helped it to recover and thrive.

The decade's most spectacular new hotel-casino, the Bellagio, was Wynn's pet project of the 1990's. Designed as high-end property, it contained a world-class art collection and an artificial lake with a dancing water fountain synchronized to music and light. At the far south end of the Strip, another high-end megaresort, Mandalay Bay, opened in March, 1999. Adjacent to the Luxor, it also was visually striking, with a gleaming gold facade and, on the inside, a shark reef and Red Square attraction.

Altogether, the new megaresorts reinvigorated Las Vegas tourism, spurred the older casinos to add new spectacular attractions and space, and set a high standard for the resort city's building boom that continued into the next century. The men who envisioned and led their construction have become players in the national arenas of business and politics.

Impact Megaresorts redefined "the Las Vegas experience." Once a scene of elegantly dressed table games and intimate lounge entertainment, megaresorts became a setting characterized by people in ordinary clothes gambling at whirring banks of slot machines. Lavish spectacle shows replaced many of the more intimate lounge acts, although Vegas entertainment still featured well-known singers and celebrities. This latter-day mode—minus most of the show-business glitz—has become the standard model for many casinos that have since opened in other states. The financial success of contemporary Las Vegas casinos has led some of its entrepreneurs to bring their money and expertise to Macau, off the coast of China, which is aiming to become the "Las Vegas of Asia."

The public's fascination with Las Vegas life is as strong as ever. Vegas-set movies and television shows continue to be produced. One other possible long-term impact of the city's economic revival is on the labor movement. Las Vegas maintains a strong labor union presence, and most of the new megaresorts have large numbers of unionized employees, typically belonging to the Culinary Workers Union. The union was strengthened in Nevada by the megaresorts' growth.

Further Reading

Gottdiener, M., Claudia C. Collins, and David R. Dickens. *Las Vegas: The Social Production of an All-American City.* Malden, Mass.: Blackwell, 1999. A sociological study of the modern city, with attention to the role of the megaresorts and their financing.

Moehring, Eugene P. *Resort City in the Sunbelt: Las Vegas, 1930-2000.* Reno: University of Nevada Press, 2000. A scholarly history of the city's growth. The epilogue summarizes developments in the megaresort era.

Smith, John L. *Sharks in the Desert: The Founding Fathers and Current Kings of Las Vegas.* Fort Lee, N.J.: Barricade Books, 2005. Biographical sketches of the past and present hard-dealing men who built Las Vegas, by the foremost columnist for the city's largest newspaper.

Emily Alward

See also Architecture; Cirque du Soleil; Hobbies and recreation.

■ LASIK surgery

Definition Laser eye surgery that corrects nearsightedness, farsightedness, and astigmatism

During the 1990's, LASIK surgery allowed many people with myopia to throw away their eyeglasses or contact lenses after undergoing a quick and relatively easy surgical procedure.

Myopia (nearsightedness) is a common visual defect. In the 1950's, Colombian ophthalmologist José Ignacio Barraquer first suggested that myopia could be solved through surgery on the cornea known as keratomileusis (derived from the Greek *keratos,* "cornea," and *mileusis,* "carving"). Surgeons and researchers were skeptical, however, particularly about the safety of the surgery. In 1977, Richard Troutman introduced keratomileusis to the United States, but the procedure remained difficult to perform correctly and easily. In 1989, Lucio Buratto performed the procedure using the excimer laser. Since a laser does not generate heat, it can sculpt extremely thin layers of tissue. Buratto's innovation allowed the cut to be made with great precision, few complications, little surgical trauma to the eye, and little stress for the surgeon. Moreover, the surgery generally took less than thirty minutes. In 1995, the U.S. Food and Drug Administration (FDA) approved laser-assisted in situ keratomileusis (LASIK) surgery for nearsightedness. By the end of the decade, more complicated LASIK procedures had been approved for hyperopia (farsightedness) and astigmatism, but they were less commonly performed.

Myopic keratomileusis aims to flatten the central cornea by increasing the radius of curvature of the anterior cornea by removing a specific amount of stromal tissue within a specific optic zone. Keratomileusis became the first operation by which a piece of an organ was removed, modified, and replaced in its original position. A computer determined the degree of surgery necessary to compensate for the defect in the eye. The surgeon numbed the patient's eye with drops before placing a suction ring over the eye to secure it and maintain pressure. The patient stared at a beam of light to keep the eye still. Using a device called a microkeratome, the doctor cut a thin layer of the cornea—about 30 percent of its thickness—forming a flap and folding it back. The laser reshaped the flawed corneal tissue, then the flap was placed back over the eye and allowed to heal without stitches over the next six to eight weeks. About 98 percent of people who underwent LASIK surgery subsequently enjoyed 20/40 vision or better. The risk of a vision-threatening complication was less than 1 percent. In the 1990's, LASIK surgery was expensive, with the cost dropping from $4,000 to $2,000 per eye over the decade. Fees were not always covered by insurance. The high cost was due to extensive training and expensive equipment.

Impact Myopia affected about 75 million Americans by 2000. Many people reported that LASIK surgery had changed their lives by giving them the ability to see clearly without corrective lenses.

Further Reading

Buratto, Lucio, and Stephen F. Brint. *LASIK: Principles and Techniques.* Thorofare, N.J.: SLACK, 1998.

Gimbel, Howard V., and Ellen E. Anderson Penno. *LASIK Complications: Trends and Techniques.* 3d ed. Thorofare, N.J.: SLACK, 2004.

Caryn E. Neumann

See also Laparoscopic surgery; Medicine; Science and technology.

■ Late night television

Definition Talk and sketch shows that appeared on network and cable television after 11:30 P.M.

With the rise of cable television, increased syndication of late night shows, and the retirement of Johnny Carson, suddenly late night was a diverse field providing viewers more choices in late night programming.

On May 22, 1992, Johnny Carson aired his last *Tonight Show* after nearly thirty years of late night ratings dominance on the National Broadcasting Company (NBC). On May 25, Jay Leno replaced him as host of *The Tonight Show.* Leno's selection as host of the show was controversial, as many critics felt the show should have gone to David Letterman, the host of the show following Carson, *Late Night with David Letterman.* Instead, Letterman moved to the Columbia Broadcasting System (CBS) to have his own 11:30 P.M. show, which initially beat Leno in the ratings and continued to have strong ratings throughout the decade. Another initial problem with Leno's version of *The Tonight Show* was that his executive producer, Helen Kushnick, would get into booking wars with other shows: banning any talent from appearing on *The Tonight Show* if they appeared on another late night show. While this eventually led to her firing, the booking wars hurt Leno's reputation among other late night hosts, such as Arsenio Hall. When Letterman left NBC, the network replaced him with then-unknown comic Conan O'Brien, and while he struggled at first, his ratings stabilized by the end of the decade. Letterman also developed a 12:30 A.M. show for CBS to go up against O'Brien, first featuring Tom Snyder, with Craig Kilborn taking over in 1999.

Syndicated Late Night For many years, syndicated shows had tried to rival Johnny Carson, but all had failed. The first to have success against Carson was *The Arsenio Hall Show,* which premiered in 1989. Featuring the first African American late night host, the show appeared hipper than Carson's and appealed to a younger audience. In 1992, Hall scored a coup when presidential candidate Bill Clinton appeared on the show. An overwhelming response led to the trend of political candidates appearing on late night television. *The Arsenio Hall Show* did not maintain long-term success, however, and ended in 1994.

Still, the success of Hall's show encouraged other syndicated efforts, such as the short-lived *Dennis Miller Show* (1992), *The Jon Stewart Show* (1993-1995), *The Keenan Ivory Wayans Show* (1997-1998), *The Magic Hour* (1998-1999; Magic Johnson), and *Vibe* (1997; hosted by Sinbad). None of these syndicated shows had the success of Hall's show.

Cable Television With more households subscribing to cable television, a new outlet for late night television emerged. Many of these shows took on a political bent: from *The Chris Rock Show* (1997-2000) on Home Box Office (HBO), to Comedy Central's *The Daily Show* and *Politically Incorrect.* Comedy Central began airing *Politically Incorrect* in 1993, and the show, which mimicked the Sunday morning pundit

Talk-show host Johnny Carson, right, and the show's announcer, Ed McMahon, shake hands during their final episode of The Tonight Show *on May 22, 1992.* (AP/Wide World Photos)

shows, was an immediate hit. Moderated by comedian Bill Maher, and featuring a mix of celebrities, former celebrities, and political figures as panelists, the show was a new take on the political issues of the day. In 1996, Maher left Comedy Central and moved the show to the American Broadcasting Company (ABC) late night.

To replace *Politically Incorrect*, Comedy Central premiered *The Daily Show*, which initially was a spoof of news shows such as the local news and *20/20*. After original host Craig Kilborn left in 1998 to move to CBS late night, new host Jon Stewart began moving the show to the political coverage and satire for which it became known.

In addition to these cable late night shows, HBO produced a comedy about fictional late night talk show host Larry Sanders (played by Garry Shandling). *The Larry Sanders Show* (1992-1998) was a hit for the network throughout the decade.

Sketch Comedy Shows *Saturday Night Live* remained the leader in late night sketch comedy throughout the decade, although it did face competition beginning in 1995 with the premiere of the Fox Network's *MADtv*. Unlike other *Saturday Night Live* challengers over the years, *MADtv* remained on the air and somewhat successful. *Saturday Night Live* began the decade strong, with Mike Myers, Dana Carvey, and Phil Hartman leading the cast, but it hit a rough patch in 1995 due to an abrupt turnover in the cast; ratings returned by the end of the decade. During the decade, many films based on *Saturday Night Live* characters were produced, including *Wayne's World* (1992), *Wayne's World 2* (1993), *Coneheads* (1993), and *A Night at the Roxbury* (1998).

Impact With the increase in late night television programming, a new type of television show emerged. With a mixture of skits, interviews, and political commentary, shows such as *The Daily Show* and *Politically Incorrect* reenergized late night and helped usher in the increase of political content on all late night shows, a trend that began in 1992 with Bill Clinton's appearance on *The Arsenio Hall Show*.

Further Reading

Carter, Bill. *The Late Shift: Letterman, Leno, and the Network Battle for Late Night*. New York: Hyperion, 1994. Excellent overview of the transition from the Carson era to the battle between Jay Leno and David Letterman. Also provides some detail about syndicated efforts at late night, such as Arsenio Hall and Dennis Miller.

Jones, Jeffrey. *Entertaining Politics: New Political Television and Civic Culture*. New York: Rowman & Littlefield, 2005. Jones examines how late night shows such as *Politically Incorrect* and *The Daily Show* have had an impact on political conversation in the United States.

Shales, Tom, and James Andrew Miller. *Live from New York: An Uncensored History of "Saturday Night Live."* Boston, Mass.: Little, Brown, 2002. Interviews with nearly every living person involved with *Saturday Night Live* throughout its run, including major 1990's stars Dana Carvey and Mike Myers.

Spring, Greg. "Tricky Times for Late-Night Contenders." *Electronic Media* 16, no. 49 (December 1, 1997): 55-57. Article looks at a number of syndicated shows going up against Letterman and Carson and discusses their chances at long-term survival.

Julie Elliott

See also Cable television; Comedians; *Larry Sanders Show, The*; Rock, Chris; Television.

■ Latin America

Definition The Western Hemisphere nations located south of the United States

The end of the Cold War led to a new strategic focus by the United States in Latin America during the 1990's.

With the collapse of communism in the Soviet Union in 1991 and the consequent end of the Cold War, the United States became the sole world hegemonic power. Relations between the United States and Latin American countries were dominated by the rise of economic liberalization and the push for regional free trade agreements in the 1990's. Latin American countries felt that the United States should start focusing more on its neighbors, and U.S. foreign policy specialists started debating the role of the United States in the region. The shift in U.S. foreign policy toward Latin America was slow and somewhat irregular. While some countries experienced improved relations with the United States in the 1990's, others did not.

Economic, Military, and Political Relations The 1990's were seen as the age of economic liberalism. Trade between the United States and Latin American countries increased considerably during this time, and Latin American countries started trading at a higher rate among themselves as well. In 1991, Brazil, Argentina, Uruguay, and Paraguay established Mercado Común del Sur (MERCOSUR), also known as the Southern Common Market, a trade organization intended to increase economic cooperation among the member nations. The North American Free Trade Agreement (NAFTA) among the United States, Canada, and Mexico came into effect in 1994 and started the trend of multilateral agreements in Latin America.

In terms of military involvement, the United States had a limited role in Latin America during the 1990's. With the exception of the Haiti intervention in 1994, the United States did not intercede with force in any other Latin American country during the decade. However, the long-lasting "war on drugs" continued, with the United States supporting Latin American countries, especially Colombia and Bolivia, in their attempts to stop drug trafficking.

Politically, the relationship between the United States and Latin America was stable during the decade. One relevant exception was the strained relationship between the United States and Cuba. The long-lasting embargo on Cuba was codified into law in 1992 and expanded in 1996 with the Helms-Burton Act, which restricted U.S. citizens from doing business in Cuba and restricted all financial support to Cuba coming from U.S. citizens. In general, even when politics was involved, the relationship between the United States and Latin America was dominated by economic interests.

Impact U.S. foreign policy toward Latin America in the 1990's had an impact beyond the decade. The rise of economic liberalization, together with U.S. military relations with Latin American states, has helped shape the national and foreign policies of most Latin American countries. With the end of the Cold War, the need for regional collaboration seemed to push the United States toward Latin America, with the focus on economic collaboration instead of military intervention.

Further Reading

Brewer, Stewart. *Borders and Bridges: A History of U.S.-Latin American Relations.* Westport, Conn.: Praeger Security International, 2006. A good starting point to understanding of U.S.-Latin America relations before, during, and after the 1990's.

Chambers, Edward J., and Peter H. Smith, eds. *NAFTA in the Millennium.* La Jolla, Calif.: Center for U.S.-Mexican Studies, University of California, San Diego, 2002. Looks at the challenges NAFTA experienced in the 1990's and at the future of the institution. A great collection of works regarding many aspects of NAFTA.

Girard, Philippe R. *Clinton in Haiti: The 1994 U.S. Invasion of Haiti.* New York: Palgrave MacMillan, 2004. Focuses on the political career of Haitian president Jean-Bertrand Aristide and the foreign policy dynamics between Haiti and the United States.

Haney, Patrick J., and Walt Vanderbush. *The Cuban Embargo: The Domestic Politics of American Foreign Policy.* Pittsburgh: University of Pittsburgh Press, 2005. Outlines the history of the Cuban embargo and discusses more recent issues surrounding it.

Hartlyn, Jonathan, Lars Schoultz, and Augusto Varas, eds. *The United States and Latin America in the 1990's: Beyond the Cold War.* Chapel Hill: University of North Carolina Press, 1993. Outlines the changes in U.S.-Latin America relations after the Cold War.

Wiarda, Howard J. "Benign Neglect: American Foreign Policy in Latin America in the Post Cold War Era." In *The Crisis of American Foreign Policy.* Lanham, Md.: Rowman & Littlefield, 2006. Focuses on the shift in U.S. foreign policy after the Cold War, with an emphasis on the economic policy prescriptions of the Washington Consensus and their consequences.

Pedro dos Santos

See also Albright, Madeleine; Bush, George H. W.; Business and the economy in the United States; Christopher, Warren; Clinton, Bill; Conservatism in U.S. politics; Foreign policy of the United States; Haiti intervention; Illegal immigration; Immigration to the United States; Latinos; Liberalism in U.S. politics; Mexico and the United States; North American Free Trade Agreement (NAFTA).

■ Latinos

Identification Americans originating from Spanish-speaking countries

During the 1990's, the United States experienced an unprecedented increase in the Latino population, affecting the country's demographics, educational system, politics, and culture.

The term "Latino" is often used interchangeably with "Hispanic." Both terms are used to identify persons of Latin American and Caribbean heritage living within the United States. The term "Hispanic" is derived from the Iberian Peninsula, which contains Spain and Portugal, the two countries which colonized Latin America. Some people dislike this term, believing it ignores Latin American indigenous heritage. The term "Latino" refers instead to Latin America, including countries that largely share the Spanish language, the Catholic religion, and a colonialist past.

The countries of origin for Latinos in the United States include all of the Latin American and Caribbean countries. The majority of Latinos can trace their heritage to Mexico. At the end of the twentieth century, Americans of Mexican descent made up 66 percent of the Latino population, Central and South Americans as a group made up 14.5 percent, Puerto Ricans 9 percent, and Cubans 4 percent.

Immigration During the 1990's, the Latino population grew from an estimated 22.4 million in 1990 to 32.8 million in 2000. The influx of immigrants can be attributed to a number of factors. Beginning in the 1980's and continuing into the 1990's, Mexico experienced economic hard times. Their national currency, the peso, dropped to half of its previous value. The North American Free Trade Agreement (NAFTA), effective January 1, 1994, led to the failure of many family farms in Mexico and Central America, as they could not compete with tariff-free corn and grains grown by corporate farms in the United States. Factory work that was available in Mexico, producing goods for the U.S. market, was at a poor rate of pay and often entailed unhealthy living and working conditions. Similar jobs in the United States would pay a worker ten times the salary received in Mexico. Instead of lowering the number of Latin American immigrants entering the United States, as predicted by President Bill Clinton, NAFTA may have actually increased the number of Mexicans crossing the border.

Demographics At the end of the twentieth century, one in eight people in the United States were Latino. Latinos live in urban areas, with 91.5 percent living in metropolitan areas, compared with 77 percent of non-Hispanic whites. States with the largest Latino populations are California, Texas, Arizona, Nevada, and New Mexico. Depending on their country of origin, Latinos tend to reside in different areas of the country. Mexicans are likely to settle in the West and the South, Cubans in the South (Florida), and Puerto Ricans in the Northeast (New York City and New Jersey).

Latinos are more likely than their white non-Hispanic counterparts (by a two-to-one ratio) to be employed in service occupations and as operators and laborers. In 1990, median family income for a Latino family was $25,064, and as of 1999 it had risen to $31,663. Median family income for a white non-Hispanic family in 1999 was $54,121.

The Latino population in the United States is much younger than that of the white non-Hispanic population. Latino immigrants are likely to be young and of childbearing years, quite different from the baby-boomer age demographics of the white non-Hispanic population in the United States. As of 1999, only 14.5 percent of Latinos were age forty-five to sixty-four, as compared to 24 percent of white non-Hispanics. Latinos sixty-five years or older made up only 5.3 percent of the Latino community, compared with 14 percent of the non-Hispanic whites. Latinos fell largely into two younger age groups, twenty-five to forty-four-year-olds (29.5 percent) and those less than eighteen (35.7 percent).

This large number of childbearing-age Latinos, with a birthrate almost double that of the non-Latino population, resulted in a large second generation of school-age Latinos. This second generation differed from their parents in many ways: They were born with U.S. citizenship and mastered the English language at a much younger age than their parents. These two factors gave the second generation opportunities in education and employment that were not available to their parents.

Education Education became the key for improving the quality of life for recent immigrant populations. In the 1970's, 30 percent of Latinos graduated from high school, rising to 40 percent in the 1980's,

50 percent in 1990, and 57 percent by 1999. Despite this increase, Latinos still fell below the national graduation rate. This lower rate of graduation can be attributed to language barriers and cultural differences. Students arriving in the United States with minimal English language skills are often held back, thus lengthening the years required to graduate. Cultural norms for education in the United States are different from those of Mexico, where an eighth-grade education may be considered sufficient for joining the labor force. Many Latino students leave high school to join the workforce to contribute to the household income.

Schools throughout the United States struggled in the 1990's with how to best serve the growing Latino student population, particularly recent immigrant, Spanish-speaking students. Bilingual education versus English-only instruction was often at the center of this debate. In the bilingual classroom, students received instruction in either Spanish or English, depending on the language in which they were most proficient. If they were Spanish speakers, additional tutoring was provided for improving English language skills. This allowed students to maintain the learning pace of their peers. Many schools did not have a sufficient number of bilingual teachers to offer bilingual instruction. In spite of the fact that researchers consistently found that bilingual education was effective in teaching students with limited English proficiency, it was opposed by its critics, who deem that bilingual education hinders students' English-speaking skills and assimilation into American culture. More radical opponents believe that bilingual education weakens national identity and divides citizens along ethnic lines. English-only classrooms offered instruction solely in English, supplemented by English-language tutoring. This method typically resulted in Latino children being held back a grade level or performing at a lower level than their peers.

For those Latino students who did graduate from high school, additional obstacles existed for continuation into higher education. Many states required undocumented residents to pay out-of-state tuition, even if they had lived in the state for most of their lives and graduated from a state high school. Even for students born in the United States with full citizenship, it proved difficult to apply for and receive financial aid if their parents were undocumented residents. By 1999, only one in eleven Latinos had completed four years or more of college.

English-Only Movement According to the U.S. Census Bureau, the number of Latinos who spoke Spanish in their homes rose from 17.3 million in 1990 to 28.1 million in 2000, an increase of nearly 62 percent. About half of these Spanish speakers said that in addition to Spanish, they speak English "very well." Seven counties in Texas were cited as having more than 80 percent of the population speaking a language other than English, essentially making Spanish the common language for commerce, education, and municipal government.

Such statistics were regarded as a potential threat to some members of the English-speaking population. They perceived this trend as threatening to the American culture and lobbied to have laws passed that would declare English as a state's official language. In the early 1990's, eighteen states had such laws. On August 1, 1996, the House of Representatives passed a bill that made English the official language of government, creating much debate about what it means to be an American citizen and the importance of the English language in defining American culture.

Politics As the Latino population grew in the 1990's, so did their political power. In 1990, President George H. W. Bush appointed Antonia Coello Novello to serve as the surgeon general of the United States, the first women and the first Latino to serve in this office. In the same year, President Bush also appointed Jimmy Gurlu as an assistant attorney general of the United States. In 1992, President Bill Clinton appointed more Latinos to senior-level positions than any other president in history. Clinton appointees included Henry G. Cisneros as secretary of housing and urban development and Federico Peña as secretary of transportation. Clinton later appointed Peña to serve as the secretary of energy in his second term, beginning in 1997. After Peña's resignation in 1998, another Latino, Bill Richardson (later elected governor of New Mexico), was named secretary of energy.

Impact The growth of the Latino population was in direct proportion to the United States' dependence on cheap, undocumented labor. Halting the flow of immigrants from Mexico would result in higher prices for produce, meat, and goods sold in the United States. The cultural impact of Latinos was evident in the popularity of Latino entertainers, music, dance, and food. Latinos benefit both financially and socially from education and proficient English language skills.

Subsequent Events In 2003, the U.S. Census Bureau announced that Latinos had officially become the largest minority in the United States, exceeding the number of African Americans. It is estimated that by the year 2020, Latinos will made up 25 percent of the U.S. population.

Further Reading

Bean, Frank D., et al. *At the Crossroads: Mexico and U.S. Immigration Policy.* Lanham, Md.: Rowman & Littlefield, 1997. Examines the economic situation in Mexico, Mexican immigration, and U.S. immigration policy.

Diaz Soto, Lourdes, ed. *The Praeger Handbook of Latino Education in the U.S.* Westport, Conn.: Praeger, 2007. Issues of Latino education, arranged in alphabetical order by topic.

Gonzalez, Juan. *Harvest of Empire: A History of Latinos in America.* New York: Penguin Books, 2000. History of Latinos and Latino immigration in the United States.

Padilla, Amanda M., et al. "The English-Only Movement: Myths, Reality, and Implications for Psychology." *American Psychologist,* 46, no.2 (February, 1991): 120-130. Article contains the history of English-only advocacy in the United States and issues relating to the bilingual education debate. Also discusses the necessity of bilingual communication in providing health care to patients with limited English skills.

Therrien, Melissa, and Roberto R. Ramirez. "The Hispanic Population in the United States: Population Characteristics." U.S. Census Bureau. http:// www.census.gov/ prod/2001pubs/p20-535.pdf. Summary of demographic trends for Latinos in the United States during the 1990's.

Elizabeth Cramer

See also Alvarez, Julia; Demographics of the United States; Illegal immigration; Immigration Act of 1990; Immigration to the United States; Latin America; Mexico and the United States; North American Free Trade Agreement (NAFTA); Novello, Antonia Coello; Race relations; Selena; Sosa, Sammy; TV Martí.

■ Lee, Spike

Identification American film director, writer, producer, and actor
Born March 20, 1957; Atlanta, Georgia

In the 1990's, Lee was the most visible, vocal, and successful of a growing group of African American filmmakers. He became the first African American producer-director to achieve international fame, working within mainstream American cinema.

Born Shelton Lee, the feisty youngster was dubbed "Spike" by his family, who moved to Brooklyn when Lee was a child. New York City would later figure as the primary setting for most of his controversial and innovative films. After graduating from a traditionally black college, Lee received graduate film training at New York University's prestigious film school. His thesis project won a student academy award and was soon followed by a hugely successful feature, *She's Gotta Have It* (1986), made on a shoestring budget. The explosive *Do the Right Thing* (1989), written, produced,

Spike Lee in 1991. (AP/Wide World Photos)

directed, and starring Lee, was nominated for the Palme d'Or at the Cannes Film Festival and propelled him into instant celebrity status, a situation the young entrepreneur embraced with gusto.

During the 1990's, Lee's prodigious output included nine theatrical films—*Mo' Better Blues* (1990), *Jungle Fever* (1991), *Malcolm X* (1992), *Crooklyn* (1994), *Clockers* (1995), *Girl 6* (1996), *Get on the Bus* (1996), *He Got Game* (1998), and *Summer of Sam* (1999); several television specials; an important documentary, *Four Little Girls* (1997); numerous television and film appearances; and a series of television commercials for Nike, in which his on-screen presence made him instantly recognizable to millions. One of only four American directors selected to participate in the French project *Lumière et compagnie* (1995) commemorating the one hundredth anniversary of the film camera, Lee enjoyed a respect previously unknown to African American filmmakers.

Many of Lee's films explore contemporary race relations and tensions within African American communities with a bluntness rare in commercial American cinema. Lee's most ambitious, thoughtful, and mature work, *Malcolm X*, is a masterpiece of biographical film. In it, the director drew a deeply moving performance of the black leader from Denzel Washington, a frequent player in Lee's films. Often criticized for the limitations of female characters in his screenplays, Lee collaborated with Pulitzer Prize-winning playwright Suzan Lori-Parks in creating a narrative of a young woman's difficult search for success in *Girl 6*, with disappointing results. In *Get on the Bus*, Lee returned to his strengths, deftly dramatizing the political, personal, and class differences among a (fictional) group of African American men traveling to the (actual) Million Man March in Washington, D.C. Lee's film topics have expanded, while his stylistic verve, his talent for directing actors, his ear for lively dialogue, and his fierce attention to the inequities of urban life continue.

Impact Through his production company, Forty Acres and a Mule, Lee provided international audiences with compelling contemporary stories told from an African American perspective, provided professional opportunities for a generation of African American actors and technical crew, and opened the doors of Hollywood for other directors of color.

Further Reading

Aftab, Kaleem, and Spike Lee. *Spike Lee: That's My Story and I'm Sticking to It*. New York: W. W. Norton, 2005.

Blake, Richard Aloysius. *Street Smart: The New York of Lumet, Allen, Scorsese, and Lee*. Lexington: University Press of Kentucky, 2005.

Donalson, Melvin. *Black Directors in Hollywood*. Austin: University of Texas Press, 2003.

Carolyn Anderson

See also Academy Awards; African Americans; Basketball; Crown Heights riot; Film in the United States; Hip-hop and rap music; Independent films; King, Rodney; Los Angeles riots; Million Man March; Police brutality; Race relations; Washington, Denzel.

■ Left Behind books

Identification Best-selling Christian fiction series
Authors Tim LaHaye (1926-) and Jerry B. Jenkins (1949-)

These novels depict characters surviving from the Rapture until the Second Coming of Jesus Christ. The blend of conservative Christian content and action-adventure plots made these books widely popular, though controversial.

Tim LaHaye and Jerry B. Jenkins began a literary industry when they published *Left Behind: A Novel of the Earth's Last Days* in 1995. *Tribulation Force: The Continuing Drama of Those Left Behind* followed in 1996, then *Nicolae: The Rise of Antichrist* in 1997, *Soul Harvest: The World Takes Sides* in 1998, and *Apollyon: The Destroyer Is Unleashed* and *Assassins: Assignment—Jerusalem, Target—Antichrist*, both in 1999.

Published by Tyndale House, the series grew to include sixteen adult novels (including three prequels) and sold more than fifty million copies; seven novels reached number one on *The New York Times* best-seller list. In addition, a series for children sold ten million copies. Related items included audiobooks, movies, graphic novels, study guides, and even clothes and collectibles. This success was a first for books with content that is staunchly Christian and conservative.

Specifically, the novels espouse dispensational premillennialism, an interpretation of the Bible—namely 1 Thessalonians 4 and the book of Revelation—developed by John Nelson Darby in the 1800's. After the Rapture, in which good Christians are taken into Heaven, those remaining on Earth, those "left behind," suffer ordeal after ordeal and the coming of the Antichrist until Jesus Christ returns to Earth and time ends. LaHaye and Jenkins take the biblical prophecies literally, including menaces such as stinging insects with human faces. The novels follow several characters with whom the reader is encouraged to identify.

Jenkins, who did the writing based on LaHaye's notes, has written over 150 books, both fiction and nonfiction, and has worked for the Moody Bible Institute, at which LaHaye also worked. LaHaye encouraged televangelist Jerry Falwell to found the Moral Majority and sat on its board of directors; he also founded various Christian conservative activist and lobbying groups himself.

Although the series appealed mostly to Christians, many did not agree with all the doctrines in the books. Some have criticized the books as being anti-Catholic. Others have criticized the depictions of violence, guns, and car chases, and the implied message that solving the world's problems is unnecessary—or, as in the case of the Antichrist promising world peace, actually bad.

Impact Perhaps fueled by the approach of the millennium, the popularity of the novels brought attention to Christian publishers, whose books often sold very well but did not generally get covered by best-seller lists. The series also gave a concrete depiction of Darbyist end times events, as believed by a significant and vocal American minority. While many critics simply dismissed the books, others examined them as religious statements, for their cultural significance and as signs of popular tastes in literature.

Further Reading

Forbes, Bruce David, and Jeanne Halgren Kilde, eds. *Rapture, Revelation, and the End Times: Exploring the Left Behind Series.* New York: Palgrave Macmillan, 2004. A collection of essays, academic but generally readable.

Shuck, Glenn W. *Marks of the Beast: The Left Behind Novels and the Struggle for Evangelical Identity.* New York: New York University Press, 2004. Thorough, especially about the theological context.

Bernadette Lynn Bosky

See also Falwell, Jerry; Grisham, John; King, Stephen; Publishing; Religion and spirituality in the United States.

■ Lewinsky scandal

The Event U.S. president Bill Clinton's sexual dalliance with White House intern Monica Lewinsky leads to his impeachment trial
Date 1995-1999

Only one president before Clinton, Andrew Johnson, was impeached. In both cases, the Congress that demanded impeachment failed to obtain the conviction that would have resulted in removal from office.

During his presidency, Bill Clinton was dogged by allegations of scandal related to his private life and legendary womanizing. At the beginning of his second term of office in January, 1997, independent counsel Kenneth Starr was involved in investigating potentially damaging charges, launched in 1994, that Clinton and his wife, Hillary, had enriched themselves substantially before they came to Washington through their involvement in the Whitewater affair,

Former White House intern Monica Lewinsky. (AP/Wide World Photos)

"I Misled People"

On August 17, 1998, President Bill Clinton testified before a grand jury regarding his relationship with former White House intern Monica Lewinsky. That evening, he delivered a televised address to the nation in which he admitted that he and Lewinsky had a relationship and explained why he was reluctant to acknowledge it:

Indeed, I did have a relationship with Miss Lewinsky that was not appropriate. In fact, it was wrong. It constituted a critical lapse in judgment and a personal failure on my part for which I am solely and completely responsible. . . .

I know that my public comments and my silence about this matter gave a false impression. I misled people, including even my wife. I deeply regret that.

I can only tell you I was motivated by many factors. First, by a desire to protect myself from the embarrassment of my own conduct.

I was also very concerned about protecting my family. The fact that these questions were being asked in a politically inspired lawsuit, which has since been dismissed, was a consideration, too.

In addition, I had real and serious concerns about an independent counsel investigation that began with private business dealings twenty years ago, dealings I might add about which an independent federal agency found no evidence of any wrongdoing by me or my wife over two years ago.

The independent counsel investigation moved on to my staff and friends, then into my private life. And now the investigation itself is under investigation.

This has gone on too long, cost too much and hurt too many innocent people.

Now, this matter is between me, the two people I love most—my wife and our daughter—and our God. I must put it right, and I am prepared to do whatever it takes to do so.

a real estate deal that smacked of unethical if not illegal machinations.

Lewinsky's Internship and Affair Monica Lewinsky became a White House intern in July, 1995. In that position, she would normally have had, at best, minimal direct contact with the president. Lewinsky, however, lost no opportunity to ingratiate herself with Bill Clinton. On November 15, 1995, their relationship became sexual and was carried on in the Oval Office and in a pantry adjoining it. Realizing the potential hazards of such an affair, Clinton, on April 5, 1996, had Lewinsky transferred to the Pentagon. Their sexual contact, however, continued sporadically until March 29, 1997, when Clinton ended it decisively.

Lewinsky once harbored the delusion that Clinton would eventually leave his wife and marry her. When it became obvious that this would not happen, she felt badly wronged. She knew few people in Washington but had developed a friendship with one of her coworkers, Linda Tripp, whose hatred of Clinton was undisguised. Tripp referred to him as "the creep," a term Lewinsky ultimately adopted in referring to the president.

As Lewinsky increasingly felt herself being pushed out of Clinton's life, Tripp became her closest confidant. They had long telephone conversations in which Lewinsky spoke frankly of the affair she had been carrying on with the president. Tripp, delighted at being able to do anything she could to discredit Clinton, recorded all of Lewinsky's telephone conversations.

The Paula Jones Affair In the midst of Bill Clinton's clandestine affair with Lewinsky, a woman by the name of Paula Jones emerged from Clinton's Arkansas past and filed a suit against the president for sexual harassment. Clinton, needing to deal with this accusation, employed Robert Bennett as his counsel and made every effort to forestall this suit until he left office, arguing that defending himself would distract him from dealing with pressing affairs of state that confronted him as president.

In January, 1996, the U.S. Court of Appeals refused to allow the president to delay answering the charges against him, so in 1997, *Jones v. Clinton* came before the U.S. Supreme Court. The president did not testify in person but, in deference to the demands upon him, was permitted to respond in writing to a series of questions submitted by Kenneth Starr's office.

Incontrovertible Evidence The Paula Jones diversion loomed over Clinton as the Lewinsky scandal began to unfold. When asked whether he had engaged in sex with Lewinsky, Clinton denied, eventually under oath, that such a relationship ever existed. Finally, however, Starr, with Tripp's help, was able to substantiate the existence of the sexual relationship that Clinton had repeatedly denied. He tracked down eleven people in whom Lewinsky had confided that such an affair had occurred.

Tripp made available to the prosecutors recordings of her telephone conversations with Lewinsky. She also revealed that Lewinsky had in her possession a blue dress with spots on it. The prosecution obtained this dress, had DNA tests run on the stains, and determined categorically that these stains were semen that was identified unquestionably as the president's.

Impeachment Starr reported his findings to Congress on September 9, 1998. The Judiciary Committee of the House of Representatives, after refusing a Democratic request that the president merely be censured, issued four articles of impeachment, of which two, perjury and obstruction of justice, were approved by the House.

Clinton's impeachment trial began on January 7, 1999, and ended on February 12. Neither of the articles brought against Clinton received the requisite majority vote that would have paved the way for his removal from office, although the charge of obstruction of justice received a split 50-50 Senate vote.

Impact One cannot underestimate the impact of the Monica Lewinsky scandal on American politics. Although President Clinton was not convicted of the charges lodged against him and removed from office, the scandal was largely responsible for the Republican victories in the following presidential and congressional elections.

Al Gore, in no way involved in the scandals, suffered from the fallout they occasioned. The impeachment and the subsequent hearings were a decisive factor in George W. Bush's winning the 2000 presidential election against Gore. The Religious Right and other conservative voting blocs reaped considerable political capital from the Lewinsky scandal.

Further Reading

Busby, Robert. *Defending the American Presidency: Clinton and the Lewinsky Scandal.* New York: Palgrave, 2001. A thorough assessment of the Lewinsky scandal, with detailed information about the impeachment and subsequent trial.

Clinton, Bill. *My Life.* New York: Alfred A. Knopf, 2004. Clinton reflects with considerable objectivity on the Lewinsky affair and its effects on his presidency.

Good, Howard, ed. *Desperately Seeking Ethics: A Guide to Media Conduct.* Lanham, Md.: Scarecrow Press, 2003. In chapter 2, "Reporters or Peeping Toms? Journalism Ethics and News Coverage in the Clinton-Lewinsky Scandal," Tanni Haas analyzes the morality of how the press covered the Clinton-Lewinsky scandal and the overall moral effects of such coverage. In chapter 8, "A New Class of Heroes: Fallout from the Clinton-Lewinsky Scandal," Clinton Collins considers the effects of the scandal on public morality.

Sternberg, Robert J. *Why Smart People Can Be So Stupid.* New Haven, Conn.: Yale University Press, 2002. Chapter 6 focuses clearly and concisely on Clinton's dalliance with Monica Lewinsky and its aftermath, including Clinton's trial and impeachment.

R. Baird Shuman

See also Clinton, Bill; Clinton, Hillary Rodham; Clinton's impeachment; Clinton's scandals; Elections in the United States, midterm; Elections in the United States, 1996; Scandals; Starr Report; Troopergate; Whitewater investigation.

■ Liberalism in U.S. politics

Definition A political ideology that tends to support progress, civil rights and liberties, reform, social justice, and using the power of the federal government to improve the general welfare of the nation

During the 1990's, liberalism experienced both successes and defeats in elections, public opinion, and public policy.

In 1990, Republican president George H. W. Bush asked a Democratic-controlled Congress to authorize the use of military force against Iraq after that country, led by President Saddam Hussein, began a full-scale invasion of Kuwait on August 2, 1990. Antiwar interest groups and most liberal Democrats in Congress opposed Bush's request, but enough Democrats joined Republicans in Congress to pass the Gulf War resolution in 1991.

With the rapid increase in the size of the federal budget deficit during the 1980's and early 1990's, competing proposals from both major parties dominated discussions of domestic spending. Liberals failed to substantially increase or create new programs to address poverty, urban decay, child care, and health care for uninsured Americans. While public opinion in the United States increasingly expressed support for more liberal policies on public education and environmental protection—that is, greater federal spending and regulations—it also expressed more conservative positions on such issues as deficit reduction, tax cuts, abortion rights, and the death penalty. Liberals hoped that the end of the Cold War meant significantly lower defense spending, decreased use of military power in foreign policy, and a greater emphasis on foreign policy focusing on human rights, the AIDS epidemic, and environmental protection. Nonetheless, it was mostly liberal Democrats in Congress who pressured Bill Clinton's administration to use military intervention for humanitarian reasons in Haiti, Somalia, and Kosovo.

Liberalism and Two-Party Politics Believing that American voters unfavorably associated liberalism with high taxes, excessive welfare spending, and weakness on crime and national defense, President Clinton did not publicly identify himself as a liberal. Instead, he ran for the 1992 Democratic presidential nomination and in the general election as a self-proclaimed centrist New Democrat who promised deficit reduction, a middle-class tax cut, tougher crime control, and an end to "welfare as we know it." With most voters dividing their support between Bush and independent presidential candidate H. Ross Perot, Clinton was elected president with 43 percent of the popular vote. Democrats lost seats but retained control of Congress in the 1992 elections.

In 1993, House Republicans led by representative Newt Gingrich of Georgia, conservative interest groups like the National Rifle Association (NRA) and the American Medical Association (AMA), the Religious Right, and conservative media commentators portrayed Clinton and the Democratic Congress as insincere, big government liberals who were increasing taxes and regulations and threatening traditional moral values. In particular, these conservative critics opposed Clinton's policy efforts on gun control, national health insurance, and gays in the military.

Meanwhile, some liberals, especially those from the environmental protection and labor movements, opposed Clinton's support for the North American Free Trade Agreement (NAFTA). They feared that NAFTA would be detrimental to global environmental protection and unionized blue-collar jobs in the United States. Likewise, some African American liberals were dismayed by Clinton's greater emphasis on crime control and prison expansion than on antipoverty programs.

These political conditions contributed to the Republicans winning control of Congress in the 1994 midterm elections. The Republican victory, however, enabled Clinton to distance himself from liberal Democrats and behave as a moderate power broker between liberals and conservatives in Congress on such issues as budget negotiations, deficit reduction, antiterrorist legislation, and welfare reform. Clinton's moderate, compromising leadership style became known as "triangulation" and was the major theme of his reelection campaign strategy in 1996. Polls indicated that most Americans agreed with Clinton's moderate leadership and his portrayal of Republicans, especially Speaker of the House Newt Gingrich, as unreasonable, right-wing ideologues. Clinton easily defeated Republican presidential nominee Bob Dole in the 1996 presidential election.

While many Americans credited Clinton with overseeing a prosperous economy and steadily reducing the budget deficit, some liberals in Congress and among interest groups like the Children's Defense Fund and Greenpeace were disappointed that Clinton had not attempted or accomplished more policy progress on poverty, environmental protection, and urban decay. Nevertheless, liberals staunchly supported Clinton when Republicans impeached, tried, but failed to convict Clinton in 1998-1999 on legal issues stemming from his sexual affair with White House intern Monica Lewinsky. Polls and voting behavior in the 1998 midterm elections indicated that there was a clear, growing division of cultural and moral values among Americans that was highlighted by the issues of impeachment and adultery. These value differences between pro-impeachment and anti-impeachment Americans became a major influence on voting behavior in the 2000 presidential election.

Impact Liberalism in U.S. politics during the 1990's was most successful in promoting stronger environmental protection compared to the 1980's; racial, ethnic, and gender diversity in Clinton's executive and judicial appointments; and the retention of noncash medical and nutritional benefits in the Personal Responsibility and Work Opportunity Reconciliation Act of 1996. Nonetheless, the Republicans controlled Congress during most of the 1990's after they negatively associated the early Clinton administration with liberalism. Liberals failed to achieve national health insurance and to reject or revise NAFTA and other free trade agreements in order to pressure U.S. trading partners to improve their environmental, labor, and human rights policies. In the 2000 presidential campaign, some liberals supported the Democratic presidential candidacy of Bill Bradley and later the Green Party presidential candidacy of Ralph Nader as alternatives to Vice President Al Gore's Democratic candidacy.

Further Reading

Drew, Elizabeth. *Showdown: The Struggle Between the Gingrich Congress and the Clinton White House.* New York: Simon & Schuster, 1996. An analysis of the conflicts and compromises between Clinton and the Republican Congress, especially on welfare reform and budget negotiations.

Germond, Jack W., and Jules Witcover. *Mad as Hell: Revolt at the Ballot Box, 1992.* New York: Warner Books, 1993. A detailed account of the events, candidates, and issues of the 1992 presidential election.

Woodward, Bob. *The Choice.* New York: Simon & Schuster, 1996. A study of the events, issues, and policies during Clinton's first term as president, including his relationship with liberals.

Sean J. Savage

See also Abortion; Albright, Madeleine; Bush, George H. W.; Clinton, Bill; Clinton's impeachment; Conservatism in U.S. politics; Crime; Don't ask, don't tell; Elections in the United States, midterm; Elections in the United States, 1992; Elections in the United States, 1996; Foreign policy of the United States; Gingrich, Newt; Ginsburg, Ruth Bader; Gore, Al; Gulf War; Gun control; Haiti intervention; Health care reform; North American Free Trade Agreement (NAFTA); Kosovo conflict; Lewinsky scandal; Reno, Janet; Republican Revolution; Somalia conflict; Welfare reform.

■ Life coaching

Definition A philosophy emphasizing unconditional support that aims to motivate individuals to achieve their life goals and life satisfaction

Life coaching began in the early 1990's as a way of helping individuals maximize their life satisfaction and potential.

Life coaching began as a movement to help chief executive officers (CEOs), top executives, and athletes achieve their professional goals. In the 1990's, the coaching principles were expanded to everyday individuals seeking advice on how to become more successful in life. Life coaching seeks to use individuals' strengths to help them achieve what they want in life. It draws heavily from schools of psychology, executive coaching, career development, sports, and behavior modification. Life coaches help their clients define and achieve their goals in the areas of career, interpersonal relationships, fiscal management, and internal motivation.

The practice of life coaching has been criticized as the application of psychotherapy without adequate therapeutic training. There is no official regulatory body for life coaching; one does not have to have any specific educational training to use the title of "life coach." In the late 1990's, the International Coach Federation (ICF) and International Association of Coaching (IAC) were established and started training programs for life coaches. Life coaches state that what they do is similar to psychotherapy, but with important differences: They do not treat mental illness, they are present-oriented rather than past-oriented, and their interventions are not aimed at "fixing" individuals or their problems. They see their approach as a supportive partnership with their clients and liken their interventions to preparing an athlete for the intensive race ahead through a process of inquiry, personal discovery, and acceptance of personal responsibility. Life coaching can be done in person or over the phone. Sessions typically last from thirty to sixty minutes and typically start at $100 per hour.

Impact In the late 1990's, life coaching was recognized as its own unique popular discipline. Books, magazines, and television shows began to discuss and explore the impact of life coaching as a pop cultural phenomenon. The discipline, its scope of topical areas, and the number of individuals it reached continued to grow in the early twenty-first century.

Further Reading

Ellis, David B. *Life Coaching: A New Career for Helping Professionals.* Rapid City, S.Dak.: Breakthrough Enterprises, 1998.

Hudson, Frederic M. *The Handbook of Coaching: A Comprehensive Resource Guide for Managers, Executives, Consultants, and Human Resource Professionals.* New York: Jossey-Bass, 1999.

Miedaner, Talane. *Coach Yourself to Success: 101 Tips from a Personal Coach for Reaching Your Goals at Work and in Life.* Chicago: Contemporary Books, 2000.

Richardson, Cheryl. *Take Time for Your Life: A Personal Coach's Seven-Step Program for Creating the Life You Want.* New York: Broadway Books, 1998.

Katherine M. Helm

See also Feng shui; Psychology.

■ Limbaugh, Rush

Identification Conservative radio talk-show host
Born January 12, 1951; Cape Girardeau, Missouri

The voice of conservatism in the 1990's, Limbaugh changed the course of talk radio for the foreseeable future.

Rush Limbaugh began taking courses at Southeast Missouri State University in 1969. After one year, he left college to pursue a career in radio. During the 1970's, Limbaugh worked as a disc jockey at several Top 40 radio stations in Pennsylvania and Kansas City, Missouri. In 1979, he took a position as promoter of the Kansas City Royals baseball team and

House Speaker Newt Gingrich, right, gestures as conservative radio talk-show host Rush Limbaugh speaks on a phone during a taping break on NBC's Meet the Press *in November, 1995. Limbaugh helped transform talk radio into one of the most politically influential forms of mass media.* (AP/Wide World Photos)

dropped out of the radio business. In 1984, Limbaugh returned to radio as a talk-show host at KFBK, an AM station in Sacramento, California.

After just over three years in Sacramento, Limbaugh began searching for a way to break into the national market. With help from friend and colleague Bruce Marr, Limbaugh began broadcasting nationally from New York on WABC on August 1, 1988. Limbaugh's audience size in 1988 was approximately 250,000 listeners, and his show was carried on fifty-six stations. Limbaugh's format was unlike any other on talk radio at the time. He did not have guests or do interviews. Rather, he addressed what he deemed relevant social and political issues as they occurred. He was told that such a format would not work, but it made him the voice of the political conservative movement by the early 1990's.

In 1992, Limbaugh began airing his "Morning Update," a ninety-second blurb on AM radio during morning rush hour. In 1993, he was inducted into the Radio Hall of Fame. By the end of the 1990's, Limbaugh's audience had grown from 250,000 per week to approximately twenty million, and the number of stations that carried him had grown to nearly six hundred.

From 1992 through 1996, Limbaugh had a syndicated half-hour television show, which he used as another vehicle to provide commentary on contemporary politics and society. He also authored two books in the 1990's, *The Way Things Ought to Be* (1992) and *See, I Told You So* (1993), both of which reached number one on *The New York Times* best-seller list.

Impact Rush Limbaugh was credited with helping the Republicans win control of Congress in 1994. By the end of the 1990's, Limbaugh's show was the most popular talk radio show in America.

Further Reading

Barker, David C. *Rushed to Judgment: Talk Radio, Persuasion, and American Political Behavior.* New York: Columbia University Press, 2002.

Limbaugh, Rush. *See, I Told You So.* New York: Pocket Books, 1993.

_______. *The Way Things Ought to Be.* New York: Pocket Books, 1992.

AWR Hawkins III

See also Abortion; Christian Coalition; Conservatism in U.S. politics; Elections in the United States, midterm; Elections in the United States, 1992; Elections in the United States, 1996; O'Reilly, Bill; Republican Revolution; Right-wing conspiracy; Talk radio; Television.

■ Line Item Veto Act of 1996

Identification Federal law authorizing the president to exercise a limited line-item veto

Date Signed into law April 9, 1996; declared unconstitutional June 25, 1998

Congress, unable to control its own spending, permitted the president to cancel specific items within appropriations and tax bills after signing the bill into law.

A line-item veto permits the executive to veto parts of a bill without vetoing the entire bill. In the 1980's, with the annual deficit and national debt rising, President Ronald Reagan proposed that the president be given the authority to discourage wasteful spending and reduce the national debt. Although Reagan's efforts were unsuccessful, the executive was subsequently given this power, however briefly, by the Line Item Veto Act of 1996. The act, which went into effect on January 1, 1997, authorized the president to "cancel" individual spending and tax benefit provisions contained in a bill within five days after signing the bill into law.

On January 2, 1997, two representatives and four senators filed a lawsuit asserting that the law unconstitutionally strengthened the presidency. Although the federal district court declared the law unconstitutional, the U.S. Supreme Court, in *Raines v. Byrd*, dismissed the lawsuit, holding that the litigants did not have standing. Shortly thereafter, President Bill Clinton canceled one provision in the Balanced Budget Act of 1997 and two provisions of the Taxpayer Relief Act of 1997. These provisions, if not canceled, would have benefited two public hospitals in New York City and a potato farmers' cooperative in Idaho. These parties filed suit in federal district court, which declared the statute unconstitutional. The Supreme Court granted expedited review.

In *Clinton v. City of New York*, decided on June 25, 1998, the justices held that the cancellation provisions set forth in the Line Item Veto Act of 1996 violated the presentment clause of Article I, section 7, clause 2 of the Constitution. Writing for six members of the Court, Justice John Paul Stevens noted that there were important differences between the presi-

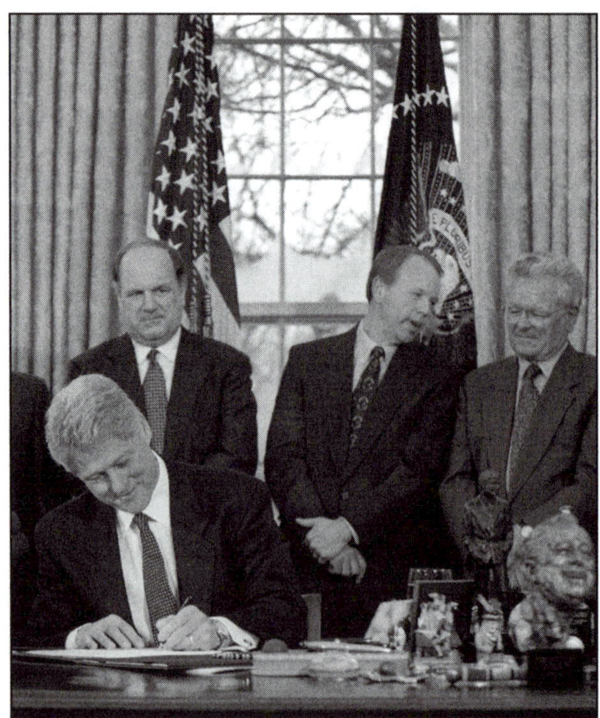

President Bill Clinton signs the Line Item Veto Act at the White House on April 9, 1996. (AP/Wide World Photos)

dent's "return" of a bill pursuant to Article I, section 7 and the president's cancellation authority pursuant to the Line Item Veto Act—most notably that the Constitution expressly authorized the president to play a role in the process of enacting statutes, but was silent on the subject of unilateral presidential action that either appealed or amended parts of duly enacted statutes. Although the Congress was willing to grant such sweeping powers to the president, the Court found it unconstitutional.

Impact The impact of the Line Item Veto Act was negligible. The act was struck down less than eighteen months after it went into effect. Prior to that, the line-item veto was employed eleven times to strike eighty-two provisions from the federal budget. Since *Clinton v. City of New York,* Congress has considered, but never proposed, a constitutional amendment that would grant line-item veto power to the president.

Further Reading

Dewar, Helen, and Joan Biskupic. "Line-Item Veto Struck Down; Backers Push for Alternative." *The Washington Post,* June 26, 1998, p. A01.

Worcester, Courtney. "An Abdication of Responsibility and a Violation of a Finely Wrought Procedure: The Supreme Court Vetoes the Line Item Veto Act of 1996." *Boston University Law Review* 78 (December, 1998): 1583-1608.

Richard A. Glenn

See also Balanced Budget Act of 1997; Clinton, Bill; National debt; Supreme Court decisions.

■ Literature in Canada

Definition Drama, prose, and poetry by Canadian authors

During the 1990's, most of the writers who had helped to establish Canada as an important literary center continued to publish outstanding works. Moreover, new writers appeared on the scene, bringing new ideas and subjects into an already rich literary culture.

Inevitably, the decade saw the departure of some writers who had played important roles in Canada's literary renaissance. Robertson Davies (1913-1995) was a journalist, critic, playwright, and novelist who had won international renown for his two trilogies. His novels *Murther and Walking Spirits* (1991) and *The Cunning Man* (1994) were the first two volumes in a projected trilogy dealing with modern Canada. Another literary leader who passed away during the 1990's was Anne Szumigalski (1922-1999), an award-winning poet and the founder of the influential Saskatchewan Writers Guild.

Many established writers produced award-winning works of fiction during the decade. Mordecai Richler (1931-2001) again found in Montreal ample subjects for satire. His novel *Barney's Version* (1997) was awarded the Giller Prize. *The English Patient* (1992), by Michael Ondaatje, won the Trillium Award, shared the Booker Prize, and was made into a film that in 1997 won nine Academy Awards, including Best Picture. Timothy Findley (1930-2002), whose experience as actor and playwright is evident in his highly dramatic novels, published four works during the 1990's. Two of them, *The Piano Man's Daughter* (1995) and *Pilgrim* (1999), which was Findley's most complex work, were finalists for the Giller Prize.

Several well-known writers ventured into new areas. After three decades as a master of the short story, Alistair MacLeod tried his hand at long fiction.

His first novel, *No Great Mischief* (1999), which like his short stories focuses on Cape Breton and the Gaelic heritage, won critical acclaim and the Trillium Award. Like MacLeod, Rudy Wiebe was known for his association with a particular place, the Canadian West, and the people who live there. Like many of his earlier works, his eighth novel, *A Discovery of Strangers* (1994), shows how English explorers were unwilling to understand the peoples they encountered. Another book that Wiebe published during the decade, however, was very different from anything he had written previously. Wiebe became interested in Yvonne Johnson, a descendant of the famous Cree chief Big Bear who had written Wiebe from prison. The result was a coauthored work, *Stolen Life: The Journey of a Cree Woman* (1998). It was a finalist for the 1998 Governor General's Award for Nonfiction.

Female Writers and the Issue of Identity Canada's female writers, too, were often extremely versatile. Anne Hébert (1916-2000) published *L'Enfant chargé de songes* (1992; *Burden of Dreams*, 1994), which won the Governor General's Award for French-Language Fiction, and three years later brought out an impressive volume of poetry. Another of Canada's most famous writers, Margaret Atwood, won a Trillium Award for a collection of short stories, *Wilderness Tips* (1991), shared a Trillium Award for her psychological novel *The Robber Bride* (1993), and two years later again shared a Trillium Award, this time for a poetry collection titled *Morning in the Burned House* (1995). Atwood's *Alias Grace* (1996), which won the Giller Prize, is a historical novel based on an 1843 murder case. Though the plotline is about the title character's guilt or innocence, the theme of the novel is the question of identity.

In works by Canada's male writers, the identity issue most often involves responding to an ethnic heritage or seeking one's place in a diverse and ever-changing society. For female writers, the issue of identity is even more complex. After centuries of being confined to rigid roles, many women were attempting to find out who they really were. It is hardly surprising that Canada's female writers made the search for personal identity one of their major themes.

There is no shortage of examples. Wendy Lill's play *Sisters* (pb. 1991) focuses on the denial of personal identity to the women assigned to teach in residential native schools. Similarly, Sandra Birdsell's fiction shows how women were deprived of a sense of self in an isolated, rural society. Her novel *The Chrome Suite* (1992) is about a young woman's venture into the past in an attempt to understand the person she has become. Most of the women in the short fiction of Alice Munro and in the novels of Carol Shields (1935-2003) also search for their identities. Both writers attained international recognition early in the decade. Munro's *Friend of My Youth* (1990) won a Trillium Award, and Shields's novel *The Stone Diaries* (1993) won the Governor General's Award and the Pulitzer Prize.

Variety and Diversity During the 1990's, all Canadian writers looked at broad psychological issues. Shields's *Larry's Party* (1997) points out how the outward appearance of a forty-seven-year old man belies the richness of his inner life. *The Selected Stories of Mavis Gallant* (1996) emphasizes the feelings of alienation that make Gallant's characters so unhappy. In her third novel, *Away* (1993), which brought her a shared Trillium Award, Jane Urquhart showed how the O'Malleys' Irish heritage haunts them in their Canadian home. In Urquhart's *The Underpainter* (1997), which won the Governor General's Award for English-Language Fiction, an elderly artist realizes that by repeatedly choosing art instead of real life, he has become alienated from humanity and even from his art.

A number of new writers gained prominence during the 1990's. Bonnie Burnard won the Giller Prize for her family saga *A Good House* (1999); Yann Martel wrote a novel called *Self* (1996), the story of an unexpected gender change; and Diane Schoemperlen produced a woodcut-illustrated short-story collection, *Forms of Devotion* (1998), which won the Governor General's Award for English-Language Fiction. Other new writers explored their own cultural identities, among them the dramatist Djanet Sears, whose play *Harlem Duet* (pb. 1997) won a Governor General's Award in 1998; the Caribbean poet Marlene Nourbese Philip; the Japanese Canadian authors Joy Kogawa and Kerri Sakamoto; the Chinese Canadian writer Wayson Choy, who shared a Trillium Award for his novel *The Jade Peony* (1995); and M. G. Vassanji, an Indian from East Africa, who won the Giller Prize for *The Book of Secrets* (1994). Another fiction writer, Rohinton Mistry, established an international reputation by re-creating the world he had known in his native Mumbai. His novel *Such a Long Journey* (1991) won the Governor General's Award for English-Language Fiction and the Trillium Award. *A Fine Balance* (1995) won numerous awards, including the Giller Prize. Both books were short-listed for the Booker Prize. *A Fine Balance* was the first Canadian work to be chosen by the popular talk-show host Oprah Winfrey for her book club.

Impact The 1990's were characterized by consolidation of the cultural gains that had been made during the previous decades, by an increasing acceptance of experimental forms, and by expansion of the subject matter of Canadian literature. Though female writers continued to recall past oppression and to emphasize the need for a sense of personal identity, they were now moving on to other subjects, including specific social problems, such as poverty, or philosophical issues, including the need to define the national spirit. During the decade, talented new writers from every province and from other parts of the world were appearing on the literary scene. At the end of the decade, it was evident that the reputation of Canada as the home of great literature would continue into the twenty-first century.

Further Reading

Gilbert, Paula Ruth, and Roseanne L. Dufault, eds. *Doing Gender: Franco-Canadian Women Writers of the 1990's.* Madison, N.J.: Fairleigh Dickinson University Press, 2001. A useful volume about an important group of writers. Bibliography and index.

Kruk, Laurie. *The Voice Is the Story: Conversations with Canadian Writers of Short Fiction.* Oakville, Ont.: Mosaic Press, 2003. Revealing discussions with ten writers, all with achievements in several genres. Biographical notes. Indexed.

Pearlman, Mickey, ed. *Canadian Women Writing Fiction.* Jackson: University Press of Mississippi, 1993. Ten essays by American and Canadian scholars, pointing out their use of such themes as family, place, memory, and identity. Includes an excellent introduction by the editor.

Schaub, Danielle, ed. *Reading Writers Reading: Canadian Authors' Reflections.* Edmonton: University of Alberta Press, 2006. Comments about books and reading by twenty-three writers, along with Schaub's photographic portraits.

Toye, William, ed. *The Concise Oxford Companion to Canadian Literature.* 2d ed. Don Mills, Ont.: Oxford University Press, 1997. Updates earlier reference works with entries on new writers and recent publications.

Williamson, Janice, ed. *Sounding Differences: Conversations with Seventeen Canadian Women Writers.* Toronto: University of Toronto Press, 1993. Each interviewee comments on her craft, on gender issues, and on her impact on social change. Includes a biographical note on each writer and an excerpt from her work.

Rosemary M. Canfield Reisman

See also Audiobooks; Book clubs; Canada and the United States; Literature in the United States; Minorities in Canada; Mistry, Rohinton; Ondaatje, Michael; Poetry; Publishing; Theater in Canada.

■ Literature in the United States

Definition Drama, prose, and poetry by American authors

In this first fully electronic decade of American history and culture, the 1990's revealed a new sense of energy and growth in several areas of literature.

Literature in the last decade of the nineteenth century was accused of decadence, escapism, and/or extreme aestheticism, reflecting, critics argued, the world-weariness that came with the end of those tumultuous hundred years. The literature of the 1890's came to be known as the "yellow decade" in England (through writers like Oscar Wilde and Bram Stoker), the "decadent decade" in France (in Arthur Rimbaud and Paul Verlaine), and the "mauve decade" in the United States (a term coined by Thomas Beer in a 1926 study of the culture surrounding writers like Henry James, Stephen Crane, and Ambrose Bierce). The 1990's, by contrast, was a period of renewed energy and production in American literature. New literary movements flourished, writers explored different genres and forms, and whatever end-of-the-century despair that appeared was soon lost in a rush of new voices.

Some of this energy can be attributed to changes in the literary marketplace. The 1990's were the first electronic decade in American culture, the first full decade when readers could go online to read books (on Project Gutenberg, for example) and order them (from Amazon.com), find out about literary matters, and even talk to authors. Audiobooks became more popular, for travel and as a substitute for reading. At the same time, large chains (notably Borders and Barnes & Noble) could do mass marketing of books that smaller bookstores could not afford. Finally, book clubs proliferated during the period, both nationally (Oprah Winfrey's book club sold hundreds of thousands of copies of recommended books) and locally. Publishers began to insert readers' "book club guides" at the end of books they hoped might become book club choices.

Long Fiction The decade began with the completion of a work begun years before: John Updike published the last volume in his Rabbit quartet, opened with *Rabbit, Run* in 1960, with *Rabbit at Rest,* which won both the Pulitzer Prize and the National Book Critics Circle Award for 1990. Other writers who had dominated the previous decades of the twentieth century were also active: Philip Roth won the National Book Award in 1995 with *Sabbath's Theater,* and the Pulitzer for *American Pastoral* in 1997. The prolific Joyce Carol Oates produced *Because It Is Bitter and Because It Is My Heart* in 1990, and followed with another two dozen volumes of fiction, drama, and poetry, including the novels *Foxfire: Confessions of a Girl Gang* (1993), *What I Lived For* (1994), *We Were the Mulvaneys* (1996), and *Broke Heart Blues* (1999). T. C. Boyle published six volumes in the decade, including *The Road to Wellville* (1993) and *The Tortilla Curtain* (1995). Barbara Kingsolver (*Animal Dreams,* 1990, *Pigs in Heaven,* 1993, and *The Poisonwood Bible,* 1998), Carol Shields (*The Stone Diaries,* 1993, which won both the Pulitzer Prize and the National Book Critics Circle Award in 1994), Mark Helprin (*A Soldier of the Great War,* 1991), Larry McMurtry (*Comanche Moon,* 1997), and other established writers continued their fictional efforts through the decade.

At the same time, newer writers were emerging, both traditional fictionists and those who were expanding literary boundaries. Jane Smiley emerged to national prominence with *A Thousand Acres,* a novel set on a farm in Iowa but built around Shakespeare's *King Lear* (pr. c. 1605-1606), and won the National Book Critics Circle Award and the Pulitzer Prize in 1991. Annie Proulx followed two years later with the best-selling *The Shipping News,* which took both the Pulitzer and the National Book Award for 1993. Richard Ford won the Pulitzer for *Independence Day* (1995), a sequel to *The Sportswriter* (1986). Charles Frazier won the National Book Award for *Cold Mountain* (1997), a novel about the Civil War that became a runaway best seller, and Michael Cunningham won the Pulitzer for *The Hours* (1998), a novel based on Virginia Woolf's *Mrs. Dalloway* (1925).

While traditional novelists continued to dominate the decade, writers who more often used the nonlinear and fragmentary tools of postmodernism continued to grow in popularity. Cormac McCarthy won the National Book Award and the National Book Critics Circle Award with *All the Pretty Horses* in 1992, a novel set in Mexico in the middle of the twentieth century and the first volume in what would become known as The Border Trilogy, with the publication of *The Crossing* in 1994 and *Cities of the Plain* in 1998, novels that sometimes lose traditional story lines in linguistic labyrinths. McCarthy became a major American writer during the decade and began to attract not only faithful readers but also scholarly interest. Don DeLillo had already established himself as a major postmodernist with his novel *White Noise* in 1985, and he confirmed that rank with *Mao II* (1991), a novel mixing themes of terrorism and writing that won the PEN/Faulkner Award, and *Underworld* (1997), a novel that covers baseball, nuclear threat, and much more in a dazzling fusion of history and fiction. Jonathan Lethem gained national prominence, and a National Book Critics Circle Award, with *Motherless Brooklyn* in 1999, and he became one of a group of younger writers (such as William Vollman and Michael Chabon) bending traditional genres—here, for example, using detective fiction (as he had used science fiction in earlier novels) in a mainstream work. Finally, Art Spiegelman broke all bounds with his *Maus* (volume 2, 1991), a graphic novel that pours family history and the Holocaust into a comic book format with cats, mice, and other animals as characters. The book was given a Pulitzer Prize Special Award.

Short Fiction The 1990's can also be noted as the decade when the short story was infused with new life. Raymond Carver died in 1988, but his popularity continued to grow during the 1990's, inspiring numerous other practitioners of short fiction with his minimalist, realist style. The decade saw the publication of important collections of stories from Robert Olen Butler (*A Good Scent from a Strange Mountain,* 1992, which won the Pulitzer Prize in 1993), John Updike (*The Afterlife, and Other Stories,* 1994), Grace

Paley (*The Collected Stories*, 1994), Rick Bass (*In the Loyal Mountains*, 1995), Andre Dubus (*Dancing After Hours*, 1996), Gina Berriault (*Women in Their Beds*, which won the National Book Critics Circle Award in 1996), Andrea Barrett (*Ship Fever, and Other Stories*, which took the National Book Award in 1996), Ann Beattie (*Park City*, 1998), and Alice Munro (*The Love of a Good Woman*, which won the National Book Critics Circle Award in 1998). Annie Proulx published *Close Range: Wyoming Stories* in 1999, a collection that included the story "Brokeback Mountain," which was made into a film in 2005. *The New York Times* at the end of 1999 included twenty-nine short-story collections in a list of 130 "Notable Books" of the previous year. The emergence of short, short fiction (also called sudden fiction, or stories of 500-1000 words) also increased the popularity of the form. The genre that after World War II (with the death of *The Saturday Evening Post, Collier's, Scribner's Monthly*, and other popular magazines that had showcased short fiction through its heyday of the 1920's through the 1940's) was dying was suddenly given new life.

The Multicultural 1990's The 1990's consolidated the movements toward inclusion and diversity in American letters that had been building during preceding decades. Both popular and academic books reflected a new awareness of the importance of issues of gender, race, age, and social class, and the very tone of the discussion of American literature was changing. To read but one barometer, *The Heath Anthology of American Literature* appeared in 1990 and quickly became one of the most popular college textbooks in the field. Its second (1994) and third (1998) editions only confirmed its importance in demonstrating the diversity and breadth of American literature, which earlier anthologies had defined much more narrowly. In the second volume (covering 1865-present) of that third edition, for example, earlier women writers (Anzia Yezierska, Tillie Olsen) were rediscovered, there was a new section on "The New Negro Renaissance" of 1920-1940, there were samples of the poetry carved in the walls of Angel Island detention center in San Francisco Bay by Chinese immigrants, and there were contemporary examples of writing from every major ethnic group in the United States. *The Heath Anthology* only clarified what was already taking place in the literary marketplace and in bookstores nationwide, and other textbook publishers soon followed Heath's lead.

Whatever question there was of the importance of women's writing in American culture was certainly settled by the 1990's. Best sellers by Oates, Proulx, Smiley, Shields, Alice McDermott (*Charming Billy* won the National Book Award in 1998), and others had long been commonplace. To cite just *The New York Times* best-seller lists from the 1990's, women dominated in every genre of literature, from celebrity memoirs (Madonna, Dolly Parton), through romances and historical fiction (Jean M. Auel, Judith Krantz, Mary Higgins Clark—even Alexandra Ripley writing a sequel to Margaret Mitchell's 1936 *Gone with the Wind*), thrillers (Anne Rice), mysteries (Sue Grafton, Sara Paretsky), humor (Erma Bombeck), political commentary (Molly Ivins), feminist theory (Deborah Tannen, Susan Sontag, Susan Faludi), and photography (Annie Leibovitz). Gender had become an accepted category of literary discussion by the 1990's, and there appeared collections of women's writing, even women's humor (such as *The Penguin Book of Women's Humor*, 1992), as well as numerous anthologies of writings by gay and lesbian writers. The more narrowly defined American literature of a half century earlier, which had assumed male heterosexual hegemony, had been broadened in all directions.

Ethnic American Literature The 1990's also confirmed the power and possibility of ethnic American literature. The emergence of modern ethnic literature accompanied the fight for identity of various groups in the second half of the twentieth century. While there had certainly been ethnic American writers earlier, theirs had often been isolated, exceptional contributions. When the movements for ethnic recognition began in the second half of the twentieth century—first the Civil Rights movement for black Americans in the 1950's, and then the American Indian Movement in the 1960's—they were accompanied by, or helped to create, new waves of ethnic literature.

By the 1990's, the essential place of ethnic writing in American culture was clearly established. The Cuban American writer Oscar Hijuelos took the Pulitzer Prize in fiction with *The Mambo Kings Play Songs of Love* (1989) in 1990, the African American novelist Charles Johnson won the National Book Award the same year for *Middle Passage*, and Ernest Gaines followed with the National Book Critics Circle Award for *A Lesson Before Dying* in 1993. Asian American writers played a major part in the cultural climate of the 1990's. Amy Tan had emerged as a major force with *The Joy Luck Club* in 1989—still on the best-seller lists in 1990—and she followed with *The Kitchen God's Wife* in 1991 and *The Hundred Secret Senses* in 1995. Another Chinese American writer, Ha Jin, ended the decade by winning the National Book Award for *Waiting* in 1999, while Jhumpa Lahiri took the Pulitzer Prize in 2000 for her stories collected in *Interpreter of Maladies* (1999). Between Tan and Lahiri, Asian American writers were everywhere: Chinese American writers Gish Jen, Gus Lee, David Wong Louie, Sandra Tsing Loh, and Fae Myenne Ng, among others, established themselves in fiction, and other Asian groups represented in the decade included Filipino American Jessica Hagedorn (*Dogeaters*, 1990), Japanese American Cynthia Kadohata (*In the Heart of the Valley of Love*, 1992), Indian American Bharati Mukherjee (*The Holder of the World*, short stories, 1993), and Korean American Chang-Rae Lee (*Native Speaker*, 1995).

Native American writers likewise emerged as a force in the decade. Louise Erdrich had already gained a critical reputation in the 1980's with novels like *Love Medicine* (1984), but she consolidated her place in the 1990's with *The Bingo Palace* (1994), *Tales of Burning Love* (1996), and *The Antelope Wife* (1998). With her husband, Michael Dorris, she also published *The Crown of Columbus* (1991). Dorris collected his short stories a few years later in *Working Men* (1993). Other Native American writers included Gerald Vizenor (*The Heirs of Columbus*, 1991), Sherman Alexie, whose collection of short stories, *The Lone Ranger and Tonto Fight in Heaven*, immediately gained critical attention in 1993, and Leslie Marmon Silko, who published *Gardens in the Dunes* in 1999.

African American writers were similarly busy during the 1990's. Toni Morrison followed her award-winning *Beloved* (1987) with *Jazz* in 1992, in the same year published *Playing in the Dark: Whiteness in the Literary Imagination*, and followed in 1998 with the novel *Paradise*. Terry McMillan produced best sellers in *Waiting to Exhale* (1992) and *How Stella Got Her Groove Back* (1996). Likewise, Walter Mosley established himself in the 1990's not only as one of the premier writers of mystery fiction (in *Devil in a Blue Dress*, for example, in 1990) but also as a writer who could deal with issues of race and urban poverty (*Always Outnumbered, Always Outgunned*, 1997, and *Walkin' the Dog*, 1999). Jamaica Kincaid (born in Antigua) published *Lucy* in 1990 and *The Autobiography of My Mother* in 1996. Edwidge Danticat (born in Haiti) published a collection of short stories, *Krik? Krak!* in 1995 and the novel *The Farming of the Bones* in 1998.

Latino fiction was likewise active. Sandra Cisneros followed her critically acclaimed *The House on Mango Street* (1984) with *Woman Hollering Creek* (1991), while Dagoberto Gilb published *The Magic of Blood* in 1993. Helena Maria Viramontes succeeded her 1985 collection of short stories, *The Moths*, with *Under the Feet of Jesus* (1995), a young adult novel concerning the plight of migrant workers in California's Central Valley. Isabel Allende published the popular *Daughter of Fortune* in 1999. Dominican American Junot Díaz was one of a number of Caribbean writers to appear in the decade, with the short-story collection *Drown* (1996). Dominican American Julia Alvarez published the popular *How the García Girls Lost Their Accents* in 1991, Oscar Hijuelos followed up his 1990 Pulitzer with *The Fourteen Sisters of Emilio Montez O'Brien* (1993) and *Mr. Ives' Christmas* (1995), and Christine Bell (also Cuban American) published the novel *The Perez Family* in 1990.

Middle Eastern writers who published in the decade included Jordanian writers Joseph Geha (*Through and Through*, short stories, 1990) and Diana Abu-Jaber (*Arabian Jazz*, 1993), and Meena Alexander (*Fault Lines*, 1993) and Chitra Banerjee Divakaruni (*The Mistress of Spices*, 1997, and *Sister of My Heart*, 1999), both from India. The emergence of new ethnic literature actually spurred recognition of older traditions that had been taken for granted. There was renewed interest in Irish American writers (T. C. Boyle, Maureen Howard, William Kennedy, Mary Gordon, Alice McDermott), Italian American authors (Gay Talese, Mario Puzo, John Fante), and Jewish American writers (Saul Bellow, Cynthia Ozick, Norman Mailer).

Globalism and Regionalism The increasing diversity in American literature could be felt in other ways as well. While American readers were discovering the breadth and depth of the American ethnic mix, they were at the same time expanding their horizons in the recognition of writers from around the globe. Writers in English had always been popular, and this included in the 1990's British writers like A. S. Byatt

(*Possession*, 1990) and J. K. Rowling (the Harry Potter series, 1997-2007), and also meant Canadian writers like Margaret Atwood (*Alias Grace*, 1996) and Alice Munro, Indian writers like Arundhati Roy (*The God of Small Things*, 1997) and Rohinton Mistry (*A Fine Balance*, 1995), and South African writers like J. M. Coetzee (*Disgrace*, 1999). The 1990's saw best sellers in the United States by world writers like Umberto Eco, whose *Il pendolo di Foucault* (1988; *Foucault's Pendulum*, 1989) was still a best seller in 1990, Gabriel García Márquez (*El general en su laberinto*, 1989; *The General in His Labyrinth*, 1990), and Laura Esquivel (*Como agua para chocolate*, 1989; *Like Water for Chocolate*, 1992).

At the same time that the literary marketplace was welcoming world writers, American writers were celebrating their regional roots. In the tumultuous pressures of the 1990's, in other words, readers were becoming both more "macro" and more "micro" in their literary tastes, expanding their reading interests worldwide, yet homing in on familiar, local geography. Of writers already cited, Jane Smiley and Louise Erdrich celebrate their Midwestern roots, Larry McMurtry and Cormac McCarthy focus on Texas and the West, Barbara Kingsolver on Arizona, Rick Bass on Montana, Charles Frazier on North Carolina, and Don DeLillo on New York City. Such geographical identifications are almost endless. Garrison Keillor mines Minnesota in his stories of Lake Wobegon, William Kennedy upstate New York, Rick Moody (*The Ice Storm*, 1994) Rhode Island, John Edgar Wideman (*Two Cities*, 1998) Pittsburgh and Philadelphia, Jim Harrison (*The Road Home*, 1998) Nebraska, Kent Haruf (*Plainsong*, 1999) the American prairie, and David Guterson (*Snow Falling on Cedars*, 1994) and Annie Dillard (*The Living*, 1992) the Northwest. There have always been writers drawing stories from their rich southern heritage, and in the 1990's they included Lee Smith (*The Devil's Dream*, 1992), Dorothy Allison (*Bastard Out of Carolina*, 1992), and Wendell Berry with stories and novels of his native Kentucky.

Nonfiction: The Creative Memoir Possibly the most noticeable literary movement in the 1990's occurred not in fiction, but in nonfiction, with the emergence of the creative memoir as a distinct and popular form. Memoirs and autobiographies have been popular for centuries, but in the 1990's the creative memoir began to emerge as a distinct genre and to compete with fiction in its storytelling power. Fiction and nonfiction had crossed lines before in the 1960's and 1970's with the New Journalism, a form of news reporting that borrowed fictional techniques (such as point of view and stream of consciousness) to present a more intimate portrait of a subject. In the 1990's, this was clearly occurring in the memoirs that began to dominate nonfiction best-seller lists. Frank McCourt's *Angela's Ashes* (1996), his gripping story of growing up in Cork, Ireland, and emigrating to America, was on the *New York Times* best-seller list for over a year. Mary Karr's *The Liars' Club* (1995) and Rick Bragg's *All Over but the Shoutin'* (1997) had attributes similar to McCourt's volume: an almost incredible amount of detail about childhood hardship, and a compelling, novelistic plot. (A few years later, this line between fiction and nonfiction would explode when James Frey's 2003 memoir, *A Million Little Pieces*, chosen for Oprah Winfrey's book club, was exposed to be significantly fictionalized.) Memoirs appeared in the 1990's from all ranks: from political figures (Jimmy Carter in 1997) to actors and entertainers (Katherine Hepburn in 1992, Howard Stern in 1993).

Ethnic autobiographies also proliferated in the decade, in part because the memoir gives the ethnic writer the perfect literary form to write about such themes as assimilation and cultural conflict, dual identity, and generation gaps. Judith Ortiz Cofer published *Silent Dancing: A Partial Remembrance of a Puerto Rican Childhood* (1990); Elmaz Abinader *Children of the Roojme: A Family's Journey from Lebanon* (1990), Victor Villaseñor *Rain of Gold* (1991), and Mary Crow Dog *Lakota Woman* (1990). Richard Rodriguez published *Days of Obligation: An Argument with My Mexican Father* in 1992, and Luís J. Rodriguez his chronicle of L.A. gang life in *Always Running* (1993); Henry Louis Gates, Jr., published *Colored People* (1994), and Bell Hooks *Bone Black* (1997); Gustavo Pérez Firmat published *Next Year in Cuba* in 1995, and Chinese American Shirley Geok-lin Lim *Among the White Moon Faces* in 1996. A new interest in people's lives is evident in the 1990's, as well as a fresh desire to tell the story of becoming American. These impulses resulted in a large number of creative memoirs.

Impact Changes in the literary marketplace—the ways in which books were distributed, read, and reviewed—helped to stimulate literary discussion and dissemination in the 1990's. Like the poetry and drama of the decade, a new energy infused the fiction and nonfiction of the 1990's and spilled over into the opening years of the twenty-first century, in literature that was more open, inclusive, and alive.

Further Reading

Heilbrun, Carolyn G. "Contemporary Memoirs: Or, Who Cares Who Did What to Whom?" *The American Scholar* 68, no. 3 (Summer, 1999): 35-42. Discussion of the development of recent women's memoirs as a unique genre.

Lauter, Paul, et al., eds. *The Heath Anthology of American Literature: Volume E—Contemporary Period, 1945 to the Present.* 5th ed. Lexington, Mass.: Heath, 2005. Still the best sampling of the diverse range of contemporary American literature.

Millard, Kenneth. *Contemporary American Fiction: An Introduction to American Fiction Since 1970.* New York: Oxford University Press, 2000. Fresh analysis and interpretation of more than thirty texts, including recent works by Roth, Updike, Jen, and Alexie.

Muller, Gilbert H. *New Strangers in Paradise: The Immigrant Experience and Contemporary American Fiction.* Lexington: University Press of Kentucky, 1999. Hijuelos, Kincaid, Tan, and Mukherjee are among the many ethnic writers Muller discusses against the historical and sociological forces shaping recent American life.

Prosser, Jay, ed. *American Fiction of the 1990's.* New York: Routledge, 2008. Collection of essays on individual writers and geographical, ethnic, technological, and sexual topics by a range of academic writers.

Rowe, John Carlos, ed. *Post-nationalist American Studies.* Berkeley: University of California Press, 2000. Nine contributors propose new approaches to the study of multiethnic American culture.

Schlager, Neil, and Josh Lauer, eds. *Contemporary Novelists.* Detroit: St. James Press, 2001. Massive project profiles hundreds of contemporary novelists, including many Americans.

David Peck

See also Albee, Edward; Alvarez, Julia; Amazon .com; Angelou, Maya; *Angels in America*; Audiobooks; Barry, Dave; Book clubs; Censorship; Chick lit; Children's literature; Faludi, Susan; Grafton, Sue; Grisham, John; Harry Potter books; Kelley, Kitty; King, Stephen; Kingsolver, Barbara; Komunyakaa, Yusef; Literature in Canada; McCourt, Frank; McMillan, Terry; McNally, Terrence; Morrison, Toni; Palahniuk, Chuck; Poetry; Project Gutenberg; Proulx, Annie; Rice, Anne; Rock Bottom Remainders, The; Roth, Philip; Sontag, Susan; Spoken word movement; Strand, Mark; Theater in the United States; Updike, John; *Vagina Monologues, The*; Wallace, David Foster.

■ Lollapalooza

The Event Touring music festival
Date 1991-1997

Unlike previous rock festivals, Lollapalooza represented a 1990's sensibility that music festivals should be accessible to audiences in a variety of locations. The eclectic tour also helped define the word "alternative" in relation to a lifestyle and not just a music genre.

At the time of the first Lollapalooza tour in 1991, American rock festivals had been around for decades. In the post-MTV 1990's, fans were more discriminating and desired another outlet besides the aging music-video format to keep them in touch with the music that defined the last generation to come of age in the twentieth century.

Lollapalooza was the creation of Perry Farrell, singer for the alternative rock band Jane's Addiction and Porno for Pyros. Although often thought of as a rock festival, Lollapalooza included a range of acts, including the hip-hop group Arrested Development, the rap-metal band Rage Against the Machine, and rap artist Ice-T's metal band, Body Count.

The precursor to Lollapalooza was A Gathering of the Tribes, a two-day music festival in California. That event paved the way for the event that Lollapalooza eventually became, with a broad range of styles offered by the performers—from Queen Latifah to Iggy Pop. Like Lollapalooza, it demonstrated itself to be a reflection of a number of American subcultures. As a result, the final form of Lollapalooza was that of a traveling show, one that would draw in hundreds of thousands of music fans from across the United States and Canada.

The Music While the musical acts featured at Lollapalooza represented a range of styles, what they all had in common was an edginess that made them relevant to audiences who were growing increasingly dissatisfied with the standard Top 40 music that dominated the industry. As a result, rappers and rock artists alike found Lollapalooza to be a venue in which they could perform to the largest number of receptive fans.

The festival was not only for established acts to connect or reconnect with a youthful contingent but also for new bands, giving them the opportunity to build a fan base. Most notably, Rage Against the Machine, which had been heard in few places outside of the West Coast prior to Lollapalooza 1992, gained a much higher profile after the tour. The band earned a great deal of radio play as result of festivalgoers from around the United States responding positively to the music.

In terms of genres, although hip-hop and techno acts were definitely a part of Lollapalooza, the festival itself was characterized and earned a reputation as a grunge, alternative rock show. Each year from 1991 to 1997, grunge acts figured prominently, although in 1991 and 1992 hip-hop acts from Ice-T and Body Count to Cypress Hill to Arrested Development and others were major draws to the festival. The tone of Lollapalooza in the 1990's was set by bands such as Red Hot Chili Peppers, Tool, Stone Temple Pilots, Violent Femmes, and Jane's Addiction.

One of the successes of Lollapalooza was that listeners of nonstandard pop music finally found a music event that related to them. It not only encapsulated what they listened to but also reflected how they lived and what they believed in, especially with regard to the environmental issues. By the 1990's, MTV had begun to limit alternative music to a late Sunday night show called *120 Minutes*; music fans who had grown up watching the network might have felt disappointed by its inability or unwillingness to continue showing cutting-edge music in prime time. Without the vehicle for edginess upon which they had relied for years, the generation who had grown up on MTV turned to a live music festival to be their avenue of musical expression.

Other Attractions and Discontent Because Lollapalooza was a lifestyle festival, there was more than just music present at the touring shows. Nonmusical acts also helped Lollapalooza differentiate itself from other festivals. Lollapalooza festivals included virtual reality games, a circus sideshow, tattoo and piercing booths, folk vendors who sold everyday items made of hemp, information kiosks where concertgoers could learn about environmental and political concerns, and, perhaps most telling and symbolic of all, a television-smashing area.

Eddie Vedder of Pearl Jam performs at Lollapalooza 1992. (Hulton Archive/Getty Images)

Before the Internet, concertgoers had to physically purchase tickets from Ticketmaster outlets, sometimes spending multiple days in front of outlets while waiting for Lollapalooza tickets to go on sale. When ticket and concession prices rose, so did fans' impatience. After the first couple of tours, reports of violence and mayhem began to be reported from the festival. It is unclear what the cause of the unrest was—a mix of displeasure at the prices or simply an outpouring of unrest that was present in the target demographic for the festival. The festival's run in the 1990's ended in 1997, with a mix of new and formerly famous bands performing on two stages (a feature present since 1992), including: Devo, Snoop Doggy Dogg, Porno for Pyros, Julian and Damian Marley, and Beck.

Impact Lollapalooza marked the first time an American music festival was run as a concert tour. With roughly a dozen acts representing the most cutting-edge performers of the time, Lollapalooza arguably picked up where MTV stopped.

Further Reading

Kendall, Gavin. "Pop Music: Authenticity, Creativity and Technology." *Social Alternatives* 18 (April, 1999): 25-28. Explores the relationship between a time period's existing technologies and the resulting pop music creativity.

Van Zandt, Steven. "Garage Rock." *Billboard* 119 (June, 2007): 24. Details the methods by which the music industry and musicians support programs that benefit the environment.

White, Timothy. *Music to My Ears: The Billboard Essays, Profiles of Popular Music in the '90's.* New York: Henry Holt, 1996. Provides detailed reviews of essential popular music artists of the 1990's.

Dodie Marie Miller

See also Alternative rock; Culture wars; Electronic music; Grunge fashion; Grunge music; Hip-hop and rap music; Love, Courtney; Marilyn Manson; Music; Nine Inch Nails; Nirvana; Tibetan Freedom Concerts; Woodstock concerts.

■ Long Island Lolita case

The Event Seventeen-year-old Amy Fisher shoots and severely wounds Mary Jo Buttafuoco, the wife of her alleged lover Joey, at the Buttafuoco home

Date May 19, 1992

Place Massapequa, Long Island, New York

The Long Island Lolita case raised the issues of the sexual exploitation of teenagers and the sexism of the mass media.

On a May morning, Amy Fisher rang the doorbell of the Buttafuoco home in Long Island and spoke to Mary Jo Buttafuoco, a thirty-seven-year-old mother of two young children and the wife of auto body shop owner Joey Buttafuoco. Fisher claimed that Joey was having an affair with her younger sister. When a skeptical Mary Jo turned to go back into her home, Fisher shot her in the head with a .25-caliber pistol.

Fisher claimed that the shooting was accidental and that she had meant only to strike Buttafuoco for refusing to take her seriously. Buttafuoco survived, with a bullet lodged in her head, deaf in one ear, and half of her face paralyzed. She described her assailant as a young woman with long, violet hair, and Joey Buttafuoco named Fisher for the Nassau County police investigating the case. Fisher was arrested and jailed on attempted murder charges, while Joey faced statutory rape charges. Fisher claimed that he had served as her pimp and had asked her to kill his wife. He initially confessed to the affair but subsequently denied it.

As soon as the story broke, the case grabbed headlines in the press. Fisher also became the butt of late-night comedians' jokes and a recurring feature on tabloid television shows. Part of the shock over the case seemed to result from Fisher's background. The term "Long Island" stood as a metaphor for white, suburban, and middle class. As a white, middle-class girl, Fisher did not fit the stereotypical image of a bad girl, yet she became a prostitute and would-be murderer. Meanwhile, Joey Buttafuoco's protestations of innocence strained the credulity of many Americans, while Mary Jo's willingness to believe her husband proved just as stunning.

In 1999, Fisher left prison after spending seven years in Albion Correctional Facility. She apologized to Mary Jo Buttafuoco and declared that she would not let the media affect her life. Joey Buttafuoco served four months for statutory rape and remained in the public eye as a minor celebrity. The Buttafuocos divorced in 2000.

Impact The Long Island Lolita case grabbed the attention of the public to the degree that between 100 and 125 million people, about half of the U.S. population, watched at least one of the three made-for-television movies about the shooting that aired during the week of December 28, 1992: *The Amy Fisher Story,* starring Drew Barrymore; *Casualties of Love: The Long Island Lolita Story,* starring Alyssa Milano; and *Amy Fisher: My Story,* starring Noelle Parker.

Further Reading

Eftimiades, Maria. *Lethal Lolita: A True Story of Sex, Scandal, and Deadly Obsession.* New York: St. Martin's Press, 1992.

Kenny, Lorraine Delia. *Daughters of Suburbia: Growing Up White, Middle Class, and Female.* New Brunswick, N.J.: Rutgers University Press, 2000.

Caryn E. Neumann

See also Bobbitt mutilation case; Crime; Journalism.

■ Los Angeles riots

The Event Four days of continuous violence, including arson, assault, looting, and shooting, erupts after the unexpected acquittal of four Caucasian Los Angeles police officers on charges of police brutality
Date April 29-May 2, 1992
Place Los Angeles, California

The largest multiracial urban disturbance of the twentieth century, the Los Angeles riots brought to the fore issues of immigrant assimilation, racism, poverty, and gang warfare.

When a private citizen brought forward a videotape of a lengthy beating of African American Rodney King by four Los Angeles Police Department (LAPD) officers on the night of March 3, 1991, television stations eagerly played the tape. The public then expected that the Caucasian officers would surely be found guilty of police brutality. The officers, however, believed that they were trying to apprehend a motorist who was resisting arrest after a high-speed highway chase.

On April 1, 1991, Los Angeles Mayor Tom Bradley, an African American, decided to set up an independent commission to determine whether King's beating was part of a pattern of racism within the police department. The report, issued on July 9, found that LAPD officers often used excessive force without being disciplined. Once again, the public expected convictions of the four officers. A key recommendation, to institute community policing, was ignored by Bradley. The report also asked Police Chief Daryl Gates to resign, but he refused.

When the four officers were arraigned on charges of excessive force, the judge moved the trial outside Los Angeles because of prejudicial pretrial publicity, including remarks by Bradley that the officers should be punished and numerous replays of the most sensational segment of the videotape on television. The venue chosen, Simi Valley, was a suburb in Ventura County. The jury, assembled from residents of a nearby community in Los Angeles, consisted of ten Caucasians, one Hispanic, and one Asian.

About a year later, on March 16, 1992, fifteen-year-old African American Latasha Harlins entered Empire Liquor Market, a convenience store owned by a Korean American immigrant family that previously experienced burglary, shoplifting, and gang terrorism. After putting a bottle of orange juice in her backpack, she approached the counter with money in her hands. Observing the bottle in her backpack but not the money, proprietor Soon Ja Du attempted to take the backpack away, whereupon Latasha knocked the woman down and put the juice bottle on the counter. As Latasha attempted to leave the store, Du shot and killed her. On March 22, Du was charged with voluntary manslaughter.

On April 21, a jury found Du guilty and recommended a sixteen-year sentence. Judge Joyce Karlin, however, reduced the sentence to five years probation, four hundred hours of community service, and a fine of $500. The verdict seemed much too light from the viewpoint of the African American community in Los Angeles.

Then, on April 29, three of the LAPD officers were acquitted and there was a hung jury for the fourth officer. Exculpatory evidence included a thirteen-second segment that had been edited out of the television broadcasts during which King got up from the ground and charged one of the officers. The officers also testified that King held all four off, but that was not on tape. Unaware of the exculpatory evidence outside the courtroom, many African American residents were incredulous of yet another apparent miscarriage of justice involving their community.

The Riots Begin Thirty minutes after the verdict was announced, about three hundred people appeared outside the downtown Los Angeles courthouse to protest; the number doubled over the next two hours. At approximately the same time, a large crowd of African Americans assembled at an intersection (Florence and Normandie) in South Central Los Angeles. Members of the group began to loot businesses and accost those with white faces. When Reginald Denny, a construction worker, stopped at the intersection, his truck was surrounded, and he was dragged from his vehicle, severely beaten, and almost murdered by the mob in the presence of a television news helicopter. However, several African

American residents rushed to the scene after watching the televised beating to prevent his death.

Construction worker Fidel Lopez, a Guatemalan immigrant, arrived at the same intersection soon afterward. Members of the mob tore him from his truck, ripped off his clothes, spray painted his body, stole nearly $2,000, and smashed his head open. Arriving on the scene as one of Lopez's ears was being severed, an African American minister took his unconscious body to the hospital, where his ear was reattached and he regained consciousness.

Although some police arrived at the fateful intersection, they were frightened by what they saw. Lieutenant Michael Moulin, the officer in charge, ordered his small unit to withdraw from the scene. Later, firefighters were also so intimidated by the mayhem that they were not on the scene to stop the burning.

One hour after the rioting began at the intersection, local businesses were completely looted and burning. The mob then moved into other areas, blocking the path of firefighters and police by positioning burning vehicles. Carjackings occurred, and drivers were beaten as they proceeded. Other mobs emerged as far away as Inglewood, not far from Los Angeles International Airport, where flight patterns were altered. The downtown protest turned more violent, with rocks thrown at windows of buildings. Police Chief Gates, assuring the public on television that rioting would soon be brought under control, went to a political fund-raiser instead of directing a response while police donned riot gear and awaited orders to act.

Within six hours after the verdict was announced, the riots were out of control. Mayor Bradley declared a state of emergency and a curfew. California Governor Pete Wilson ordered two thousand members of the National Guard to mobilize; they arrived the following day (April 30). Korean Americans, many of whom had served in the military, organized to defend Koreatown in open gun battles as mobs moved north toward Hollywood and northwest toward Beverly Hills. California Highway Patrol officers were flown in. President George H. W. Bush also pledged to bring support.

Calm Gradually Returns On the third day (May 1), the burning and looting continued while the National Guard presence swelled to 4,000, and 1,700 federal law-enforcement officials arrived. Rodney King, interviewed on television, asked "Can we all get along?" To assure African Americans that their cries for justice were being heard, President Bush assured that a federal grand jury investigation would consider civil rights charges against the four officers.

On the fourth day (May 2), 4,000 active-duty soldiers arrived with tanks and armed personnel carriers. A peace rally attracted 30,000 people. Calm returned to the city, though there was a lone incident on May 3. The riots were quelled before reaching Beverly Hills and Hollywood.

On Monday, May 4, Bradley canceled the curfew and banks and schools opened, but sporadic criminal activities continued for several days. California National Guard personnel left on May 14. Federal troops exited on May 27.

In all, fifty-three people died in the riots. Gunfire from rioters killed twenty-five persons, and National

A fire rages near Vermont Avenue in Los Angeles on April 30, 1992, during the riots. (AP/Wide World Photos)

Guard and law-enforcement personnel shot ten dead. Six were killed in car crashes. The rest died from stabbings, strangulation, or beatings. Five women died. Among the dead were twenty-five African Americans, sixteen Hispanics, eight Caucasians, two Asians, and two Middle Easterners. Some 4,000 were wounded. The Empire Liquor store and about 2,000 Korean-owned businesses were burned to the ground. Among the 12,000 arrested for looting and other crimes, Latinos were the most numerous. There was approximately $1 billion in property damage, mostly from the destruction of a thousand buildings. Koreatown resembled a war zone because of the burning after the looting.

Observers have called the event an "urban disturbance" rather than a "race riot." The main reason is that many participants simply took advantage of the chaos to loot nearby stores, with little interest in the political overtones that began the riots.

Impact The Los Angeles riots made it clear that class conflict complicates racial conflict in the United States, involving immigrant Asians and Hispanics as well as the black-white conflict. Observers commented that resentment builds when some immigrants with limited English ability succeed while some articulate African Americans do poorly in American society, and indeed there were mini-riots in sixteen other American cities after the verdict. The looting by some of the poorest Latino immigrants brought to light the way in which the demographics of Los Angeles had become increasingly complex throughout the 1990's.

The United States struggles to find a coherent concept of how to deal with a burgeoning multicultural, multiracial population. Riots are possible anywhere when events bring to the fore reminders of injustice. Indeed, disturbances continued beyond the 1990's, notably in Cincinnati during 2001.

The 1992 riots also brought to light the practice of racial profiling, that is, the tendency of white police officers to stop black motorists and pedestrians more frequently than Asians or whites. The Rodney King incident also made television media realize the viewing potential of film car chases, and the public realized the importance of private videotaping. Subsequently, Hollywood films capitalized on the theme of race relations in Los Angeles. The film *Grand Canyon,* released in 1992 after the King beating but before the riots, promoted racial cooperation. In *American History X* (1998), the character played by actor Edward Norton speculates that there would have been no Los Angeles riots in 1992 if Gates's successor, African American Willie Williams, had been the police chief. *Crash* (2005) suggests that nothing had improved in race relations since 1992.

Subsequent Events On April 17, 1993, the verdict in the federal civil rights trial found two of the police officers guilty; they were sentenced to thirty months in prison. Three were fired and one resigned from LAPD. Gates resigned after Bradley's office released unfavorable information about him. Williams tried to restore confidence in LAPD by establishing community policing as he had done while Philadelphia police chief. Bradley did not seek reelection. King was awarded $3.8 million in compensation, largely to pay his attorneys, but he was arrested several times thereafter. Koreatown was rebuilt. While some Koreans moved to homes outside the city, many Latino immigrants moved into their former Koreatown apartments. Some $1.4 billion was used from the Rebuild Los Angeles project, but South Central Los Angeles observers found little evidence of any major reconstruction besides a Home Depot, Wal-Mart, and new grocery stores. The Multicultural Collaborative and other groups emerged to bring African Americans and Korean Americans together.

Further Reading

Cannon, Lou. *Official Negligence: How Rodney King and the Riots Changed Los Angeles and the LAPD.* New York: Crown, 1998. The definitive account of the trials of the four Los Angeles police officers, including the impact of the missing thirteen seconds of videotape on the jury, with a conclusion about the way in which a new mayor and police chief tried to correct the city's many problems regarding law enforcement.

Report of the Independent Commission on the Los Angeles Police Department. Los Angeles: Independent Commission on the Los Angeles Police Department, 1991. After reviewing five years of reports, the commission concluded that many LAPD officers used excessive force against the public in violation of written guidelines, while complaints were dismissed without corrective action. The commission was chaired by well-respected Los Angeles business executive Warren Christopher, who later became secretary of state.

Tervalon, Jervey, ed. *Geography of Rage: Remembering*

the Los Angeles Riots of 1992. Los Angeles: Really Great Books, 2002. A collection of essays written by Los Angeles residents who reflect on what happened ten years earlier.

Williams, Willie L., with Bruce Henderson. *Taking Back Our Streets: Fighting Crime in America.* New York: Scribner, 1996. The former police chief in Los Angeles and Philadelphia explains how community policing can restore the morale of police officers while building trust with the public.

Michael Haas

See also African Americans; Christopher, Warren; Crime; Crown Heights riot; Hate crimes; King, Rodney; Mount Pleasant riot; Police brutality; Race relations.

■ Louima torture case

The Event Arrest and subsequent mistreatment of Abner Louima by four New York City police officers

Date August 9, 1997

Place Brooklyn, New York

The outrageous nature of the allegations of physical abuse by NYPD officers after they arrested Louima galvanized the public and focused intense attention during the subsequent trial proceedings on the police use of force.

Abner Louima was a Haitian immigrant arrested during a brawl outside a social club in Brooklyn, New York, during the early morning hours of August 9, 1997. One of the police officers called to the scene was struck and identified Louima as his assailant (this charge was later dropped). Louima was handcuffed and taken to the seventieth police precinct in Brooklyn. During that drive, it was alleged that the officers stopped and beat Louima. Once at the station, he was strip searched and then taken from the holding cell to a bathroom where the assault continued. The most heavily publicized aspect of this assault occurred when one officer used a plunger to sodomize Louima, later sticking the handle into his mouth and breaking several of his teeth. This was accompanied by racial slurs; he was eventually returned to the holding cell.

The next morning, Louima was taken by ambulance to a local hospital emergency room, where police told staff that he had been injured as the result of homosexual behavior. A nurse at the hospital did not believe this and notified Louima's family and the New York Police Department (NYPD) Internal Affairs Bureau. The latter did not act on these allegations until his relatives called them thirty-six hours after the arrest. Louima remained hospitalized for two months, during which time the NYPD applied disciplinary measures (including transfer, suspension, and modified assignment) to fifteen officers and filed misconduct charges against the four officers involved in the initial incident. On February 27, 1998, following an investigations by the U.S. Attorney's Office, the Federal Bureau of Investigation (FBI), and the NYPD's own Internal Affairs Division, the arresting officers were charged with civil rights violations and a supervisor was charged with trying to cover up the assault. The NYPD filed additional charges in October, 1998, against the officers, claiming that they had lied to FBI agents investigating the case. Two of the officers received prison terms (one for thirty years), while Louima himself received \$8.75 million—the largest police brutality settlement in New York City history.

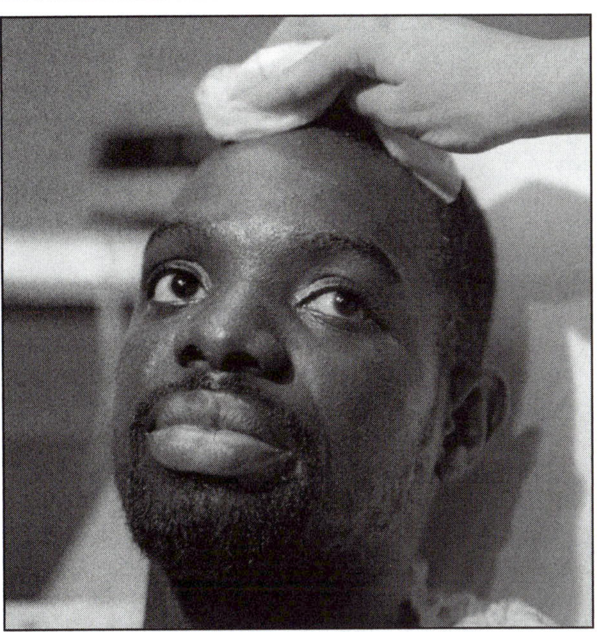

A nurse wipes the forehead of Abner Louima, the victim of police torture, at Coney Island Hospital in Brooklyn, New York, on August 14, 1997. (AP/Wide World Photos)

Impact This incident sparked outrage in the Haitian community, which joined with thousands of other citizens in several high-profile protests in New York City and Washington, D.C., against police brutality. Mayor Rudolph Giuliani created a task force to investigate the brutality allegations and promised to review recommendations from an Amnesty International report in June, 1996, that highlighted accusations of police brutality and excessive force in the NYPD. The resistance of police personnel to the investigation itself and the allegations of a cover-up prompted many recommendations for reform in NYPD procedures and supervisory structures. This included a proposal by Richard Emery, a prominent civil rights lawyer, that police station houses be equipped with video cameras to record all proceedings, including interrogations.

Further Reading

Alfieri, Alfred V. "Prosecuting Race." *Duke Law Journal* 48, no. 6 (1999): 1157-1264.

Kleinig, John. "Civil Rights and Civil Liberties: Videotaping the Police." *Criminal Justice Ethics* 17, no. 1 (1998): 42-49.

Eric W. Metchik

See also Diallo shooting; Giuliani, Rudolph; Hate crimes; King, Rodney; Police brutality.

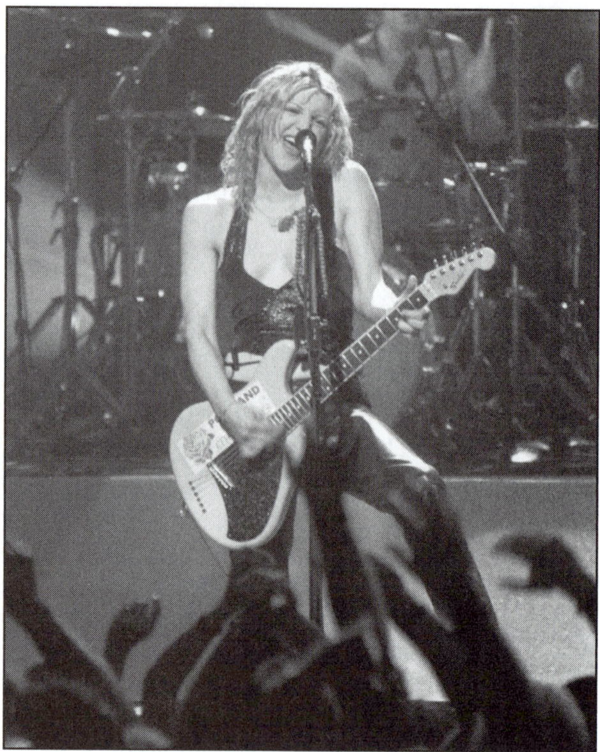

Courtney Love performs with her alternative rock band, Hole, at the MTV Video Music Awards in September, 1998. (AP/Wide World Photos)

■ Love, Courtney

Identification Rock musician, actor, and wife of Nirvana lead singer Kurt Cobain

Born July 9, 1964; San Francisco, California

During the 1990's, Love achieved notoriety as a rock musician. Much of her success as a musician, however, was overshadowed by her lifestyle and her status as the wife, and later widow, of Cobain.

Courtney Love spent much of her childhood living in communes with her mother. As a teenager, she developed an appreciation for punk rock music and, in 1989, formed the band Hole in Los Angeles. Shortly after forming her band, Love met her future husband, Nirvana front man Kurt Cobain, at a club in Portland, Oregon. The two began a courtship that would last the next couple of years. During this time, Hole's first album, *Pretty on the Inside*, was released in 1991 to favorable reviews by many underground music critics. Love and Cobain made their relationship official with a wedding on Waikiki Beach, Hawaii, on February 24, 1992. Less than six months later, on August 18, Love gave birth to the couple's daughter, Frances Bean Cobain.

Prior to the birth of their daughter, Love and Cobain already had reputations as partying, drug-using rock stars, identities they did little to discourage. However, Love's negative public image increased as a result of a 1992 article in *Vanity Fair* that revealed that Love had used heroin during her pregnancy. Over the next several years, Love and Cobain struggled with parenthood, superstardom, and drug addiction, all under the watchful and ever-present eye of the mainstream media. As a result of his inability to deal with many of his problems, Cobain committed suicide on April 5, 1994. Shortly after his body was found, Love read Cobain's suicide note to fans at a memorial service in Seattle.

Love's musical career would continue despite Cobain's death. Only four days after Cobain's body was discovered, Hole's breakthrough second album, *Live Through This*, was released. The album was such a commercial and critical success that *Rolling Stone* magazine declared it best album of the year. In 1996, Love starred in the film *The People vs. Larry Flynt,* a performance that earned her a Golden Globe nomination. Her career successes continued with the release of Hole's third and final album, *Celebrity Skin,* which was also released to wide critical acclaim in 1998.

Impact Despite Courtney Love's many career milestones following Kurt Cobain's death, her public image never recovered or improved following Cobain's death. In the latter part of the 1990's, Love found herself the subject of many tabloid photographs, appearing drunk or stoned onstage or passed out in various venues. In addition, she had a reputation for being sexually promiscuous and found herself arrested several times for disorderly conduct and drug use. At the end of the decade, however, Love's career continued to flourish despite her flawed public image.

Further Reading

Brite, Poppy Z. *Courtney Love: The Real Story.* New York: Simon & Schuster, 1997.

Coates, Norma. "Moms Don't Rock: The Popular Demonization of Courtney Love." In *"Bad" Mothers: The Politics of Blame in Twentieth-Century America,* edited by Molly Ladd-Taylor and Lauri Umansky. New York: New York University Press, 1998.

Lindsay Schmitz

See also Alternative rock; Drug use; Film in the United States; Grunge music; Lollapalooza; Music; Nirvana.

■ Lucid, Shannon

Identification American astronaut
Born January 14, 1943; Shanghai, China

Lucid served as a mission specialist on four space shuttle flights before her most famous spaceflight in 1996 on the Russian Mir space station. On that mission, she earned the U.S. single-mission endurance record of 188 days in space and the international endurance record for any female astronaut at the time.

The National Aeronautics and Space Administration (NASA) selected Dr. Shannon Lucid in 1978 as one of six women out of thirty-five in the first astronaut class to accept women. After two space shuttle flights in 1985 and 1989, Lucid's third spaceflight was a nine-day mission from August 2-11, 1991, on the space shuttle *Atlantis.* On this mission of 142 orbits, she and the crew conducted thirty-two experiments related to extended spaceflights. Her fourth spaceflight was a fourteen-day mission on the space shuttle *Columbia* from October 18 to November 1, 1993, lasting a record 225 orbits. She and the crew conducted sixteen engineering tests and twenty extended-duration medical experiments on themselves and on forty-eight rats. With this flight, Dr. Lucid had logged 838 hours and 54 minutes in space to achieve the record for American women in space.

After a year of training in Star City, Russia, Lucid began her last and most famous spaceflight from Kennedy Space Center, Florida, on March 22, 1996, aboard the space shuttle *Atlantis.* She was transferred to the Mir space station, where she served as a board engineer 2 with Russian cosmonauts Yuri Onufrienko and Yuri Usachev. She conducted many science experiments during her six months in space

Shannon Lucid. (NASA)

and became the first American to conduct a spacewalk on Mir. Her return was scheduled for July 31 but was delayed nearly two months because of mechanical and weather problems with shuttle launches. She finally returned to Kennedy Space Center aboard *Atlantis* on September 26, 1996, after traveling more than 75 million miles in space.

Impact Shannon Lucid's career in space demonstrated that female astronauts could equal or surpass their male counterparts. When no one expressed interest in an extended trip on the sparse Mir space station, she volunteered and established several space records. After six months of weightlessness, she surprised experts by walking on her own from the space shuttle to the medical transporter. Over the next three years, she was NASA's most important source of data for the effects of space on the human body. In December of 1996, she became the tenth astronaut to receive the Congressional Space Medal of Honor, and in February of 1997 she won the Free Spirit Award from the Freedom Forum.

Further Reading

Bredeson, Carmen. *Shannon Lucid: Space Ambassador.* Brookfield, Conn.: Millbrook Press, 1998.

Lucid, Shannon W. "Six Months on Mir." *Scientific American,* May, 1998, pp. 46-55.

Shayler, David, and Ian Moule. *Women in Space: Following Valentina.* New York: Springer, 2005.

Joseph L. Spradley

See also Astronomy; Bondar, Roberta; Glenn, John; Science and technology; Space exploration; Space shuttle program; Women in the workforce.

McCaughey septuplets

Identification The world's first living set of septuplets

Born November 19, 1997; Des Moines, Iowa

News media worldwide celebrated the birth of Bobbi McCaughey's septuplets as a medical miracle. Conception had been facilitated by infertility treatment, and advances in medical technology assured the septuplets' survival.

On November 19, 1997, Kelsey, Brandon, Nathan, Joel, Alexis, Natalie, and Kenneth McCaughey were delivered nine weeks early by cesarean section at Iowa Methodist Medical Center in Des Moines, Iowa. Their birth weight ranged from two pounds, five ounces, to three pounds, four ounces. Like their older sister, Mikayla, the septuplets were conceived with the help of Metrodin, an ovulation-stimulating fertility drug.

Early in the course of Bobbi McCaughey's second pregnancy, a sonogram revealed the presence of seven babies. Pregnancies with a high number of fetuses pose a significant health risk to both the mother and her unborn children. A reduction in the number of fetuses by selective abortion was discussed with the expecting parents, but this was an option that Kenny and Bobbi McCaughey, fundamentalist Christians, refused. On October 15, the expecting mother was hospitalized so that her high-risk pregnancy could be closely monitored. Two weeks later, on October 29, the press received word of the pending delivery and poured into town. The McCaugheys appointed a spokesperson to help them deal with the onslaught of requests for interviews and statements.

Impact Forty health care workers, including nurses, respiratory therapists, neonatologists, anesthesiologists, and obstetricians, attended the babies' delivery. The news media closely informed the general public about the birth and progress of the septuplets, and this led to an avalanche of congratulations and gifts. U.S. president Bill Clinton chatted with the mother over the phone. Iowa's governor committed to the construction of a larger home for "The Seven from Heaven." The citizens of Carlisle, Iowa, home of the McCaughey family, provided housekeeping, cooking, and day-and-night child care services. Donations to the family included diapers for life, one year of free groceries, university scholarships, and a fifteen-seat van. The birth was celebrated as a medical miracle. There was little discussion of the financial burden to society: The cost of the birth and prolonged hospitalization of the seven has been estimated at $1.2 million. The injudicious use of a fertility drug responsible for higher-order pregnancies also escaped media scrutiny.

Subsequent Events The news media's initial claim that seven healthy babies had been born was not entirely accurate. Two of the babies relied on feeding tubes until they were four years old. Another suffered seizures, and two were diagnosed with cerebral palsy.

Further Reading

Halvorson, George, and George Isham. "Miracles Cost Money." In *Epidemic of Care. A Call for Safer, Better, and More Accountable Health Care*, edited by George Halvorson and George Isham. San Francisco: Jossey-Bass, 2003.

Klotzko, Arlene. "Medical Miracle or Medical Mischief? The Saga of the McCaughey Septuplets." *Hastings Center Report* 28, no. 3 (May/June, 1998): 5-8.

Pence, Gregory. "The McCaughey Septuplets: God's Will or Human Choice?" In *Bioethics: An Anthology*, edited by Helga Kuhse and Peter Singer. Malden, Mass.: Blackwell, 2006.

Elisabeth Faase

See also Abortion; Health care; Journalism; Medicine.

■ McCourt, Frank

Identification American author
Born August 19, 1930; Brooklyn, New York

McCourt's artful, emotionally wrenching first memoir won the Pulitzer Prize in biography in 1997 and was a best seller for over three years. The book is credited with generating an increase in popularity of the memoir genre.

In the early 1990's, after retiring from teaching high school in New York City for thirty years, Frank McCourt sat down to write a memoir. What resulted from this project was an account of his childhood that was an unprecedented literary and commercial success. The book, titled *Angela's Ashes* (1996), centers on the first eighteen years of McCourt's life, which was spent primarily in Ireland, in extreme poverty. His sensitive prose, combined with a conversational and engaging style, elevated the genre of memoir to a new level.

Upon its publication, *Angela's Ashes* received great critical and public acclaim, winning such prestigious accolades as the Pulitzer Prize, National Book Critics Circle Award, *Salon* Book Award, American Library Association Award, *Los Angeles Times* Book Award, and many other book of the year awards from magazines and newspapers across the United States. McCourt enjoyed instant stardom as a first-time author at the age of sixty-five. The book was distributed in eighteen countries and became a modern classic.

Angela's Ashes relates the life of an impoverished Irish family in the 1930's and 1940's from a child's perspective. An alcoholic father who eventually abandons the family, two brothers and a sister who die in infancy, and his mother, Angela, who tries to hold everything together, make for a captivating tale, told with humor, grief, and every emotion in between. As the boy Frank matures, he takes on more responsibilities for the family and learns some hard lessons along the way.

In 1998, McCourt, his brother Malachy, and nephew Conor teamed up to produce a documentary film titled *The McCourts of Limerick.* A sequel, *The McCourts of New York,* was produced the following year. McCourt published a second memoir, *'Tis,* in 1999. It centers on McCourt's experiences as a young man returning to America, trying to carve out a life for himself and find a better future, and the challenges he faces as a person caught between the cultures of Ireland and America. This book was also a critical and commercial success, shooting to the top of the best-seller lists immediately after it was published. In 1999, a film titled *Angela's Ashes,* based on McCourt's first memoir, was released.

Impact Frank McCourt's contribution to American letters, especially in the memoir genre, generated a new interest in biography, memoir, and the immigrant experience. Few authors are so admired by both their peers and the public.

Further Reading

McCourt, Frank. *Angela's Ashes.* New York: Scribner, 1996.

_______. *Teacher Man.* New York: Scribner, 2005.

_______. *'Tis.* New York: Scribner, 1999.

Kris Bigalk

See also Book clubs; Film in the United States; Literature in the United States; Publishing.

Frank McCourt. (Gasper Tringale/Scribner)

■ McEntire, Reba

Identification American country music singer
Born March 28, 1954; Chockie, Oklahoma

Reba McEntire was the most successful female country music recording artist of the decade.

By 1990, Reba McEntire was already a popular country music singer with a large fan following. Her music contract, signed in 1984 with MCA Nashville Records, had successfully propelled her to the status of being among the best-selling country music artists of all time. In 1990, she gave birth to her son, Shelby Stephen, and released her fifteenth album, *Rumor Has It*, which contained the number one hit "You Lie" and what would become her signature song, "Fancy." Tragically, on March 16, 1991, seven of her band members and her road manager were killed in an airplane crash. One week after the accident, amid criticism, McEntire performed the song, "I'm Checking Out," at the Academy Awards in honor of her band members. In October 1991, she released her sixteenth album, *For My Broken Heart*, which was also dedicated to her band members.

In December, 1992, she released her seventeenth album, *It's Your Call*, which went triple platinum. The song "The Heart Won't Lie," which was performed as a duet with country singer Vince Gill, reached number one on the country music charts in April, 1993. Another duet on the album "Does He Love You," which she performed with Linda Davis, also reached number one on the country charts in November, 1993. In April, 1994, she produced her eighteenth album, *Read My Mind*, as well as her nineteenth album, *Oklahoma Girl*. *Read My Mind* produced five country chart singles and went triple platinum. Her twentieth album, *Starting Over*, was released in October, 1995, and marked the singer's twentieth anniversary in the music industry. In November, 1996, she released her twenty-first album, *What If It's You*, in 1998 she released her twenty-second album, *If You See Him*, and in November 1999, she released her twenty-third album, *So Good Together*.

In addition to producing nine albums during the 1990's, McEntire also toured with her band to promote her music. In 1994 and 1995, her stage shows earned more money than any other concert tour in country music at the time. As if her music did not keep her busy enough, in 1994, she published her autobiography, *Reba: My Story*. She also starred in several television movies during the decade, including *The Gambler IV* (1991), with Kenny Rogers, *The Man from Left Field* (1993), with Burt Reynolds, and *The Secret of Giving* (1999). Throughout the 1990's, McEntire also won numerous awards for her music, including several American Music Awards, People's Choice Awards, and Academy of Country Music Awards.

Reba McEntire performs at the Country Music Association Awards in Nashville, Tennessee, on October 4, 1995. (AP/Wide World Photos)

Impact With diligence and hard work, Reba McEntire became a country music superstar during the 1990's. She produced nine studio albums and two compilation albums, performed hundreds of stage shows, wrote her autobiography, and starred in several television movies. She revolutionized the stereotypical image of a female country music star. Her upbeat songs, elaborate stage shows, and vibrant personality proved that a female country music star could be as glamorous as any other music diva.

Further Reading

Keel, Beverly. "Reba McIntire." In *Popular Musicians*, edited by Steve Hochman. Vol. 3. Pasadena, Calif.: Salem Press, 1999.

McEntire, Reba. *Comfort from the Quilt*. New York: Bantam Books, 2000.

McEntire, Reba, and Tom Carter. *Reba: My Story*. New York: Bantam Books, 1994.

Bernadette Zbicki Heiney

See also Brooks, Garth; Country music; Lang, K. D.; Music.

■ McGwire, Mark

Identification American baseball player
Born October 1, 1963; Pomona, California

McGwire broke the single-season home run record in 1998 and helped rejuvenate interest in Major League Baseball.

Mark McGwire was one of the best power hitters of the 1980's and 1990's. Over the course of sixteen seasons, McGwire hit 583 home runs, drove in 1,414 runs, and was a twelve-time all-star. In 1987, his first full year in the major leagues, McGwire hit forty-nine home runs, a rookie record, and won the American League Rookie of the Year Award as first baseman for the Oakland Athletics. In 1997, after he had spent nine seasons in Oakland, the Athletics traded McGwire to the St. Louis Cardinals, where he became a national sports icon.

After finishing the 1997 season with fifty-eight home runs, McGwire began the 1998 season by hitting home runs in each of his first four games. Despite McGwire's hot start, by June, Chicago Cubs outfielder Sammy Sosa and McGwire were neck and neck for the league lead in home runs. For the rest of the season, McGwire and Sosa pursued the single-season home run record set by Roger Maris with sixty-one home runs in 1961. On September 8, McGwire hit his sixty-second home run, and after hitting five home runs in his last three games, he finished the season with seventy home runs to Sosa's sixty-six. For his achievements, McGwire won the Silver Slugger Award and finished second to Sosa in the voting for National League Most Valuable Player.

Impact The home run chase between McGwire and Sosa in 1998 was one of the events that attracted widespread interest and helped repair baseball's image after the damage it suffered in the wake of the 1994-1995 baseball strike. Fans returned to games in droves, and attendance rose by seven million fans between the 1997 and 1998 seasons. Indicative of the cultural significance of the home run race, McGwire's seventieth home run ball sold for over $3 million.

However, McGwire's accolades were short-lived. During the 1998 season, an Associated Press story revealed that McGwire's locker contained androstenedione, a muscle-building substance legal for use in Major League Baseball but banned by most other sports organizations.

Subsequent Events Despite the furor over the supplement, McGwire's reputation remained mostly intact until 2005, when José Canseco alleged that he

Mark McGwire hits his sixty-first home run of the 1998 season, tying Roger Maris's single-season record. (AP/Wide World Photos)

and McGwire had used steroids while teammates in Oakland. At a congressional hearing, McGwire's refusal to answer questions about his steroid use left many fans and sportswriters suspicious about his history with performance-enhancing drugs. Although considered a future hall of famer upon his retirement, McGwire was not elected to the National Baseball Hall of Fame during his first year of eligibility. The taint of steroid use has made him the only eligible player with five hundred home runs to not be a member of the Hall of Fame.

Further Reading

Fainaru-Wada, Mark, and Lance Williams. *Game of Shadows: Barry Bonds, BALCO, and the Steroids Scandal That Rocked Professional Sports.* New York: Gotham Books, 2006.

Golenbock, Peter. *The Spirit of St. Louis: A History of the St. Louis Cardinals and Browns.* New York: Spike Books, 2000.

Paisner, Daniel. *The Ball: Mark McGwire's Seventieth Home Run Ball and the Marketing of the American Dream.* New York: Viking Press, 1999.

Jacob F. Lee

See also Baseball; Baseball realignment; Baseball strike of 1994; Home run race; Griffey, Ken, Jr.; Ripken, Cal, Jr.; Sosa, Sammy; Sports.

■ McMansions

Identification Large mass-produced houses for a family market

The growth of entire communities of large faux-luxury homes during the 1990's drew withering criticism for the houses' mixed stylistic elements, wasted space, and high energy requirements. Their popularity, however, showed the extreme home centeredness of many of the decade's families, seeking ways to incorporate indoor leisure pursuits with individuals' needs for "personal space."

When the first mass-produced housing developments appeared after World War II, the typical tract house was small. Levittown, Long Island's 17,500 new houses averaged only 750 square feet each. With two bedrooms, one bathroom, a small living room, and kitchen, these quickly sold out to young families as new home owners. As prosperity spread and baby-boom children became teenagers and then adults, the average home size also increased, although not dramatically. As late as 1984, the first New American Home, an ideal model sponsored by the housing industry, still contained only 1,500 square feet and two bedrooms, although with two and a half baths.

In the preceding forty years, however, residential construction had changed from the bailiwick of individual small builders and contractors to an industry dominated by large-scale corporate builders. Aided by new techniques such as five-way wooden trusses (allowing larger open interior spaces to be built cheaply), such builders adapted tract, predesigned methods to larger, upscale housing. The 1990's growing prosperity, falling mortgage rates, and new cultural patterns brought eager buyers for such new, lavish "McMansions." Their most usual locale was the outer suburbs of American cities. The name comes from the word "mansion" with the use of "Mc," which conjures the common concepts surrounding the McDonald's fast-food franchise—assembly-line process, quick and generic, mass appeal.

Most McMansions featured striking front facades; they might mix styles and decorative elements such as gables, stone inlays, and lavish windows. Inside, two-story entrance atriums allowed light to flood into the house for immediate impact. The ground floor typically included little-used formal living and dining rooms, a large open area incorporating a giant kitchen flowing into an informal dining area and/or a family room, and perhaps special purpose rooms. Upstairs, a master suite usually included a lavish bathroom and multiple closets, and there were additional bedrooms and baths. Attached garages provided space for at least three cars.

These homes were roundly condemned for their heavy energy demands, for using unneeded space, and for the aesthetic imbalance between large house "footprints" and small surrounding yards. Reasons for their popularity were less remarked. Besides serving as a status symbol, the new space possibilities appealed to extreme commuters, blended families, and immigrant extended families. Seldom-used formal living areas were not a new phenomenon. Since the advent of family rooms, most Americans have preferred to concentrate the messy activities of everyday living and television watching in a kitchen-family room nexus and to keep the front areas pristine for important visitors. Except for gardeners, many middle-class families confined their yard use to the barbecue patio and the swimming pool. Even children played outdoors less than formerly.

Impact McMansions remained part of the urban and suburban housing stock. Their greater impact may be in the features that have become expected in any new middle-class dwelling: a master bedroom suite, an open-plan kitchen-family room core, and rooms wired for various electronic connections.

Further Reading

McGinn, Daniel. *House Lust.* New York: Doubleday, 2007.

McGuigan, Cathleen. "The McMansion Next Door." *Newsweek,* October 27, 2003, 85-86.

Emily Alward

See also Architecture; Sustainable design movement.

■ McMillan, Terry

Identification African American novelist
Born October 18, 1951; Port Huron, Michigan

In novels that accurately describe the lives of upwardly mobile African American women, McMillan provided a voice for an important segment of the population.

Terry McMillan. (©Marion Ettlinger)

Terry McMillan's novels dramatize the plight of African American professional women struggling with relationships. Some of McMillan's heroines have never been married, others have been deserted by their lovers, and still others are divorced. Those who have never had children fear that they are growing too old to establish a family. Others, rearing children alone, desperately try to be good parents without jeopardizing their careers. One of her goals in writing about the trials of these single mothers, McMillan has said, is to show how the structure of the African American family has altered.

Like her earlier fiction, the novels that McMillan wrote during the 1990's reflect her own experiences. For *Waiting to Exhale* (1992), the author drew on years of frustration in her continuing search for someone with whom she could share her life. The novel is about four African American women, all of whom have trouble either finding or keeping a good man. Although the book was extremely popular with women, African American men insisted that the author had treated them unfairly, that the book simply reflected her own prejudices. The tone of McMillan's next novel, *How Stella Got Her Groove Back* (1996), was very different. Like McMillan herself, the fictional Stella went on a Jamaican vacation, met a local man half her age, and brought him to California, where at the end of the novel they expect to live happily ever after. Unfortunately, McMillan's own Jamaican romance ended in disillusionment and divorce.

McMillan's fiction is as authentic in style as it is in content. Perhaps more than any other writer of the decade, McMillan captured the rhythms of African American conversation, complete with idiomatic expressions. Late in the 1990's, book-length critical studies of McMillan began to appear, indicating that she was not just a popular writer but also a major figure in American literary history.

Impact Finding in McMillan's novels a genuine understanding of their lives, African American women flocked to bookstores to buy her books. McMillan is credited with creating a new reading audience. Moreover, her success stimulated other African American women to produce similar realistic fiction. Thus, it has been said that she established a new genre. Her emergence in the 1990's as the voice of upwardly mobile African American women made her one of the most important writers of the decade.

Further Reading

Nunez, Elizabeth, and Brenda M. Greene, eds. *Defining Ourselves: Black Writers in the 90s.* New York: Peter Lang, 1999.

Patrick, Diane. *Terry McMillan: The Unauthorized Biography.* New York: St. Martin's Press, 1999.

Richards, Paulette. *Terry McMillan: A Critical Companion.* Westport, Conn.: Greenwood Press, 1999.

Rosemary M. Canfield Reisman

See also African Americans; Chick lit; Literature in the United States; Marriage and divorce; Race relations; Women's rights.

■ McNally, Terrence

Identification American playwright
Born November 3, 1939; St. Petersburg, Florida

McNally achieved huge success in the 1990's with his books for musicals and his plays grappling with gay issues.

American playwright Terrence McNally is one of the most respected and prolific playwrights since Tennessee Williams. His straight plays often contain gay characters and themes, while his writing for musicals leans heavily toward work that embraces dreamers trying to forge a better life.

McNally's work does not shy away from gay themes. In 1990, he won an Emmy Award for the televised broadcast of *Andre's Mother,* a play that deals with a woman trying to cope with her son's death from AIDS. The following year, he wrote *Lips Together, Teeth Apart,* which also deals with the disease, although this time from the perspective of two heterosexual couples vacationing on Fire Island and afraid to go in a pool owned by a man who died of AIDS.

McNally wrote the book for the 1992 musical *Kiss of the Spider Woman,* for which he won the Tony Award for Best Book of a Musical. The following year, his India-themed *A Perfect Ganesh* opened to moderate reviews. The year 1994 brought critical acclaim in the form of *Love! Valour! Compassion!*—a look at the relationships of eight gay men during summer weekends at a Dutchess County getaway. In 1995, it won the Tony Award for Best Play and the Drama Desk Award for Outstanding Play, as well as the New York Drama Critics' Circle Award for Best American Play. It was adapted to film in 1997.

In 1995, McNally's look at famed opera diva Maria Callas in his play *Master Class* opened on Broadway and won the Tony Award for Best Play. In 1996, his collaboration with Lynn Ahrens and Stephen Flaherty produced *Ragtime,* which won him his fourth Tony Award of the decade. This victory ensured his position as America's foremost playwright during the 1990's.

McNally's most controversial play, *Corpus Christi,* opened in October, 1998. The story of a gay Jesus Christ and Apostles living in modern-day Texas, its allusions to Judas betraying Jesus out of sexual jealousy proved too much for many theatergoers. Fearing public safety concerns, the Manhattan Theatre Club, producer of the work, canceled the opening. A nationwide censorship debate followed, and the production was rescheduled. The new opening followed the death of gay Wyoming student Matthew Shepard and continued the dialogue of religion, art, and gay politics.

Impact By the end of the decade, McNally was hailed as one of America's most prominent and important American playwrights.

Further Reading

Drukman, Steven. "Terrence McNally." In *Speaking on Stage: Interviews with Contemporary American Playwrights,* edited by Philip C. Kolin and Colby H. Kullman. Tuscaloosa: University of Alabama Press, 1996.

Frontain, Raymond-Jean. "'All Men Are Divine': Religious Mystery and Homosexual Identity in Terrence McNally's *Corpus Christi.*" In *Reclaiming the Sacred: The Bible in Gay and Lesbian Culture.* 2d ed. New York: Haworth Press, 2003.

Zinman, Toby Silverman, ed. *Terrence McNally: A Casebook.* New York: Garland, 1997.

Tom Smith

See also Broadway musicals; Censorship; Homosexuality and gay rights; Literature in the United States; Mapplethorpe obscenity trial; Theater in the United States.

■ McVeigh, Timothy

Identification Domestic terrorist responsible for the 1995 Oklahoma City bombing
Born April 23, 1968; Pendleton, New York
Died June 11, 2001; Terre Haute, Indiana

McVeigh committed the deadliest terrorist attack on U.S. soil up to that time and the deadliest example of domestic terrorism ever in the United States.

Timothy McVeigh was the middle child born to William McVeigh and Mildred Noreen Hill in Pendleton, New York. His parents divorced when he was ten, and he went to live with his father while his two sisters went to live with their mother in Florida. In May of 1988, he enlisted in the Army. He served in the Gulf War and was awarded a Bronze Star. He then began training for the Army's Special Forces (Green Berets) but dropped out after a couple of days.

On April 17, 1995, in Junction City, Kansas, McVeigh rented a Ryder truck, which he and Army friend Terry Nichols packed with a two-ton bomb. McVeigh then drove to Oklahoma City, where he parked the truck a few blocks from the Alfred P. Murrah Federal Building. On the early morning of April 19, McVeigh drove to the federal building, lit the five-minute fuse, and parked the truck in a drop-off zone. At 9:02 A.M., the truck bomb exploded, hitting the northern face of the building and leaving a third of the building in ruins and downtown Oklahoma City devastated. The blast was felt over fifty miles away and measured about 3.0 on the Richter scale, damaging over three hundred surrounding buildings.

Preparation for this event began around September, 1994. McVeigh was angry at the government's handling of the incidents at Ruby Ridge, Idaho, in 1992 and Waco, Texas, in 1993. He had traveled to Waco during the siege to distribute antigovernment pamphlets. McVeigh thought that certain Bureau of Alcohol, Tobacco, and Firearms (ATF) agents whom he blamed for the Waco incident had their offices in the Alfred P. Murrah Federal Building and felt that that building was an easy target.

Oklahoma City bombing suspect Timothy McVeigh is escorted by law-enforcement officials on April 21, 1995. In 1997, he was found guilty on eleven counts of murder and conspiracy and was sentenced to death by lethal injection. (AP/Wide World Photos)

About an hour after the bombing, a police officer pulled over McVeigh about sixty miles from Oklahoma City for not having a rear license plate. When the officer approached the car, he noticed a bulge in McVeigh's jacket, which was the gun McVeigh brought with him in case the bomb failed to ignite. He admitted to the officer that he had a concealed weapon and was arrested. When they searched his car, police discovered documents that revealed the motivations behind the bombing. They connected the vehicle identification number on the Ryder truck to McVeigh, then began searching for his accomplices.

In the largest criminal case ever, McVeigh was convicted on all eleven counts against him, including eight counts of first-degree murder, use of a weapon of mass destruction, destruction by explosives, and conspiracy to use a weapon of mass destruction. He was executed on June 11, 2001, in Terre Haute, Indiana.

Impact One hundred sixty-eight lives were lost and over eight hundred people were injured in the Oklahoma City bombing. The incident shocked the American public, creating an increased fear of potential future attacks.

Further Reading

Kight, Marsha, comp. *Forever Changed: Remembering Oklahoma City, April 19, 1995.* Amherst, N.Y.: Prometheus Books, 1998.

Linenthal, Edward T. *The Unfinished Bombing: Oklahoma City in American Memory.* New York: Oxford University Press, 2001.

Roleff, Tamara L. *The Oklahoma City Bombing.* San Diego, Calif.: Greenhaven Press, 2004.

Sheryl L. Van Horne

See also Columbine massacre; Crime; Militia movement; Montana Freemen standoff; Oklahoma City bombing; Olympic Park bombing; Ruby Ridge shootout; Terrorism; Unabomber capture; Waco siege.

■ Madonna

Identification American singer, songwriter, producer, actor, and entertainer
Born August 16, 1958; Bay City, Michigan

Madonna's use of sexual and religious themes in her work provoked controversy in the 1990's, and her work in film and music brought her a number of awards.

Madonna starred as Breathless Mahoney in the 1990 film adaptation of the well-known *Dick Tracy* comic strip. She released the album *I'm Breathless* in the same year to accompany the film. It included the Stephen Sondheim song "Sooner or Later," which won an Academy Award for Best Original Song. *I'm Breathless* was a great hit in the United States, Europe, and Australia, and sold over five million copies worldwide.

Controversial Music From April to August of 1990, Madonna toured Japan, the United States, and Europe on her Blond Ambition World Tour, featuring sexual and religious themes and creating controversy over her performance of "Like a Virgin." In November, she released her first greatest hits album, *The Immaculate Collection,* including two new songs, "Justify My Love" and "Rescue Me." The music video for "Justify My Love" showed suggestive scenes of Madonna with her lover, actor Tony Ward, as well as scenes of sadomasochism between gay and lesbian characters. It was considered too explicit for MTV, which banned it from the station. However, when Warner Bros. released "Justify My Love" as a video single, it became the best-selling video of all time.

The album *Erotica,* released in October of 1992, contained only three overtly sexual songs out of fourteen. Although the title song was panned by critics, "Erotica" topped the charts around the world. Madonna's soft-core book *Sex* was published around

Madonna performs during her Blond Ambition World Tour in July, 1990, in London. (AP/Wide World Photos)

the same time and featured many erotic photos of Madonna. The book became an international best seller and one of the most controversial books of the decade. In 1993, the highly erotic film *Body of Evidence,* starring Madonna, was released and subsequently bombed at the box office.

In 1993, The Girlie Show Tour featured the singer as a whip-wielding dominatrix surrounded by topless dancers. Her performance in Puerto Rico incited controversy over her vulgar use of the Puerto Rican flag, and her show was protested by Orthodox Jews at her first performance in Israel.

Later Hits The 1996 film *Evita,* based on the 1978 stage musical by Andrew Lloyd Webber with lyrics by Tim Rice, was Madonna's most critically successful film. It stars Antonio Banderas as Ché, an Argentinean everyman, and Madonna as Eva Perón, the charismatic wife of Juan Perón (played by Jonathan Pryce) who became the most powerful woman in Argentina during her husband's presidency. Madonna, who took voice lessons to extend her range for the movie, performs the music flawlessly and is convincing as Evita, the poor, urban child who converts herself into a nightclub singer, radio star, voluptuous mistress, and political leader.

The sound track of the film became Madonna's twelfth platinum album and included two songs that became hit singles: "Don't Cry for Me Argentina" and "You Must Love Me," which was written for the film. The following year, "You Must Love Me" won an Academy Award and a Golden Globe Award for Best Original Song. Madonna also won a Golden Globe Award for Best Actress in a Comedy or Musical for her performance in *Evita.*

In 1998, Madonna released the album *Ray of Light,* which indicated a new musical direction. It blended introspective and personal lyrics about motherhood and spirituality with electronic instrumentation, strings by Craig Armstrong, and Eastern music. Many of the songs were written in collaboration with British electronic musician William Orbit, whose work Madonna admired. *Ray of Light* was recorded over four and a half months in 1997, the longest Madonna had ever worked on an album. Since she had taken singing lessons for *Evita,* Madonna's voice was easy to record, and many of her vocal tracks required only one take. The recording was plagued with technical difficulties, however, as Orbit preferred to work with computers and synthetic sounds rather than live musicians, and the computers frequently broke down.

Madonna earned rave reviews for *Ray of Light,* which many reviewers considered her most successful album to date. It won three Grammy Awards in 1999 for Best Dance Recording, Best Pop Album, and Best Recording Package. The title track also won a Grammy for Best Short Form Music Video. Three years later, *Rolling Stone* readers voted *Ray of Light* as the twenty-ninth greatest album of all time.

Impact Madonna ranks among the best-selling female artists in pop music, having sold over 300 million records. More than just a performer, Madonna is a cultural icon who has pushed the boundaries of religion and sexuality in her work, influencing popular culture and other artists.

Further Reading

Guilbert, Georges-Claude. *Madonna as Postmodern Myth: How One Star's Self-Construction Rewrites Sex, Gender, Hollywood, and the American Dream.* Jefferson, N.C.: McFarland, 2002. An analysis of Madonna's influence on American culture, including other artists and feminists. Appropriate for cultural studies professors and students.

Paglia, Camille. *Sex, Art, and American Culture: Essays.* New York: Vintage Books, 1992. The first two sections, "Madonna I: Animality and Artifice" and "Madonna II: Venus of the Radio Waves," offer an incisive discussion of the cultural meaning of Madonna's excesses by an accomplished journalist.

Sexton, Adam, ed. *Desperately Seeking Madonna: In Search of the World's Most Famous Woman.* New York: Delta, 1993. An anthology of cartoons, articles, quotations, and poetry that the music journalist Sexton has collected from such sources as the *National Review, Christianity and Crisis, Rolling Stone,* Ellen Goodman, Art Buchwald, Helen Gurley Brown, and others. Illuminates the many sides of Madonna.

Sheila Golburgh Johnson

See also Academy Awards; Broadway musicals; Censorship; Electronic music; Film in the United States; Music; Rock and Roll Hall of Fame Museum.

■ Mafia

Identification Criminal organization that traces its history back to immigrant ethnic groups, usually of Italian descent, and that operates illegal businesses or corrupt legal enterprises in many American cities

The serious challenge mounted by various law-enforcement agencies to the Mafia's ability to conduct criminal activities and continue its involvement in a number of legitimate industries changed the landscape for organized crime during the 1990's. Mafia leaders were forced to enter into partnerships with other organized crime groups and engage in some activities they had avoided in the past.

A veteran New York City crime reporter once referred to the 1990's as "the twilight of the Mob." For more than a hundred years, the organization that had its roots in the Italian immigrant communities of the late nineteenth century had been a major criminal force in American cities, conducting criminal operations, causing serious problems for legitimate businesses, and often injecting a sense of fear into communities where it had notable influence. Mafia "families," normally working independently but often joined in loose alliances to maximize their ability to generate profits by agreeing to limit competition among themselves, had operated until the 1970's with little real threat from conventional law-enforcement agencies.

In 1970, however, the federal government passed the Racketeer Influenced and Corrupt Organizations (RICO) Act, which made it a crime simply to be involved in certain illegal activities. Under RICO, government prosecutors could prosecute Mafia leaders as well as those who actually committed crimes at their direction. Additionally, stiff penalties for individuals convicted under this law, as well as longer sentences imposed for a number of crimes committed by subordinates in the organization, helped to break down the notion of *omertà*. For decades this "code of silence" had virtually guaranteed leaders immunity from prosecution, since underlings would simply accept jail sentences—which were usually brief—rather than testify against their bosses. RICO was used successfully during the 1980's, especially in New York City, where U.S. attorney Rudolph Giuliani mounted a campaign against all five of the major crime families in the city.

Government Crackdown The tone for the 1990's was set early in the decade when federal agents arrested John Gotti, the flamboyant head of New York City's Gambino crime family. Gotti was convicted of murder and other crimes and sentenced to life in prison. Prosecutors were able to get convictions against Gotti and others because they had finally convinced Mafia members to testify for the government in exchange for reduced sentences for crimes they may have committed. Additionally, the government began making extensive use of sting operations in which Mafia members were caught red-handed.

During the 1990's, heads of Mafia groups in New York, as well as in other American cities such as Boston, Philadelphia, Chicago, Detroit, Cleveland, New Orleans, and Kansas City, began feeling intense pressure from federal agencies. Among the more notable figures sent to prison was Vincent "The Chin" Gigante of New York's Genovese family, considered by many the most influential of New York's crime bosses. Even though leaders who remained free tried to keep a low profile and restrain activities of their subordinates, law-enforcement officials kept up the pressure. A coordinated national effort launched in 1996 by the Federal Bureau of Investigation (FBI) resulted in the arrest and conviction of hundreds of Mafia members and the seizure of millions of dollars in assets. By the end of the decade, membership in the Mafia had declined by as much as eighty percent.

The New Face of Organized Crime In addition to pressure from law enforcement, Mafia leaders began seeing their traditional territories and business activities threatened by new criminal gangs, often with international ties. Many of these gangs were engaging in activities the Mafia had largely avoided, such as white-collar crime or drug trafficking. When pressure from law enforcement began making it more difficult for Mafia groups to continue realizing significant profits from traditional businesses such as prostitution, gambling, loan sharking, or bid rigging of government or private contracts for construction and transportation, leaders found themselves forced to consider new criminal activities or partnering with groups already carrying on such trade. As a result, while the number of Mafia members declined during the decade, those who remained within the organizations across American cities were now part of a worldwide network of organized crime that engaged in drug smuggling, stock market fraud, cyber crime, human trafficking, and even international terrorism.

Impact Unquestionably, the efforts of law-enforcement agencies to eradicate the influence of those groups traditionally designated as "the Mafia" in America did serious damage to well-established organizations that had conducted numerous illegal operations for a century. Unfortunately, the rise of other organized crime cartels both in the United States and abroad tended to serve as a counterweight to the effectiveness of government initiatives in eradicating the kinds of illicit activities for which the Mafia had long been famous. The resiliency of the new generation of Mafia leaders also played a significant role in the organization's ability to adapt to changing conditions in the global marketplace, allowing these criminal elements to join forces with others bent on taking advantage of both disadvantaged groups and new industries where safeguards had not yet been established to protect against infiltration by criminal groups.

Further Reading

Lunde, Paul. *Organized Crime: An Inside Guide to the World's Most Successful Industry.* New York: Dorling Kindersley, 2004. A lengthy chapter outlines the history of the American Mafia. Includes numerous photographs.

Raab, Selwyn. *Five Families: The Rise, Decline, and Resurgence of America's Most Powerful Mafia Empires.* New York: Thomas Dunne, 2005. Extensive, detailed accounts of the history of Mafia activity in New York City and interactions of its groups with others across the nation. Also describes law-enforcement efforts to eradicate organized crime during the 1990's.

Reppetto, Thomas A. *Bringing Down the Mob: The War Against the American Mafia.* New York: Henry Holt, 2006. Traces activities of federal, state, and local agencies to wipe out organized crime in America. Describes the changing nature of organized crime during the 1990's as its leaders reacted to pressure from law enforcement and responded to new opportunities in other parts of the world.

Ryan, Patrick J. *Organized Crime: A Reference Handbook.* Santa Barbara, Calif.: ABC-Clio, 1995. Useful summaries of the activities of Mafia groups, outlining the organization of groups in cities throughout America and abroad. Contains brief biographies of key leaders, describes efforts by law enforcement to eliminate Mafia activities, and provides a chronology of law-enforcement efforts directed against organized crime groups.

Laurence W. Mazzeno

See also Business and the economy in the United States; Crime; Giuliani, Rudolph.

■ Magic Eye pictures

Definition Computer-generated optical illusions that hide three-dimensional images in seemingly random patterns

Manufacturer N. E. Thing Enterprises (renamed Magic Eye Inc. in 1996)

A fad that became a multimillion-dollar worldwide industry in a few short years, Magic Eye pictures swept the globe in the early 1990's, gracing posters, newspapers, greeting cards, advertisements, and books.

Although three-dimensional (3-D) images had been around since the 1830's, early incarnations required mechanical devices, such as View-Masters or 3-D glasses, in order to be viewed. In the late 1950's, a neuroscientist named Béla Julesz generated a random dot stereogram, which used two sets of slightly offset dots to produce a 3-D image that did not require a viewing device. Instead, the viewer could focus his or her eyes beyond the surface of the image, tricking the mind into perceiving depth and thus revealing a hidden 3-D image.

In 1990, an entrepreneur named Tom Baccei saw an example of a random dot stereogram in *Stereo World,* a magazine about 3-D images. Baccei quickly realized the endless marketing possibilities for the technology and created a company called N. E. Thing Enterprises in response. With the help of an artist and a computer programmer, Baccei refined the technique and contracted out the production of posters and a calendar utilizing the hidden images. He then began giving away samples and running advertisements, hoping that the gimmick would catch on.

Before long, other entrepreneurs noticed what Baccei was doing and decided to exploit the images as well. A company named Nvision set up kiosks and carts in shopping malls across the United States to sell posters, which turned out to be the best possible advertising for the fledgling enterprise. Because not everybody could immediately see the 3-D images, people gathered to coach each other, creating a congenial atmosphere and a willing customer base.

Baccei wisely allowed Nvision to concentrate on the posters and, in the meantime, coined the phrase "Magic Eye" to market a series of books from publisher Andrews and McMeel. The books quickly topped various best-seller lists in the United States and elsewhere, leading to licensing deals featuring Disney, Looney Tunes, Garfield the cat, and *Star Wars* characters in books and on greeting cards, cereal boxes, and lunch boxes. N. E. Thing Enterprises even began running a syndicated newspaper feature, with a different hidden image each week. In 1996, Baccei renamed the company Magic Eye, Inc. in order to capitalize on the brand name recognition that he had worked so hard to achieve.

Impact The Magic Eye pictures became one of the most widespread, lucrative, and enduring popular culture phenomena of the twentieth century. Although the peak of the pictures' popularity occurred in the mid-1990's, Baccei's company and its competitors continue to seek out or invent new niches for this technology, including custom-made images for companies or individuals, neckties, and puzzles, proving that this multimillion-dollar industry was not merely a simple fad that would quickly run its course and fade away.

Further Reading

Grossman, John. "In the Eye of the Beholder." *Inc.* 16, no. 10 (October, 1994): 60-67.

N. E. Thing Enterprises. *Magic Eye: A New Way of Looking at the World: 3D Illusions.* Kansas City, Mo.: Andrews and McMeel, 1993.

Amy Sisson

See also Advertising; Beanie Babies; CGI; Fads; Science and technology.

■ Mall of America

Identification The second-largest shopping and entertainment complex in North America
Date Opened on August 11, 1992
Place Bloomington, Minnesota

Since its opening, the Mall of America has regularly attracted over forty million visitors annually to the more than five hundred shops within it that are housed in an enclosed area of approximately 4.2 million square feet. With parking facilities for 12,550 cars (later increased to 20,000 cars), the mall employs some twelve thousand people, making it a significant factor in Minnesota's economy.

Strategically located at the intersection of Interstate 494 and Highway 77 close to the Minneapolis-St. Paul International Airport in Minnesota, the Mall of America is the most visited megamall in the United States, attracting annually more visitors than the Statue of Liberty and the Washington Monument combined. Although it is not the largest mall in North America—a distinction held by the West Edmonton Mall in Alberta, Canada, whose square footage is 5.2 million—the Mall of America attracts more visitors than any mall in North America. It is the third-largest enclosed mall when measured by its retail space, but it is the largest in the United States when measured by its total enclosed area.

The Architectural Plan The sprawling Mall of America is essentially rectangular. Three sides of the rectangle have three levels with over five hundred shops facing the pedestrian passageways on its sides. There is a fourth level on the remaining side of the rectangle, much of it devoted to restaurants, bars, cocktail lounges, and other service facilities. The mall is subdivided into four zones, each distinctive in its decor. Because of Minnesota's harsh winters, the mall is totally enclosed so that visitors are not subjected to the extreme weather. The design is also environmentally friendly: Hundreds of skylights provide illumination as well as solar-generated heat.

Only the entrances to the mall are heated. Some of the heat needed to make the mall comfortable is generated by its lighting fixtures, and a great deal more comes from the body heat of people working in or visiting the mall. It amazes many people to learn that in the dead of winter, it is often necessary to cool the mall artificially to make it comfortable.

Aside from more than five hundred retail stores that occupy three levels of the mall, each of the corners of the mall is occupied by a so-called anchor store, a large department store with a well-known name. In the Mall of America, the anchor stores are Bloomingdale's, Macy's, Nordstrom, and Sears.

An inside view of the Mall of America in Bloomington, Minnesota. (AP/Wide World Photos)

An Accessible Location The Mall of America is ideally situated for accessibility by the populations of Minneapolis and St. Paul. Its proximity to an international airport has made it possible for the mall, in cooperation with various airlines, to offer special inducements to fly people from abroad to Minnesota for shopping sprees at the legendary mall. The site on which the mall was constructed was originally occupied by the Metropolitan Sports Arena and Met Stadium, where the Minnesota Twins baseball team played for many years. One seat from the Met Stadium was placed in the Mall of America at the spot it originally occupied to mark the 520-foot home run hit by Harmon Killebrew, who went on to be enshrined in the Baseball Hall of Fame.

The Bloomington Port Authority contracted with the Triple Five Group, the Canadian concern that built the West Edmonton Mall, to construct a megamall in Bloomington. Ground was broken for the Mall of America on June 14, 1989, and some three years later, on August 11, 1992, the mall opened its doors to its first customers.

Impact The Mall of America has become an American icon. Within its walls are a fourteen-screen movie theater, a wedding chapel, a church, an eighteen-hole miniature golf course, and an alternative high school, the Metropolitan Learning Alliance. The Hiawatha Light Rail connects the mall to the nearby international airport and to downtown Minneapolis.

The economic impact of the Mall of America has been substantial. It has turned suburban Bloomington, the third-largest city in Minnesota, into a thriving metropolis with a workforce of thousands of people who have jobs ancillary to those of the twelve thousand people employed directly in the mall itself. Visitors from around the world have come to Minnesota, the northernmost of the forty-eight contiguous states, to visit and shop in the mall.

Further Reading

Herwig, Oliver. *Dream Worlds: Architecture and Entertainment.* New York: Prestel, 2006. A well-illustrated volume especially valuable for its chapter titled "Southdale Mall and the Mall of America: A Shopping Universe."

Lysloff, René T. A., and Leslie C. Gay, Jr. *Music and Technoculture.* Middletown, Conn.: Wesleyan University Press, 2003. Especially relevant is chapter 13, "Sounds Like the Mall of America: Programmed Music and the Archtectonics of Commercial Space."

Nelson, Eric. *The Mall of America: Reflections of a Virtual Community.* Lakeville, Minn.: Galde Press, 1998. An extremely valuable resource that covers the history of the Mall of America as well as the social implications of such an enterprise.

Rubenstein, Harvey. *Pedestrian Malls, Streetscapes, and Urban Spaces.* New York: John Wiley & Sons, 1992. One of the best sources on the types of malls found worldwide. The historical perspective of this book is broad and, although it was published shortly before the Mall of America was established, the book is worth referring to for its overall portrayal of malls throughout the world.

R. Baird Shuman

See also Architecture; Business and the economy in the United States; Employment in the United States; Recession of 1990-1991; Ventura, Jesse.

■ Malone, Karl

Identification American basketball player
Born July 24, 1963; Summerfield, Louisiana

Characterized by consistency and durability, Malone's nineteen-year National Basketball Association (NBA) career flourished in the 1990's. During the decade, he received two Olympic gold medals and two Most Valuable Player Awards and led the Utah Jazz to successive appearances in the NBA Finals.

On January 27, 1990, allegedly disgruntled by his exclusion from the starting lineup of the Western Conference All-Star Team, Karl Malone scored a career-high (and Utah Jazz franchise record) sixty-one points against the Milwaukee Bucks. The effort was part of his strongest statistical season and was a harbinger of Malone's decade-long dominance of the power forward position. In the 1990's, he was the only player selected to the All-NBA First Team each season and made a total of eleven appearances on the team over the course of his career.

Malone finished his career as the second-highest all-time scorer in NBA history, behind Kareem Abdul-Jabbar. Malone's total was augmented by his fortuitous partnership with point guard John Stockton, the NBA's career assists leader. The two were teammates for sixteen seasons and utilized the pick-and-roll to confound opponents and produce unprecedented success for the Jazz franchise. Beginning in 1992, the Jazz advanced to the Western Conference Finals five times in seven years. "When we play the game like we're supposed to play it, it is pretty easy. Making the extra pass, making the simple play, it's not about between your legs, behind your back, and all of that, it's just about scoring the bucket," Malone said, highlighting the team's work ethic.

In 1997, Malone received the first of his two Most Valuable Player (MVP) Awards and guided the Jazz into the NBA Finals against the team of the decade, Michael Jordan's Chicago Bulls. With the series tied after four games, Jordan, sick with the flu, scored thirty-eight points to help Chicago win game five in Utah. In a close game six, the Bulls eliminated the Jazz. The following year, the two teams finished with identical 62-20 regular-season records and met again in the NBA Finals. With his team down three games to one, Malone had his strongest Finals performance—thirty-nine points, nine rebounds, and five assists—to force a game six. With time expiring in game six, Jordan made a twenty-foot jump shot that gave Chicago a 87-86 lead and its sixth championship of the 1990's. Malone returned once more to the NBA Finals—in 2004, his only season with the Los Angeles Lakers—but was hampered by a knee injury; as evidence of his integral role with the team, his inability to contribute cost the Lakers the championship.

Malone's durability—he played in at least eighty games in all but two seasons—was partly attributable to his fitness regimen. He cultivated an intimidating physique and employed a physical playing style. Opponents often accused Malone of playing dirty; on one occasion, Isiah Thomas required forty stitches above his eye because of contact with one of Ma-

Utah Jazz power forward Karl Malone, left, defends against the Chicago Bulls' Michael Jordan during game two of the 1997 NBA Finals. (AP/Wide World Photos)

lone's notorious elbows. Malone's willingness to improve was also responsible for his longevity: Over the course of his tenure, he sharpened his passing ability as well as his free throwing and perimeter shooting.

Impact In the 1990's, Malone won two Olympic gold medals—one with the 1992 "Dream Team." His career statistics rival Abdul-Jabbar's, and though he retired without an NBA championship, he was a worthy adversary for Jordan, Hakeem Olajuwon, and other dominant players of the decade. Malone's success was heightened by the fact that he played for a small-market franchise. His on-court demeanor and his conspicuous musculature are indelible images of the NBA in the 1990's.

Further Reading

Hareas, John. *NBA's Greatest.* New York: Dorling Kindersley, 2003.

Kalb, Elliott. *Who's Better, Who's Best in Basketball? Mr. Stats Sets the Record Straight on the Top Fifty NBA Players of All Time.* Chicago: Contemporary Books, 2004.

Latimer, Clay. *Special Delivery: The Amazing Basketball Career of Karl Malone.* Lenexa, Kans.: Addax, 1999.

Lewis, Michael C. *To the Brink: Stockton, Malone, and the Utah Jazz's Climb to the Edge of Glory.* New York: Simon & Schuster, 1998.

Christopher Rager

See also African Americans; Barkley, Charles; Basketball; Dream Team; Johnson, Magic; Jordan, Michael; Olympic Games of 1992; Olympic Games of 1996; O'Neal, Shaquille; Sports.

■ Mapplethorpe obscenity trial

The Event A highly publicized trial over the display of allegedly obscene art
Date September 24-October 5, 1990
Place Cincinnati, Ohio

The acquittal of the Cincinnati Contemporary Arts Center and its director Dennis Barrie on charges of pandering obscenity was a reaffirmation of freedom of speech protection, particularly with regard to homoerotic art, and set off a national controversy about the public funding of artworks.

In 1990, the Cincinnati Contemporary Arts Center (CAC) exhibited popular American photographer Robert Mapplethorpe's (1946-1989) highly erotic *The Perfect Moment* to great public outrage, due in part to the openly homosexual nature of much of Mapplethorpe's work. The display resulted in the unsuccessful prosecution of director Dennis Barrie on charges of pandering obscenity. Mapplethorpe, who was highly regarded for his large-scale, black-and-white portraits of celebrities and photos of flowers and nudes, photographed the human body in a manner that combined formal beauty and sexuality and included in his work homoerotic imagery and sadomasochistic acts. He was best known for his 1978 sexually explicit Portfolio X series, which resulted in national outrage because it was displayed at publicly funded exhibitions.

It should be remembered that in the early 1990's, the pendulum was swinging toward a more politically and socially conservative America. In 1990, the National Endowment for the Arts (NEA) had one of its highest budgets ever, $170 million, and Republicans made plans to eliminate the agency entirely. The opposition of the American Family Association and other religious organizations to Mapplethorpe's work led to a direct attack on the NEA, which funded the Mapplethorpe exhibit. Also, since the exhibit began its national tour almost a year before it reached Cincinnati, those in that city who objected to the exhibition had plenty of time to prepare an attempt to close the exhibit under Ohio's obscenity statute, which made it illegal to display obscene material.

The Trial A watchdog group, Citizens for Community Values, organized a protest against Mapplethorpe's exhibit. Hours after the opening on April 7, 1990, the CAC and Barrie were indicted by the Hamilton County Grand Jury for criminal violations of the Ohio obscenity statute for pandering obscenity and illegally displaying photographs of nude children. The trial began on September 24, with a jury made up of four men and four women and Judge F. David J. Albanese presiding. The lawyers for the CAC and Barrie were Marc D. Mezibov and H. Louis Sirkin; the prosecutors were Richard A. Castellini, Frank H. Prouty, Jr., and Melanie J. Reising.

At issue were 7 of 175 photographs, also referred to as the "Dirty Pictures" (and the name of the 2000 film about the trial), which depict children with exposed genitals and men in sadomasochistic poses. The cross-examination of witnesses by the prosecution, led by Prouty, concluded that what some peo-

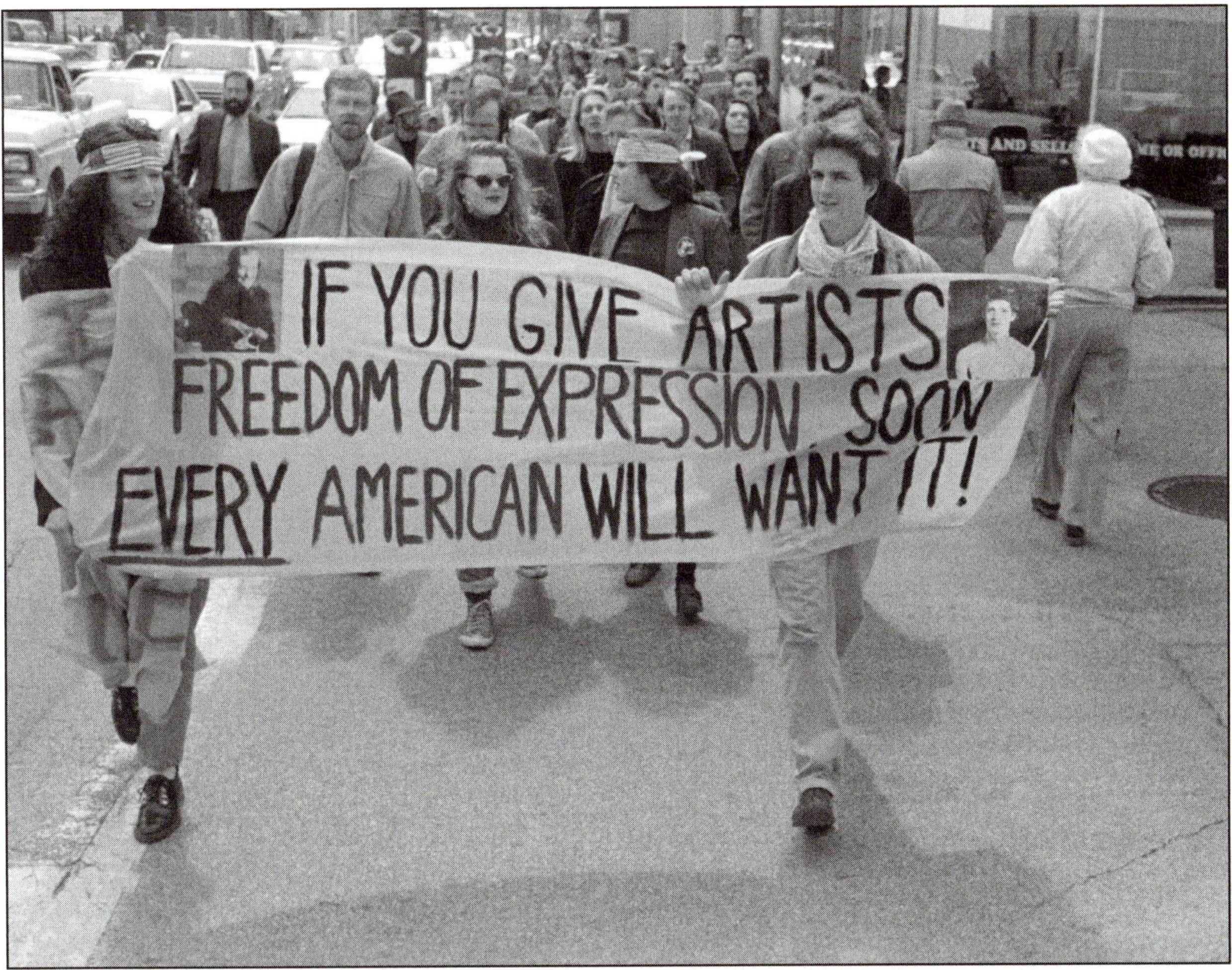

Demonstrators in support of the late Robert Mapplethorpe's controversial exhibit, The Perfect Moment, *march through downtown Cincinnati on April 6, 1990.* (AP/Wide World Photos)

ple view as pornography, others view as art. The prosecutors had to convince the jury that the pictures were "obscene," as defined by the Supreme Court in the 1973 case *Miller v. California.* The defense witnesses, made up of art experts, saw the pictures in the light of artistic freedom. Janet Kardon, a defense witness, viewed the photographs themselves as symmetrical and classically composed figure studies, while witnesses for the prosecution viewed the photographs as deeply offensive sexually explicit merchandise.

This debate led to the decisive questions: Who determines art and how does one know if something is art? Ultimately, Barrie and the CAC were acquitted in a much-publicized trial six months after the indictment.

Impact The acquittal of the defendants was a reaffirmation of freedom of speech. Also, the obscenity trial served to illustrate the struggle between the liberal and conservative values of early 1990's America. As an issue, public arts funding remained in the forefront throughout the decade, and politicians continued the debate about the government's need to sponsor art. Indeed, some argue that the Mapplethorpe trial was a catalyst for bringing about the culture wars.

The Cincinnati Institute of Fine Arts temporarily dropped funding for the CAC. Between 1990 and 1995, the NEA saw the abolishment of twenty categories of grants. Consequently, funding plummeted and attempts were made to eliminate the agency. Ultimately, however, the Mapplethorpe trial brought arts advocates together and galvanized support for the NEA and the federal role for arts support in the United States. Indeed, state legislatures across the country granted arts councils $292 million in 2000. Still, those who brought the 1990 obscenity charges against the Contemporary Arts Center claim that the trial worked to their advantage simply because their primary intention was not to close art museums but merely to force them to act responsibly in their selection of art, which, they argue, was the ultimate outcome.

Further Reading

Danto, Arthur C. *Playing with the Edge: The Photographic Achievement of Robert Mapplethorpe.* Berkeley: University of California Press, 1996. Offers a lucid discussion of Mapplethorpe's works. Illustrated.

Gurstein, Rochelle. "Current Debate: High Art or Hard-Core? Misjudging Mapplethorpe—the Art Scene and the Obscene." *Tikkun* (November/December, 1991): 70-80. Gurstein, who teaches history and other subjects at Bard Graduate Center in Manhattan, argues against avant-garde artists such as Mapplethorpe who she believes invoke free speech rights to justify what she considers violent, dehumanizing, or pornographic works.

Merkel, Jayne. "Art on Trial." *Art in America* (December, 1990): 41-46. Not only details the events of the Mapplethorpe obscenity trial but also argues that it was not so much Mapplethorpe on trial as art in America.

M. Casey Diana

See also Art movements; Censorship; Child pornography; Conservatism in U.S. politics; Culture wars; *Holy Virgin Mary, The*; Homosexuality and gay rights; National Endowment for the Arts (NEA); Photography; Republican Revolution.

■ Marilyn Manson

Identification Industrial metal band
Date Formed in 1989

The band established itself in the American music scene by courting controversy through provocative lyrics and shock metal antics during its shows. Thematically, the band grapples with the subjects of death, violence, drug use, youth alienation, and American religious culture.

Marilyn Manson is an industrial metal band influenced by the shock rock bands of Kiss and Alice Cooper and by the glam rock of David Bowie. The band was established to be shocking to the public as a whole, as demonstrated by the stage names the band adopted for its early acts. The idea behind the stage names was to reflect the dichotomy of good and evil in American popular culture. For example, "Marilyn Manson" links Hollywood sex symbol Marilyn Monroe to serial killer Charles Manson; "Gidget Gein," stage name of one of the band's bassists in the 1990's, combines the names of the television character Gidget and serial killer Ed Gein. The early stage act in Fort Lauderdale, Florida, had band members dressing in androgynous costumes on a stage decorated with bloody crosses, naked women, and animal parts. In 1992, Trent Reznor of the industrial band Nine Inch Nails helped to popularize Marilyn Manson by coproducing its first three albums. The band's debut album, *Portrait of an American Family* (1994), had limited commercial success. Following its first headlining tour, the band released the extended play record *Smells Like Children* (1995), which contained the hit single remix "Sweet Dreams (Are Made of This)." With *Antichrist Superstar* (1996), the band became popular in the mainstream.

A considerable portion of the band's popularity derived from the protest of parents and religious groups who found *Antichrist Superstar* obscene and anti-Christian. Singles from the album, including "The Beautiful People" and "Tourniquet," contributed to the protests, as did the lead singer, Marilyn Manson (Brian Warner), who stoked protests with provocative comments about the need to end Christianity. To promote the album, the band headlined the Dead to the World tour, which featured an elaborate goth-inspired stage show, which was picketed by protesters and even banned in some cities. In 1998, the band released *Mechanical Animals,* which featured the hit singles "The Dope Show," "I Don't Like the Drugs (But the Drugs Like Me)," and "Rock Is Dead." As the band began its Rock Is Dead tour in 1999 with Hole (led by Courtney Love) and Monster Magnet, the Columbine massacre caused the band to cancel the rest of the tour dates out of respect for the victims. In the immediate aftermath, Marilyn Manson and its music was often cited as a contributing factors in the rampage.

Impact Marilyn Manson, a self-proclaimed advocate for individuality and self-expression, became the symbol for all that is wrong with American culture during the mid- to late 1990's, especially because of the band's seeming promotion of violence, drug abuse, and generally antisocial, anti-Christian behavior.

Further Reading

Brackett, Nathan, and Christian Hoard, eds. *The New Rolling Stone Album Guide.* 4th ed. New York: Simon & Schuster, 2004.

Manson, Marilyn, and Neil Strauss. *The Long Hard Road out of Hell.* New York: HarperCollins, 1998.

John P. Cryderman

See also Alternative rock; Censorship; Columbine massacre; Drug use; Love, Courtney; Music; Nine Inch Nails; Religion and spirituality in the United States; School violence; Wal-Mart.

■ Marriage and divorce

Definition Social institution under which two people become legally united and the legal dissolution thereof

Complex historical and social trends created significant cultural changes since the 1960's, establishing diverse family and household compositions and unique challenges for marriage in the 1990's.

Until the 1960's, the divorce and remarriage rates in the United States changed jointly. As one increased or decreased, so did the other. However, beginning in the 1960's, marriage, divorce, and remarriage patterns changed dramatically. First marriage rates began to fall, and divorce rates rose. The remarriage rate initially increased in response to the rising divorce rate but ultimately declined. The divorce rate remained relatively unchanged at high levels during the 1970's and 1980's—dropping slightly at the end of the second decade. First marriage rates and remarriage rates continued to decrease through the 1970's and 1980's. In the 1990's, demographic indicators pertaining to marriage and divorce stabilized as compared to the previous two decades. Marriage and remarriage rates continued a long-term decline, but more gradually, and divorce rates dropped slightly.

From 1990 to 2000, crude marriage rates (number of marriages per year per 1,000 population) declined from 9.8 to 8.5. This modest decline could suggest that individuals are simply marrying at later ages than in earlier decades or choosing an alternative such as single parenting or cohabitation over marriage. The low marriage rate during the mid-1990's was similar to rates experienced during the Great Depression.

Age at marriage increased throughout the 1990's. In 1980, the median age of marriage was 24.7 for men and 22.0 for women. By 1990, men married at a median age of 26.1 and women at 23.9. By 2000, the median age had risen to 26.7 for men and 25.1 for women. Women often postponed marriage because of economic and opportunity costs of early marriage and child rearing, while men delayed marriage because of a more restricted pool of women to marry.

The crude divorce rate (number of divorces per year per 1,000 population) peaked in the United States at 5.3 in 1970 and 1983. Liberalizing divorce laws and lessening social stigma associated with divorce contributed to high rates of divorce. Additionally, as women's economic opportunities improved, divorce also increased because women could be financially independent.

In 1990, the divorce rate stood at 4.7 and dropped to 4.0 by 2000, still at one of the highest levels in the industrialized world. Fewer marriages, resulting in less opportunity for divorce, and older average age at marriage contributed to the slight decline of the divorce rate.

Lower marriage rates and increased childbearing out of wedlock resulted in a decline in the growth of family households (families maintained by married couples or a man or woman living with other relatives—children may or may not be present). Between 1980 and 1990, household growth rate slowed from 1.7 million per year to 1.3 million per year and dropped even further to 1.1 million in the 1990's.

Postponement of marriage and lower remarriage rates after divorce coupled with changing social norms led to a larger percentage of births to unmarried woman in the 1990's than ever before reported. Women spent less time in marriages, and thus the opportunity for nonmarital childbearing increased.

Social Issues While divorce, marriage, and remarriage trends are important indicators of marriage and family change, throughout the 1990's the emergence of cohabitation and same-sex marriage demonstrated the shifting meaning of marriage and family in the United States. Cohabitation grew during the 1990's and became a more socially accepted familial alternative to traditional marriage. The number of cohabiting couples in the United States grew from 2.8 million in 1990 to 4.5 million in 2000. The escalation of cohabitation helped account for lower remarriage rates.

Court decisions appeared to set the stage for legal same-sex marriages. The Hawaii Supreme Court ruled in 1993 that restricting marriages to opposite-sex partners violated the equal protection clause in the state constitution. However, in 1998, Hawaiian voters gave the state legislature power to block same-sex marriages, which it quickly did. The 1996 Defense of Marriage Act signed by President Bill Clinton denied federal recognition to same-sex couples. However, the Vermont Supreme Court ruled in 1999 that the state must allow same-sex couples to marry or permit them the same rights of married couples. In April, 2000, Vermont began to recognize civil unions.

Impact Economic and cultural changes since the 1960's increased the prevalence of and tolerance for diverse family forms. A weakening of social bonds and norms that traditionally defined people's behavior in the family led to negotiation of new family roles and in new types of families. The traditional, biological two-parent family was no longer the idealized or most common family form. Birthrates dropped, people delayed marriage, cohabitation rates soared, and divorce rates increased.

Further Reading

Cherlin, Andrew J. "The Deinstitutionalization of American Marriage." *Journal of Marriage and Family* 66, no. 4 (2004): 848-861. Examines the changing significance of marriage in society, including practical implications for economic well-being and childrearing as well as symbolic meanings of marriage in the United States.

Fields, Jason, et al. *America's Families and Living Arrangements.* Washington, D.C.: Government Printing Office, 2001. Reports trends about households, families, and living arrangements in the United States.

Kreider, Rose M., et al. *Marital Status 2000: Census 2000 Brief.* Washington, D.C.: U.S. Government Printing Office, 2003. Presents U.S. Census data on marital status from 1950-2000.

Martin, Teresa Castro, et al. "Recent Trends in Marital Disruption." *Demography* 26, no. 1 (1989): 37-51. Examines the reduction in marital stability in the United States, with emphasis on the decline in divorce rates in the 1980's and the leveling off in the 1990's.

Norton, Arthur J., et al. *Marriage, Divorce, and Remarriage in the 1990's.* Washington, D.C.: U.S. Government Printing Office, 1992. Includes analysis of data from several surveys explaining patterns of marriage, divorce, remarriage, and redivorce.

Teachman, Jay D., et al. "The Changing Demography of America's Families." *Journal of Marriage and Family* (2000): 1234-1246. An overview of changes in American families related to declining prevalence of early marriage, increasing levels of marital dissolution, and the growing tendency to never marry.

Barbara E. Johnson

See also Blended families; Demographics of the United States; Defense of Marriage Act of 1996; Domestic partnerships; Homosexuality and gay rights.

■ Mars exploration

Definition The intensive study of Mars by spacecraft

In the 1990's, NASA began an ambitious, decade-long program to explore Mars by flying two spacecraft to the planet every twenty-six months. This program resulted in high-quality photographic imaging of most of the surface of Mars as well as the deployment of the first rover, a small, semiautonomous laboratory that performed chemical analysis of rocks and soil.

Mars is the most Earth-like planet in the solar system, so it provides insights into how Earth-like planets evolved and, possibly, how life originated. The major objective of the National Aeronautics and Space Administration's (NASA) Viking 1 and 2 spacecraft, which landed on Mars in 1976, was to search for evidence of life, possibly in the form of microorganisms in the soil. Unfortunately, the reactive chemistry of the Martian soil interfered with these analyses.

After a hiatus of more than fifteen years, NASA resumed its exploration of Mars with the launching of the Mars Observer on September 25, 1992. This large observatory was intended to study the geology and climate. On August 21, 1993, just three days before it was scheduled to enter orbit, radio contact was lost. A review panel determined that a fuel-line rupture in the propulsion system during preparation for orbital insertion probably caused its failure.

Mars Pathfinder Following the failure of the Mars Observer, NASA shifted its Mars exploration efforts to more frequent but smaller spacecraft. Mars Pathfinder, the second of NASA's low-cost Discovery missions, was designed to test a new way to deliver payloads to the Martian surface. Pathfinder was launched by a Delta II rocket on December 4, 1996, and landed on Mars on July 4, 1997, directly entering the Martian atmosphere using a small parachute to slow its descent and a system of air bags to cushion its impact. Pathfinder hit the surface at forty miles per hour, bouncing five hundred feet into the air. It bounced sixteen times before coming to rest after 2.5 minutes, about 0.6 mile from its initial impact. The landing site, Ares Vallis, was selected because photographs from the Viking spacecraft indicated it was an ancient floodplain containing a variety of different types of rocks.

The six-hundred-pound Pathfinder carried the twenty-two-pound Sojourner rover, named after the civil rights crusader Sojourner Truth. The six-wheeled rover rolled onto the surface of Mars on July 6. It was controlled from Earth, but the ten-minute time delay for communication required autonomous control of some rover activities. Mars Pathfinder took 16,500 images of the surface and monitored weather. Sojourner took 550 images and analyzed 15 rocks. The results suggest that Mars was once warm and wet with a thick atmosphere. Communications with Pathfinder and Sojourner were lost, for unknown reasons, on September 27, 1997.

Mars Global Surveyor Launched on November 7, 1996, aboard a Delta II rocket, the Mars Global Surveyor was a fast, low-cost spacecraft to perform most of the science planned for Mars Observer. The spacecraft entered a highly elliptical orbit around Mars on September 12, 1997, and began sixteen months of aerobraking, repeatedly passing through the upper atmosphere to reduce the high point of the orbit, putting it into a nearly circular, two-hour polar orbit. This orbit allowed the Surveyor to observe each spot on Mars every seven days. Beginning in March, 1999, Surveyor performed high-resolution mapping, studied the gravitational field, investigated the role of water and dust on the atmosphere, and mapped the Martian magnetic field. Some images showed bright, new deposits in two gullies, suggesting that water may still flow, at least sporadically, on the Martian surface. High-resolution images of the Cydonia Region showed that the "face on Mars," a formation resembling a human face in lower-resolution Viking images, was simply a natural rock formation. After studying Mars for four times as long as planned, the Mars Global Surveyor ceased transmitting in November, 2006, probably resulting from a computer error leading to battery failure. The Surveyor was one of the first spacecraft in NASA's planned, decade-long exploration of Mars, with launches every twenty-six months.

Mars Global Surveyor prior to a second launch attempt on November 7, 1996. (NASA Kennedy Space Center)

Mars Climate Orbiter and Polar Lander Launched on December 11, 1998, by a Delta II rocket, the Mars Climate Orbiter carried instruments to study weather, atmospheric ozone, distribution and transport of dust and water, effects of topography on atmospheric circulation, and atmospheric response to solar heating. The spacecraft reached Mars on September 23, 1999, and fired its engine to enter orbit. Radio contact was not reestablished after the spacecraft passed behind Mars. A failure review board determined that some commands were sent in imperial instead of metric units and that the spacecraft was destroyed by atmospheric stresses when it came too close to Mars.

The Mars Polar Lander, launched aboard a Delta II rocket on January 3, 1999, was targeted to land near the edge of the south polar ice cap. The spacecraft was designed to record weather conditions, analyze samples of polar deposits for water and carbon dioxide, and determine soil composition. The last radio signal from the lander was sent just prior to atmospheric entry on December 3, 1999. When the Mars Climate Orbiter was lost, the task of relaying communications from the Polar Lander was shifted to the Mars Global Surveyor, but no communications were received from the surface. The Polar Lander carried two soil penetrators, intended to separate from the spacecraft just before atmospheric entry to measure thermal conductivity of the surface, but these were lost as well.

Impact Indications that Mars was once warm, wet, and had a dense atmosphere suggest that it was Earth-like in the past, raising the question of how it evolved into an inhospitable planet. The successes of Mars Pathfinder and Mars Global Surveyor set the stage for more ambitious exploration in the twenty-first century, possibly including human exploration of Mars. The Sojourner rover marked the beginning of a program of ever more ambitious Mars rovers in the twenty-first century. However, the failures of the Mars Observer, Mars Climate Orbiter, and Mars Polar Lander emphasized the difficulty of planetary exploration.

Further Reading

Bizony, Piers. *The Exploration of Mars: Searching for the Cosmic Origins of Life.* London: Aurum Press, 1998. A well-illustrated, two-hundred-page account of the search for life on Mars.

Mishkin, Andrew. *Sojourner: An Insider's View of the Mars Pathfinder Mission.* New York: Berkeley, 2004. A firsthand account of the Mars Pathfinder probe by a systems engineer at the Jet Propulsion Laboratory. Illustrated.

Shirley, Donna. *Managing Martians.* New York: Broadway Books, 1998. An account of the development of Sojourner by the first woman to manage a NASA spaceflight program.

George J. Flynn

See also Science and technology; Space exploration; Space shuttle program.

■ Matrix, The

Identification Science-fiction action film
Directors Larry Wachowski (1965-) and Andy Wachowski (1967-)
Date Released on March 31, 1999

This highly influential and popular film reflected popular concerns about the relationships among technology, cyberspace, and humanity.

The Matrix tells the story of Thomas "Neo" Anderson (Keanu Reeves), a weary computer programmer for a megacorporation by day and a computer hacker by night. When he follows the advice of unusual strangers, Neo learns the truth of his existence: It is not 1999 as he and most humans believe, but nearly two hundred years later. Machines rule the world and have created a virtual reality—the Matrix—to pacify humans. The rebels free Neo and train him to manipulate the Matrix, hoping he will be the hero who will save the human race.

The story's mystery is heightened by the philosophical questions it overtly raises: What is reality? Does a self exist? How do images relate to reality? How are humans and machines related? The almost constant allusions to literature, philosophy, theory, film, and popular culture provide resonance and sometimes humor. For example: Neo must follow the white rabbit to find the rebels and then go down the "rabbit hole" (Lewis Carroll's *Alice's Adventures in Wonderland,* 1865). Neo's understanding that his "life" in 1999 is an illusion exemplifies Plato's "Allegory of the Cave." The names Zion and Nebuchadnezzar come from the Bible, and Neo may be "the One," a clear symbol for Christ. Film buffs will recog-

nize allusions to *Star Wars* (1977), *Ghost in the Shell* (1995), and *The Wizard of Oz* (1939).

Although clearly much of the film is derivative, the cyberpunk visual style is memorable, from the vertically falling "rain" of data on rebel computer screens to the extremely violent, stylized kung fu fighting sequences enhanced with wirework and computer-generated images. The bullet-time effect (in which computer graphics enhance simulations of hyperslow and hyperfast speeds) is particularly striking, not only producing breathtaking images but also expressing the heightened perceptions of the main characters while in the Matrix.

Impact This film reflects many of the concerns of the 1990's: worries about pollution, the approaching millennium, and the increasing electronification of American lives (proliferation of cell phones and surveillance technology, miniaturization of electronic devices, and increased reliance on computers and the Internet) that might lead to social alienation. *The Matrix* became a modern myth as viewers engaged with both the themes and the style. The film's visual style was much copied, especially the sophisticated fight scenes and special effects.

The success of *The Matrix* prompted the completion of the trilogy (*The Matrix Reloaded* and *The Matrix Revolutions* in 2003). *The Matrix* is also the base of a large transmedia franchise that includes *The Animatrix* (2003), a video game, comics, and an online game; each of these contributes information valuable to the story as a whole. *The Matrix* is taught in a variety of college courses, including courses focusing on philosophy, science fiction, media, and psychology.

Further Reading

Irwin, William, ed. *The Matrix and Philosophy: Welcome to the Desert of the Real.* Chicago: Open Court, 2002.

Kapell, Matthew, and William G. Doty, eds. *Jacking in to the Matrix Franchise: Cultural Reception and Interpretation.* New York: Continuum, 2004.

Kathryn A. Walterscheid

See also CGI; Computers; Film in the United States; Hackers; Internet; Reeves, Keanu.

Medicine

Definition Medical discoveries and advances as well as newly recognized illnesses during the decade

During the 1990's, medicine was characterized by a mixture of both medical successes and setbacks. The eradication of poliomyelitis in the Western Hemisphere was announced by the World Health Organization, while the introduction of a new generation of therapeutic drugs offered additional weapons against illness or disease. At the same time, new outbreaks of diseases such as Ebola and hantavirus respiratory infections took place.

The 1990's represented a period during which newer technologies were introduced or underwent increased development and application. New generations of drugs were approved, both for treatment of infectious disease as well as for palliative measures in dealing with chronic problems or illnesses.

Palliative Treatments The use of rectal or oral thermometers as currently recognized dates to the latter half of the nineteenth century. The use of mercury within the instrument, as well as the discomfort and time associated with their use, was problematic. In 1990, new forms of thermometers were introduced, with one type inserted into the ear canal, and a second type placed on the forehead. Each produced a relatively rapid reading, though their accuracy was later called into question.

In 1999, new forms of painkillers were introduced. Treatment of arthritis or other forms of inflammation or pain had previously relied on nonsteroid drugs such as ibuprofen or aspirin. Bleeding and possible organ damage were occasional side effects, albeit rare when these drugs were properly used. The drug Celebrex was the first of the cyclooxygenase-2 (COX-2) inhibitors to be approved, inhibiting the enzyme pathway that results in production of inflammatory chemicals.

The use of hysterectomy as a means to treat uterine problems such as bleeding or fibroids, the most common benign tumors in the reproductive tract of young women, remained controversial. During the 1990's, approximately 600,000 hysterectomies were carried out annually. In the mid-1990's, an alternative treatment for dealing with fibroids was introduced: myomectomy, a method that removes the fibroids while allowing the uterus to remain intact.

Unfortunately, in almost half these cases, fibroids returned. Nevertheless, the issue of research into alternative treatments for bleeding or fibroids was brought to the public's attention.

Infectious Disease The last "natural" case of poliomyelitis in the United States had been diagnosed in 1979. The introduction of the first inactivated poliomyelitis vaccine developed by Jonas Salk in the mid-1950's, subsequently followed by the oral poliomyelitis vaccine developed by Albert Sabin in the mid-1960's, had resulted in control of what had been annual devastating epidemics. The last case of polio in the Western Hemisphere occurred in Peru in 1991, and in 1994 the Pan American Health Organization within the World Health Organization announced the eradication of the disease in the West. Both Salk and Sabin died during the decade, Salk in 1995 at age eighty, and Sabin in 1993 at age eighty-six.

Meanwhile, a newly recognized disease appeared in the southwestern United States in 1993. In March, the first case of acute respiratory distress syndrome (ARDS) was diagnosed in the Native American area near the Four Corners region. By June, sixteen patients, twelve of whom had died, had been diagnosed, with another twenty-five persons likely infected. In the period between 1993 and 1995, forty-five deaths were attributed to the infection. The etiological agent was identified in 1993 as a member of the hantavirus group, first described during the Korean War. The reservoirs for the agent were the deer mouse and cotton rat, as well as other regional rodents. Isolated infections by the same family of viruses were subsequently reported in other regions of the country.

While stomach ulcers were not normally classified as infectious illnesses, Australian gastroenterologist Dr. Barry Marshall proposed in 1983 that a bacterium he had isolated from the stomachs of patients, *Helicobacter pylori*, was the likely agent underlying development of ulcers. Marshall's work was confirmed by others during the 1990's, resulting in possible treatment of ulcers using antibiotics.

The first examples of "extensively drug-resistant" (XDR) cases of tuberculosis were reported in the United States during the 1990's. Between 1993 and 1999, over 111,000 culture-confirmed cases of the disease were reported by the National Tuberculosis Surveillance System (NTSS). Thirty-two of these cases were due to infection by XDR strains of *Mycobacterium tuberculosis*. Antibiotic-resistant strains of other bacteria were likewise becoming an increasing problem. In 1996, vancomycin-resistant strains of *Staphylococcus aureus*, previously found to be resistant to other commonly used antibiotics such as methicillin, were isolated from infected patients.

The incidence of acquired immunodeficiency syndrome (AIDS) in the United States peaked in the mid-1990's, with 257,000 cases reported between 1993 and 1995. Approximately 600,000 cases were reported during the decade, though the numbers were inflated from the previous decade in part as a result of redefining the disease to include additional opportunistic infections. In 1996, the incidence of new cases began to decline, in part the result of increased emphasis on altering risk behaviors. Approximately two-thirds of persons diagnosed with AIDS since its recognition in 1981 had died by the end of the 1990's. Among the persons diagnosed in 1991 as being HIV-positive was Los Angeles Lakers basketball player Magic Johnson. However, in 1996, the first of a new generation of anti-human immunodeficiency virus (HIV) drugs was introduced and approved by the Food and Drug Administration. A series of protease inhibitors received "fast-track" approval and were incorporated into drug cocktails, combinations of anti-AIDS drugs acting at different targets of viral infection. Despite the development of new forms of treatment, the isolation of a drug-resistant virus was reported by the end of the decade.

Cancer The incidence of breast cancer in women continued to rise during the 1990's, surpassing 100 cases per 100,000 women, with approximately 180,000 cases diagnosed annually; by age eighty-five, a woman had one chance in eight of developing the disease. However, the "good" news was that the death rate attributed to breast cancer in women declined by greater than 6 percent, with a decline of nearly 10 percent in women under the age of sixty-five. Several explanations accounted for these results. First, emphasis on early detection resulted in earlier diagnosis and treatment. The proportion of women who reported having undergone a yearly breast examination, including mammography, increased to nearly 40 percent, a tenfold increase when compared with surveys in the 1970's. Improved treatment also had an impact. For example, use of the hormone tamoxifen was found to reduce by 40 percent the chance of the second breast developing cancer in women previously diagnosed with the disease. However, the drug was also linked to increased risk of developing uterine cancer. Funding by Congress for research into the disease was increased to over $300 million.

The rate of cancer mortality in general dropped during the 1990's, reversing a trend that had shown an increase in the death rate during the previous twenty years. The mortality rate for prostate cancer among men of all ages dropped by greater than 6 percent; in men under age seventy-five, mortality was reduced by 7.5 percent. The improvement was a direct result of earlier diagnosis, with emphasis on yearly digital examinations and increased reliance on the blood test that measured prostate specific antigen (PSA) levels.

Similar emphasis on examination and early detection also accounted for decreased mortality of other forms of cancer, including that of colorectal cancer (7 percent), with improved diet being a contributing factor, and several forms of lymphoma. Even the trend associated with lung cancer, the most common form of malignancy, showed improvements. While persons over the age of sixty-five showed an increase greater than 14 percent in mortality associated with lung cancer, the direct result of an increase in smoking associated with this generation, the mortality in both men and women under age sixty-five showed a leveling in the rate, and by the end of the decade, a slight reduction (4 percent) in the mortality rate of the disease. In 1994, the FDA argued that tobacco companies "manipulated" the concentration of nicotine in cigarettes, with the purpose being to establish an addiction to cigarettes. That year, the former head of research at one of the major tobacco companies supported the FDA contention by providing documentary evidence that not only the nicotine content had been manipulated but also that additional chemicals had been added to cigarettes to boost the addictive effects of the nicotine.

One alleged cause of cancer was eliminated during the decade. A report in 1992 had initially linked the presence of electromagnetic fields (EMF) associated with power lines with increased risk of development of a malignancy. Further analysis within the Department of Health and Human Services showed that no such relationship existed, and EMF posed no cancer risk.

Health Care Reform The increase in research costs during the 1990's reflected a general increase in costs of health care. However, estimates projected that over thirty-seven million Americans had no health insurance, with the number climbing as unions lost much of their power and as jobs were eliminated as a result of outsourcing. For businesses, the cost of health care was estimated as greater than $4,500 per year per employee. In 1993, President Bill Clinton placed health care reform as one of America's highest priorities. The costs associated with the pharmaceutical industry were among the areas open to criticism. Clinton observed that on an annual basis, pharmaceutical companies spend over $1 billion more for advertising than they do on research into newer drugs. President Clinton appointed his wife, First Lady Hillary Rodham Clinton, to head a commission with the job of reforming the system.

Among the opponents of reform as President Clinton saw it was the health insurance industry. Shortly after the commission was established, the Health Insurance Agency of America began a series of television advertisements that made light of the attempted reforms. In the end, little was accomplished in the area of health care reform, and the issue continued into the new century.

Impact The decline in most forms of cancer continued into the twenty-first century. Mortality due to breast cancer decreased an average of 2 percent annually, with a decline averaging greater than 3 percent in women under the age of fifty. Most of this improvement was the result of improved methods of diagnosis; the five-year survival after diagnosis approached 90 percent by 2005. While the incidence rate for diagnosis of prostate cancer in men remained unchanged between 1990 and 2005, the mortality associated with the disease was reduced among white males from nearly 26 to 20 per 100,000. Rates remained significantly higher among African Americans but still demonstrated an improvement, from 48 to 35 per 100,000. Mortality rates associated with colorectal cancer leveled off during the ensuing years but was half that reported during the 1970's.

The safety of COX-2 analgesics was eventually called into question. Both Celebrex, manufactured by Pfizer, and Vioxx, produced by Merck, were associated with increased risk of heart disease or stroke.

In 2004, Vioxx was removed from the market. While Celebrex remained available, the FDA recommended that other forms of nonsteroid analgesics such as acetaminophen be substituted when indicated.

Further Reading

Harper, David, and Andrea Meyer. *Of Mice, Men, and Microbes: Hantavirus.* San Diego, Calif.: Academic Press, 1999. Description of the hantavirus outbreak that took place in the Four Corners region of southwestern United States in the early 1990's.

Nuland, Sherwin. *How We Die: Reflections on Life's Final Chapter.* New York: Vintage Books, 1995. Discussion of methods by which both physicians and their patients deal with impending death.

Sampson, Wallace, and Lewis Vaughn, eds. *Science Meets Alternative Medicine: What the Evidence Says About Unconventional Treatments.* Amherst, N.Y.: Prometheus Books, 2000. Collection of articles that address the quality and efficacy of alternative medical treatments such as holistic medicine, alternative healing, and therapeutic touching.

Stine, Gerald. *AIDS Update 2007.* San Francisco: Benjamin Cummings, 2007. Yearly update on research into the AIDS virus, as well as information about biological events that follow infection. Discussion about the progress of treatment is also included. Preventives undergoing testing, such as "pre-exposure prophylaxis," are also described.

Richard Adler

See also AIDS epidemic; Alzheimer's disease; Antidepressants; Attention-deficit disorder; Autism; Cancer research; Carpal tunnel syndrome; Clinton, Bill; Clinton, Hillary Rodham; Depo-Provera; Drug advertising; Drug use; Elders, Joycelyn; Fen-phen; Genetic engineering; Genetically modified foods; Genetics research; Health care; Health care reform; Human Genome Project; Johnson, Magic; Kevorkian, Jack; Laparoscopic surgery; LASIK surgery; McCaughey septuplets; Nicotine patch; Novello, Antonia Coello; Pharmaceutical industry; Physician-assisted suicide; Science and technology; Silicone implant ban; Stem cell research; West Nile virus outbreak.

■ Men Are from Mars, Women Are from Venus

Identification Best-selling self-help book
Author John Gray (1951-)
Date Published in 1992

One of the biggest-selling books of the decade and one of the most widely read books about relationships ever published in America, Gray's book dominated the best-seller charts for over half of the 1990's.

John Gray's subtitle for *Men Are from Mars, Women Are from Venus* states his purpose succinctly: to provide his readers with *A Practical Guide for Improving Communication and Getting What You Want in Your Relationships.* What distinguished Gray's work from that of other authors with similar goals was his approach, one derived from cultural anthropology and linguistics rather than purely from psychology and conventional wisdom. Gray encourages his readers to interpret conflict between the sexes as the result of cultural differences not unlike those that confuse people from one civilization when they interact with representatives from another. Just as people sometimes misunderstand or offend people from other societies because of the contrasting values and customs of the two groups, men ("Martians") and women ("Venusians") likewise annoy each other because they tend to operate according to different sets of assumptions, habits, and concerns.

Since both sexes are ignorant of these gender-based cultural contrasts, men and women take offense where none is intended and so need to study the cultural values and customs of the opposite gender. Therefore, Gray advises readers about various differences he perceives in male and female behavior, especially in regard to politeness and language. For example, women, claims Gray, tend to talk as a way of thinking through a problem and of relieving negative emotions, while men tend to talk primarily to exchange information. As a result of these habits, a wife may talk to her husband about problems at her workplace as a means of venting her frustrations. The wife assumes that her husband understands that she needs to talk in order to express her feelings; however, he assumes, based on typically male conversational motives, that she is asking for his advice and so promptly gives it. The wife is then offended because she interprets his behavior as interruptive and domineering; the husband is offended because she apparently has rejected what he meant as an attempt to help.

Impact With its novel approach to gender-based conflicts, eye-catching title, and aggressive marketing campaign, Mars/Venus became a publishing phenomenon, spawning numerous sequels, a line of videos, a series of television programs, and even a board game. As popular as the book was with readers, many found its portrayal of gender differences sexist and outdated, seemingly depicting men as active and women passive. Nevertheless, Gray's anthropological/cultural approach to gender conflict offered Americans of the 1990's a nonjudgmental, nonhierarchical interpretation of differences between the sexes that did not overtly "bash" or belittle one gender in favor of the other.

Further Reading

Gray, John. *Men Are from Mars, Women Are from Venus: A Practical Guide for Improving Communication and Getting What You Want in Your Relationships.* New York: HarperCollins, 1992.

Tannen, Deborah. *You Just Don't Understand: Women and Men in Conversation.* New York: Ballantine, 1990.

Thomas Du Bose

See also Domestic partnerships; Marriage and divorce; Publishing; *Rules, The.*

Lyle, left, and Erik Menendez in a courtroom in Santa Monica, California, in August, 1996. The brothers were found guilty of the first-degree murder of their parents on March 20, 1996. (AP/Wide World Photos)

■ Menendez brothers murder case

The Event Lyle and Erik Menendez kill their wealthy parents and are convicted of first-degree murder

Date Murders took place on August 20, 1989; brothers convicted on March 20, 1996

Place Beverly Hills and Van Nuys, California

The Menendez trials were covered extensively in popular magazines and on television, reflecting and expanding on the American public's interest in sensational crimes and how media coverage impacts the legal system.

On the evening of August 20, 1989, film company executive Jose Menendez and his wife, Kitty, were murdered in their Beverly Hills home, each suffering multiple shotgun blasts. Police inquiries focused initially on Jose's business relationships. Jose, a driven and brutal executive whose personal estate was worth $14 million, had been sued by a former business associate with rumored links to organized crime. However, the police turned their attention to Jose and Kitty's sons Lyle, age twenty-one, and Erik, age eighteen, in the weeks following the murders, as the brothers gave up their plans to attend college and spent thousands of dollars on new cars, designer clothes, and jewelry.

In October, 1989, Erik confessed to his psychologist, Jerome Oziel, that he and Lyle had killed Jose because he had been too domineering and had planned to disinherit them; they had murdered Kitty because she was unhappy in her marriage. Five months later, Oziel's girlfriend Judalon Smyth contacted police, saying she had overheard the confession and that Oziel had recorded it on audiotape. Based on Oziel and Smyth's evidence, police arrested the brothers in March, 1990, charging each with suspicion of murder. Their trial was delayed by arguments over whether Oziel's information was protected by therapist-client confidentiality. Ultimately, juries were allowed to hear portions of Oziel's audiotapes.

The brothers were tried together, but with separate juries. Lyle and Erik testified that Jose had psychologically and sexually abused them for years and that they had feared he was planning to kill them. Neither jury could agree on a verdict. At a second trial, before a single jury, Lyle and Erik were found guilty of first-degree murder and conspiracy to commit murder. Each was sentenced to two consecutive terms of life in prison without parole.

Impact During the first trial, the Court TV network provided live coverage of the trial. Attorneys and witnesses made dramatic statements outside the courtroom, knowing they would appear on national television. Combined with the court's inability to render a verdict, the transformation of a murder trial into entertainment raised questions about the impact of increasing media coverage on the American justice system.

Further Reading

Dunne, Dominick. "Nightmare on Elm Street." In *Justice: Crimes, Trials, and Punishments*. New York: Crown, 2001.

Scott, Gini Graham. "When Rich Kids Kill." In *Homicide by the Rich and Famous: A Century of Prominent Killers*. Westport, Conn.: Praeger, 2005.

Soble, Ron, and John Johnson. *Blood Brothers: the Inside Story of the Menendez Murders*. New York: Onyx, 1994.

Maureen Puffer-Rothenberg

See also Crime; Ramsey murder case; Simpson murder case; Television; Versace murder.

■ Metallica

Identification American heavy metal band
Date Formed in 1981

Considered by many to be the foremost heavy metal band of the 1990's, Metallica is known for bringing heavy metal to mainstream audiences.

Formed by guitarist James Hetfield and drummer Lars Ulrich in Los Angeles in 1981, Metallica became one of the top thrash metal bands of the 1980's, releasing *Kill 'Em All* (1983), *Ride the Lightning* (1984), *Master of Puppets* (1986), and *... And Justice for All* (1988). Other principal members of the group in the 1980's and 1990's included lead guitarist Kirk Hammett and bassist Jason Newsted, who replaced Cliff Burton after Burton was killed in a bus accident in 1986.

The band met commercial success in 1991 with the release of its self-titled album, dubbed by fans as the "Black Album." Although the band became synonymous with heavy metal music during the 1990's, Metallica ironically sacrificed a number of heavy metal tropes, such as lengthy heavy metal jam sessions found on its earlier albums. The inclusion of the ballads "Nothing Else Matters" and "The Unforgiven" on *Metallica* distanced the band from some heavy metal purists but set the tone for its next release, *Load*

The members of Metallica (from left)—Jason Newsted, Lars Ulrich, Kirk Hammett, and James Hetfield—stand with their award for Favorite Artist: Heavy Metal/Hard Rock at the 1997 American Music Awards. (AP/Wide World Photos)

(1996). The music on this album bordered between the alternative and heavy metal genres, and the entire Metallica image underwent significant reform with band members cutting their trademark long hair and remaking the signature jagged-edged Metallica logo into a blocky, simpler form.

This change in image, which seemed to fit the rock fashions made popular by MTV, carried into the band's next album, *ReLoad* (1997), which was originally intended for release as a double CD with *Load* and bore similar artwork and music as the previous album. A testament to its continued popularity, Metallica was given a star on San Francisco's Walk of Fame the year after the release of *Garage Inc.* (1998), a collection of cover songs, including the popular rendition of Bob Seger's "Turn the Page." Metallica rounded out the decade in collaboration with the San Francisco Symphony Orchestra, performing songs with the symphony in April, 1999. The performance was released on CD and DVD later that year as *S&M.*

Impact Metallica pushed the boundaries of the heavy metal genre into new territory in the 1990's, often raising questions as to whether it could justly be called a heavy metal band. Nevertheless, the staccato rhythms and power chords characteristic of Metallica's first four albums were incorporated into the more traditional song structures that would make up later albums, exposing heavy metal sounds to a broader audience. Because Metallica's popularity continued to grow throughout the 1990's and its sound was continually reshaped, it is hard to say exactly what sounds other bands have borrowed. Metallica's influence, rather, is more appropriately seen in paving the way on MTV and the radio for such "nu metal" bands as Korn, Limp Bizkit, and Linkin Park.

Further Reading

Berlinger, Joe, and Greg Milner. *Metallica: This Monster Lives.* New York: St. Martin's Press, 2004.

Chirazi, Steffan. *So What! The Good, the Mad, and the Ugly.* New York: Broadway Books, 2004.

Crocker, Chris. *Metallica: The Frayed Ends of Metal.* New York: St. Martin's Press, 1993.

Lawrence Schwegler

See also Alternative rock; Grunge music; Lollapalooza; MP3 format; Music; Nine Inch Nails; Nirvana; Woodstock concerts.

■ MetLife scandal

The Event The nation's largest life insurer and the second-largest insurance company misleads thousands of its customers who had purchased policies disguised as retirement plans or saving accounts

Date 1994

MetLife sales agents were alleged to have misrepresented facts about policies and deceived nearly forty thousand customers who had bought insurance policies that were disguised as high-interest retirement savings accounts. Although MetLife denied wrongdoing, over a billion dollars was refunded to most of the plaintiffs who filed a civil action.

During the fall of 1994, it was discovered that sales agents at the Metropolitan Life Insurance Company (MetLife) in the Tampa, Florida, had sold life insurance policies disguised as retirement savings plans or investment products. The word "insurance" was never mentioned in these particular policies. Furthermore, an industrywide practice known as churning was purposely used by some of MetLife sales agents to persuade customers to exchange old policies for newer ones, with the false claim that the newer policies were more cost-effective and offered more comprehensive coverage. It was later asserted that the underlying goal of these agents was to obtain high-end commissions at the expense of their customers. Most of the victims of the agents' actions in Tampa were nurses and other health care professionals who resided in the state.

Aside from the practice of churning, other customers alleged that MetLife also sold policies with so-called vanishing premiums, in which the premium would not have to be paid after a given number of years. For some customers, this premium never disappeared as promised, leading to more allegations and subsequent civil suits filed against the company. Although MetLife publicly claimed no wrongdoing and that deceptive practices were never used by its employees, it did provide thousands of customers with monetary refunds for the miscommunication that took place between MetLife agents and their customers.

Impact By the end of 1994, some fifteen states, including New York, California, Texas, Pennsylvania, and West Virginia, had followed in Florida's footsteps by opening up investigations of their own. Nearly forty thousand customers alleged that they had fallen victim to the deceptive sales tactics of some of MetLife's agents. Those customers, including many working-class families along with thousands of senior citizens who did not receive MetLife refunds, opted to pursue the matter in civil court. From 1994 through 1999, thousands of customers filed civil actions against MetLife. The company agreed to pay $1.7 billion to settle customer lawsuits regarding the deceptive sales practices.

Further Reading

Brewer, Geoffrey, and Nancy Arnott. "Can MetLife Insure Honest Selling?" *Sales and Marketing Management* 146, no. 3 (March, 1994): 8-9.

Hartley, Robert F. *Business Ethics: Mistakes and Successes.* New York: John Wiley & Sons, 2005.

Meier, Barry. "Metropolitan Life in Accord for Settlement of Fraud Suits." *The New York Times*, August 19, 1999, p. A1.

Paul M. Klenowski

See also Advertising; Archer Daniels Midland scandal; Business and the economy in the United States; Crime; Health care; Health care reform; Scandals; Stock market; Tobacco industry settlement; Wigand, Jeffrey.

■ Mexico and the United States

Definition Diplomatic relations between the two countries

During the 1990's, political leadership in both the United States and Mexico changed, with numerous significant consequences.

At the beginning of 1993, Bill Clinton, a Democrat, became the U.S. president. He replaced George H. W. Bush, a Republican, and remained in office until early 2001. In Mexico, the six-year presidency of Carlos Salinas de Gortari ended in 1994. His successor, Ernesto Zedillo (replacing a previously nominated candidate who was assassinated), remained in office until 2000. Both Salinas and Zedillo were members of the Institutional Revolutionary Party (PRI), which held a grip on power for most of the century, although it climactically lost that hold by the end of the decade.

NAFTA and Financial Crisis On January 1, 1994, a most significant event in U.S.-Mexican economic relations occurred. The North American Free Trade Agreement (NAFTA) went into effect, removing tariffs on trade among Canada, the United States, and Mexico. The treaty spewed a cornucopia of American goods at reduced prices into Mexico, benefiting Mexican consumers. Mexican producers, however, at a competitive disadvantage, suffered losses. Moreover, U.S. labor saw jobs lost as companies moved to Mexico to lower their cost of wages. After 1995, U.S. companies that built assembly plants in Mexico and then shipped the lower-cost goods back to the United States, called maquiladoras, appeared at a rate of one a day. They accounted for one-fourth of the Mexican gross domestic product (GDP) and nearly one-fifth of its jobs. On the day that NAFTA took effect, Maya Indian rebels in Chiapas, the Zapatistas, staged an uprising.

In December, 1994, just after the inauguration of President Zedillo, Mexico devalued its currency, the peso. Financial panic ensued, and capital fled the country. Fearing bankruptcy, Mexico appealed for international aid. President Clinton engineered a multinational response to the appeal, providing $20 billion from the United States toward a $50 billion international bailout for the country. The financial shock wave that rippled other countries was known as the "tequila effect."

Immigration and Trafficking Issues of illegal immigration and drug smuggling into the United States swelled during the 1990's. The United States experienced economic expansion and widespread job growth. Mexico had a surplus of workers. From 1950 to 2000, the Mexican population soared from 25 to 100 million people, and average life expectancy extended to more than seventy years. Young job-seekers flocked to the United States because even low American wages were higher than average Mexican incomes. They concentrated in U.S. states along the Rio Grande border. The advancing influx pushed farther north, however, settling in areas previously without Hispanic populations.

By decade's end, one-third of the 30 million foreign-born residents of the United States were from Mexico, and 10 million of the foreign-born were undocumented, with half from Mexico. Thus, it was estimated that one of two Mexicans in the

United States, the largest foreign group in the country, was undocumented.

Drug smuggling and gang warfare magnified the border violations. Major and expanding Mexican drug cartels operated from Tijuana, Juarez, and the Gulf of Mexico. Smaller, competing groups emerged throughout Mexico. Cartels compromised the police and military, using bribery, blackmail, and assassinations. In 1997, General Jesús Gutiérrez Rebollo, Mexico's antidrug czar, was arrested for accepting cartel money. Raul Salinas, the brother of the president, was widely alleged to court financial advantages from the cartels. In 1997, President Clinton sent his antidrug czar, General Barry McCaffrey, to confer with President Zedillo. From Fort Bliss, Texas, the Pentagon expanded its military monitoring that supported interagency antidrug operations along the border.

Border Culture By decade's end, 10 percent of Mexico's population lived along the U.S. border. Moreover, the U.S. border population was the fastest-growing in the country, attracted to the Sunbelt. These mutually increasing populations augmented the character of a hybrid culture growing across the region since the middle of the twentieth century.

Mexicans living in Baja California but working in Southern California were described as "Mexifornians." The number of speakers of Spanglish, combining Spanish and English, increased. Chicano studies and literature expanded, and U.S. trade publishers launched unprecedented lines of books in Spanish.

"Tex-Mex" described people living along or between Texas and Mexico and a cuisine that they developed characterized by the ingredients of cheese, beef, beans, and chilies. Tejano music, intermixing rock and *cumbia*, evolved with the Houston-based group La Mafia. The group added electronic instruments and created a bicultural pop-country genre. It also launched the career of the Grammy-winning Tejano artist Selena, whose murder by a fan in 1995 made national headlines.

Impact The 1990's were a decade in which problems and opportunities in U.S.-Mexican relations grew and an evolving hybrid culture became more widely recognized and accepted.

Further Reading

Anderson, Joan B, and James Gerber. *Fifty Years of Change on the U.S.-Mexico Border: Growth, Development, and Quality of Life*. Austin: University of Texas Press, 2008. Examines U.S.-Mexican relations during the 1990's within a broader frame beginning in the 1950's. Includes photos.

Castañeda, Jorge G. *The Mexican Shock: Its Meaning for the United States*. New York: New Press, 1995. A prominent Mexican intellectual reflects on his country in the mid-1990's, finding it extraordinarily polarized. He believes, however, that NAFTA will offer the opportunity to mold the agreement into one of "growth with justice."

Davidow, Jeffrey. *The U.S. and Mexico: The Bear and the Porcupine*. Princeton, N.J.: Markus Wiener, 2004. The author was U.S. ambassador to Mexico from 1998 to 2002. He examines recent U.S.-Mexican relations, characterizing perceptions of the United States as overbearing and of Mexico as prickly or oversensitive.

Folsom, Ralph Haughwout. *NAFTA and Free Trade in the Americas in a Nutshell*. 2d ed. St. Paul, Minn.: West, 2004. A concise assessment of NAFTA in the first ten years following its enactment. Provides an overview of contemporary free trade policies and practices in the context of the Western Hemisphere. Includes the text of NAFTA.

Otero, Gerardo, ed. *Mexico in Transition: Neoliberal Globalism, the State, and Civil Society*. Black Point, N.S.: Fernwood, 2004. Examines the effects of neoliberalism on Mexican economics, politics, society, and culture, concentrating specifically on the consequences of NAFTA.

Payan, Tony. *The Three U.S.-Mexico Border Wars: Drugs, Immigration, and Homeland Security*. Westport, Conn.: Praeger Security International, 2006. Summarizes recent decades of history for the three most contentious elements of relations between the United States and Mexico, examining economic, sociopolitical, and ethnic conditions.

Edward A. Riedinger

See also Business and the economy in the United States; Demographics of the United States; Health care; Immigration Act of 1990; Immigration to the United States; Latinos; North American Free Trade Agreement (NAFTA); Selena.

■ Michelangelo computer virus

Definition A destructive piece of computer code designed to make a person's computer unusable and trigger on March 6 of a given year

The Michelangelo virus was hyped by the media to proportions that far exceeded its actual distribution and caused panic among computer users. The incident also damaged the credibility of many of the industry experts.

The Michelangelo computer virus was first discovered in 1991. It overwrote the boot sector of a computer's hard drive running an operating system based on DOS (Disk Operating System) as well as floppy disks inserted into an infected machine. The boot sector contains the information that a computer needs to start. This virus would have made the computer unusable and the data irretrievable for the average user. The name is derived from the virus's activation date of March 6, the birthday of Italian Renaissance artist Michelangelo.

Leading Edge, a major computer manufacturer at the time, accidently shipped five hundred computers infected with the virus in January of 1992. This prompted the manufacturer to start shipping all new computers with antivirus software preinstalled. A computer virus expert wrongly called the Michelangelo virus the third most commonly distributed virus after the announcement. Soon after, about nine hundred infected floppy disks were shipped by another vendor in the computer industry. The two incidents brought the virus to the forefront of media attention. The infection numbers were further inflated to five million possible computers worldwide by the antivirus industry, and the media also reported, incorrectly, that the virus could be spread through computer bulletin boards.

A few reporters and industry experts remained skeptical about the claims of millions of infected computers, but by the end of February, 1992, the media had fueled the public's fears and the experts were largely ignored. The antivirus industry added to the furor by offering free detectors that could be downloaded. Symantec, another industry leader, placed a full page ad in *Computerworld* in order to take advantage of the media attention. The days leading up to the virus activation date saw the virus receiving constant media reports, including speculation that damages could be in the millions. March 6, 1992, brought a mere ten to twenty thousand cases of reported data loss. The low rates of infection were touted as a success by the antivirus industry and media coverage. Analysts, however, saw nowhere near the initial reported rates of infection. The virus dropped from the headlines by the following day. The first report about the virus surfaced a full two weeks after the virus release date and criticized the industry and the media for the whole incident.

Impact The media hype and poor reporting about the Michelangelo virus caused a panic among computer users. Antivirus experts inflated claims of infection and companies that produced antivirus programs took advantage of the hysteria to sell their products. The poor handling of the reporting damaged the reputation of computer-virus experts for some time to come, and the media lost a measure of credibility.

Further Reading

Caldwell, Wilma R., ed. *Computer Security Sourcebook.* Detroit, Mich.: Omnigraphics, 2003.

Erbschloe, Michael. *Trojans, Worms, and Spyware: A Computer Security Professional's Guide to Malicious Code.* Boston: Elsevier Butterworth Heinemann, 2005.

Furnell, Steven. *Cybercrime: Vandalizing the Information Society.* Boston: Addison-Wesley, 2002.

James J. Heiney

See also America Online; Computers; Hackers; Internet; Microsoft; Science and technology; World Wide Web; Y2K problem.

■ Microsoft

Identification Computer software company

As manufacturer of Windows, the leading microcomputer operating system, Microsoft came under fire for alleged antitrust violations.

At the beginning of the 1990's, Microsoft was one of the leading computer software companies. During the second half of the 1980's its Disk Operating System, often called MS-DOS, had come to dominate the home computer market, displacing earlier systems such as CP/M. However, it was a command-line interface, which required users to memorize commands and type them exactly at the C-prompt. A mistyped command could destroy hours or even days of work.

By contrast, the Macintosh Operating System, or Mac OS, pioneered by Apple for its Macintosh line of computers, used a graphical user interface, or GUI, based on the metaphor of a desktop. Using a mouse, the user pointed and clicked upon files and folders to work on them. One of the reasons that kept MS-DOS users from defecting to this simple, intuitive interface was the high price point, maintained by Apple's steadfast refusal to license their technology to clone makers.

To protect their market share, Microsoft developed a shell program called Windows that would give users a simplified interface. The earliest version, released in 1985, gave the user a set of tiled windows with buttons representing the options for opening application software and working with files. However, successive versions delivered a smoother and more flexible interface, although Mac users still lambasted Windows 3.1, released in 1990, as still not up to Macintosh standards. This was in spite of a 1988 copyright suit by Apple alleging that Microsoft had infringed upon the Mac OS with an earlier version of Windows, which was settled only because the judge knew that both Microsoft and Apple had drawn upon the work of the Xerox Palo Alto Research Center in creating their interfaces.

Throughout the first half of the 1990's, Microsoft continued to promise the successor to Windows 3.1 would be finished and shipped, yet the actual date kept moving into the future. In 1995, the date finally came, as Windows 95 was revealed to have undergone a complete revamping of the user interface to make it more Mac-like. Yet again Apple made angry noises about copyright infringement, but by this time Apple was in serious financial trouble, having become committed to multiple overambitious products and a muddled product line. However, their complaints drew the attention of the United States Department of Justice.

For years, rival software companies had been complaining that Microsoft was taking unfair advantage of its position as manufacturer of Windows to promote their own office suite, Microsoft Office. When Novell owned WordPerfect, they alleged that Microsoft used their intimate knowledge of the inner workings of Windows to tweak Microsoft Word to perform better than any other company's word-processing software could hope to attain. Netscape became annoyed when Microsoft not only released its own Web browser, Internet Explorer, but also made it the default browser in Windows. The final straw was a licensing agreement Microsoft made with a number of computer hardware manufacturers that stipulated that, in order to license Windows to be preinstalled on their computers, they had to agree to have it preloaded with a startup screen that identified several other Microsoft products as preferred options.

Throughout 1998, Microsoft fought the Department of Justice suit with various tactics that many observers regarded as disingenuous. One of the most memorable moments in the investigation was Bill Gates's testimony, in which he was cornered about an aspect of his company's activities and responded that the answer depended upon the definition of the word "is."

In the end, Microsoft executives realized that although they might win in the legal arena, the loss of public goodwill would only ensure an endless series of battles, until the company was exhausted by the legal expenses and the drain of intellectual capital away from the company's real work of designing and producing software. Gates transferred the day-to-day responsibility of running Microsoft to Steve Ballmer and concentrated on keeping Microsoft innovative. He also worked on improving Microsoft's image with such gestures as a deal with Steve Jobs, which saved Apple, and the creation of the Bill and Melinda Gates Foundation to focus upon charitable giving.

Impact The 1990's marked the period in which Microsoft solidified dominance in the personal computer operating-system market. Although MS-DOS and Windows were to be found on almost every desktop in the nation, resentment about the way in which Microsoft did business began to solidify. Many people regarded Microsoft as taking unfair advantage of their position and treating its customers poorly. The resulting efforts to bring legal judgment against Microsoft for monopolistic practices led to a reorienting of Microsoft's efforts, although even in the first decade of the twenty-first century there were complaints that the Vista operating system was poorly designed and inordinately restricted users' options to install and run non-Microsoft applications.

Further Reading

Bank, David. *Breaking Windows: How Bill Gates Fumbled the Future of Microsoft.* New York: Free Press,

2001. Highly critical of Gates's management, particularly during the antitrust suit crisis.

Edstrom, Jennifer, and Marlin Eller. *Barbarians Led by Bill Gates: Microsoft from the Inside—How the World's Richest Corporation Wields Its Power.* New York: Henry Holt, 1998. A critical look at Microsoft at the time of the antitrust suit.

Rohm, Wendy Goldman. *The Microsoft File: The Secret Case Against Bill Gates.* New York: Times Business, 1998. Details of Microsoft's actions to dominate the microcomputer operating-system market.

Slater, Robert. *Microsoft Rebooted: How Bill Gates and Steve Ballmer Reinvinted Their Company.* New York: Portfolio, 2004. Microsoft's response to the antitrust suit.

Wallace, James, and Jim Erickson. *Hard Drive: Bill Gates and the Making of the Microsoft Empire.* New York: John Wiley & Sons, 1992. Extensive biography of both Gates the man and Gates the business tycoon.

Leigh Husband Kimmel

See also Apple Computer; Business and the economy in the United States; Computers; Gates, Bill; Internet; Jobs, Steve.

■ Middle East and North America

Definition Actions and events that shaped, and were shaped by, relations between governments and peoples in the Middle East and North America

Events in the Middle East and related events inside the United States during the 1990's deepened, expanded, and changed the direct and overt involvement of the United States, especially militarily, in Middle Eastern affairs.

Prior to 1979 few Americans knew or even cared much about events or peoples in the Middle East. Western stereotypes of Middle Easterners abounded, although they did not fit the facts of the region. While Americans identified Middle Easterners with Arabs and Arabs with Muslims, in fact almost half of the people in the Middle East are not Arab (for example, the Turks in Turkey and Persians in Iran) and fewer than one-fourth of the world's Muslims are Arabs. The complacence and lack of awareness of Americans about the Middle East changed with the advent of the Islamic Revolution in Iran and the emergence of power of the Ayatollah Khomeini in 1979. The overthrow of Iran, an American political ally, and the subsequent takeover of the U.S. embassy in Iran's capital, Tehran, brought the region's social and political unrest to the attention of many Americans, even though other important relevant events had also taken place that same year, such as the signing of the Camp David peace agreement between Egypt and Israel.

Another important event that occurred in 1979 was the assuming of political and military control of Iraq by Saddam Hussein. While the majority of Iraqis were Shia Muslims, Hussein represented the ruling Sunni Muslims, and he maintained a brutal regime. Iran was predominantly Shia Muslim, and Hussein was concerned about the expansion of Iran's Islamic Revolution, particularly in light of Khomeini's calls for "Western-oriented" Arab leaders (such as Hussein) to be overthrown. An immediate result of the rise of Khomeini and Hussein was the Iran-Iraq War, which lasted from 1980 to 1988. This war engaged the United States in particular because of the interruption of oil exports from the region, resulting in the United States "reflagging" Kuwaiti oil tankers late in the war.

The Gulf War A consequence of the eight-year-long Iran-Iraq War was that both nations exhausted their economic resources. In 1990, because of this and reports exposing that the United States, under President Ronald Reagan's administration, secretly had been providing weapons to both countries while publicly declaring its opposition to Iran (an episode that came to be known as the Iran-Contra scandal), Hussein declared that other Arab nations, particularly the oil-rich U.S. ally of Kuwait, owed Iraq economic restitution, since Iraq had depleted its resources protecting Arabs from Persians (Iranians) and Sunnis from the Shia revolution. Neither the United States nor the leaders of the nations neighboring Iraq fully agreed with Hussein. Despite multiple diplomatic efforts and interpretations, in August, 1990, Iraq attacked Kuwait. Immediately, the United States formed a coalition of nations to send troops to the region and repel the invasion. The effort was dubbed Operation Desert Shield, which included troops, equipment, and financial resources from thirty-four countries from around the world, including Canada and many Middle Eastern nations. The stated mission was to defend Kuwait,

Saudi Arabia, and other neighboring nations. In early 1991, Operation Desert Shield ended and was followed by Operation Desert Storm, with the stated mission of liberating Kuwait. Operation Desert Storm was a dramatically swift success, with the coalition forces routing the Iraqi forces in only a few weeks.

A result of Operation Desert Storm was that Iraq was effectively stripped of its military might. Hussein retained his official status as the nation's leader, but the United States established no-fly zones in the southern third of the country, where most of the Shia Iraqis lived, and in the northern third of the country, where ethnic Kurds lived. The no-fly zones prevented Iraqi military operations in those areas and provided much more autonomy to them than they had enjoyed prior to 1991. Bill Clinton became U.S. president in 1992, and under his administration the no-fly zones were maintained throughout the 1990's and into the first several years of the twenty-first century.

Israel and Palestinians The state of Israel, as a sovereign political entity, was established by the United Nations in 1948 by parceling out part of the land of Palestine. From that time up to the 1990's, the region experienced continuing and ongoing conflict, with Palestinians and neighboring Arab states claiming that Palestinian territory had been illegally stolen and Israelis claiming that they were subject to military attacks and were defending themselves. Over the course of several decades, multiple Israeli-Arab wars ensued, in 1948, 1956, 1967, 1973, and 1982.

In 1991, following the events of the Gulf War and Operation Desert Storm, many world leaders urged U.S. president George H. W. Bush to set a peace agreement between Israel and its neighbors, including Palestinians, as a top priority for U.S. foreign policy. With the collapse of the Soviet Union at the end of the 1980's and with many Arab leaders insisting that Middle Eastern unrest would continue and worsen without some resolution to the "Palestinian problem," the United States was seen as the only world power that could broker a genuine and lasting peace accord. As a result, multilateral peace talks began in Madrid, Spain, to deal with this issue. Over the next several years, progress was slow to nonexistent, in part because a new administration, under Bill Clinton, took office in 1992, with a subsequent refocusing of U.S. foreign and domestic priorities and policies. In 1993, it became public that, in spite of slow progress in Madrid, the Israeli government and the Palestinian leadership (under the name of the Palestine Liberation Organization, or PLO, later to be recast as the Palestine National Assembly, or PNA) had been holding secret meetings in Oslo, Norway, and negotiations had been hopeful. The result was the Oslo Accords, which led to a Declaration of Principles for Palestinian self-rule and recognition by the PNA of Israel's sovereign status. A consequence of this apparent progress was that, in 1994, Jordan became the second Arab state (after Egypt) to sign an official peace treaty with Israel.

Hopes for further movement toward ending the conflicts were dashed in 1995, with the assassination of Israeli prime minister Yitzhak Rabin by an Israeli Orthodox Jew, who believed that Rabin was aiding the enemies of Israel. A result of this was the election of Benjamin Netanyahu as Rabin's successor and a hardening by both Israelis and Palestinians toward each other. In 1999, a new Israeli prime minister was elected, Ehud Barak. In his final years in office, President Bill Clinton worked closely with Barak and Palestinian leader Yasir Arafat to sign a final peace agreement. These close talks and negotiations broke down, however, over several final, important issues, such as the status of East Jerusalem as the capital of Palestine, questions about the final borders of Israel and Palestine, security guarantees, and questions concerning Palestinians returning to land now inside of Israel as well as Israelis living in settlements in Palestinian territories. The 1990's ended with no peace agreement between the Israelis and Palestinians.

Events in North America Several dramatic events connected to U.S. actions and policies related to the Middle East took place outside the region during the 1990's. Within the United States, in 1993 a car bomb was detonated beneath Tower One of the World Trade Center in New York City. Six people were killed and more than a thousand were injured in the attack. It was the first such attack within the United States that most Americans identified as an act of terrorism connected to the Middle East. In the subsequent trial, main perpetrator, Ramzi Yousef, openly acknowledged this as an act of terrorism and that it was directly related to U.S. policies and actions in the Middle East.

A second event that took place, not in North America but that was directly related to U.S. actions and policies in the Middle East, was the bombing of U.S. embassies in Kenya and Tanzania on August 7, 1998. The bombings were coordinated, as they occurred simultaneously, together killing more than two hundred people and injuring thousands. Subsequent investigation showed these attacks were planned by a group known as al-Qaeda. These bombings brought to the world for the first time the name of their primary planner, Osama Bin Laden.

A third event that occurred was the crash of EgyptAir Flight 990 sixty miles south of Nantucket Island, Massachusetts, in October, 1999. The plane was headed from New York to Cairo, and the crash killed more than two hundred people. Transcripts from flight information indicated that the airplane crashed shortly after relief pilot Gamil el-Batouti took control of the airplane and was reported to have said, "I made my decision now. I put my faith in God's hands." Investigators stated that the crash was the result of human, not mechanical, error. Although there was never concrete proof that the crash was a deliberate act of terrorism, many Americans came to that conclusion.

Impact Events in the Middle East during the 1990's were a mixture of both stasis and change. What remained static were the relations between Israel and the Palestinians, with another decade gone by without a peace agreement or final status for either party. In addition, the United States continued to be seen as the one external party that could break the deadlock on progress, but without any significant results. What changed was the level and types of U.S. involvement in the Middle East. The primary change was the direct military involvement by U.S. forces in Iraq. Another major change was the taking of center stage for U.S. foreign affairs of Middle Eastern issues. With the Cold War over at the end of the 1980's, many officials saw the 1990's as the emergence of a clash of civilizations between the West and a revived Islamic Middle East. Although others downplayed such a clash, a marked focus on the Middle East, for both government officials and for Americans generally, was a definite consequence.

Subsequent Events Events in the Middle East, particularly as they related to U.S. action and policies, led to even more dramatic events in the first years of the new millennium. Barely into the twenty-first century, the world witnessed the attacks of September 11, 2001, and the subsequent "war on terrorism" and invasion of Iraq in 2003. U.S. foreign policy became dominated by concerns related to the Middle East, with an important carryover to domestic issues, both political and economic.

Further Reading

Barber, Benjamin R. *Jihad vs. McWorld.* New York: Ballantine, 1995. A very readable examination of the impact of Western culture on traditional Middle Eastern societies.

Barboza, Stephen. *American Jihad: Islam After Malcolm X.* New York: Image Books, 1994. A close look at the rise of Islam in America during the second half of the twentieth century, particularly among African Americans.

Gerner, Deborah J., and Jillian Schwedler. *Understanding the Contemporary Middle East*, 2d ed. Boulder, Colo.: Lynne Rienner, 2004. An excellent overview of contemporary Middle Eastern culture and societies, going beyond merely politics and history.

Kamalipour, Yahya R., ed. *The U.S. Media and the Middle East: Image and Perception.* New York: Praeger, 1997. A fine collection of essays focused on portrayals of the Middle East and how those portrayals both shape and are shaped by popular and political values.

Roberts, John. *Visions and Mirages: The Middle East in a New Era.* Edinburgh, Scotland: Mainstream Publishing, 1995. A thorough and accessible look at contemporary Middle Eastern societies, particularly social and cultural changes over the past century.

Rugh, William. *American Encounters with Arabs: The "Soft Power" of U.S. Public Diplomacy in the Middle East.* New York: Praeger, 2005. An in-depth and "on the ground" review of public diplomacy practiced by the United States over the past century in relation to nations in the Middle East.

Schoenbaum, David. *The United States and the State of Israel.* New York: Oxford University Press, 1993. An unflinching look at the history and ongoing web of relations between the United States and Israel and how they impact general U.S. policies in and toward the Middle East.

Sifry, Micah L., and Christopher Cerf, eds. *The Gulf War Reader.* New York: Doubleday, 1991. An expansive and rich collection of material, written from multiple perspectives, documenting the 1990-1991 Gulf War and Operation Desert Storm.

Spencer, William J. *Global Studies: The Middle East.* 11th ed. Dubuque, Iowa: McGraw-Hill, 2007. A superb and comprehensive survey of Middle Eastern nations, with information on each individual country, as well as data on the region as a whole.

Taylor, Alan. *The Superpowers and the Middle East.* Syracuse, N.Y.: Syracuse University Press, 1991. A detailed look at the history of international relations involving nations in the Middle East and their relationships to the United States, Europe, and Soviet diplomacy and policies.

David Boersema

See also Clinton, Bill; CNN coverage of the Gulf War; EgyptAir Flight 990 crash; Foreign policy of the United States; Gulf War; Israel and the United States; Terrorism; U.S. embassy bombings in Africa; World Trade Center bombing.

■ Midnight basketball

Identification Crime-prevention program designed for youths
Date Began in 1985

Later considered a secondary program for attempting to control inner-city crime, midnight basketball, like other neighborhood-oriented programs in the United States, lost community support and necessary funding for its survival.

The concept of midnight basketball was first proposed in the mid-1980's. However, it was not until the early 1990's that midnight basketball gained notoriety as a possible crime-prevention program. President Bill Clinton's 1994 crime bill provided funding for neighborhood crime-prevention strategies. The primary rationale for funding neighborhood programs such as midnight basketball was a proactive approach by the government and community leaders to deter crime by providing youths with character-building activities. Police chiefs, city mayors, and even *Sports Illustrated* praised midnight basketball for its success in aiding in the decline of violent offenses, property crimes, and nonviolent juvenile offenses.

The major flaw with midnight basketball was not found in the concept itself but rather was evident in the era in which such programs were established. The 1990's witnessed an increase in violent crimes, especially by inner-city youth. Also, the national consensus in the 1990's was to "get tough on crime" and punish offenders with incarceration. Midnight basketball was seen by some as a poorly developed scheme. Senator Bob Dole, the 1996 Republican presidential candidate, many members of Congress, and even radio personality Rush Limbaugh criticized governmental spending for a crime-prevention program aimed at urban neighborhoods as a waste of money and as having a potentially racist undertone.

Communities that started midnight basketball programs, such as those in Maryland, saw a 60 percent drop in youth drug-related crime. Inner-city public housing neighborhoods saw as high as a 78 percent reduction in juvenile crime. This trend was seen in Atlanta; Kansas City, Missouri; and Fort Worth, Texas.

The goal of midnight basketball programs was to remove youth from the streets and allow them to become attached to a formal group rather than criminal elements. Along with governmental funding, community support from police, businesses, and private donors funded such programs. The goal was twofold: keep participants busy and provide positive role models, and keep participants crime-free while providing job skills. Guidelines were strict, and participation in crime would often bar an individual from playing midnight basketball. Although many inner-city programs were developed in the early 1990's, federal cutbacks and lack of city funding limited the potential growth of the midnight basketball in the early twenty-first century.

Impact The desire for midnight basketball programs had not declined by the late 1990's, but federal and local spending for programs deemed "expendable" had shifted to other crime-prevention programs. Nevertheless, even if the intended impact of midnight basketball was not found on a large scale, testimonials of a small percentage of Americans, including some National Basketball Association (NBA) athletes, praised midnight basketball for its positive influence on their lives.

Further Reading

Farrell Walter, et al. "Redirecting the Lives of Urban Black Males: An Assessment of Milwaukee's Midnight Basketball League." *Journal of Community Practice* 2, no. 4 (May, 1996): 91-107.

Kennedy, P., et al. "Round Midnight." *Sports Illustrated* 85, no. 8 (August, 1996).

Keith J. Bell

See also African Americans; Basketball; Clinton, Bill; Crime; Limbaugh, Rush; Sports.

■ Militia movement

Definition A paramilitary movement that emerged in the United States in the 1990's

Collectively, the militias constituted the largest right-wing movement in the United States in the decade.

Paramilitary groups are not a recent right-wing phenomenon in the United States. In the 1930's, a group called the Christian Front was created to defend the United States. Then, in the 1960's, the Minutemen was created to provide a citizen army to fight communists, both domestic and foreign. There were two catalysts for the 1990's citizen militia movement: the events at Ruby Ridge, Idaho, and Waco, Texas. Both were government standoffs involving federal weapons violations, and both ended with charges that federal officials had acted incorrectly. At Ruby Ridge, Randy Weaver, a survivalist and Christian Identity church member, bought sawed-off shotguns from an undercover agent in 1989. Weaver failed to appear in court to face the charges. When federal marshals attempted to arrest Weaver in 1992, a shoot-out occurred at Weaver's isolated cabin. A federal marshal and Weaver's wife and fourteen-year-old son were killed. Later, Weaver was acquitted of all charges except for failure to appear in court, and the federal government lost a civil suit in the case.

In Waco, Texas, four federal agents were killed in February, 1993, when the Bureau of Alcohol, Tobacco, and Firearms (ATF) raided the Branch Davidian compound of cult leader David Koresh in search of illegal weapons. Following a fifty-one-day siege, the Federal Bureau of Investigation (FBI) used armored vehicles and tear gas to end the standoff; however, a fire broke out and seventy-six men, women, and children from the religious sect were killed. This event, like Ruby Ridge, was seen by the radical right as an example of the federal government using unjustified force to stifle dissent. In fact, an article in *Modern Militiaman* magazine asserted that the militia movement was conceived at Ruby Ridge in 1992 and born at Waco in 1993.

On January 1, 1994, the Militia of Montana (MOM) was officially started by John Trochman, a friend of Randy Weaver, in Noxon, Montana. Trochman's militia became a major supplier of propaganda documents, paramilitary supplies, and paramilitary manuals for the movement in the 1990's. In April, the Michigan Militia was formed by gun shop owner Norm Olson. This group became one of the largest organizations, with an estimated membership of six thousand.

Militia groups grew rapidly throughout 1994, but few Americans were aware of the militias until the bombing of the Oklahoma City federal building in April, 1995, that killed 168 people. This bombing, by Timothy McVeigh, occurred on the second anniversary of the Waco fire and was at first incorrectly linked to the militias. In June, 1995, members of militia groups were called to testify before the U.S. Senate Judiciary Committee. As Americans became more aware of the militias' presence, militias continued to grow. By early 1996, there were paramilitary groups in most states and an estimated membership of forty thousand. Overall, the Southern Poverty Law Center estimated that there were 370 militia groups in the United States in 1996, most of which operated autonomously. The militia movement began to decline in late 1996 because of arrests and less hard-core members dropping out. There were numerous arrests of militia members on charges of conspiracy and of possession of illegal weapons and explosives. By 1997, the Southern Poverty Law Center estimated there were only 221 militia groups, with the strongest support coming from the midwestern and western states.

Issues There were several major issues that resulted in individuals becoming involved in militias. The first issue was gun control. Militia members were opposed to federal laws, such as the Brady bill, that were seen as limiting the rights of citizens to keep and bear arms. Many felt that such measures were the first steps toward government confiscation of all firearms. Second, militia members were suspicious of government, especially the federal government, because of events such as Ruby Ridge and Waco. Some believed that no government was legitimate above the county level. Third, many militia members believed that there was a conspiracy to create a "New World Order" that would result in a one-world socialist government. They were especially suspicious of the United Nations and international agreements between the United States and foreign governments, especially those dealing with free trade. Some militia groups were also racist and anti-Semitic; however, there were also some militias with African American and Jewish members.

Impact The militia movement tended to attract rural, lesser-educated, blue-collar males who owned guns and were suspicious of the actions of the federal government. Many of them disliked government policies linked to gun control, environmental protection, free trade, smoking bans, and affirmative action for women and minorities. The militias were formed to protect themselves from what they perceived as illegal and illicit practices of government. Some groups actually planned terrorist actions against the government. In fact, in the three years following the Oklahoma City bombing, twenty-five major domestic terrorist conspiracies were thwarted by law-enforcement officials. While militia activity decreased in the latter part of the decade, domestic terrorism remained a major concern for government officials. As illegal immigration became more of an issue in the early part of the twenty-first century, some militia group members became involved in private patrol movements along the U.S.-Mexico border.

Further Reading

Levitas, Daniel. *The Terrorist Next Door: The Militia Movement and the Radical Right.* New York: St. Martin's Press, 2002. The definitive history of the origins and impact of the militia movement.

Sonder, Ben. *The Militia Movement: Fighters of the Far Right.* New York: Franklin Watts, 2000. A short journalistic account of the militia movement.

Stern, Kenneth S. *A Force upon the Plain: The American Militia Movement and the Politics of Hate.* New York: Simon & Schuster, 1996. An early work on the militia movement written after the Oklahoma City bombing by the American Jewish Committee's expert on hate groups and hate movements.

William V. Moore

See also Conservatism in U.S. politics; Gun control; Illegal immigration; McVeigh, Timothy; Montana Freeman standoff; Oklahoma City bombing; Ruby Ridge shoot-out; Terrorism; Waco siege.

■ Milli Vanilli

Identification Pop music group
Date Formed in 1988

Initially notable for its immense popularity, the duo known as Milli Vanilli became infamous for lip-synching, in videos and onstage, to the vocals of other singers and thus inspiring litigation from fans who believed they had been deceived and from studio singers who believed they were not being duly recognized or monetarily compensated for their performances.

The story of Milli Vanilli began in the 1970's, when Frank Farian, a white German performer discouraged by his record company from recording "black" music, formed Boney M, a quartet whose members hailed from Jamaica and Aruba and contributed little to Boney M's recordings. By the mid-1980's, after a decade of international popularity, Boney M ap-

Rob Pilatus, left, and Fabrice Morvan of Milli Vanilli pose after winning the Best New Artist Grammy on February 21, 1990. (AP/Wide World Photos)

peared to have run its course, and Farian, in the role of producer, recorded songs for a new project using the studio singers John Davis, Brad Howell, twin sisters Jodie and Linda Rocco, and Charles Shaw. Convinced that the group needed a more video-friendly appearance, and buoyed by his success at having gotten away with masking performances before, Farian hired photogenic German models and dancers Fabrice "Fab" Morvan and Rob Pilatus to "perform" the new songs as Milli Vanilli (a name taken from a Turkish advertising slogan).

Milli Vanilli, whose music was a catchy blend of high-tech, postdisco dance music and R&B that included a little rap, became an instant success. *Girl You Know It's True*, the group's debut album, sold over six million copies upon its U.S. release in 1989, and all four of its singles ("Baby Don't Forget My Number," "Blame It on the Rain," "Girl I'm Gonna Miss You," and the title track) reached the top five on *Billboard*'s pop singles chart.

Even after a technical gaffe at a July, 1989, performance revealed Morvan and Pilatus to have been lip-synching onstage, the ruse might have continued. However, as criticism over their live nonsinging grew, Morvan and Pilatus began pressuring Farian to allow them to sing on future Milli Vanilli recordings, and, in November, 1990, nine months after Milli Vanilli had won a Grammy Award for Best New Artist, Farian responded by officially unmasking the duo as a fraud.

In 1993, Morvan and Pilatus attempted a comeback by releasing *Rob & Fab*, but the album failed. In 1996, Pilatus was convicted of vandalism, attempted robbery, and assault and served a brief jail term. Following a stint in a drug rehabilitation program, Pilatus returned to Germany and committed suicide there on April 2, 1998.

Impact After the scandal, the practice of using nonsingers to pose as a song's actual performers (a practice that, in fact, was not widespread but that showed signs of becoming prevalent) came to an end. In the wake of lawsuits filed by the singer Martha Wash against the acts C+C Music Factory, Black Box, and Seduction, each of whom had disguised her contributions to their music with more fashionably presentable lip-synching performers, legislation was passed requiring all recordings to accurately credit their participants.

Further Reading

Bogdanov, Vladimir, Stephen Thomas Erlewine, and Chris Woodstra, eds. *All Music Guide to Rock: The Definitive Guide to Rock, Pop, and Soul.* 3d ed. Milwaukee: Hal Leonard, 2002.

Popyk, Bob. "How Can They Call This Junk Music? Or, How Seeing Milli Vanilli in Concert Made Me Feel Ready for the Geriatric Ward." *Music Trades* 138, no. 9 (October, 1990): 89-90.

Arsenio Orteza

See also African Americans; Hip-hop and rap music; Music; Scandals.

■ Million Man March

The Event African American men participate in a massive rally

Date October 16, 1995

Place The National Mall in Washington, D.C.

The Million Man March was composed of African American men and others who supported its stated goals of "unity, atonement, and brotherhood." The rally was also political, as its leaders were critical of the conservative Republican leadership that rose to power in the 1994 congressional elections.

Louis Farrakhan, the leader of the Nation of Islam, conceived the idea for the Million Man March. Farrakhan was born Louis Eugene Walcott and later assumed a Muslim name. Recognized as a powerful and inspirational speaker, he was a controversial figure because some of his comments were viewed as racist, sexist, or anti-Semitic. Republican leader and Speaker of the House Newt Gingrich criticized the gathering for supporting Farrakhan. President Bill Clinton supported the march but was critical of Farrakhan's comments, as were many African Americans. Farrakhan defended his remarks by stating that they were taken out of context.

Although Farrakhan's primary role in the Million Man March was the subject of great controversy, most Americans respected the importance of the issues addressed by the event. The program agenda and thousands of discussions on the National Mall focused upon fundamental social issues important to African American males. Besides Farrakhan, many others played important roles in the Million Man March. Benjamin Chavis, Jr., served as the national director for the event, and about sixty people spoke or entertained, including the Reverend Jesse Jackson, activist Rosa Parks, comedian Dick Gregory, poet Maya Angelou, and singers Isaac Hayes, Hammer, and Stevie Wonder.

The numbers attending the Million Man March have been in dispute since the event. The estimates range from less than a half-million to more than one and a half million. Boston University used aerial photographs to estimate the crowd at 837,000, with a 20 percent margin for error. In any case, the gathering was one of the largest and most peaceful gatherings on the National Mall and was much larger than the gathering for Martin Luther King, Jr.'s "I Have a Dream" speech in 1963, which was presented to 250,000 during the March on Washington for Jobs and Freedom.

Goals of the March The tone for the Million Man March was summed up by Farrakhan, who asked attendees to pledge to the following beliefs:

To love my brother as I love myself
To strive to improve myself spiritually, morally, mentally, socially, politically and economically
To build businesses, hospitals, factories, and conduct international trade
To never use a gun or a knife to harm any human being other than in self-defense
To never abuse one's wife or children physically or sexually
To never use the "b" word to describe any female, especially black women.
To never again abuse one's body with drugs or other things that are self-destructive
To support black media and artists who have clean acts and show respect for themselves and others

While most African American women supported the goals of the march, many were bothered by the fact that women were not welcome to attend the event. Activist Angela Davis provided one view of the sexist aspect of the Million Man March by saying, "No march, movement or agenda that defines manhood in the narrowest terms and seeks to make women lesser partners in this quest for equality can be considered a positive step." While other women were less strident in their view, they were still critical of the male-only march, even though some women were featured on the program.

Impact The goals established at the Million Man March motivated and inspired many African American men who adhered to the pledge that they made on October 16, 1995. While some fell short of the pledge, efforts continued to attract African Americans to the widely accepted goals that were initiated

"We Got to Get Back to the Houses of God"

On October 16, 1995, Louis Farrakhan addressed his audience at the Million Man March, held in Washington, D.C. Farrakhan urged blacks to join organizations that seek to uplift the people:

Everyone of you, my dear brothers, when you go home, here's what I want you to do. We must belong to some organization that is working for, and in the interests of, the uplift and the liberation of our people. Go back, join the NAACP if you want to, join the Urban League, join the All African People's Revolutionary Party, join us, join the Nation of Islam, join PUSH, join the Congress of Racial Equality, join SCLC, the Southern Christian Leadership Conference. But we must become a totally organized people and the only way we can do that is to become a part of some organization that is working for the uplift of our people. . . .

I know that the NAACP did not officially endorse this march. Neither did the Urban League. But, so what? So what? Many of the members are here anyway. . . . These are our brothers and we're not going to stop reaching out for them simply because we feel there was a misunderstanding. We still want to talk to our brothers because we cannot let artificial barriers divide us. . . .

No, we must continue to reach out for those that have condemned this, and make them to see that this was not evil, it was not intended for evil, it was intended for good. Now, brothers, moral and spiritual renewal is a necessity. Every one of you must go back home and join some church, synagogue or temple or mosque that is teaching spiritual and moral uplift. . . . The men are in the streets, and we got to get back to the houses of God.

at the march. An immediate impact was felt in elections, as voter registration statistics reveal that one and a half million African American men registered to vote in the months following the march. Although the Million Man March is not the only impetus for this increase in voter registration, it is viewed as being a major contributing factor.

In addition, the National Association of Black Social Workers reported a surge in the adoption of black children after the march. While not solely responsible, the Million Man March appears to have served as inspiration for both organizations and individuals to adopt black children.

Subsequent Events The Million Man March inspired a tenth-anniversary commemoration called the Millions More Movement, which was also initiated by Farrakhan. A second march was held from October 14 to 17, 2005, in Washington, D.C. This movement has continued to address issues of importance to African American men. Among them are many themes initiated during the Million Man March, including unity, spiritual values, education, economic development, political power, reparations, prison issues, health, artistic and cultural development, and peace. The group has developed many state affiliates and maintains a national contact office in Chicago.

Further Reading

Bennett, LaRon D., Sr. *The Million Man March: The Untold Story.* Brunswick, Ga.: Bhouse, 1996. The author's personal narrative of the event. Describes the march from the point of view of participants.

Cottman, Michael. *Million Man March.* New York: Crown, 1995. A beautifully photographed book with text by Cottman.

Madhubuti, Haki R., and Maulana Karenga, eds. *Million Man March/Day of Absence: A Commemorative Anthology.* Chicago: Third World Press, 1996. Contains speeches, commentary, photography, poetry, illustrations, and documents related to the march.

Terry, Roderick, and Cliff Giles. *One Million Strong: A Photographic Tribute of the Million Man March and Affirmations for the African-American Male.* Edgewood, Md.: Duncan & Duncan, 1996. A pictorial work that features quotations from famous African American men and the Million Man March pledge.

Douglas A. Phillips

See also African Americans; Angelou, Maya; Elections in the United States, midterm; Farrakhan, Louis; Gingrich, Newt; Hip-hop and rap music; Promise Keepers; Race relations; Religion and spirituality in the United States.

■ Minimum wage increases

The Event U.S. federal minimum wage increases four times during 1990's

Following nearly a decade of no change and the continued erosion of its real value due to inflation, the minimum wage began to increase in the 1990's.

The minimum wage, the lowest hourly rate that employers can legally pay employees, became law in the United States for most workers with the passage of the Fair Labor Standards Act of 1938. The act was the outgrowth of the exigencies created by falling wages during the Great Depression and of the "living wage movement," which argued that workers in a democratic society were not truly citizens if their work could not provide a minimal standard of living. Opposition to the act was strongest in the South, where it was argued that a minimum wage would lead to job losses. Since the act did not provide for automatic increases in the minimum wage, similar debates emerge each time the issue is raised.

With no increase since 1981, by 1989 the real value of the U.S. federal minimum wage was at its lowest level since 1950. Soon after becoming president in 1989, George H. W. Bush expressed a willingness to increase the minimum wage to $4.25 per hour if the bill included the provision for a training wage of 85 percent of the minimum for six months for new hires. After vetoing a bill put forward by U.S. House and Senate Democrats raising the minimum to $4.55, President Bush approved an increase in the minimum wage from the existing $3.35 to $4.25 in two stages. The first increase occurred April 1, 1990, to $3.80. The second increase occurred on April 1, 1991, to $4.25. The legislation also included the provision for a training wage for new hires under age twenty for their first ninety days of employment. Despite this 27 percent increase, the real value of the minimum wage remained relatively low compared to the previous thirty-five years.

By 1995, the real value of the minimum wage had sunk nearly to the level it had been in 1989, before the previous increase. Support was once again building for an adjustment. In the years since the minimum wage had last been raised, the political environment had changed. The Democratic Party now controlled the White House and the Republican Party controlled Congress. Despite being in the minority, congressional Democrats were able to build sufficient support for raising the minimum wage, which was approved by President Bill Clinton. The legislation again involved a two-stage increase. The first occurred on October 1, 1996, raising the wage to $4.70 per hour. The second increase on September 1, 1997, raised the wage to $5.15. A $4.25 training wage for ninety days was included for new hires under age twenty. Although the increase represented a real gain over the earlier increase, the real value of the new minimum wage was still less than it had averaged during each of the previous three decades.

In addition to the federal minimum wage, states have the right to set a higher minimum wage. During the 1990's, a number of states had a minimum wage above the federal one. This differs slightly from the policy in Canada, where there is no federal minimum wage and each province and territory has the authority to set its own minimum wage.

Minimum Wage Debate The movement to increase the minimum wage during the 1990's received wide support from the public but still faced serious challenges in getting implemented. The main argument against raising the minimum wage was based on the classical economics view that a government-imposed wage rate above the market wage rate will reduce the number of available jobs because workers lack the skills to justify higher wages. As a result, an increase will hurt those it is intended to help. The primary argument for increasing the minimum was to be found in the view that a full-time worker should be able to raise a family without living in poverty.

Since most minimum-wage employees were found to be part-time workers under age twenty-five, never married, and living in households with incomes well above the U.S. Census Bureau's poverty threshold, it was argued that increasing the minimum wage would reduce employment opportunities for teenagers without having much impact on poverty. However, research conducted following the increases in the minimum wage during the 1990's found little evidence of its leading to increased unemployment.

Welfare reforms aimed at reducing the number of individuals receiving benefits implemented during the Clinton administration strengthened arguments that full-time work should keep families out of poverty. The increases in the minimum wage during the 1990's were sufficient to keep a single individual above the U.S. Census Bureau's poverty threshold, but not a family of three as it had during the 1960's and 1970's.

Impact The 1990's provided minimum-wage workers with their first increase since 1981. With increases in prices during the intervening years, the purchasing power of the minimum wage had fallen to its lowest level in four decades. Since increases in the minimum wage tend to also increase wages for those earning slightly above the minimum, the increases in the 1990's represented a real gain for millions of low-wage workers. Despite these gains, however, the purchasing power of the minimum wage for the decade was at its lowest level since the 1940's.

Further Reading

Ehrenreich, Barbara. *Nickel and Dimed: On (Not) Getting By in America.* New York: Metropolitan Books, 2001. A compelling look at one woman's sojourn into the world of low-wage work and the struggles she encountered.

Levin-Waldman, Oren M. *The Case of the Minimum Wage: Competing Policy Models.* Albany: State University of New York Press, 2001. A multidisciplinary presentation of the forces that have shaped minimum wage laws in the U.S.

Waltman, Jerold. *The Case for the Living Wage.* New York: Algora Publishing, 2004. The book presents a well-reasoned argument advocating the role that the minimum wage could play in reducing poverty.

_______. *The Politics of the Minimum Wage.* Urbana: University of Illinois Press, 2000. A thought-provoking look at the political maneuvering that has guided and will likely continue to guide minimum wage policy.

Randall Hannum

See also Clinton, Bill; Income and wages in Canada; Income and wages in the United States; Poverty; Welfare reform.

Minorities in Canada

Definition Racial, ethnic, cultural, and linguistic segments of the Canadian population

The population of Canada, about 26 million at the beginning of the 1990's, reached about 31 million by the end of 1999. Visible minorities accounted for 3.5 million people at the end of the decade, or 13 percent of the total population.

Under the Employment Equity Act of Canada adopted in 1986, minorities are identified as "visible" minorities, people whose race is non-Caucasian and who are not white. Ten such groups constitute visible minorities in Canada: Arabs, blacks, Chinese, Filipinos, Japanese, Koreans, Latin Americans, Pacific Islanders, South Asians (Indians and Pakistanis), Southeast Asians, and West Asians.

Aboriginal peoples—American Indians, Inuit (known colloquially as Eskimos), and Metis (persons of mixed native and Old World genetic heritage)—were guaranteed unique rights under the Constitution Act of 1982, part of the Canadian Charter of Rights and Freedoms. Because aboriginal populations were the first peoples occupying Canada, they are not considered minorities but are accorded a separate status in Canadian legislative processes.

The Role of Immigration Between 1991 and 2000, Canada welcomed 2.2 million immigrants, the highest number for any decade during the twentieth century. While European nations such as the United Kingdom, Germany, Italy, and the Netherlands were the most common sources of immigrants to Canada up to the 1960's, immigration from Asia had become increasingly important, with 58 percent of all immigrants to Canada in the 1990's arriving from Asia, and with only 20 percent coming from Europe, 11 percent from Central and South America and the Caribbean, 8 percent from Africa, and 3 percent from the United States. Asian immigrants originated mostly from the People's Republic of China, India, the Philippines, Hong Kong, Sri Lanka, Pakistan, and Taiwan. These countries and territories constituted more than 40 percent of all immigrants to Canada in the decade.

New immigrants to Canada in the 1990's were overwhelmingly attracted to large metropolitan areas, with 73 percent of them settling in or near Toronto, Vancouver, and Montreal. This pattern was probably the result of the greater economic opportunity that cities provide and the immediate benefit derived from moving into a community in which minorities were already well established. Toronto was home to 25.8 percent of the nation's visible minorities in 1991, and 31.6 percent in 1996. Vancouver had 24 percent of Canada's visible minorities in 1991, 31.1 percent in 1996, and by the end of 1999 had overtaken Toronto as the nation's center of minority residence.

Language and Culture In the process of integration of new immigrants, communication in one of the two official languages in Canada, English and French, is very important. However, because of its political history—the amalgamation of a dominant English and an intensely nationalistic French population following the French defeat in 1763—Canada embraces a multiculturalism that also encourages immigrant minorities to maintain their traditional cultures and languages. The tension between these sometimes contradictory goals of integration and cultural maintenance has resulted in much linguistic diversity. During the decade, the desire to perpetuate minority group languages was accommodated by the creation of individual language courses, by having schools teach the minority languages as part of their curricula, and by the founding of clubs and organizations in which the language was spoken.

Census studies during the 1990's showed that 88 percent of Chinese reported speaking a nonofficial language at home and 29 percent were unable to speak an official language, while 15 percent of immigrants from India and 13 percent of those from Taiwan were unable to converse in either English or French. In the census completed in 2001, three-quarters of these minorities were able to speak English, but still one in ten remained incapable of self-expression in either official language. The nonofficial languages spoken by visible minorities were Chinese (31 percent), Punjabi (7.3 percent), Arabic (5.1 percent), Spanish (4.7 percent), Tagalog (Filipino) and Russian (4.5 percent), Persian (Farsi) and Tamil (4.2 percent), Urdu (3.4 percent), and Korean (3.3 percent).

Chinese, South Asians, and blacks accounted for almost two-thirds of the visible minorities. The number of Chinese in Canada approached one million; Chinese immigration is very old, with the first major wave beginning during the late 1850's in British Columbia after the first Gold Rush. Vancouver, the preferred port of entry for people coming from China because of its location on the West Coast, housed an immigrant population of which 57 percent spoke Chinese in the 1990's, compared to 28.9 percent in Toronto and 13.8 in Montreal. South Asians and blacks were more abundant in the eastern provinces of Canada. Many Canadians of African descent have been part of Canada for a very long time, and they are proportionally more important in Quebec and the Atlantic provinces (Nova Scotia, New Brunswick, Prince Edward Island, and Newfoundland and Labrador).

During the 1990's, minority groups were very heterogeneous not only in their origins and distribution within Canada but also in their patterns of integration. There was a marked increase (25 percent over the decade) in the number of marriages between visible minority and nonminority individuals. Blacks were more likely than any other visible minority group to intermarry, while Chinese ranked second, increasing the number of their mixed marriages during the 1990's by more than 50 percent.

Impact The influx of visible minorities transformed Canada's population greatly by increasing its cultural diversity as well as it multiethnicity. The history of these immigrant peoples has been, and will continue to be, an experiment in the production of a functioning multicultural society as the forces of integration and those of cultural maintenance and/ or isolation seek to achieve a workable equilibrium in the lives of all Canadians.

Further Reading

Beaujot, Roderic, and Don Kerr, eds. *The Changing Face of Canada: Essential Readings in Population.* Toronto: Canadian Scholars' Press, 2007. A study of the Canadian population and the implications of population changes in sociology, economics, and geography.

Jones, Beryle Mae. "Multiculturalism and Citizenship: The Status of 'Visible Minorities' in Canada." *Canadian Ethnic Studies Journal,* March 22, 2000. Examines the Canadian population in the 1990's, including location, political representation, languages, and the integration of visible minorities.

Mackey, Eva. *The House of Difference: Cultural Politics and National Identity in Canada.* Toronto: University of Toronto Press, 2002. Examines the national identity of the multiethnically diverse Canadian population through interviews.

Denyse Lemaire and David Kasserman

See also Immigration to Canada; Race relations.

■ Mississippi River flood of 1993

The Event Flooding along the Mississippi River and its tributaries inundates vast regions of the Midwest

Date April-October, 1993

Place Particularly Minnesota, Iowa, Missouri, and Illinois

The flooding of the Mississippi River and its tributaries was unprecedented in its scope and duration and ranks as one of the greatest natural disasters in U.S. history.

During the spring and summer of 1993, an abnormal pattern of upper-level and lower-level steering winds prevented weather systems from following their normal track across the central plains. Instead, they followed a more northerly course, generating a series of persistent storms. The recurrent storms resulted in heavy rainfalls on soils already saturated by the wet autumn of the previous year. Record amounts of precipitation fell across nine states, with some locations recording up to four feet of rain. Minnesota, Iowa, Missouri, and Illinois were among the hardest hit states. North Dakota, South Dakota, Nebraska, Kansas, and Wisconsin also were affected. The rainfall amounts ran 200 to 350 percent of normal for the impacted regions. Many locations experienced precipitation for twenty or more days in July compared to the normal average of eight to nine days.

The runoff sent streams and rivers spilling over their banks, as over 1,000 of 1,300 levees failed to hold back the overflows. However, the larger cities like St. Louis, where the Mississippi reached a record crest of 49.47 feet, were protected by massive floodwalls. The Mississippi remained over flood stage at St. Louis for nearly two months. Across the state, the Missouri River crested at Kansas City at a record 48.9 feet. At one stage, close to 600 river forecast stations, stretching along nearly 150 major streams and tributaries, were above flood stage. Altogether, over ninety locations set record crests. At one point, the flooding disabled a major water plant

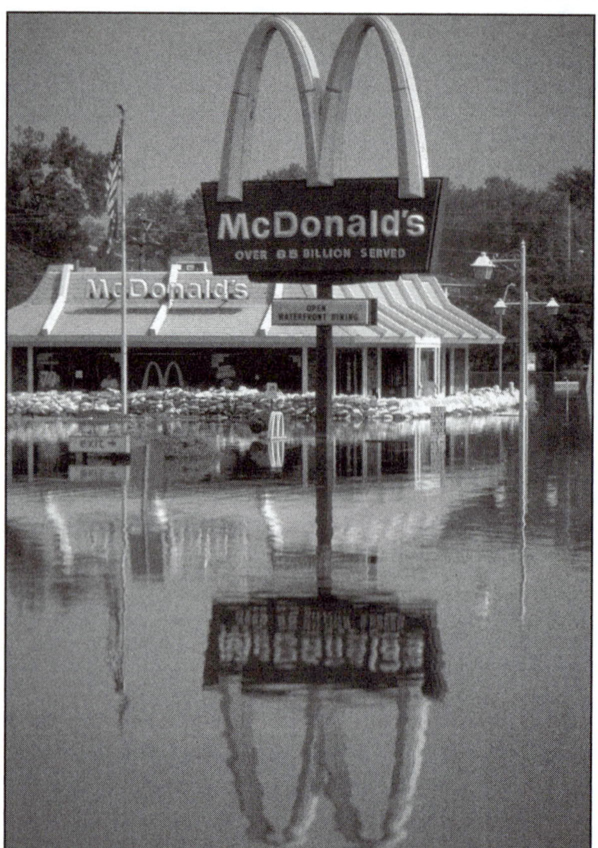

The severity of the Mississippi River flooding can be seen in this July 9, 1993, photo taken in Festus, Missouri. (Federal Emergency Management Agency)

near Des Moines, Iowa, leaving the city without safe drinking water. Following the flood, the U.S. Army Corps of Engineers had to inspect affected docks, dams, and levees for damage.

The overall economic impact of the flooding was monumental. Approximately fifty thousand homes were either destroyed or damaged. Tens of thousands of residents were forced to evacuate. Over fifteen million acres of farmland and at least seventy-five towns ended up under water. In addition, railroad and barge traffic was brought to a standstill for extended periods. Bridges, highways, and several major commercial airports also were shut down. Total damage was estimated around $15 billion. Over fifty people died in the flooding.

Impact In addition to its massive economic impact, the devastation wrought by the Mississippi River flood led to an extensive review and revision of the nation's flood-control measures. Special emphasis was placed on the forecasting of river flows during periods of extensive runoffs.

Further Reading

Changnon, Stanley Alcide, ed. *The Great Flood of 1993: Causes, Impacts, and Responses.* Boulder, Colo.: Westview Press, 1996.

Lauber, Patricia. *Flood: Wrestling with the Mississippi.* Washington, D.C.: National Geographic Society, 1996.

William H. Hoffman

See also Agriculture in the United States; Natural disasters; Perfect Storm, the; Storm of the Century.

■ Mistry, Rohinton

Identification Canadian novelist
Born July 3, 1952; Bombay (now Mumbai), India

In novels describing the lives of poor or middle-class Indians, Mistry explores the human condition.

Though he has lived in Canada since 1975, Rohinton Mistry chose the India he knew in his youth for the setting of the two novels he wrote during the 1990's. *Such a Long Journey* (1991) is set in Bombay in the 1970's, and most of *A Fine Balance* (1995) takes place between 1975 and 1977 in an unnamed city that resembles Bombay. Because he uses such meticulous detail in describing the daily routines of his characters and the small crises that are the stuff of everyday life, Mistry is often compared to nineteenth century realists like the English novelists Charles Dickens and George Eliot. Like them, he sees life as a precarious matter.

At the beginning of *Such a Long Journey,* Gustad Noble, a Parsi bank clerk, is giving thanks to his deity, Ahura Mazda, for his good health and his happy family life. However, his older son soon rebels against him, his young daughter becomes seriously ill, and Noble finds himself innocently involved in transactions involving corrupt government officials that could cost him his job and even his life. Though he escapes, Noble will never again face life so confidently.

A Fine Balance is an even darker novel. After fate brings them together, the four protagonists settle into a seemingly secure life. Though the widow Dina Dalal still misses her young husband, her sewing business permits her to live independently. Her employees, the low-caste Ishvar and Omprakash Darji, are delighted to have jobs. The fourth member of the little family is Dina's boarder, Maneck Kohlah, a college student. However, their happiness is short-lived. Government officials bulldoze the slum shanties and remove the residents, including the two Darjis, to be forcibly sterilized; afterward, they become beggars. Another government ruling deprives Dina of her home and her business, and she becomes a drudge in her brother's household. Disillusioned with life, Maneck kills himself.

Though Mistry admits that chance plays a role in the lives of his characters, what they have to fear most is the cruelty of other human beings, as reflected in the caste system, the greed of government officials, and religious intolerance. The only power one has, Mistry suggests, is to will to be good rather than evil.

Impact *Such a Long Journey* won the 1991 Governor General's Literary Award for Fiction and the Commonwealth Writers Prize and was short-listed for the Trillium Award. *A Fine Balance* won the 1995 Giller Prize, the Canada-Australia Literary Prize, the Winifred Holtby Memorial Prize, and the Commonwealth Writers Prize for Best Book. Both books were short-listed for the Booker Prize. Thus, with his first two novels, Rohinton Mistry established himself not only as a superb realist but also as one of Canada's finest writers.

Further Reading

Allen, Brooke. *Twentieth-Century Attitudes: Literary Powers in Uncertain Times.* Chicago: Ivan R. Dee, 2003.

Bahri, Deepika. *Native Intelligence: Aesthetics, Politics, and Postcolonial Literature.* Minneapolis: University of Minnesota Press, 2003.

Morey, Peter. *Rohinton Mistry.* Manchester, England: Manchester University Press, 2004.

Rosemary M. Canfield Reisman

See also Immigration to Canada; Literature in Canada; Minorities in Canada.

■ Montana Freemen standoff

The Event Standoff between federal agents and a right-wing extremist group
Date March 25-June 13, 1996
Place Justus Township ranch, in Brusett, Montana

The patient approach of the Federal Bureau of Investigation (FBI) in negotiating with the Montana Freemen led to the surrender of the Freemen without the violence that had been anticipated and that had marked FBI confrontations with several other extremists in the 1990's.

The Montana Freemen were one of many extremist groups established in the 1990's that were part of the Patriot movement. Like other Patriot groups, the Freemen perceived the federal government as having been corrupted and controlled by a Jewish conspiracy. In addition to strong anti-federal government beliefs, the Freemen espoused a Christian Identity religious doctrine, which holds that Caucasians are the descendants of the biblical Adam, Jewish people are the descendants of Satan, and ethnic minority groups are subhuman.

The Freemen standoff had its origins in a January, 1994, incident in which twenty-six Freemen

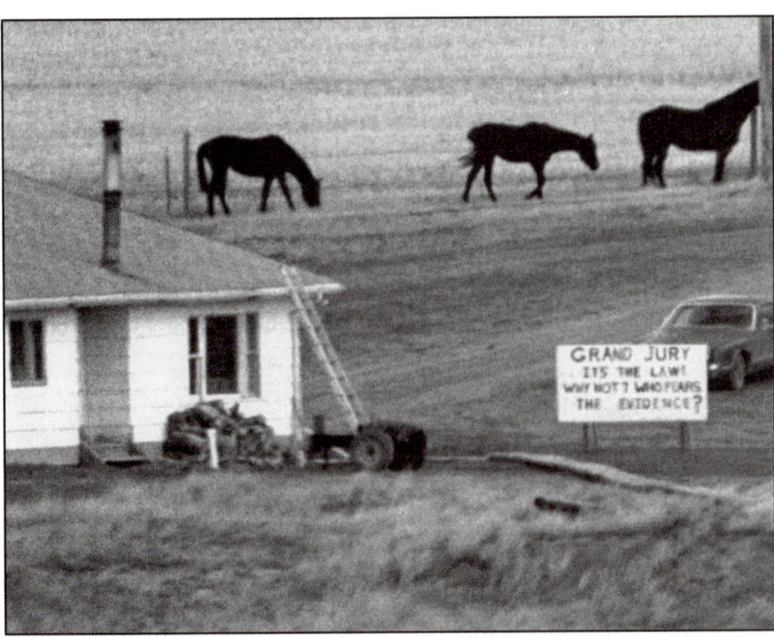

A sign erected at the Montana Freemen compound reads, "Grand Jury. It's the law! Why not? Who fears the evidence?" The antigovernment militants were demanding that they be tried by a jury of their own choosing. (AP/Wide World Photos)

briefly took over a county courthouse in Montana and proclaimed the establishment of their own government and court. Many of the Freemen who faced charges from the incident refused to appear in court and took refuge on ranches in Roundup and Brusett, Montana. Fearing violence with the armed Freemen, local law enforcement did not seek to take the ranches by force. In addition to the conflict with local law enforcement, several Freemen faced conflict with the federal government for threatening a federal judge, tax evasion, and bank fraud. The Freemen had been printing fake money orders with which they defrauded banks, credit card companies, and other businesses for over one million dollars. Like local enforcement, the FBI sought to avoid an armed conflict with the Freemen, but federal agents maintained surveillance around the ranches.

In 1995, the Freemen abandoned the ranch in Roundup and combined their forces at the ranch in Brusett. They named the ranch Justus Township and proclaimed it an independent state, free from the jurisdiction of the federal government. In March, 1996, two of the Freemen leaders, LeRoy Schweitzer and Daniel Peterson, were arrested after being lured to a secluded location by an undercover FBI agent who had infiltrated the fringe group. Eighty-one days after the arrest of Schweitzer and Peterson, the remaining Freemen surrendered peacefully. Schweitzer was sentenced to twenty-two years in prison, and Peterson to fifteen years. Several other Freemen were also sentenced to lengthy prison terms.

Impact After the violent standoffs between the FBI and the Branch Davidians in Waco, Texas (1993), and the Weaver family in Ruby Ridge, Idaho (1992), it was feared that a standoff between the FBI and the heavily armed Freemen would also end in violence. The patient and relatively hands-off approach of the FBI and the subsequent peaceful surrender of the Freemen ended what could have been a deadly conflict. The surrender of the Freemen also effectively marked the end of their organization.

Further Reading

Crothers, Lane. *Rage on the Right: The American Militia Movement from Ruby Ridge to Homeland Security.* Lanham, Md.: Rowman & Littlefield, 2003.

Neiwert, David. *In God's Country: The Patriot Movement and the Pacific Northwest.* Pullman: Washington State University Press, 1999.

Damon Mitchell

See also McVeigh, Timothy; Militia movement; Oklahoma City bombing; Ruby Ridge shoot-out; Waco siege.

■ Moore, Judge Roy

Identification Former chief justice of the Alabama Supreme Court

Born February 11, 1947; Gadsden, Alabama

Moore was dubbed the "Ten Commandments Judge" for his controversial display of the Ten Commandments in his courtroom.

Moore graduated from U.S. Military Academy at West Point and studied law at the University of Alabama School of Law. Following law school, he be-

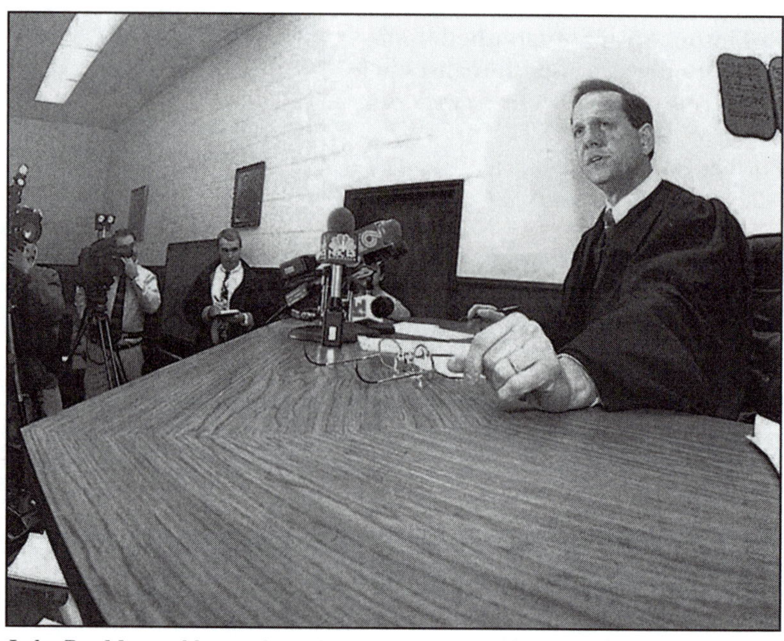

Judge Roy Moore addresses the media during a news conference in his Etowah County courtroom in February, 1997. Behind him is the controversial wood carving of the Ten Commandments. (AP/Wide World Photos)

came the first full-time deputy district attorney for Etowah County, Alabama. In 1982, he ran an unsuccessful campaign for circuit court judge of Etowah County. Moore returned to Gadsden, where he established a private practice. In 1986, he ran another unsuccessful campaign, this time for district attorney. He remained politically inactive until his appointment by Governor Guy Hunt as Etowah County judge. Upon taking his position, Moore decorated his courtroom with various state and legal symbols. He also placed a handmade wooden Ten Commandments plaque behind his bench "to reflect [his] belief in the Supreme Lawgiver of the universe . . . [and] to acknowledge God." Moore also opened his court with prayer every day.

In June, 1993, Joel Sogol, an attorney with the Alabama American Civil Liberties Union (ACLU), threatened to file suit against anyone who conducted public prayer in court, but Moore was not deterred. The ACLU recorded Moore's prayer in June, 1994, and continued to threaten lawsuit. During that summer, Moore began campaigning for circuit judge, facing opposition led by the ACLU regarding his public prayer and Ten Commandments display. November witnessed his election by nearly 60 percent of those voting. The ACLU filed suit in U.S. district court against Moore regarding his prayer and Ten Commandments plaque, declaring the prayer a "religious test." However, on July 7, 1995, the judge dismissed the case, determining that the plaintiffs lacked standing. The ACLU filed complaint again in 1996, and trial began in September of that year. The judge in the trial declared the plaque constitutional but the prayer unconstitutional; though prayers had to cease, Moore's display was permissible as part of a historical display. In February, 1997, the judge from the trial visited Moore's courtroom and determined that the display must be removed. An appeal set before the Alabama Supreme Court was ultimately dismissed in January, 1998. Increasingly confident, Moore declared his campaign for chief justice of the Alabama Supreme Court on December 7, 1999.

Impact Moore's case brought renewed national attention to issues of religion and politics and new fervor to the church-state debate.

Subsequent Events Judge Moore was sworn in as chief justice of the Alabama Supreme Court on January 15, 2001. Justice Moore installed a two-ton monument of the Ten Commandments in the rotunda of the Alabama Judicial Building on July 31, 2001. He faced legislation from the ACLU and Southern Poverty Law Center in the federal courts in 2002 and 2003. The monument was removed from the rotunda by order of a judge, and Roy Moore was removed from his position as chief justice.

Further Reading

Feldman, Noah. *Divided by God: America's Church-State Problem—and What We Should Do About It.* New York: Farrar, Straus and Giroux, 2005.

Moore, Roy, with John Perry. *So Help Me God: The Ten Commandments, Judicial Tyranny, and the Battle for Religious Freedom.* Nashville: Broadman & Holman, 2005.

Meredith Holladay

See also Censorship; Christian Coalition; Conservatism in U.S. politics; Religion and spirituality in the United States; Right-wing conspiracy; Supreme Court decisions.

■ Morissette, Alanis

Identification Canadian singer-songwriter
Born June 1, 1974; Ottawa, Ontario, Canada

Morissette gave voice to a new generation of young women who felt both aggrieved and empowered with respect to the social situation in the 1990's. She became one of the most popular singers of the latter half of the decade.

Alanis Morissette, the daughter of a Canadian man (Anglophone despite the French surname) and a woman who had been a refugee from the suppression of the Hungarian rebellion in 1956, was a child star during the 1980's and early 1990's. She was promoted by various producers, at least one of whom pursued a romantic relationship with her, to which she later referred in her songs. Importantly, Morissette wrote or cowrote her own songs after the age of fifteen. Morissette released two albums in the early 1990's. These were only limited successes. These were followed by her 1995 breakout, *Jagged Little Pill*, cowritten with producer Glen Ballard.

Female singers had become increasingly prominent during the 1990's, but Morissette was one of the youngest and most unconventional of these to gain wide acclaim. The first single from *Jagged Little Pill*, "You Oughta Know," concerns a woman in the after-

Alanis Morissette receives the Album of the Year award for Jagged Little Pill *at the 1996 Grammy Awards. She also won Best Female Rock Vocal Performance, Best Rock Song (both for "You Oughta Know"), and Best Rock Album.* (AP/Wide World Photos)

math of a bitter breakup with a boyfriend and contains graphic references to sexual situations, conveying a palpable sense of regret and disgust. The second and third singles, "Hand in My Pocket" and "You Learn," incarnated more constructive attempts to deal with romantic setbacks. The fourth single, the more lyrical "Ironic," spoke of life's bittersweet juxtapositions and incongruities (and was the subject of much controversy as to whether the word "ironic" was used aptly therein). The fifth single, "Head over Feet," bouncily reassured a lover that he had already won the singer's love without totally being sure of it. The very fact that one album in itself produced five hit singles is remarkable. *Jagged Little Pill* became the best-selling rock album of the 1990's and the second best-selling album of the decade.

Morissette toured widely to support her album. Its success meant that she was on the road for longer than anticipated. Exhausted, Morissette sought spiritual relief in December, 1996, by traveling to India and practicing yoga. She paid tribute to this experience on "Thank U," the first single from her next album, *Supposed Former Infatuation Junkie* (1998). "Unsent," the album's second single, paid poignant tribute to former boyfriends and tantalized the listener with the sense that it was referring to real relationships. Earlier in 1998, Morissette had released "Uninvited." This song, originally composed for a movie sound track, was sad and plaintive. It also became a major hit and received wide airplay. Though Morissette's second album was not the pop culture phenomenon the first had been, it sold millions of copies. *Supposed Former Infatuation Junkie* confirmed Morissette's rank as a major rock star of the 1990's.

Impact Although the first wave of the "riot grrrl" movement had passed by the time *Jagged Little Pill* was released, Morissette's angry yet introspective songs confirmed the visibility of young women in the media. Morissette helped ensure that the 1990's was a decade as associated with the prominence of women and girls in popular culture as the 1980's had been with more masculine presences.

Further Reading

Cantin, Paul. *Alanis Morissette.* New York: St. Martin's Press, 1998.

Tomashoff, Craig. *You Live, You Learn: The Alanis Morissette Story.* New York: Berkley, 1998.

Nicholas Birns

See also Alternative rock; *MTV Unplugged*; Music; Women's rights.

■ Morris, Dick

Identification Political strategist
Born November 28, 1948; New York, New York

A powerful bipartisan political strategist during the 1990's, Morris assisted U.S. president Bill Clinton in winning a second term in office during the 1996 presidential election. During the campaign, he gained notoriety when his relationship with a prostitute became public knowledge.

After attending Columbia University, Dick Morris began what would become a very successful and lucrative career as a political strategist. Throughout the 1970's and 1980's, he assisted various Republican and Democratic politicians with their political campaigns. In 1977, Arkansas attorney general Bill Clinton hired Morris as a political adviser for his upcoming 1978 gubernatorial race in Arkansas. Clinton won the election, but the campaign was the beginning of a turbulent professional relationship between the two men.

In 1992, Clinton was elected as president of the United States. Then, in 1994, the Republicans took control of both the House of Representatives and the Senate. In response, Clinton secretly hired Morris to help him with his 1996 reelection campaign. Morris's three-pronged approach to winning the presidential election for Clinton involved campaigning on the same issues that the Republicans used to gain control of Congress in 1994, implementing an early but aggressive television advertising campaign, and relying heavily on political polling to guide his campaign strategy.

On August 29, 1996, the same day that Clinton accepted the Democratic presidential nomination, *Star* magazine published an article about Morris having a long-term paid relationship with Sherry Rowlands, a high-priced prostitute. The ensuing scandal destroyed Morris's reputation as a political adviser, and he resigned from the Clinton campaign. Morris rebounded from the scandal by using his talents as a campaign strategist to reinvent himself. In 1997, he published *Behind the Oval Office*, an inside account of Clinton's reelection campaign. In 1999, he published *The New Prince*, a guide to political strategy. Morris also established himself as a political commentator and by 1998 was appearing regularly on the Fox News Channel. That year, he was hired to write a weekly political column for the *New York Post*. In 1999, he was also hired to write a syndicated political column for United Feature Syndicate, Inc.

Impact During the 1996 presidential campaign, Morris worked for President Clinton as his confidential campaign strategist. His brilliant political insights and campaign strategy helped Clinton win a second term in office. Unfortunately, Morris also became notorious for his long-term paid relationship with a prostitute. Ultimately, he used his talents as a campaign strategist to transform himself publicly from a disgraced political adviser to a celebrity political commentator.

Further Reading

Morris, Dick. *Behind the Oval Office: Winning the Presidency in the Nineties.* New York: Random House, 1997.

_______. *The New Prince: Machiavelli Updated for the Twenty-first Century.* Los Angeles: Renaissance Books, 1999.

Weisberg, Jacob. "Who Is Dick Morris?" *New York* 28, no. 31 (August, 1995): 34-26, 86.

Bernadette Zbicki Heiney

See also Cable television; Clinton, Bill; Elections in the United States, midterm; Elections in the United States, 1992; Elections in the United States, 1996; Journalism; Republican Revolution; Scandals.

■ Morrison, Toni

Identification African American novelist
Born February 18, 1931; Lorain, Ohio

In 1993, Morrison was awarded the Nobel Prize in Literature, becoming the first African American woman to win the prize.

In the press release announcing Toni Morrison as the 1993 winner of the Nobel Prize in Literature, the Swedish Academy noted both the uniqueness of Morrison's vision as well as her connections to the American tradition: "One can delight in her unique narrative technique, varying from book to book and developed independently, even though its roots stem from [William] Faulkner and American writers from further south." The statement hints at the importance of the Morrison's work for the American canon. Morrison bridges chasms that have long divided Americans: black and white, male and female, urban and rural, lowbrow and highbrow. The importance of her work grows directly from what it provides all Americans and all human beings: a way to view the world and its far-from-tranquil history with realism, humanity, and humor. She unflinchingly examines the most painful circumstances of American life—slavery, discrimination, even incest and infanticide—and yet still manages to find something redeeming and even humorous in human beings and in the American experience.

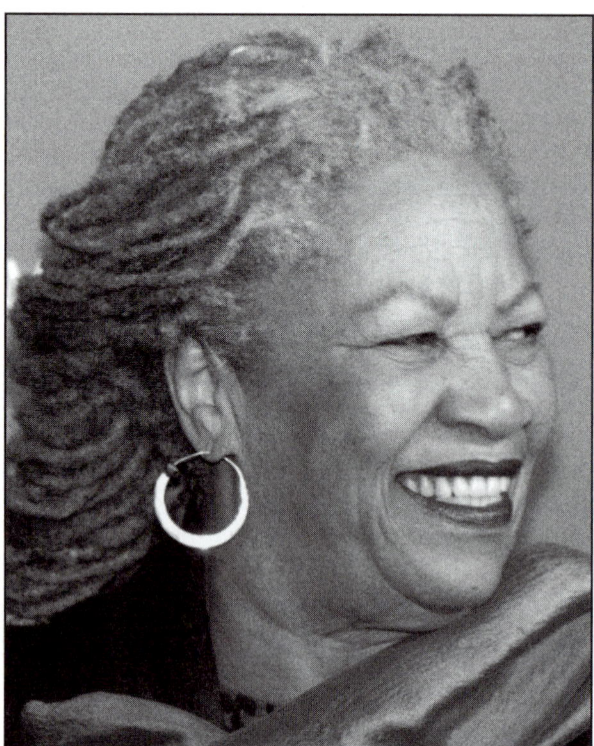

Toni Morrison. (Stephen Chernin/Reuters/Landov)

Morrison's work in the 1990's continued to provide Americans with profound questions about themselves, their culture, and most importantly their history. One year before she won the Nobel Prize, Morrison published her first book-length volume of literary criticism: *Playing in the Dark: Whiteness and the Literary Imagination.* Therein, she explores the way in which the American literary tradition has always contained an unacknowledged African presence. She explores this theme in canonical American writers, such as Mark Twain, Herman Melville, Willa Cather, and Edgar Allan Poe. Later in the decade, she produced *Paradise* (1997), a novel that completed the trilogy started in 1987 with *Beloved* and included the 1992 novel *Jazz.* Each of these novels grows out of a specific point in African American history, often a specific and relatively unknown historical event. *Beloved* is based on the newspaper account of Margaret Garner's partially successful attempt to kill her children upon the return of her slave master. *Paradise* is based on an advertisement for an all-black township in the West: "Come Prepared or Not at All." In *Beloved,* she addresses the unexplored reality of the life of an average slave, not a slave who survived to write and speak about slavery. In *Paradise,* she examines that most persistent of American and human obsessions—the attempt to create paradise—and turns the matter on its head: What if paradise depends upon the absence of white people? In these three novels—*Beloved, Jazz,* and *Paradise*—Morrison takes her readers from the 1850's to the 1970's, essentially rewriting and reexamining the history of American and African American life.

Impact Toni Morrison's literary achievement enables Americans to understand themselves on deeper, more realistic levels. Further, it deepens and broadens the shared language of black and white, male and female, educated and uneducated.

Further Reading

Beaulieu, Elizabeth Ann, ed. *The Toni Morrison Encyclopedia.* Westport, Conn.: Greenwood Press, 2003.

Morrison, Toni. *Playing in the Dark: Whiteness and the Literary Imagination.* Cambridge, Mass.: Harvard University Press, 1992.

Rice, Herbert William. *Toni Morrison and the American Tradition: A Rhetorical Reading.* New York: Peter Lang, 1996.

Weinstein, Philip. *What Else but Love: The Ordeal of Race in Faulkner and Morrison.* New York: Columbia University Press, 1996.

H. William Rice

See also African Americans; Literature in the United States; Nobel Prizes; Publishing; Winfrey, Oprah.

■ Mount Pleasant riot

The Event A two-day civil disturbance in the Mount Pleasant neighborhood of Washington, D.C.
Date May 5-6, 1991
Place Washington, D.C.

The Mount Pleasant riot in Washington, D.C., in May, 1991, highlighted the tensions between the primarily English-speaking African American metropolitan police force and the primarily Spanish-speaking residents of the Mount Pleasant neighborhood. It further exposed various procedural and communications failures of the police department and widespread violation of civil rights by members of the metropolitan police force.

The Mount Pleasant riot is categorized as an urban commodity riot in which members of a lower socioeconomic urban group riot against property owners and symbols of public authority, represented by the police. On May 5, 1991, during a Cinco de Mayo neighborhood festival, an African American English-speaking female police officer attempted to arrest a Spanish-speaking male for drinking alcohol in public. The police officer initially stated that the male suspect threatened her with a knife. The officer shot the man in the chest. She later stated she thought the male suspect had a knife in his possession.

The crowds of Hispanics celebrating in the streets of Mount Pleasant heard about the shooting and quickly turned violent against other police on duty at the festival. Widespread communications equipment failures among members of the metropolitan police force, lack of specific information about what actually happened, no Spanish-speaking officers available to respond quickly, and an overall lack of coordinated police response contributed to an escalation of the violence. Few additional police officers were deployed to the neighborhood, and some police cars and neighborhood stores were damaged. Rain in the early hours of the morning helped break up crowds of angry Hispanic young men in the streets.

Washington, D.C., mayor Sharon Pratt Kelly met with Hispanic community leaders on May 6 to ask them to help restore order. By nightfall, however, the metropolitan police force had deployed more than one thousand police in riot gear in the four-square-mile Mount Pleasant area. This heavy police presence infuriated the Mount Pleasant residents. Local news stations carried extensive coverage of the disturbance. The news coverage attracted a number of young men from outside the Mount Pleasant neighborhood who simply wanted to participate in the disturbance and fight with the police. Larger-scale rioting and property damage ensued. Mayor Kelly declared a state of emergency not only in Mount Pleasant but also in the surrounding neighborhoods of Adams Morgan and Columbia Heights, which was not lifted until May 9, 1991. This curfew upset many of the residents of the wealthier neighborhood of Columbia Heights. The vast majority of residents stayed inside after the mayor declared the state of emergency. Small groups of young men continued to engage the police and threw rocks and bottles at them, but little additional property was damaged. The statistics are significant: 230 people were arrested for curfew violations and looting; 50 police officers were injured; 60 police cars and at least 20 city buses were damaged or burned. Property damage totaled several hundred thousand dollars.

The U.S. Commission on Civil Rights investigated police conduct during the Mount Pleasant riot. In its 1993 report, the commission found the metropolitan police department guilty of widespread police misconduct both leading up to and during the disturbance, including the use of racist language against Hispanics, excessive force, harassment of Hispanics for possible immigration violations, and a failure to investigate previous charges of police misconduct against Hispanic members of the community.

Mayor Kelly accepted the commission's findings. She acknowledged that members of the Hispanic community had long-standing, legitimate complaints against the metropolitan police force, including repeated police failures to respond to emergency calls in Spanish. The police force immediately began efforts to recruit bilingual Spanish-English candidates for police officers and emergency dispatchers. To help regain the trust of the Hispanic community, the police further agreed to cease asking any questions regarding a person's immigration status. The police force agreed to place as many Spanish-speaking officers as possible in predominantly Spanish-speaking neighborhoods and to institute a type of community policing that deployed the same officers in the same areas so both police officers and community residents could get to know one another.

Mayor Kelly disputed the accusation that the police acted in a heavy-handed manner in Mount Pleasant at the request of newer and wealthier residents. The accusation was that these newer residents wanted the police to get tough on groups of Hispanic men who were causing problems such as littering and public consumption of alcohol.

Impact As a result of police behavior during the Mount Pleasant riot, the U.S. Department of Justice took over investigations of metropolitan police misconduct as the police force itself was deemed unable to conduct impartial investigations. Mayor Kelly was criticized for hesitating in her response to the first night of disturbances, for not holding the police to high standards of professional conduct, for their lapses in its training methods, for their faulty internal investigatory procedures, and for not adequately funding the police department at a level that would permit it to purchase fully functioning communications equipment. In her defense, Mayor Kelly stated that problems in and with the metropolitan police force occurred long before her tenure as mayor. Mayor Kelly subsequently left politics.

The police force did establish community liaisons within the Hispanic community in order to have ongoing channels of communications. They also made a sustained effort to recruit, train, and hire more bilingual police officers. The Mount Pleasant neighborhood has seen an influx of wealthier non-Hispanic residents move in and gentrify the neighborhood. Rising housing prices have pushed portions of the Hispanic community into less expensive areas of the city.

Further Reading

Fuchs, Lawrence. *The American Kaleidoscope: Race, Ethnicity, and the Civic Culture.* Middletown, Conn.: Wesleyan University Press, 1990. A sociological study of the conditions necessary in order for riots and other types of civil disturbances to occur.

Waddington, David. *Public Order Policing: Theory and Practice.* London: Willan Publishing, 2007. A scholarly study and classification of all types of civil disturbances around the world. Includes a brief analysis of the Mount Pleasant riot.

Victoria Erhart

See also African Americans; Demographics of the United States; Illegal immigration; Immigration to the United States; Latin America; Latinos; Los Angeles riots; Police brutality; Race relations.

■ Mozart effect

Definition A temporary effect whereby listening to a Mozart sonata leads to improved performance on a spatial-temporal task

The broader interpretation of the Mozart effect—the idea that just listening to Mozart can make one smarter—caught both researchers' attention and the public's imagination in the 1990's.

Specifically, the Mozart effect refers to a finding published by Frances H. Rauscher, Gordon L. Shaw, and Katherine N. Ky in a 1993 issue of *Nature.* Rauscher and her colleagues found that just listening to a Mozart sonata led to temporary improvement in undergraduate students' performance on a spatial-reasoning task. In this research, college undergraduates listened to different kinds of music (and silence, in one condition) for ten minutes. Afterward, they were administered a mental paper-folding and -cutting test getting at spatial-reasoning ability. In comparison to the other conditions, students who listened to Mozart showed improved performance on their immediate test. Since this listening effect was only temporary (about fifteen minutes), there were few implications for education. Further, the numerous follow-up studies have been mixed as to the phenomenon's existence.

Nevertheless, in the 1990's, a Mozart effect industry developed, and numerous books and classical music CDs were marketed toward parents who wanted to enhance their children's intelligence. Indeed, in 1998, Georgia governor Zell Miller went so far as to propose a budget that would spend $105,000 so that a classical music CD could be sent to every newborn in the state.

On another front, the Mozart effect has sometimes been associated with additional research findings as to the potential cognitive benefits of music instruction. Again, in an early study, Rauscher and her colleagues found that preschoolers who received music instruction did better on a puzzle test than did a comparison group who did not receive music instruction. The music instruction effect has been more consistently supported by subsequent research and has more implications for education since the benefits seem to last longer. That is, children who receive music instruction may end up higher in spatial-reasoning ability than those who do not. Rauscher and her colleagues have further concluded that music instruction can lead children to score higher in hand-eye coordination and arithmetic. It is important to note that the music instruction effect is a more general effect and is not limited to the music of Mozart.

Impact In the 1990's, the Mozart effect grew from an obscure research finding to a well-known (if somewhat confused) phenomenon. While the purported, temporary listening effect has limited educational implications, the value of music instruction holds more promise.

Further Reading

Hetland, Lois. "Listening to Music Enhances Spatial-Temporal Reasoning: Evidence for the 'Mozart Effect.'" *The Journal of Aesthetic Appreciation* 34 (2000): 105-148.

Rauscher, Frances H., and Sean C. Hinton. "The Mozart Effect: Music Listening Is Not Music Instruction." *Educational Psychologist* 41 (2006): 233-238.

Rauscher, Frances H., Gordon L. Shaw, and Katherine N. Ky. "Music and Spatial Task Performance." *Nature* 365 (1993): 611.

Russell N. Carney

See also Classical music; Education in the United States; Music; Psychology.

■ MP3 format

Definition Digital audio-encoding format

MPEG Audio Layer 3, also known as MP3, is a method of digital audio compression that significantly decreases the size of an audio file while minimizing reduction of sound quality. The late 1990's saw the release of portable music players that used this revolutionary digital audio-encoding format. The technology allowed for improved storage of audio data and faster online transmission of music, facilitating the development of computer-based music distribution centers like Napster and amazingly small music players like Apple Computer's revolutionary iPod.

The first portable music systems tapped into a desire for mobility in the music-listening public in the 1980's, as seen with the immense popularity of the Walkman cassette player, introduced by Sony in 1979, and the D-50 Discman compact disc (CD) player, in 1984. Throughout the 1980's, music lovers saw continuing improvements to media-storage methods that would not only allow better sound reproduction but also eliminate the tendency of CD players to "skip" when the players were subjected to vibration. The Fraunhofer Institute for Integrated Circuits IIS in Erlangen, Germany, was founded in 1985 to research audio- and video-source coding, among other commercial projects. Initially headed by Dr. Deiter Seitzer, and later by Drs. Heinz Gerhaeuser and Karlheinz Brandenburg (the "father" of the MP3), the Fraunhofer team started developing a digital audio-encoding format under the project name of EUREKA.

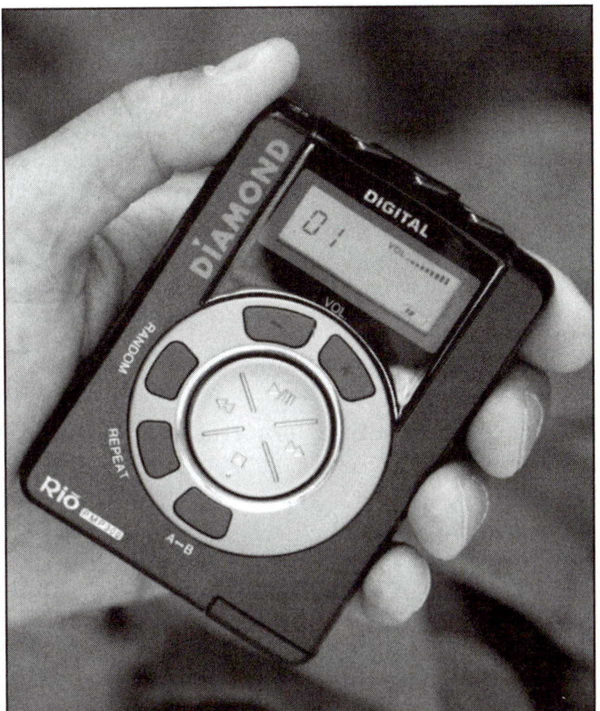

The Rio PMP300 digital portable music player, the first device to use the MP3 format. (AP/Wide World Photos)

In 1993, Fraunhofer researchers formally named their audio-encoding format "MP3" as a simplified file name extension. MP3 was then selected by the WorldSpace satellite broadcasting system as that system's coding format of choice. Then, on July 7, 1994, 13enc, a software MP3 encoder developed by the Fraunhofer Society, was released to the general public as a generic audio format. The format had immediate appeal to users because of its small size (it took up little computer memory) and its broad range of use in a variety of music players (as opposed to such proprietary formats as Vorbis and Windows Media Audio, or WMA). In 1998, the Rio PMP300, the first music player capable of handling the new encoding format, was released and became the forerunner of many new players that would be able to hold hundreds, if not thousands, of audio recordings in digital format. The music player contained 32 megabytes of memory, enough to hold about twelve songs.

Impact The streamlined nature of the MP3 format made it possible for online file servers to act as virtual storehouses of audio files and to support a newly observed trend toward commercial online music sharing. Napster, one of the most prolific file-sharing services, attracted a great deal of media attention as well as massive numbers of online users before a lawsuit by the Recording Industry Association of America (RIAA) led to its shutting down in 2001. The RIAA continued to try to limit the explosion of pirated music files from music-sharing services in the early twenty-first century.

Further Reading

Ewing, Jack. "How MP3 Was Born." *BusinessWeek,* March 5, 2007, 17.

_______. "An Idea Incubator Tries to Grow Cash." *BusinessWeek,* March 12, 2007, 61.

Julia M. Meyers

See also Apple Computer; Computers; Digital audio; Jobs, Steve; Internet; Inventions; Microsoft; Music; Science and technology; World Wide Web.

■ *MTV Unplugged*

Identification Television concert series
Date Began airing in 1989

MTV Unplugged *became the first television concert series revolving around popular musicians performing in acoustic settings. The program spawned a series of best-selling sound-track CDs and VHS/DVD releases, which, in some cases, have left a seminal impact on the modern-day entertainment industry.*

The roots of "unplugged" music, acoustic music performed by musicians who typically play with electric instruments, date back to Elvis Presley's *'68 Comeback Special* and the Beatles' 1970 documentary *Let It Be.* Though the trend occasionally crept into concert performances during the early to mid-1980's, it truly hit a stride in 1989 when Jon Bon Jovi and Richie Sambora (both of the band Bon Jovi) performed stripped-down versions of their hard rock hits "Livin' on a Prayer" and "Wanted Dead or Alive" during the MTV Video Music Awards.

Following the initial broadcast, the network was flooded with positive feedback over what was still considered an unconventional medium, inspiring MTV producers to brand an entire program around the concept. Though *MTV Unplugged* debuted in fall, 1989, with an episode led by English rockers Squeeze, the concept did not fully catch on until the following year, becoming a mainstay of the subsequent decade and attracting a cavalcade of marquee names.

One of the series' most popular 1990 episodes featured guitarists Stevie Ray Vaughan and Joe Satriani, two of the most recognizable electric guitar players who proved equally proficient in acoustic contexts. Having those major names on the series landed instant credibility to the program, which soon attracted the likes of Don Henley, Elton John, and Aerosmith. In addition to revisiting the songbooks of already-established stars, the program also introduced new acts of the time, such as metal men Damn Yankees (comprised of Ted Nugent with members of Styx and Night Ranger).

The blockbuster first year also attracted Paul McCartney for one of 1991's most-viewed episodes, which focused on solo material and several rarely performed Beatles treasures. After inciting extreme fan demand for copies of the recording, he and the network eventually compiled *Unplugged: The Official Bootleg* (1991), launching the first of several episode sound tracks.

The Glory Years The momentum from McCartney's appearance carried over into 1992, which began with an emotional performance from Eric Clapton (who had just lost his young son in an accident). The famed rock guitarist performed "Tears in Heaven," a tribute to his son; several blues tunes; and a reimagined "Layla" as a jangle-based ballad. Once again, the television audience rapturously received the performance, which led to an audio and video sound-track release. That process was also duplicated by soulful pop star Mariah Carey the same year, followed by Bruce Springsteen, though he was the first artist to tinker with the show's tried and true formula. "The Boss" and his solo band of that time period performed an intimate concert, but outside of one acoustic selection, ran through the rest of the set with amplified instruments, in turn rebranding that sound track's title *In Concert/MTV Plugged,* released in the United States in 1997.

Additional attention came in 1993, when entirely acoustic albums were released by 10,000 Maniacs, Neil Young, and Rod Stewart with Ron Wood. Yet Nirvana's appearance became one of the most critically acclaimed concerts to date, in part because of the band's inventive reworking of its alternative rock pedigree and possibly because the album *MTV Unplugged in New York* was released shortly after singer Kurt Cobain's 1994 suicide. As *MTV Unplugged* proved its longevity, producers sought to include an even wider variety of genres and generations and sought out entertainers who would embark on additionally experimental tendencies. The 1994 season featured artists as diverse as vintage swinger Tony Bennett, ex-Led Zeppelin members Jimmy Page and Robert Plant, electronic artist Björk, and folk troubadour Bob Dylan.

The 1995 season highlight came from Kiss, not only because the band reunited all four original members but also because it was the band's first-ever concert appearance without its trademark makeup. In fact, public reaction was so rabid over the taping and sound track that it prompted a full-fledged Kiss reunion tour. The following year was best known for a notorious episode involving the English rock band Oasis, whose lead guitarist, Noel Gallagher, substituted vocals for his temporarily estranged brother Liam.

Tapings remained regular throughout 1997 (including a sound track from Bryan Adams), but the production schedule slowed down considerably as the decade came to a close. Despite the network pumping most of its promotion into the music-video countdown show *Total Request Live*, there was still considerable interest in Björk's 1998 return to the series, along with 1999 performances by the Corrs, Shakira, and Alanis Morissette. As a result of the groundwork built throughout the 1990's, *MTV Unplugged* remained a visible brand via occasional episodes throughout the 2000's, relaunching with regularity for a full 2007 season.

Impact While the concept of unplugged music first seemed risky and unconventional, this program shaped the performance style into a mainstream phenomenon. In doing so, *MTV Unplugged* helped springboard the careers of several newcomers, while simultaneously reviving public awareness of older artists and introducing them to younger audiences. Though the show's popularity fluctuated at various points of its lengthy run, the concept lingered on and earned a revival with an entirely new generation.

Further Reading

Gundersen, Edna. "MTV Flips the Switch Back on for 'Unplugged.'" *USA Today*, September 20, 2007, 18D. An article tracing the birthing and revival of *MTV Unplugged*, including an analysis of key episodes and a sidebar of its best-selling sound tracks.

McGrath, Tom. *MTV: The Making of a Revolution.* Philadelphia: Running Press, 1996. This historical documentation of the famed music channel features coverage of *MTV Unplugged*, including information about several famous episodes and the show's overall contributions to the music industry at large.

MTV. *MTV Uncensored.* New York: Pocket Books/MTV, 2001. Compiles a series of interviews, quotes, and sound bites featured on various programs, including *MTV Unplugged*. Focuses on the network's most outrageous and outlandish guests, incidents, and bloopers.

Andy Argyrakis

See also Alternative rock; Cable television; Carey, Mariah; Lollapalooza; Morissette, Alanis; Music; Nirvana; Television; Woodstock concerts.

■ Mulroney, Brian

Identification Prime minister of Canada, 1984-1993

Born March 20, 1939; Baie-Comeau, Quebec, Canada

During the 1990's, Mulroney negotiated Canada's membership in the North American Free Trade Agreement. He also sought to resolve underlying constitutional problems.

At the beginning of the 1990's, Brian Mulroney was in his second term of office as Canadian prime minister and leader of the Progressive Conservative Party. He had been reelected unexpectedly in 1988 on the Canada-United States Free Trade Agreement platform, despite massive criticism of government corruption, patronage, and his abrasive personal style. His economic policies were close to those of Ronald Reagan (1981-1989) in the United States and Margaret Thatcher (1979-1990) in the United Kingdom.

Negotiations on the extension of the Canada-United States Free Trade Agreement to include Mexico went ahead in 1990, again with considerable opposition from Liberals, who had once been free trade proponents. Mulroney's internationalism even caused him to suggest in September, 2000, that all border posts between the United States and Canada should be abolished, a suggestion rebuffed by the United States. The North American Free Trade Agreement (NAFTA) was passed by all three governments in 1992 and came into effect in 1994.

Constitutional Issues With the passage of the Constitution Act of 1982, Canada assumed full control over its constitution, ending British legislative authority over Canada. Sovereignist Quebec, however, refused to approve the new constitution. In 1987, Mulroney, a committed federalist, proposed the Meech Lake Accord to settle outstanding difficulties, especially concerning Quebec as well as First Nations (Canada's Native American population) over the Charter of Rights and Freedoms section of the Constitution Act. In the spring of 1990, it was clear that no unanimity was to be achieved over the accord, with Manitoba and Newfoundland refusing to sign. By June, it was dead. Consequently, in 1992 Mulroney pushed through a document known as the Charlottetown Accord, which seemed to have general agreement from all parties. However, when put to a national referendum, it too failed, leaving the constitutional issue over Quebec unresolved.

What was worse for Mulroney was the breakaway of Mulroney's senior Québécois partner, Lucien Bouchard, to form his own Bloc Québécois, with the object of gaining the province's independence. On a positive note, just before his resignation in the early summer of 1993, Mulroney legislated for the formation of Nunavut as a new territory to be formed out of the Northwest Territories by 1999. Nunavut would include most of the Inuit population.

Other Issues One of Mulroney's new tax initiatives in the 1990's was the Goods and Services Tax (GST), to replace the Manufacturers' Sales Tax. Legislated in 1989 and imposed in 1991, the GST was similar to the European value-added tax (VAT) in that services as well as goods were taxed, but at a rate set at 7 percent, considerably less than the European model and more in line with sales tax rates. However, because its range was wider than the old tax, and because it was added in a much more visible way, the GST became instantly unpopular, particularly in Alberta, where there had been no previous sales tax. Some of the Alberta Conservative members of Parliament deserted the party for the Reform Party, which, in the 1993 election, had great support in western Canada. In that election, the Liberals, under Jean Chrétien, campaigned against the tax; however, once the Liberals were in power, it was retained as a significant source of revenue.

Brian Mulroney. (AP/Wide World Photos)

On the international front, Mulroney's record is less controversial. With the collapse of the Iron Curtain and the emergence of newly independent states across Eastern Europe, Mulroney was particularly supportive of such states. Also, through membership of the British Commonwealth, Mulroney had been a fierce opponent of apartheid in South Africa and saw its crumbling with the installation of a new leadership under Nelson Mandela. Both Reagan and Thatcher admired Mulroney's international role.

Life After Politics In the spring of 1993, Mulroney realized his unpopularity would severely handicap the party at the upcoming elections and resigned as party leader and hence effectively as prime minister, just as Thatcher had done in the United Kingdom in 1990. After the election, he retired from politics and returned to the practice of law, becoming a senior partner in the Montreal law firm of Ogilvy Renault. He also sat on the boards of various major companies.

Impact The beneficial effect of NAFTA on the Canadian economy was pronounced. The recession at the beginning of the 1990's began to lift by 1993, largely as a result of the agreement. Trade with the United States especially continued to grow, and by 2004 the United States and Canada were the biggest trade partners in the world; trade between the two countries was worth some $700 billion annually.

Mulroney's Progressive Conservative Party lost all but two of its parliamentary seats in the 1993 elections. The change of leadership to Kim Campbell, Canada's first female prime minister, had no effect at all on the party's unpopularity, which remained for many years. Reassessment of Mulroney's national and international contributions has varied widely, and he remains a controversial figure. His recognition of the independence of postcommunist countries has been praised, especially by the Ukraine, as has his help in ending apartheid in South Africa. His environmental policies, also, have come out as forward-looking.

Further Reading

Blake, Raymond B., ed. *Transforming the Nation: Canada and Brian Mulroney.* Montreal: McGill-Queen's University Press, 2007. Leading Canadian politicians and scholars discuss the major policy debates of Mulroney's period of office.

McDonald, Marci. *Yankee Doodle Dandy: Brian Mulroney and the American Agenda.* Toronto: Stoddart, 1995. One of a number of books and articles highly critical of the influence of big business on Mulroney.

Mulroney, Brian. *Memoirs: 1939-1993.* Toronto: McClelland & Stewart, 2007. Mulroney's own account of his political life until his resignation.

Savoie, Donald J. *Thatcher, Reagan, Mulroney: In Search of a New Bureaucracy.* Pittsburgh: University of Pittsburgh Press, 1994. Examines the common beliefs of all three conservative leaders toward privatization and the reduction of state bureaucracy.

David Barratt

See also Bloc Québécois; Business and the economy in Canada; Campbell, Kim; Canada and the British Commonwealth; Canada and the United States; Charlottetown Accord; Chrétien, Jean; Elections in Canada; Foreign policy of Canada; North American Free Trade Agreement (NAFTA).

■ Murphy Brown

Identification Television comedy series
Date Aired from 1988 to 1998

This groundbreaking series won eighteen Emmy Awards, including two for Outstanding Comedy Series during its ten-season run and five for star Candice Bergen.

When it premiered in 1988, *Murphy Brown* was a very funny series, similar to *The Mary Tyler Moore Show,* but with a more cynical Mary as its protagonist and with topical news headlines incorporated into many of the story lines. Candice Bergen played Murphy, a recovering and world-weary alcoholic reporter, just back from the Betty Ford Center in the first episode, who works for the Washington, D.C.-based magazine television show *FYI.* The supporting cast included Grant Shaud as emotional yuppie producer Miles Silverberg; Charles Kimbrough as stuffy Jim Dial, anchor on *FYI*; Faith Ford as former model but now flighty reporter Corky Sherwood; Joe Regalbuto as macho correspondent Frank Fontana; and, perhaps most important, Robert Pastorelli as the moody beatnik housepainter Eldin Bernecky, who serves as Murphy's sounding board and nanny. Plotlines covered everything from romance to friendship, national politics to office politics, with a running joke throughout the series being the revolving door of secretaries that Murphy has. One episode had John F. Kennedy, Jr., showing up to publicize his new magazine, *George,* with Murphy mistaking him for her new secretary.

Perhaps the most controversial story line involved Murphy's pregnancy. The father is her ex-husband, Jake Lowenstein, a political activist who was unable to commit to fatherhood. The pregnancy was heavily criticized by family values groups and then vice president Dan Quayle, who accused single mom Murphy of being a poor example of a parent, public comments that ignited a firestorm of discussion on the importance of marriage and legitimacy. However, the fact that the vice president criticized the series showed the degree to which it was a bellwether of the period in which it ran.

In its hour-long finale, George Clooney, then the star of *ER,* appeared as a silent member of the medical team helping Murphy face her breast cancer ordeal. After the take, Clooney asked Bergen if she was okay. Bergen opened her mouth to speak, then turned away to cry. This final episode also included cameos from Julia Roberts (as herself) and Bette Midler (as "No. 93" in the long line of Murphy's temp secretaries). Robert Pastorelli reprised his role as Eldin after an earlier departure from the series, and Murphy even nabbed the ultimate interview, with God (comedian Alan King in a dream sequence).

Impact *Murphy Brown,* with its career woman star, built on the success of the earlier television comedy hits such as *That Girl* and *The Mary Tyler Moore Show,* but with more of an edge. Story lines explored life situations that these earlier series (products of the 1960's and 1970's, respectively) could only mention, if even that. Most notable was Murphy's breast cancer and pregnancy and her decision to raise the child as a single mother.

Further Reading

Alley, Robert S., and Irby B. Brown. *Murphy Brown: Anatomy of a Sitcom.* New York: Delta, 1990.

Dow, Bonnie J. *Prime-Time Feminism: Television, Media Culture, and the Women's Movement Since 1970.* Philadelphia: University of Pennsylvania Press, 1996.

The F.Y.I. news team from the television series Murphy Brown *(from left): Corky Sherwood (Faith Ford), Jim Dial (Charles Kimbrough), Murphy Brown (Candice Bergen), Frank Fontana (Joe Regalbuto), and Miles Silverberg (Grant Shaud).* (CBS/Landov)

Klein, Allison. *What Would Murphy Brown Do? How the Women of Prime Time Changed Our Lives.* Emeryville, Calif.: Seal Press, 2006.

Lowe, Denise. *Women and American Television: An Encyclopedia.* Santa Barbara, Calif.: ABC-Clio, 1999.

Martin J. Manning

See also Clooney, George; *ER*; Journalism; Quayle, Dan; Television; Women in the workforce; Women's rights.

■ Music

Definition The many styles of popular music and its subgenres

The 1990's, in terms of popular music, was the decade in which subgenres of all styles that had developed in previous decades rose to mainstream prominence. Additionally, technological advances at the end of the decade influenced the way musicians shared their work with fans, and how fans shared music with one another. The rise of new genres challenged the way rock, pop, and rap music were classified. Further, in regard to performers, the 1990's gave rise to iconoclastic female performers, boy bands, and a new generation of teen performers whose looks and sounds separated them from their counterparts of previous decades.

By the 1990's, rock music was forty years old, and popular music in all its forms had become such a part of the North American entertainment landscape that individuals from a variety of ethnicities and social and political designations wanted to represent their style and need for expression in the new varieties of music that began during the decade. As a result, the demographics of popular performers were beginning to more closely resemble that of the United States and North America as a whole.

The 1990's were seemingly a time for all popular music genres to reinvent themselves. By 1990, Music Television (MTV) was almost a decade old. Audiences expected to see their favorite performers and up-and-coming acts on the video channel. In short, what had been new and important in the previous decade was at risk of becoming irrelevant in the new decade.

Like the previous decade, pop music as a dance- and fashion-oriented genre remained popular throughout the 1990's. However, new performers created dances to go with their songs in a number of crazes that swept through club scenes and wedding receptions. The new dances punctuated beats from drum machines that were harsher than those of the 1980's, and the high-energy dances were often more strictly aerobic than their smoother counterparts of the previous decade. Relevant to the musical style revolution of the 1990's is techno, a type of electronic dance music that was invented in the United Kingdom in the 1980's, and house music, a form of electronic music that is a hybrid of American funk and soul combined with European techno, featuring strong, often anthemic vocals. These styles entered the mainstream via chart-topping singles.

Guitar-oriented rock music underwent a revolution as well. The 1990's were ushered in by an underground rock sound that, prior to 1990, was known mostly around the Seattle, Washington, area of the United States. It was called "grunge." Typified by heavy guitar riffs, reminiscent of punk rock, but played at a slower tempo, with energetic drums and rough-edged vocals that often grew into sounds that resembled screams, grunge at first was difficult to define. A number of bands became popular as grunge moved from the West Coast to all of North America.

Even rap music, the relative newcomer to the popular music scene, underwent a metamorphosis to remain relevant to a changing audience base and the music industry—which at one time in the 1980's had disparaged it as a fad because of its apparent lack of live instruments—and as a result became one of definitive genres of the 1990's.

While genres as a whole made changes, individual performers, especially in the genres of rhythm and blues, pop, and rap, and in particular those whose careers began in previous decades, also revised their styles, or in some cases, switched from their typical genres to maintain their place in music history throughout the 1990's. In addition, the teen performers of the 1990's displayed an adult sensibility that was largely absent in their counterparts of the previous decade.

Rock While the public backlash against disco as early as 1980 allowed Top 40 Pop and various forms of rock music to dominant the decade and in effect bring about the extinction of disco, arguably, it was heavy metal's inability to develop and, as a result, parody itself that made it possible for grunge to take over as the hard rock sound of the 1990's.

Of all the bands and variations of grunge and alternative sounds that came out of the Seattle movement, the first and perhaps most famous was Nirvana. In 1992, Nirvana's single, "Smells Like Teen Spirit" was played on radio stations across the United States, and the song's video aired on MTV. While clearly noticeable as a rock song, the single caught audience's attention by failing to be categorized by any previously existing genre. What was obvious was a punk sensibility (grunge can be defined as punk rock played slowly) and a tone of disaffected or antisocial lyrics. Further, the video medium allowed the band to make fun of the typical American high school social scene. The result was that the generation who had grown up on MTV and had defined themselves with an underground, or non-mainstream type of music, now had a genre of hard rock with which they could identify.

Other bands from the Seattle scene, or who at least helped define the sound, were Soundgarden, Pearl Jam, Mudhoney, Alice in Chains, and Temple of the Dog—comprised of members of Soundgarden and Pearl Jam. The Seattle scene not only had its own bands but also a movie and a dress code. The movie *Singles* (1992) illustrated the Seattle scene and the professional and social lives of young adults of a new generation. The dress code for those who wished to identify with the Seattle music scene consisted chiefly of heavy lace-up boots, jeans, and flannel shirts.

Even though in many ways grunge was like punk rock, it was also influenced by heavy metal. However, the new, heavy sound was at odds with heavy metal of the 1980's. Those 1980's bands were still around, but because the new sound was the most novel subgenre to develop in nearly a decade, heavy metal was quickly usurped in popularity by grunge. Diehard fans, however, supported their favorite older acts by attending shows such bands would play in small clubs throughout the 1990's. This was a dramatic shift from the bands' abilities to sell out large arenas in the previous decade.

One possible reason for heavy metal being replaced by grunge was that audiences' priorities were changing. Perhaps audiences had grown tired of songs that in large part detailed substance abuse and physical relationships. On the other hand, grunge and similar alternative rock forms paid attention to, and protested against, human rights abuses, environmental concerns, and other socio-political themes, establishing hard rock with a message as a relevant genre for the 1990's.

The Rise of Gangsta Rap Although thought marginalized because of its predominantly African American performers, who wrote songs about their communities' issues, rap increased its popularity in a subgenre known as gangsta rap. Defined by its focus on street life—or means of survival in neighborhoods and communities marked by rampant drug trade, prostitution, and street gangs—by 1993, gangsta rap was as popular with suburban youth as it was with urban youth who had perhaps experienced the songs' themes firsthand.

Before the 1990's, the category of rap seemed to be a broad category of music that simply meant a performer, known as an emcee, talking rhythmically over prerecorded beats, or music samples. With a growing number of groups who had street life stories to tell, the genre began, and separated itself from more mainstream, or party-oriented, or positive-themed rap, such as that of Will Smith.

Sonically, gangsta rap was darker than most mainstream rap. While rap that had managed to break into the pop charts before 1990 was relatively light and danceable, gangsta rap was dark and brooding, with heavy bass underscoring the pessimistic lyrics. The result was an ominous sound that coincided with a social culture that included customizing older cars, outfitting them with an array of bass speakers through which to play gangsta rap loudly.

Key to the development of gangsta rap was Ice Cube, a former member of the rap group N.W.A. from Compton, California. In 1990, Ice Cube's album *Amerikkka's Most Wanted* was released. With it, he continued to detail the Compton community's antagonistic relationship with the Los Angeles Police Department. The sentiments, however, resonated in African American communities across the United States, especially with youth who felt unjustly profiled and harassed by law-enforcement officers. Other groups such as Geto Boys, Bone Thugs-N-Harmony, and solo artists such as Dr. Dre and Snoop Doggy Dogg contributed to the genre. In 1991, Ice Cube starred in *Boyz 'N the Hood*, a movie that exemplified the pluralities of inner-city life and the choices that young men are forced to make in drug- and crime-ridden areas.

While there were clearly shifts in performance styles and lyrical content, the other important development in terms of rap was a geographic shift. Previously, the East Coast of the United States represented the home base of rap, but when California-based Ice Cube and others began to rap unabashedly about their dissatisfaction with America's criminal justice system, it resonated in communities similar to Compton throughout the United States, and eventually found its way to suburban listeners.

Other Rap Genres In the 1990's, other forms of rap continued to exist that had their roots in previous decades. Jazz-rap and alternative rap became popular because of artists such as Digable Planets and Arrested Development. After 1993, it became obvious that neither the West Coast nor the East Coast had a particular claim to rap music: Artists from across the United States and Canada were putting their particular spin on the genre, creating many subgenres, including trip-hop. It was during this time that a new brand of hip-hop was created. Hip-hop involves using a turntable on which to push a vinyl album by hand to create a scratching sound to mix two different sounds. Scratching causes the turntable to perform like a drum or other percussion instrument. Often, prerecorded music samples are included in the mixing. Throughout the 1990's, hip-hop evolved to include singers who performed with the rappers, and who might also sing over melody samples from prerecorded samples.

Even though it was a predominantly African American art form, there were Caucasian rappers who were quite popular during the 1990's. From Canada, there was Snow, a rapper from Toronto whose reggae-inflected songs were often performed rapidly and told of problems with the police and his hardscrabble upbringing. Vanilla Ice was another Caucasian rapper who earned fame in the early 1990's. His brand of dance rap was largely about urban scenes in Miami. His videos featured the rapper and backup dancers performing choreographed moves. In the late 1990's, Eminem was featured with veteran rapper Dr. Dre in Dre's comeback single, "Forgot About Dre." Eminem, however, had his own brand of self-deprecating rap that catapulted him to fame through the end of the decade. In 1992, the Beastie Boys released *Check Your Head*, which went double platinum in the United States. This was followed by *Ill Communication* (1994), which included the hit song "Sabotage," and *Hello Nasty* (1998); both albums went triple platinum.

By the middle of the decade, there was a form of hip-hop that was street-life oriented but also included harmony in the vocal performance and contained the heavier bass associated with gangsta rap. This form of rap would come to define hip-hop. An example of this is Bone Thugs-N-Harmony from Cleveland, Ohio. Considered by some critics to be particularly dangerous because of their willingness to depict graphic violence in detail, Bone Thugs-N-Harmony nonetheless became famous for their rapid-fire delivery, which was sometimes sung, and the limber, yet dark, rhythmic bass that accompanied it.

Inevitably, sometimes the street life that many rappers illustrated in their songs became a part of their real life. In a feud whose origin is unknown, rappers from the East Coast began to grow at odds with rappers from the West Coast, and vice versa. The most famous, and arguably most tragic, example of the feuding was when onetime friends Tupac Shakur and Notorious B.I.G., also known as Biggie Smalls, created songs that taunted each other. Things came to an end when Tupac Shakur was gunned down in Las Vegas in 1996. A short time later, in March, 1997, Biggie Smalls was ambushed by gunfire. Shakur was represented by the West Coast record company Death Row Records, while Smalls recorded with New York-based Bad Boy Records. Both murder cases remain unsolved.

Female Performers Female groups were popular in the 1990's as they had been at no other time in music history, except perhaps the 1960's. Throughout the decade, female groups with pop sensibilities, regardless of the genre to which they actually belonged, were popular with audiences who desired a more radio- and dance-friendly sound than could be found in most rap.

En Vogue was a quartet who sang in harmony. Comprised of African Americans, the group sometimes created a sound that hearkened back to earlier times in rhythm-and-blues (R&B) history. SWV, or Sisters with Voices, was an African American trio who had radio-friendly hits and contemporary-sounding melodies. While women dominated the pop R&B charts, they also excelled as rap artists. Throughout the 1990's, performers such as MC Lyte, Queen Latifah, Salt-n-Pepa, and TLC proved that women could rap while providing socially positive messages and a danceable beat with memorable hooks.

In the late 1990's, Destiny's Child came into national prominence with their single, "No, No, No." The group was an example of the fashion-consciousness that would mark contemporary R&B and pop for years to come. Also, the superfast delivery of clean but clever lyrics made them radio-ready immediately.

While groups of female performers were integral to the changing scheme of popular music, the 1990's were also the years of the single performer, typically a sultry singer who sang about love. Characterized by arguably stunning physical features and distinctive voices, these performers—such as Shakira, Jennifer Lopez, Christina Aguilera, and Britney Spears—created models of dance music that would change audiences' expectations for female singers for the rest of the decade.

Teen Acts New in the 1990's was the phenomena of teen acts who performed music exactly as their adult counterparts did. In a departure from previous decades' packaging popular teen performers as innocents, the 1990's allowed underage performers the opportunity to express mature sentiments, sometimes with controversial results. The rise of teen stars was seen in a cross-section of musical genres: in country music, there was LeAnn Rimes; in pop, there was Britney Spears; and in hard rock, there was Silverchair. Additionally, the 1990's continued the trend of boy bands. Typically, these were groups of four or five young men with an urban sense of choreographed dance, soulful lyrics, and pop hooks. Boy bands were definitely popular with the teen demographic but, unlike in previous decades, were also well-received by adult listeners. Examples of 1990's boy bands were Backstreet Boys, *NSYNC, and Soul Decision. Arguably, Motown's Boyz to Men could have been considered a boy band, but the seriously romantic tone of the group's music and the almost built-in audience of Motown fans (which was the band's label) separate them from other all-male singing groups of the era. The opportunity for teens to interact with audiences like adult performers was indicative of fact that the decade was a time for redefining previously held conventions.

Veteran Performers Reinvention in the music industry was not limited to child stars performing like adults. Adult stars from previous decades were either continuing to enjoy success previously earned or were crossing over to new genres. Most notably, Cher became a techno singer and was widely known for the single "Believe." Madonna remained nearly as popular in the 1990's as she was in the 1980's. She even sparked a dance craze by taking a move from the gay dance scene, the Vogue, and created a single of the same name. Veteran rock acts such as Van Halen (albeit with a new lead singer) were popular as well. Perhaps most notable was the 1999 release of *Supernatural* by Carlos Santana, formerly of 1970's supergroup Santana. On this release, Santana performed with a number of contemporary young artists with a range of musical styles, from rap to rock. The meshing of styles on the recording, in essence, symbolizes what the 1990's had to offer audiences, which was a mixing of styles, instead of confining styles to the genre designations created in decades past.

Country Music Previously ignored by mainstream audiences, country music underwent musical and cosmetic changes to garner a significant share of audiences in the 1990's. Like the rest of the music industry during the decade, country music was given to anthemic songs that were accompanied by a dance. In the early 1990's, Billy Ray Cyrus entered the national music consciousness with a song called "Achy Breaky Heart." The catchy, rhyming lyrics, and the resulting line dance, made the song an instant hit that would remain popular throughout the early 1990's. With movie star looks and sporting a "mullet," or a hockey haircut popular with rock stars and fans in the 1980's, Cyrus was just unexpected enough to make certain audiences rethink their perception of country music.

Female country performers enjoyed a makeover and retail success as well. Canadian Shania Twain paved the way for other female country stars of the era to embrace a sophisticated look in terms of fashion and cosmetics, while singing a brand of country that some critics claimed was simply retooled 1970's light rock. Regardless of criticism, the new country had a pop sensibility that caused the genre to be played on Top 40 stations all over North America.

Sultry Sounds The 1990's were a time for both groups and individual artists to enjoy success. Artists who were considered R&B, or soul performers, often ensured their popularity with sensuous love songs. Singers such as Toni Braxton, Adina Howard, Mariah Carey, Keith Sweat, R. Kelly, and 1970's romance king Barry White all had chart-toppers that had a particularly sensual quality to them. However, because of the pop influence that could be heard in a variety of music markets, the songs not only fared well in R&B markets but sometimes on Top 40 charts as well.

Impact In the 1990's, the soundscape of American popular music changed in ways that moved beyond style or genre. Furthermore, toward the end of the decade, there were also changes in the way in which music was shared between listeners. The increasing popularity of the Internet allowed for new musical artists to reach potential audiences more quickly than through the traditional means of previous decades and for most of the 1990's.

The 1990's also saw genres once on the periphery of mainstream music commanding a great deal of attention. Country music, especially female artists of that genre, enjoyed a great deal of success due in large part to the revamping of country music in terms of the look of artists and the redesigning, and redefinition of the country sound. Other genres that would remain a part of American music culture—Latin, gangsta rap, and techno music—underwent significant evolutions in the 1990's, either by way of their creation, increased popularity, or ability to change from the decade's beginning to its end. Similarly, rock music added subgenres that helped the aging form maintain its relevance forty years after its inception.

Further Reading

Bell, Thomas L. "Why Seattle? An Examination of an Alternative Rock Culture Hearth." *Journal of Cultural Geography* (Fall/Winter, 1998): 35-48. Details the history of the Seattle sound, and how the youth culture of one region became a cultural phenomenon.

Harding, Cortney. "Back to the Future." *Billboard* 120 (April, 2008): 24-24. Discusses how particular rock acts of the 1990's returned to their independent roots.

Touré. *Never Drank the Kool-Aid.* New York: Picador, 2006. A collection of articles and essays by urban-music insider and journalist Touré. Illustrates the real people behind the recordings and artistic personas.

Dodie Marie Miller

See also Alternative rock; Boy bands; Carey, Mariah; Censorship; Coffeehouses; Country music; Death Row Records; Digital audio; Ecstasy; Electronic music; Grunge fashion; Grunge music; Heroin chic; Hip-hop and rap music; Internet; Latinos; Lollapalooza; Love, Courtney; McEntire, Reba; Madonna; Milli Vanilli; Morissette, Alanis; MP3 format; *MTV Unplugged*; Nine Inch Nails; Nirvana; O'Connor, Sinéad; Rock and Roll Hall of Fame Museum; Selena; Shakur, Tupac; Smith, Will; Tibetan Freedom Concerts; Woodstock concerts.

■ Myers, Mike

Identification Canadian comedian and actor
Born May 25, 1963; Scarborough, Ontario, Canada

Myers's characters on Saturday Night Live *as well as the* Austin Powers *spy spoof films became cultural touchstones for teenagers and young adults in the 1990's.*

A former child actor in commercials, Mike Myers joined *Saturday Night Live* in 1989 and quickly created several popular featured characters: Wayne Campbell, the teenage host of the Aurora, Illinois,

Mike Myers plays the British superspy Austin Powers in the 1997 film of the same name. (Reuters/Landov)

cable access television show *Wayne's World*, *Coffee Talk* host Linda Richman (based on his mother-in-law), and Dieter, the host of *Sprockets*. Each character had a popular catchphrase—Wayne's "Excellent!" and "Not!" Richman's "It's like buttah," and Dieter's "Would you like to touch my monkey?"—that soon entered the teenage lexicon. The *Wayne's World* sketch was made into a 1992 feature film and became the only film based on a *Saturday Night Live* skit to gross more than $100 million.

Wayne's World, with Myers as Wayne and Dana Carvey as his sidekick, Garth Algar, became the most famous of Myers's *Saturday Night Live* creations. Still, some were concerned about how the sketch would fare. Carvey thought "we'd be nailed as doing a Bill and Ted ripoff"—referring to the popular comedy *Bill and Ted's Excellent Adventure* (1989). Then-show writer Conan O'Brien even tried to dissuade Myers from submitting the idea for the sketch. Both O'Brien and Carvey were shocked at its success. On one occasion, in 1992, the skit caused a minor political furor when Myers's character mocked Chelsea Clinton's looks and compared her unfavorably to Vice President Al Gore's daughters. Myers later apologized to First Lady Hillary Clinton for the sketch.

Wayne's World 2 (1993) was less successful than the original film, as was his next comedy, *So I Married an Axe Murderer*, released the same year. After leaving *Saturday Night Live* in 1995, Myers created the satirical character of 1960's British spy Austin Powers. A spoof of the James Bond films, *Austin Powers: International Man of Mystery* (1997) was a cult hit, and two successful sequels followed in 1999 and 2002.

Impact Myers, with his work on *Saturday Night Live* and the *Austin Powers* movies, along with Jim Carrey, another comedian who went from television to film, was a major comedy force of the 1990's.

Further Reading

Shales, Tom, and James Andrew Miller. *Live from New York: An Uncensored History of "Saturday Night Live."* Boston: Little, Brown, 2002.

Sydney, Leah. "The Very Groovy Life of Mike Myers." *Biography* 3, no. 6 (June, 1999): 96-101.

Julie Elliott

See also Carrey, Jim; Comedians; Film in the United States; Late night television; Television.

■ Nanotechnology

Definition Fabrication of functional systems at the molecular level between 1 and 100 nanometers (one billionth of a meter)

During the 1990's, nanotechnology posed the possibility of improving human life with better materials and tools to provide breakthroughs in medicine, artificial intelligence, and the conquest of space.

The first book about nanotechnology, *Engines of Creation*, was published by Eric Drexler in 1986. In 1991, International Business Machines (IBM) endorsed the use of nanotechnology to produce electronic and mechanical devices atom by atom. Later that year, carbon nanotubes were discovered. Possessing remarkable tensile strength and varying electrical properties, they proved useful as molecular components.

Drexler published the first nanotechnology textbook, *Nanosystems*, in 1992. In it, he outlined how to design, analyze, and manufacture high-performance machines from the molecular lattice of carbon. That same year, Drexler testified before a U.S. Senate committee about the implications, applications, and major scientific benefits of nanotechnology. He pointed out that products of unprecedented quality and performance could be constructed by precisely guiding the assembly of molecules.

In 1993, the first Feynman Prize in Nanotechnology was awarded to Charles Musgrave for modeling a hydrogen abstraction tool useful in nanotechnology. The first industrial analysis of military applications of nanotechnology was released by Hughes Aircraft Company in 1995. In 1996, the National Aeronautics and Space Administration (NASA) began work in computational nanotechnology. NASA researchers proposed the use of a single carbon nanotube as the tip of an atomic force microscope (AFM).

The first nanotech company, Zyvex, was founded in 1997 in Richardson, Texas. Zyvex proposed using nanotubes for scanning force microscope (SFM) probes and pursued the production of nanorobots that could break the chemical bonds of cheap ingredients and reassemble them into sophisticated, useful products. Federal funding of nanotechnology research began in earnest in the late 1990's. In 1998, researchers at New York University published a paper showing a molecular mechanical system that was constructed from branched DNA molecules. Other research focused on nanotechnology design that mimics the process of biological evolution at the molecular scale. The first safety guidelines addressing the potential positive and negative consequences of nanotechnology were released by the Foresight Institute in 1999.

Impact Nanotechnology research is focused on developing programmable, molecular-scaled systems that can precisely and inexpensively produce nanostructured materials and devices that are permitted by the laws of physics. This approach has led to the manufacture of polymers based on molecular structure and the design of computer chip layouts based on surface science. Commercial applications of nanotechnology have taken advantage of colloidal nanoparticles in bulk form to produce protective coatings, antireflective and antifogging glass, stain-resistant and water-repellent clothing, and some lines of sunscreens, cosmetics, and paints. Nanotubes, quantum dots, and other nanomaterials show promise for providing universal clean water supplies, molecular-engineered food, cheap and powerful energy generation, drastically improved formulation of drugs and organ replacements, greater information storage and communication capacities, and long-term life preservation.

Further Reading

Drexler, Eric. *Engines of Creation*. New York: Anchor Books, 1986.

King, Vernon B. *Nanotechnology Research Advances*. New York: Nova Science, 2007.

Wiesner, Mark R., and Jean-Yves Bottero. *Environ-*

mental Nanotechnology: Applications and Impacts of Nanomaterials. New York: McGraw-Hill, 2007.

Wolf, Edward L. *Nanophysics and Nanotechnology: An Introduction to Modern Concepts in Nanoscience.* New York: Wiley-VCH, 2004.

Alvin K. Benson

See also Computers; Genetic engineering; Genetically modified foods; Genetics research; Inventions; Medicine; Science and technology; Space exploration.

■ National debt

Definition The national debt is the total amount of unrepaid money borrowed by the federal government since it was created

The national debt increases the cost of government as it is forced to pay interest to those who have loaned money to the government. During the 1990's the growth of the national debt slowed.

During the 1980's, federal budget deficits had swelled the national debt beyond $2 trillion. As the decade of the 1990's began, the debt and deficit became a potent political issue. President George H. W. Bush negotiated a budget agreement with the Democratic Congress intended to reduce the budget deficit and slow the growth of the national debt. The agreement, though, proved politically unpopular, and the debt issue ignited the third-party candidacy of billionaire H. Ross Perot. The election of Bill Clinton, with Perot's help, was based partly on his promise to reduce the deficit and with it the national debt.

Clinton administration In 1993, Clinton pushed through a series of tax increases with some of the additional revenue going to reduce the deficit. Clinton also reduced spending, mostly in defense, as part of the "peace dividend" that was to save the federal government money after the collapse of communism. During his first term, Clinton slashed defense spending by more than $30 billion or 10 percent. Yet even with his tax increases and budget cuts, Clinton only slowed the growth of the national debt during his first term. From just under $3 trillion in 1992, the debt exceeded $3.7 trillion by 1996, a nearly 25 percent increase. This was the smallest percentage increase in the debt since Richard M. Nixon's first term and represented a measure of success.

Clinton's inability to seriously reduce the deficit during his first two years in office made the national debt an issue in the 1994 midterm elections. Republican candidates promised deficit reduction, mostly through budget cuts, and a constitutional amendment mandating a balanced budget. The Republican sweep in 1994 turned the Congress over to the party for the first time in forty years.

Republican Congress In 1995, Congress passed a series of measures to reduce or eliminate the budget deficit and to gain control of the national debt. A constitutional amendment mandating a balanced budget was offered in the House of Representatives but did not pass with the necessary two-thirds majority. The amendment would have forced Congress to pass a balanced budget every fiscal year but provided little direction on how the amendment would be enforced. Also in 1995, Congress passed a stringent budget for the 1996 fiscal year, cutting some federal programs and holding others to zero growth. The result was a swiftly declining deficit and a flattening of the national debt. Finally, Congress gave the president greater authority in making spending cuts. The line-item veto was approved, and it allowed the president to eliminate excessive spending in a bill.

Clinton's second term saw a flattening of the national debt. At the start of his administration, the debt totaled more than $4 trillion, rising to $5.25 trillion by the time of his reelection, but by the end of the decade, the debt had increased less than 10 percent to a total just above $5.5 trillion. The Asian financial crisis contributed to a $130 billion increase in the debt, the largest in four years.

The reduction in the debt led to changes in the interest costs for government borrowing. The Treasury Department announced that it was discontinuing the long-term thirty-year bonds. The decision reduced government's interest costs as the thirty-year bond enjoyed a higher interest rate than the ten-year bonds. The demise of the thirty-year bond further lowered the interest paid by the federal government as high-interest bonds from the 1970's and 1980's were retired and replaced by shorter-term bonds and notes costing less. The Treasury also introduced inflation-sensitive bonds. The bonds' interest rates were adjusted to include the inflation rate but, because inflation was relatively low during the 1990's, the bonds cost less in interest than the regular EE bonds.

In his 2000 state of the union address, President Clinton announced the national budget enjoyed a $184 billion surplus, some of which would be used to pay off a portion of the national debt. Yet in his announcement of a budget surplus, Clinton left unsaid that some $160 billion came from the Social Security trust fund. Starting in 1984, the retirement program ran a surplus because of higher payroll taxes. The Social Security funds were then loaned to the federal government, artificially lowering the deficit. Also contributing to the budget surplus were the ever-increasing tax revenues from the skyrocketing stock market. By 2000, cracks had developed in the market, a warning of a future crash and a significant reduction in the taxes paid.

Impact The reduction of the national budget deficit calmed political fears of an out-of-control debt and removed the national debt as a political issue in the 2000 presidential race.

Further Reading

Berman, William C. *From the Center to the Edge: The Politics and Policies of the Clinton Presidency.* New York: Rowman & Littlefield, 2001. An examination of the Clinton administration and its economic and foreign policy. Includes discussions of his budget policies and his achievements in reducing the budget deficit.

Christensen, Jane. *The National Debt: A Primer.* Hauppauge, N.Y.: Nova Science Publishers, 2004. A wide-ranging examination of the debt, who owns the debt, how it has grown, and the cost in interest payments.

Kelly, Robert, and Nelson Benton. *The National Debt of the United States, 1941-2008.* Jefferson, N.C.: McFarland, 2008. A detailed analysis of the national debt and its growth through the latter years of the twentieth century. Particular attention is paid to the Clinton administration and the president's attempt to reduce the budget deficit.

Douglas Clouatre

See also Balanced Budget Act of 1997; Bush, George H. W.; Clinton, Bill; Contract with America; Defense budget cuts; Line Item Veto Act of 1996; Social Security reform; Stock market.

■ National Endowment for the Arts (NEA)

Identification U.S. public agency that supports projects in the arts

During the 1990's, the NEA awarded thousands of grants but struggled economically as a result of controversial budget cuts.

The NEA is the largest national funder of the arts in the United States. Its mission is to support works of artistic excellence, advance learning in the arts, and strengthen the arts in communities.

Funding Controversies From 1990 to 1995, Congress granted the NEA between $152 and $175 million annually. In 1996, however, Congress cut NEA funding to $99.5 million because of pressure from conservative groups, such as the Reverend Donald Wildmon's American Family Association. The Religious Right criticized the agency for funding such controversial artists as Robert Clark Young, Andres Serrano, Robert Mapplethorpe, and the "NEA Four"—Karen Finley, Tim Miller, John Fleck, and Holly Hughes—whose proposed grants had been vetoed by NEA chairperson John E. Frohnmayer in 1990.

Congress also voted to phase out funding for the agency over a two-year period, and the House of Representatives announced a plan to eliminate the endowment. Congress placed specific limitations on the NEA. Except for the literature fellowships, all individual grants were eliminated, but the honorific National Heritage Fellowships and American Jazz Masters awards were kept. Congress also prohibited the seasonal or general operating support grants, allowing only project support to organizations. Restrictions were imposed on allowing grantees to subgrant to third-party organizations and artists. As a result of the budget reduction, the agency was forced to organize itself and the staff was cut by 47 percent, from 279 to 148. The NEA suffered further reductions in its budget with a 1999 budget of $98 million.

Chairs The 1990's opened with a change in the chair of the NEA. At the very end of 1989, Frohnmayer was appointed by President George H. W. Bush to lead the agency. His leadership was challenged by the Religious Right, however, and after two years of controversies, especially those surrounding its funding of projects by polarizing

National Endowment for the Arts Funding

Funding and Grants	*1990*	*1995*	*1999*	*2000*	*2001*
Funds available (in millions)	170.8	152.1	85.0	85.2	94.0
Grants awarded (number)	4,475	3,685	1,675	1,882	2,093

Source: U.S. National Endowment for the Arts, *Annual Report.*

figures such as photographer Mapplethorpe, he was forced to resign.

In 1993, Jane Alexander, an American actor and author, was appointed to head the NEA by President Bill Clinton. During her four years in this position, she faced unsuccessful attempts by Congress to shut down the program. In May, 1998, Bill Ivey became the seventh chair of the NEA. Appointed by President Clinton, he was given the task of leading the organization into the new century. In 1999, Ivey launched a five-year strategic plan that became the basis for Challenge America, a new national program to expand the reach and impact of NEA activities.

Grants and Awards The NEA awards grants in three areas: art projects, leadership initiatives, and partnership agreements. In 1996, it established the Open Studio project in partnership with the Benton Foundation, to bring free public Internet access to arts organizations around the United States. In 1997, thanks to a $225,000 leadership initiative, the NEA helped the Young Men's Christian Association (YMCA) to establish literary arts centers in neighborhoods across the country. The NEA also published *The Accessible Museum* (1993), a guide to creating accessibility programs for museums in collaboration with the American Association of Museums and the Institute of Museum Services, and it continued to fund ventures such as the Sundance Film Festival.

Additionally, the NEA awards individual fellowships in literature. A number of recipients of NEA Creating Writing Fellowships during the 1990's, including Jeffrey Eugenides and Annie Proulx, have won National Book Awards, National Book Critics Circle Awards, or Pulitzer Prizes in fiction and poetry.

In January 23, 1995, the series *American Cinema* premiered on public television as part of the NEA's millennium celebration of American art in the twentieth century.

Impact During the 1990's, the National Endowment for the Arts awarded about forty thousand grants, totaling in excess of $1 billion, that brought art to Americans by supporting regional theater, opera, ballet, symphony orchestras, museums, and other art organizations.

Further Reading

Alexander, Jane. *Command Performance: An Actress in the Theater of Politics.* New York: PublicAffairs, 2000. Alexander recounts her experience as head of the NEA from 1993 to 1997.

Binkiewicz, Donna M. *Federalizing the Muse: United States Arts Policy and the National Endowment for the Arts, 1965-1980.* Chapel Hill: University of North Carolina Press, 2004. A study on the U.S. national arts policy that refutes the assumption that the NEA has had a liberal agenda.

Campbell, Mary Schmidt, and Randy Martin, eds. *Artistic Citizenship: A Public Voice for the Arts.* New York: Routledge, 2006. Essays by artists and scholars address the role of art and artists in civic life.

National Endowment for the Arts. *National Endowment for the Arts, 1965-2000: A Brief Chronology of Federal Support for the Arts.* New York: Author, 2000. An overview of the first thirty-five years of the NEA.

Reiss, Alvin H. "For Long-Term NEA Survival, Arts Must Reach Unreached Constituencies." *Fund Raising Management* 28, no. 4 (June 1, 1997): 1-36. Focuses on the aftermath of the 1996-1997 controversies.

Zeigler, Joseph Wesley. *Arts in Crisis: The National Endowment for the Arts Versus America.* Pennington, N.J.: A Cappella Books, 1994. Extremely helpful for understanding the underlying problems of a government-funded arts system.

Concepcion Saenz-Cambra

See also Art movements; Bush, George H. W.; Censorship; Classical music; Clinton, Bill; Culture wars; Education in the United States; Gardner Museum art theft; Gehry, Frank; Holocaust Memorial Museum; Literature in the United States; Mapplethorpe obscenity trial; Music; Photography; Poetry; Project Gutenberg; Sundance Film Festival; Theater in the United States.

■ Native Americans

Definition Members of any of the aboriginal peoples of the United States

Despite the economic success of casinos on certain Native American reservations, Native Americans as a whole continued to be one of the most disadvantaged segments of American culture during the 1990's.

Early English settlers, such as the Pilgrims at Plymouth and the subsequent Puritan settlers at Massachusetts Bay Colony, divided Native Americans into "good Indians" and "bad Indians." Early American novelists, such as James Fenimore Cooper, provided the same simplistic analysis, celebrating the virtues of the "good Indians" while portraying the "bad Indians" as sly and untrustworthy. From the Native American point of view, European contact created similar divisions. Some tribal members became "reservation Indians," Native Americans who depended on government handouts for survival, often falling prey to that most destructive of the white man's gifts—alcohol. Others, such as the famed Sioux warrior Crazy Horse, lived the old way. They were known as "traditionals." Even in the protests of the 1970's and 1980's, this division in Native American life continued. In organizing protests, such as the occupation of Mount Rushmore in 1971, the American Indian Movement (AIM) became the organization that represented traditionals. On the other side of Native American life were those who sought to accommodate themselves to American culture. Some of them became victims of alcohol or drugs. Others figured out ways to make large sums of money through casinos. Significantly, the divisions lasted into the 1990's, and Native Americans remained a population of people who were divided, discriminated against, and disadvantaged.

Indian Gaming In the 1999 afterword to the reprint of his 1991 book *Black Hills White Justice*, Edward Lazarus points out the stark irony of the phenomenal rise of gaming on Native American reservations: "But such benefits and success provide cold comfort to the vast majority of Native Americans, who like the Sioux, reap little money from gaming and will suffer immeasurably from a growing popular perception—what Senator Ben Nighthorse Campbell (the sole Native American in Congress) has called 'the Foxwoods myth'—that Indians all over the country are now getting rich by exploiting the vices of the white man." Statistics support Lazarus's observation.

The improved economic status for tribes that have introduced and profited from gaming is undeniable. In an essay from *Legalized Casino Gaming in the United States* (1999), Carl Boger, Jr., and colleagues report that the Foxwoods Resort Casino in Connecticut, opened in 1986, had created 9,500 jobs by 1993. With an average salary of $35,000 per year, these jobs paid some $2,000 more per year than the average job in the area. Moreover, each casino job created roughly 1.23 noncasino jobs through the increased flow of people into and out of the area. Each of those jobs decreased reliance of those in the area on government programs and increased area home values. Boger and colleagues estimate that for every 1,000 new jobs, 175 recipients of Aid to Families with Dependent Children (AFDC) were removed from government rosters. These statistics reflect the impact of one casino, the Foxwoods casino that Senator Campbell alluded to in his statement. Precise measurement of the economic impact of casinos on Native American life is impossible since Native Americans are not required to report their earnings. Nonetheless, that gaming has been a boon to those tribes that have developed casinos is undeniable.

Still, the other side of the issue is significant. Casinos divide tribes and divide the Native American population as a whole. Casinos bring with them increased crime rates and an abandonment of traditional ways, much to the dismay of some tribal members. Further, for Native Americans as a whole, they create a division between rich and poor. Lazarus points out that most of the tribes that have profited from gaming are small tribes near major cities, a relatively small segment of the Native American population. During the same period of economic expansion for the Mashantucket Pequot tribe, proprietors of the Foxwoods casino, the Sioux on the Pine Ridge Reservation in South Dakota, site of the famous AIM protests of the 1970's and the notorious Wounded Knee Massacre of 1891, remained among the poorest people in America. Three out of four people were unemployed. Lazarus quotes tribal vice president Milo Yellow Hair: "It is like living at the bottom of a well, . . . the Great White Father looks down and says 'Here's a few dollars.'"

Complicating matters further, the federal government has continued to fail to take responsibility for the long-standing mistreatment of Native Americans. In the 1830's, during President Andrew Jackson's administration, infamous for the Trail of Tears, a trust fund was established by the federal government to manage income from federal use of Native American land and other assets. Royalties were supposed to be passed along to the tribes. Though up to $350 million has been deposited into that account each year, the money has not been distributed in an equitable fashion to the tribes in question. When Keith Harper, attorney for the Native American Rights Fund, sued the federal government on behalf of 300,000 Native Americans in the late 1990's, government officials were unable to explain what happened to the disbursements. Furthermore, after U.S. district judge Royce C. Lamberth demanded an explanation from federal authorities, the U.S. government disclosed that in 1998, 162 boxes of records had been shredded, making reconstruction of what happened to the money almost impossible. Though the shredding was apparently a part of a routine purging of government records, the documents destroyed contained information on the disbursement of funds between 1900 and 1958. Furthermore, the shredding of documents was revealed only after an attempt on the part of government officials to cover up the matter.

Impact In 1990, 30.9 percent of Native Americans lived in poverty, compared to 13.1 percent of the U.S. population as a whole. In 2000, 25.7 percent of Native Americans lived in poverty, compared to 12.4 percent of the total U.S. population. Similar discrepancies continue to exist in educational opportunities: 9.3 percent of Native Americans were college-educated in 1990, whereas 20.3 percent of whites were; by 2000, 11.5 percent of Native Americans were college-educated, compared to 26.1 percent of whites. Despite the popular perception that gaming has been a panacea for Native Americans, the majority of Native Americans continue to be an underprivileged people, seemingly forgotten and abandoned by the federal government.

Further Reading

Hsu, Cathy H. C., ed. *Legalized Casino Gaming in the United States: The Economic and Social Impact.* Binghamton, N.Y.: The Haworth Hospitality Press, 1999. Though Hsu's book covers gambling throughout the United States and not just on Native American reservations, three chapters provide detailed analyses of the impact of gambling on Native American reservations. The book as a whole gives useful perspectives on gaming in the United States, both its history and its impact.

Jackson, Robert L. "Officials Destroyed Records on Native Americans." *Los Angeles Times*, December 5, 1999, p. 5. Jackson reports on the ongoing suit concerning the trust fund the federal government established for income from Native American land and assets.

Lazarus, Edward. *Black Hills White Justice: The Sioux Nation Versus the United States, 1775 to the Present.* Reprint. Lincoln: University of Nebraska Press, 1999. The most complete account available of what is arguably the most famous treaty violation in the history of U.S.-Native American relations. Since the matter of the broken 1868 treaty granting the Black Hills to the Sioux is still not resolved, the book is well worth reading for those interested in the continuing failure of the United States to make good on its promises to Native Americans.

Staurowsky, Ellen J. "American Indian Imagery and the Miseducation of America." *Quest* 51, no. 4 (1999): 382-392. Presents the continuing debate about team mascots.

H. William Rice

See also *Dances with Wolves*; Demographics of the United States; Employment in the United States; Income and wages in the United States; Minorities in Canada; Nunavut Territory; Poverty; Race relations.

Natural disasters

Definition Meteorologic and geologic events resulting in significant loss of life or property

During the 1990's, 3,397 people in the United States and 54 people in Canada died as a result of natural disasters.

Natural disasters are conceptually divided into geologic disasters (earthquakes, avalanches, landslides, and volcanic eruptions) and climatic disasters (floods, hurricanes, tornadoes, heat waves, blizzards, droughts, and wildfires).

Earthquakes In the 1990's, Canada experienced no earthquake of significance. No one was killed in any of the very small earthquakes that occurred, and only minimal damage resulted. On the other hand, the United States had eight major earthquakes during the decade.

The worst earthquake of the decade occurred on January 17, 1994, in Northridge, one of the northern suburbs of Los Angeles. Felt as far away as 400 kilometers from the epicenter, the earthquake had an impact over 200,000 square kilometers, including the heavily populated areas of Santa Monica, Malibu, Santa Clarita, the Simi Valley, and west and central Los Angeles. Fifty-seven people were killed, sixty thousand buildings were damaged, six major bridges collapsed, and five freeway overpasses fell. The cost of this earthquake exceeded $20 billion.

On February 28, 1990, an earthquake injured thirty people and caused $12.7 million in damages in the city of Upland in Southern California. Another small earthquake affected the area around Alamo in Northern California at the end of March, 1990. A year later, on June 28, 1991, an earthquake struck near Pasadena in Southern California, resulting in property damage equaling $33.5 million, the deaths of two people, and injuries to another hundred. On April 25, 1992, a quake in the Cape Mendocino area of Northern California caused $75 million in damage and injured ninety-four people. Two months later, the town of Landers in Southern California was severely damaged by an earthquake, killing one, injuring three hundred, and causing destruction amounting to $100 million. It also triggered a second large earthquake that day in the mountain resort town of Big Bear. Outside California, the town of Klamath Falls in Oregon was hit in 1993 by an earthquake that killed two, displaced three thousand people, and caused $7.5 million in damage. The last earthquake of significance of the decade occurred on December 26, 1994, in Eureka, affecting 225 people and causing $2.1 million in damage.

Avalanches and Landslides During the 1990's, the United States ranked second among all nations in the number of deaths caused by avalanches, with about 17 percent of the world avalanche fatalities. Canada ranked sixth, with about 8 percent of the fatalities. The number of people killed in avalanches was the highest in Alaska, Colorado, and Utah and increased steadily during the decade as the number of snowmobiles grew and imprudent people explored more remote areas in the wilderness.

During the winter of 1997, several large landslides occurred in California along Highway 50 between Placerville and South Lake Tahoe. Called the Mill Creek landslide, this event forced authorities to close the well-traveled highway for four weeks.

Landslides occur regularly during the rainy season on the bluffs and hillsides of Seattle and other areas of the Puget Sound region. During the decade, there were 334 landslides within the northwest of the United States. In 1990, 1996, and 1997, winter storms triggered landslides. About 70 percent of the landslides occurred in 1997, and it is not surprising that the heaviest damage took place that year as well, causing the deaths of four people on Bainbridge Island in Washington during a heavy winter storm.

In Canada, British Columbia suffered severe damage from landslides in Donna Creek (1992), Chisca River (1995), Buckinghorse River (1995), Chilliwack River (1997), Bear River Valley (1997), Capricorn Creek (1998), Five Mile Creek (1999), and Clanwilliam (1999). In Ontario, the South Nation River Valley landslide of 1993 was similarly destructive.

Floods In the 1990's, there were fifty-five major floods in the United States and Canada. Forty-nine of these floods happened in the United States, killing four hundred, while the remaining six, in Canada, killed twenty-five. The worst of these floods took place in 1993, affecting the Mississippi River and 150 major rivers and tributaries that flow into it, causing fifty fatalities and costing almost $15 billion. This flood was one of the most severe ever recorded in the United States. It was caused by intense late spring precipitation in the eastern Dakotas, southern Minnesota, Kansas, Wisconsin, Iowa, southern Nebraska, and Missouri. The rainfall totals were 12 inches above normal. Hundreds of levees broke along the Missouri and Mississippi rivers, severely disrupting both land transportation, through the flooding of highways and the destruction of bridges, and barge traffic, with hazardous waterways making movement impossible for more than seven weeks.

In Canada, the twelve provinces and territories experienced 170 floods during the twentieth century, with 62 percent of the disasters occurring in Manitoba, Ontario, New Brunswick, and Quebec. In the last decade of the century, floods affected the eastern regions of Canada, northwestern and southwestern British Columbia, and southern Manitoba. Most of the flooding in the 1990's happened in the southern part of Ontario and Quebec, where the population is highly concentrated. In the west, Manitoba and the city of Winnipeg suffered flooding in 1993, when three episodes of intense rainfall occurred from July 25 to August 14, causing extensive damage to agricultural land infrastructure, roads, homes, and power lines. Four years later, the Winnipeg, Red, and Assiniboine rivers again overtopped their banks between April and May, 1997, as a result of the spring melting of snow. It took seven weeks for the 7,000 military personnel sent to the rescue to help relocate more than 25,000 people who had been evacuated from their homes.

Hurricanes and Tornadoes During the decade, 1,653 people in the United States and 29 people in Canada lost their lives as a result of wind storms, which have their most dramatic expression in hurricanes, tornadoes, and tropical storms.

Nineteen hurricanes affected the United States in the 1990's: Bob and Grace in 1991; Andrew, Axel, and Iniki in 1992; Emily and Wylie in 1993; Alberto in 1994; Opal and Erin in 1995; Fran in 1996; Danny in 1997; Bonnie, Frances, and George in 1998; and Brett, Floyd, Irene, and Dennis in 1999. The worst of them was Hurricane Andrew, which caused extensive damage to Florida, Louisiana, and the Bahamas. Forty-four people perished, fifty-five were injured, and a quarter million were left homeless after the passage of the storm. The total property loss exceeded $30 billion. Hurricane Floyd destroyed property worth $4.5 billion, followed (in cost) by Fran with $3.2 billion in losses, Opal with $3 billion, Bob with $1.5 billion, Bonnie with $720 million, Erin with $700 million, and Alberto and Frances with $500 million each.

More than 95 percent of the tornadoes of the world occur in the United States. Tornadoes are a yearly event in Tornado Alley, stretching from Texas through Indiana and into Ohio. An unusual concentration occurred, however, when a swarm of tornadoes hit fifteen states between May 16 and 19, 1995, causing $10 billion in damage, killing three people, and injuring sixty-seven. In Canada, there were two tornadoes the 1990's. On August 5, 1994, a tornado near Ottawa injured four people and affected another three hundred, and on July 6, 1999, a tornado in Drummondville (Quebec) two hundred people were left homeless and four thousand more reported damages.

Extreme Temperatures During the 1990's, five heat waves (1990, 1993, 1995, 1998, and 1999) killed 1,116 people in North America and cost over $5 billion in energy usage, crop damage, and water usage.

Periods of record cold temperatures affected the United States in 1990, 1993, 1994, and 1995 in Washington, Ohio, Illinois, Indiana, Pennsylvania, Tennessee, Kentucky, North Carolina, South Carolina, New Jersey, New York, and Connecticut. During these colder periods, blizzards affected a large area of the center of the United States. Winter weather was ranked second after floods by the number of fatalities caused in 1996 and in 1997, and 1996 had the record number of blizzards with twenty-eight. These blizzards, which combined very cold temperatures and blowing snow, caused more than $500 million in damage. Among the cities that sustained the largest number of casualties were Atlanta, Detroit, Philadelphia, Chicago, and Milwaukee, where forty people lost their lives. In 1998, a large-scale ice storm caused $4.2 billion in damage in Ontario and Quebec.

Drought and Wildfires During the decade, two significant periods of drought were reported in the United States. A seven-month period in 1991 produced droughts that affected California, Pennsylvania, and Maryland and cost $1.3 billion. In the summer of 1999, Kentucky, Maryland, Ohio, Pennsylvania, and Virginia suffered a drought resulting in $800 million in damage. While drought in Canada has been the most expensive natural disaster over the past two hundred years, no significant events were reported in the 1990's.

Wildfires affected California repeatedly every

year of the 1990's except for 1995. California's one quiet year was not so in Canada, however, where wildfires in Saskatchewan cost of $89.5 million and those in British Columbia cost $120 million.

Impact By the 1990's, it seemed apparent that, despite continuing debate over its causes and rate, global climate change was occurring. This change almost certainly promised to increase the number and severity of climatic disasters, as what was considered normal was altered and extreme weather increased in frequency worldwide. Meanwhile, the growing world population put more people and property at risk. Even geological disasters, which can be expected to remain relatively unchanged in frequency, became significantly more expensive as more people crowded into more of the world's less stable areas.

The natural disasters that occurred during the decade served as reminders that these events are, for the most part, inevitable and can produce devastating costs, prompting calls for improvements in preparation efforts, such as better engineering, better site usage, better event prediction, and better emergency-response systems.

Further Reading

Bolin, Robert, and Lois Stanford. *The Northridge Earthquake: Vulnerability and Disaster.* New York: Routledge, 1998. Presents details about the Northridge earthquake, providing the reader with excellent photographic documents.

Greenberg, Michael. *Disasters.* Sudbury, Mass.: Jones and Bartlett, 2006. A compendium of natural and human-made catastrophes.

Hough, Susan Elizabeth. *Earthshaking Science: What We Know (and Don't Know) About Earthquakes.* Princeton, N.J.: Princeton University Press, 2002. Presents basic information about earthquakes for the nonscientific reader.

_______. *Finding Fault in California: An Earthquake Tourist's Guide.* Missoula, Mont.: Mountain Press, 2004. Provides readers with pertinent observations on faults.

Spignesi, Stephen J. *Catastrophe! The One Hundred Greatest Disasters of All Time.* New York: Citadel, 2005. Gives a brief synopsis of each of the one hundred greatest disasters of the last two thousand years.

Yeats, Robert S. *Living with Earthquakes in California: A Survivor's Guide.* Corvallis: Oregon State University Press, 2001. Provides suggestions on how to live safely in earthquake-prone country.

Denyse Lemaire and David Kasserman

See also Chicago heat wave of 1995; Hurricane Andrew; Mississippi River flood of 1993; Northridge earthquake; Oakland Hills fire; Oklahoma tornado outbreak; Perfect Storm, the; Storm of the Century.

■ NC-17 rating

Definition Certification mark prohibiting children seventeen years of age and younger from attending such films

Date Established September 26, 1990

Created to replace the original X rating, which had acquired the stigma of pornography, the NC-17 rating enjoyed a brief flurry of acceptability before falling into disfavor.

When the classification and rating system was first introduced in 1968 for motion pictures released in the United States, the letter *X* was reserved for films considered inappropriate—because of sex, violence, and/or aberrational behavior—for viewers seventeen years old and younger. Although the other ratings—initially G (general audiences), M (mature audiences), and R (restricted), and later PG (parental guidance suggested), which essentially replaced M, and PG-13 (parents strongly cautioned)—were trademarked by the Motion Picture Association of America (MPAA), the X rating was not, and soon it was appropriated by hard-core pornography, which proudly proclaimed itself XX, XXX, and higher. As a result, some newspapers and television stations would not allow advertisements for X-rated films, and some theaters refused to show such films. Serious motion pictures in danger of receiving the X rating were usually self-censored, with producers trimming footage deemed too graphic or offensive.

The issue came to a head in early 1990, when two serious art films—*The Cook, the Thief, His Wife, and Her Lover* (1989; Great Britain) and *Tie Me Up! Tie Me Down!* (1990; Spain)—were both rated X. At the same time, two lawsuits were filed that challenged the constitutionality of the X rating, and a petition to the MPAA was signed by major film directors, advocating a new rating that might signal the presence of themes or images unsuitable for minors, albeit without the X stigma.

Accordingly, on September 26, 1990, the MPAA replaced X with NC-17, intending that the rating be applied not to pornography, but only to films that many parents would not want their children to see. The first film so labeled was *Henry and June* (1990), a sexually explicit account of the affair between writers Henry Miller and Anaïs Nin. Other notable films of the 1990's rated NC-17 included *Showgirls* (1995), *Crash* (1996), and *Two Girls and a Guy* (1997)—all for explicit sexual content.

Impact During its first two years, the NC-17 rating was given to 41 pictures, or roughly 3.5 percent of all films that were rated by the MPAA in 1990 and 1991. However, these numbers quickly declined. From 1992 through 1999, only 35 pictures were rated NC-17, representing less than one percent of the 5,292 films that were rated during these eight years. Because the NC-17 rating is usually applied to sexual, rather than violent, content, it carries much the same pornographic stigma as the former X. By eliminating a large part of a film's potential audience (those seventeen and under), the NC-17 rating is rarely welcomed by filmmakers, theater owners, and viewers.

Further Reading

Sandler, Kevin S. "The Naked Truth: *Showgirls* and the Fate of the X/NC-17 Rating." *Cinema Journal* 40, no. 3 (Spring, 2001): 69-93.

Vaughn, Stephen. *Freedom and Entertainment: Rating the Movies in an Age of New Media.* New York: Cambridge University Press, 2006.

James I. Deutsch

See also *Basic Instinct*; Censorship; Film in the United States; *Showgirls*; TV Parental Guidelines system.

■ Nicotine patch

Definition A transdermal patch intended to help smokers quit

Date Introduced in the United States in 1992

Introduction of the nicotine patch, also known as transdermal nicotine replacement therapy, offered hope to millions of smokers who wanted to break a life-threatening addiction.

For most of the twentieth century, smoking was acceptable, and even glamorous, but in 1964, the U.S. surgeon general reported that smoking was dangerous to health. By the 1970's, the deaths of millions of Americans were attributed to smoking-related illnesses—lung cancer and other respiratory and cardiovascular diseases. In 1988, Surgeon General C. Everett Koop called smoking "the chief, single, avoidable cause of death" in America, highlighting its highly addictive nature. Cigarette companies denied the dangers of smoking, but secret documents, leaked to the public in 1994, revealed that they had repeatedly lied to Congress and manipulated the contents of cigarettes to increase addiction. In 1995, the Food and Drug Administration (FDA) declared that cigarettes were drug-delivery devices and proposed restrictions on marketing and sales. Cigarette advertising was banned from television, and smoking was banned on airplanes and in most public places. By the end of the decade, taxes on cigarettes had increased dramatically, and cigarette companies settled lawsuits with most states for smoking-related illnesses.

Most people knew that smoking was harmful and wanted to quit. When, in 1992, four drug companies introduced nicotine patches (available by prescription only), the demand for the patch far exceeded the supply. The palm-sized circular patch, attached to the skin on the back or upper arm every twenty-four hours, delivered a steady dose of nicotine to help satisfy physical cravings and reduce withdrawal side effects. After a month, ex-smokers could wean themselves by using successively smaller patches. Studies comparing the patch to a placebo patch showed that it doubled the odds of quitting for at least six months, whether used alone or in combination with other interventions. However, only 26 percent of those wearing the patch quit smoking, as opposed to 12 percent using the placebo. Many smokers continued to smoke while using the patch, leading to toxic, and occasionally, dangerous health risks. The patch became available over the counter in 1996.

Impact Demand for the patch spurred pharmaceutical companies and therapists to increase public awareness of the dangers of smoking and to develop other aids to help smokers quit. Limited success underscored the complexity of addiction to tobacco and challenged researchers in the field. Although not a cure-all, the patch still offered a one-in-four chance of quitting—roughly the odds of dying from a tobacco-related illness if one continues to smoke.

Subsequent Events Meta-analyses of numerous studies have shown that the patch doubles the chances of quitting smoking. However, only 20 percent of patch users have actually broken the habit. Tobacco use has decreased among adults but increased among teenagers, whom the tobacco industry targets. In 2000, the Supreme Court ruled that the FDA has no authority to regulate tobacco as a drug. The FDA has subsequently revoked its restrictions on the sale of cigarettes to minors.

Further Reading

Kranz, Rachel. *Straight Talk About Smoking*. New York: Facts On File, 1999.

Sherman, Carl. "Kicking Butts." *Psychology Today* 27, no. 5 (September/October, 1994): 40-46.

Edna B. Quinn

See also Cancer research; Drug use; Health care; Health care reform; Medicine; Psychology; Tobacco industry settlement.

■ Nine Inch Nails

Identification Industrial rock band
Date Founded in 1988

Nine Inch Nails influenced and popularized industrial rock in the 1990's.

Although he regularly tours with a band, Trent Reznor is the sole member of Nine Inch Nails, acting as singer, songwriter, instrumentalist, and producer. Nine Inch Nails garnered recognition and acclaim in the 1990's through the continued popularity of 1989's *Pretty Hate Machine* and the subsequent release of 1992's *Broken* and 1994's groundbreaking *The Downward Spiral*. *Broken*, influenced by Reznor's touring in 1991, was harder and more raw than the pop- and New Wave-influenced *Pretty Hate Machine*, though it still featured existential and personal lyrics. Songs from *Broken* earned Reznor his only Grammy Awards, but his work would receive more nominations.

Nine Inch Nails' second full-length album, *The Downward Spiral*, was much anticipated and entered the *Billboard* 200 at number two following its release in 1994. Following a central character's mental path toward collapse, *The Downward Spiral* featured more textures of sound than any previous Nine Inch Nails album while maintaining the electronic beat-driven hallmarks of Reznor's previous work. "Closer" was the album's most popular single in spite of (perhaps because of) the explicit sexual refrain and launched Nine Inch Nails fully into mainstream radio play as it blended pop sensibility and taboo subject matter. Reznor's Self-Destruct Tour supporting the album included a stop at Woodstock '94, where the Grammy-winning performace of "Happiness in Slavery" was filmed as well as beamed into twenty-four million homes. Reznor would not release another album with new material for five years, a delay due to his admitted difficulties with perfectionism, substance abuse, and writer's block.

When the much-anticipated double-CD *The Fragile* arrived in 1999, it debuted at number one on *Billboard*'s 200. The epic album was thematically similar to *The Downward Spiral*, featuring layered soundscapes and a continuous narrative; however, *The Fragile* was hailed as a more mature and subtle effort, a richer evolution of Reznor's distinctive sound. The album received positive reviews but fell off the charts quickly. It was nominated for a Grammy for Best Alternative Music Performance in 1999.

Reznor has worked as a producer for movie sound tracks, including one for *Natural Born Killers* (1994), and other artists, notably Marilyn Manson, whom he

Nine Inch Nails lead singer Trent Reznor, caked in mud, performs at Woodstock '94. (AP/Wide World Photos)

helped introduce to the mainstream. Nine Inch Nails is also well known for its remix material.

Impact Nine Inch Nails combined techno beats and hard rock guitar and brought this sound to mainstream acceptance, while connecting with fans through introspective and risqué lyrics. Trent Reznor proved to be an intriguing front man: tortured, withdrawn, and explosive on stage.

Further Reading

Huxley, Martin. *Nine Inch Nails.* New York: St. Martin's Press, 1997.

Udo, Tommy. *Nine Inch Nails.* London: Sanctuary Records, 2002.

Alan Haslam

See also Alternative rock; Electronic music; Grunge music; Lollapalooza; Marilyn Manson; Music; Woodstock concerts.

■ Nirvana

Identification Alternative rock band

Nirvana and grunge icon Kurt Cobain initiated the alternative music explosion in the early 1990's.

Nirvana in its ultimate incarnation featured singer-guitarist Kurt Cobain, bassist Krist Novoselic, and drummer Dave Grohl. After the independent release of 1989's *Bleach,* Nirvana signed with Geffen Records and recorded the hugely successful *Nevermind* (1991). While *Bleach* was heavily influenced by punk rock, *Nevermind* fused grunge-era guitar rock with pop hooks and melody. *Nevermind* was more polished and accessible than *Bleach,* and though the band expressed some dissatisfaction with the postproduction of the album, its radio-friendliness was a main factor in its widespread popularity. *Nevermind* shifted popular rock music away from the glam and arena rock of the 1980's toward alternative rock.

In January, 1992, *Nevermind* was selling about 300,000 copies per week, and the album reached number one on the *Billboard* charts. The album's popularity was boosted by heavy rotation on MTV of the music video for the hit single "Smells Like Teen Spirit." The music video begins in a surrealistic high school pep rally where Nirvana plays to uninterested students and cheerleaders wearing anarchist symbols and ends with the students destroying the set and the band's equipment. *Nevermind* spawned three other hit singles and music videos that cemented the grunge look and sound into the public consciousness.

In 1993, amid much hype and press, Nirvana released *In Utero,* and listeners were shocked as they were introduced to a radically different Nirvana. *In Utero* harked back to Nirvana's punk roots, almost an intentional move to alienate Nirvana's brand-new legion of fans as quickly as they had come. The album was raw, dissonant, and difficult, yet featured many of Nirvana's hallmark melodies and hooks. In September, 1993, *In Utero* debuted at number one on the *Billboard* 200 but did not enjoy the lasting power of *Nevermind.*

Nirvana front man Kurt Cobain. (AP/Wide World Photos)

Kurt Cobain As important as Nirvana's music was for the burgeoning grunge scene in the early 1990's, Kurt Cobain was equally important as the personification of the angst-ridden, identity-lacking, and disillusioned Generation X. Born in 1967, Cobain lived near the depressed logging town of Aberdeen, Washington, for most of his life. When Cobain was seven years old, his parents divorced, an event that profoundly affected him and contributed to the rebellious tendencies that eventually attracted him to the Pacific Northwest punk scene, where he met and befriended many of the musicians who would influence him for years to come. Cobain received his first guitar as a gift at the age of fourteen and finally convinced Krist Novoselic, fellow denizen of Aberdeen and devotee of punk rock, to begin playing with him in 1985.

In 1992, Cobain married Courtney Love of the band Hole. They were immediately hailed as the next Sid Vicious and Nancy Spungen because of their copious heroin use and "live fast, die young" rock-star behavior. Cobain turned to drug use early in his life as a response to depression and chronic pain due to an undiagnosed stomach condition for which he tried to find a cure for most of his life. Heroin dominated his adult life, and although he would occasionally enter a drug rehabilitation program, he always relapsed. Cobain's habit contributed to his grunge hero status as he slurred and sometimes nodded off on stage and during interviews and photo shoots, but he would often perform and speak lucidly even while under the influence. As with so many other artists, heroin would prove to be his final undoing.

On April 8, 1994, Cobain's body was discovered in a room above the garage of his Lake Washington home. Cobain had fled rehab just days before. The official cause of death was a self-inflicted shotgun blast to the head; a suicide note was found nearby, and heroin was in his system. Seven thousand mourners attended a vigil on April 10 in Seattle. Cobain's death spawned conspiracy theories, but none were ever deemed probable.

Post-Cobain Nirvana In November, 1993, Nirvana taped a popular and critically acclaimed performance on *MTV Unplugged*, and an album of the show was released in November, 1994. A "plugged-in" concert compilation, *From the Muddy Banks of the Wishkah*, was released in 1996, named for the river that flows through Cobain's hometown.

Grohl's career flourished after Nirvana as he became front man and the creative force behind the Foo Fighters. Novoselic continued to be involved in recording and playing live music and became increasingly involved in politics.

Impact Nirvana inaugurated a new musical era and managed to occupy the rare space of achieving commercial success and critical acclaim while maintaining artistic integrity. Cobain's suicide rendered him a John Lennon-esque figure for Generation X and fostered a myth around his life.

Further Reading

Azerrad, Michael. *Come as You Are: The Story of Nirvana.* New York: Doubleday, 1993. Members of Nirvana contributed to this biography, which was amended in a 1994 reprint to include information on Nirvana's final tour and Cobain's death.

Cross, Charles R. *Heavier than Heaven: A Biography of Kurt Cobain.* New York: Hyperion, 2001. Cross conducted more than four hundred interviews over four years for the book and was granted exclusive interviews and access to Cobain's private journals, lyrics, and photos by Courtney Love.

True, Everett. *Nirvana: The Biography.* New York: Omnibus Press, 2006. Includes nearly full transcripts of many interviews with Nirvana members and their acquaintances and offers somewhat more exhaustive details of the controversy surrounding Cobain's death and Nirvana's place in grunge music and the culture of the 1990's than previous biographies of the band.

Alan Haslam

See also Alternative rock; Drug use; Grunge fashion; Grunge music; Heroin chic; Lollapalooza; Love, Courtney; *MTV Unplugged*; Music.

Nobel Prizes

Definition Prizes awarded each year for achievements in chemistry, economic sciences, literature, peace, physics, and physiology or medicine

In the 1990's, North Americans dominated the scientific and economic Nobel Prizes. North Americans were awarded about 60 percent of the Nobel Prizes of the decade, with Canadians constituting about 10 percent of the North American total.

The Nobel Prize award signifies international praise for scientific and cultural achievements. Nobel laureates bring prestige to their country and its institutions and attract the attention of students and funding bodies to their work.

Chemistry Prizes were awarded in chemistry for a diverse group of achievements. Elias James Corey was honored for work on the methodology of organic chemical synthesis, and George Olah for studies of positively charged carbon ions. Walter Kohn developed density functional theory and John Pople developed new computational methods for quantum mechanics. Rudolph A. Marcus elucidated electron transfer reactions in chemical systems, while Ahmed Zewail employed femtosecond spectroscopic techniques to study transition states in reactions.

Mario J. Molina and F. Sherwood Rowland shared a prize for studies of ozone depletion in the atmosphere. Richard Smalley and Robert Curl were honored for work on the structure and properties of fullerenes: carbon cage molecules.

On the biochemical side, Kary B. Mullis shared a prize with Michael Smith; Mullis developed the polymerase chain reaction (PCR), and Smith was honored for protein studies using oligonucleotide-based, site-directed mutagenesis. Paul D. Boyer shared a prize for work on the mechanism of synthesis of adenosine triphosphate (ATP).

Literature and Peace Writer Toni Morrison was awarded the prize for her novels, such as *Beloved* (1987), which speak to aspects of American reality. She was the first African American woman to win the Nobel Prize in Literature. Derek Walcott was honored for his luminous poetry with its historical vision.

The Nobel Peace Prizes were awarded to Joseph Rotblat and the Pugwash Conferences on Science and World Affairs in 1995 for efforts to ban nuclear weapons proliferation, and in 1997 to Jody Williams and the International Campaign to Ban Landmines for efforts to ban antipersonnel land mines.

Physics Scattering of electrons by protons and bound neutrons formed the basis of studies by Jerome I. Friedman, Henry W. Kendall, and Richard E. Taylor, which earned their award. Bertram N. Brockhouse was honored for developing neutron-scattering techniques in the study of condensed matter. He shared the prize with Clifford G. Shull, who concentrated on neutron diffraction. Condensed matter also figured in the prize awarded to David M. Lee, Douglas D. Osheroff, and Robert C. Richardson, who discovered superfluidity in helium-3. A prize was shared by Martin L. Perl for discovery of the tau lepton and by Frederick Reines for detection of the neutrino. Steven Chu and William D. Phillips shared a prize for cooling and trapping atoms with laser light. Robert B. Laughlin, Horst L. Störmer, and Daniel C. Tsui were honored for discovery of a new type of quantum fluid. Russell A. Hulse and Joseph H. Taylor, Jr., were awarded the prize for discovering a new type of pulsar, important in the study of gravitation.

Physiology or Medicine Joseph E. Murray and E. Donnall Thomas shared the Nobel Prize for discoveries related to organ and cell transplantation. Edmond H. Fischer and Edwin G. Krebs were honored for studies on reversible protein phosphorylation. Phillip A. Sharp shared a prize for the discovery of split genes. Alfred G. Gilman and Martin Rodbell shared a prize for the discovery of G proteins and their role in cellular signaling. Edward B. Lewis and Eric F. Wieschaus shared a prize for discoveries concerning genetic control of embryonic development.

Stanley B. Prusiner won a prize for the discovery of prions, a new principle of infection. Robert F. Furchgott, Louis J. Ignarro, and Ferid Murad were honored for discoveries related to nitric oxide as a signaling agent in the cardiovascular system. Günter Blobel won his prize for discovering the signals proteins have that govern their transport and localization in the cell.

Economic Sciences Harry M. Markowitz, Merton H. Miller, and William F. Sharpe were awarded the 1990 prize for work on the theory of financial

North American Nobel Prize Winners, 1990-1999

Year	*Chemistry*	*Economic Sciences*	*Literature*	*Peace*	*Physics*	*Physiology or Medicine*
1990	Elias James Corey	Harry M. Markowitz Merton H. Miller William F. Sharpe			Jerome I. Friedman Henry W. Kendall Richard E. Taylor	Joseph E. Murray E. Donnall Thomas
1991		Ronald H. Coase				
1992	Rudolph A. Marcus	Gary S. Becker	Derek Walcott			Edmond H. Fischer Edwin G. Krebs
1993	Kary B. Mullis Michael Smith	Robert W. Fogel Douglass C. North	Toni Morrison		Russell A. Hulse Joseph H. Taylor, Jr.	Phillip A. Sharp*
1994	George Olah	John C. Harsanyi John F. Nash, Jr.*			Bertram N. Brockhouse Clifford G. Shull	Alfred G. Gilman Martin Rodbell
1995	Mario J. Molina F. Sherwood Rowland*	Robert E. Lucas, Jr.		Joseph Rotblat Pugwash Conferences on Science and World Affairs	Martin L. Perl Frederick Reines	Edward B. Lewis Eric F. Wieschaus*
1996	Robert Curl Richard Smalley*	William Vickrey*			David M. Lee Douglas D. Osheroff Robert C. Richardson	
1997	Paul D. Boyer*	Robert C. Merton Myron S. Scholes		Jody Williams International Campaign to Ban Landmines	Steven Chu William D. Phillips*	Stanley B. Prusiner
1998	Walter Kohn John Pople	Amartya Sen			Robert B. Laughlin Horst L. Störmer Daniel C. Tsui	Robert F. Furchgott Louis J. Ignarro Ferid Murad
1999	Ahmed Zewail	Robert A. Mundell				Günter Blobel

*Prize shared with non-North American.

economics. Ronald H. Coase won in 1991 for work on transaction costs and property rights for the institutional structure and functioning of the economy. Gary S. Becker extended microeconomic analysis to a wide variety of human behavior. Robert W. Fogel and Douglass C. North shared a prize in 1993 for applying economic theory and quantitative methods to explain changes in the economy and institutions. John C. Harsanyi and John F. Nash, Jr., shared a prize for analysis of noncooperative games. Robert E. Lucas, Jr., was honored for transforming macroeconomic analysis by developing the hypothesis of rational expectations. William Vickrey shared a prize for contributions to an economic theory of incentives under asymmetric information. Robert C. Merton and Myron S. Scholes were honored for a new method for determining the value of derivatives. Amartya Sen was the winner of the 1998 prize for contributions to welfare economics. Robert A. Mundell won in 1999 for analysis of monetary and fiscal policy under differing exchange-rate regimes.

Impact During the 1990's, North Americans were particularly prominent in the Nobel Prizes in Economic Sciences, Physiology or Medicine, Physics, and Chemistry, and sparsely in Literature and Peace. The only two female winners were in the latter areas.

Particularly significant work included the polymerase chain reaction of Mullis, which is important in DNA testing; Molina and Rowland's studies that revealed the pollutants that threaten the ozone layer and that led to a worldwide ban on chlorofluorocarbons; and the discovery of fullerenes by Smalley and Curl, which contributed to the important field of nanotechnology.

Further Reading

Feldman, Burton. *The Nobel Prize: A History of Genius, Controversy, and Prestige.* New York: Arcade, 2000. Prizewinners are classified in various ways, and stories are told of unexpected controversies.

Morrison, Toni. *Beloved.* New York: Alfred A. Knopf, 1987. The novel that won the author a Pulitzer Prize concerns the emergence of a woman from the evils of slavery.

Roberts, Shawn, and Jody Williams. *After the Guns Fall Silent: The Enduring Legacy of Landmines.* Washington, D.C.: Vietnam Veterans of America Foundation, 1995. An account of the land mines remaining around the world and the danger they pose for children and others.

Zewail, Ahmed. *Voyage Through Time: Walks of Life to the Nobel Prize.* Cairo: American University of Cairo, 2002. Personal reminiscences of the 1999 prizewinner in chemistry.

John R. Phillips

See also Air pollution; African Americans; Asian Americans; Astronomy; Genetics research; Inventions; Jewish Americans; Literature in Canada; Literature in the United States; Medicine; Morrison, Toni; Nanotechnology; Poetry; Science and technology.

■ Noriega capture and trial

The Event U.S. forces arrest Panama's military dictator, General Manuel Noriega, who is subsequently tried for drug trafficking and money laundering
Date 1990-1992
Place Panama and Miami, Florida

The surrender and capture of Noriega brought an end to his de facto regime that had ruled for nearly six years. The removal of Noriega from power put a stop to the human rights abuses that were associated with his ruling, allowed a new Panamanian government to take over, and greatly helped the U.S. "war on drugs" in the region.

Manuel Antonio Noriega was a soldier for most of his life; he trained on U.S. military bases and slowly rose among the ranks of his own government in Panama. Noriega became a close informant for the U.S. Central Intelligence Agency (CIA), and the death of Panamanian leader Omar Torrijos helped to launch his career as the next Panamanian leader.

Noriega was not elected to his position but rather became the de facto leader by succeeding a man who removed himself from the presidential race. Noriega promoted himself to the position of general and took power in 1983. He continued his good relations with the United States by giving the United States more access to the Panama Canal and by helping U.S. interests in the region. Noriega allowed presidential elections in the following year, but when it appeared that he might lose, he halted the elections to ensure he stayed in power.

It was about this time, when Noriega assumed his role as a dictator, that he was first accused of being involved in drug trafficking. In addition, the general was suspected of murdering one of his critics, and the news of this brought the Panamanian public into the streets to protest his leadership. Despite these accusations, Noriega remained in the good graces of the United States until he was finally indicted on drug charges in 1988.

The Capture and Trial Investigations took place into Noriega's activities and his alleged deals with drug cartels to allow the transportation of cocaine over the Panamanian border. After enough evidence had been compiled proving that Noriega was, in fact, involved in the trafficking of millions of dollars worth of narcotics, the U.S. government called for his resignation. Noriega fervently refused to comply, and tensions between U.S. troops that were stationed in Panama and Noriega's troops intensified.

The United States placed economic sanctions on Panama, and on December 16, 1989, the situation reached a climax when a U.S. Marine was shot in an altercation. President George H. W. Bush responded by sending American forces to invade Panama and to depose Noriega. The general managed to avoid capture by U.S. forces for nearly a month. Surrendering on January 3, 1990, he was immediately transported to Miami, Florida, where he would face trial.

General Noriega was tried on eight counts of drug trafficking, money laundering, and racketeering. He was found to have been supplying information and assistance to drug cartels in the region while at the same time pledging to help the United States fight the so-called war on drugs in Panama. Noriega was ultimately convicted of his crimes and was sentenced on July 10, 1992, to serve forty years in a U.S. state penitentiary.

Impact A onetime ally of the U.S. administration, in particular the CIA, Noriega slowly distanced himself from his northern neighbors. His involvement in the transportation of cocaine across the Panamanian border made him a target in the U.S. war on drugs. His capture and eventual conviction was a success for the Drug Enforcement Administration (DEA), which saw his imprisonment as a step toward severely depleting drug trafficking into the United States and in helping end the reign of large drug cartels with which Noriega had been involved.

Subsequent Events Though Noriega's capture did not win the war on drugs for the United States, it certainly stopped a great deal of the flow of illegal drugs through Panama. In March, 1999, his forty-year sentence was reduced to thirty. There have been repeated attempts by his lawyers to have him released. However, if released, Noriega may still serve time for his 1995 convictions of human rights abuses and murder in Panama. Also, the French government has attempted to have Noriega extradited so that he may serve time for a 1999 money-laundering conviction on French soil. In 2004, Noriega suffered a small stroke and was briefly hospitalized.

Further Reading

Behar, David S., and Godfrey Harris. *Invasion: The American Destruction of the Noriega Regime in Panama.* Los Angeles: Americas Group, 1990. Describes the events leading up to the invasion of Panama by the United States. Behar pays a great deal of attention to the invasion itself and the steps that were taken to ultimately bring down Noriega's government.

McMillan, Robert R. *Global Passage: Transformation of Panama and the Panama Canal.* Charleston, S.C.: Booksurge, 2006. Focusing on the historical context of the Panama Canal, this book explains the effect the creation of the canal has had on the developing country. The author refers to Noriega throughout the text in relation to his negotiations about canal expansion and usage.

Murillo, Luis E. *The Noriega Mess: The Drugs, the Canal, and Why America Invaded.* Berkeley, Calif.: Video-Books, 1995. Murillo investigates the uneven politics in Panama, the vindictive nature of Noriega, and the history and circumstances that allowed the general to rise to power. The book is a truthful tale of the harsh realities of Panama and the extenuating circumstances that led to the U.S. invasion.

Jennifer L. Titanski

See also Bush, George H. W.; Crime; Foreign policy of the United States; Latin America.

North American Free Trade Agreement (NAFTA)

Identification Trade agreement reducing barriers to the flow of goods, services, and investment among Canada, Mexico, and the United States

Date Signed in 1992; ratified in 1993; implemented in 1994

This agreement allowed for increased economic interactions among the three nations. The treaty was highly debated with regard to its merits and flaws both before and after its implementation.

On January 1, 1994, the North American Free Trade Agreement (NAFTA) came into effect. The United States, Canada, and Mexico entered a new era in their economic history by promising to remove most tariffs on products traded among them and to phase out all tariff barriers over the next fifteen years. This agreement was an expansion of the Canada-United States Free Trade Agreement of 1988 and resulted from trade talks among U.S. president George H. W. Bush, Canadian prime minister Brian Mulroney, and Mexican president Carlos Salinas de Gortari. While NAFTA was ratified by all the legislatures, January 1, 1994, was the date set for the agreement to begin; the actual treaty had been signed in December, 1992, and ratified by the legislatures of all three countries in 1993. Ratification was not an easy task, however, as strong opposition to the treaty existed in different areas of society, including labor unions in the United States and Canada and farmers in Mexico.

Preamble to the North American Free Trade Agreement

The Government of Canada, the Government of the United Mexican States and the Government of the United States of America, resolved to:

STRENGTHEN the special bonds of friendship and cooperation among their nations;

CONTRIBUTE to the harmonious development and expansion of world trade and provide a catalyst to broader international cooperation;

CREATE an expanded and secure market for the goods and services produced in their territories;

REDUCE distortions to trade;

ESTABLISH clear and mutually advantageous rules governing their trade;

ENSURE a predictable commercial framework for business planning and investment;

BUILD on their respective rights and obligations under the General Agreement on Tariffs and Trade and other multilateral and bilateral instruments of cooperation;

ENHANCE the competitiveness of their firms in global markets;

FOSTER creativity and innovation, and promote trade in goods and services that are the subject of intellectual property rights;

CREATE new employment opportunities and improve working conditions and living standards in their respective territories;

UNDERTAKE each of the preceding in a manner consistent with environmental protection and conservation;

PRESERVE their flexibility to safeguard the public welfare;

PROMOTE sustainable development;

STRENGTHEN the development and enforcement of environmental laws and regulations; and

PROTECT, enhance and enforce basic workers' rights.

The Debate over NAFTA Proponents of the trade agreement included U.S. and Canadian politicians who favored free trade, transnational corporations, a number of economists, and other proponents of a liberal system in which trade barriers are limited among countries. The arguments used to support NAFTA included increased trade among the three countries and increased job growth and economic output, as well as a reduction of poverty, especially in Mexico.

Opponents of the trade agreement included labor unions in the United States and Canada, which feared that manufacturing jobs would move away from their countries into Mexico because of lower wage costs; Mexican farmers, who feared that agriculture subsidies provided to American farmers would put them at a further disadvantage and run them out of business; advocacy groups focusing on the environment and social justice; and human rights groups, which feared that the impact of the treaty would lead to noneconomic negative consequences, especially in Mexico.

Impact NAFTA was one of the most significant agreements signed in the 1990's by the United States and Canada, and the consequences of this trade agreement could be seen throughout the decade. While the main goal of NAFTA was to change the economic picture of North America, the agreement affected much more than just the economies of these countries. While numbers show that trade among them increased, many economists claim that such a change did not help the economy as a whole: Instead of creating new markets, NAFTA simply diverted trade from countries that are not members of the agreement. Also, the increased number of *maquiladoras* (Mexican factories that take in imported raw materials and produce goods for export) raised many questions about the hiring practices and work conditions of these industries.

NAFTA was the topic of many heated political debates of the 1990's in all three of the signatory countries, and the economic, political, social, and cultural changes prompted by the trade agreement helped change the relationship between Mexico and North America in many ways during this period.

Further Reading

Chambers, Edward J., and Peter H. Smith, eds. *NAFTA in the Millennium.* La Jolla: Center for U.S.-Mexican Studies, University of California, San Diego, 2002. Examines the challenges that NAFTA experienced in the 1990's and the future of the treaty. A great collection of essays on many aspects of the agreement.

Hufbauer, Gary Clyde, and Jeffrey J. Schott. *NAFTA Revisited: Achievements and Challenges.* Washington, D.C.: Institute for International Economics, 2005. One of the most comprehensive analyses of NAFTA to date, this book examines the first seven years of the trade agreement and outlines the new challenges that NAFTA may encounter in the future.

McKinney, Joseph A., and M. Rebecca Sharpless, eds. *Implications of a North American Free Trade Region: Multidisciplinary Perspectives.* Waco, Tex.: Program for Regional Studies, Baylor University, 1992. Written before the implementation of NAFTA, this book discusses the debate regarding the agreement and what effects it would have on the economy, politics, law, culture, and society.

Villers, David R. Dávila, ed. *NAFTA, the First Year: A View from Mexico.* Lanham, Md.: University Press of America, 1996. A collection of papers presented at the First Forum of the Americas, whose main objective is to evaluate NAFTA on a yearly basis. Provides an in-depth analysis of the impact that NAFTA had in Mexico in the first year of its inception and discusses the proposition of creating other trade agreements, focusing especially on those targeting Latin America.

Pedro dos Santos

See also Agriculture in Canada; Agriculture in the United States; Bush, George H. W.; Canada and the United States; Clinton, Bill; Foreign policy of Canada; Foreign policy of the United States; Mexico and the United States; Mulroney, Brian.

■ North Hollywood shoot-out

The Event A shoot-out between police officers and two heavily armed men wearing body armor
Date February 28, 1997
Place A district of Los Angeles

Although this confrontation was shocking to many, some in law enforcement had feared its occurrence, believing that law enforcement had been greatly limited in its ability to contend with heavily armed suspects. The event was also aired live on television, allowing millions of viewers to witness the inability of hundreds of law enforcement officers to quickly restrain two men.

Shortly after 9 A.M. on February 28, 1997, Larry Phillips, Jr., and Emil Matasareanu entered a Bank of America in the North Hollywood section of Los Angeles, California. The two men wore body armor and carried automatic weapons, including AK-47s, a fully automatic Bushmaster rifle, a semiautomatic H&K, and a semiautomatic 9-millimeter Beretta handgun. A Los Angeles Police Department (LAPD) officer driving down the street had seen the two enter the bank, and police had the bank surrounded by the time Phillips and Matasareanu attempted to leave.

When officers attempted to stop Phillips and Matasareanu, the bank robbers shot the cars of the officers, who were only carrying 9-millimeter pistols and revolvers. The bullets shot by police would simply ricochet off the suspects' body armor, while the suspects were able to injure several officers and civilians. Shortly thereafter, the two gunmen attempted to drive away in the getaway car, which was soon rendered inoperable due to heavy police fire. Phillips then left the protection of the getaway car and brazenly walked down the street firing at officers and television news helicopters. He was finally shot and killed by officers.

After Phillips was killed, Matasareanu attempted to escape in an abandoned pickup truck, only to find that the owner had taken his keys with him when he fled. Matasareanu then encountered special weapons and tactics (SWAT) members who shot underneath the truck into his unprotected legs, badly injuring him. He died from loss of blood on the street as officers were attempting to secure the scene. Before their deaths, the suspects fired over 1,100 rounds, injuring

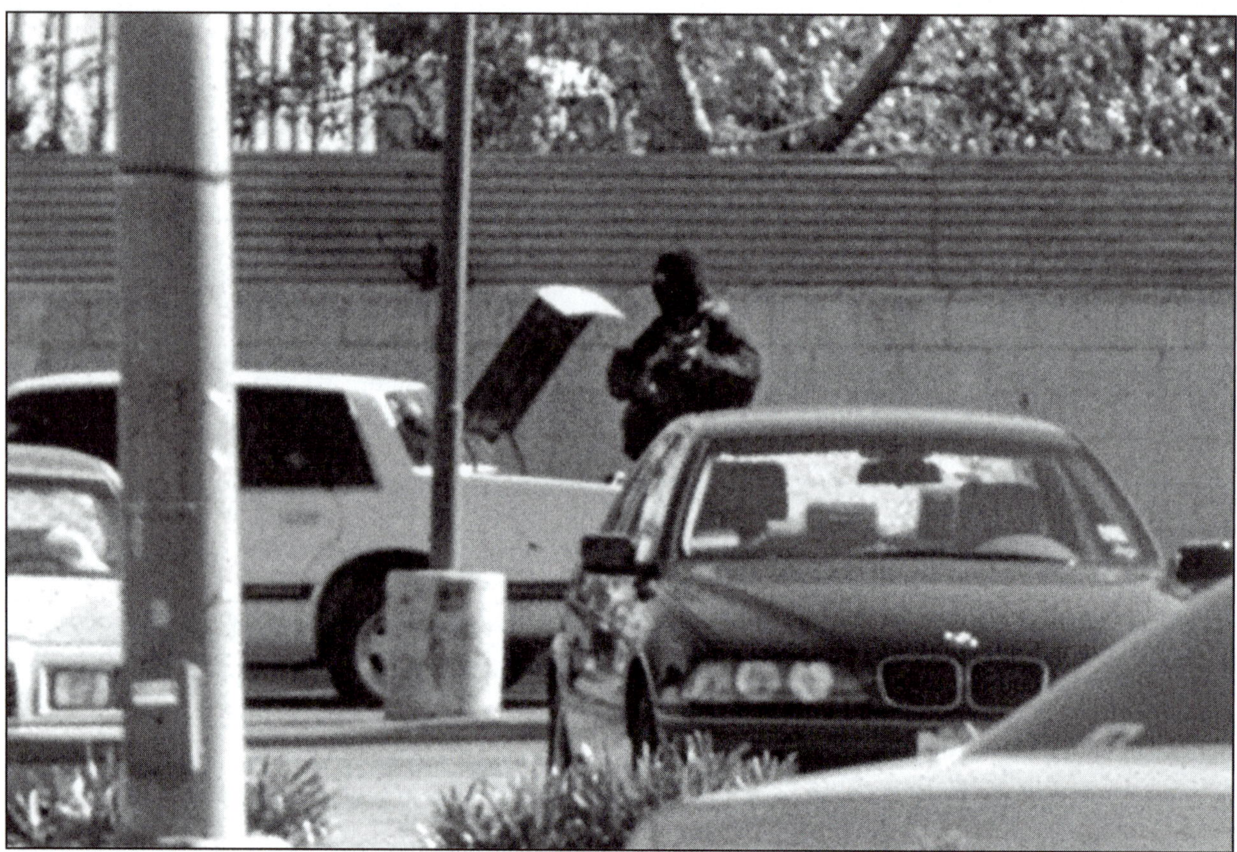

One of the two armed gunmen stands in a parking lot across the street from the Bank of America in North Hollywood on February 28, 1997. Following a botched bank heist, the robbers fired hundreds of rounds in a gun battle that injured several police officers and civilians and ended in the robbers' deaths. (AP/Wide World Photos)

eleven officers and six civilians and destroying several police cars.

Impact Although individual police officers received high praise for their heroic actions on the day of the shoot-out, the event resulted in criticism of the police response overall and a debate about policies surrounding automatic weapons and the weapons that police carry. While many concluded that such events would occur with more frequency in the future if police did not increase their weaponry, others contended that drastic policy change should not be the result of media sensationalism surrounding a few infrequent events.

Further Reading

Rehder, William J., and Gordon Dillow. *Where the Money Is: True Tales from the Bank Robbery Capital of the World.* New York: W. W. Norton, 2003.

Robinson, Paul. *Would You Convict? Seventeen Cases That Challenged the Law.* New York: New York University Press, 1999.

Brion Sever

See also Crime; Gun control; Los Angeles riots; Police brutality.

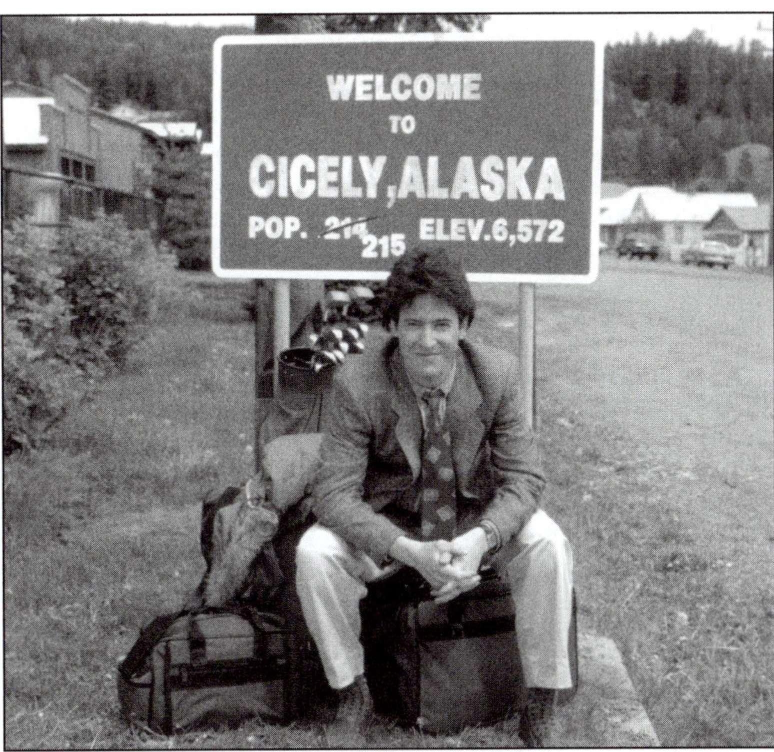

Rob Morrow as Dr. Joel Fleischman in Northern Exposure. (CBS/Landov)

■ Northern Exposure

Identification Television series
Producers Joshua Brand (c. 1952-) and John Falsey (1945-)
Date Aired from July 12, 1990, to July 26, 1995

This series was an early example of the "dramedy"—a realistic blending of sitcom and dramatic series—but mixed with a dose of Magical Realism. Its characters were an exceptionally diverse mix of ages, ethnicities, and sexual orientations. Aging and death were presented as natural parts of life.

Northern Exposure first appeared on the Columbia Broadcasting System (CBS) network as a summer replacement in 1990 and resumed in the spring of 1991. Well accepted by critics and audiences, it became a regular series in the fall of 1991. For its first full three seasons, it was among the top twenty shows in the United States, was honored with two Peabody Awards, and won three Emmys, two Golden Globes, and one Directors Guild Award.

The show found Dr. Joel Fleischman (Rob Morrow) unexpectedly assigned to the isolated town of Cicely, Alaska, to fulfill his debt for a medical school loan. Fleischman, a Jew from Manhattan, is angry about the assignment and unable to relate to the town's 215 residents. The townspeople, however, accept his churlishness nonchalantly.

The townspeople are not the typical "rubes" commonly depicted in shows that mix urban and rural characters: Maurice Minnifield (Barry Corbin), a former astronaut, is a wealthy land developer; former felon Chris Stevens (John Corbett) has started over in Cicely as an artist and the radio station's morning disc jockey, mixing eclectic musical selections with philosophical musings and readings from Walt Whitman, Carl Jung, and others; Maggie O'Connell (Janine Turner), a former debutante from a prominent family in Grosse Pointe, Michigan, is a bush pilot; widow Ruth-Anne Miller (Peg Phillips) retired to Cicely and is now the town's postmistress and runs the general store.

Impact *Northern Exposure* featured many scenarios that were unusual or daring for network television in the early 1990's. Two homosexual couples were featured in several episodes: Ron (Doug Ballard) and Erick (Don R. McManus), proprietors of a local inn, were married on the show, a first for prime-time television. This was not accepted in many quarters: Two network affiliates refused to air the episode, and one sponsor pulled out. Other episodes discuss the town's founding by a lesbian couple, Roslyn and Cicely.

Ethnic diversity on a show starring white characters was also uncommon. *Northern Exposure* featured two Native Americans—naïve, loveable Ed Chigliak (Darren E. Burrows) and Marilyn Whirlwind (Elaine Miles), Fleischman's receptionist—and Chris's half brother, Bernard Stevens (Richard Cummings, Jr.), was African American. Ruth-Ann was another unique character for television: a feisty, independent septuagenarian who interacted with the townspeople as an equal, not a frail, doddering senior citizen.

Further Reading

Chunovic, Louis. *The "Northern Exposure" Book*. New York: Citadel Press, 1993.

Williams, Betsy. "'North to the Future': *Northern Exposure* and Quality Television." In *Television: The Critical View*, edited by Horace Newcomb. 5th ed. New York: Oxford University Press, 1994.

Irene Struthers Rush

See also Cable television; Television.

■ Northridge earthquake

The Event A 6.7 magnitude earthquake strikes a densely populated area in Southern California, resulting in fifty-seven deaths

Date January 17, 1994

Place The San Fernando Valley of Los Angeles

The Northridge earthquake was among the largest quakes ever to occur directly beneath a major urban area in the United States. Building design and reinforcement programs were credited with preventing catastrophic loss of life. Many structures in the region, including freeway bridges, had been designed using standards implemented after a 1971 earthquake within the San Fernando Valley. However, economic losses were estimated to have exceeded $20 billion, making the quake the costliest in U.S. history at that time.

Located twenty miles northwest of downtown Los Angeles, the community of Northridge lies within the suburban San Fernando Valley. At 4:30 A.M. on the morning of January 17, 1994, an earthquake with a Richter scale magnitude of 6.7 shook the region, causing widespread damage, especially to wood-framed buildings and freeway overpasses. The National Geophysical Data Center estimated the quake's epicenter at ten miles below the ground surface. Although located in the vicinity of the San Andreas fault, the quake occurred along a previously unknown blind thrust fault within the Oak Ridge fault system. Thirty-eight accelerographs positioned throughout Southern California were used to measure movement associated with the quake. For a period of eight seconds, the rupture moved upward and northwest along the fault plane at two miles per second. At the surface, vertical movements lifted structures off their foundations while horizontal accelerations shifted walls laterally. With shaking lasting twenty seconds in some areas, the quake caused deformation within the Earth's crust across an area of more than fifteen hundred square miles. The quake's tremendous force caused the Santa Susana Mountains and much of the San Fernando Valley to be pushed upward more than a foot. Hundreds of aftershocks continued for months, with the largest recorded at 4.0 on the Richter scale.

Damage Among buildings suffering total collapse was a four-level parking facility at California State University, Northridge. Inside buildings, severe shaking damaged sprinkler pipes, interior partitions, ceilings, and air-handling systems. Throughout the region, about one hundred buildings designed to withstand severe ground motion experienced failure of their steel frames or reinforced concrete.

In contrast to other seismic events, the legacy of the Northridge earthquake was not calamitous damage but that more severe destruction and loss of life had been adverted. Experience with prior earthquakes had prompted building codes and the reinforcement of existing structures in order to reduce damage and threats to building occupants. Despite close proximity to the quake's epicenter, many buildings experienced minimal damage. However, the quake caused severe damage to large wood-

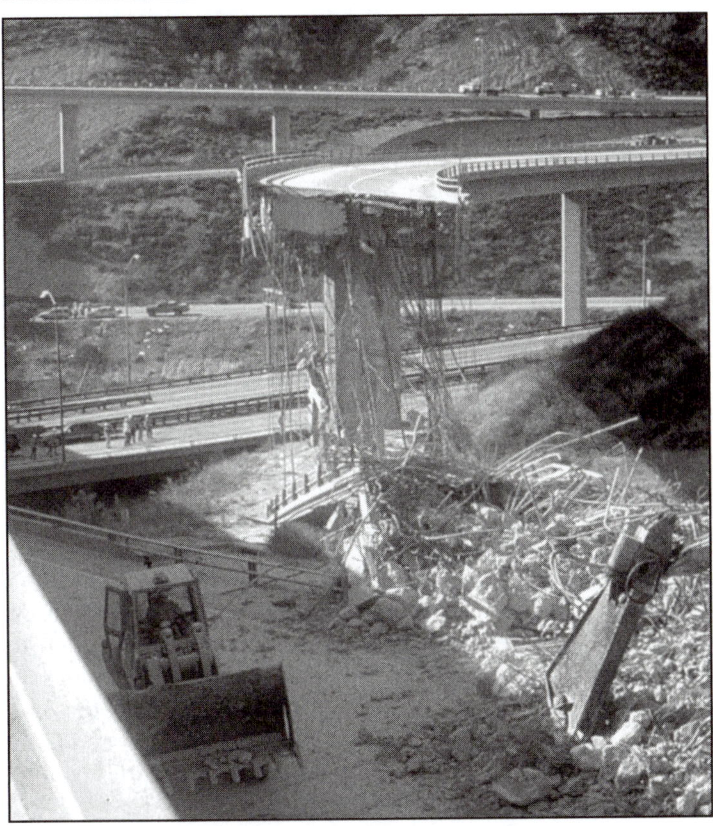

A collapsed connector structure at the Interstate 5 and State Route 14 interchange. (National Oceanic and Atmospheric Administration)

framed buildings, including many apartment complexes. Damage to streets was considerable in some areas, especially in western parts of the San Fernando Valley and within the cities of Simi Valley, Sherman Oaks, and Santa Monica. Significant damage to freeways occurred within twenty miles of the epicenter, affecting sections of Interstates 5 and 10 and State Route 14. The interchange connecting Interstate 5 and State Route 14 located between Newhall and San Fernando experienced a complete collapse.

A total of 170 freeway bridges experienced damage that affected traffic for months following the quake. In addition to damage to structures, the quake caused landslides that destroyed homes and utility lines and blocked roads and streams. In contrast to other large earthquakes such as the 1964 Alaska and 1989 Loma Prieta quakes, liquefaction and ground failure did not cause massive destruction. This was due to the relatively arid climate and dry soil in the Northridge area.

Human Toll The death toll for the quake included fifty-seven persons, with eleven thousand others injured. A majority of persons killed were in multifloor wood-frame structures. The early morning timing of the quake contributed to the low number of persons killed. Had the quake occurred just hours later, the loss of life on freeways would have been considerably higher. Immediately following the quake, more than nine thousand homes and businesses were without power. Responding to the disaster, the American Red Cross established forty-seven shelters for persons displaced from their homes.

Impact Information collected from the Northridge earthquake represents among the most detailed data sets on shaking intensity ever recorded in the United States. Scientific research based on data collected during the quake led to new building codes for the construction of steel-framed buildings. The quake also affected policy making. Damage to local hospitals prompted the California state legislature to pass a law requiring emergency and acute care facilities to be built to higher standards. As a result of enormous recovery payouts, many insurance companies discontinued earthquake coverage for property owners. To address this problem, the California Earthquake Authority was created as a publicly managed but privately funded agency offering minimal earthquake coverage.

Further Reading

Bolin, Robert C., and Lois Stanford. *The Northridge Earthquake: Vulnerability and Disaster.* New York: Routledge, 1998. A look at the effects of urbanization, population movement, and other sociodemographic factors on the vulnerability of Southern California to major disasters.

Bolt, Bruce A. *Earthquakes.* New York: W. H. Freeman, 1999. Provides a well-illustrated reference about earthquakes, with topics ranging from ground acceleration to earthquake forecasting. Several examples are provided from quakes, including Northridge in 1994 and Kōbe in 1995.

Hough, Susan E. *Finding Fault with California: An*

Earthquake Tourist's Guide. Missoula, Mont.: Mountain Press, 2004. A guidebook to major faults and earthquakes in the state of California. In addition to explaining characteristics of faults, the book provides profiles of geologists and the methods they use to study seismic activity.

Palm, Risa I., and Michael E. Hodgson. *After a California Earthquake: Attitude and Behavior Change.* Chicago: University of Chicago Press, 1992. Through twenty-five hundred interviews, the authors examine the attitudes of home owners regarding vulnerability to a major earthquake.

Stein, Seth, and Michael Wysession. *An Introduction to Seismology, Earthquakes, and Earth Structure.* Malden, Mass.: Blackwell, 2003. Provides an excellent reference for understanding the role of plate tectonics and seismic waves and their relationship to earthquakes.

Thomas A. Wikle

See also Natural disasters.

■ Novello, Antonia Coello

Identification Surgeon general of the United States, 1990-1993

Born August 23, 1944; Fajardo, Puerto Rico

Novello was the first woman as well as the first Hispanic to be appointed U.S. surgeon general.

Antonia Coello Novello was appointed U.S. surgeon general by President George H. W. Bush on March 9, 1990. Dr. Novello had a background in pediatric medicine and in public health care policy. Novello joined the Public Health Service Commissioned Corps in 1978. As a minority woman, Novello was very concerned that all federal health care policy decisions include the health care concerns of women, most especially minority women. While surgeon general, Novello led workshops and conferences to form the National Hispanic/Latino Health Initiative, which addressed problems non-English-speaking patients have accessing health care information and providers.

Novello also insisted that children's medical issues be of paramount importance in the allocation of federal health care dollars. Novello developed the Healthy Children Ready to Learn Initiative, which tied basic pediatric health care, including immunizations, with programs to promote proper nutrition. She believed that children who are physically as well as mentally healthy are able to perform well in school. Novello developed a program to address pediatric acquired immunodeficiency syndrome (AIDS), a health care problem that began to grow substantially during her term in office.

Novello also targeted the health care problems of older children, particularly teenagers. Novello repeatedly urged the U.S. Department of Health and Human Services to develop national programs to combat underage drinking, including banning the advertising of alcohol and alcohol-related products in various types of media. She campaigned against cigarette advertising that used Joe Camel, designed specifically to appeal to a younger audience.

Novello resigned as surgeon general on June 30, 1993, and accepted the position as special representative for health and nutrition to the United Nations Children's Fund (UNICEF). Novello continued to work as an advocate for children's medical issues on a global basis until 1996, when she accepted a one-year visiting professorship in health policy and management at The Johns Hopkins School of Hygiene and Public Health, the institution at which she earned her master's degree in public health in 1982. Novello then served as commissioner of health for the state of New York until her retirement in 2007.

While commissioner of health, Novello continued her campaign to ban tobacco advertising aimed at children and teenagers. She supported youth antismoking initiatives. Novello also worked to support the design and delivery of healthcare support programs to human immunodeficiency virus (HIV) and AIDS patients throughout New York.

Impact Much of U.S. health care policy and funding concentrated primarily on the medical conditions, problems, and diseases of adult males. Novello forced changes in federal health care policies to address the needs of women, especially minority women, and children.

Further Reading

"Antonia Novello." In *Notable Hispanic American Women,* Book 2, edited by Joseph M. Palmisano. Detroit: Gale Research, 1998.

Hawxhurst, Joan C. *Antonia Novello, U.S. Surgeon General.* Brookfield, Conn.: Millbrook Press, 1993.

Victoria Erhart

See also AIDS epidemic; Bush, George H. W.; Elders, Joycelyn; Health care; Joe Camel campaign; Latinos; Medicine; Tobacco industry settlement.

■ Nunavut Territory

Definition Canada's largest and newest territory
Date Created on April 1, 1999, by division of the Northwest Territories

Nunavut, meaning "our land," came into existence as a result of the political initiative of the Inuit people, who felt aboriginal interests in the Canadian Arctic were increasingly threatened by nonaboriginal policymakers and developers.

Composed of the central and eastern portions of the Canadian Arctic, Nunavut has 31,000 residents in twenty-eight communities spread over about 735,000 square miles, one-fifth of Canada's total land area. Specifically, the territory includes the eastern mainland, much of the Arctic archipelago, and all of the islands in the Hudson, James, and Ungava Bays.

The legal basis for its creation dates from the Canadian Supreme Court decision in 1973 that ruled in favor of aboriginal title claims to traditional lands. The Canadian government began negotiating land claims settlements with the indigenous peoples in 1974, and in 1982 the Inuit lent their overwhelming support to a plebiscite to divide the Northwest Territories. The Nunavut Land Claims Agreement Act, passed by the Canadian parliament in June, 1993, gave the Inuit people title to more than 136,000 square miles of land, of which 14,000 square miles include mineral rights; one billion dollars in capital transfer payments over fourteen years; representation for Inuit on several resource and environmental boards; and creation of a new territory, Nunavut, with a system of self-government. All residents of the territory can participate in the election of the government, regardless of ethnicity or origin; there are no political parties; and decisions are made by consensus within a unicameral legislative assembly and are based heavily on the wisdom and values of Inuit elders. A premier and commissioner lead the territorial government, there are three internal administrative districts, and Iqaluit, formerly Frobisher Bay, is the largest city (about 6,000 residents) and the territorial capital.

Nunavut's inhabitants, or Nunavummiut, are about 85 percent Inuit, and Inuktitut, the Inuit language, is the primary language of government and internal communication. Hunting, trapping, and fishing remain important activities for the local food supply, and minerals such as lead, zinc, and gold are valuable components of the territory's resource base. Arts and crafts are significant industries, and tourism is likely to grow as a result of three new national parks.

Impact The creation of Nunavut Territory represents an important milestone in the history of indigenous peoples in Canada. Pride in Inuit culture and history has experienced a rebirth. The Nunavut Land Claims Agreement Act transferred jurisdiction over property taxation, land-use planning, and natural resource management to the territorial government. Outside interests in energy and resource development have posed a threat, but the citizens of Nunavut have a strong voice in the protection of their fragile Arctic environment. Still, Nunavut's residents are faced with daunting problems of high unemployment, dependency on Ottawa for federal funding, environmental limits and vulnerabilities, and a cost of living about twice that of southern Canada.

Further Reading

Bennett, John, and Susan Rowley, eds. *Uqalurait: An Oral History of Nunavut.* Montreal: McGill-Queen's University Press, 2004.

Kulchyski, Peter Keith. *Like the Sound of a Drum: Aboriginal Cultural Politics in Denendeh and Nunavut.* Winnipeg: University of Manitoba Press, 2005.

Ann M. Legreid

See also Chrétien, Jean; Demographics of Canada; Elections in Canada; Employment in Canada; Minorities in Canada; Mulroney, Brian; Native Americans.

■ Nye, Bill

Identification Television personality, science educator, comedian, engineer, author and inventor
Born November 27, 1955; Washington, D.C.

Best known as "Bill Nye the Science Guy," Nye earned national acclaim by combining his talents for science and entertaining on the small screen, creating a popular television program that made science exciting and accessible for young audiences.

William Nye first realized his talent for teaching while tutoring his schoolmates in mathematics during high school. Always being interested in how things worked, Nye went on to earn a degree in mechanical engineering from Cornell University, which in turn led him to Seattle, Washington, where he took a position as an engineer for the Boeing Company.

While Nye maintained a successful career as an engineer, he also fostered an additional interest in comedic performance, being particularly inspired by the work of Steve Martin. Before long, he found himself juggling both passions at once. Soon after winning a Steve Martin look-alike contest, he began moonlighting as a stand-up comedian himself and quickly launched into the entertainment industry. Nye eventually left engineering as a profession and took on a position as performer and writer on *Almost Live*, a late night Seattle comedy show, where he would earn the well-known title of "Bill Nye the Science Guy."

In 1993, armed with his trademark bow ties, Nye left the show to pursue a different venture, one that would ultimately make him famous: an educational program aimed at reaching preteen audiences that would inspire an enthusiasm and appreciation for the world of science and that would encourage youths to get personally involved in kid-friendly scientific experiments. Nye worked to demystify a wide array of challenging subjects such as ecology, physics, chemistry, and biology. The show quickly became a success among young audiences, as well as stimulated interest in many adults, teachers, and college students. The show originally aired on the Public Broadcasting Service (PBS) from 1993 to 1997, totaling one hundred episodes in all; reruns were later released to such channels as Noggin and the Disney Channel.

In 1998, Nye devoted his scientific skills to the collaborative development of the MarsDial: a small sundial designed as a camera calibration target to be mounted on each rover for the Mars exploration missions. Among other inventions, Nye went on to

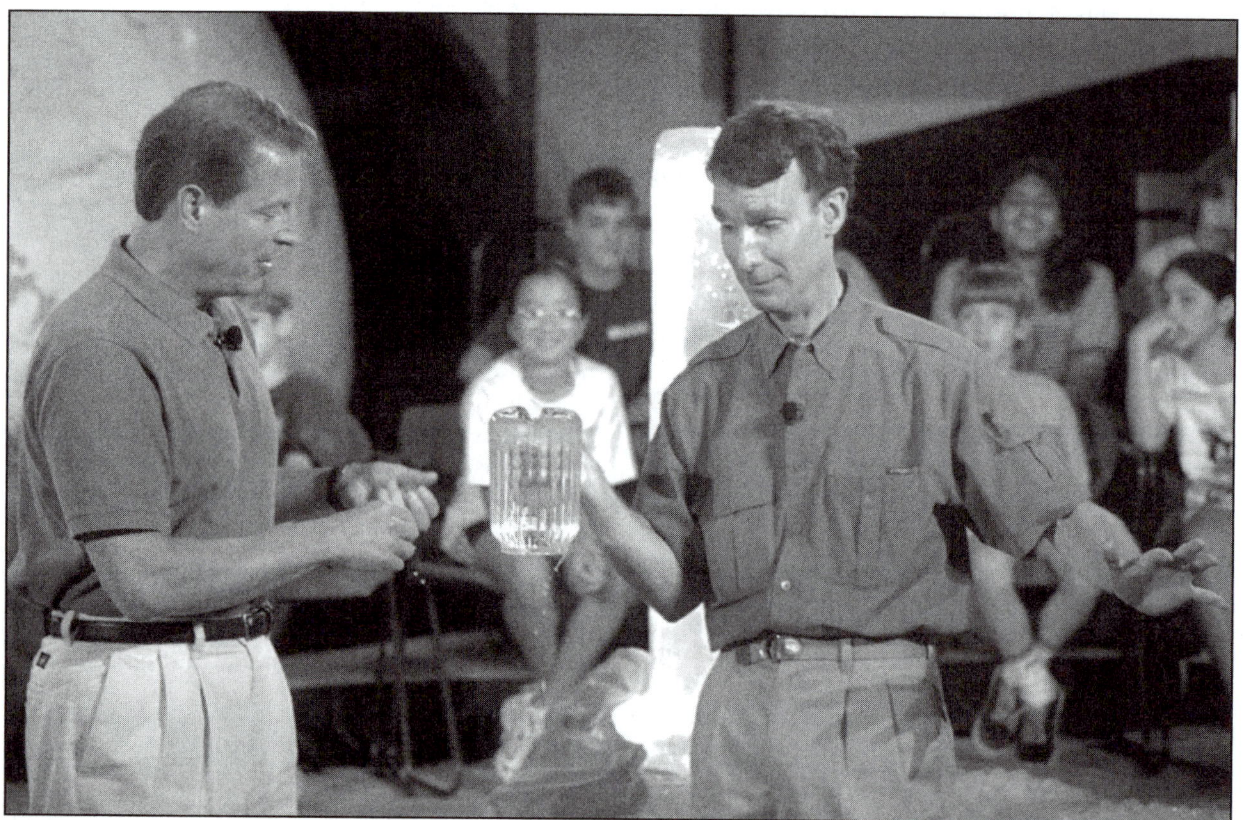

Bill Nye, right, and Vice President Al Gore use a pitcher of water to discuss global warming with summer camp students at the National Geographic Society in Washington, D.C., in 1999. (AP/Wide World Photos)

develop several patents, including a ballet toe shoe and a ball-throwing training device.

Impact The series *Bill Nye the Science Guy* won multiple awards, including seven Emmy Awards for production, performance, and writing. It remained in syndication until 2008 and continued to be widely used in classrooms as an educational resource. Nye has also written several children's books, which inspire an appreciation for science in young audiences nationwide.

Further Reading

Haven, Kendel, and Donna Clark. *One Hundred Most Popular Scientists for Young Adults: Biographical Sketches and Professional Paths.* Westport, Conn.: Libraries Unlimited, 1999.

Nye, Bill. *Bill Nye The Science Guy's Big Blast of Science.* New York: Basic Books, 1993.

_______. *Bill Nye's Great Big Book of Science: Featuring Oceans and Dinosaurs.* New York: Hyperion, 2005.

Danielle A. DeFoe

See also Children's television; Mars exploration; Science and technology; Space exploration; Television.

The cast of NYPD Blue *pose in New York in 1993. From left: David Caruso, Dennis Franz, Amy Brenneman, James McDaniel, Sherry Stringfield, and Nicholas Turturro.* (Hulton Archive/Getty Images)

■ *NYPD Blue*

Identification Television drama series
Creators Steven Bochco (1943-   ) and David Milch (1945-   )
Date Aired from September 21, 1993, to March 1, 2005

This program redefined acceptable limits for broadcast television in the areas of language, violence, and nudity. It also presented an extremely realistic view of police life and important social issues, while retaining the occasional comedic element.

Created by Steven Bochco and David Milch, *NYPD Blue* was partly based on an earlier series by Bochco, *Hill Street Blues*, and both programs generally had a single episode that followed one day's events in a police precinct house. Bochco was a devoted advocate of gritty realism, so the scripts for *NYPD Blue* were reviewed by a former police officer for accuracy. The program was a schedule mainstay of the American Broadcasting Company (ABC) for twelve years and won many honors and recommendations, including four Golden Globe Awards.

The program's main character was Detective Andy Sipowicz, portrayed for all twelve seasons by veteran character actor Dennis Franz. Sipowicz had a kind heart and a keen sense of justice, both of which he hid behind a coarse and gruff personality. The tragedies he suffered through and survived, including but not limited to being shot, beaten, having cancer, and the murders of his son and wife, would have destroyed a weaker person. The program was not exclusively about Sipowicz, however. No viable topic was considered too inflammatory or offensive, and episodes dealt with such diverse topics as organized crime, gangs, sexual perversion, and racial hatred.

It was the frank and open treatment of obscenity and nudity, along with the fine scripts and acting, which truly differentiated *NYPD Blue* from the myriad other police and drama programs. The program routinely featured adult language, which until then had been heard only on cable and satellite television. This did offend many viewers, and ABC was often threatened with boycotts and other forms of retribution.Others, however, felt the program was only reflecting the way police officers really spoke, and the consistently high ratings appeared to indicate most viewers were not too upset. It was its treatment of nudity that was most upsetting to the drama's most vocal detractors, however. Both sexes appeared in various forms of undress on a fairly regular basis. Full-frontal nudity was avoided, but little else was left to the imagination. Like the obscenity, though, the use of nudity was not gratuitous but seemed to flow naturally from the plots.

Impact *NYPD Blue* changed the standards and mores of dramatic broadcast television. For better or worse, it opened the doors for a host of increasingly more explicit programs that followed. Its main appeal, though, was that it featured outstanding ensemble acting, intriguing scripts, and story lines that millions of viewers found to be entertaining.

Further Reading

Collins, Max Allan. *NYPD Blue: Blue Blood—NYPD (NYPD Blue)*. New York: Signet, 1997.

Nelson, Robin. *TV Drama in Transition, Values, and Cultural Change.* New York: St. Martin's Press, 1997.

Thomas W. Buchanan

See also *GoodFellas*; *Pulp Fiction*; Television.

■ Oakland Hills fire

The Event One of the most destructive urban fires in American history
Date October 19-20, 1991
Place Oakland-Berkeley Hills, California

The fire was one of a series of 1990's events that demonstrated the vulnerability of California residents to natural disasters—in this case, an inadequately suppressed grassland fire, which reignited the following day and tore through affluent residential neighborhoods, resulting in destruction, death, and injury.

In 1991, Northern California was suffering from five years of drought, which meant that the Oakland-Berkeley Hills were covered with dried vegetation and the fire risk was extremely high. This was a region that had experienced previous wildfires, the most extensive conflagration in 1923 and a smaller one in 1970. However, despite these earlier events, fire-resistant building and landscaping practices still had not been fully implemented in the neighborhoods. Also, in the years since 1970, residential development had moved higher into the hills, creating increased urban-grassland interface areas and escalating challenges for fire-control strategies.

On October 19, 1991, emergency crews suppressed a small brush fire in the Oakland-Berkeley Hills and left the scene. Unfortunately, windy conditions the following morning fanned the embers, and the increasing gusts drove the flames into the adjacent residential neighborhoods. Firefighting services were rapidly mobilized, ultimately deploying approximately fifteen hundred individuals. It was soon apparent, however, that the wildfire was too fast and hot to be controlled and that local residents needed to be evacuated quickly. The police and other emergency-response teams moved into action, but in most locations people had little or no warning before they had to leave their homes, attempting to flee with family members, pets, and limited possessions. Some residents, disoriented by smoke, struggling to help others, or with no available path to safety, never made it out of their community and perished in the fire. Most people managed to escape the blaze, but many of them lost their pet companions, their homes, and all their possessions.

The End of the Day By evening on October 20, the winds lessened and the fire burnt at a reduced ferocity, no longer spreading rapidly. It was completely suppressed on its third day. The final damage tally was not calculated until weeks later, but the extensive wildfire had destroyed approximately 1,600 residential acres, including roughly 3,800 homes and apartment units. Twenty-five people were killed in the blaze (including two emergency workers), another 227 individuals required medical treatment, mostly for smoke-related injuries, and thousands were left homeless.

Long-Term Effects In the coming months, people dealt with grief and the psychological challenges of coping with a disaster of such magnitude. By the end of November, approximately 3,700 individuals had accessed counseling and mental health services through the American Red Cross. Presumably, many more people obtained mental health assistance on their own. Emotional difficulties are a common outcome of a natural disaster. In the case of this fire, these challenges also contributed to the logistical and financial difficulties experienced by the Oakland-Berkeley population after the catastrophe, including finding new accommodations, dealing with insurance paperwork, replacing necessary items, and returning to work, educational pursuits, or other activities.

The unique geographic and cultural context of the Oakland-Berkeley Hills also resulted in some distinctive reactions by residents to the disaster. The area is located on the outskirts of San Francisco, an eclectic American city, highly supportive of the arts and diversity in general. The neighborhood population is middle class to upper class, fairly well educated, and numbers high proportions of academics, writers, and artists, many of whom work or attend the University of California, Berkeley. In the years following the fire, people wanted to memorialize the event in a manner that reflected the unique character of the residents and paid tribute to their losses. Given this context, it was not surprising that a number of literary and visual remembrances were published or displayed in local galleries. In addition, an official memorial was created by the city, which featured tiles painted by local residents.

Impact The fire had a major impact on many aspects of urban life in the Oakland-Berkeley area and California in general. The fatalities, injuries, and losses of pets and possessions affected individual families and neighborhoods. The rapidity with which the fire moved across the residential district resulted in improvements in many areas of emergency response and in neighborhood strategies to protect homes and key transportation links, such as the reduction of flammable vegetation in selected zones.

Further Reading

Adler, Patricia, et al., eds. *Fire in the Hills: A Collective Remembrance.* Berkeley, Calif.: Patricia Adler, 1992. A poignant recollection through words and photographs of the Oakland Hills fire by residents, rescue workers, authors, and artists.

Beebe, Grant S., and Philip N. Omi. "Wildland Burning: The Perception of Risk." *Journal of Forestry* 91, no. 9 (1993): 19-24. A consideration of fire-control policies, including public awareness of residential protective strategies and the effects

Beyond the charred foreground stand the chimneys of homes destroyed in the 1991 Oakland Hills fire. (AP/Wide World Photos)

of media reporting about the Oakland Hills fire.

Hoffman, Susanna M. "The Monster and the Mother: The Symbolism of Disaster." In *Catastrophe and Culture: The Anthropology of Disaster,* edited by Susanna M. Hoffman and Anthony Oliver-Smith. Santa Fe, N.Mex.: School of American Research Press, 2002. A consideration of the Oakland Hills fire's effects on the community by an anthropologist who lost her home, two pets, and all of her possessions.

Oliver-Smith, Anthony. "Anthropological Research on Hazards and Disasters." *Annual Review of Anthropology* 25 (1996): 303-328. A review of disaster research, with brief reference to the Oakland Hills fire and some broader themes for understanding its context.

Shusterman, Dennis, Jerold Z. Kaplan, and Carla Canabarro. "Immediate Health Effects of an Urban Wildfire." *Western Journal of Medicine* 158 (1993): 133-138. An examination of the effects of the Oakland Hills fire on human health, documented by coroner and hospital records.

Susan J. Wurtzburg

See also Chicago heat wave of 1995; Hurricane Andrew; Mississippi River flood of 1993; Natural disasters; Northridge earthquake; Oklahoma tornado outbreak.

■ O'Connor, Sinéad

Identification Pop singer
Born December, 8, 1966; Dublin, Ireland

Sinéad O'Connor is a Grammy Award-winning international recording artist whose successful career has been sprinkled with controversy.

Sinéad Marie Bernadette O'Connor was born in Dublin, Ireland, to Jack and Marie O'Connor. The O'Connors had five children, of whom Sinéad is the middle child. At eight years old, her parents divorced, and she lived with her physically and mentally abusive mother. Her father later became a barrister to protect the rights of children and divorced fathers.

At age thirteen, O'Connor was sent to a reform school after incidents of shoplifting and truancy. Unhappy at Sisters of Our Lady of Charity, O'Connor enrolled at the liberal Newtown School, in 1983. Her musical talents were recognized at once, and by 1984, O'Connor had formed a band called Ton Ton Macoute. She gained the attention of Fachtna O'Ceallaigh, former head of U2's Mother Records, who helped produce her first album in 1987, *The Lion and the Cobra,* which contained the college radio hits "Mandinka" and "I Want Your (Hands on Me)." The album received tremendous praise and earned O'Connor a Grammy nomination for Best Female Rock Vocal Performance.

In 1990, O'Connor released *I Do Not Want What I Haven't Got,* which contained her biggest hit, Prince's "Nothing Compares 2 U." The song's international success was aided by the haunting video directed by John Maybury, which primarily featured O'Connor's face. Her striking shaved head and large eyes, coupled with her raw emotional and powerful delivery of the song's lyrics, resonated with fans and made the song a number one hit internationally.

O'Connor's career was not without controversy, as she made her political, social, and religious beliefs known throughout her career. This came to a head in 1992, when she performed on *Saturday Night Live.* During a live performance of Bob Marley's "War," O'Connor replaced the lyric "racism" with "child abuse" in a protest against the sexual molestation scandals plaguing the Catholic Church, and she culminated the performance by holding up a photo of Pope John Paul II to the camera and tearing it to pieces while saying "fight the real enemy." *Saturday Night Live* never aired the incident again, choosing instead to air rehearsal footage. The reaction to the performance was mixed; some radio stations refused to play her music, and people destroyed her albums, others praised her for her passion and bravery.

By the end of the decade, O'Connor was more comfortable with herself and her background. In 1996, she married John Waters, a journalist, and they had a daughter named Roisin. She also appeared in Irish director Neil Jordan's *The Butcher Boy* (1997).

Impact Sinéad O'Connor's music and convictions inspired music lovers throughout the 1990's and beyond. She appeared on compilation albums and performed in several benefit concerts. Her devotion to her beliefs and causes comes through in her lyrics and music, offering inspiration to her fans.

Further Reading

George-Warren, Holly. *The Rolling Stone Encyclopedia of Rock and Roll.* New York: Fireside, 2001. A comprehensive history of rock and roll.

Jeffries, Stan. *Encyclopedia of World Pop Music: 1980-2001.* Westport, Conn.: Greenwood Press, 2003. A thorough look into the music that defined the 1990's.

Struthers, Irene. "Sinéad O'Connor." In *Popular Musicians,* edited by Steve Hochman. Vol. 3. Pasadena, Calif.: Salem Press, 1999. Four-column summary of O'Connor's life and career.

Woodstra, Chris. *All Music Guide to Rock: The Definitive Guide to Rock, Pop, and Soul.* San Francisco: Backbeat Books, 2002. A complete guide to all things music.

Sara Vidar

See also Alternative rock; Electronic music; Grunge music; Love, Courtney; Madonna; Morissette, Alanis; Music; Nine Inch Nails; Nirvana; Rock and Roll Hall of Fame Museum; Rock the Vote.

■ Oklahoma City bombing

The Event A terrorist attack kills 168 people and injures 842
Date April 19, 1995
Place Oklahoma City, Oklahoma

This was the deadliest terrorist attack in the United States until the attacks on September 11, 2001.

On April 19, 1995, the nine-story Alfred P. Murrah Federal Building in Oklahoma City, Oklahoma, was destroyed by a bomb, killing 168 people and injuring 842 others. The conspiracy began a year earlier, when a man named Timothy McVeigh and others met in a trailer in Kingman, Arizona. Investigators later learned that McVeigh hated the government for its raid on the Branch Davidian compound on April 19, 1993, in Waco, Texas, as well as the incident at Ruby Ridge, Idaho, in 1992. He chose the two-year anniversary of the Waco siege to carry out his attack. The other man involved in the bombing was Terry Nichols, an Army friend of McVeigh from Michigan.

The Bombing Two days before the bombing, using false identification with the name "Robert D. Kling," Timothy McVeigh rented a Ryder truck in Junction City, Kansas, 270 miles from Oklahoma City. He and Nichols packed 108 bags of ammonium nitrate fertilizer, three fifty-five-gallon drums of liquid nitromethane, and several crates of explosives into the Ryder truck and moved it to Geary County State Lake, where they mixed the materials; a dual-fuse ignition system finished the truck bomb. At this point, Nichols left for Herington, Kansas, while McVeigh drove the truck to Oklahoma City.

Carrying quotes from white supremacist William Luther Pierce's *The Turner Diaries* (1978), McVeigh drove toward the Alfred P. Murrah Federal Building on the morning of April 19. At 8:57 A.M., he lit a five-minute fuse before parking the truck in front of an employee day-care center on the north side of the federal building. He then walked back to his getaway vehicle, which he had parked there days before.

At 9:02 A.M., the bomb discharged, destroying a third of the building and leaving a thirty-foot-wide crater. The explosion damaged more than three hundred other buildings; the blast could be felt more than fifty miles away and measured approximately 3.0 on the Richter scale. The victims, nineteen of whom were children, ranged in age from three months to seventy-three years.

The Aftermath At 9:25 A.M., State Emergency Operations Center (SEOC) specialists arrived on the scene. In addition, representatives from the Air Force, the Civil Air Patrol, the American Red Cross, the Oklahoma National Guard, and the Department of Civil Emergency Management were quickly on hand. Fifty people were rescued from the building and treated at local hospitals. Meanwhile, news trucks arrived en masse and began broadcasting. Initial stories speculated that there was a Middle Eastern connection to the bombing, given that the 1993 World Trade Center bombing was masterminded by Islamic terrorists.

Similarly, agents of the Federal Bureau of Investigation (FBI) initially believed the Oklahoma City bombing to be an outside terrorist attack on the United States and immediately sent government investigators to Oklahoma City. They soon found a piece of metal that turned out to be the truck axle. It was etched with a vehicle number that was quickly traced to Junction City, Kansas. In addition, a nearby bank videotape showed the Ryder truck parked in front of the building. They were well on their way to capturing the perpetrators. Composite sketches

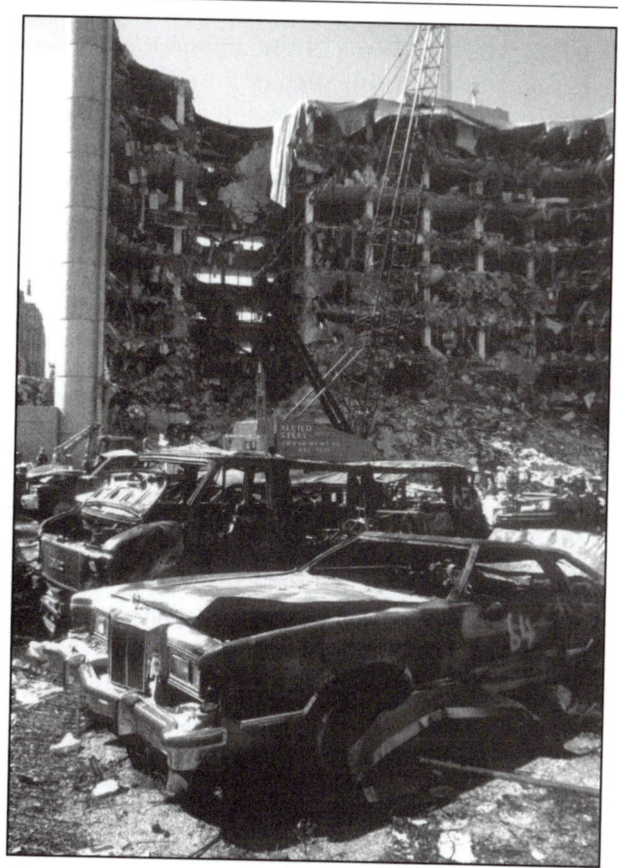

The remains of the Alfred P. Murrah Federal Building following an explosion on April 19, 1995, that killed 168 people. Timothy McVeigh was convicted of the terrorist act. (U.S. Department of Defense)

were soon broadcast around the country, and a motel owner in Junction City quickly identified McVeigh.

While all of this activity was occurring at the bombing site, however, McVeigh and Nichols were not making their way across country in an escape attempt or going underground to safety. Indeed, McVeigh was already in custody just sixty miles away, pulled over while traveling north out of Oklahoma City on Interstate 35 near Perry, Oklahoma, after a state trooper stopped him because his car was lacking a license plate. The police officer arrested him for carrying a concealed weapon. Just before McVeigh was scheduled to be released after a hearing, federal agents arrived. McVeigh's real driver's license led to a Michigan farm owned by James Nichols, the brother of Terry Nichols, who gave himself up two days after the bombing.

While McVeigh was making his failed getaway, at 9:45 A.M. Oklahoma governor Frank Keating declared a state of emergency. Later that day, President Bill Clinton declared a federal emergency and consoled the nation. The whole country, and indeed the world, responded to the people of Oklahoma City and donated so many supplies that drop-off centers had to be set up to collect and disperse donations. Citizens helped by donating blood, and restaurants provided meals. Americans donated more than $15 million to help the victims. In all, 12,000 people helped in relief and rescue efforts. K-9 units searched for survivors and bodies, while about 200 tons of rubble were removed every day for ten days in an attempt to uncover additional bodies. Recovery efforts ceased on May 4, and on May 23 the building was demolished.

In 1996, the image of firefighter Chris Fields holding the dying infant Baylee Almon won the Pulitzer Prize for Spot News Photography. Five years later, on April 19, 2000, the Oklahoma City National Memorial was dedicated, and the victims are remembered annually on April 19 at 9:02 A.M.

The Trial The investigation, known as OKBOMB and led by FBI Special Agent Weldon L. Kennedy, was the nation's largest criminal case in history. On August 10, 1995, a grand jury indicted McVeigh and Nichols. They were charged with one count of conspiracy to use weapons of mass destruction and one count of death and injury, in addition to charges of malicious destruction of federal property and the murder of eight federal employees. An Army friend of McVeigh and Nichols named Michael Fortier confessed to charges of conspiracy and became the prosecution's star witness.

McVeigh and Nichols pleaded not guilty to all charges, and the defense dismissed the prosecutor's case as "thin" and "circumstantial" by claiming that the real bombers died in the explosion. It also contended that Fortier could not be believed because he had earlier lied to the FBI. The defense argued for a change of venue, and the trial was moved to Denver, Colorado.

Joseph Hartzler led the government's prosecution, which called 137 witnesses. Fortier and his wife Lori testified about McVeigh's plans to blow up the Alfred P. Murrah Federal Building. McVeigh's sister Jennifer McVeigh testified about his hatred for the government. The defense, which presented twenty-five witnesses, was led by Stephen Jones. In spite of the defendant's wish that his lawyer claim the bombing was meant to protect future incidents such as Ruby Ridge and Waco, Jones attempted to create reasonable doubt by arguing that McVeigh could not have acted alone. Dr. Frederic Whitehurst, a witness for the defense, was highly critical of the FBI's poor handling of evidence. Traces of explosives on the shirt that McVeigh wore on April 19, however, were particularly damning.

On June 2, 1997, McVeigh was found guilty on eleven counts of murder and conspiracy; he was later sentenced to death by lethal injection. On June 11, 2001, he was executed at the U.S. penitentiary in Terre Haute, Indiana, exactly three months before the September 11, 2001, attacks. On August 9, 2004, Nichols was sentenced to life in prison without the possibility of parole. Michael Fortier was given a twelve-year sentence and a fine of $200,000 for failing to warn the U.S. government.

The Motive Immediately after the Oklahoma City bombing occurrred, Americans expected to find that foreign terrorists were responsible and were deeply shocked when pictures of Midwestern Americans McVeigh and Nichols flashed across television screens. How, they wondered, could such seemingly everyday Americans, indeed U.S. Army veterans, be responsible for such a heinous crime? Soon it became apparent that McVeigh and Nichols were members of an antigovernment militia group and intent on attacking the U.S. government in retribution for the deaths in Waco, Texas, and Ruby Ridge, Idaho.

Many Americans were surprised to discover that various militia groups existed throughout the United States and regularly practiced military exercises. While some groups advocated white supremacy, others believed that the federal government conspired to deprive them of their rights as Americans. Another group, The New World Order, was highly suspicious of the United Nations, which they believed wanted to take over America. The militia groups shared the opinion, however, that they had the right to bear firearms, a right granted by the U.S. Constitution's Second Amendment. Thus, they considered any form of gun control legislation to be anti-American. Many militia group members viewed the raid by the government at Waco against the Branch Davidian religious cult and the 1992 raid at Ruby Ridge against white supremacist Randy Weaver and his family as acts of murder.

Impact The Oklahoma City bombing shook America to its core and deeply affected the country's sense of security. As a result of the bombing of the Alfred P. Murrah Federal Building, the government took legislative measures, notably the Antiterrorism and Effective Death Penalty Act of 1996 and the Victim Allocution Clarification Act of 1997, in an effort to prevent future terrorist attacks. In 1995, Clinton, who criticized promoting hatred of the government and violence against authority, signed a bill increasing the number of federal antiterrorist agents, making the planning of a terrorist act a crime, lessening restrictions on information gathering on terrorist groups, and increasing funds for counterterrorism efforts. In addition, all federal buildings were surrounded with protective barriers and engineering improvements were made to construct safer buildings.

Until the attacks of September 11, 2001, the Oklahoma City bombing was the deadliest act of terror against the United States on American soil. Although the bombing brought Americans together in expressions of grief, the revelations about militia movements divided the country. Some argued that militia members were simply obeying the law and strongly believing in the constitutional right to bear firearms. Others saw militia members as traitors, terrorists, and fanatics intent on destroying the U.S. government.

Further Reading

Davis, Jayna. *The Third Terrorist: The Middle East Connection to the Oklahoma City Bombing.* Nashville: WND Books, 2004. Suggests that McVeigh and Nichols were not alone in the Oklahoma City bombing but were part of a greater conspiracy involving Islamic terrorists.

Kight, Marsha, comp. *Forever Changed: Remembering Oklahoma City, April 19, 1995.* Amherst, N.Y.: Prometheus Books, 1998. A compilation of seventy-nine essays, including testimonies from survivors.

Serrano, Richard A. *One of Ours: Timothy McVeigh and the Oklahoma City Bombing.* New York: W. W. Norton, 1998. Provides a compelling profile of McVeigh in an attempt to understand how and why an American man became a terrorist.

Wright, Stuart A. *Patriots, Politics, and the Oklahoma City Bombing.* New York: Cambridge University Press, 2007. Demonstrates the rise of domestic terrorism. Suggests that the U.S. armed forces may indirectly serve as training camps for future terrorists such as McVeigh.

M. Casey Diana

See also Clinton, Bill; Gun control; McVeigh, Timothy; Militia movement; Montana Freemen standoff; Ruby Ridge shoot-out; Terrorism; Waco siege; World Trade Center bombing.

■ Oklahoma tornado outbreak

The Event Tornadoes take forty-seven human lives and cause immense property damage
Date May 3, 1999
Place Central and northern Oklahoma, as well as Kansas

The many tornadoes that hit Oklahoma and Kansas would have cost more lives had scientific weather forecasting, technologically advanced communications, and alert television and radio reporting not given most residents adequate warning.

At 8:00 A.M. on Monday, May 3, 1999, the Storm Prediction Center (SPC) in Norman, Oklahoma, issued a notice that the risk for thunderstorms was slight. As the day advanced, the SPC raised the risk to moderate, then to high. At 4:45 P.M., it issued a tornado watch to alert much of the state and part of Kansas that atmospheric conditions might lead to supercell thunderstorms, which generate tornadoes. At 4:47 P.M., the National Weather Service issued a tornado warning, and soon a small tornado touched the ground in northern Comanche County, Oklahoma. Television and radio stations were quick to inform their audiences of the general danger; as events proceeded, the efforts to warn residents proved valuable.

Metropolitan Oklahoma City The worst of the tornadoes began at 6:23 P.M. in rural Grady County, Oklahoma, near the small town of Amber, and, as tornadoes usually do in North America, moved northeast—in this case, toward metropolitan Oklahoma City. At about 6:54 P.M., as the tornado left the community of Bridge Creek, near the South Canadian River, mobile Doppler radar measured its rotating wind speed on the ground at 301 miles per hour (484 kilometers per hour), plus or minus 20 miles per hour (32 kilometers per hour). A tornado with a rotational speed that high is capable of causing such extreme damage that it would be rated as an F5, the highest category of the Fujita scale used then to indicate tornadic severity. It was the highest wind speed ever measured at the Earth's surface.

Immediately north of the McClain County town of Newcastle, near the Interstate 44 bridge across the South Canadian, the tornado entered Cleveland County and the southernmost part of Oklahoma City, from which it moved on to the large suburb of Moore, crossing Interstate 35 at its junction with Shields Boulevard. After further movement through Moore, the tornado reentered Oklahoma City and crossed the Oklahoma County line, then proceeded into Del City and past Tinker Air Force Base. Having already slackened enough to become an F4, the tornado eventually disappeared over Midwest City, north of Interstate 40 and east of Sooner Road. It had traveled 38 miles (61 kilometers) and lasted 85 minutes.

Stroud, Mulhall, and Metropolitan Wichita Although the F5 tornado in Grady, Cleveland, and Oklahoma counties was the most powerful, it was only one among dozens from eleven supercell thunderstorms in Oklahoma and Kansas in the late afternoon and night of May 3. An F3 tornado hit Stroud, Oklahoma, on Interstate 44 in Lincoln County, midway between Oklahoma City and Tulsa. More powerful was the F4 tornado that struck the small town of Mulhall, Oklahoma, in northern Logan County. Mobile Doppler radar measured the distance between the highest speeds on either side of that enormous tornado at 1.0 mile (1.6 kilometers) and measured a diameter of 4.3 miles (7.0 kilometers) between points where gusts exceeded 96 miles per hour (155 kilometers per hour). Farther north, another F4 hit Haysville, Kansas, and moved into Wichita.

Impact Altogether, at least seventy-one tornadoes struck Oklahoma on May 3, and a total of ninety-six occurred on the Great Plains that day and the next. Property damage was immense. Tornadoes destroyed 2,314 houses and damaged 7,428 others. As for apartments, 473 were destroyed in Cleveland and Oklahoma counties. Among the total of 164 destroyed businesses were all 53 in Stroud's Tanger Factory Outlet Center, a shopping mall that has not been rebuilt. Additionally, the tornado outbreak destroyed four public buildings, two schools, and five churches. The estimate of the total property damage was $1.2 billion.

In contrast to the immense damage, the human death toll was low. Of the forty-seven fatalities, five were in Sedgwick County, Kansas, and the other forty-two were in eight Oklahoma counties. The F5 tornado that began in Grady County and ended in Oklahoma County claimed thirty-eight lives. As almost everyone knew beforehand, mobile homes, as in Bridge Creek, are death traps in tornadoes. As many people learned because of this outbreak, overpasses create wind tunnels during tornadoes and therefore prove unsafe places for shelter. Three persons who tried to take cover at overpasses along interstate highways in Oklahoma died from their injuries: one each in McClain, Cleveland, and Payne counties. Along with the high number of injuries, the number of deaths did have the positive result of encouraging people in Oklahoma, where basements are rare, to have storm cellars or safe rooms built at their houses, and the total of injuries and deaths should have reminded Oklahomans, Kansans, and others of the need for solid construction and of the threat tornadoes pose.

Further Reading

Bluestein, Howard B. *Tornado Alley: Monster Storms of the Great Plains.* New York: Oxford University Press, 1999. A meteorologist's depiction of tornadoes through text and photographs and a history of relevant research.

Bradford, Marlene. *Scanning the Skies: A History of Tornado Forecasting.* Norman: University of Oklahoma Press, 2001. Traces the history of tornado forecasting and the technological advances that helped improve it.

Grazulis, Thomas P. *The Tornado: Nature's Ultimate Windstorm.* Norman: University of Oklahoma Press, 2001. A meteorologist's thorough, statistically rich account of tornadoes in general, with a page about the Oklahoma outbreak of 1999.

Mathis, Nancy. *Storm Warning: The Story of a Killer Tornado.* New York: Simon & Schuster, 2007. A mixture of the stories about meteorologists and tornado victims, with an emphasis on the tornado that struck metropolitan Oklahoma City in 1999.

National Oceanic and Atmospheric Administration. National Weather Service. Weather Forecast Office. "The Great Plains Tornado Outbreak of May 3, 1999." http://www.srh.noaa.gov/oun/storms/19990503/. A short account, with a map and photographs.

Victor Lindsey

See also Business and the economy in the United States; Chicago heat wave of 1995; Global warming debate; Natural disasters; Perfect Storm, the; Science and technology; Storm of the Century.

■ Olympic Games of 1992

The Event The staging of XVI Winter and XXV Summer Olympiads, international athletic competitions, held every four years

Date Winter Games, February 8-23, 1992; Summer Games, July 25-August 9, 1992

Place Winter Games, Albertville, France; Summer Games, Barcelona, Spain

The 1992 Olympics marked the end of a decade of political boycotts and the first Games to be held after the Iron Curtain had come down. They were also the last Olympics in which Winter and Summer Games were held in the same year.

Albertville, France, had been selected to host the 1992 Winter Olympics out of eight bids, including Anchorage, Alaska, and Lillehammer, Norway. Lillehammer actually staged the next Winter Olympics, held just two years later in 1994.

Sixty-four nations were represented, fielding some 1,801 athletes: 1,313 men and 488 women. Seven sports were included, generating fifty-seven separate events. The sports included figure skating, speed skating, alpine and Nordic skiing, and ice hockey. Freestyle skiing, short-track speed skating, and women's biathlon were held as medal competitions for the first time. Curling was included for the first time as a demonstration sport. Of the fifty-seven events, eighteen were held in Albertville, the remainder being held at nearby resorts in the French Alps.

The Games were opened by French president François Mitterrand in a ceremony featuring dancers and acrobats. The Olympic torch was lit by French soccer star Michel Platini and a local boy, François-Cyrille Grange. The Olympic Oath was taken on behalf of the athletes by figure skater Surya Bonaly and the Official Oath by alpine skier Pierre Bornat.

Leading Medal Winners of the 1992 Winter Olympics

Country	Gold	Silver	Bronze	Medals Won
Germany	10	10	6	26
Unified Team (former Soviet Union)	9	6	8	23
Norway	9	6	5	20
Austria	6	7	8	21
United States	5	4	2	11
Italy	4	6	4	14
France	3	5	1	9
Finland	3	1	3	7
Canada	2	3	2	7
South Korea	2	1	1	4

Leading Medal Winners of the 1992 Summer Olympics

Country	Gold	Silver	Bronze	Medals Won
Unified Team (former Soviet Union)	45	38	29	112
United States	37	34	37	108
Germany	33	21	28	82
China	16	22	16	54
Cuba	14	6	11	31
Spain	13	7	2	22
South Korea	12	5	12	29
Hungary	11	12	7	30
France	8	5	16	29
Australia	7	9	11	27

The Olympics of 1992 were held soon after the collapse of the communist Soviet Union (December, 1991), which quickly produced a number of newly independent states, and the unification of East and West Germany (October, 1990). As many of the new states had not had time to organize themselves for the Olympics, they were allowed to compete as the former Soviet team, but under the title of the Unified Team (UT, or EUN). On the other hand, the two Germanies had managed to unite and for the first time since 1960 competed as a single nation. This led them to immediate success, and they headed the medal table with ten gold medals and twenty-six medals in all, outstripping the UT team, which gained nine golds and twenty-three medals in all. Frequently, the host country does very well, but this was not the case in 1992. France, one of the dominating skiing countries, could only manage three gold medals and nine medals in all. Of the smaller countries, Norway did unexpectedly well, finishing with nine golds and twenty medals in all. The United States earned five gold medals and a total of eleven.

Of individual performances, that of Raisa Smetanina of the UT was one of the most outstanding. At thirty-nine years old, she was the oldest woman ever to win a cross-country skiing gold medal in the 4-by-5-kilometer relay race, bringing her total haul of Olympic medals to ten. Another outstanding winner was the Austrian skier Petra Kronberger, who won golds in both the slalom and giant slalom events. Close behind her in the medals tally came the veteran Italian skier Alberto Tomba, who won gold in the giant slalom for a record-breaking second time and silver in the slalom.

Among other outstanding individual performances was that of Canadian skier Kerrin Lee-Gartner, who won the women's downhill skiing. She had not won in six years, and only came out of retirement to compete in the Winter Olympics, having had reconstructive knee surgery. Behind her, in silver medal position, was another surprise in Hilary Lindh of the United States, comprehensively breaking the Alpine countries' stranglehold over the event. In figure skating, American Kristi Yamaguchi won gold, with Nancy Kerrigan taking the bronze. Paul Wylie of the United States gained a silver medal in the men's figure skating, behind Viktor Petrenko of the UT.

In the team sports, Canada won the women's 3,000-meter relay in speed skating, with the U.S. team taking silver. Canada started favorites in the ice hockey but were beaten in the final by the UT. Canada also gained the silver in the men's 500-meter speed skating relay.

The Summer Olympics For the twenty-fifth Olympiad, Barcelona, in the Catalonian region of Spain, had been chosen over five other cities in an International Olympic Committee (IOC) meeting in 1986. Catalonia was fittingly the birthplace of IOC president Juan Antonio Samaranch. Some 169 nations participated, a record number, and 9,356 athletes competed: 6,652 men and 2,704 women. Thirty-two sports were represented in 286 separate events. Baseball, badminton, and women's judo were added as new sports, and slalom canoeing returned after twenty years. The demonstration sports were roller hockey and tae kwon do as well as the local Spanish sports of Basque pelote and Valencian pilota.

King Juan Carlos I of Spain presided over the opening ceremony in the newly constructed Olympic Stadium, and Spanish paraplegic archer Antonio Rebollo shot a flaming arrow to ignite the Olympic torch. The Olympic Oath was read by the veteran Spanish sailor Luis Doreste Blanco. The theme song "Barcelona" could only be played as part of a recorded travelogue, as Freddie Mercury (of the British rock band Queen), the song's composer and one of the singers, had recently died. The other theme song, Andrew Lloyd Webber's "Amigos para Siempre" (always friends), was sung at the closing ceremony.

As with the Winter Games, the former Soviet team competed as the Unified Team using the Olympic flag and anthem, while the Germans competed as a single team. The breakup of Yugoslavia presented difficulties for the constituent parts of that country. Because of U.N. sanctions against their country, Yugoslav athletes were allowed to compete under the Olympic flag, but not their own. Newly independent Croatia and Slovenia, who had been invited by the IOC to Albertville, made their Summer Olympic debuts, while Bosnia and Herzegovina competed for the first time. South Africa was able to compete for the first time in several decades, the IOC having decided the notorious apartheid policy of that country had been dismantled sufficiently to bring it into compliance with Olympic rules.

Under Samaranch, the financial basis of the Olympics had been secured during the 1980's by allowing commercial sponsorship and sale of broadcasting rights. This continued at the 1992 Summer Olympics. The rules that sought to ensure that all athletes were nonprofessionals were relaxed. In the case of basketball, the International Basketball Federation (FIBA) allowed any professional to participate, and thus the United States was able to field its "Dream Team" of leading professional basketball players, easily securing the gold medal. Cycling and soccer also eased the professional rules considerably. After the 1988 drug scandal surrounding Canadian sprinter Ben Johnson, drug testing was for the first time rigorously monitored.

Outstanding Performances Every Olympic Games produces its crop of outstanding performances, sur-

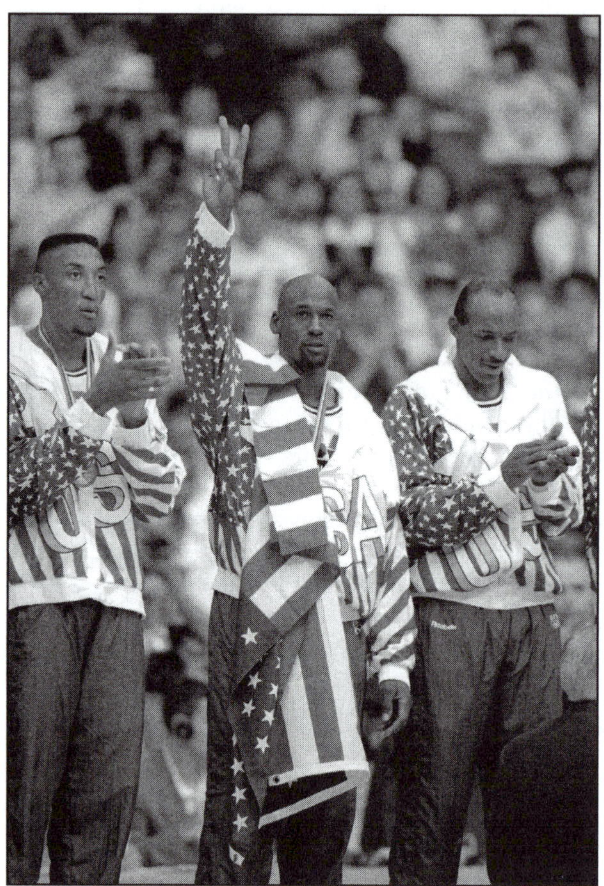

Dream Team members Scottie Pippen (left), Michael Jordan, and Clyde Drexler rejoice after defeating Croatia for the gold. (AP/ Wide World Photos)

prises, and disappointments. The Barcelona Games were no exception. Probably the most extraordinary success was in men's gymnastics, in which the UT gymnast Vitaly Scherbo took six gold medals, four of them on a single day. He won in the men's all-around, still rings, pommel horse, vault, parallel bars, and in the team all-around. In swimming, Hungary's Krisztina Egerszegi became a triple champion in the 100-meter backstroke, 200-meter backstroke, and the 400-meter individual medley. Egerszegi had first won Olympic gold at Seoul when she was just fourteen. She became the world record-holder over both 100-meter and 200-meter backstroke. The UT swimmer Alexander Popov won golds in both the 50-meter and 100-meter freestyle, beating strong U.S. challenges.

In rowing, the great British oarsman Steve Redgrave won another gold medal, this time rowing with Matthew Pinsent in the coxless pairs, a victory to be repeated in Atlanta four years later. Redgrave went on to win golds in no fewer than five Olympics, Pinsent in four. The German oarsman Thomas Lange retained his 1988 title in the single sculls. In the track-and-field events, the great Cuban high jumper Javier Sotomayor finally gained a gold medal, having been forced to boycott the previous two Olympics. In the sprints, the U.S. dominance was broken by the win of the British 100-meter sprinter Linford Christie and the arrival of sprinters from Africa, particularly Namibia and Nigeria. At thirty-two, Christie was the oldest sprint champion on record. Hassiba Boulmerka, the Algerian winner of the women's 1,500-meter, became the first female medalist from a Muslim country, having run despite great criticism from some of her fellow Muslims.

The host country is thought to have an advantage in winning medals. This proved particularly true for Spain, normally regarded as quite an average country in world sport, and was nowhere better seen than in the men's 1,500-meter, in which a relatively unknown Spaniard, Fermin Cacho, won the race of a lifetime in an impeccably timed race. The Spanish also gained golds in soccer, the men's 20-kilometer walk, and their first ever in a swimming event. Spain came an astonishing sixth in the unofficial medals table, with 13 gold and 22 medals altogether. The UT team won the most medals, with 45 gold and 112 altogether, ahead of the United States with 37 gold and 108 altogether.

Technology continued to play a significant role in a number of sports, ranging from improved materials in the construction of poles for pole vaulting to the materials for canoes, kayaks, and boats. Perhaps the most dramatic technological innovation was in cycling, in which British rider Chris Boardman sported a revolutionary new bicycle designed using the latest aerodynamic technology—though his bicycle was still within Olympic specifications. He won the 4000-meter individual pursuit event, beating world champion Jens Lehmann. Later, allegations were made that he would not have won had it not been for the new bicycle, allegations proved wrong when, after the Olympics, he won similar pursuit races using a conventional bicycle.

The most dramatic event marking the return of South Africa to the Olympics was the women's 10,000-meter, in which South African Elana Meyer battled the whole race with Ethiopian Derartu Tulu, with Tulu just beating Meyer to the finish. The two athletes ran the lap of honor hand in hand, black and white athlete together.

Another dramatic event was in the men's 400-meter. In the semifinal, the British runner Derek Redmond suddenly pulled a hamstring on the final bend. Struggling to continue, Redmond found his father jumping on to the track to support his son to the finish.

Probably the greatest disappointment was in the men's pole vault, in which the UT jumper Sergei Bubka was widely expected to win, having taken gold at Seoul in 1988 and setting a new Olympic record. Bubka in fact totally failed to make any height, though just a month later he set a new world record.

U.S. Achievements The U.S. contingent consisted of 578 athletes, compared to 494 from the UT and 486 from the united German team. Canada's contingent amounted to 304 athletes, on a level with Australia, with 295 athletes.

During the first week, the swimming and diving events were held. In these, Americans took eleven golds, more than any other country. Mike Barrowman, who had finished fourth in Seoul in the men's 200-meter breaststroke, broke his own world record in that event despite the death of his father shortly before. The win in the men's 4-by-100-meter freestyle relay gave Matt Biondi his seventh Olympic gold, though he was well beaten in other events. In the men's medley relay, the U.S. team beat two world records in their win. The other outstanding U.S.

swimmer was Pablo Morales, who won the men's 100-meter butterfly. In the women's competitions, Summer Sanders won the 200-meter butterfly, but elsewhere the challenge from Hungary, China, and the UT was too strong. However, in the second week, the synchronized swimming events took place, and the U.S. teams proved unrivaled there.

The gymnastics events were also held the first week. Shannon Miller emerged as the most successful American gymnast, earning silver medals in the women's all-around and the balance beam and bronze medals in the uneven bars and floor exercise. The only U.S. gold was won by Trent Dimas in the men's horizontal bar.

The athletics events were held the second week, and, as usual, U.S. athletes excelled. Gail Devers was seeking to become the first woman since Fanny Blankers-Koen in 1948 to win the 100-meter and the 100-meter hurdles double, despite having been seriously ill for several years before the Olympics. She had only resumed training in March, 1992. She managed to win the 100-meter but found the hurdles race, held later in the week, beyond her. In the 200-meter, Gwen Torrence edged out two Jamaicans to win, and in the women's 4-by-100-meter relay, Evelyn Ashford won her fourth Olympic gold, with Torrence adding a second. The other outstanding female athlete on the U.S. team was Jackie Joyner-Kersee, who won the heptathlon.

Among the men, the veteran Carl Lewis won the long jump at his first attempt, setting up an American clean sweep of medals. He then added an eighth gold to his overall tally in the 4-by-100-meter relay to bring an outstanding Olympic career to an end. Mike Marsh was also in the relay team, whose time was a new world record. Marsh had previously taken gold in the 200-meter, with an Olympic record time in the semifinals. Michael Johnson, the 200-meter favorite, had been surprisingly knocked out at that stage.

Other U.S. triumphs in track and field included Quincy Watts's victory in the men's 400-meter, with the United States also taking silver. In the 400-meter hurdles, Kevin "Spiderman" Young set a new world record time to win gold. The 4-by-400-meter men's relay was also a U.S. victory. A new world record was set in the triple jump, in which the U.S. team took both gold and silver, as they did in the shot put, with Mike Stulce's outstanding performance beating the heavily favored Swiss Werner Gunther.

In other sports, the Dream Team won the men's basketball competition, defeating Croatia in the final game, and Jennifer Capriati won the women's singles tennis gold, beating the much-favored German Steffi Graf in the final. Elsewhere, successes were more moderate. In boxing, for example, U.S. boxers gained only three medals in all, a bronze, silver, and gold, finishing behind Cuba and Germany in the boxing medals count. In men's volleyball, the team that had won at Seoul was knocked out in the first round. The baseball team also failed to make a great impression. Overall, however, it was a good Olympics for the United States, narrowly behind the UT in the medals count, but well ahead of the Germans.

Impact The Summer and Winter Games were great successes, both in terms of records broken and outstanding performances achieved, but also because they were not marred by boycotts or any great controversies. Drug problems were minimal, and a disqualification of the Moroccan winner of the 10,000-meter was quickly overturned on appeal. The Games were well organized and the financial backing secure. It marked a particular triumph for IOC president Juan Antonio Samaranch on his home turf.

Further Reading

Goldstein, Gabriella, and Brad Lewis, eds. *Olympic Results, Barcelona 1992: A Complete Compilation of Results from the Games of the XXV Olympiad.* New York: Garland, 1993. This volume of the Garland Reference Library is one of the most comprehensive results lists available.

Hargreaves, John. *Freedom for Catalonia? Catalan Nationalism, Spanish Identity, and the Barcelona Olympic Games.* Cambridge, England: Cambridge University Press, 2000. An investigation into the wider political and cultural forces at work in the Olympics of recent years.

Rendell, Matt, ed. *The Olympics: Athens to Athens 1896-2004.* London: Weidenfeld & Nicholson, 2004. A pictorial survey of the Summer Olympiads, picking out the highlights from each of the Games.

U.S. Olympic Committee. *The Olympic Century: XXIV Olympiad, Seoul 1988, and Albertville 1992.* Tonawanda, N.Y.: Firefly Books, 1997. Includes the official report on the 1992 Winter Olympics from the U.S. point of view.

_______. *The Olympic Century: XXV Olympiad, Barcelona 1992, and Lillehammer 1994.* Tonawanda,

N.Y.: Firefly Books, 1996. Includes the official U.S. report of the Barcelona Olympics.

Wallechinsky, David. *The Complete Book of the Olympics, 1992.* New York: Little, Brown, 1992. A complete preview of that year's Olympic Games, with full descriptions of leading athletes and events.

David Barratt

See also Barkley, Charles; Baseball; Basketball; Boxing; Browning, Kurt; Dream Team; Hockey; Johnson, Magic; Jordan, Michael; Kerrigan, Nancy; Malone, Karl; Olympic Games of 1994; Olympic Games of 1996; Olympic Games of 1998; Olympic Park bombing; Salt Lake City Olympics bid scandal; Soccer; Sports; Stojko, Elvis; Tennis; Yamaguchi, Kristi.

■ Olympic Games of 1994

The Event The staging of the XVII Winter Olympiad, an international athletic competition held every four years

Date February 12-27, 1994

Place Lillehammer, Norway

These Games marked the first time that the Winter and Summer Olympics were not held in the same year. Norway performed exceptionally well, as did Russia and Germany.

Despite that Lillehammer was a town of only twenty-five thousand inhabitants, it beat rival bids from Anchorage, Alaska; Östersund in neighboring Sweden; and Sofia, Bulgaria, for the 1994 Olympics. The city put in a great number of resources, even moving the jumping hills to accommodate the Columbia Broadcasting System (CBS).

Sixty-seven nations participated—with 1,737 athletes, 1,215 men and 522 women—statistics comparable with the previous Winter Games. This time, the former Soviet bloc countries competed separately, rather than under the Unified Team banner of the previous Games. These included Russia, Ukraine, Uzbekistan, Kazakhstan, and Belarus. Sixty-one events were slated across six sports, one less sport (curling) than the previous games, at nine separate locations.

King Harald V of Norway presided over the opening ceremony. The Olympic Oath was taken by cross-country skier Vegard Ulvang and the Official Oath by figure skater Kari Karing. The Olympic torch was lit by Crown Prince Haakon in the Lysgårdsbakkene Stadium. The theme for the opening spectacular was based on Norwegian folklore.

The day of the opening was marred by the theft of Norway's iconic painting *The Scream,* by Edvard Munch, from the National Museum in Oslo. The thieves reckoned on everyone being distracted and off guard because of the opening ceremony. The painting was recovered several years later.

Outstanding Achievements The host country is seen to have an advantage, and its athletes often gain unexpected success. In these Games, Norway's athletes performed outstandingly, gaining more medals than any other country overall and gaining ten gold medals in all, only one fewer than Russia. Their total medal count of twenty-six equaled the combined total of the U.S. and Canadian teams, who gained thirteen medals each. On the opening day, for example, Norwegian Johann Koss earned a gold medal in the men's 5,000-meter speed skating, setting a world record, though downhill champion Kjetil Aamodt, widely expected to win, could only attain silver. Koss went on to pick up two other golds in speed skating, again setting new world records.

In cross-country skiing, Italian Manuela Di Centa gained a medal in every one of the women's events.

Leading Medal Winners of the 1994 Winter Olympics

Country	*Gold*	*Silver*	*Bronze*	*Medals Won*
Russia	11	8	4	23
Norway	10	11	5	26
Germany	9	7	8	24
Italy	7	5	8	20
United States	6	5	2	13
South Korea	4	1	1	6
Canada	3	6	4	13
Switzerland	3	4	2	9
Austria	2	3	4	9
Sweden	2	1	0	3

She gained the gold in the toughest of the races, the 30-kilometer, in which Russian Lyubov Yegorova, who had already won three golds and a silver, was favored. Yegorova finished fifth. The famous Alberto Tomba failed in his bid to win a third successive gold for Italy in the men's slalom, having to settle for the silver.

The figure skating usually produces a number of outstanding performances. By 1994, the rules had been relaxed, in keeping with certain other sports, to allow professionals to compete, though on an amateur basis. This meant that the British dancers Jayne Torvill and Christopher Dean, previous gold medalists at Sarajevo (1984), could compete again, as could Germany's Katarina Witt. However, the judges seemed at odds with the new rules and awarded Torvill and Dean a very controversial bronze, behind two Russian dance pairs. At a later press conference, the judges admitted that they had made mistakes in the scoring. Witt also placed very poorly.

Equally controversial was the gold awarded to the young Ukrainian Oksana Baiul. Her gold was a fairy-tale ending for her, as her coach had previously left her, she had no funding, and she had been helped only by her fellow Ukrainian, former gold medalist Viktor Petrenko, and his coach. However, many felt that the gold should have gone to American Nancy Kerrigan, the more mature of the skaters. Moreover, a few months earlier, Kerrigan had been clubbed in the knee by an assailant linked to rival Tonya Harding; thus, there was a large sympathy vote for Kerrigan. The incident certainly produced the largest-ever American viewing audience for the women's figure skating events.

U.S. and Canadian Successes Besides Kerrigan's silver, Canadian Elvis Stojko won a silver medal in men's figure skating, and many felt that he, too, should have received the gold with his athletic brilliance. Canada gained gold in the women's 7.5-kilometer biathlon, breaking the European stranglehold over this event. However, in ice hockey, Canada was defeated by Sweden in the final on a penalty shoot-out.

For the United States, American speed skater Dan Jensen finally won a gold medal in the men's 1000-meter, setting a world record, having failed to gain a medal in four Olympic attempts at the 500-meter. Yet he had won at the world championships a few weeks earlier at the shorter race, breaking his own world record. In women's speed skating, Bonnie Blair won the 1000-meter, making it a U.S. double. Canada took the silver.

U.S. success began on the first day of the Games, when Tommy Moe from Alaska beat the Norwegian favorite in the downhill. Moe later gained silver in the men's super giant slalom. In the women's version, Diann Roffe won for the United States, making another double.

Impact International Olympic Committee president Juan Antonio Samaranch declared the 1994 Games the "best Winter Games ever" in his closing speech, but he also reminded his audience of the 1984 Sarajevo Games and the fact that Bosnia and Herzegovina was in the midst of a war in 1994. The peaceful and reconciling work of the Games was still needed.

Further Reading

Klausen, Arne Martin, ed. *Olympic Games as Performance and Public Event: The Case of the XVII Winter Olympic Games in Norway.* New York: Berghahn Books, 1999. A sociological series of essays on the Games.

U.S. Olympic Committee. *The Olympic Century: XXV Olympiad, Barcelona 1992, and Lillehammer 1994.* Tonawanda, N.Y.: Firefly Books, 1996. Includes the official U.S. report of the 1994 Winter Games.

Wallechinsky, David. *The Complete Book of the Winter Olympics, 1994.* New York: Little, Brown, 1993. A preview of the 1994 Winter Games.

Wukovits, John. *The Encyclopedia of the Winter Olympics.* New York: Franklin Watts, 2002. A compendium of information on all the Winter Olympics.

David Barratt

See also Hockey; Kerrigan, Nancy; Olympic Games of 1992; Olympic Games of 1996; Olympic Games of 1998; Sports; Stojko, Elvis.

■ Olympic Games of 1996

The Event The staging of the XXVI Summer Olympiad, an international athletic competition held every four years

Date July 19-August 4, 1996

Place Atlanta, Georgia

The 1996 Olympic Games demonstrated that there was tremendous fan interest in the Olympics, as two million visitors came to Atlanta and another 3.5 billion spectators watched the Games through mass media.

In September, 1990, during the ninety-sixth International Olympic Committee (IOC) session in Tokyo, it was announced that Atlanta, by a vote of fifty-one in favor and thirty-five against, would be the host city for the 1996 Olympic Games. The 1996 Games would mark the centennial anniversary of the Olympic Games. Several other cities had submitted proposals to host the Games, including Athens, Belgrade, Manchester, Melbourne, and Toronto. Many thought that Athens would get the bid since it was in Athens where the inaugural 1896 Olympic Games took place. However, in part because of the unstable economic conditions in Greece, the committee selected Atlanta. The year 1996 marked the fourth time that the Summer Games were held in the United States: 1904 in St. Louis, 1932 and 1984 in Los Angeles.

On July 19, 1996, the opening ceremony to the twenty-sixth Summer Olympics took place in the host city, Atlanta. The opening ceremony was attended by a crowd of 83,000 at the Olympic stadium. President Bill Clinton officially opened the Games, and boxing great Muhammad Ali lit the Olympic torch. The Games were presided over by IOC president Juan Antonio Samaranch.

The 1996 Games were not burdened with the political and economic strife that plagued the Games in the 1970's and 1980's, but 1996 was not free of tragedy. On July 27, a pipe bomb located at the Centennial Olympic Park exploded during a concert, killing one spectator and wounding 111.

Economics of the Games In funding the $1.8 billion Games, which were the most expensive to date, Atlanta received considerable contributions from the private sector. Corporate sponsors such as Atlanta-based companies Coca-Cola and the Cable News Network (CNN) provided considerable support. The six-year preparation for the Games included revitalizing the downtown area with hotel expansion, addition of new restaurants and businesses, and $500 million to construct new athletic facilities and improve existing facilities. More than two million visitors came to Atlanta during the Olympic Games, and an estimated 3.5 billion people watched the 1996 Olympics on television worldwide. The IOC had negotiated a television contract with the National Broadcasting Company (NBC) for $456 million to give NBC the rights to broadcast the Games. The overall economic impact on the city was $5.14 billion, and as a result, the Games made a profit. More significant was the impact of the Games in revitalizing Atlanta's downtown area and moving Atlanta forward as a modern city.

Olympic Venues More than twenty-five different athletic sites were used for competition. Many of the top spectator events of the Olympics, including the

Carl Lewis jumps just over eight meters on June 17, 1996, at the Olympic track trials in Atlanta. He later won the gold in the long jump. (AP/Wide World Photos)

opening and closing ceremonies, were located at sites located within the downtown area of Atlanta. As a result, there were numerous traffic problems, which became a major criticism of the Games. A twelve-acre Olympic Centennial Park was developed in the heart of the downtown area. The 85,000-seat Olympic Stadium was constructed for the opening and closing ceremonies and to be used for the track-and-field competitions. At the conclusion of the Olympic Games, the stadium was modified to become the home of the Atlanta Braves baseball team.

Existing facilities were used to accommodate the competition of several sports. The Atlanta-Fulton County Stadium was used for baseball competition; the Omni Coliseum, home of the National Basketball Association (NBA) Atlanta Hawks, was used for volleyball matches. The Georgia Dome, with a seating capacity of 69,000, was used for men's and women's basketball as well as artistic gymnastics and team handball. Neighboring colleges and universities provided their facilities for competition. For the first time in Olympic history, all four of the aquatics sports—diving, swimming, synchronized swimming, and water polo—were held at the same venue: the Georgia Tech Aquatic Center. In addition, Georgia Tech's Alexander Memorial Coliseum, home to Georgia Tech's basketball team, was used for boxing matches. The campus of Georgia State University was used for badminton competition. The Georgia World Congress Center was used for fencing, judo, table tennis, weight lifting, and wrestling. Although many of the competitive sports were conducted at facilities located in the downtown area, there were several competitive events that were located elsewhere. Canoe and kayak events were held on the Ocoee River in Cleveland, Tennessee. Columbus, Georgia, was the site for the softball events. Soccer matches were played in Miami, Orlando, Washington, D.C., and Birmingham, Alabama, and finals were held at the University of Georgia campus located in Athens, Georgia.

Medals A total of 10,318 athletes (3,512 women, 6,806 men) from 197 nations participated in the 1996 Olympic Games. A record-setting seventy-nine nations won medals and fifty-three won gold. Three new sports were introduced: mountain biking, softball (women), and beach volleyball. In addition, women's football (soccer) made its first Olympic appearance. Cycling professionals were permitted for the first time, and each soccer team that qualified was allowed to have three professional soccer players. A total of 1,933 medals were awarded. The top four nations with medal accumulations and gold medals won were the following: The United States won the most medals, 101, and the most gold medals, 44; Russia had a total of 63 medals and 26 gold; Germany had 65 total medals and 20 gold; China had a total of 50 medals and 16 gold. There were seventeen Olympic records in track-and-field events and two world records. In aquatics, twelve Olympic and four world records were established.

Leading Medal Winners of the 1996 Summer Olympics

Country	*Gold*	*Silver*	*Bronze*	*Medals Won*
United States	44	32	25	101
Russia	26	21	16	63
Germany	20	18	27	65
China	16	22	12	50
France	15	7	15	37
Italy	13	10	12	35
Australia	9	9	23	41
Cuba	9	8	8	25
Ukraine	9	2	12	23
South Korea	7	15	5	27

Athletic Achievements In track and field, Donovan Bailey of Canada won the gold medal in the men's 100 meters with a world record of 9.84 seconds. Michael Johnson of the United States won gold medals in the men's 200 and 400 meters, setting a new world record in the 200 meters with a time of 19.32 seconds. Gail Devers of the United States won the gold in the women's 100 meters. Marie-José Pérec received gold medals in the women's 200 and 400 meters. This was the second Olympic Games in which she won a gold medal in the 400 meters; it was the first time that a runner of either sex won the 400 meters twice. The United States won gold medals in the men's 110-meter hurdles (Allen Johnson) and the 400-meter hurdles (Derrick Adkins). Canada achieved the gold medal in the men's 4-by-100-meter relay, with the United States winning the silver. The U.S. men won the gold in the 4-by-400-meter relay. U.S. women achieved gold medals in both relays. Carl Lewis, at the age of thirty-five, won the gold medal in the long jump; he was one of only three athletes ever to win the same individual event four times. This was the last Olympics for Lewis. During his Olympic career, he compiled a total of nine gold medals, becoming one of only four Olympic athletes to achieve this feat.

Men and women swimmers from the United States won gold medals in all of the relay events, with a world record in the men's 4-by-100-meter medley. Amy Van Dyken of the United States won four gold medals in swimming; she was the first American woman to win four titles in a single Olympics. World records were established in men's 100-meter breaststroke by Belgium's Fred Deburghgraeve and in women's 100-meter breaststroke by Penelope Heyns of South Africa. Russia's Denis Pankratov set a world record in the men's 100-meter butterfly. Gary Hall, Jr., of the United States and Alexander Popov of Russia each won four medals in swimming, two gold and two silver.

In gymnastics, Alexei Nemov of Russia compiled a total of six medals, the most of any athlete during the 1996 Olympics. U.S. women won the gold medal in women's gymnastics, and Kerri Strug became the heroine as she had to endure an injury during her final event. Another U.S. athlete who had to overcome an injury during competition was wrestler Kurt Angle, who won the gold medal in the 100-kilogram weight class while suffering a fractured neck. In tennis, Andre Agassi of the United States won the gold medal in men's singles, and fellow American Lindsay Davenport won the women's gold medal.

In basketball, U.S. men's and women's teams won gold medals. On April 7, 1989, the international basketball rules were changed to allow professional basketball players to compete in the Olympic Games. In 1992 in Barcelona, the first "Dream Team" of NBA superstars represented the United States. In 1996, another Dream Team was gathered, which consisted of NBA players and was coached by Lenny Wilkins, the NBA's all-time winning coach. The team was undefeated at 8-0, and the attendance on the average was 32,263 fans when they played. In baseball, Cuba won the gold medal, Japan the silver, and the United States the bronze. The United States won the gold medal in the debut sport of softball. With players such as Mia Hamm, Brandi Chastain, and Julie Fowdy, the U.S. women's soccer team won the gold medal.

Impact The hosting of the 1996 Olympic Games proved to be an economic success for Atlanta. The Games served as a significant force to the revitalization of the downtown area in Atlanta. Corporate sponsors played a major role in contributing to the financial support for hosting the Games; however, there was criticism that the Games were overcommercialized as a result of corporate involvement.

Further Reading

Albertson, Lisa H., ed. *Athens to Atlanta: One Hundred Years of Glory.* Salt Lake City, Utah: Commemorative Publications, 1996. Provides an overview of the 1996 Olympic Games.

Guttmann, Allen. *The Olympics: A History of the Modern Games.* 2d ed. Urbana: University of Illinois Press, 2002. A look at the political and social climate of the Olympic Games.

Miller, David. *Athens to Athens: The Official History of the Olympic Games and the IOC.* Edinburgh: Mainstream, 2003. Definitive history of the Olympics, including engaging stories of competitors.

Payne, Michael. *Olympic Turnaround: How the Olympic Games Stepped Back from the Brink of Extinction to Become the World's Best Known Brand.* Westport, Conn.: Praeger, 2006. Provides a business perspective on the Olympics by the IOC's first marketing director.

Pound, Richard W. *Inside the Olympics: A Behind-the-Scenes Look at the Politics, the Scandals, and the Glory of the Games.* Etobicoke, Ont.: John Wiley & Sons Canada, 2004. A well-written inside look at the Games from a former IOC vice president.

Wallechinsky, David. *The Complete Book of the Summer Olympics.* Woodstock, N.Y.: Overlook Press, 2000. Packed with statistics and records from the 1896 Olympics through the 1990's.

Alar Lipping

See also Bailey, Donovan; Basketball; Dream Team; Hamm, Mia; Malone, Karl; Olympic Games of 1992; Olympic Games of 1994; Olympic Games of 1998; Olympic Park bombing; O'Neal, Shaquille; Salt Lake City Olympics bid scandal; Soccer; Strug, Kerri.

■ Olympic Games of 1998

The Event The staging of the XVIII Winter Olympiad, an international athletic competition held every four years
Date February 7-22, 1998
Place Nagano, Japan

The first Winter Olympics held in Japan since 1972, these Games had a record number of athletes participating. Events such as ice hockey and women's figure skating were among the most watched.

Nagano had been chosen as the site of the 1998 Games, beating bids from Aosta, Italy; Jaca, Spain; Salt Lake City, Utah; and Östersund, Sweden. Seventy-two nations took part, five more than in the 1994 Games. A record 2,176 athletes participated, 1,389 men and 787 women, about 400 more than in the previous Winter Games. Sixty-eight events took place in eight sports. Curling returned to the list of sports, having been dropped at Lillehammer in 1994, and snowboarding made its debut. There were 32,000 volunteers and 8,329 accredited media personnel.

Nagano lies two hundred miles northwest of Tokyo, across a high mountain range called "the roof of Japan." Mount Happo'one was chosen for the site of the downhill races. The Japanese built a new bullet train track to make the city more accessible and added new roads, the total investment amounting to $10 billion. A new stadium was built in the shape of a cherry blossom.

The Games were officially opened by Emperor Akihito, with the Olympic Oath being taken by Nordic skier Kenji Ogiwara and the Official Oath by figure skater Junko Hiramatsu. The Olympic torch was lit by figure skater Midori Ito. There was also a purification ceremony performed by Japan's leading sumo wrestler, Akebono. As in the Lillehammer Games, the opening ceremony focused on mythic and folkloric themes.

Outstanding Achievements Norwegian cross-country skier Björn Daehlie achieved golds in the 10-kilometer and the 50-kilometer race, then gained another gold in the team event. He also gained a silver in the combined pursuit event, bringing his total number of Olympic medals to twelve, eight of which were gold, and making him the most successful Nordic skier in Olympic history.

In the downhill, the Austrian favorite, Hermann Maier, had a spectacular crash on a very difficult course. The race had been postponed several times because of snowstorms. However, Maier recovered to win both the super giant slalom and the giant slalom. Germany's Katja Seizinger was one of the outstanding athletes, successfully defending her gold medal in the women's downhill. Another was the Italy's Deborah Compagnoni, who won her third Olympic gold in the giant slalom and super giant slalom events.

Though the host country usually has some advantage over its competition, this was not the case for Masahiko Harada. Widely expected to win the ski-jumping competition, he made a poor second jump and lost all medal chances. This was a repeat of a similar loss at Lillehammer. However, Harada did win bronze in the new large-hill ski jump, which his compatriot Kazuyoshi Funaki won. Both skiers took part in the team event, gaining another gold for Japan. Japan also won the men's 500-meter speed skating.

The country that made a name for itself in speed skating was the Netherlands. The Dutch claimed that new technology and new clothing gave them a one-third-second advantage per lap. Results proved they were right, for example in the men's 1000-meter and 10,000-meter, in which they made a clean sweep of all the medals.

Leading Medal Winners of the 1998 Winter Olympics

Country	*Gold*	*Silver*	*Bronze*	*Medals Won*
Germany	12	9	8	29
Norway	10	10	5	25
Russia	9	6	3	18
Canada	6	5	4	15
United States	6	3	4	13
Netherlands	5	4	2	11
Japan	5	1	4	10
Austria	3	5	9	17
South Korea	3	1	2	6
Italy	2	6	2	10

U.S. and Canadian Successes For the first time, ice hockey allowed professionals to participate in the Olympics. Both Team USA and Team Canada were made up of National Hockey League (NHL) professionals, and one of the teams was expected to win. However, Canada was eliminated during the semifinals, and the United States lost to a brilliant team from the Czech Republic, many of whose players were also from the NHL. In women's ice hockey, the United States beat Canada in the final game.

In figure skating, U.S. success was concentrated in the women's event, where Michelle Kwan went head-to-head with fifteen-year-old Tara Lipinsky. Many felt that Kwan was unlucky to have to skate first while Lipinsky skated last, which may have tipped the scales in Lipinsky's favor. She thus became the youngest figure skater in Olympic history to win a gold medal. In men's figure skating, Russian Ilia Kulik just edged out Elvis Stojko of Canada and Todd Eldredge of the United States for the gold.

Canadian snowboarder Ross Rebagliati won the gold in the men's giant slalom, had it denied to him by failing a drug test, then had it reinstated on appeal. Other Canadian victories were in the women's curling event, in which Denmark was defeated in the final. The men's team, however, lost to Switzerland in the final. Catriona LeMay Doan won the 500-meter speed skating, breaking the Olympic record. In the bobsleigh, Canadian Pierre Lueders shared the gold with Italy, the first time a gold had been shared in the event.

For the United States, Picabo Street won the women's super giant slalom, quite unexpectedly beating the Europeans. She then confirmed her skills by winning the gold medal in downhill. The United States won golds in both the men's and the women's aerial freestyle skiing.

Impact The most successful country in the unofficial medals table was Germany, with twelve gold medals and twenty-nine total, even though the Germans did not have any of the most successful athletes. This showed the broad range of skills the country still possessed even after the dissolution of the communist East German sports machine. Canada did very well, as did the Netherlands.

The Columbia Broadcasting System (CBS) alone paid $375 million for a major share of the television rights to the Olympics, but the huge audience generated by the ice hockey events and the women's figure skating justified the scale of such expenditure and ensured the continued economic viability of the Games.

Further Reading

International Olympic Committee. *The Official Olympic Games Companion: The Complete Guide to the Olympic Games, 1998.* Drexel Hill, Pa.: Brassey's, 1997. The official pre-Games guide.

Wallechinsky, David. *The Complete Book of the Winter Olympics, 1998.* New York: Little, Brown, 1997. One of a series of pre-Games guides.

Wukovits, John. *The Encyclopedia of the Winter Olympics.* New York: Franklin Watts, 2002. A full account of all the Winter Games.

David Barratt

See also Hockey; Olympic Games of 1992; Olympic Games of 1994; Olympic Games of 1996; Salt Lake City Olympics bid scandal; Sports; Stojko, Elvis.

■ Olympic Park bombing

The Event A terrorist bombing at the 1996 Summer Olympics kills one and injures 111
Date July 27, 1996
Place Atlanta, Georgia

The Centennial Olympic Park bombing, a terrorist act committed by Eric Robert Rudolph, shocked America and increased concern about domestic terrorism and security.

In the early morning of July 27, 1996, about fifty thousand people were gathered at AT&T's Global Village in Atlanta to hear the band Jack Mack and the Heart Attack when an explosion occurred. Shortly before the explosion, a backpack placed underneath a bench was discovered by thirty-three-year-old security guard Richard Jewell, who warned authorities and also called 911 before he and fellow officers began clearing the area for federal explosives experts from the Bomb Management Center at Dobbins Air Reserve Base. Although attempts were made to evacuate the noisy crowd, the bomb, made up of three separate pipe bombs surrounded by nails, exploded and killed a forty-four-year-old Georgia woman, Alice Hawthorne. A Turkish cameraman, Melih Uzunyol, suffered a fatal heart attack as he ran to capture the action.

Centennial Olympic Park in Atlanta, Georgia, after an explosion during the 1996 Summer Olympics killed one person and injured more than one hundred people. (AP/Wide World Photos)

The Aftermath and Subsequent Bombings The nation was horrified, and the White House vowed to bring those responsible to justice. Although officials considered closing down the Olympic Games, the decision was made to allow the athletes to compete. Desperate to find the culprit, officials looked in the wrong direction. *The Atlanta Journal-Constitution* ran a story saying that security guard Richard Jewell, who had earlier been regarded as a hero, was being investigated. Although Jewell was never arrested, he suffered greatly at the hands of the media, and two of the victims even brought lawsuits against him. Three months later, he was cleared and issued a public apology by Attorney General Janet Reno. Jewell said publicly: "I am not the Olympic Park bomber. I am a man who has lived eighty-eight days afraid of being arrested for a crime I did not commit." Before his death in 2007, he settled libel lawsuits against various television networks and a former employer.

While Jewell was wrongfully accused in the bombing case, the real culprit, Eric Rudolph, was free. On January 16, 1997, a bomb exploded at the Atlanta Northside Family Planning Clinic, an abortion clinic, and another bomb exploded on February 21 at the Otherside Lounge, a lesbian nightclub in northeast Atlanta. Both bombs were similar in design to the Olympic Park bomb. On January 29, 1998, another bomb exploded at the New Woman, All Women Health Care Clinic, an abortion clinic in Birmingham, Alabama, which resulted in the death of police officer Robert Sanderson but also provided a partial license plate number that identified thirty-year-old Rudolph.

Despite a $1 million reward for his arrest, Rudolph managed to escape capture in the heavily wooded hill country of the North Carolina Appalachian Mountains for five years. Finally, on May 31, 2003, Rudolph was arrested behind a Save-A-Lot grocery store in Murphy, North Carolina.

Federal grand juries in Atlanta and Birmingham had indicted Rudolph on November 15, 2000. In an effort to avoid the death penalty, he pleaded guilty in 2005 to the Olympic Park bombing and the three other bombings, claiming his purpose in the 1996 bombing was to punish the government for legalizing abortion and to ensure that the canceled Olympic Games would lose money. On August 22, 2005, Rudolph was sentenced to three concurrent life sentences without the possibility of parole. At his sentencing, he apologized to the Olympic Park bombing victims and their families and stated that he was angry at the government, not them. He was sent to the supermax federal prison in Florence, Colorado. At Centennial Olympic Park, the Quilt of Remembrance stone mosaic memorializes the bombing victims.

Impact Before the 1996 Summer Olympic Games commenced, chief organizer Billy Payne stated that "the safest place on this wonderful planet will be Atlanta, Georgia, during the time of our Games." However, the occasion that was to bring people together in international fellowship was marred by an act of terrorism. While the Olympic Park bombing did not lead to the cancellation of the Games, government officials became increasingly concerned about terrorism on U.S. soil. The bombing also led to increased domestic surveillance and heightened security at places such as shopping malls, parks, and airports. At the closing ceremonies, the president of the International Olympic Committee, Juan Antonio Samaranch, called the Atlanta Games "most exceptional"—instead of the customary declaration at the end of each Olympics, "the best Olympic Games ever"—out of respect for the bombing victims.

Further Reading

Schuster, Henry, and Charles Stone. *Hunting Eric Rudolph.* New York: Berkley, 2005. Account of the five-year hunt for the man behind the 1996 Atlanta Olympic Park bombing by Schuster, a CNN senior producer, and Stone, the former head of the Georgia Bureau of Investigation Anti-Terrorist Force.

Turchie, Terry D., and Kathleen M. Puckett. *Hunting the American Terrorist: The FBI's War on Homegrown Terror.* Palisades, N.Y.: History Publishing Company, 2007. Focuses primarily on the cases of Theodore Kaczynski (Unabomber), Timothy McVeigh (Oklahoma City bomber), and Eric Rudolph.

Vollers, Maryanne. *Lone Wolf: Eric Rudolph—Murder, Myth, and the Pursuit of an American Outlaw.* New York: HarperCollins, 2006. The author of *Ghosts of Mississippi* (1995) was the only journalist with whom Rudolph corresponded. The book attempts to understand the mind of the Olympic Park bomber.

M. Casey Diana

See also Abortion; Clinton, Bill; Homosexuality and gay rights; Oklahoma City bombing; Olympic Games of 1996; Reno, Janet; Terrorism; Unabomber capture; World Trade Center bombing.

■ Ondaatje, Michael

Identification Canadian novelist and poet
Born September 12, 1943; Colombo, Ceylon (now Sri Lanka)

During the 1990's, Ondaatje published the poetry collection The Cinnamon Peeler *(1991) and the novel* The English Patient *(1992), for which he is now most celebrated.*

Michael Ondaatje was born to an English mother and a Burgher (European-native) father in Ceylon. The family split because of his father's alcoholism, and young Michael and his mother moved to England in 1954, then to Canada in 1962. There he earned a bachelor's degree at the University of Toronto in 1965 and a master's degree at Queen's University in 1967. He began teaching at the University of Western Ontario, and then moved to his current post at Glendon College, York University, in 1971. Ondaatje wrote amusingly about his childhood in *Running in the Family* (1982), but he became known principally as a poet.

The English Patient takes place in the waning days of World War II, bringing together two Canadians, a nurse and a soldier; an Indian sapper from the British army; and a mysterious, badly burned man recovering in a deserted Italian villa. The characters ruminate on their past as they endure the tension of their isolation and uncertainty about the postwar world. (Interestingly, the two Canadian characters were introduced in Ondaatje's 1987 novel, *In the Skin of a Lion.*) *The English Patient* was a worldwide best seller and won the Booker Prize, the Canada-Australia Prize, and the Canadian Governor General's Award.

In 1996, *The English Patient* was released as a feature film, with the screenplay adapted by director Anthony Minghella. The film highlighted the romance between a beautiful Englishwoman and the Hungarian archaeologist who becomes "the English patient." The young nurse was prominently featured—indeed, Juliette Binoche won the Oscar for Best Supporting Actress for the role—but the Indian sapper was reduced to a minor character. Ondaatje, however, pronounced himself satisfied with the changes represented in the cinematic version. The film earned nine Academy Awards, two Golden Globes, and six BAFTAs from the British Academy of Film and Television Arts. It won Best Picture in each competition.

Ondaatje was named an Officer of the Order of Canada in 1988. The citation hailed his "extraordinarily visual" writing and his "interest in film as a complement to literature."

Impact Ondaatje is the author of more than a dozen books of poetry, several novels, a memoir, and numerous films, anthologies, and works of criticism. *The English Patient* brought him worldwide acclaim that solidified his reputation as a fiction writer, and his subsequent novels have been well received. *Anil's Ghost* (2000) returned to Sri Lanka to investigate the brutal guerrilla war between the government and the Tamil Tigers.

Further Reading

Barbour, Douglas. *Michael Ondaatje.* New York: Twayne, 1993.

Jewinski, Ed. *Michael Ondaatje: Express Yourself Beautifully.* Toronto: ECW Press, 1994.

Jan Hall

See also Academy Awards; Film in the United States; Literature in Canada; Poetry.

■ O'Neal, Shaquille

Identification Professional basketball player
Born March 6, 1972; Newark, New Jersey

During the 1990's, O'Neal was a dominant force on the basketball court and became a media personality through film and music.

Shaquille O'Neal starred in basketball at Robert G. Cole High School in San Antonio, Texas, from 1987 to 1989. Louisiana State University (LSU) won the recruiting battle for the seven-foot, one-inch, 301-pound center's services. Coach Dale Brown was impressed with O'Neal's tremendous work ethic, quickness, and tenacious rebounding. As an LSU freshman in 1990, O'Neal led the Southeastern Conference (SEC) in rebounds. He earned College Player of the Year honors and made consensus All-American in 1991. Besides pacing the nation in rebounds, O'Neal became the first player to lead the SEC in scoring, rebounding, field-goal percentage, and blocked shots in the same season. The 20-10 Tigers shared the SEC crown. A repeat All-American as a junior in 1992, O'Neal ranked first in blocked shots and second in rebounds and scoring nationally. During his three-year LSU career, O'Neal scored 1,941 points (21.6-point average), converted 61 percent of his field goals, made 1,217 rebounds (13.5 average), and blocked 412 shots (4.6 average) in 90 games. He made three National Collegiate Athletic Association (NCAA) tournament appearances and trails only David Robinson in NCAA career blocked shots average.

The Orlando Magic selected O'Neal as the first overall pick in the 1992 National Basketball Association (NBA) draft. O'Neal, who played for Orlando from 1992 to 1996, garnered NBA Rookie of the Year and All-Rookie First Team honors and finished second in rebounding and blocked shots in 1993. He collected a career-best 28 rebounds and 15 blocked shots against the New Jersey Nets on November 20, 1993. Besides lifting the Magic to the NBA Playoffs for the first time in the franchise's history in 1994, he led the NBA in field-goal percentage and ranked second in points and rebounds. The following season, O'Neal topped the NBA in scoring with 2,315 points (29.3-point average). Orlando captured the Atlantic Division and reached the NBA Finals. O'Neal holds Orlando career records for rebounds (3,691) and blocked shots (824).

In 1996, O'Neal made the NBA's Fiftieth Anniversary All-Time Team and starred on the gold-medal-winning U.S. Olympic basketball team, dubbed the "Dream Team." After signing with the Los Angeles Lakers in July, 1996, O'Neal attained All-NBA First Team accolades in 1998 and led the NBA in scoring with 1,289 points (26.3-point average) in 1999.

Impact O'Neal took advantage of his larger-than-life size and charismatic personality to expand into music and films during the decade. He released the rap albums *Shaq Diesel* (1993), *Shaq-Fu: Da Return* (1994), *You Can't Stop the Reign* (1996), and *Respect* (1998) and starred in a handful of films, including *Blue Chips* (1994), *Kazaam* (1996), and *Steel* (1997).

Subsequent Events O'Neal enjoyed his most productive years with the Lakers under coach Phil Jackson, winning three consecutive NBA championships from 2000 through 2002. In 2000, O'Neal led the NBA in scoring with 2,344 points (a career-high 29.7-point average) and was chosen as the regular-season and NBA Finals Most Valuable Player. He posted a career-high 61 points against the Los Angeles Clippers on March 6. O'Neal was traded to the Miami Heat in July, 2004, and helped Miami capture the 2006 NBA title. He was traded again, this time to the Phoenix Suns, in 2008.

Further Reading

Nelson, Murry R. *Shaquille O'Neal: A Biography.* Westport, Conn.: Greenwood Press, 2007.

O'Neal, Shaquille. *Shaq Talks Back.* New York: St. Martin's Press, 2001.

O'Neal, Shaquille, with Jack McCallum. *Shaq Attaq!* New York: Hyperion, 1993.

David L. Porter

See also African Americans; Barkley, Charles; Basketball; Dream Team; Film in the United States; Hip-hop and rap music; Johnson, Magic; Jordan, Michael; Malone, Karl; Olympic Games of 1996; Sports.

■ O'Reilly, Bill

Identification Broadcast journalist and political commentator

Born September 10, 1949; New York, New York

A prominent broadcast journalist during the 1990's, O'Reilly launched the popular but controversial cable news program The O'Reilly Factor *on the Fox News Channel.*

Bill O'Reilly earned a bachelor's degree in history from Marist College in 1971 and a master's degree in broadcast journalism from Boston University in 1976. O'Reilly then spent the next two decades working as a news reporter and/or anchor at numerous television news stations across the United States, including WNEP-TV in Scranton, Pennsylvania, and KATU-TV in Portland, Oregon. Following a three-year stint as a news correspondent for *ABC World News Tonight,* O'Reilly was hired in 1989 by King World Productions as a correspondent for the newly created syndicated program *Inside Edition.* The program, which competed with other tabloid news programs such as *Hard Copy* and *A Current Affair,* included a mix of crime stories, investigative news stories, and celebrity reporting. Shortly after the program's inception, O'Reilly replaced the show's original anchor, David Frost.

Bill O'Reilly, seen here in 1993, hosted the tabloid news show Inside Edition *from 1989 to 1995.* (Hulton Archive/Getty Images)

O'Reilly was popular with television audiences during the 1990's, and his reports about working-class issues brought a legitimacy to the television show and solidified his professional status as a news anchor. In 1995, he left the television show to attend the Kennedy School of Government at Harvard University, where he earned his master's degree in public administration. In 1996, Roger Ailes, the chief executive officer of the fledgling Fox News Channel, hired O'Reilly to produce and host his own television show, *The O'Reilly Report.* It premiered on October 7, 1996, and his first guest was General Barry McCaffrey, director of the Office of National Drug Control Policy. Shortly after the show debuted, its name was changed to *The O'Reilly Factor.* Maintaining complete creative control of the hour-long news program, O'Reilly declared his show to be the "no spin zone," where news reports contained just the facts without any political spin. Both liberal and conservative guests were invited to his program in an attempt to fairly cover the issues. His confrontational interview style and strong political commentary also made him popular with viewers and set his show apart from competing news programs, such as the Cable News Network's (CNN) *Larry King Live.* In 1998, O'Reilly published his first book, *Those Who Trespass,* a fictional story about the world of broadcast journalism.

Impact Through diligence and hard work, Bill O'Reilly became a leading news anchor during the 1990's. His strong opinions and aggressive interviewing style, while controversial, made him popular with the American public. With the launch of *The O'Reilly Factor* in 1996, he helped change the way news was delivered to American television audiences.

Further Reading

Kitman, Marvin. *The Man Who Would Not Shut Up: The Rise of Bill O'Reilly.* New York: St. Martin's Press, 2007.

O'Reilly, Bill. *The O'Reilly Factor: The Good, the Bad, and the Completely Ridiculous in American Life.* New York: Broadway Books, 2000.

_______. *The No Spin Zone: Confrontations with the Powerful and Famous in America.* New York: Broadway Books, 2001.

Bernadette Zbicki Heiney

See also Cable television; Conservatism in U.S. politics; Journalism; Liberalism in U.S. politics; Limbaugh, Rush; Talk radio; Television.

■ Organic food movement

Definition Agricultural and consumer movement

The organic food movement of the 1990's affected agriculture and grocery stores and launched a rapidly expanding industry.

The environmental movement of the 1960's and 1970's laid the foundation for the increased support for the organic food movement in the 1990's. Following grassroots advocacy for organic standards in the 1980's, the U.S. government passed the Organic Foods Production Act (OFPA), Title XXI of the Food, Agriculture, Conservation, and Trade Act of 1990. The purpose of the OFPA was to establish national standards for the marketing of certain agricultural products as organic; to assure consumers of a consistent organic standard; and to facilitate interstate commerce in organically produced food. The act established standards for organic products and criteria for certifying a farm or part of a farm as organic.

During the 1990's, the organic food industry experienced sustained growth. Major chains such as Whole Foods Market and Wild Oats Markets grew rapidly and incorporated smaller chains and independent organic grocery stores. These large organic grocery chains helped to bring the prices of organic food down, although it remained more expensive than conventional food in part because of increased production costs in some areas and higher expenses due to smaller-scale production, and because of the costs associated with governmental certification. These large chains marketed organic food to consumers as a moral and enjoyable alternative to conventionally grown food products.

Community-Supported Agriculture Organic gardening and community-supported agriculture (CSA) increased in popularity during the 1990's. Home gardeners used organic techniques to grow fruits and vegetables as well as ornamentals. Home gardeners and some small organic farmers also focused on growing heirloom varieties.

Community-supported agriculture was a way for small farmers to have a successful closed market. In a

National Standards for Organic Certification

The U.S. Department of Agriculture's National Organic Program published a fact sheet in October, 2002, that explains the national standards for the certification of organic products laid out in the 1990 Organic Foods Production Act:

The national organic standards address the methods, practices, and substances used in producing and handling crops, livestock, and processed agricultural products. The requirements apply to the way the product is created, not to measurable properties of the product itself. Although specific practices and materials used by organic operations may vary, the standards require every aspect of organic production and handling to comply with the provisions of the Organic Foods Production Act (OFPA). Organically produced food cannot be produced using excluded methods, sewage sludge, or ionizing radiation.

Crop standards

The organic crop production standards say that:

> Land will have no prohibited substances applied to it for at least 3 years before the harvest of an organic crop. The use of genetic engineering (included in excluded methods), ionizing radiation and sewage sludge is prohibited. Soil fertility and crop nutrients will be managed through tillage and cultivation practices, crop rotations, and cover crops, supplemented with animal and crop waste materials and allowed synthetic materials.
>
> Preference will be given to the use of organic seeds and other planting stock, but a farmer may use non-organic seeds and planting stock under specified conditions. Crop pests, weeds, and diseases will be controlled primarily through management practices including physical, mechanical, and biological controls. When these practices are not sufficient, a biological, botanical, or synthetic substance approved for use on the National List may be used.

Livestock standards

These standards apply to animals used for meat, milk, eggs, and other animal products represented as organically produced.

The livestock standards say that:

> Animals for slaughter must be raised under organic management from the last third of gestation, or no later than the second day of life for poultry. Producers are required to feed livestock agricultural feed products that are 100 percent organic, but may also provide allowed vitamin and mineral supplements. Producers may convert an entire, distinct dairy herd to organic production by providing 80 percent organically produced feed for 9 months, followed by 3 months of 100 percent organically produced feed. Organically raised animals may not be given hormones to promote growth, or antibiotics for any reason. Preventive management practices, including the use of vaccines, will be used to keep animals healthy. Producers are prohibited from withholding treatment from a sick or injured animal; however, animals treated with a prohibited medication may not be sold as organic. All organically raised animals must have access to the outdoors, including access to pasture for ruminants. They may be temporarily confined only for reasons of health, safety, the animal's stage of production, or to protect soil or water quality.

CSA system, consumers subscribed to a weekly share of food products and accepted whatever was seasonal. Some CSA farms encouraged subscribers to work on the farm in exchange for part of membership costs. The system reduced risk to the farmer and provided consumers with a way to obtain fresh, local food. Not all CSA farms were organic, but many were, and CSA systems were closely tied to the local food movement, founded on similar principles.

Criticism and Controversy Consumers wanted organic food for a variety of reasons. These included concerns about pesticide residues on conventionally grown plants and artificial hormones given to livestock; the belief that organic food tastes better; and a desire to lessen environmental impact. All of these reasons have been criticized as incorrect or unfounded, but evidence remains inconclusive.

The organic food movement has been criticized

for being antitechnological and unsustainable. Some studies have shown organic farming to result in lower yield and higher impact than conventional farming; others have shown comparable or higher yields for organic techniques in certain parts of the world. Critics argue that conventional techniques produce more food per acre and have lower impact because they preserve more nonagricultural land; proponents of organic agriculture claim that small farms are more efficient overall, although they do not produce large volumes of single crops the way monoculture farms do.

Critics have also claimed that organic food is too expensive for low-income families and poorer countries and thus a luxury available only to the elite. Others contend that the cost of synthetic fertilizers and pesticides is prohibitively expensive to poorer countries and that application of organic farming methods would improve crop yield. The many variables involved in measuring agricultural yield make it difficult to determine definitively the effectiveness of organic farming as compared to conventional methods.

Impact The organic food movement of the 1990's changed how many Americans viewed food and widely affected agricultural and marketing practices. The enormous success of organic food chains like Whole Foods Market and Wild Oats Markets proved that organic food could be profitable to retailers and producers as well as appealing to the general public.

The impact of the growth in the organic food industry reverberated throughout the decade and continued to arouse public debate in the twenty-first century. The increased popularity of organic agriculture brought up many issues, such as the relative impacts of different agricultural methods on the environment; food safety and public health; whether industrial organic agriculture is in keeping with the ideals of the organic food movement; and socioeconomic topics.

Further Reading

DeGregori, Thomas R. *Origins of the Organic Agriculture Debate.* Ames, Iowa: Blackwell, 2004. DeGregori discusses two historically contrasting views, the technological view that led to modern agriculture and the "vitalist" view that supports organic agriculture. The author is a proponent of responsible use of technology and argues that resources are not finite but rather created by technology.

Fromartz, Samuel. *Organic Inc.: Natural Foods and How They Grew.* Orlando, Fla.: Harcourt, 2006. Addresses the history of the organic movement and its connections to industry, assessing the compromises the movement has made to reach mainstream consumers.

Groh, Trauger, and Steven McFadden. *Farms of Tomorrow Revisited: Community Supported Farms, Farm Supported Communities.* Junction City, Oreg.: BioDynamic Farming and Gardening Association, 1998. Provides an introduction to, history of, and argument for community-supported agriculture.

Kristiansen, Paul, Acram Taji, and John Reganold. *Organic Agriculture: A Global Perspective.* Ithaca, N.Y.: Cornell University Press, 2006. The authors critically examine the successes and limitations of the organic agriculture movement worldwide, including in the United States.

Lipson, Elaine Marie. *The Organic Foods Sourcebook.* Chicago: Contemporary Books, 2001. Covers the history of the organic food movement, profiles influential people and companies, and provides a list of resources.

Norberg-Hodge, Helena, Todd Merrifield, and Steven Gorelick. *Bringing the Food Economy Home: Local Alternatives to Global Agribusiness.* London: Zed Books, 2002. Examines global food issues from multiple angles in an argument for local food.

Melissa A. Barton

See also Agriculture in Canada; Agriculture in the United States; Earth Day 1990; Food trends; Genetically modified foods; Global warming debate; Kyoto Protocol; Science and technology.

■ Outsourcing

Definition The business practice of subcontracting labor to external sources for greater efficiency or cost saving

During the 1990's, outsourcing rapidly expanded beyond manufacturing and clerical functions to include business and knowledge processes, resulting in the offshoring of white-collar jobs. This trend not only helped American and

European corporations to become more efficient and profitable but also globalized and integrated the world economy in unprecedented ways.

Although outsourcing has long existed prior to the 1990's, until the late 1980's most of the outsourcing work by corporations based in the United States, Canada, or Europe occurred domestically. Toward the end of the 1980's and early 1990's, outsourcing turned to offshoring technology-assisted white-collar jobs, qualitatively changing the nature of business and the structure of the world economy.

Contributing Factors Outsourcing through offshoring in the 1990's was triggered by a coincidence of several economic and political changes that occurred worldwide. The initial impetus for outsourcing information technology (IT) jobs in the late 1980's, most of which went to India, was the millennium bug crisis, also known as the year 2000 problem (Y2K). Corporations could not cope with the Y2K compliance work without external assistance. Also, the early 1990's witnessed a number of global economic and political changes that facilitated outsourcing. They included the collapse of communism in the former Soviet Union and the liberalization of socialist economies in India and Eastern Europe; China's transition to market capitalism; the explosive growth of information technology; the rise of dot-com companies, spurring global entrepreneurship; and the availability of a large, well-trained, and inexpensive workforce in developing nations.

In addition to wanting to take advantage of inexpensive foreign labor, global companies turned to outsourcing in order to keep abreast of the best practices in areas outside their core competencies and functions, thereby leveraging their profit-making capacity and improving customer service. As a result, during the 1990's outsourcing quickly grew into business process outsourcing (BPO), the subcontracting of many back-office business functions that included billing, accounting, finance, payroll, human resources, procurement, accounts payable, accounts receivable, collections, customer service, and call center operations. Because some of these operations required original research and development as well as knowledge management, some have used the term "knowledge process outsourcing" (KPO) to describe some aspects of the process. The nations that served as major destinations for outsourcing in the 1990's included India, China, the Philippines, Vietnam, Dubai, Hungary, Romania, Poland, and Mexico, where skilled technical labor was available at relatively cheaper rates. Among them, India soon emerged as the leader, thanks to its large pool of highly educated, English-speaking engineers, technicians, and entrepreneurs.

Impact The success of outsourcing convinced global companies that virtually every business process could be outsourced in order to create value for customers, to increase market share, and to achieve innovation. For instance, International Business Machines (IBM), which was on the verge of collapse in the early 1990's, reversed its decline as a result of outsourcing many of its operations to India, where it also found new markets. With its substantial investment and a large Indian workforce, IBM launched its expansion to other developing countries, including China, Brazil, and Russia. Through outsourcing, companies also learned that their success depended on pursuing their core competencies and specializations while shifting the burden of routine management tasks to others who specialize in such operations. Some companies outsourced a single business process such as customer service, while others outsourced multiple processes that included human resources, finance, and accounting. During the 1990's, the typically outsourced BPO was human resources.

Subsequent Events Since the 1990's, outsourcing has affected areas beyond businesses. For instance, higher education has recognized the need for internationalization in areas such as business, engineering, information technology, and cultural studies. As companies move their operations from country to country seeking greater value and profitability, there is pressure on skilled and white-collar professions in the United States and Europe to innovate. Outsourcing has spurred such innovation not only in client countries but also in the provider countries such as India and China.

The success of outsourcing through offshoring has caused controversy. Concerns have been raised about the loss of jobs in the United States and Europe as companies began to ship jobs abroad. Some have questioned the wisdom of sharing technology and equipment with countries such as India and China that are potential competitors to the United States and Europe. Others are concerned about the security and privacy of data, intellectual property rights, potential political instability, and the possibility of losing control over core functions and operations. Some of these concerns appeared to be unfounded. For instance, in the 1990's, the loss of IT-related jobs in the United States due to outsourcing was approximately one percent, and although that percentage has since grown modestly, IT employment has also grown robustly in the United States, suggesting that outsourcing has not had a significant negative impact on IT job growth in the United States.

Outsourcing has created for global companies a workforce that "never stops working": At every hour of the day or night, some people somewhere in the world are working for them, contributing to their unprecedented growth productivity. There has emerged a corporate mindset that work should flow to places where products and services can be delivered most efficiently. Perhaps more than any other factor in recent decades, the new turn in the outsourcing trend that began in the 1990's has compelled the world economy to become more interdependent and integrated.

Further Reading

Brown, Douglas, and Scott Wilson. *The Black Book of Outsourcing: How to Manage the Changes, Challenges, and Opportunities.* Hoboken, N.J.: John Wiley & Sons, 2005. Excellent overview of the outsourcing process, including practical advice for managers interested in outsourcing.

Halvey, John K., and Barbara M. Melby. *Business Process Outsourcing: Process, Strategies, and Contracts.* 2d ed. Hoboken, N.J.: John Wiley & Sons, 2007. A useful guide to the world of BPO, the emerging market, and choosing providers.

Power, Mark J., Kevin Desouza, and Carlo Bonifazi. *Outsourcing Handbook: How to Implement a Successful Outsourcing Process.* Philadelphia: Kogan Page, 2006. Offers tools to assess the potential for outsourcing success as well as practical strategies to avoid common mistakes.

Robinson, Marcia, and Ravi Kalakota. *Offshore Outsourcing: Business Models, ROI, and Best Practices.* Alpharetta, Ga.: Mivar Press, 2005. Clear introduction to offshoring business processes, using examples of successful companies.

Mathew J. Kanjirathinkal

See also Business and the economy in Canada; Business and the economy in the United States; China and the United States; Computers; Dot-coms; Downsizing and restructuring; Employment in Canada; Employment in the United States; Health care; Income and wages in Canada; Income and wages in the United States; Mexico and the United States; Science and technology.

■ Palahniuk, Chuck

Identification American author
Born February 21, 1962; Pasco, Washington

Palahniuk gained recognition and a cult following with the publication and film adaptation of Fight Club *(1996) in the 1990's.*

Chuck Palahniuk's *Fight Club*, published in 1996, won both the 1997 Pacific Northwest Booksellers Association Award and the 1997 Oregon Book Award for Best Novel. However, *Fight Club*'s and Palahniuk's fame would truly skyrocket after the release of David Fincher's 1999 film adaptation starring Brad Pitt and Edward Norton. *Fight Club* struck a chord with audiences for its critique of consumerism and the state of masculinity in America and for its highly realistic depiction of violence, for which it was sometimes criticized. "Fight Club" refers to a network of secret, underground fighting rings that serve as radical psychotherapy for the disconnected males of Palahniuk's world.

Palahniuk led a varied life before becoming a published author, attending the University of Oregon and then working as a journalist for a local paper after graduation. Unsatisfied with journalism, Palahniuk worked as a diesel mechanic and technical writer and volunteered to help care for terminally ill patients, bringing them to and from the type of support group meetings that figure heavily in *Fight Club*. In his mid-thirties, Palahniuk began attending fiction-writing workshops. The first novel he submitted for publication was *Invisible Monsters*, which was rejected by publishers as too disturbing. He wrote *Fight Club* next, intending to shock the publishers even more, but it was accepted for publication.

After *Fight Club*, Palahniuk penned *Survivor*, published in February, 1999, which relates the story of Tender Branson, the last member of a suicide cult, and deals with themes such as identity, free will, commercialism, consumerism, and nihilism, themes that recur in much of Palahniuk's work. In September of 1999, *Invisible Monsters* was finally published. Perhaps Palahniuk's most disturbing work to hit readers up to that point, it tells the story of Brandy Alexander's search for a new future. She is a formerly beautiful, now disfigured young model who has lost the ability to speak. Palahniuk revisits familiar themes in *Invisible Monsters*, but under more shocking circumstances.

Palahniuk is sometimes criticized for the absurdity of the situations and characters in his novels; critics allege that he is interested in nothing more than shock value and that his characters are treated ironically and humorously rather than with true humanity. Palahniuk has refuted this viewpoint.

Impact Chuck Palahniuk's fiction pushed the boundaries of popular fiction even in a decade when everything seemed acceptable, and he captured the angst of disillusioned young men with his vision of *Fight Club*. His unconventional rise to success as a writer influenced many other writers, and his Web site has maintained a large community of writers since its inception in 1999.

Further Reading

Grayson, Eric M., ed. "Special Issue: The Fiction of Chuck Palahniuk." *Stirrings Still: The International Journal of Existential Literature* 2, no. 2 (Fall/Winter, 2005).

Palahniuk, Chuck. *Fight Club*. New York: W. W. Norton, 1996.

Alan Haslam

See also Film in the United States; Literature in the United States; Pitt, Brad.

■ Paltrow, Gwyneth

Identification American actor
Born September 27, 1972; Los Angeles, California

Although her first film role was not until 1991, by the end of the decade Paltrow had won an Academy Award for Best Actress, cementing her reputation as one of the most talented young actors of her generation.

Gwyneth Paltrow assumed from a young age that she would be an actor, playing several small roles as a child at the Williamstown Theatre Festival alongside her parents, director Bruce Paltrow and actor Blythe Danner. In 1991, Paltrow enrolled at the University of California at Santa Barbara, but her performance in the play *Picnic* convinced her parents that she should pursue acting full time. That same year, she landed a small role as the young Wendy in Steven Spielberg's *Hook,* followed by parts in *Malice* (1993) and *Flesh and Bone* (1993).

Although Paltrow was given increasingly larger parts in several films during the mid-1990's, including *Seven* (1995) with Brad Pitt, her talent was not widely recognized until she won the coveted title role in *Emma* (1996), a remake of the classic Jane Austen novel. Paltrow's performance as the incurable matchmaker was praised for her comedic timing and authentic British accent, and she followed that film's success with no fewer than five movies released in 1998: *Sliding Doors, Great Expectations, Hush, A Perfect Murder,* and *Shakespeare in Love.*

In *Shakespeare in Love,* perhaps best described as period romantic comedy, Paltrow portrayed Viola de Lesseps, a fictional noblewoman whose star-crossed romance with William Shakespeare inspires him to write the play *Romeo and Juliet* (pr. c. 1595-1596). *Shakespeare in Love* won the Academy Award for Best Picture, and Paltrow's luminous performance earned her both an Academy Award and a Golden Globe. In the summer of 1999, she returned triumphantly to the Williamstown Theatre Festival, where she earned rave reviews as Rosalind in Shakespeare's *As You Like It* (pr. c. 1599-1600).

Having won an Academy Award at such a young age, Paltrow felt free to pursue projects that interested her without concern about commercial success. At the same time, she had already begun to slow the frantic pace of her career, due in part to her highly publicized broken engagement with Brad Pitt in 1997 as well as to her father's cancer diagnosis. Paltrow rounded out the decade with *The Talented Mr. Ripley* (1999) and also began filming a long-delayed project directed by her father titled *Duets,* which was ultimately released in 2000. Although the film flopped commercially, Paltrow was widely praised for her vocal talents. In addition, although she found the experience emotionally difficult in light of her father's continuing health issues, she relished the opportunity to work with him before his death in 2002.

Impact Gwyneth Paltrow's career experienced an almost meteoritic rise during the 1990's, from her first small movie roles in 1991 to an Academy Award for Best Actress in 1999 at the age of twenty-six. Her consistently strong performances earned both critical and popular acclaim, and in 2000 she was named one of *Premiere* magazine's "Power Elite" on the strength of her work in the 1990's.

Gwyneth Paltrow receives the Academy Award for Best Actress for her role in the 1998 film Shakespeare in Love. (AP/Wide World Photos)

Further Reading

Hill, Anne E. *Gwyneth Paltrow.* Philadelphia: Chelsea House, 2002.

Milano, Valerie. *Gwyneth Paltrow.* Toronto: ECW Press, 2000.

Amy Sisson

See also Academy Awards; Film in the United States; Pitt, Brad.

■ Patriot missile

Identification American air-defense missile system

Deployed during the Gulf War, the Patriot missile attracted great interest based on the U.S. Army's claims that the system was capable of shooting down other missiles. The effectiveness of the system has since come into question.

The Patriot missile (officially designated by the U.S. Army as the MIM-104) is a ground-launched missile designed to shoot down airborne targets. Development of the Patriot system began in 1964, when the Department of Defense initiated the Surface-to-Air Missile Development (SAM-D) project to replace the existing Homing All the Way Killer (HAWK) surface-to-air missile. After successful initial tests in 1976, the Army renamed the SAM-D the Patriot, an acronym for "phased array tracking radar to intercept of target." After prolonged development, the Patriot system became operational in 1984. Patriot introduced several new technologies to the battlefield. Instead of a traditional rotating radar system, Patriot used a stationary phased array system that "aimed" the radar beam. Once in flight, the Patriot missile engaged its target using track-while-scan, with which the missile received radar information from the ground and also tracked the target with its own onboard radar. The missile constantly compared the two radar images to ensure a hit. The missile also came packaged in its launch container, requiring no maintenance from the operating crew.

Patriot made its combat debut in the 1991 Gulf War. Deployed initially to Saudi Arabia and other friendly Persian Gulf states, the Patriot system performed its designed task of air defense against Iraq's air force. The Iraqi use of Soviet-made SS-1 Scud missiles, however, forced the U.S. Army to use the Patriot as an antiballistic missile weapon, a task for which it was not designed. Over the course of the conflict, the Patriot engaged more than forty Iraqi Scuds fired at Saudi Arabia and Israel. The military credited the success of the Patriot in downing Iraqi Scuds with preventing damage to coalition forces and defeating Iraq's hopes of provoking Israel into entering the war.

Impact Although claimed at the time to be a technological miracle, the success rate of the Patriot provoked some dispute. The system failed to intercept one Scud attack on Dhahran, Saudi Arabia, that caused the death of twenty-eight U.S. soldiers. While the Army claimed a 70 percent success rate, some observers claimed the Patriot was not nearly as accurate as the Army claimed. Despite the controversy, the U.S. military continued to use the Patriot as an antiballistic missile weapon, with the latest Patriot Advanced Capability-3 (PAC-3) upgrade to the Patriot capable of defending four times as much airspace with vastly improved accuracy.

Further Reading

Hildreth, Steven A. *The Patriot Air Defense System and the Search for an Antitactical Ballistic Missile System.* Washington, D.C.: Congressional Research Service, 1991.

Mitchell, Gordon R. *Strategic Deception: Rhetoric, Science, and Politics in Missile Defense Advocacy.* East Lansing: Michigan State University Press, 2000.

Steven J. Ramold

See also Arnett, Peter; Cheney, Dick; CNN coverage of the Gulf War; Defense budget cuts; Gulf War.

■ PDAs

Definition Personal digital assistants are computers small enough to be held in the hand, generally with a simplified operating system and application software

Manufacturer Apple Computer, 3Com, Research In Motion

The development and proliferation of these small computer devices led to the increasing ubiquity of computing.

A computer that could fit in the palm of one's hand and be carried everywhere had long been a staple of science fiction. The earliest realization of the idea was the pocket calculator of the early 1970's, but it was limited to purely mathematical functions. After the development of the microprocessor, which put the circuitry of a computer's central processing unit on a single chip, computers were able to become smaller, lighter, and less expensive. Pocket calculators began to go beyond basic arithmetic into advanced mathematical functions such as trigonometry. Some even included larger screens that could graph functions or the capacity to program equations into them, which could be recalled and used later.

At the same time, the earliest electronic organizers were beginning to appear for business users. These devices generally had a date book and an address book but little in the way of installable software. Some had the capacity to synchronize with a desktop computer, but many were stand-alone devices; the only input was through their tiny keyboards. As a result, the earliest generation of electronic organizers were regarded as little more than expensive toys by many consumers.

In 1993, Apple Computer's chief executive officer (CEO), John Sculley, announced that Apple would be producing a new kind of handheld computer, which he called a personal digital assistant, or PDA. This device, which Apple would sell under the name of MessagePad, would not use a keyboard. Instead, the user would write directly on its touch-sensitive screen with a plastic stylus (a device like a pen but without ink) and the computer's "electronic ink" would write the letters. It would be particularly suitable for people who needed to use a computer while walking around and thus found a laptop too bulky and awkward.

The initial response to the MessagePad was enthusiastic, but once the device actually shipped, the excitement quickly waned. The handwriting recognition, which had been promoted so heavily, was problematic, often turning one's messages into incomprehensible messes. The processor was slow, and synchronization with a desktop machine, even Apple's own Macintosh, was inconsistent. Worst of all, the battery life was notoriously short, and users often lost all their data when the batteries suddenly died. As a result, the MessagePad, often called Newton after its operating system (OS), proved to have disappointing sales figures. Although the Newton went through multiple revisions over the next several years, none of them was able to create an acceptable combination of price and performance. In 1997, Steve Jobs put an end to the Newton as part of his program to simplify Apple's product line.

However, even as Apple was struggling with the MessagePad and the Newton OS, Jeff Hawkins was creating his own pen-based handheld computer. Initially called a Zoomer, it was later renamed the Palm Pilot, or simply the Palm. In order to strike a balance between battery life and processor power, Hawkins decided to abandon true handwriting recognition in favor of a simplified alphabet called Graffiti. As a result, the Palm made a respectable, if not spectacular, showing that allowed its company to grow and expand. While Apple had sought to produce a perfect product, Palm was satisfied to make one that would make a practical difference in people's lives while staying within the constraints of workable technology.

In 1998, another contender entered the PDA field when the Canadian company Research In Motion (RIM) introduced the BlackBerry. Originally a two-way pager with some organizer functions, it was distinct from pen-based PDAs, such as the Newton and the Palm, because it had a tiny keyboard on which one typed, using the thumbs. This feature reminded one of the designers of the seeds in a strawberry; however, a linguist suggested that "straw" sounded slow, and as a result, the official name became BlackBerry. Because the BlackBerry's organizer functions were closely integrated with its wireless connection, it was notable for the smoothness with which a user could contact someone. As a result, later BlackBerry models began to expand their organizer functions until they effectively became full-service PDAs with wireless connectivity.

The success of the BlackBerry led Palm to investigate the possibility of a PDA with wireless Internet connectivity. The first attempt, the Palm VII, debuted as the 1990's gave way to the twenty-first century. However, it used a proprietary network and "web clippings," miniature Web pages that had to be acquired from Palm.

Impact In spite of the commercial failure of the Apple Newton, it proved the viability of the idea of the handheld computer sufficiently enough that other companies were willing to produce their own designs. By using less ambitious software, these were able to keep costs down to the point that they could sell enough to make the venture economical. With the addition of wireless connections that enabled the user to remain connected with either a base computer or the Internet while moving around, PDAs became indispensable for executives and others who needed computing not bounded by location. As a result, by the beginning of the twenty-first century a convergence began to develop between PDAs and cellular telephones.

Further Reading

Butter, Andrea, and David Pogue. *Piloting Palm: The Inside Story of Palm, Handspring, and the Birth of the Billion-Dollar Handheld Industry.* New York: John Wiley & Sons, 2002. A history of the Palm PDA.

Kounalakis, Markos. *Defying Gravity: The Making of Newton.* Hillsboro, Oreg.: Beyond Worlds Publishing, 1993. The history of the Apple Newton in words and pictures.

Malone, Michael S. *Infinite Loop: How Apple, the World's Most Insanely Great Computer Company, Went Insane.* New York: Doubleday, 1999. Places the Newton into the context of Apple's confused business model during the middle of the 1990's.

Swedin, Eric G., and David L. Ferro. *Computers: The Life Story of a Technology.* Greenwood Technographies. Westport, Conn.: Greenwood Press, 2005. A basic overview that puts the PDA in perspective as part of the larger computer revolution.

Leigh Husband Kimmel

See also Apple Computer; Cell phones; Computers; Internet; Jobs, Steve; MP3 format; Science and technology.

■ Perfect Storm, the

The Event An unusual combination of three weather systems produces a severe single storm
Date October 28-November 1, 1991

This huge storm caused havoc along the eastern seaboard of North America, killing twelve people and causing hundreds of millions of dollars worth of damage.

The moniker the "Perfect Storm" was coined by author and journalist Sebastian Junger after a comment made by a National Weather Service (NWS) deputy. The term refers to the combination of three lesser weather events into a single massive storm that was far more damaging than if the storms had stayed separate. The Perfect Storm is also referred to as the "1991 Halloween Nor'easter" or colloquially as the "No-Name Storm" in New England.

On October 28, 1991, a mass of warm air from over the Atlantic Ocean and a flow of cool dry air from Canada created a classic weather event called a nor'easter. The event was typical for the time of year, although larger than average. The nor'easter was located a few hundred miles east of Nova Scotia. The resulting low pressure system pulled the remnants of Hurricane Grace into the storm on October 29. Hurricane Grace had already been generating ten- to fifteen-foot swells, and with the added energy, the Perfect Storm was generating hurricane-force gusts up 65 knots (74.9 miles per hour) and wave heights of thirty-nine feet by its peak on October 30 according to the NWS. The storm itself was over fifteen hundred miles wide, well over five times the size of a typical hurricane. Although the NWS has no data to support it, waves at sea were reported to be as high as one hundred feet by eyewitness accounts. A Canadian weather buoy also recorded similar readings. The storm at this time had drifted southward and was about 350 miles south of Halifax. The storm was so large that waves ten to thirty feet high were common from North Carolina to Nova Scotia.

By October 31, the storm had stalled and started moving backward toward the west. It lost energy over the next few days but did not dissipate. Instead, it gained energy from the warm waters of the Gulf Stream and developed into a hurricane by November 2. It made landfall in Nova Scotia and quickly degenerated into a tropical depression. It dissipated within ten hours of landfall, and no damage was reported. The hurricane was never named to avoid confusion between the unnamed hurricane and the Halloween Nor'easter.

Rescue Efforts and Aftermath Because of the unexpected formation and severity of the storm, fishing and sailing vessels were caught unawares in the four-story-high waves. The Coast Guard cutter *Tamaroa* rescued three people from the sailing vessel *Satori* on October 30. That day, a New York National Guard helicopter had to ditch because of lack of fuel after trying to rescue a solo sailor 250 miles southeast of Long Island. A Coast Guard helicopter tried to rescue the downed crew members, but the winds were so strong that the rescue basket threatened to blow into the tail rotor. The *Tamaroa* arrived on the scene, and the helicopter assisted by dropping flares and using its searchlight to help the ship locate the crew members. The *Tamaroa* threw a cargo net over the side of the ship to assist the crew members in climbing aboard, but a fifth member of the crew was lost to the storm despite the efforts. The *Andrea Gail* was a seventy-two-foot fishing vessel returning from a fishing expedition and was caught in the storm. On October 28, the last transmission from the ship reported waves of thirty feet and wind gusts up to 80 knots (92.2 miles per hour) The ship was reported overdue on October 30, and after a massive search, the six-member crew was presumed dead, missing at sea. Debris from the ship was later found on Sable Island. Overall, the storm was responsible for twelve deaths.

Beach erosion and flooding were widespread. There were reports of damage from the Bahamas to northern Canada, with the worst effects seen in the New England states. There was a record-high tide in Ocean City, Maryland, that reached 7.8 feet; in Boston, the tide reached 14.1 feet above the mean low water. Lighthouses, homes, and businesses were damaged by the lengthy storm. Piers and seawalls were destroyed, and in an area where fishing is vital to the economy, numerous small boats and lobster traps were also destroyed. Federal disaster sites were declared for seven counties in Massachusetts, five counties in Maine, and one county in New Hampshire.

Impact The Perfect Storm was a rare and massive combination of three separate weather events that created a front hundreds of miles wide. It affected an area that encompassed the entire eastern seaboard of the United States and Canada and affected areas as far south as Puerto Rico. It caused hundreds of millions of dollars of damage, and the impact on the New England coast has been referred to as "the worst in living memory."

Further Reading

Houghton, Gillian. *The Wreck of the "Andrea Gail": Three Days of a Perfect Storm.* New York: Rosen Central, 2003. An account of the Perfect Storm that focuses on the ship, *Andrea Gail*, and its crew.

Junger, Sebastian. *The Perfect Storm: A True Story of Men Against the Sea.* New York: W. W. Norton, 1997. A riveting account of the Perfect Storm that was the basis for the 2000 film adaptation.

Sargent, William. *Storm Surge: A Coastal Village Battles the Rising Atlantic.* Hanover, N.H.: University Press of New England, 2004. Focuses on the regional effects of storms, with a section on the Perfect Storm.

U.S. Department of Commerce. National Oceanic and Atmospheric Administration. National Weather Service. *The Halloween Nor'easter of 1991: East Coast of the United States . . . Maine to Florida and Puerto Rico, October 28 to November 1, 1991.* Natural Disaster Survey Report. Silver Spring, Md.: Author, 1992. The official account of the Perfect Storm by the National Weather Service.

James J. Heiney

See also Global warming debate; Hurricane Andrew; Natural disasters; Oklahoma tornado outbreak; Storm of the Century.

■ Perlman, Itzhak

Identification Israeli American musician
Born August 31, 1945; Tel Aviv, Palestine (now in Israel)

Perlman became an ambassador for classical music in the 1990's with his engaging personality and ability to appeal to popular audiences.

From the 1960's through the 1980's, Itzhak Perlman developed a reputation as one of the finest classical violinists in the world, despite having survived a childhood bout with polio that left him partially paralyzed. Possessed of an accessibility and sense of humor that endeared him to popular audiences, Perlman had also increased public awareness and appreciation of classical music through numerous television and radio appearances and by the 1990's had become the face of classical music to many audiences who previously had had little or no exposure to the genre. In addition to historic visits to former Soviet-bloc nations in the early 1990's and to China and India in 1994, Perlman raised the profile of classical music in the United States, appearing on such popular American television programs as *Mister Rogers' Neighborhood* and *Late Show with David Letterman.* He appeared frequently on programs broadcast by the Public Broadcasting Service (PBS) and in 1994 hosted the U.S. broadcast of a performance by the Three Tenors, viewed by millions of Americans.

Perlman continued to perform frequently during the 1990's and released a prolific body of recorded

Renowned violinist Itzhak Perlman performs with the klezmer group Brave Old World at New York's Radio City Music Hall, on July 2, 1996. Perlman helped raise awareness of classical music among popular audiences. (AP/Wide World Photos)

classical music during the decade, winning a Grammy Award in 1991 for his recording of *Brahms: The Three Violin Sonatas* and an Academy Award for his work on the score of the 1993 film *Schindler's List.* Perlman had also begun to explore music from other genres, collaborating with jazz pianist Oscar Peterson on the 1994 album *Side by Side* and performing traditional Jewish klezmer music. His forays into other musical genres led some classical music purists to conclude that his best work was behind him; yet his appeal among popular audiences continued to grow.

Throughout the 1990's, Perlman also maintained a long-standing dedication to classical music education for children. In 1995, he founded the Perlman Summer Music Program, which sponsors the instruction of musically gifted children, and often participated personally in this program as a teacher and conductor. His appearances on children's television programs also raised awareness of classical music among young Americans. In addition, Perlman supported aid and musical education for disabled children through several foundations and scholarship programs, and he advocated for the rights of the disabled by speaking out against lags in implementation of the Americans with Disabilities Act of 1990 and by insisting upon performing only in concert halls offering full accessability to disabled patrons and performers.

Impact Through numerous television appearances and charitable projects, Perlman exposed classical music to a wider audience during the 1990's, conveying a public image that contradicted the popular stereotype of the elitist classical musician. His virtuosity and prominence in the American media also served to dispel stereotypes of disabled persons and call attention to issues affecting the disabled. At the end of the twentieth century, Perlman remained a vibrant force both in classical music and in American popular culture.

Further Reading

Behrman, Carol H. *Fiddler to the World: The Inspiring Life of Itzhak Perlman.* White Hall, Va.: Shoe Tree Press, 1992.

Morin, Alexander. *Classical Music: Third Ear—The Essential Listening Companion.* San Francisco: Backbeat Books, 2001.

Michael H. Burchett

See also Americans with Disabilities Act of 1990; Classical music; Jewish Americans; Music; *Schindler's List.*

■ Perot, H. Ross

Identification American businessman and U.S. presidential candidate in 1992 and 1996
Born June 27, 1930; Texarkana, Texas

Although not endorsed by either of the two major political parties in the United States, Perot had a substantial following among fiscal and social conservatives in his runs for the presidency as an independent in the election of 1992 and as a candidate of the Reform Party in the election of 1996.

A self-made billionaire when the decade of the 1990's dawned, H. Ross Perot made his fortune as the founder of a multibillion-dollar data-processing organization that grew into a corporation with more than seventy thousand employees. After General Motors bought him out in 1984 for over two and a half billion dollars, Perot became the largest shareholder in General Motors and served on its board of directors.

The ever-restless Perot established a computer service company in 1988, but he now set his sights on attempting to alter significantly the political scene in the United States. Rich and influential, he attracted an enthusiastic following of conservatives who rankled at government interference in businesses and who were suspicious of the close ties that many high-level politicians established with influential contributors to their political campaigns. It seemed obvious that executives of corporations that contributed substantially to politicians' war chests expected reciprocity once their candidates were elected.

Perot, able and willing to finance his own presidential campaign, appeared to many to represent a new direction in American politics. Even though Perot had no political experience and had never held an elective office, people were convinced that his business acumen compensated for his lack of such experience and that his ability to manage a corporation with more than seventy thousand employees demonstrated his strong administrative ability.

The 1992 Presidential Election In 1992, the Republican incumbent, George H. W. Bush, sought a second term as president. His Democratic opponent, Bill Clinton, was a newcomer to the national political scene. Perot, appalled by the looming federal debt the Bush administration was incurring, called for a drastic reduction in the budget deficit that was developing at an alarming rate.

Perot's bid for the presidency began in February, 1992, when he announced his intention to run for the nation's highest office if his name appeared on the ballots of all fifty states before the November presidential election. It was obvious that Perot had the means to finance his own campaign, thereby enabling him to avoid having ties with corporate contributors.

Staffed by a strong cadre of volunteers, the Perot campaign went well, but in July, 1992, the candidate

Ross Perot on the Economy

During the third presidential debate of 1992, Perot spoke further of his plan to eliminate the budget deficit:

Our challenge is to stop the financial bleeding. If you take a patient into the hospital that's bleeding arterially, step one is to stop the bleeding. And we are bleeding arterially.

There's only one way out of this, and that is to stop the deterioration of our job base, to have a growing, expanding job base, to give us the tax base—see, balancing the budget is not nearly as difficult as paying off the $4 trillion debt and leaving our children the American Dream intact.

We have spent their money. We've got to pay it back. This is going to take fair, shared sacrifice. My plan balances the budget within six years. We didn't do it faster than that because we didn't want to disrupt the economy. We gave it off to a slow start and a fast finish to give the economy time to recover. But we faced it and we did it, and we believe it's fair, shared sacrifice.

The one thing I have done is lay it squarely on the table in front of the American people. You've had a number of occasions to see in detail what the plan is, and at least you'll understand it. I think that's fundamental in our country, that you know what you're getting into.

announced that he did not think he could win and was withdrawing from the competition. Despite this retreat, the volunteers working for Perot persisted and saw to it that their candidate's name was eventually on the ballots of all fifty states. These volunteers considered Perot an outsider in a field dominated by one insider, Bush, and by a novice on the national scene, Clinton, who, they feared, would sell out to special interest groups to finance his campaign. His campaign seemingly stalled, Perot changed his mind and, in October, 1992, announced that he would run for the presidency in the upcoming election. He chose retired vice admiral James Stockdale as his running mate.

Given the on-and-off nature of Perot's campaign, it is surprising that he managed to receive approximately 19 percent of the popular vote in an election that brought Clinton into office but failed to give Perot any electoral votes. Perot and Clinton both benefited from public discontent with the Bush administration.

The Election of 1996 After his defeat in 1992, Ross Perot founded the Reform Party. He became its standard bearer in his 1996 bid for the presidency, running with Pat Choate, an economist, as the vice presidential candidate.

Perot wrote several books during the 1990's that expounded his political and social philosophies. In 1993, almost immediately after the 1992 election, he published *Not for Sale at Any Price: How We Can Save America for Our Children,* which presented a clear impression of what Perot stood for. This book was written for an electorate that he hoped would join his Reform Party movement and sweep him into office in 1996.

Bill Clinton's first term was a popular success. Government spending was brought under reasonable control, and the budget deficit decreased. Much that Perot hoped to achieve was already being achieved by the incumbent. In November, 1996, Clinton scored an easy victory, and Perot won just 8 percent of the popular vote.

Impact Ross Perot was the quintessential self-made man. He succeeded impressively in the corporate world. He had a strongly held vision for an America that would limit government intrusion into the lives of citizens and that would strictly control government spending with a resultant decrease in the national budget deficit.

Perot stood for principles that many Americans espoused, but his views were shared by people from both major political parties. In regard to the economy, Perot's principles were not substantially different from those of Clinton, who had the advantage of having served as governor of a state that provided him with experience that served him well as president.

Further Reading

Perot, H. Ross. *Not for Sale at Any Price: How We Can Save America for Our Children.* New York: Hyperion, 1993. Includes his plan for resolving the budget deficit.

_______. *Ross Perot: My Life and the Principles for Success.* Arlington, Tex.: Summit, 1996. A clear statement of Perot's political posture and his conviction that drastic political change is urgently needed.

_______. *United We Stand: How We Can Take Back Our Country.* New York: Hyperion, 1992. A lucid preelection statement of what Perot stands for.

Posner, Gerald. *Citizen Perot: His Life and Times.* New York: Random House, 1996. The most complete and authoritative assessment of Perot and of his contributions to the American political scene.

R. Baird Shuman

See also Bush, George H. W.; Clinton, Bill; Conservatism in U.S. politics; Dole, Bob; Elections in the United States, 1992; Elections in the United States, 1996; Recession of 1990-1991; Republican Revolution; Stockdale, James.

■ Pharmaceutical industry

Identification Industry involved in the manufacture and sale of medicinal drugs

The pharmaceutical industry in the 1990's introduced a wide variety of new medications for use by the general public, as well as adding to the advertisements of the decade.

During the 1990's, the use of medication to treat a variety of illnesses, both serious and nonserious, increased dramatically. The pharmaceutical industry nearly doubled posted profits between 1990 and 1996, and what was already a multibillion-dollar industry continued to expand. At the same time, pharmaceutical industries contributed millions of dollars to politicians.

New Drugs Several types of medications were introduced and approved by the Food and Drug Administration (FDA) in the 1990's, including some so-called blockbuster drugs, those that post earnings of more than $1 billion in a year. Some of these drugs were Lipitor (approved in 1996), a drug for lowering cholesterol, which became the top-selling medication of all time; Viagra (1998), a drug originally designed to increase circulation and used to treat erectile dysfunction; and Effexor (1993), a drug that treats anxiety and depression and is used for pain management, though this last use is off-label (not an approved treatment according to the FDA). In addition, many drugs were developed for rheumatoid arthritis, asthma, depression, and other medical problems.

Drugs Withdrawn Several drugs were withdrawn during the 1990's, most notably Fen-phen, a drug manufactured by Wyeth. Designed to be a weight-loss aid, Fen-phen was linked by the Mayo Clinic to heart disease in several women. The FDA requested Fen-phen's withdrawal in 1997. Most of the drugs withdrawn from the market during the 1990's were not widely used. Some drugs approved during the 1990's were withdrawn at a later date. Vioxx, a drug used to treat osteoarthritis, was approved in 1999 but withdrawn from the market in 2004, after reports of increased risk of heart disease.

Research Research in the 1990's focused on several primary avenues. Medication designed for heart disease was responsible for a large amount of research, as was medication to treat anxiety and depression. Research also focused on antiretrovirals to halt the duplication of the human immunodeficiency virus (HIV) and acquired immunodeficiency syndrome (AIDS); highly active antiretroviral therapy (HAART) was developed in 1996, allowing many HIV/AIDS patients to have their symptoms stabilized.

Drug research also focused on antidiabetic drugs, as diabetes rates continued to increase alongside obesity rates. As diagnoses of Alzheimer's disease increased, so did research for drug therapy to slow and stop the onset of the disease, as well as to treat patients already in advanced stages.

As diagnoses of attention-deficit disorder (ADD) and attention-deficit/hyperactivity disorder (ADHD) increased, so did prescriptions for drugs to treat the conditions; most drugs used to treat ADD/ADHD are amphetamines, such as methylphenidate hydrochloride, commonly known by its brand name Ritalin. Adderall was introduced in 1996 as a mixture of amphetamines and dextroamphetamines to treat ADD/ADHD.

Drug Advertising and Business Growth Direct-to-consumer (DTC) advertising of pharmaceuticals was approved in 1997 by the FDA. Prescription drug advertising was placed under the direct surveillance of the FDA, rather than the Federal Trade Commission, which oversees over-the-counter medication advertising. This permission for DTC advertising came under much criticism from both doctors and politicians, as some saw this advertising as a method to sell medications to people who did not need them. Critics have also called for an end to drug marketing to physicians, claiming that physicians may become biased in prescribing drugs.

Toward the end of the 1990's, drug lobbying in Washington reached new levels as the pharmaceutical industry outspent all other industries in lobbying; at the same time, drug companies donated large amounts of money to politicians, primarily Republicans, though Democrats also received donations.

With the development of blockbuster drugs, drug advertising, and increased political contributions, the moniker of "Big Pharma" was introduced to refer to pharmaceutical companies that posted yearly profits in excess of $3 billion. Many of the most well-known companies, like Johnson & Johnson, Merck, AstroZeneca, GlaxoSmithKline, Pfizer, Eli Lilly, and Bristol-Myers Squibb are included under the term.

Impact During the 1990's, the pharmaceutical industry experienced a period of rapid growth and expansion; this was assisted by looser regulations for advertising of drugs directly to the consumers as well as the development of blockbuster drugs. With the introduction of numerous medications for a variety of illnesses and disorders, pharmaceuticals became a multibillion-dollar industry vital not only to the economy but also to the health of patients.

Further Reading

Anderson, Stuart, ed. *Making Medicine: A Brief History of Pharmacy and Pharmaceuticals.* Grayslake, Ill.:

Pharmaceutical Press, 2005. A history of the profession of pharmacy from the time of the ancient civilizations to 2005.

Cohen, Jillian Clare, Patricia Illingworth, and Udo Schuklenk, eds. *The Power of Pills: Social, Ethical, and Legal Issues in Drug Development, Marketing, and Pricing.* London: Pluto Press, 2006. Essays discuss the development, pricing, and distribution of drugs worldwide, with a focus on the lack of access by one-third of the world population to pharmaceuticals and on what drives new drug research.

Hilts, Philip J. *Protecting America's Health: The FDA, Business, and One Hundred Years of Regulation.* Chapel Hill: University of North Carolina Press, 2003. This history of the FDA tracks the agency responsible for drug approval from its inception during Theodore Roosevelt's administration into the twenty-first century.

Ruschmann, Paul. *Prescription and Non-prescription Drugs.* Point/Counterpoint. New York: Chelsea House, 2007. Discusses the legal issues of regulation and access to pharmaceuticals, presenting arguments for different sides of regulation of the drug industry.

Emily Carroll Shearer

See also Advertising; Antidepressants; Attention-deficit disorder; Cancer research; Depo-Provera; Drug advertising; Drug use; Fen-phen; Health care; Viagra.

■ Philadelphia

Identification Academy Award-winning film
Director Jonathan Demme (1944-)
Date Released on December 23, 1993

This groundbreaking film dealt openly with homophobia and discrimination and was one of the first motion pictures to deal with HIV/AIDS in the workplace.

The film *Philadelphia* was written by Ron Nyswaner, who based the screenplay partly on the story of Geoffrey Bowers, an attorney who, after having been wrongfully terminated in 1987 from his law firm, Baker and McKenzie, filed one of the earliest AIDS-discrimination lawsuits. In the film, Tom Hanks plays Andrew Beckett, a young, successful lawyer trying to live a normal life despite having recently been diagnosed with acquired immunodeficiency syndrome (AIDS). Since he works for a very conservative law firm and an openly homophobic boss, the University of Pennsylvania graduate has kept his sexual orientation (and his partner) secret from his friends and colleagues. Unfortunately, when his disease begins to become apparent to his colleagues, Beckett finds that any goodwill he might have enjoyed among them has vanished and he is no longer welcome. His work on a major case is sabotaged, leading to his prompt dismissal from the firm. Angered by his callous treatment, Beckett decides to sue his company for illegal dismissal, lost earnings, and punitive damages, but he is shocked to discover that none of the attorneys he approaches are willing to take an AIDS patient as a client. Only Joe Miller, played by Denzel Washington, is willing to give Beckett a chance to take his case to court.

Their case is not an easy one by any stretch of the imagination. Over time, both individuals come to respect each other's tenacity. Miller's task—to prove that Beckett has been fired solely because of his homosexuality and HIV status—is difficult because of the inherently controversial nature of Beckett's disease. Further, the partners of Beckett's firm prove themselves only too willing to defame their former colleague and openly lie on the stand. Fortunately, their perjury does not, ultimately, sway the opinion of the jury; the firm is ordered to pay Beckett \$140,000 in back pay, \$100,000 for pain and suffering, and \$4 million in punitive damages even as he, suffering the final ravages of his disease, lies dying.

Impact *Philadelphia* was not the first film to deal with the treatment of AIDS sufferers in mainstream society—the made-for-television movie *And the Band Played On* (based on the 1987 book by Randy Shilts), starring Alan Alda and Matthew Modine, had previously been released in 1993—but it was equally groundbreaking in its realistic depictions of homosexual characters. Hanks won an Academy Award for Best Actor, and Bruce Springsteen earned an Academy Award for Best Original Song for "Streets of Philadelphia." *Philadelphia* was part of a general trend in the 1990's toward increased visibility of homosexuality in television, film, and the media.

Further Reading

Cante, Richard C. "Afterthoughts from *Philadelphia* . . . and Somewhere Else." In *Gay Men and the*

Forms of Contemporary U.S. Culture. London: Ashgate, 2008.
Harty, K. J. "The Failures of Jonathan Demme's *Philadelphia.*" *Four Quarters* 8, no. 1 (Spring, 1994): 13-20.

Julia M. Meyers

See also Academy Awards; AIDS epidemic; Domestic partnerships; Don't ask, don't tell; Film in the United States; Hanks, Tom; Homosexuality and gay rights; Washington, Denzel.

■ Phoenix, River

Identification American actor
Born August 23, 1970; Madras, Oregon
Died October 31, 1993; Los Angeles, California

In addition to earning unusual accolades for such a young actor, Phoenix became a role model for many young Americans because of his outspoken views, before his ironic and tragic death from a drug overdose at the age of twenty-three.

Following a breakout performance in the drama *Stand by Me* (1986), River Phoenix quickly cemented his reputation as a serious and talented young actor when he was nominated for a Best Supporting Actor Oscar for his role in *Running on Empty* (1988). Never one to pursue huge blockbuster projects, and eager to shed his teen idol image, Phoenix continued his career into the 1990's with a series of offbeat roles. In 1991, Phoenix starred alongside Keanu Reeves in *My Own Private Idaho,* an independent film about personal discovery and rebellion based loosely on William Shakespeare's *Henry IV, Part I* (pr. c. 1597-1598). Phoenix's edgy portrayal of a gay narcoleptic earned Best Actor awards from both the Venice Film Festival and the National Society of Film Critics.

Phoenix followed up with a role in another critically acclaimed independent film, *Dogfight* (1991), before returning briefly to a more mainstream project, the 1992 thriller *Sneakers,* which boasted an impressive ensemble cast including Robert Redford and Sidney Poitier. Phoenix's next film, *The Thing Called Love* (1993), was the first to showcase his musical ability; Phoenix performed his own vocals as an aspiring country singer who falls in love with another would-be Nashville star played by Samantha Mathis, whom Phoenix began dating during the filming.

In addition to acting, Phoenix became well known for his passionate views on animal compassion and the environment. As a vegan, he consumed no animal products of any kind, even refusing to wear costumes made of leather. Although he smoked, he advocated clean living and spoke forcefully against junk food and drug use. For those reasons, his death from an accidental drug overdose on October 31, 1993, while accompanied by Mathis and his brother, Joaquin, was a tremendous shock. After the fact, Hollywood insiders speculated that Phoenix's intensity may have led to either depression or a dangerous tendency to identify too much with the often-troubled characters he played.

Impact River Phoenix's intensity and passion, both on- and offscreen, not only earned him a reputation as one of Hollywood's most promising young actors but also made him a role model in the eyes of many

River Phoenix poses in a 1993 photo shoot. (Hulton Archive/Getty Images)

young Americans who subscribed to his views on veganism and clean living. Ironically, the unaccustomed pressure of that role may have contributed to Phoenix's substance abuse and untimely death, which shocked the acting world and garnered comparisons to the tragic death of James Dean.

Further Reading

Glatt, John. *Lost in Hollywood: The Fast Times and Short Life of River Phoenix.* New York: Donald I. Fine, 1995.

Robb, Brian J. *River Phoenix: A Short Life.* New York: HarperPerennial, 1994.

Stempel, Penny. *River Phoenix.* Philadelphia: Chelsea House, 1999.

Amy Sisson

See also Academy Awards; Drug use; Film in the United States; Reeves, Keanu.

■ Photography

Definition An art form whereby images are produced through the manipulation of technology

During the 1990's, advancements in technology brought forth a whole new revolution in photography. With the introduction of digital imaging, both professional and amateur photographers were able to have more control over the final image.

Technology resulted in much progress in photography during the twentieth century, and the 1990's saw several revolutionary advances. During the 1980's, Kodak introduced the Disc camera, which became the precursor to digital imaging. In 1985, Minolta produced the first autofocus single-lens reflex (SLR) system camera known as Maxxum. With these advancements in technology, it was becoming almost unnecessary for anyone to be knowledgeable about the mechanical end of photography. The cameras had the capacity seemingly to handle all technical issues for the user. With the introduction of digital photography, the medium was dramatically altered forever.

These advancements changed not only the way in which individuals would take photographs but also what they could do with the images. Since digital cameras allowed for immediate results, images would appear in an instant on the camera's screen. If the image was not satisfactory, then it could be easily deleted. The photographer did not have to worry about wasting film because there was no film. The best digital images could be loaded onto a computer. Once the images were saved, it was possible with the use of various computer programs to alter, retouch, and crop each image as desired.

Digital Revolution In 1990, Adobe Photoshop introduced Photoshop 1.0 for the Macintosh operating system used on Apple computers. This computer graphics editing program allowed images to be manipulated. It was not until 1992 that a version of Photoshop could work with Microsoft Windows operating systems. By 2007, Photoshop was in its tenth iteration. In 1991, Kodak released a photo CD system that allowed photographers to store their digital images for the first time.

The next year, Kodak introduced the DCS-100 digital SLR camera, the first digital SLR to be made commercially available. During the 1990's, several other companies also released digital SLR cameras, including Nikon, Canon, Pentax, Panasonic, Olympus, and Fujifilm. A consortium of manufacturers released the Advanced Photographic System (APS) in 1996. By this same year, the prices on mass-market digital cameras had become competitive with more conventional cameras. The first megapixel camera that could be used by the public was introduced in 1998. By 2000, digital photography was being adopted by more and more professional photographers. The price for these professional digital cameras, however, remained at several thousand dollars. For the public, digital cameras eventually became less expensive. Depending on the desired camera features, an easy-to-use, high-quality digital camera could be bought for less than five hundred dollars by the end of the decade.

As a strong indicator of the trend toward market dominance of digital cameras, close to 80 percent of the cameras sold by both Nikon and Canon were digital cameras by 2003. Taking this trend to heart, most major manufacturers of cameras increased the number of digital models available for sale by the turn of the twenty-first century.

Exhibitions, Publications, Media Events The Museum of Modern Art (MOMA) in New York put on the exhibit *Photography Until Now* in 1990. In the same year, documentary filmmaker Ken Burns made use of historic photographs from the American Civil War for his highly regarded series *The Civil War,* shown on the Public Broadcasting Service (PBS). Robert Mapplethorpe's traveling exhibition *The Perfect Moment* created controversy in 1990 because of its sexual imagery. The Whitney Museum of American Art in New York presented a major retrospective of Richard Avedon photographs in 1994 entitled *Richard Avedon: Evidence, 1944-1994.* In 1997, Getty Images, Inc., was founded. That year, the twenty-seventh photography festival held in Arles, Frances, devoted a significant portion of the festival to digital images. The Barbican Gallery in London presented the *Native Nations: Journeys in American Photography* exhibition in 1998.

During the 1990's, several extraordinarily courageous photojournalists—including Gideon Mendel, Stephanie Welsh, Lucian Perkins, Kevin Carter, and Paul Weston—continued the tradition of going into harm's way to photograph the horrors of war, rare animals in their habitat that were on the verge of extinction, the tragic consequences of disease, and the frightening circumstances surrounding natural disasters.

In the 1990's, many museums, publishers, galleries, libraries, and picture archives believed that it was advantageous for storage and access purposes to digitize their photographic images. By doing so, the images could be easily linked to the Internet, which allowed millions of people to have access to rare photographic collections.

Impact The advancements in digital technology during the decade dramatically changed the world of photography. Images could be manipulated with ease on the computer. With the introduction of digital imaging, photographs could be altered beyond all recognition. Both the professional and the amateur photographer were now capable of creating startling images. The photographer could focus more on the images that could be created and less on documenting reality. A commercial market for artistic photography blossomed during the 1990's. With the emergence of this new outlet, photographers felt emboldened to experiment more with the photographic process.

Historically, photographers had been attempting to alter photographs since the early twentieth century. Retouching and cropping had become common practices employed by photographers to enhance "reality." With the introduction of assemblages, various art forms could be merged. Photography, painting, printmaking, and sculpture were being combined in order for an artist to fulfill his or her imagination. With the photographic advancements of the 1990's, photographers and other artists had their artistic options dramatically expanded. It seemed that the nature of an image was now limited only by the imagination of the photographer.

Further Reading

Hoy, Anne H. *The Book of Photography.* Washington, D.C.: National Geographic, 2005. A fascinating look at the creative spirit that is at the heart of photography.

Mora, Gilles. *Photo SPEAK: A Guide to the Ideas, Movements, and Techniques of Photography, 1839 to the Present.* New York: Abbeville Press, 1998. A wonderful overview of the technological advancements in photography and the impact that they have had on the art world.

Parr, Martin, and Gerry Badger. *The Photobook: A History Volume II.* New York: Phaidon Press, 2006. This volume shows the extraordinary expansion of the art of photography since the introduction of digital technology.

Rosenblum, Naomi. *A World History of Photography.* 3d ed. New York: Abbeville Press, 1997. A solid explanation of what photography is and where it is going.

Wands, Bruce. *Art of the Digital Age.* New York: Thames and Hudson, 2006. Includes beautiful examples of how digital technology has revolutionized photography.

Jeffry Jensen

See also Art movements; Digital cameras; Internet; Mapplethorpe obscenity trial; World Wide Web.

■ Physician-assisted suicide

Definition Termination of a patient's life by administration of lethal drugs with a physician's direct or indirect assistance

In 1994, Oregon voters endorsed the country's only program that permits persons who meet certain conditions to enlist physicians to help them terminate life. The issue engendered debate about mercy killings, the sanctity of life, and medical ethics.

In November, 1994, voters in Oregon approved the Death with Dignity Act by a margin of 51 to 49 percent. The act permitted physicians to provide drugs to induce death in qualified patients. This was the first (and still the only) law of its kind. A similar measure had been defeated in Washington in 1991 and in California the following year, both by a 55 to 46 percent margin.

According to the act, a candidate for physician-assisted suicide must be an adult and an Oregon resident and has to personally initiate the request to be aided by a physician in inducing death. The suicide candidate has to be free of documented depression and has to be diagnosed by two doctors as terminally ill, with a reasonable expectation of no more than six months to live. Physicians have to inform the suicide applicants of the prognosis regarding their condition; alternative options, including hospice care; potential risks of the procedure (there have been reports of prolonged periods between taking the drugs and death); and medication that would control pain. The law also establishes a fifteen-day waiting period between the patient's request and the signing of a consent form. Thereafter, the doctor can prescribe lethal doses of drugs that the patient is required to self-administer.

Oregon is a relatively secular state. A 1995 survey found that 60 percent of the 2,761 Oregon doctors responding had no ethical objections to prescribing deadly drugs, and a sizeable number indicated that in treating terminally ill patients in the past they had prescribed drugs to control pain that also hastened death.

Court and Congressional Action Injunctions held up implementation of the results of the 1994 Oregon Death with Dignity referendum. Meanwhile, citizens in New York (in *Vacco v. Quill*, 1997) and Washington (in *Washington v. Glucksberg*, 1997) challenged the right of their legislatures to ban physician-assisted suicide. The Supreme Court upheld the states' prohibition on assisted suicide. The Court emphasized that the states are the proper forum for the approval or disapproval of assisted-suicide laws. The Court also declared that were a state to pass a law endorsing physician-assisted suicide, this would not violate the constitutional requirements of due process and equal protection. A second referendum was called for by the Oregon legislature seeking the repeal of the original measure. It failed in the November, 1997, vote by a 60 to 40 percent margin.

Congressional disavowal of physician-assisted suicide was expressed in the federal Assisted Suicide Funding Restriction Act of 1997, which forbade the use of federal moneys to support such programs. This was followed in 1997 by a declaration from the federal Drug Enforcement Administration (DEA) stating that it would initiate actions under the Controlled Substances Act to revoke the license of any physician who prescribed death-inducing drugs. That action, however, was overturned by the Department of Justice on the ground that it was beyond the authority of the DEA.

The Oregon Health Division monitors the physician-assisted suicide program. Its initial report covered the period from November, 1997, through December, 1998. During that time, twenty-three patients had applied for physician-assisted suicide and fifteen had died by its use, while six died of their illness, and two were still alive. Most patients were suffering from cancer. Their average age was sixty-nine, and all were white. In 1999, there were thirty-three applications and twenty-seven deaths by physician-assisted suicide. The average age that year was seventy-one, and in both reports the patients were about evenly divided by gender. Neither financial considerations nor pain were said to underlie the decision to seek death but rather the issue of personal autonomy and control over the method of dying.

Pros and Cons Civil liberties advocates have generally hailed the Death with Dignity Act as providing freedom from religious doctrines that insisted that suicide was immoral because it represented a usurpation of divine prerogative to determine matters of life and death. The American Medical Association argued against physician-assisted suicide on the grounds that it violated a doctor's obligation to protect and preserve human life. Other opponents of the process regard it as a "slippery slope," an entry point to authorize physicians to kill elderly incapacitated persons and children born with disabilities. It is also argued that the Oregon law might encourage some persons to give up rather than to fight to construct what could be a fulfilling existence. Also, the desire to save money might result in pressure exerted on terminally ill persons to end their lives.

Impact The physician-assisted program has had more symbolic than practical importance outside of

Oregon. No other jurisdiction has adopted the measure, though many legislatures have debated the subject.

Further Reading

Hillyard, Daniel, and John Dombrink. *Dying Right: The Death with Dignity Movement.* New York: Routledge, 2001. A comprehensive examination of the "death with dignity" movement in the United States and worldwide, including an in-depth consideration of the Oregon experience.

McKhann, Charles F. *A Time to Die: The Place for Physician Assistance.* New Haven, Conn.: Yale University Press, 1999. McKhann, a cancer surgeon, bases his recommendations on interviews with terminally ill patients.

Smith, Wesley J. *Forced Exit: The Slippery Slope from Assisted Suicide to Legalized Murder.* Dallas: Spence, 2003. The author argues that physician-assisted suicide reflects the failure of contemporary society to care for and respect elderly, dying, and disabled persons.

Snyder, Lois, and Arthur L. Caplan, eds. *Assisted Suicide: Finding Common Ground.* Bloomington: Indiana University Press, 2002. A collection of well-reasoned papers presented at a symposium at the University of Pennsylvania Center for Bioethics.

Weir, Robert F., ed. *Physician-Assisted Suicide.* Bloomington: Indiana University Press, 1997. Weir provides valuable historical background and a sophisticated discussion of legal and policy issues involved in physician-assisted suicide.

Gilbert Geis

See also Alzheimer's disease; Cancer research; Elder abuse; Health care; Heaven's Gate mass suicide; Kevorkian, Jack; Liberalism in U.S. politics; Medicine; Supreme Court decisions.

■ Pitt, Brad

Identification American actor
Born December 18, 1963; Shawnee, Oklahoma

Beginning in the 1990's, Pitt proved himself to be among the most effective, conscientious, and versatile actors in Hollywood.

Brad Pitt spent the 1990's consciously molding his career in ways that would reflect his extraordinary acting ability. Driven by a compelling work ethic, Pitt acted in several undistinguished films and a number of television shows before 1991, when he appeared for a fleeting fifteen minutes as J. D. in *Thelma and Louise,* which won an Academy Award for Best Original Screenplay.

Brad Pitt poses with his Golden Globe Award at the 1996 awards ceremony. He won Best Supporting Actor for his role in Twelve Monkeys. (AP/Wide World Photos)

Although Pitt's role was small, his performance, particularly his love scene with Geena Davis, projected his sexuality and charisma so authentically that he clearly established his star quality. Remarkably handsome, the blond-haired, blue-eyed Pitt with his perfect physique quickly became a sex symbol, but this is precisely what Pitt feared and struggled to thwart. He could have had a comfortable career playing shallow pretty-boy roles, but he was too serious an actor to do so.

In 1991, Pitt starred as a guitar-playing teen icon with his hair in a huge pompadour in *Johnny Suede.* Pitt attracted the attention of actor-director Robert Redford, who cast him in the role of Paul MacLean, a champion fly fisherman, in *A River Runs Through It*

(1992). In the same year, Pitt played a police officer in the partially animated film *Cool World.* Critics thought that Pitt was the only saving grace in *Johnny Suede* and had little good to say about *Cool World,* a film with special effects that bewildered Pitt, who had won the role over more than two hundred auditioning actors. In all of these films, Pitt played drastically different roles, none of which emphasized his good looks. Pitt worked hard to bring authenticity to his roles, learning fly fishing for *A River Runs Through It,* and frequently ending up with fishhooks in his scalp.

In the 1990's, Pitt acted in several films, including *Kalifornia* (1993), *Interview with the Vampire* (1994), *Legends of the Fall* (1994), *Seven Years in Tibet* (1997), and *Fight Club* (1999). Each provided him with dramatic roles that advanced his acting accomplishments, and none were dependent upon his looks. He won the Golden Globe Award for *Twelve Monkeys* (1995), which also earned him an Oscar nomination.

Ever the consummate professional, Pitt did most of his stunts himself. In 1995, his role as a homicide detective in *Seven* was much heralded. In doing his own stunts in that movie, he fell through the windshield of a car and badly injured his arm, but the filming went on. The following year, *People* magazine named Pitt the Sexiest Man Alive. A cottage industry sprang up around tracking his romances.

Impact Brad Pitt set a high standard for professionalism in the film industry. Versatility distinguished his stellar career in the 1990's and beyond.

Further Reading

Dempsey, Amy. *Brad Pitt.* Philadelphia: Chelsea House, 1998.

Robb, Brian J. *Brad Pitt: The Rise to Stardom.* London: Plexus, 1996.

R. Baird Shuman

See also Cruise, Tom; Film in the United States; Paltrow, Gwyneth; Palahniuk, Chuck; *Thelma and Louise.*

■ Pixar

Identification American computer animation and film studio

In the 1990's, Pixar was at the center of the computer revolution transforming communications in America. Largely owned by computer pioneer Steve Jobs, Pixar was a leader in creating software and hardware to render computer-generated images onto film. Combining their technological progress with artistic imagination, Pixar animators made three feature-length, fully computer-animated films that took Hollywood by storm.

In 1990, Pixar was a five-year-old computer company with a limited market for its expensive Pixar Image Computers, narrowly staving off bankruptcy by producing computer-animated commercials. Its owner, chairman of the board, and eventual chief operating officer was Steve Jobs, the creative cofounder of Apple Computer. With Pixar's computer-animated short film *Knick Knack* (1989) winning numerous prizes, Pixar and Walt Disney Studios in 1991 entered into a $26 million agreement to produce and distribute three feature-length computer-animated films.

As Pixar continued to make award-winning commercials and develop computer-imaging technologies through its RenderMan development team, Pixar animator John Lasseter took charge of developing Pixar's first feature film. Although beginning with hand-drawn sketches, Lasseter's team rendered each frame of the film on computers. It was a laborious, multistep process but promised the ability to show three-dimensional representation of lighting, perspective, and tactile surfacing in a realistic manner beyond the capabilities of traditional animation.

The First Computer-Animated Film On Thanksgiving, 1995, *Toy Story* opened in theaters, the first completely computer-animated feature film in history. In a thoroughly charming story, the memorable lead characters—toys cowboy Woody and space ranger Buzz Lightyear—overcome their rivalry for the attention of their owner, nine-year-old Andy, to save each other from threatened destruction. The talented actors Tom Hanks and Tim Allen dexterously supply the voices of Woody and Buzz, respectively. The other toys, such as grouchy Mr. Potato Head (Don Rickles), self-centered piggy bank Hamm (John Ratzenberger), loyal Slinky Dog (Jim Varney), and angst-ridden dinosaur Rex (Wallace Shawn), have personalities rooted in their aspects as toys. Randy Newman and Lyle Lovett composed and sang the musical score, carefully calibrated to each character and including the Academy Award-nominated song "You've Got a Friend in Me," perfectly capturing the theme of the film.

Pixar's union of technological achievement and dramatic skill is well demonstrated in the first moments of the film. Andy is playing with his toys, twirling them around and speaking their words so as to give them a semblance of life. Andy then leaves the room and all is still. Suddenly the toys spring to life, the film audience for the first time seeing fully realized, three-dimensional animation of inanimate objects. From that opening to the last rousing scene when the toys are joyfully reunited, *Toy Story* was a critical and popular hit, the largest revenue-grossing film of 1995. To make *Toy Story,* Pixar animators filled over one thousand CD-ROMs with 110,000 individually rendered frames. Woody himself required one hundred animation variables, or "avars," to animate his face and fifty-nine motion controls to animate his mouth alone.

Pixar directors and animators never allowed their technological skills to overwhelm the film's plot and human—or perhaps better said, toy—warmth and authenticity. The Online Film Critics Society ranked *Toy Story* as the greatest animated film of all time. The American Film Institute included it as one of the one hundred greatest American films ever made.

Pixar Animation Studio In 1995, Pixar became a publicly traded company, raising $140 million in the biggest initial public offering (IPO) of the year. With the success of *Toy Story,* it was clear that Pixar's future lay with its animation studio. Pixar's animated short film *Geri's Game* (1997), an ingenious tale of a chess-playing senior citizen in a park matching wits against himself, reflected dramatic improvements in the ability to computer-animate human skin and clothing. Pixar showed its new techniques to good effect in its next two films. *A Bug's Life* (1998) is a stirring story of a colony of ants and a troupe of comical bugs learning to stand up to a bullying grasshopper. In *Toy Story 2* (1999), the friendship of Woody and Buzz is deepened as they team up to save other toys from exile to a collector's museum. A sequel that measured up to the high dramatic and artistic standards of the original, *Toy Story 2* grossed over $485 million worldwide. Demonstrating the genius of the Pixar-Disney collaboration, Woody, Buzz, and the poignant toy cowgirl Jessie of *Toy Story 2* (voiced by Joan Cusack) joined the pantheon of Disney icons in Disney parades, ice shows, and amusement parks.

Steve Jobs, CEO of Pixar, which created the animated film "Toy Story." (Hulton Archive/Getty Images)

By the end of the 1990's, it was evident that Pixar had become not only a technological leader in computer development and animation but also one of the finest film studios in American history. Every Pixar film was charming, witty, wholesome, and an artistic success, the exquisite details rendered in its computer-animated frames outdone only by the care and attention Pixar animators lavished on character and story. The inspiring message of each film: the willingness of humans—although enacted by animated toys and bugs—to sacrifice for their friends.

Impact Pixar, based in Emeryville, California, was one of the most creative, innovative, and in the end successful companies of the 1990's. It pioneered three-dimensional computer-animated technology. As a computer hardware, software, and media company, it represented the successful return of entrepreneur Jobs and shared in the glory and rising stock prices of the dot-com craze. However, Pixar's greatest impact was derived not only by looking forward but also by looking to the past. Its three high-grossing feature films, *Toy Story, A Bug's Life,* and *Toy Story 2,* and the entertaining shorts it showed before each one, recalled the golden age of Hollywood, now rendered through digital technology. With compelling stories, engaging dialogue, attention to detail, stirring music, and a commitment to warm and wholesome entertainment, Pixar Animation Studios created the films in the 1990's that were perhaps most destined to endure as classics in the decades to come.

Further Reading

Deutschman, Alan. *The Second Coming of Steve Jobs.* New York: Broadway Books, 2000. Conversational biography of Jobs, with a chapter on his success with Pixar, thereby putting himself in the center of the computer industry for a second time.

Paik, Karen. *To Infinity and Beyond! The Story of Pixar Animation Studios.* San Francisco: Chronicle Books, 2007. Beautifully illustrated, carefully documented, definitive history of Pixar animation, with forewords by founder Steve Jobs, technology director Ed Catmull, and animator John Lasseter.

Price, Daniel. *The Pixar Touch.* New York: Alfred A. Knopf, 2008. Inspiring story of Pixar's corporate success, emphasizing its role as the most important film studio of the modern era.

Rubin, Michael. *Droidmaker: George Lucas and the Digital Revolution.* Gainesville, Fla.: Triad, 2005. Narrates the history of Pixar from its first days as an outgrowth of George Lucas's computer-generated imagery (CGI) technology.

Howard Bromberg

See also Advertising; Amazon.com; Apple Computer; CGI; Computers; Dot-coms; Film in the United States; Internet; Jobs, Steve; Science and technology; Stock market; Toys and games.

■ *Planned Parenthood v. Casey*

Identification U.S. Supreme Court decision
Date Decided on June 29, 1992

The Supreme Court upheld the central holding of Roe v. Wade, *the 1973 case that held that a woman's choice of whether to have an abortion was protected by the constitutional right of privacy.*

Of the nine Supreme Court justices who had participated in *Roe v. Wade,* six had left the Court by 1992. All six replacements had been appointed by Republican presidents, and of the three remaining on the Court, two, William H. Rehnquist and Byron White, had dissented in *Roe.* These circumstances created an expectation that *Roe* might be overturned. An opportunity for reversal arose when five provisions of the Pennsylvania Abortion Control Act of 1982 were challenged by Planned Parenthood of Southeastern Pennsylvania, an abortion provider. The district court held all five provisions to be unconstitutional. The U.S. Court of Appeals for the Third Circuit held only the spousal notification provision to be invalid. The Supreme Court essentially affirmed the holding of the court of appeals.

In *Planned Parenthood v. Casey,* the Court rejected the rigid trimester structure created in *Roe,* substituting instead an "undue burden" test, in which a restriction on the abortion right would be invalid if it "has the purpose or effect of placing a substantial obstacle in the path of a woman seeking an abortion of a nonviable fetus." Applying this test, the Court upheld provisions requiring a minor seeking an abortion to notify at least one of her parents; requiring abortionists to provide information to a woman requesting an abortion regarding the nature and risks of abortion and childbirth; requiring a twenty-four-hour waiting period after the woman's receipt of the mandated information, after which her consent for the abortion would become valid; and requiring certain recordkeeping. The Court struck down a provision of the Pennsylvania law that required physicians to refrain from performing an abortion on a married woman unless she had notified her husband of her decision to abort.

Impact The Supreme Court reaffirmed both the right of a woman to choose to have an abortion before fetal viability without undue governmental interference and the state's power to restrict abortions after viability so long as exceptions are made for pregnancies that endanger the woman's life or health. That a majority in *Casey* reaffirmed the fundamental nature of the abortion right makes it less likely that the right will be overturned in the future. Four justices in *Casey*, however, would have overturned *Roe*, and Samuel Alito, who while on the Third Circuit opined that all the provisions of the Pennsylvania statute should be upheld, was later nominated associate justice of the United States in 2005 and assumed office the following year.

Further Reading

Baird, Robert M., and Stuart E. Rosenbaum, eds. *The Ethics of Abortion: Pro-Life vs. Pro-Choice.* 3d ed. Amherst, N.Y.: Prometheus Books, 2001.

Glenn, Richard. *The Right to Privacy: Rights and Liberties Under the Law.* Santa Barbara, Calif.: ABC-Clio, 2003.

Mersky, Roy M., and Suzanne F. Young, comps. *A Documentary History of the Legal Aspects of Abortion in the United States: Planned Parenthood v. Casey.* Littleton, Colo.: Fred B. Rothman, 1996.

Howard C. Ellis

See also Abortion; Marriage and divorce; Medicine; *Rust v. Sullivan*; Supreme Court decisions; Thomas, Clarence; Women's rights.

■ Plasma screens

Definition Screens consisting of thousands of gas-filled cells that are sandwiched between two glass plates, two sets of electrodes, and protective layers

Plasma screen development led to the production of television sets and monitors that can produce bright, clear pictures on large screens that are only a few inches thick.

In an effort to develop effective displays for educational purposes, the plasma screen display was invented in the 1960's at the Coordinated Science Laboratory at the University of Illinois by Donald Bitzer, Gene Slottow, and Robert Wilson. Because of their relatively large screen size and thin profile, the original monochrome displays were popular in high-profile places like lobbies, airport lounges, and stock exchanges. In 1987, Larry F. Weber formed a company called Plasmaco to produce plasma screens. The company manufactured monochrome plasma computer displays until 1993.

When liquid crystal display (LCD) screens that produced color started taking over the market, Weber began the development of a color plasma display. He produced a flat-panel display consisting of tiny, colored phosphors that were sandwiched between two glass panels and illuminated to different intensities by a mixture of noble gases that were electrically converted into the plasma state. The excited phosphors emitted light of varying colors to generate an overall image. By 1994, Weber demonstrated the brightness and contrast ratios available with such screens.

In 1996, Plasmaco was purchased by Matsushita Electrical Industries. Weber was retained as the president of Plasmaco. Pioneer started selling the first plasma screen televisions to the public in 1997. In 1998, plasma display panels (PDPs) were used for televising Olympic events. It was a huge success. Through the efforts of Weber and Bill Schindler, a 60-inch plasma screen prototype was unveiled in 1999. It had the best contrast ratio of any screen in the industry. After the price of plasma screen televisions began to fall in the later part of 1999, they became increasingly popular.

Impact Consumers are shifting from the traditional cathode-ray tube (CRT) televisions to flat-panel plasma and LCD televisions that provide a better television-viewing experience. With their high resolution of images, exceptional color accuracy, image depth, widescreen aspect ratio, uniform screen brightness, wide viewing angle, and slim, space-saving design, plasma screen displays have revolutionized every aspect of television viewing. Plasma screens have universal display capability. They can accept any video format, including high-definition television (HDTV), digital television video (DTV), DVD video, computer video, and digital satellite broadcasts. Plasma screens have dominated in the larger television sizes, particularly 40 inches and above. The largest plasma screen display in the world, 103 inches, was shown at the Consumer Electronics show in Las Vegas, Nevada, in 2006. Over time, plasma screen manufacturers have devised ways to greatly reduce the problem of screen burn-in, the retention of images shown for a prolonged period of time on plasma screens.

Further Reading

Mitchell, Mitch. *Visual Effects for Film and Television.* Woburn, Mass.: Focal Press, 2004.

Whitaker, Jerry C. *Standard Handbook of Video and Television Engineering.* New York: McGraw-Hill, 2003.

Alvin K. Benson

See also Computers; DVDs; Inventions; Science and technology; Television.

■ Poetry

Definition A form of concentrated expression through meaning, sound, and rhythm

While poetry of the 1990's was certainly engaged with the theme of the fin de siècle—the end of the twentieth century as well as the beginning of the new millennium with its promises of yet more endings and uncertainties—there were also bold, frequently controversial new approaches to the art during the decade.

Diversity characterizes American poetry of the 1990's as a whole. Anthologists of 1990's literature disagreed vigorously on what poetry was "best." Poetic experiments based on information-age technology along with the rich assortment of political, ethnic, social, and aesthetic principles presented a challenge to any editor of poetry.

U.S. Poets The culmination of transcendental poet A. R. Ammons's career received a great deal of recognition in the 1990's, including the National Book Award. Ammons's main achievement for the decade was *Garbage* (1993), a defense of meaning and connection. Louise Glück's Pulitzer Prize-winning volume *The Wild Iris* (1992) combines confession, metaphysics, and the mundane. Yusef Komunyakaa's jazz-inspired Pulitzer Prize winner *Neon Vernacular* (1993) is grounded in his Vietnam War experience. *The Best American Poetry 1996* editor Adrienne Rich made politically oriented choices for the volume, including Alberto Álvaro Ríos's "Domingo Limón," a mix of realism and surrealism. Literary critic Harold Bloom's anthology, *The Best of the Best American Poetry, 1988-1997*, features seventy-five important poems, including W. S. Merwin's "The Stranger." In 1998, Merwin wrote *Folding Cliffs: A Narrative*, an epic in verse about Hawaii. His *Lament for the Makers* (1996) eulogizes poets who have influenced his poetry.

Pulitzer Prize winners of the decade were Charles Simic, *The World Doesn't End* (1989), Mona Van Duyn, *Near Changes* (1990), James Tate, *Selected Poems* (1991), Louise Glück, *The Wild Iris*, Yusef Komunyakaa, *Neon Vernacular*, Philip Levine, *The Simple Truth* (1994), Jorie Graham, *The Dream of the Unified Field* (1995), Lisel Mueller, *Alive Together: New and Selected Poems* (1996), Charles Wright, *Black Zodiac* (1997), and Mark Strand, *Blizzard of One* (1998).

Poets laureate to the Library of Congress included Mark Strand, 1990-1991; Joseph Brodsky, 1991-1992; Mona Van Duyn, 1992-1993; Rita Dove, 1993-1995; Robert Hass, 1995-1997; and Robert Pinsky, 1997-2000. From 1999-2000, the special bicentennial consultants were Rita Dove, Louise Glück, and W. S. Merwin.

Canadian Poets Margaret Atwood's 1996 *Morning in the Burned House* takes an elegiac approach to feminism. Métis writer Joanne Arnott's *Wiles of Girlhood* (1991), based on her experience as a mixed-race person, won the Gerald Lampert Award. Gary Barwin, who also writes for children, offered *Cruelty to Fabulous Animals* (1995) and *Outside the Hat* (1998). Retrospectives of note included metaphysical poet Margaret Avison's *Selected Poems* (1991) and Ted Plantos's *Daybreak's Long Waking: Poems Selected and New* (1997).

Among French Canadian poets, Gilles Vigneault enjoyed commercial success in 1992 with the elegant *Bois de marée.* Madeleine Gagnon won the Governor General's Award for Poetry in 1990 with *Chant pour un Québec lointain.* Her volume *La Terre est remplie de langage* (1993) dealt with meaning, while Louise Dupré treated the themes of time and death in *Noir déjà* (1993). Robert Melançon brought beauty to ordinary objects in *L'Avant-printemps à Montréal* (1994). In 1998, performance poets like Stéphane Despatie found a venue in Les Intouchables, a new publishing firm.

Likely to be overlooked by the dichotomy of English/French is work by ethnic groups such as the Southeast Asian Canadians. Surjeet Kalsey, writing in both English and Punjabi, published *Glimpses of Twentieth Century Punjabi Poetry* (1992) as well as two volumes of her own poetry, *Behind the Palace Doors* and *Woman, Words, and Shakti* (both in 1999).

Experimental Poetry Out of earlier Black Mountain experiments with multilayered texts, "new media poetry"—that is, cyberpoetry or digital poetry—made aesthetic use of hypertext and other computer technologies to produce interactive poetry. Also important were Language and performance poetry. Experimental writers in the 1990's included David Antin, Rae Armentrout, Tina Darragh, Hedwig Gorski, Adolfo Guzman-Lopez, Erica Hunt, Maggie Estep, P. Inman, Ron Silliman, Edwin Torres, Carla Harryman, Fanny Howe, Jackson Mac Low, Bernadette Mayer, Harryette Mullen, Steven McCaffery (Canadian), Ricardo Sanchez, Hannah Weiner, Saul Williams, and Emanuel Xavier, creator of the Glam Slam poetry competition in New York.

Impact The 1990's were important for poetry in at least two ways. Publicly accessible poetry was made possible by the exponential rise of Web usage. Also, in the United States more than in Canada, the trend was toward a more democratized and accessible poetry. There was a degree of acceptance in the public mind of poetic experiments that went far beyond the printed page. Institutions such as the National Endowment for the Arts did not make changes that supported performance poetry, although the presence of Language poets in university writing programs during the 1990's demonstrates acceptance of some experimental approaches.

Further Reading

Bloom, Harold, and David Lehman, eds. *The Best of the Best American Poetry, 1988-1997.* New York: Scribner, 1998. Assembles a large number of poems from the 1990's and criticizes Adrienne Rich's contribution to this series.

Glazier, Loss. *Digital Poetics: Hypertext, Visual-Kinetic Text and Writing in Programmable Media.* Tuscaloosa: University of Alabama Press, 2001. Celebrates the arrival of digital poetry, its contribution to theories that recognize texts as problematic; hypertext; interactive poetry; and more.

Lang, Robert, ed. *Contemporary Canadian Authors.* Vol. 1. New York: Gale Canada, 1996. This resource has both Canadian poets' biographies and lists of works.

Morris, Adalaide, and Thomas Swiss, eds. *New Media Poetics: Contexts, Technotexts, and Theories.* Cambridge, Mass.: MIT Press, 2006. The articles maintain that the new poetics is a vast digital break from traditional written poetry.

Rich, Adrienne, and David Lehman, eds. *The Best American Poetry 1996.* New York: Scribner, 1996. Includes some overlooked poets from the 1990's.

Schaub, Thomas, ed. *Contemporary Literature* 42, no. 2 (Summer, 2001). This issue is titled "American Poetry of the 1990's," a resource for those who would like to explore a fin de siècle theme of loss.

Silliman, Ron, ed. *In the American Tree.* Orono, Maine: National Poetry Foundation, 2001. Anthology of 1990's poetry.

Suzanne Araas Vesely

See also Alvarez, Julia; Angelou, Maya; Komunyakaa, Yusef; Literature in Canada; Literature in the United States; National Endowment for the Arts (NEA); Ondaatje, Michael; Spoken word movement; Strand, Mark; Updike, John.

■ Pogs

Definition Children's game of milk caps

Playing Pogs became a major national fad for school-age children of the early-middle 1990's. While a game of the simplest nature, it inspired a contentious disagreement over rights to use the name "Pog" itself.

The game of Pogs, which children played with small cardboard wafers, or milk caps, was a sidewalk activity popular for decades in Hawaii. In 1993, after it caught on in California, Pogs gave rise to a national, multimillion-dollar industry.

Once introduced, Pogs easily gained popularity at schools, where the milk caps themselves could be carried unobtrusively in pockets. The game's popularity was enhanced by the ease with which it could be turned to gambling, prompting some school administrations to ban it from campuses. Pogs was otherwise regarded in favorable light by educators, it being a group activity in contrast to the video and computer games massively popular since the prior decade.

The game entered the marketplace in the form of "collector Pogs," featuring various licensed characters from comic strips, television, or films. Due to the ease of their manufacture, advertising Pogs also quickly appeared.

The name of the cardboard disks and the game itself originated in Hawaii, where a Maui beverage company, Haleakala Dairy, made a juice drink of passion fruit, orange, and guava, marketed under the Pog name. The cardboard disks found on these drinks provided the original playing pieces.

Numerous variants of the game existed, most involved stacking the disks facedown in a pile. Players took turns with "slammers," larger disks of plastic or metal, which they brought down onto the stack in such a way as to upset it, the aim being to make as many Pogs as possible land faceup instead of still facedown. Players "won" or gained points from faceup Pogs.

Disagreement over rights to the "Pog" name arose in 1994. One firm believed "Pog" was a generic term chosen by children at play and not by a manufacturer. The World Pog Federation of Costa Mesa, California, however, won exclusive rights to the name in November, 1994, due in part to Haleakala Dairy being 14 percent owner of the Costa Mesa federation.

The move may have helped the fad falter, since competitors such as the Universal Pogs Association, which afterward became Universal Slammers, Inc., were forced to use generic terms such as "milk caps," which appealed less to children.

Impact Although primarily a fad of the early-middle decade, Pogs achieved nearly universal recognition among all age groups and became one of the symbols of the times.

Further Reading

Derolf, Shane. *The WPF Official Pog Collector.* New York: Random House, 1995. A useful guide for gaining insight into how Pogs were seen by youths who played the game.

Lewis, Tommi, and Craig C. Olsen. *Pogs: The Milkcap Guide.* Kansas City, Mo.: Andrews McMeel, 1994. A guide to game history, rules, and tournaments, with color illustrations.

Page, Jason. *The Unofficial POG and Cap Players' Handbook.* London, England: Bloomsbury Publishing, 1995. Useful for its international perspective upon an American-originating game.

Mark Rich

See also Fads; Hobbies and recreation; Pokémon franchise; Toys and games.

■ Pokémon franchise

Identification Gaming phenomenon
Date Created in 1995

Pokémon became one of Nintendo's most successful franchises, branching out of the original video game to television, film, manga, and other merchandise, and influencing a large group of the youth population.

Pokémon, also known as Pocket Monsters, was created in 1995 by Japanese game designer Satoshi Tajiri. It was originally a role-playing game released in Japan for Nintendo's Game Boy personal gaming system. After success in Japan, the video game was released in the United States. In the game, the player creates a character and battles with other characters by using a captured Pokémon.

In 1998, United Paramount Network (UPN) began airing Pokémon anime in the United States. The main character was known as Ash and was given Pikachu, the yellow creature often seen in Pokémon advertising, as his first Pokémon. Later games were based on Ash, including *Pokémon Yellow,* which was the first Pokémon game created for Nintendo's Game Boy Color.

Pokémon continued to expand. *Pokémon: The First*

A boy hugs an oversized Pikachu doll at the premiere of the animated feature Pokémon: The First Movie *on November 6, 1999, in Los Angeles.* (AP/Wide World Photos)

Movie was released in Japan to ecstatic reception and then in the United States in 1999. Game publisher Wizards of the Coast also released the first edition of the Pokémon Trading Card Game. Several collections of manga based on both the anime and the trading card game were also released in the late 1990's. In 1999, Pokémon sound tracks were released on compact disc. Several films and sound tracks followed.

Controversy erupted over Pokémon and the popularity the game and series enjoyed. The "evolution" that Pokémon experience in the game was said to run counter to Judeo-Christian creationism; in addition, many believed that Pokémon contained occult themes and promoted violence, especially toward animals. The claim that Pokémon was anti-Christian was refuted by the Vatican.

Several episodes of the television series were banned in the United States for a variety of reasons; one included the villain James of Team Rocket cross-dressing in a woman's bathing suit with inflatable breasts, while another featured guns being pointed at characters. More notable was a 1997 episode that caused over six hundred Japanese children to experience seizures because of a scene's strobe effects. The episode was banned in the United States, as well as in other countries around the world.

Impact The cult status of Pokémon has left a mark on popular culture. Pikachu, the main Pokémon from the original anime series, has become a widely recognized figure, even featured as a balloon in the Macy's Thanksgiving Day Parade. Pokémon is the second most successful game franchise in history, behind only Mario, another Nintendo property.

Further Reading

Allison, Anne. *Millennial Monsters: Japanese Toys and the Global Imagination.* Berkeley: University of California Press, 2006.

Kelts, Roland. *Japanamerica: How Japanese Pop Culture Has Invaded the U.S.* New York: Palgrave MacMillan, 2006.

Emily Carroll Shearer

See also Children's television; Television; Toys and games; UPN television network; Video games.

■ Police brutality

Definition Excessive use of force accompanied by bodily injury and/or death

High-profile cases in the 1990's led to greater societal awareness and media attention. Calls for greater accountability have led to restructuring and the creation of citizen boards and watchdog groups.

The 1990's witnessed increased attention to the potential problem of systemic police brutality. While isolated instances of police brutality have occurred throughout history, the number of cases, the severity of beatings and/or shootings, and the increased media attention in the 1990's brought the problem to the forefront of societal awareness. This was helped in part by new technologies that allowed citizens to record incidents of violence that traditionally went unreported.

The cause or scope of police brutality is not certain, but many commentators have speculated that a number of factors converged in the 1990's that made the use of excessive force seem an almost natural outcome. First was the increased militarization of police forces to combat more sophisticated weaponry and violent criminals. This militarization created an "us against them" mentality that led to anyone outside the force being viewed as a potential enemy. Second was a movement to "get tough on crime." Along with policy changes such as mandatory sentencing, truth in sentencing, and three-strikes laws, the push to get tough on crime advanced the notion of zero tolerance that gave tacit authorization for police officers to do whatever is necessary to get criminals off the streets. Third is the fact that police officers enjoy a tremendous amount of discretion, limited supervision, and fairly low visibility. Finally, while not all officers engage in police brutality, another important factor that allowed for the spread of power abuse was the "Blue Wall of Silence." Working closely with one another in a high-stress/high-risk profession creates something of a closed society wherein individuals within are charged with looking out for one another. Even those who do not commit abuse are reluctant to turn in their brethren—thus allowing the cases to go unreported and allowing those with a tendency toward violence to remain on the job. Between fellow officers looking the other way and victims being afraid to come forward because of the extreme power they believe officers hold, most cases of police brutality have traditionally gone unreported.

Key Incidents Three cases were particularly troubling and were national news for quite some time: the beating of Rodney King in 1991, the torture of Abner Louima in 1997, and the shooting of Amadou Diallo in 1999.

King was pulled over by Los Angeles Police Department (LAPD) officers on March 3, 1991, after a high-speed chase. King, who had a history of drunk driving and other crimes, resisted arrest. Three officers used force to get King to assume a prone position, but they continued to kick him, stomp on him, and hit him with metal batons after he was down—while their supervisor watched. The incident happened to be caught on tape by a bystander, George Holliday, who witnessed the event. Media outlets began airing the tape immediately, and the entire nation witnessed what was clearly an excessive use of force.

On August 9, 1997, New York Police Department (NYPD) officers were dispatched to investigate a disturbance outside a city nightclub, Club Rendez-Vous. A fight broke out, and one of the officers, Justin Volpe, was hit. Abner Louima, a Haitian immigrant, was identified as the assailant and was booked on a number of charges. Officers beat Louima on the way to the precinct and carried on the savagery once inside. At one point, he was stripped to the waist and sodomized with a bathroom plunger that was then shoved into his mouth, breaking some of his teeth. He required medical attention, and an ambulance was called. Police initially stated that he was a homosexual and that they had "found" him. An anonymous tip from within the hospital brought the *Daily News* onto the scene, and the Louima case would, like the King beating, make national headlines.

On February 4, 1999, four plainclothes members of the NYPD Street Crimes Unit (a special unit created to target violent crime) approached Amadou Diallo, an immigrant from West Africa, because he loosely resembled a rape suspect. Upon their approach, Diallo reached into his back pocket to pull out a wallet. Fearing that he was reaching for a gun, the officers shot Diallo forty-one times. The sheer volume of gunfire left many wondering whether police were quick to pull the trigger and whether less lethal methods could have been employed. Regardless, this was yet another case that made national headlines and put the issue of excessive force in the minds of the general public.

Impact Public attention and embarrassment on the part of many police departments in the 1990's led to a number of changes designed to hold law enforcement accountable. One such change was an increasing number of citizen review boards created and charged with monitoring police activities. Another change has been the installation of monitoring devices in patrol cars that can keep an accurate record of what transpires between the time an officer encounters a suspect and the time the suspect is taken into custody. While isolated cases of abuse are bound to continue, law enforcement has apparently bent to public outcry and agreed to mechanisms that help society to "police the police."

Further Reading

Juarez, Juan Antonio. *Brotherhood of Corruption: A Cop Breaks the Silence on Police Abuse, Brutality and Racial Profiling.* Chicago: Chicago Review Press, 2004. Written by a former Chicago policeman, this work provides an insider's view into the behind-the-scenes actions of some police officers and how the "wall of silence" can perpetuate problems.

McArdle, Andrea, and Tanya Erzen, eds. *Zero Tolerance: Quality of Life and the New Police Brutality in New York City.* New York: New York University Press, 2001. Collection of articles that highlight the inherent tensions created with zero-tolerance and tough-on-crime policies that pit police against society.

Winters, Paul A., ed. *Policing the Police.* San Diego, Calif.: Greenhaven Press, 1995. An anthology that provides different insights into the problem of police brutality. Includes a good bibliography.

Jeffrey S. Ashley

See also African Americans; Conservatism in U.S. politics; Crime; Diallo shooting; Giuliani, Rudolph; Gun control; Hate crimes; Immigration to the United States; King, Rodney; Los Angeles riots; Louima torture case; Mount Pleasant riot; Race relations; Scandals; Sharpton, Al.

■ Popcorn, Faith

Identification Marketing consultant
Born February 11, 1947; New York, New York

Named the "Nostradamus of marketing" by Fortune *magazine in the early 1990's, Popcorn was the most famous prognosticator of trends in that decade.*

The head of the market analysis firm BrainReserve, Faith Popcorn achieved success through advising powerful corporate clients on consumer behavior, consolidating her reputation as a baby-boom prophet with her 1991 national best seller *The Popcorn Report*. She was famous for her identification of such trends as "cocooning," the inclination to withdraw into the security of home, which pointed to the growth in home delivery, home business, and home shopping. Popcorn was also adept at formulating colorful words and phrases—such as her own catchy, invented surname—that captured the imagination of the public; additionally, her identification of trends appealed to a general wish on the part of her readers for greater clarity and control over their lives.

As much intuitive and emotional as scientific, Popcorn later in the decade published a second book, *Clicking* (1996), with Lys Marigold, which identified such tendencies as a suspicion of authority, or "icon toppling," and the search for a spiritual dimension to life, or "anchoring." The identification of the latter trend demonstrated the way in which Popcorn's analyses of cultural developments moved beyond market trends and addressed issues that were less secular in nature.

Impact Popcorn's identification of trends not only had a major impact on the business decisions of her corporate clients but also spoke to the baby-boom generation as it entered middle age and pondered the upcoming new millennium.

Further Reading

Popcorn, Faith. *The Popcorn Report: Faith Popcorn on the Future of Your Company, Your World, Your Life.* New York: Doubleday, 1991.

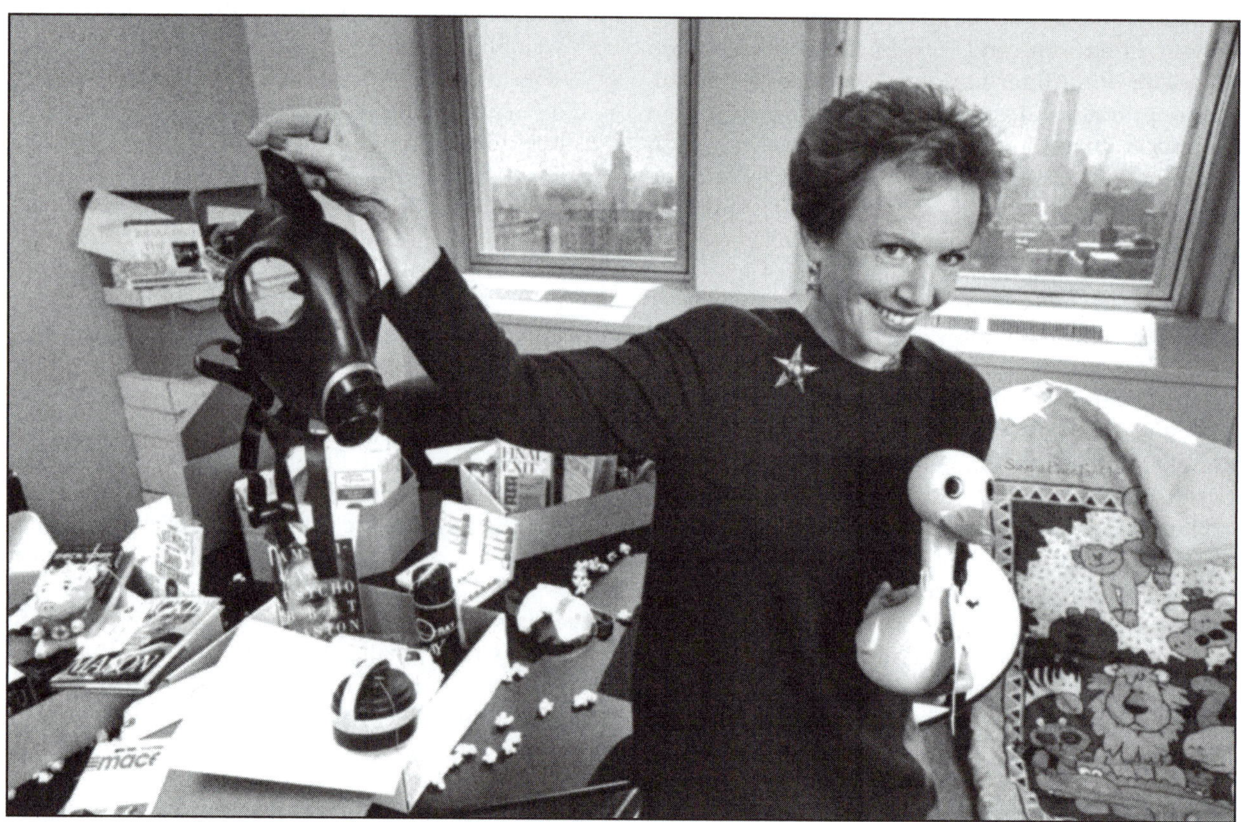

Faith Popcorn. (Hulton Archive/Getty Images))

Sherdan, William A. *The Fortune Sellers: The Big Business of Buying and Selling Predictions.* New York: John Wiley & Sons, 1998.

Margaret Boe Birns

See also Advertising; Business and the economy in the United States; Jewish Americans; Religion and spirituality in the United States.

■ Poverty

Definition A relative measure of income below a certain threshold

In the 1990's, Canada based its response to national poverty on a tax-transfer system that stabilized national poverty rates. The U.S. government relied on a distributive system that widened the inequality chasm between the wealthy and the poor.

Economically, both countries shared common experiences during the 1990's. At the beginning of the decade, both countries suffered through an economic recession. By the end of the 1990's, Canada and the United States had increased trade with other nations. Technological advancements catapulted both countries beyond their expectations. The definition of poverty was adjusted periodically to include such quantifiable and qualitative variables as social exclusion, economic growth rates, family composition, and access to jobs. U.S. and Canadian leaders supported some level of devolution—a shift of political and economic responsibilities from the national government to the individual states. Their policies, particularly regarding those living below the national poverty lines, had both similar and differing impacts on their citizens.

Canadian Policies for the Poor As Canada's national income increased, so did the salaries and wages of its citizens, yet these financial and social gains did not eradicate poverty. Canada relied on a statistical formula called low-income cut-off (LICO) to determine level of poverty and need for governmental support. This formula was very popular among the Canadian public and officials at all levels of government. It linked the percentage that an average Canadian household spent on basic necessities to the amount that a person currently earned and qualified to receive in government subsidies. The median income, however, remained stagnant throughout the decade. An increasing number of Canadians who were once part of the middle class were falling behind the national income average. The LICO standard for assistance was established too low to assist working-class families who were once part of the middle class. Poverty increased throughout all major cities and rural provinces, particularly among women, single-parent households, children, racial minorities, and laborers.

It was estimated that those living in poverty would need to work seventy-three hours more hours weekly in order to overcome poverty. Women were more likely than men to live below the poverty line, especially those who were mothers of children less than seven years of age. Child mortality rates among poorer families were twice the amount of those born to middle- and upper-class families. Furthermore, these children were more likely to have lower birth weights and to die from childhood injuries. They were much more likely to suffer from psychiatric and/or learning disabilities than were other children. Racial minorities were more likely to live in poverty than were Caucasians. The longer they remained in poverty, the more likely they were to remain in it and remain dependent on governmental subsidies. The only escape existed through obtaining additional education. Similar situations existed in the United States.

U.S. Response to National Poverty Though the United States remained the wealthiest country in the world and its antipoverty programs alleviated many social problems, it had the highest level of poverty among all industrialized nations. In 1990-1991, a recession occurred and slowed growth. These economic problems caused many Americans to support Arkansas governor Bill Clinton's economic and welfare reform plans in his bid for the presidency in 1992. Later in the decade, the United States expanded economic opportunities, advanced social policies, and increased foreign trade. Welfare reform, tax relief for the poor, earned-income tax credits, and educational opportunities were several programs created to decrease poverty in the United States. These measures increased aftertax income among all Americans during the remainder of the decade.

The same variables that contributed to poverty in Canada existed in the United States. Persons who

Number of U.S. Families Below the Poverty Level and Poverty Rate, 1990-1999

Year	*Number of Poor Families (in millions)*	*Poverty Rate for Families*	*Number of Poor Families with Female (NSP)* Householder (in millions)*	*Poverty Rate for Families with Female Householder*
1990	7.1	10.7	3.8	33.4
1991	7.7	11.5	4.2	35.6
1992	8.1	11.9	4.3	35.4
1993	8.4	12.3	4.4	35.6
1994	8.0	11.6	4.2	34.6
1995	7.5	10.8	4.1	32.4
1996	7.7	11.0	4.2	32.6
1997	7.3	10.3	4.0	31.6
1998	7.2	10.0	3.8	29.9
1999	6.8	9.3	3.6	27.8

*No spouse present.
Source: U.S. Census Bureau, Housing and Household Economic Statistics Division.

lived in poverty would be required to work the equivalent of two full-time jobs in order to overcome poverty. Women were more likely to live in poverty than were men, with single mothers with children experiencing higher poverty rates. Childhood morality and disability rates were higher among children living in poverty than among their middle- or upper-class counterparts. African Americans and Hispanics were more likely to live in poverty than were Caucasians.

Impact The debate over how to address poverty expanded throughout the decade to include topics such as basic human rights, the encouragement of self-reliance, the elimination of disability and discrimination in the workplace, and money flow into poverty-stricken households. Despite efforts to fight poverty, more than 3.6 million Canadians and 32.8 million Americans lived in poverty by the late 1990's. In both countries, higher-wage earners owned more wealth than those who lived at or below the poverty lines. The economic distance between the "haves" and "have-nots" grew. Canada narrowed the distance between these two groups, however, by creating a tax-transfer system that offset and stabilized the redistribution of income, while the United States experienced rising inequality between the groups.

Further Reading

Casper, Lynne M., Sara S. McLanahan, and Irwin Garfinkel. "The Gender-Poverty Gap: What We Can Learn from Other Countries." *American Sociological Review* 59, no. 4 (1994): 594-605. Examines eight industrialized countries' poverty rates and the factors affecting rates between men and women.

Myles, John. "How to Design a 'Liberal' Welfare State: A Comparison of Canada and the United States." *Social Policy and Administration* 32, no. 4 (1998): 341-364. Aims to show how differences in the two otherwise "liberal" welfare systems have generated substantially different patterns of welfare state retrenchment and distributive outcomes since the 1970's.

Osberg, Lars. "Poverty in Canada and the United States: Measurement, Trends, and Implications." *The Canadian Journal of Economics* 33, no. 4 (2000): 847-877. Explains why Canadian economic, social, education, and health care policies remain distinct from U.S. policies.

Dwight Vick

See also Business and the economy in Canada; Business and the economy in the United States; Clinton, Bill; Employment in Canada; Employment in the United States; Health care reform; Income

and wages in Canada; Income and wages in the United States; Recession of 1990-1991; Welfare reform.

■ Powell, Colin

Identification Chairman of the Joint Chiefs of Staff, 1989-1993

Born April 5, 1937; New York, New York

General Powell's leadership during the Gulf War catapulted him into the national spotlight and caused many to think of him as a suitable candidate for major national office.

Colin Powell's distinguished military career began in 1958 and included valorous combat service and a succession of increasingly responsible command and staff positions, frequently in the offices of high-ranking political figures. In 1987, he was named national security adviser to President Ronald Reagan. His appointment as chairman of the Joint Chiefs of Staff (JCS) in October, 1989, made him the highest-ranking military official in the new administration of President George H. W. Bush and put him in the forefront of several key issues that would dominate the national agenda for the next four years.

Powell was called on almost immediately to orchestrate a military intervention in Panama to oust dictator Manuel Noriega. The lessons learned from this operation were important when he was called on to marshal U.S. forces against Iraq's Saddam Hussein, who invaded neighboring Kuwait in August, 1990. For the next seven months, Powell was the public face of the U.S. military buildup aimed at protecting Saudi Arabia, Kuwait's neighbor, and evicting Iraq from Kuwait. Powell promoted a strategy that would commit overwhelming force to the operation once the American public was solidly behind the effort. The United States' unqualified success solidified the American public's esteem for Powell, whose candor and integrity made people feel confident in his abilities.

Both during and after the Gulf War, Powell was active in developing a new strategic mission for the U.S. military, reducing force size and eliminating many nuclear weapons. Meanwhile, although he was still on active duty, Powell was approached by both Republican and Democratic political strategists regarding his willingness to serve in high political offices. Then and later, Powell turned down such opportunities. When Bill Clinton was elected president in 1992, Powell remained in his position as JCS chairman and almost immediately became embroiled in debates about Clinton's wish to permit gays and lesbians to serve openly in the military. In 1993, Powell retired from active duty, although not before engaging in confrontations with members of Clinton's cabinet over potential U.S. involvement in Somalia and Bosnia.

After retiring, Powell committed himself to public speaking and writing his autobiography, *My American Journey*, which became a best seller in 1995. Pressure to become a candidate for president continued, fueled in part by Powell's immense popularity. Finally, in 1995, Powell made a public announcement that he would not run, effectively quelling efforts by both parties to have him be their standard-bearer. Two years later, he founded America's Promise, a nonprofit organization committed to improving educational and employment opportunities for American youth.

Colin Powell. (U.S. Air Force)

Impact In 2001, Powell became secretary of state under President George W. Bush. His four-year tenure in the position was marred by constant squabbling with more conservative members of the president's cabinet. Further, his public image was damaged when, in an attempt to convince the United Nations Security Council to declare war against Iraq in 2003, he asserted that Iraq possessed weapons of mass destruction, a claim later proven to be false.

Further Reading

DeYoung, Karen. *Soldier: The Life of Colin Powell.* New York: Alfred A. Knopf, 2006.

Powell, Colin, with Joseph E. Persico. *My American Journey.* New York: Random House, 1995.

Steins, Richard. *Colin Powell: A Biography.* Westport, Conn.: Greenwood Press, 2003.

Laurence W. Mazzeno

See also Bosnia conflict; Bush, George H. W.; Cheney, Dick; Clinton, Bill; CNN coverage of the Gulf War; Cold War, end of; Defense budget cuts; Don't ask, don't tell; Elections in the United States, 1996; Gulf War; Noriega capture and trial; Schwarzkopf, Norman; Somalia conflict; Wolfowitz, Paul.

■ Project Gutenberg

Definition Text digitization project

As a pioneer nonprofit volunteer project to digitize published works in the public domain, Project Gutenberg has amassed a collection of tens of thousands of e-books. Making them freely available on the Internet, it has prompted numerous similar projects around the world and changed the nature of publishing and libraries.

Project Gutenberg (named after the fifteenth century craftsman Johannes Gutenberg, who revolutionized the printing of books) began at the University of Illinois at Urbana-Champaign in 1971. A student at the school, Michael Hart, was allotted a grant for use of a university computer and conceived the idea of storing public domain literary works as electronic texts freely accessible by anyone. Entering the Declaration of Independence as his first document, Hart used 7-bit (Plain Vanilla) ASCII, elementary coding that would allow any type of computer to access materials. By 1989, Hart had succeeded in storing ten works, keying in the entries as continuous text (not page) files.

With the development of the Internet, mushrooming capacity for computer storage, and mass commercial acquisition of personal computers, Project Gutenberg experienced a quantum advance. During the 1990's, the project accumulated more than two thousand electronic books, both in English and other languages. Hart established monthly production targets with exponential annual increments: one text per month during 1991; two per month in 1992; three in 1993; and reaching one hundred e-books by 1994. To accelerate this pace, Hart began to attract and coordinate a corps of volunteers, who produced over the rest of the decade a monthly average of about three dozen texts.

With the collection growing, a categorization of holdings was devised: reference literature for encyclopedias and dictionaries; "heavy" literature denoting works of classical authors such as Dante, William Shakespeare, and Miguel de Cervantes; and "light" literature for works such as Lewis Carroll's *Alice's Adventures in Wonderland* (1865) or James Barrie's *Peter and Wendy* (1911). As the project entered into the twenty-first century, it surpassed more than ten thousand digitized or scanned texts, had enrolled hundreds of volunteers worldwide, and spawned Gutenberg projects in Europe, Australia, Canada, Portugal, and the Philippines.

Impact Project Gutenberg pioneered an impressive innovation. Nonetheless, by the following decade, e-books had become a commonplace of publishing and reading. The Google search engine enterprise initiated a project to scan millions of books from the world's leading libraries. Commercial enterprises, such as NetLibrary, offered full-text retrieval of books still in copyright. Full-text retrieval of articles from scholarly journals began with JSTOR (University of Michigan) and Project MUSE (The Johns Hopkins University). E-texts have definitively changed how publishers and libraries produce, store, and make accessible the printed word.

Further Reading

Fairhead, Elizabeth. "The Final Workshop of the Gutenberg-e Project." *Perspectives on History* 44, no. 5 (2006): 12-15.

Hans, Paula J. "Project Gutenberg Progresses: This Resource, Developed in 1971, Has Experienced

Its Share of Progress and Growing Pains." *Information Today* 21, no. 5 (2004): 28.
Hart, Michael S. "The Linear File: Project Gutenberg—Access to Electronic Texts." *Database* 13, no. 6 (December, 1990): 6.

Edward A. Riedinger

See also Audiobooks; Book clubs; Computers; E-mail; Internet; Literature in Canada; Literature in the United States; Publishing; World Wide Web.

■ Promise Keepers

Identification Christian men's movement
Date Founded in 1990

The 1990's saw a growing concern over male identity among men themselves, partly in reaction to the feminist and gay movements of previous decades, as well as a growth of interest in a specifically male spirituality. Promise Keepers was a spontaneous Christian response, particularly from the growing evangelical churches, to these concerns, manifesting itself mainly in mass rallies and in a specific agenda of "promises" that defined a male role.

Promise Keepers (PK) was formed by a group of evangelical Christian laymen led by the head football coach at the University of Colorado at Boulder. Bill McCartney was a highly successful coach who was involved with the Fellowship of Christian Athletes (FCA), among other Christian ventures. He had a vision of a men's movement that would disciple Christian men. Behind the vision was the awareness of both the success of the FCA in promoting a "muscular Christianity" and the insecurity of male identity both culturally and in the church, after several decades of feminism, gay rights activism, and successful Christian women's movements. By contrast, male spirituality seemed fragmented, uncertain, and lacking direction and leadership.

Establishing Promise Keepers A group of seventy-two laymen met at Boulder in 1990. They called the incipient movement "Promise Keepers," since one of the planks would be a specific list of promises. The seven promises were to honor Jesus Christ; to be in a small accountability group of other men; to practice purity; to build strong marriages; to honor their pastors; to reach beyond denominational and racial boundaries; and to obey the "Great Commandment" (Mark 12:30-31) and the "Great Commission" (Matthew 28:19-20). There was also a doctrinal minimum, which was basically that of conservative evangelicalism, holding to a belief in the Trinity, the Bible, salvation by faith in Christ alone, and his virgin birth and Second Coming. There was to be no membership as such. It was also to be a men's-only organization, with sons included.

The organization arranged large rallies in stadiums around the country and encouraged attendees to organize themselves into accountability groups based on their local churches. The first such big rally was held in July, 1991, in Boulder's Folsom Field, with 4,200 men in attendance. From that point, the movement mushroomed over the next five years. The year 1993 saw one rally, again at Folsom Field, but with 50,000 attending. In 1994, six rallies saw more than 270,000 attending. The total attendance for 1995 was 738,000 at thirteen rallies, and in 1996, twenty-two rallies included a total of 1.1 million men. The conferences were held over two days and cost $60 per person. Rallies consisted of inspirational messages, testimonies, and times of reconciliation and repentance. The atmosphere was often highly charged emotionally. In 1994, McCartney resigned his coaching job, though he refused to take a Promise Keepers salary.

Standing in the Gap The high point of the movement came during the Stand in the Gap rally on October 4, 1997, in Washington, D.C. There had already been some seventeen other rallies that year, attracting some two million men. It was hoped that this one-day rally at the capital would attract one million men, a parallel to the Million Man March held in Washington two years before and organized by Louis Farrakhan and the Nation of Islam. The Promise Keepers rally saw a 700,000-plus turnout comparable to the Million Man March. Men from every state in the union were in attendance, as were Native American representatives. PK organizers had invited men from fifty-seven other countries as well. At the rally, it was announced that all future events would be free, and the Promise Keepers substituted volunteers for many of the paid staff.

Criticism The most outspoken criticism of the Promise Keepers came from the National Organization for Women (NOW). NOW's president, Patricia Ireland, saw Promise Keepers as a thinly disguised attempt to reinstate old-fashioned patriarchy and rob women of hard-won rights. Other women's groups criticized NOW for such a sweeping attack and recognized the family-values agenda as helpful to women. Gay rights and pro-choice groups attacked the Promise Keepers' antiabortion and antigay stances. Civil rights activist Jesse Jackson and others feared that the organization could divert black voters away from the Democratic Party.

At the other end of the political spectrum, fundamentalist Christian groups attacked Promise Keepers for not being doctrinally specific, for welcoming Roman Catholics, and for being merely "feel-good" Christianity. None of this criticism was particularly heard by PK members. If anything, the movement's leaders responded much more to charges of commercialism.

Impact The main goal of the Promise Keepers was to change the style of male spirituality, to help men become more confident as Christians, sharing their faith with other men and becoming more aware of their roles as fathers and husbands. There were real efforts to bridge the color divide, and speakers from the black community were frequently invited to conferences. Branches of Promise Keepers were formed in Canada, Australia, and New Zealand. Sociologists and church historians are still assessing its lasting impact.

By the end of the decade, the Promise Keepers movement was in decline. Although rallies continued, their attendance dropped. The agenda to form a huge network of accountability groups never materialized; many local churches were happy to send their men to rallies, but not to have the groups as part of the church network. With the growth of male spirituality, the felt need for a movement like Promise Keepers lessened. However, the movement continued into the next century.

Further Reading

Brickner, Bryan W. *The Promise Keepers: Politics and Promises.* Lanham, Md.: Lexington Books, 1999. Explores the ideology of the evangelical movement.

Clausen, Dane S., ed. *The Promise Keepers: Essays on Masculinity and Christianity.* Jefferson, N.C.: McFarland, 2000. A varied collection of academic essays on the movement, some critical, some supportive.

Gutterman, David S. *Prophetic Politics: Christian Social Movements and American Democracy.* Ithaca, N.Y.: Cornell University Press, 2005. Gutterman explores four Christian social movements, including the Promise Keepers.

Novosad, Nancy. *Promise Keepers: Playing God.* Amherst, N.Y.: Prometheus Books, 2000. A feminist critique of the Promise Keepers movement.

Williams, Rhys H., ed. *Promise Keepers and the New Masculinity: Private Lives and Public Morality.* Lanham, Md.: Lexington Books, 2001. Essays examine the movement in the contexts of history, gender, and race relations.

David Barratt

See also Farrakhan, Louis; *Iron John*; Million Man March; Religion and spirituality in the United States.

■ Proulx, Annie

Identification American fiction writer
Born August 22, 1935; Norwich, Connecticut

Proulx's fiction described the beauty of remote areas of North America and celebrated the courage and tenacity of ordinary human beings.

It was not until Annie Proulx published her first novel in 1992 that she was recognized as a writer of major importance. Her characters are always involved in a struggle for survival, often against nature, which though magnificent is also unforgiving, and often against equally merciless human beings. However, Proulx's grimly realistic assessments of the human condition are expressed in such exuberant prose, lightened with such flashes of humor, and brightened by so many evidences of the strength of the human spirit that they are ultimately more optimistic than pessimistic.

In *Postcards* (1992), the main character flees the family farm in backwoods Vermont because he has accidentally killed his fiancé. Over the next four decades, he wanders throughout the West, periodically reporting his activities in postcards sent to the family, whose lives prove to be as precarious as his. When *Postcards* won the 1993 PEN/Faulkner Award, Proulx became the first woman writer to be so honored.

The hero of her second novel, *The Shipping News* (1993), is a bumbling journalist who, after his wife's death, moves to his ancestral home in a remote

Newfoundland village. *The Shipping News* won numerous awards, including a 1994 Pulitzer Prize, and was adapted into a 2001 film. In *Accordion Crimes* (1996), Proulx traces the adventures of an accordion as it moves from owner to owner over the course of a century. Though each of the nine owners is a member of a different ethnic group and lives in a different part of America, they are all new immigrants and thus subject to harassment, discrimination, and cruelty.

In 1999, Proulx returned to short fiction with *Close Range: Wyoming Stories,* in which ranchers and cowhands are pitted against nature and their own frailties. One of the stories in the collection, "Brokeback Mountain," was made into a 2005 film.

Impact Unlike many earlier women writers, Proulx does not focus merely on issues related to gender. The subject of her novels is the heroism of ordinary human beings, both women and men, whether they are confronted by an inhospitable natural environment or, as in the case of the immigrants, by an equally inhospitable social order. This breadth of focus, along with her masterful characterization and her brilliant style, guarantee Proulx's standing as one of the most significant writers of the 1990's.

Further Reading

Bilton, Alan. *An Introduction to Contemporary American Fiction.* New York: New York University Press, 2003.

Rood, Karen Lane. *Understanding Annie Proulx.* Columbia: University of South Carolina Press, 2001.

Steinberg, Sybil. "E. Annie Proulx: An American Odyssey." *Publishers Weekly* 243, no. 23 (June 3, 1996): 57-58.

Rosemary M. Canfield Reisman

See also Literature in the United States.

Pulitzer Prize-winning author Annie Proulx on her property in Vershire, Vermont, in April, 1994. (AP/Wide World Photos)

■ Psychology

Definition The scientific study of human mental processes and behaviors

With its myriad specialties and branches, psychology in the 1990's explored a range of topics, including language acquisition; emotional intelligence; prescription privileges; memory acquisition, retention, and retrieval; and social influences on cognition.

In the waning years of the 1980's, President George H. W. Bush encouraged American citizens to become more involved in giving back to their communities, a call to action that the psychology community embraced. In 1990, psychology professionals began using magnetic resonance imaging (MRI) on the brain to study human cognition; in the same year, a committee from the American Psychological Association (APA) discussed possibilities for the up-and-coming branch of psychology called pharmapsychology, or behavioral biology. Interdisciplinary approaches began forming during the early part of this "Decade of the Brain," a time when psychologists researched cognition, language acquisition, memory, and aging. Mental health professionals began studying a cluster of illnesses, known as Gulf War syndrome, that some Gulf War combat veterans experienced.

During the early 1990's especially, psychology became more accepting of the possibility of genetic influences on human cognition, so much so that some psychologists needlessly worried that focus would shift away from social dynamics toward genetic factors, and social influences would become irrelevant. In truth, social psychology reached maturity during this decade, and today it remains integral to the field as a whole.

As mid-decade approached, psychologists continued to examine the individual's behavior and the elusive subject of human consciousness and automaticity, or how certain human processes become automatic over time. Ever mindful of their quest toward unified theories about how humans know and appreciate the world, researchers turned to reading comprehension and image cognition, then to educational and mathematical psychology, also called psychological economics, particularly later in the decade. Ecopsychology, previously known as environmental psychology, also originated during this time, offering another example of psychology's tendency during the 1990's to return its focus to the way in which the human psyche intersects with its surroundings. Other (re)emerging fields, such as evolutionary psychology, which situates psychology as a subfield of biology, also evinced psychology's intersectionality. Transpersonal psychology, with its attention to religious and spiritual issues, received scholarly attention and renewal in the early part of the decade.

In 1994, the American Psychiatric Association released the fourth edition of its *Diagnostic and Statistical Manual of Mental Disorders* (*DSM-IV*), the reference book psychologists and psychiatrists use to diagnose patients. Exacerbated by the ongoing AIDS epidemic and millennial anxieties, the United States was a hotbed for psychological and psychiatric conditions, and the increase of patients in psychologists' offices led to higher demands for trained mental health professionals. By the mid-1990's, the exciting field of psychology had become the most popular science major for undergraduate university students, and with the United States' multiethnic population expanding, educators began emphasizing multicultural and global approaches in the psychology classroom. The disciplinary shift toward educational psychology led later in the decade to increased research and publication concerning teacher-student interaction.

The Second Half of the Decade At the 1995 American Psychological Association convention, psychologists gained prescription privileges, contingent upon the profession's developing legal protocols and proposing training curricula. Shortly thereafter, former Walter Reed pharmacology fellow U.S. Navy Commander John L. Sexton was the first psychologist to prescribe medication. Later that same year, the APA created a new division for the study of men and masculinity.

During the second half of the 1990's, "emotional intelligence" surfaced as one of psychology's most popular terms. Made widely recognizable in the academic community by journals and conferences, the term also caught the popular imagination, finding its way into newspapers and magazines around the world. The American Dialect Society named it one of the most useful new phrases of the decade. Through this positive publicity, the typically academic field of psychology began forming alliances with mainstream culture, inspiring the popular psychology movement.

In 1998, APA president Martin Seligman chose the theme "positive psychology" for his term as president and thereby introduced a new branch of psychology to the field. Positive psychology refigures the aim of mental health counseling from its previous intent—treating mental illness—to a more optimistic goal: making life more fulfilling. After a long decade of soaring antidepressant statistics, the American public along with television and radio personalities embraced positive psychology and the onslaught of self-help books that ensued.

Impact Over the decade, the fragmented field of psychology remained malleable, capable of allying itself with economics, literature, and a number of sciences. The interdisciplinarity of psychology made it accessible to students interested in diverse aspects of the human condition, which therefore made psychology a popular subject to study in school. In tandem with the increasing demand for trained psychologists—particularly those capable of distributing pharmaceuticals—psychology's likability increased its visibility both in America and abroad.

Further Reading

Freedheim, Donald K., and Irving B. Weiner. *Handbook of Psychology Volume 1: History of Psychology.* Hoboken, N.J.: John Wiley & Sons, 2003. Organized topically over four volumes.

Pickren, Wade E., and Donald A. Dewsbury, eds. *Evolving Perspectives on the History of Psychology.* Washington, D.C.: American Psychological Association, 2002. Academic essays that explore methods and disciplinary divisions across time.

Schultz, Duane P., and Sydney Ellen Schultz. *A His-*

tory of Modern Psychology. 9th ed. Florence, Ky.: Wadsworth Cengage Learning, 2007. Focused primarily on the late nineteenth and twentieth centuries. Contains an epilogue centered on late twentieth century psychological developments.

Ami R. Blue

See also AIDS epidemic; Alzheimer's disease; Americans with Disabilities Act of 1990; Antidepressants; Attention-deficit disorder; Genetics research; Gulf War syndrome; Health care; Pharmaceutical industry; Religion and spirituality in the United States; Science and technology.

■ Publishing

Definition The business of the commercial production and distribution of literature

The 1990's was a time of transition for the publishing industry. With the advent of the Internet, the industry had a new method for content delivery but also a competitor for its audience's leisure time.

Large chain bookstores such as Barnes & Noble and Borders were becoming increasingly popular in the 1990's, and as their sales grew, more independent bookstores began to close. The impact this had on the publishing industry was determined by the kind of materials the big bookstores wanted—namely, books by big-name authors and celebrities. While major authors and celebrities were offered large advances by the publishing houses, these titles did not always sell well. Millions of dollars were being lost because of these advances in combination with a high rate of returns (unsold copies returned to publishers for a refund).

Not all books sold poorly. Textbook sales increased during the 1990's, as did the sales of audiobooks. Audiobooks had initially been sold through direct mail, but as the 1990's progressed, they became more popular and widely available, first through libraries and then bookstores.

The landscape of the book publishing industry changed significantly during the 1990's, with over six hundred mergers and acquisitions among publishing companies taking place during the decade. Large media conglomerates acquired or created publishing companies: For instance, the Walt Disney Company established its publishing branch, Hyperion, and CBS/Viacom purchased Simon & Schuster. The consolidation of the industry into a few major players concerned bookstore owners across the country; booksellers claimed that they had less contact with publishing representatives and that larger publishing houses were putting all of their resources into best sellers and major chain bookstores. The result—they claimed—was a blander, less robust literary scene.

Internet In July of 1995, Amazon.com opened for business. The site became a very popular venue for the purchase of books and other media, and as its sales took off, more online bookstores followed, including online outlets of chain stores Barnes & Noble and Borders. The Internet not only was a new forum from which to sell books but also became another competitor for readers' (and viewers') leisure time. With home computers and the Internet taking off, publishers experimented with different methods of content distribution, such as CD-ROMS, e-books, and print on demand (POD)—in which books are printed only after an order has been placed. By printing only what is needed, publishers using POD technology could save money. Experimentation with content distribution would continue into the next decade.

Harry Potter, Left Behind, and Oprah In 1996, Oprah Winfrey started her book club. Once a month, she selected a new title that would be discussed in a later episode of her show. Oprah's Book Club took off, with her selections (many by unknown authors) becoming best sellers. In 1997, British author J. K. Rowling's *Harry Potter and the Philosopher's Stone* (published in the United States as *Harry Potter and the Sorcerer's Stone* in 1998) became a phenomenon with children and adults alike, and Rowling's popular sequels continued to be published into the following decade. Christian fiction also surged in popularity and sales during the 1990's, notably the Left Behind series by Tim LaHaye and Jerry B. Jenkins, beginning with *Left Behind: A Novel of the Earth's Last Days* in 1995.

Impact The introduction of the large chain bookstore and Internet bookstores such as Amazon.com changed the publishing industry. Because of their size and dominance of the market, these large companies were able to sell books at a steep discount, making it more difficult for smaller, independent bookstores to remain in business. With the consolidation of the publishing industry through mergers and acquisitions, the majority of top-selling books came from fewer publishers every year, and the number and types of books published also diminished.

Further Reading

"Book Sales Flat in '90's—Report." *Publishers Weekly* 244 (October 27, 1997): 14. Provides an overview of the publishing industry up to 1996, including areas of strong sales, the impact of chain bookstores, and return rates.

Greco, Albert N. *The Book Publishing Industry.* 2d ed. Mahwah, N.J.: Lawrence Erlbaum Associates, 2005. Examines the major issues in the book publishing industry: return rates, mergers, and the Internet. Provides a good historical overview, but much of book deals with the post-2000 industry. Has an excellent glossary of publishing terms.

Jones, Margaret. "Mergers-and-Acquisition Aftershocks." *Publishers Weekly* 246 (September 20, 1999): 25-28. Provides an overview of the aftermath of the major mergers of the 1990's.

Lofquist, William S. "Economic Outlook for the U.S. Printing and Publishing Industry." *Publishing Research Quarterly* 12, no. 3 (Fall, 1996): 22-28. Examines the state of the publishing industry up to 1996 and anticipates the impact the Internet will have on the industry.

Whitten, Robin. "Growth of the Audio Publishing Industry." *Publishing Research Quarterly* 18, no. 3 (Fall, 2002): 3-11. Covers the growth of the audiobook industry in the 1990's.

Julie Elliott

See also Amazon.com; Audiobooks; Bezos, Jeff; Blogs; Business and the economy in the United States; Harry Potter books; Internet; Left Behind books; World Wide Web.

■ *Pulp Fiction*

Identification American crime film
Director Quentin Tarantino (1963-)
Date Released on October 14, 1994

Drawing on the conventions of hard-boiled pulp fiction, auteur Tarantino brought independent film to the forefront of the American imagination with this stark, complicated crime drama.

Quentin Tarantino, a video store clerk turned writer-director, fused *Pulp Fiction* together from a wide array of influences: undervalued American crime fiction, samurai films, the French New Wave, the work of directors Martin Scorsese and Brian De Palma, blaxploitation films, and 1950's, 1960's, and 1970's pop culture. The film, cowritten with Roger Avary, was successful, in part because it was an homage to Tarantino's favorite writers, directors, and singers. It was also challenging in a time when Hollywood was pushing safe, formulaic blockbusters, and it stood out because it relied heavily on dialogue and challenged standard conventions of storytelling.

Pulp Fiction was also a tremendous success for the actors and actresses involved. John Travolta, the star of one of Tarantino's favorite films—Brian De Palma's *Blow Out* (1981)—had long been resigned to mediocre Hollywood fare and made his comeback with this film, playing the type of character he had played early in his career. *Pulp Fiction* also served as a breakthrough for Samuel L. Jackson, who built an entire career around his performance as Jules Winnfield. The film also solidified Uma Thurman's place as Tarantino's muse and showcased Bruce Willis, who was recovering from a series of commercial flops, as a punchy boxer straight out of a classic film noir.

Pulp Fiction won the Palme d'Or (Golden Palm) at the 1994 Cannes Film Festival, and it grossed $107.93 million at the U.S. box office, making it the first independent film to surpass $100 million. It was also nominated for several Academy Awards, including Best Picture and Best Director. The decision by the Academy of Motion Picture Arts and Sciences to award the Best Picture Oscar to *Forrest Gump,* a film that was the polar opposite of *Pulp Fiction* in both intention and execution, spoke to a divide in the American consciousness and revealed a hesitation to give highest honors to a film that reveled in vulgarity, dark humor, and B-movie conventions. Tarantino and Avary did, however, receive the award for Best Original Screenplay.

Impact *Pulp Fiction* inspired a generation of young filmmakers to forego film school and to simply make their own movies, and it had a deep impact on the conventions of crime films, as more and more writers and directors began to experiment with time and point of view. It also helped to launch a prolific decade for independent films, and Tarantino, who re-

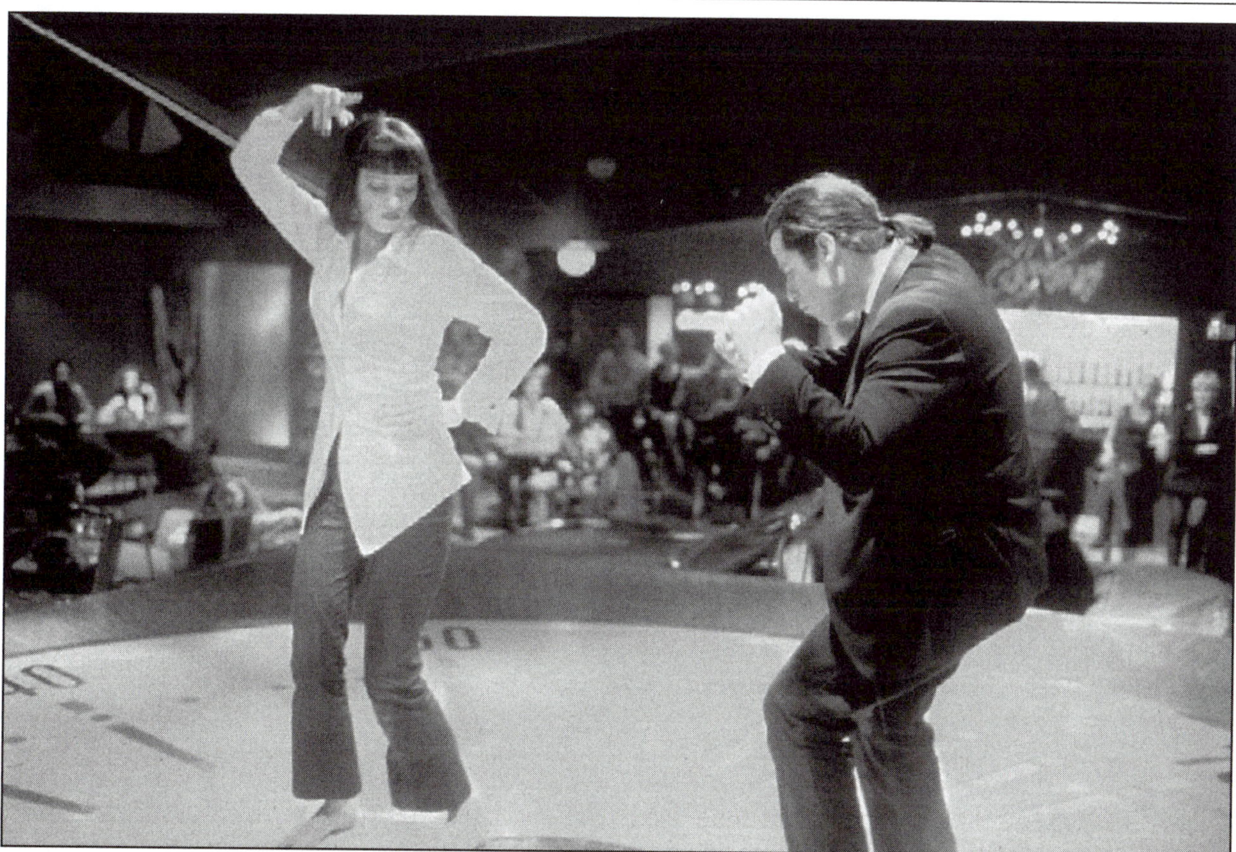

Mia Wallace (Uma Thurman) and Vincent Vega (John Travolta) dance at Jack Rabbit Slim's in the film Pulp Fiction. (Reuters/Landov)

ceived his big break at the Sundance Film Festival, opened doors for filmmakers like Robert Rodriguez (with whom he later collaborated), Christopher Nolan, and others.

Further Reading

Bernard, Jami. *Quentin Tarantino: The Man and His Movies.* New York: HarperPerennial, 1995.

Clarkson, Wensley. *Quentin Tarantino: The Man, the Myths, and His Movies.* London: John Blake, 2007.

Peary, Gerald, ed. *Quentin Tarantino: Interviews.* Jackson: University Press of Mississippi, 1998.

William Boyle

See also Academy Awards; DVDs; Film in the United States; *Forrest Gump*; Independent films; Literature in the United States; Music; Sundance Film Festival; Tarantino, Quentin; Travolta, John.

Q

■ Quayle, Dan

Identification Vice president of the United States, 1989-1993

Born February 4, 1947; Indianapolis, Indiana

Though Quayle was an intelligent and capable politician, his single term as vice president is unfortunately best remembered for his verbal malapropisms and the huge amount of scorn and ridicule heaped upon him by the media and political adversaries.

Dan Quayle was born into a wealthy family and enjoyed a privileged lifestyle. He graduated from DePauw University and Indiana University School of Law—Indianapolis. A conservative by inclination, he was recruited by the Republican Party, and he sought a seat in the U.S. House of Representatives from the Fourth District of Indiana. He won handily in 1976 and was reelected in a landslide in 1978. In 1980, at the age of thirty-three, he won a seat in the Senate and was easily elected to a second term in 1986.

As a senator, Quayle was reliably conservative and unfailingly ingratiating. In 1988, George H. W. Bush, the Republican presidential candidate, surprised the nation by choosing Quayle to be his running mate. Quayle's nomination was met with a wave of derision and opposition. His giddy enthusiasm about being chosen for the nomination seemed like immature behavior to many observers. In a debate between rival vice presidential nominees, Democrat Lloyd Bentsen delivered a memorable retort to Quayle's comparison of himself to John F. Kennedy in terms of congressional experience, stating that Quayle was "no John Kennedy." Despite Quayle's campaign mistakes and the unrelenting criticism by the media, the Bush-Quayle team won the election, and Quayle became the forty-fourth vice president of the United States.

As vice president, he competently chaired the National Space Council and the Council on Competitiveness and occasionally presided over the Senate, but the attacks and derision continued, fueled by his ongoing verbal gaffes, such as "the future will be better tomorrow." After a brief period of high poll ratings due to the Gulf War, the economy failed to flourish, and President Bush disastrously broke an often repeated campaign promise by raising taxes. When the Bush-Quayle team sought reelection in 1992, they were soundly defeated.

Impact While vice president, Quayle had chided fictional television character Murphy Brown for giving birth out of wedlock and thus setting a bad moral example. Although Quayle was criticized for these

President George H. W. Bush, left, and Vice President Dan Quayle pose at the White House in 1989. (NARA)

remarks, many believed he had a valid point about the irresponsibility of mainstream media. The unending criticism he drew apparently ended his political career, thus revealing again the power and influence of the media.

Further Reading

Quayle, Dan. *Standing Firm.* New York: HarperCollins, 1994.

Woodward, Bob, and David S. Broder. *The Man Who Would Be President: Dan Quayle.* New York: Simon & Schuster, 1992.

Thomas W. Buchanan

See also Bush, George H. W.; Elections in the United States, 1992; Gulf War; *Murphy Brown.*

■ Quebec referendum of 1995

The Event Quebec votes against secession from Canada
Date October 30, 1995
Place Quebec Province, Canada

The Quebec referendum of 1995, sponsored by the Parti Québécois government of Jacques Parizeau, was the second referendum on Quebec sovereignty to be held in fifteen years. Voters rejected the plan, but only by the narrowest of margins.

Historians cite a variety of reasons for the resurgence of French Canadian nationalism in the early 1990's. Prominent among them were the ambivalent outcome of Quebec's first referendum on sovereignty in 1980; Quebec's opposition to the Constitution Act of 1982; controversial Supreme Court rulings on Quebec's language and commerce laws; and failure of the Meech Lake (1987) and Charlottetown accords (1992).

On September 12, 1994, Jacques Parizeau, leader of the Parti Québécois and longtime advocate of the sovereignty movement, was elected premier of Quebec. During the electoral campaign, he had promised voters that, if elected to the premiership, he would formulate a new plan for Quebec sovereignty and organize a referendum on the issue. He was joined in his effort by Lucien Bouchard, leader of the Bloc Québécois, and Mario Dumont, leader of Action Démocratique du Québec. On June 12, 1995, the three men drafted the outline of a new bill and agreed on a mutually acceptable platform for the referendum. Bill 1, the so-called Sovereignty Bill, was placed before the province's National Assembly in early September with a referendum scheduled for October 30.

The campaigns for and against secession received heavy media coverage and were emotionally charged. Quebec Liberal Party leader Daniel Johnson, Labor Minister Lucienne Robillard, and Prime Minister Jean Chrétien were among the most outspoken opponents of the plan. Each contended that the referendum question was confusing, even disingenuous.

With the future of Quebec at stake, Canadians were wrought with anxiety on referendum day. Voter participation rose to a surprising 93.5 percent. In the final tally, 50.58 percent of Quebec's citizens voted against the government's plan. The measure was thus defeated by less than 1 percent of the popular vote. In a referendum night concession speech, Premier Parizeau sparked indignation when he blamed his defeat on "money and the ethnic vote" yet failed to acknowledge that approximately 40 percent of the francophone community had rejected his party's sovereignty plan.

Impact Following the referendum, Parizeau resigned as Quebec premier and was replaced by Bouchard. Most observers felt that the 1995 referendum had failed to resolve any of the tough political issues at hand. In a gesture of reconciliation, Chrétien's federal government hastened to recognize Quebec as a "distinct society" with its own language, culture, and legal system. However, Canada's parliament also passed the Clarity Act of 2000, stipulating that any future referendum on independence must be founded on a clear and unambiguous question and must obtain a clear majority approval before negotiations with the federal government could be initiated.

Further Reading

Cardinal, Mario. *Breaking Point Quebec/Canada: The 1995 Referendum.* Montreal: Bayard Canada Books, 2005.

Jedwab, Jack, et al. *À la prochaine? Une Rétrospective des référendums Québécois de 1980 et 1995.* Montreal: Éditions Saint-Martin, 2000.

Young, Robert Andrew. *The Struggle for Quebec: From Referendum to Referendum?* Montreal: McGill-Queen's University Press, 1999.

Jan Pendergrass

A huge Canadian flag is shown among a crowd on October 27, 1995, in Montreal, where thousands of people rallied in support of the Quebec referendum. (AP/Wide World Photos)

See also Bloc Québécois; Business and the economy in Canada; Charlottetown Accord; Chrétien, Jean; Minorities in Canada; Mulroney, Brian.

■ Queer Nation

Identification Gay and lesbian activist organization

Date Founded in 1990

Queer Nation's founding marked the first large-scale reclamation of the word "queer" for the gay and lesbian community. It also introduced a new style of activism for lesbians and gays, a shift away from assimilation-based efforts that preceded the group.

In the spring of 1990, a small group of activists for gay and lesbian equality joined together in New York's Greenwich Village to start a new movement. They were disenchanted with the state of most large-scale gay and lesbian rights organizations, which had turned so much of their focus to AIDS or tolerance models of inclusion. Of these organizations, those who were concentrating on broader issues of gay and lesbian equality focused on a goal of assimilation of gays and lesbians with the heterosexual mainstream. Groups such as the Human Rights Campaign espoused that lesbians and gays were just like heterosexuals and thus should be treated equally. Much like ACT UP (AIDS Coalition to Unleash Power), Queer Nation rejected this moderate position, choosing instead to promote the unique qualities of gay and lesbian people in order to be celebrated (rather than just tolerated) because of these attributes.

Fundamentally opposed to the way organizations

of the time framed themselves, these activists came together to form Queer Nation. In the tradition of reclamation, they chose to refer to themselves as "queer," a word that had been used pejoratively to label homosexuals, and by doing so empowered themselves as individuals who were proud to reside outside the heteronormative structure. The act of using such a powerful term that had negative connotations to so many people was only the first of many "in-your-face" political actions of the organization.

The New York chapter of Queer Nation, as well as those in major cities around the country, began to actively engage the mainstream culture through radical rhetoric and action, hosting sit-ins against companies who openly discriminated against gays and lesbians, organizing kiss-ins in traditionally heterosexual spaces, and protesting activities that catered to heterosexual audiences. Unlike the organizations that had come before it, Queer Nation was loud and abrupt, coining the popular slogan "We're here, we're queer, get used to it."

By the organization's first anniversary, chapters had been established in many major cities around the United States, including Albuquerque, Atlanta, Houston, and San Francisco. However, by that time, the organization was already beginning to experience an identity crisis. Founding members quickly found themselves burned out with such direct activism. It was at this time that members of the group began trying to make Queer Nation a platform for their own particular causes. The combination of these factors saw some of the chapters begin to dissolve in early 1991, while others lasted well into the mid-1990's. Queer Nation as a whole has never officially disbanded, though no active chapters are currently in existence.

Impact Queer Nation moved facets of the gay and lesbian movement into a new territory—that of aggressive disobedience. The organization will be best remembered for reclaiming the word "queer" and for resisting assimilation in favor of celebrated diversity.

Further Reading

Baker, James N., et al. "What Is Queer Nation?" *Newsweek*, August 12, 1991, 24-25.

Slagle, R. Anthony. "In Defense of Queer Nation: From Identity Politics to a Politics of Difference." *Western Journal of Communications* 59, no. 2 (Spring, 1995): 85-102.

Needham Yancey Gulley

See also AIDS epidemic; Domestic partnerships; Don't ask, don't tell; Hate crimes; Homosexuality and gay rights; Transgender community.

■ Race relations

Definition Social, political, and economic interactions among persons associated with different racial and ethnic groups, often involving patterns of prejudice, discrimination, and subordination

In both the United States and Canada, the 1990's saw significant controversies, changes, and developments in race relations.

During the 1990's, social scientists and journalists wrote numerous books and articles about continuing conflict, negative stereotypes, and discriminatory treatment. Activists with liberal and left-wing perspectives often argued that aggressive steps were needed in order to reduce the continuing effects of institutional racism and "white privilege." Moderates and conservatives, in contrast, tended to be satisfied with the goal of promoting equal opportunities for individuals, and they sometimes focused on allegations of "reverse discrimination." Although radical right-wing organizations had much less public support than in the past, the Ku Klux Klan and other white identity groups continued to denounce the idea of racial integration and to proclaim the inherent superiority of persons of European ancestry.

The United States Throughout the 1990's, American society was growing increasingly diverse in race and ethnicity. By the end of the century, African Americans made up about 12.1 percent of the population, whereas the growing Hispanic population reached 12.5 percent, of which almost half also classified themselves as white. Persons of Asian ancestry represented 3.6 percent, and Native Americans made up less than 1 percent. The conceptualization of a binary black-white society was clearly anachronistic, even though most discussions of race relations tended to focus on that aspect of the topic.

The Supreme Court issued a number of decisions that were more conservative than in previous decades. When considering court-ordered busing to desegregate schools, for example, the Court allowed communities to terminate mandatory programs after making good-faith efforts at desegregation. A Harvard University study, directed by Gary Orfield, found that largely because of these decisions, classrooms were becoming increasingly segregated. White students were particularly segregated by race; by 1999, they attended schools in which more that 80 percent of the students were white and less than 20 percent were from other racial groups. Experts disagreed about the consequences of this renewed segregation. Many conservatives argued that racial integration had little to do with the quality of education, whereas most liberals insisted that segregation inevitably meant less equality in funding schools and fewer opportunities for children of diverse backgrounds to learn to live and work together.

The decade saw much controversy over the matter of equal opportunity versus parity in employment and admissions to competitive schools. One contentious issue was the use of employment qualifications that had a "disparate impact" on historically disadvantaged groups. After the Supreme Court modified its previous, more liberal rulings, Congress reacted with the Civil Rights Act of 1991, which required employers to demonstrate that all qualifications were closely connected to performing the particular job. Affirmative action programs, which usually included limited preferences for minorities and women, were often denounced by opponents as unfair to white males. In the case of *Adarand Constructors v. Peña* (1995), the Supreme Court ruled that all racial preferences in government-financed programs were inherently suspect and must be evaluated by the criteria of "strict scrutiny," which made it much more likely that they would be struck down as unacceptable. In California, voters approved a 1996 referendum, Proposition 209, which outlawed all race-based preferences in state-sponsored activities. Two years later, voters in Washington State passed a similar law. Although affirmative action programs continued in much of the country, most polls indicated that about 60 percent of whites and 35 percent of blacks opposed racial preferences.

Numerous instances of racial violence took place. In 1990, Congress passed a law requiring the Federal Bureau of Investigation (FBI) to keep records of hate crimes. In 1996, a rather typical year, the agency reported 8,769 such occurrences, with about 63 percent based on race. The decade's most highly publicized racial hate crime was the 1998 murder of African American James Byrd, Jr., when three white supremacists dragged his mangled body behind a pickup truck in Jasper, Texas. Although black-white conflict tended to attract the headlines, in Los Angeles and many other cities confrontations between Hispanics and blacks, often organized into hostile gangs, was a growing problem. Two significant race riots occurred. In 1991, when a car driving a Hasidic Jewish leader struck and killed a black child in the Brooklyn community of Crown Heights, the result was four nights of rioting, in which one Jewish student was murdered, 188 persons were injured, and more than 150 were arrested. That same year, several police officers were taped beating Rodney King following a high-speed chase and his refusal to obey their orders. The next year, after three of the officers were acquitted of using excessive force, rioting and looting broke out in Los Angeles, resulting in fifty-three deaths, ten thousand arrests, and the destruction of about four thousand buildings.

The sensational murder trial of O. J. Simpson demonstrated that African Americans and European Americans tended to perceive American society from radically different perspectives. For the latter, the evidence against Simpson appeared overwhelming. In addition to DNA tests and the bloody glove found on his property, he had a motive, time to commit the murders, and a history of violent behavior. Yet, Johnnie Cochran achieved an acquittal by convincing the predominantly black jury that Mark Furman and other white police officers had planted evidence because of their desire to destroy a successful black man. When the jury announced that Simpson was not guilty, one juror raised his fist in a black-power salute. Over national television, a group of black law students at Howard University cheered in delight. Following the trial, 85 percent of blacks said they agreed with the verdict, compared with some 24 percent of whites.

Canada In comparison with the U.S. population, a much larger majority of Canada's peoples were of European ancestry. According to official statistics, racial minorities constituted only about 9.4 percent of Canadians in 1991, but largely because of immigration, they grew to include almost 14 percent by the end of the decade. Despite the country's global reputation for toleration and equal rights, it had many of the racial and ethnic inequalities found in other modern societies. In employment and education, racial minorities were significantly underrepresented in prestigious positions, and a number of studies indicated that discrimination continued to be practiced against minorities. There were significant differences, however, among the various groups, with Asian Canadians showing more gains than black Canadians or aboriginal peoples. Statistics also showed even greater variation in the criminal justice system. Whereas black Canadians in 1996 made up about 2.2 percent of the country's population, they comprised over 6 percent of prison inmates. Asian Americans, in contrast, made up 7.2 percent of the population but only 2.4 percent of persons incarcerated.

At the beginning of the decade, Canada already had strong federal and provincial human rights legislation prohibiting discrimination on the basis of race or ethnicity. In 1995, the Parliament revised and strengthened the Employment Equity Act, declaring that no person should be "denied employment opportunities or benefits for reasons unrelated to ability." The statute further announced the goal of correcting the "conditions of disadvantage" of minorities in employment equity, which "means more than treating persons in the same way but also requires special measures and the accommodation of differences." In 1996, the federal government proclaimed the Canadian Race Relations Foundation Act, designed to focus its efforts on eliminating all racism against minorities, with particular emphasis on systematic discrimination in education and employment.

Public opinion polls by the Centre for Research and Information on Canada (CRIC) usually showed growing support for the concept of racial and ethnic diversity, even though many French-speaking people in Quebec feared that multiculturalism posed a challenge to the survival of French culture. A minority of Canadians agreed with Neil Bissoondath's *Selling Illusions: The Cult of Multiculturalism in Canada*

(1994), which argued that multiculturalism promotes social conflict and a diminished sense of Canadian identity. In contrast, Will Kymlicka, in *Finding Our Way: Rethinking Ethnocultural Relations in Canada* (1998), argued that the multiculturalism had not decreased the rate of integration by immigrants. His statistics showed considerable levels of political participation, rates of intermarriage, and the ability of new Canadians to speak an official language, French or English.

Canadians experienced considerably less ethnic violence than persons living in the United States, although violent incidents did occasionally take place. The most highly publicized event occurred in the town of Oka, Quebec, during the summer of 1990, when the town announced plans to expand a golf course into an area near the Mohawk community of Kanesatake. The disputed area included a traditional burial ground and a grove of pine trees that was considered sacred. After losing a court battle, members of the Mohawk community erected a barricade around the area. At the request of the town mayor, the provincial police of Quebec intervened, and they attacked the barricade, deploying tear gas and flash-bang grenades to create confusion in the Mohawk ranks. One police officer was killed during the resulting fifteen-minute gunfight. Native American groups in Canada and the United States then joined the conflict. In solidarity, several Mohawks from another community, Kahnawake, blockaded a bridge between Montreal and a southern suburb, resulting in large traffic jams and angry anti-Mohawk crowds. The federal government then brought in the Royal Canadian Mounted Police (RCMP) as well as 2,500 members of the Canadian armed forces. Most citizens of Quebec expressed outrage with the Mohawk actions. After lasting seventy-eight days, the crisis finally ended when the federal government agreed to spend $5.3 million to purchase the disputed land. One consequence of the dispute was passage of the First Nations Policing Policy, which allowed aboriginal peoples more control over their police services.

Impact In 1997, U.S. president Bill Clinton sponsored a national discussion on racial issues, which was called One America in the Twenty-first Century: The President's Initiative on Race. The announced goal of the initiative was to promote appreciation for the nation's growing diversity as it entered the new century. Although the initiative produced a number of interesting conferences, most observers were disappointed with its results. Native Americans and other minority groups protested their lack of inclusion in the initial organization, and some conservative white Americans bitterly complained that their ideas and perceptions about issues like affirmative action were not taken seriously.

As the twentieth century ended, in both the United States and Canada there were many indications of improvements in race relations. In the United States, for instance, 12.1 percent of the new marriages were between persons of different races, compared with only 3 percent in 1970. A Pew Carter poll of 1999 found that 63 percent of respondents said that interracial marriages were good "because they helped break down racial barriers." Many businesses and educational institutions tried to improve race relations with sensitivity training—with mixed results. Although growing numbers of disadvantaged minorities were achieving middle-class status, the U.S. Census Bureau reported in 1999 that African Americans, in comparison with non-Hispanic whites, were three times more likely to be poor and six times more likely to serve prison terms. Although overt racial discrimination was illegal and increasingly rare, most experts agreed that covert discrimination, often encouraged by negative stereotypes, continued to be widespread.

Further Reading

CQ Research Staff. *Issues in Race, Ethnicity and Gender.* Washington D.C.: CQ Press, 2002. Balanced discussions of controversies relating to Native Americans, African Americans, Latinos, and Asian Americans at the end of the twentieth century, with bibliographical essays.

Feagin, Joe R., and Clairece B. Feagin. *Racial and Ethnic Relations.* 7th ed. New York: Prentice Hall, 2002. A popular, one-sided textbook asserting that American institutions continue to be white supremacist, racially hierarchical, and oppressive of minority groups.

Li, Peter S., ed. *Race and Race Relations in Canada.* 2d ed. New York: Oxford University Press, 1999. An interesting collection of essays about issues of discrimination, multiculturalism, and the status of visual minorities.

Marger, Martin. *Race and Ethnic Relations: American and Global Perspectives.* 5th ed. Belmont, Calif.:

Wadsworth, 1999. A comparative approach that emphasizes racial groups in the United States and includes a good chapter on Canada.

Swain, Carol. *The New White Nationalism in America: Its Challenge to Integration.* New York: Cambridge University Press, 2002. Argues that contemporary multiculturalism with its emphasis on racial pride has the unintended consequence of promoting virulent forms of white racism.

Thernstrom, Stephan, and Abigail Thernstrom. *America in Black and White: One Nation, Indivisible.* New York: Simon & Schuster, 1997. A scholarly work that opposes affirmative action and argues that the country has made significant progress toward ending racial discrimination.

Thomas Tandy Lewis

See also African Americans; Asian Americans; Byrd murder case; Cochran, Johnnie; Civil Rights Act of 1991; Crown Heights riot; Demographics of Canada; Demographics of the United States; Diallo shooting; Hate crimes; Illegal immigration; King, Rodney; Latinos; Los Angeles riots; Mount Pleasant riot; Native Americans; Sharpton, Al; Simpson murder case.

■ Ramsey murder case

The Event The murder of a six-year-old and its investigation
Date December 26, 1996
Place Boulder, Colorado

JonBenét Ramsey's murder generated sensational press coverage, largely focused on JonBenét's appearances in child beauty pageants. This media attention reflected Americans' rising interest in criminal investigation and the American justice system.

Six-year-old JonBenét Ramsey, daughter of Patsy and John Ramsey, was found dead in the basement of her parents' home in Boulder, Colorado, on the morning of December 26, 1996. A blow to the head had fractured her skull; she had been strangled with a cord tied around her neck and tightened with a garrote.

Patsy Ramsey had called police early that morning to report JonBenét missing. Patsy had found a ransom note demanding $118,000 and promising that the kidnappers would contact the Ramseys before 10:00 A.M. After several hours had passed with no contact from the kidnappers, Boulder Police detective Linda Arndt asked John Ramsey and his friend Fleet White to search the house. Ramsey found JonBenét's body lying on the floor of a small basement room. The first uniformed officer on the scene had searched the house but had not opened the latched door to that room; a friend had opened the door in a later search but had not entered the room and seen the body.

John Ramsey was president and chief executive officer of Access Graphics, a wholesale computer parts company owned by Lockheed Martin. Patsy Ramsey was involved with community and charitable activities, and the Ramseys regularly attended Boulder's St. John's Episcopal Church. The couple also maintained large homes in Atlanta, Georgia, and Charlevoix, Michigan. Patsy was a former Miss West Virginia and Miss America contestant, as was her sister Pam. Along with Patsy's mother, they had begun entering JonBenét in child beauty pageants, and she had already won several titles. Patsy spent thousands of dollars on singing and dancing lessons for JonBenét, as well as custom-made costumes. News stories distributed photographs and video showing six-year-old JonBenét posing and performing wearing elegant, flamboyant showgirl outfits, high heels, and makeup. Investigators wondered if a child molester or pornographer might have found JonBenét's pageant appearances sexually provocative, leading to a pursuit of the child resulting in her death.

Boulder Police and District Attorney Investigators were divided as to whether John and Patsy Ramsey should be considered suspects. Handwriting experts eliminated more than seventy people as possible writers of the ransom note, but could not definitely say Patsy had not written it. The garrote used to strangle JonBenét was made with the broken handle of an artist's paintbrush belonging to Patsy.

Boulder was an affluent, politically liberal community whose police had little experience with murder cases. District attorney Alex Hunter preferred to negotiate plea bargains rather than prosecute defendants in court. The police failed to completely search the Ramsey home, interview the Ramseys, or secure the crime scene, and later rejected offers of help from both the Federal and Colorado Bureaus

The adorned gravesite of JonBenét Ramsey. (AP/Wide World Photos)

of Investigation. While Boulder detectives assembled a case against Patsy Ramsey, Hunter's office hired its own investigators, allowed the Ramsey attorneys to review police files and physical evidence, and insisted detectives treat the Ramseys as victims rather than suspects.

Ramsey supporters argued that an intruder had entered the Ramsey home through a broken basement window. The layout of the home was complex; Boulder detectives argued that an intruder could not have maneuvered through the mansion in the dark to locate JonBenét's bedroom or the basement room where her body was found. Hunter's investigators believed JonBenét could have been killed by anyone already familiar with the home. Neither the duct tape on JonBenét's mouth nor the cord used to strangle her could be matched to anything belonging to the Ramseys.

In 1998, Boulder County convened a grand jury to decide if there was sufficient evidence to support any indictment. After thirteen months, the grand jury ruled no charges could be filed based upon the evidence.

Impact The Ramsey case generated intense public scrutiny and tabloid coverage. The Ramseys were unable to counter images of Patsy as a stage mother and JonBenét as an oddly mature-looking child beauty queen. Boulder's legal officials could not collaborate to solve a murder among the city's elite. Detailed in countless media outlets, their failure contributed to the American public's growing concern about the effectiveness of the American justice system.

Subsequent Events Patsy Ramsey died of ovarian cancer on June 24, 2006. In August, 2006, an American substitute teacher named John Mark Karr confessed to killing JonBenét. Witnesses placed him in Alabama at the time of the murder, however, and Boulder authorities announced that he would not be charged. In July, 2008, the Boulder district attorney's office announced that new deoxyribonucleic acid (DNA) sampling and testing techniques had cleared all members of the Ramsey family.

Further Reading

Bardach, A. L. "Missing Innocence: The JonBenét Ramsey Case." *Vanity Fair,* no. 446 (October, 1997): 322. Bardach's frequently cited overview of problems within the investigation and relevant political connections in the Boulder district attorney's office.

Douglas, John E., and Mark Olshaker. "The JonBenét Ramsey Murder." In *The Cases That Haunt Us.* New York: Charles Scribner's Sons, 2000. Federal Bureau of Investigation profiler once employed by the Ramseys argues that an intruder killed JonBenét.

Gentile, Don, and David Wright, eds. *JonBenét: The Police Files.* Boca Raton, Fla.: American Media, 2003. Includes transcripts of police interviews with the Ramseys.

Ramsey, John, and Patsy Ramsey. *The Death of Innocence: The Untold Story of JonBenét's Murder and How Its Exploitation Compromised the Pursuit of Truth.* Nashville: Thomas Nelson, 2000. The Ramseys' account of their loss and their struggles with the media and Boulder police.

Schiller, Lawrence. *Perfect Murder, Perfect Town.* New York: HarperCollins, 1999. Often cited as a definitive account in spite of occasional inaccuracies and the author's decision to draw no conclusions; later editions include index.

Thomas, Steve, with Don Davis. *JonBenét: Inside the Ramsey Murder Investigation.* New York: St. Martin's Press, 2000. Lead detective on the Ramsey case argues that the Boulder district attorney's office protected the Ramseys.

Maureen Puffer-Rothenberg

See also Crime; Klaas kidnapping and murder case; Simpson murder case.

■ *Real World, The*

Identification Reality television show
Creators Mary-Ellis Bunim (1946-2004) and Jonathan Murray (1955-)
Date Premiered on May 21, 1992

The series mixed documentary and soap opera elements, spawning a new era of television programming, the reality show.

The Real World, created by Mary-Ellis Bunim and Jonathan Murray, first aired on May 21, 1992, on MTV. Bunim, who had produced soap operas for sixteen years, and Murray, with a background in journalism, became partners in 1992 and created the 24/7 documentary series about seven strangers ages eighteen to twenty-five living together in New York City and having their lives filmed. The house was filled with cameras, the residents wore recording packs, and camera crews followed them whenever they left the house. Each subsequent year, the show moved to a new city with seven new housemates.

Impact *The Real World* became the model for future reality television series. It enjoyed enormous popularity, becoming the longest-running MTV show of the 1990's and continuing its success into the twenty-first century. Despite the show's popularity, many critics believed that what began as a legitimate look at young people as they tried to find their way in the world became increasingly voyeuristic, self-referential, and orchestrated. When the series began, serious issues such as prejudice, politics, morality, sexuality, and personal growth were explored honestly and openly. Many subjects taboo on network shows were routinely presented. Then the show gradually changed, providing casts with weeklong vacations, ready-made employment situations, and fantasy housing, which increased the show's artificiality. Cast members were chosen to ensure conflict and controversy, and some participants seemed to have serious medical and emotional problems. Instead of locating the casts in cities with varied cultural and employment opportunities, producers started placing them in resort communities, with cast members becoming overly self-aware and too focused on sex, fame, and binge drinking.

Further Reading

Hill, Annette. *Reality TV: Factual Entertainment and Television Audiences.* New York: Routledge, 2005.
Murray, Susan, and Laurie Ouellette, eds. *Reality TV: Remaking Popular Culture.* New York: New York University Press, 2004.

Leslie Neilan

See also Cable television; Television.

■ Recession of 1990-1991

The Event U.S. economic contraction
Date Lasted from July, 1990, to March, 1991

Although the recession of 1990-1991, the only recession of the 1990's, was considered to be mild in terms of its duration and the reduction in output experienced, President George H. W. Bush claimed that the Federal Reserve's response to it was the reason that he was not reelected in 1992.

Market economies experience periods of economic expansion and contraction, often referred to as business cycles. Difficult to predict, these periods of economic contraction are called recessions. By common usage, a recession is said to occur if real gross domestic product (GDP) falls for two or more consecutive quarters. Real GDP is a measure of the market value of the output produced in a country that ignores the impact of inflation on prices, and a quarter is a three-month period of time. The National Bureau of Economic Research (NBER), the organization that assigns the beginning and ending dates to recessions, does not use this definition, instead defining a recession as "a significant decline in activity spread across the economy, lasting more than a few months," which may be seen through a number of economic indicators, one being real GDP. A recession is said to have ended when the economy begins to expand.

The recession of 1990-1991 ended the second-longest period of economic expansion up to that point in the twentieth century and was followed by the longest period of economic expansion in U.S.

history. At only eight months in length, the economic contraction of 1990-1991 was less than the average of nearly eleven months for the nine recessions that occurred during the twentieth century after 1945, and with a drop in real GDP of about 1.3 percent, the 1990-1991 recession recorded the second-lowest drop in real GDP among these nine recessions.

Cause of Recession The causes of recessions are the subject of numerous disagreements, and the 1990-1991 recession is no exception. The disagreements arise as a result of differences in how economists view the workings of the economy. Since a recession occurs when the economy produces less output, this may result from two basic sources: one being that less output is demanded, causing producers to produce less, and the other being that producers supply less output as a result of a reduction in the availability of resources. John Maynard Keynes (1883-1946), the founder of macroeconomics, built his theory regarding the cause of recessions on a reduction in the demand for output. Although many economists have continued in this tradition, others have developed theories based on the role reduced supply plays in explaining recessions. While there is general agreement among economists that reductions in either the demand for output or the supply of output may lead to recessions, there is less agreement about which has led to a specific recession and what factors caused either a reduction in demand or a reduction in supply to occur.

These differing views can be seen in some of the explanations economists have offered for the cause of the 1990-1991 recession. Viewing a reduction in demand as the cause, some economists have argued that the recession may have been brought on by a reduction in consumer purchases due to concerns about the economy. Others suggest that a decline in demand for output may have been due to efforts by the Federal Reserve to reduce the growth of the money supply in the year prior to the recession. Still others argue that the increase in oil prices that accompanied Iraq's invasion of Kuwait reduced the supply of output. As a result, no agreed-upon explanation has emerged regarding the cause of the 1990-1991 recession.

The Federal Reserve, the central bank of the United States, is responsible for monetary policy in the United States and as such often takes the lead in dealing with recessions. Under the leadership of Federal Reserve chairman Alan Greenspan, the Fed began taking steps to increase the money supply once there were signs that the economy was contracting. Increasing the money supply tends to lower interest rates and thereby increase the demand for output. President George H. W. Bush criticized these efforts as insufficient and cited them as the reason he was not reelected in 1992.

Impact Effects of the recession can be seen in the impact that it had on the unemployment rate and wages during the early 1990's. Just prior to the start of the recession, the June, 1990, unemployment rate was 5.2 percent. Over the course of the next two years, it reached a high of 7.8 percent in June, 1992. The economy did not achieve an unemployment rate of 5.2 percent again until August, 1996. The increase in the unemployment rate was accompanied by a slight reduction in average hours worked per week and wage rates that remained stagnant during the first several years of the decade.

While the 1990's will be better remembered for its long uninterrupted period of economic growth, the 1990-1991 recession is a reminder that recessions are an inevitable part of market economies. Occurring between two of the longest periods of economic expansion in U.S. history, the 1990-1991 recession is often dismissed as a minor deviation from the slow but steady growth of the U.S. economy. Nevertheless, this recession, though mild in comparison to other post-World War II recessions, did adversely impact life in the United States.

Further Reading

Heilbroner, Robert, and Lester Thurow. *Economics Explained.* Rev. ed. New York: Touchstone, 1998. A concise overview of key economic concepts such as unemployment, inflation, and recessions and how they have affected society.

Knoop, Todd A. *Recessions and Depressions: Understanding Business Cycles.* Westport, Conn.: Praeger, 2004. A comprehensive look at recessions in the United States and a review of the difficulties encountered in trying to predict and prevent them.

Woodward, Bob. *Maestro: Greenspan's Fed and the American Boom.* New York: Simon & Schuster, 2000. An engaging look at the workings of the Federal Reserve during the 1990's under the guidance of Alan Greenspan.

Randall Hannum

See also Bush, George H. W.; Business and the economy in the United States; Clinton, Bill; Downsizing and restructuring; Elections in the United States, 1992; Employment in the United States; Greenspan, Alan; Income and wages in the United States.

■ Reeve, Christopher

Identification American actor and activist
Born September 25, 1952; New York, New York
Died October 10, 2004; Mount Kisco, New York

An established actor, Christopher Reeve became internationally recognized for his courageous advocacy of rights for the disabled after a horse-riding accident left him nearly completely paralyzed.

A working actor since fourteen, Christopher Reeve had found his hunky good looks and self-deprecating charisma a fortunate combination as first a villain on the soap opera *Love of Life* and then most prominently as Superman in a trilogy of highly successful films in the 1980's. Gifted with financial security but restless for professional challenges, Reeve by the early 1990's was selecting film and theater roles that worked against the Superman persona. In addition, Reeve, a lifelong athlete, pursued high-risk hobbies including piloting, scuba diving, and most notably horse riding, particularly eventing, a demanding three-day competition that combines the finesse of dressage with the speed of cross-country racing.

It was on May 27, 1995, during an eventing competition in Culpepper, Virginia, that Reeve was thrown forward off his horse when it froze before a rail jump. Reeve landed headfirst, shattering the uppermost vertebrae in his spine (actually severing his skull from the column). Instantly paralyzed, Reeve was unable to breathe, and only urgent neurological care saved his life. Rehabilitation over the next months was an excruciating and frustrating regimen: Reeve was confined to an electric wheelchair, nearly completely immobilized and compelled to use a ventilator except for brief periods.

His medical trauma, however, received international coverage, and within a year of his injury Reeve began making public appearances—most notably at the 1996 Academy Awards—to advocate for the rights of the disabled and increased funding for spinal cord injury research. Along with his wife, Dana, Reeve established the Christopher Reeve Paralysis Foundation in 1996, which led efforts both to protect the insurance coverage of victims of such injuries and to promote controversial stem cell research as the best hope for genuine advances toward cures for spinal cord injury. In 1997, Reeve returned to filmmaking, directing the Home Box Office (HBO) film *In the Gloaming*, a sobering look at AIDS. It was nominated for five Emmy Awards. Reeve's performance the following year as the Jimmy Stewart character in a remake of Alfred Hitchcock's 1954 classic *Rear Window* earned him a Screen Actors Guild Award for best television actor.

Reeve published two inspirational best sellers that urged victims of spinal cord injuries to live as independently as possible even as he had begun to reclaim limited muscle response in his fingers and to feel hot and cold sensations. Despite his heroic re-

Christopher Reeve accepts the 1996 National Courage Award from the Courage Center in Bloomington, Minnesota. After suffering a spinal injury from a horse-riding accident that rendered him a quadriplegic, Reeve became an advocate for the disabled. (AP/Wide World Photos)

covery, Reeve struggled constantly to ward off infections. On October 10, 2004, he succumbed to a heart attack after being treated with an antibiotic for sepsis, a blood infection.

Impact Immediately after his accident, Reeve later admitted, he considered suicide. That he refused to surrender, that he maintained his courage—and grace—under such catastrophic pressure made him an international symbol of the human spirit. Perhaps more important, however, was Reeve's determination to raise awareness about the promise of controversial medical research and his campaign to protect the rights of victims of catastrophic accidents.

Further Reading

Havill, Adrian. *Man of Steel: The Career and Courage of Christopher Reeve.* New York: Signet, 1996.

Karp, Gary, and Stanley D. Klein, eds. *From There to Here: Stories of Adjusting to Spinal Cord Injuries.* Horsham, Pa.: No Limits Communication, 2004.

Reeve, Christopher. *Nothing Is Impossible: Reflections on a New Life.* New York: Random House, 2002.

Joseph Dewey

See also Academy Awards; Americans with Disabilities Act of 1990; Audiobooks; Cable television; Film in the United States; Genetic engineering; Health care; Health care reform; Stem cell research; Television.

■ Reeves, Keanu

Identification Canadian American actor
Born September 2, 1964; Beirut, Lebanon

An actor who enjoys experimenting with roles, Reeves helped reshape audience expectations for action and science-fiction blockbusters in the 1990's.

While Keanu Reeves's first widely known film was *Bill and Ted's Excellent Adventure* (1989), in which his portrayal of a time-traveling party lover earned a cult following, the young Canadian actor had already starred in several movies after moving to the United States in the mid-1980's. He followed his first big commercial success with a sequel, *Bill and Ted's Bogus Journey* (1991), as well as *Point Break* (1991), a buddy-cop film with Patrick Swayze set among the California surfing scene; *My Own Private Idaho* (1991), a quirky independent film on which Reeves became close to costar River Phoenix; *Bram Stoker's Dracula* (1992); and *Much Ado About Nothing* (1993), based on William Shakespeare's play. With this eclectic mix, Reeves hoped not to be pigeonholed as the airheaded Ted, and he was successful to some degree, earning particularly good reviews for *My Own Private Idaho.*

It was not until the movie *Speed* (1994), however, that Reeves became a household name. Reeves bulked up and got a buzz haircut for the role of police officer Jack Traven, thus creating an Everyman action-hero persona popular with both male and female audiences. Reeves's on-screen chemistry with the not-yet-widely-known Sandra Bullock, as well as the movie's fast-paced, clever plot and dazzling special effects, made *Speed* wildly popular, and Reeves began earning multimillion-dollar salaries. In spite of this success, Reeves did not partake of the glamorous Hollywood lifestyle, in part because of his grief over River Phoenix's death from a drug overdose in October of 1993.

Following the universally panned *Johnny Mnemonic* (1995), Reeves continued to experiment with roles, including the romantic *A Walk in the Clouds* (1995), the offbeat *Feeling Minnesota* (1996), and the creepy *The Devil's Advocate* (1997), which costarred Al Pacino. Reeves's next big breakthrough occurred with the action-filled yet cerebral science-fiction film *The Matrix* (1999), in which he played Thomas Anderson, a corporate drone by day and a hacker named Neo by night, who discovers that the entire world is a virtual reality environment created by machines who have enslaved what is left of the human race. Reeves's understated confusion fit the role perfectly, and his facility during the groundbreaking kung fu fight scenes was impressive. *The Matrix* was an instant cult favorite and a huge financial success, cementing Reeves's reputation as a reliable box-office draw.

Impact Keanu Reeves's career throughout the 1990's, while varied in both the genre and the success of his chosen projects, contained two unmistakable high points that widely influenced the industry: *Speed,* which led audiences to expect smarter action movies with more everyday heroes than the industry had previously seen, and *The Matrix,* which introduced revolutionary special effects and showed that audiences' interest in high-concept science fiction had not ended with the *Star Wars* and *Terminator* movies.

Further Reading

Brown, Scott. "The Man Who Would Be Keanu." *Entertainment Weekly*, no. 736 (November 7, 2003): 24-28.

Grossman, L. "The Man Who Isn't There." *Time*, February 21, 2005, 54-56.

Membery, York. *Keanu Reeves*. Philadelphia: Chelsea House, 1998.

Amy Sisson

See also Film in the United States; *Matrix, The*; Phoenix, River.

■ Reform Party

Identification "Radical center" third-party movement

Date Established in 1995

The Reform Party's rise and successes demonstrated the dissatisfaction felt by many Americans with two-party politics as usual, especially on economic issues.

Although the Reform Party was not officially established until 1995, many citizens' dismay at the major parties' disregard of their concerns spurred the rise of several independent political movements during the 1990's. Of these, the most spectacular were the two attempts by Dallas software billionaire H. Ross Perot to win the presidency. The Reform Party, established as a vehicle for Perot's 1996 campaign, continued as a viable political entity through the rest of the decade.

The Antecedents At the beginning of the decade, a manifesto titled "Grassroots Petition" was published by retired financial planner Jack Gargan. Gargan's outrage was fueled by the political system's "dirty little secrets" that the major news media seldom covered. A national debt of $3 trillion, self-enacted congressional raises, depleting of the Social Security system to cover the deficit, and lobbyists' inordinate influence due to their political contributions, were among his complaints. Enough response greeted Gargan's petition to start an organization called Throw the Hypocritical Rascals Out (THRO). In fall, 1990, Ross Perot, who agreed with Gargan's complaints about the system, contacted Gargan. Perot had long meddled in high-level politics himself. Among other efforts, he had founded United We Stand during Richard M. Nixon's administration to aid the cause of American prisoners of war in North Vietnam.

When Perot announced his independent run for the presidency in February, 1992, he had a ready-made structure in place, made up of his own Electronic Data Systems (EDS) employees, Gargan's THRO lists, and grassroots volunteers. Under the aegis of United We Stand America, Perot ran an unconventional but remarkably successful campaign. Despite a two-month shutdown during summer, 1992, he reentered the race on October 1, keeping most of his supporters. His folksy plain speaking and colorful charts made him the star of the candidates' debates. In the 1992 election, he won 19 percent of the vote, a new record for a third party.

The Party Although Perot was initially coy about making another presidential run, his dismay about the enactment of the North American Free Trade Agreement (NAFTA), the lack of genuine campaign finance reform, and other disappointments meant that this remained a live option. In September, 1995, appearing on the *Larry King Live* show, Perot announced the creation of a new party "for the independent voters." Its convention was held in Long Beach, California, in August, 1996, with a second session held a week later in Valley Forge, Pennsylvania.

Unlike the relatively disciplined 1992 movement, these events were preceded by infighting and a fair amount of chaos in Reform Party ranks. Perot had a challenger, former Colorado governor Richard Lamm. To no one's surprise, Perot's selection as the party's nominee was announced in Valley Forge. His 1996 campaign largely emphasized the same issues of economic nationalism and citizen access on which he had run before. This time, however, much of the electorate's attention had returned to two-party rivalries, and some anger had been deflected by the Clinton administration's budget-balancing success and the nation's rising prosperity. The Reform Party won approximately 8 percent of the presidential vote in 1996.

This was enough, however, to qualify the party for federal matching funds in 2000. During the intervening years, as Perot removed himself from the party's active leadership, the gap between the EDS and party activists and its local volunteers widened. State organizations went their own way, adding to the fragmentation. In Minnesota, former professional wrestler and suburban mayor Jesse Ventura won the support of one of the more robust state Reform Party organizations in a run for governor. His outspoken advocacy of ideas like smaller classes in public schools, a light-rail system for the Twin Cities, freezing property taxes, and a medical approach to drug addiction came as a fresh approach to politics. The entire nation was shocked when he won Minnesota's governorship in 1998. Ventura's victory was largely attributed to his appeal to younger voters and to working-class citizens, who liked his combination of fiscal sobriety and a libertarian stance on cultural issues. Elsewhere, there were several Reform Party candidates for Congress and for local offices in 1998, but they had little success.

The prospect of $12 million in federal matching funds led to a contentious struggle for the party's 2000 presidential nomination. Ventura's victory made him a major force within the party, but he declined to run, throwing his support to Jack Gargan, the "godfather" of early movement efforts. Meanwhile, pundit Pat Buchanan set out to capture the party's nomination. He brought his own supporters into the party, added goals drawn from his own isolationist hard-right ideology, and outmaneuvered several attempts to stop him with short-lived candidacies such as that of entrepreneur Donald Trump. Neutralizing both the Perot and the Ventura factions, Buchanan entered the 2000 presidential election season as the Reform Party's candidate. Buchanan succeeded in turning the party's platform in a totally different direction from its "radical center" origins and presided over its disintegration as a force in the nation's political life.

Impact At its height, the Reform Party served the traditional function of American third parties: bringing neglected issues into the mainstream and forcing the major parties to confront them. President Bill Clinton's deficit-reduction measures were, arguably, made possible by the Reform Party's highlighting of the problem. Others among the party's issues, however, remained unaddressed or even worsened.

The party's meteoric rise and successes also showed the gap between many citizens' expectations and the "issues" that most politicians want to talk about. Even after the party's near-demise, this gap remains, perhaps providing ammunition for future reform efforts.

Further Reading

Edwards, Tamala M. "The Ventura Way: If It Isn't Fun, I Quit." *Time*, August 9, 1991, p. 8. Reporting from the trenches of the party's national convention, showing the rivalries and stresses that shaped its downfall.

Jelen, Ted G., ed. *Ross for Boss: The Perot Phenomenon and Beyond*. Albany: State University of New York Press, 2001. A collection of articles on aspects of Perot's campaigns and on the Jesse Ventura phenomenon.

Sifry, Micah L. *Spoiling for a Fight: Third Party Politics in America*. New York: Routledge, 2002. Examines the rise and fall of the Reform Party and other third parties that sprang up during the 1990's. Emphasizes the forces working against the party's long-term survival.

Emily Alward

See also Balanced Budget Act of 1997; Buchanan, Pat; Bush, George H. W.; Business and the economy in the United States; Clinton, Bill; Elections in the United States, midterm; Elections in the United States, 1992; Elections in the United States, 1996; North American Free Trade Agreement (NAFTA); Perot, H. Ross; Stockdale, James; Ventura, Jesse.

■ Religion and spirituality in Canada

Identification Organized and nonorganized expressions of spiritual belief and practice among Canadians

Traditionally characterized by the Roman Catholic, Anglican, and United Church of Canada denominations, religion in Canada in the 1990's also embraced an increasing variety of religious faiths and spiritualities.

Reflecting a long-term trend, Canada's religious life in the 1990's was marked by its increasing pluralism, sharing the increasing multiculturalism of Canada. At the same time, there was a seeming decline in formal religious membership, accompanied by a reduced role for the religious perspective in civic life.

Demographics of Religion Unlike the United States, Canada asks about religious preference in its census data. The 1991 Canadian census indicated that Canadians were 45 percent Roman Catholic, 35 percent Protestant, and 1.4 percent Eastern Orthodox. Jews represented about 1.2 percent of the Canadian population. Reflecting the changing sources of immigration and Canada's increasingly multicultural society, these demographics changed significantly over the decade of the 1990's. The total number of Christians in percentage terms declined from 81 percent in 1991 to 74 percent in 2001, with Catholics falling to 43.6 percent of the population and Protestants to 29 percent of the population. Meanwhile, there was a significant increase in adherents of Islam (doubling in population over the 1990's to become 2 percent of the Canadian population). Likewise, there was a large increase of adherents to Hinduism and Sikhism (both increasing by 89 percent) and Buddhism (increasing by 84 percent), with all three of these religions growing to about 1 percent each of the Canadian population by decade's end. This increase is largely explained by the large number of adherents of these religions who were part of the 1.8 million immigrants to Canada during the 1990's.

The most influential faiths in Canada have traditionally been Roman Catholic, Anglican, and the United Church of Canada (formed by a union of Presbyterian, Methodist, Congregational, and other churches in 1925).These three denominations were traditionally granted special prerogatives under Canadian law, especially in the field of education, and played a dominant role in Canadian society. All three underwent significant changes in the latter half of the twentieth century, including the 1990's. While the number of adherents and the traditions of Catholicism did not diminish, the same cannot be said of the influence on society of the Catholic hierarchy and priests, especially in Quebec. (Particularly damaging to the Catholic Church in Canada were disclosures of abuse at the Mount Cashel Boys Home in Newfoundland, which was closed in 1990.) The Anglican and United Churches seemed to show a decline in both numbers and influence. It seems that the progressive social attitudes of the mainline Protestant denominations on such issues as homosexual and abortion rights did not draw more adherents to these churches. In fact, the Protestant groups that showed the most growth were those of an evangelical and freestanding character. A vivid example is the "Toronto Blessing" revival that began in the Toronto Airport Vineyard Fellowship in January, 1994, and attracted millions of participants to its physically charismatic worship services.

The heartland of Canadian Catholicism has always been French-speaking Quebec. The Quiet Revolution of the 1960's and 1970's had already seen the secularization of the once clericalist Quebec society. This trend was to continue through the 1990's. A symbol of this changed status occurred in 1990. The chairman of the Montreal Catholic School Commission called upon the Quebec provincial government to encourage immigration by people who shared Judeo-Christian values. This call was immediately repudiated by the provincial leaders as conflicting with Quebec's secular character.

Another sign of Canada's determination to accommodate a broader faith experience than the traditional Catholic and Protestant religions inherited from the mother countries of France and England was illustrated in a debate over national prayer. The federal parliament in Canada traditionally began its daily sessions with a prayer dedicated in part to Jesus Christ. In February, 1994, the Canadian Parliament voted unanimously to substitute the nondenominational reference to "Almighty God" for the Christian reference.

The Canadian government traditionally funded, at least to some extent, Catholic and Protestant schools; this led to controversy in the 1990's. In 1991, protesters took over an Amherstburg public school to protest the increasing jurisdiction of the Catholic school system over formerly public schools. In 1994, a suit by Jewish parents to obtain public funding for their schools was rejected by the Ontario Court of Appeal. In 1996, the Supreme Court in its *Adler v. Ontario* decision upheld the Province of Ontario in funding Catholic schools to the exclusion of Jewish schools as part of the political compromise that made the 1867 confederation possible. While accepting the advantages granted to Canada's largest denominations in school funding, however, the courts were eager to show that Canada welcomed all faiths. In the same year, for example, in the case of *Ross v. New Brunswick School District No. 15*, the Supreme Court found that a school board was liable for discrimination for failing to take action against a teacher who made vituperative comments against Jewish people during his off-duty time.

Despite these debates over Canada's increasingly pluralistic and even secularized approach to faith and spirituality, there is an academic consensus on the different role that religion plays in Canadian political life from that of its southern neighbor, the

United States. In the last decades of the twentieth century, religion played a potent, persuasive, and at times divisive role in U.S. politics, but organized religion did not play a similar role in Canada during the 1990's. Despite Canada's traditional conservatism, a consensus had emerged accepting Canada's diverse and personalized approach to religion, separated from the tumult of politics.

Impact Religion in Canada in the 1990's reflected the changes in Canadian society. From its French and English roots, Canadian religion took on a more diverse character, with the greatest increases registered among non-Christian religions and among religious nonadherents. Whether because of the declining influence of the Catholic Church in Quebec, the sometimes extreme stands of the Protestant mainline churches, or the more personal, expressive faith of the evangelical denominations, Canadian religion did not seem to play a major role in Canadian politics of the 1990's.

Further Reading

Choquette, Robert. *Canada's Religions: An Historical Introduction.* Ottawa: University of Ottawa Press, 2004. Part of the Religion and Beliefs series, this volume traces the history of religion in Canada as shaped by traditional beliefs and modern practices.

Menendez, Albert. *Church and State in Canada.* Amherst, N.Y.: Prometheus Books, 1996. An update on Canadian church-state relations in the mid-1990's, critical of the role of religion in Canadian life.

Murphy, Terrence, and Roberto Perin, eds. *A Concise History of Christianity in Canada.* Toronto: Oxford University Press, 1996. A comprehensive history of the institutions of Canada's Christian denominations and their social and political impact.

Howard Bromberg

See also Abortion; Canada and the United States; Dead Sea scrolls publication; Demographics of Canada; Education in Canada; Elections in Canada; Homosexuality and gay rights; Immigration to Canada; Minorities in Canada; Religion and spirituality in the United States.

■ Religion and spirituality in the United States

Identification Organized and nonorganized expressions of spiritual belief and practice among Americans

Religion and spirituality played an important, if at times contradictory, role in political and social life of the United States in the 1990's.

Like much of American history, the 1990's were marked by both religious and spiritual dynamism and by growing secularism. These somewhat paradoxical tendencies are well exemplified in the results of a public opinion data poll that identified 1992 as both the "Year of the Evangelical" and the "Year of the Secular." New religious movements and spiritualities partook both of traditional devotions and a practical, entrepreneurial spirit that has always been an American characteristic. America's ability to harmonize the conflicting strands of religiosity and secularism in the 1990's was perhaps nowhere better illustrated than in politics. Although the United States prides itself on separation of church and state, changing religious affiliations played a crucial role in national and local politics.

Demographics Most American adults identify themselves with one particular religion or denomination. There is no quicker way of understanding the social landscape of the 1990's than by surveying the demographics of religious adherence in the United States. Although the U.S. Census does not ask about religious affiliation, the Graduate School of the City University of New York conducted a National Survey of Religious Identification in 1990, one of the most extensive surveys of religious affiliation ever undertaken. This comprehensive survey found that of the total adult civilian population of approximately 175 million Americans, 86 percent were identified as Christian. The largest Christian denomination was Roman Catholic, with approximately 46 million adult adherents, a little more than a quarter of the adult population. The largest Protestant denomination was Baptist, with about 34 million adherents, or about one-fifth of the adult population. About 17 million American adults—one-tenth of the population—were identified as nondenominational Protestants. The next largest Protestant denominations were Methodist, with approximately 14 million adult members, Lutheran with 9 million, Presbyterian with 5 million, Pentecostal with 3 million, Episcopalian with 3 million, and the Church of Jesus Christ of Latter-day Saints (Mormon), with about 2.5 million adult members.

Other non-Christian religions surveyed in 1990 were much smaller in comparison. Approximately 3 million adults were identified as Jewish, about 2 percent of the population. In addition, 527,000 adults were identified as Muslim, 401,000 as Buddhist, 227,000 as Hindu, 47,000 as belonging to Native American religions, 45,000 as Scientologist, 28,000 as Baha'i, 23,000 as Taoist, and about 20,000 as New Age adherents. Nonbelieving or nonclassified adults constituted about 10 percent of the population. From this it can be seen that the United States entered the 1990's as a nation in which the vast majority of adults identified themselves as belonging to Christian denominations. Although the nation had a large number of adherents of almost every other religion in the world, making the United States the most religiously diverse country on earth, their numbers remained small in comparison with Christianity. Immigration patterns of the 1990's would play an important role in religious demographics. In 1990, 7.2 million Americans, or 2.9 percent of the population, were of Asian origin. Increased immigration from Asia and Africa accounted for most of the rise in numbers of non-Christian religions.

Politics and Religion The influence of the Religious Right in American politics continued unabated in the 1990's. At the beginning of the decade, Pat Robertson founded the Christian Coalition to assert the values of conservative Christianity in local and national politics. By 1995, the Christian Coalition under its director Ralph Reed had become remarkably active, claiming 1.7 million members in local chapters nationwide. These chapters registered and educated millions of voters and lobbied legislators in support of their principles. These principles were summarized in the Coalition's Contract with the American Family, introduced on the steps of the U.S. Capitol. Likewise, the Reverend Jerry Falwell spoke of reviving his Moral Majority organization, a political force in the 1980's, if the federal government pushed for abortion and homosexual rights. The Supreme Court decision in *Lee v. Weisman* (1992), which prohibited nonsectarian prayer at public school graduations, illustrated the federal judiciary's push toward secularization.

Since September 1, 1960, when presidential candidate John F. Kennedy delivered a major address distinguishing between his private religious beliefs and his political actions, candidates for the presidency had followed an unwritten rule. Religion was not to be an issue, and matters of faith were not relevant in political campaigns. This unwritten code was stretched to the limit in the 1992 presidential race between President George H. W. Bush and Bill Clinton. As political columnist William Safire noted, no presidential campaign in American history was more explicit in invoking the name and blessings of God than the 1992 campaign. For example, President Bush often invoked the religious and Christian heritage of the United States, especially in appearances before conventions of America's largest Protestant denomination, the Southern Baptists, and before evangelical groups, which were becoming increasingly active and influential in American politics. His challenger Bill Clinton was competing for the same votes and in his speeches often quoted from the Bible and referred to the "new covenant" he wanted to make with America and the "crusade" he would carry out to reform government. Even third-party candidate H. Ross Perot found religious demographics to be one of the chief determinants of the presidential campaign. The votes for Perot came almost exclusively from one demographic category: white Protestants. As a result, the famous 1990's pollster George Gallup, Jr., was well able to conclude that religious affiliation was one of the most accurate of political indicators.

Religion and the Media The 1990's saw the continued visibility of religious figures on the most dominant media of the decade—television. Using the new capabilities of cable television, Paul Crouch built the Trinity Broadcasting Network and Mother Mary Angelica built her Eternal Word Television Network into international media empires. Pat Robertson, already a significant voice through his Christian Broadcasting Network featuring *The 700 Club*, founded International Family Entertainment in 1990 to promote and distribute family-oriented programming to cable television. The Reverend Billy Graham, perhaps the best-known and most-respected religious figure in the United States, increasingly reached out to groups beyond his fundamentalist roots. His ecumenical evangelistic crusades attracted millions of Americans. Perhaps the most influential American Catholic prelate of the 1990's was Joseph Cardinal Bernardin of Chicago, who developed the "seamless garment" ethic to moral questions involving human life. But certainly the most forceful and telegenic personality for American Catholics was Pope John Paul II, whose worldwide travels, charisma, and personal holiness made him a vivid presence. Traveling to the United States in the years 1993, 1995, and 1999, Pope John Paul II called on Americans to return to their moral roots, while working for a more peaceful, pluralistic, and economically just world. Under his leadership, the United States Conference of Catholic Bishops reaffirmed its vigorous opposition to the practice of abortion, euthanasia, and capital punishment.

Religious broadcasting on both television and radio figured significantly in the ongoing "culture wars." Religious leaders, networks, and groups chose sides in the bitter ethical and political debates over issues such as abortion, divorce, homosexuality, and public education. Other religious leaders stirred up different kinds of controversies, which inevitably received the widest publicity on television news and talk shows. Allegations of clergy abuse of parishioners were mushrooming into a nationwide scandal. Televangelists Jimmy Swaggert, Mike Warnke, and Robert Tilton were exposed for scandalous behavior in 1991. Minister Louis Farrakhan, leader of the Nation of Islam sect and organizer of the successful Million Man March on October 16, 1995, was accused of making anti-Semitic statements.

Religious Pluralism As the United States became a more pluralistic society through the 1990's, its religious life became more diverse as well. Religions other than Christianity and Judaism had entered the mainstream. For example, during this decade the U.S. Navy commissioned its first Muslim chaplain and opened its first mosque. The 2001 American Religious Identification Survey, a follow-up to its 1990 survey by the Graduate School of the City University of New York, revealed that over the course of the decade the proportion of American adults identifying themselves as Christian had declined by 7 percent of the population. Meanwhile, adherents of non-Christian religions had increased during the 1990's from 3.5 percent to 5.2 percent of the total population, with the number of Muslims in the United States increasing 109 percent, Buddhists 170 percent, and Hindus 237 percent. The number of those reporting no adherence to religion increased to 15 percent of the population; it is likely that many of these nonadherents still counted themselves as spiritual but followed a syncretistic mix of religious and spiritual beliefs.

The United States has been a nation of remarkable dynamism, with its ingenuity, inventiveness, and productiveness admired throughout the world. The American approach to religion has likewise been characterized by the rapid and easy birth of new religions, denominations, and spiritual traditions, a process that defined the 1990's as well. Promise Keepers was founded by Bill McCartney in 1990 to encourage men to commit to responsible and biblical relationships. Kwanzaa, an African American spiritual holiday, grew in popularity and was commemorated by a U.S. postal stamp in 1997.

Perhaps the most remarkable American phenomenon was the rise of the New Age movement. New Age beliefs represented a distinctly American and eclectic synthesis of Asian meditation practices, insights from modern science, and a search for a holistic balance of mind and body. One of its leading practitioners, Dr. Deepak Chopra, founded the Chopra Center for Wellbeing in La Jolla, California, in 1996.

America's innovative approach to religion had a dark side as well, with the proliferation of several dangerous cults. In 1993, in response to the killing of four federal agents, a Federal Bureau of Investigation (FBI) siege of the Branch Davidian compound in Waco, Texas, resulted in the deaths of seventy-six cult members. In 1997, thirty-nine members of the Heaven's Gate sect in San Diego, California, committed suicide after the sighting of the Hale-Bopp comet.

Impact In American politics, religion seemed to play a largely conservative role, as evangelical Protestants helped move local elections toward a more traditional footing and forced presidential aspirants to answer to their concerns. In spiritual and moral terms, the United States saw a resurgence in traditional religion perhaps best symbolized by the ecumenical appeal of the Reverend Billy Graham and Pope John Paul II. At the same time, the United States saw an increasingly eclectic and practical approach to the spiritual quest undertaken by many Americans. In the end, it is hard to say whether the

1990's was an age in which religion shaped American beliefs and values or whether American pragmatism reshaped American religion.

Further Reading

Eck, Diana. *A New Religious America: How a "Christian Country" Has Become the World's Most Religiously Diverse Nation.* San Francisco: HarperCollins, 2002. Explores the growth of non-Christian religions in modern America.

Kosmin, Barry, and Seymour Lachman. *One Nation Under God: Religion in Contemporary American Society.* New York: Harmony Books, 1993. Sociological analysis based on a comprehensive demographic analysis of American religion.

McGraw, Barbara. *Rediscovering America's Sacred Ground: Public Religion and Pursuit of the Good in a Pluralistic America.* Albany: State University of New York Press, 2003. Academic analysis of religion and the culture wars in America at the end of the twentieth century.

Porterfield, Amanda. *The Transformation of American Religion: The Story of a Late Twentieth-Century Awakening.* New York: Oxford University Press, 2001. Places recent American religiosity in its historical context, with an emphasis on religious pluralism.

Roof, Wade Clark, ed. *Contemporary American Religion.* New York: Macmillan Reference USA, 2000. Over five hundred articles on various facets of the modern religious and spiritual life of the United States.

Wald, Kenneth. *Religion and Politics in the United States.* Lanham, Md.: Rowman & Littlefield, 2003. Argues that despite America's increasingly secularized society, religion continues to play an important political role.

William, Martin. *With God on Our Side: The Rise of the Religious Right in America.* New York: Broadway Books, 1996. The accompanying text to a PBS television series, this book examines the confluence of religious faith and political life in modern America.

Wuthnow, Robert. *After Heaven: Spirituality in America Since the 1950's.* Berkeley: University of California Press, 1998. Finds the trend of modern American religious faith to be practice-oriented, personalized, and ephemeral.

Howard Bromberg

See also Bernardin, Joseph Cardinal; Chopra, Deepak; Christian Coalition; Conservatism in U.S. politics; Culture wars; Dead Sea scrolls publication; Demographics of the United States; Elections in the United States, 1992; Falwell, Jerry; Farrakhan, Louis; Heaven's Gate mass suicide; Holocaust Memorial Museum; Jewish Americans; Kwanzaa; Promise Keepers; Waco siege; WWJD bracelets.

■ Reno, Janet

Identification Attorney general of the United States, 1993-2001

Born July 21, 1938; Miami, Florida

Reno was the first female attorney general of the United States. Her tenure as the highest-ranking law-enforcement official was marked by controversial, high-profile decisions.

After his inauguration as president in 1993, Bill Clinton turned his immediate attention to filling cabinet positions. He identified two women as possible candidates to be attorney general, but both withdrew. Having twice visited the drug court Janet Reno established in Florida, Clinton was impressed by the success of this visionary project that spared first offenders from prison terms.

Clinton examined Reno's credentials, which included considerable judicial experience in Florida and a law degree from Harvard University. He asked his aide, Vince Foster, to interview Reno. Foster was impressed by the candidate and recommended that she become attorney general. Clinton nominated Reno on February 11. On March 11, the Senate confirmed her appointment unanimously.

The first crisis in a tenure that involved innumerable crises was already raging when Reno assumed office. In February, 1993, a group of heavily armed religious fundamentalists, the Branch Davidians, barricaded themselves inside their compound near Waco, Texas. Following a shoot-out between Davidian members and agents from the Bureau of Alcohol, Tobacco, and Firearms (ATF) that left four agents and an undetermined number of Davidians dead, a siege led by the Federal Bureau of Investigation (FBI) lasted for fifty-one days.

The FBI pressured Reno to end the standoff, which deployed dozens of agents who were needed elsewhere, by storming the compound. Reno took the proposal to Bill Clinton, who reluctantly assented. On April 19, the assault occurred. The compound went up in flames, killing seventy-six Da-

Janet Reno. (AP/Wide World Photos)

vidians, including twenty-one children. This event evoked questions about religious freedom. Critics of the Clinton administration hurled barbed vituperations at both Clinton and Reno.

Meanwhile, many other crucial matters occupied Reno. She brought action against Microsoft for violations of the Sherman Antitrust Act, led the prosecution of twenty-one radicals in Montana for staging an eighty-one-day standoff, and oversaw the arrest and conviction of the Unabomber (Theodore Kaczynski) and of Timothy McVeigh and Terry Nichols for engineering the 1995 Oklahoma City bombing.

In the Elián González proceeding in 1999, the father of a young Cuban boy being cared for by relatives in Miami sought custody of his son. Public sentiment deplored the boy's return to Cuba, but the law favored the father. Reno ordered armed guards to seize Elián and return him to Cuba.

Impact Janet Reno was the first (and to date only) female attorney general of the United States. That Reno weathered the numerous storms that occurred during her tenure and was the longest-serving U.S. attorney general in the twentieth century speaks volumes for her strength of character.

Further Reading

Anderson, Paul. *Janet Reno: Doing the Right Thing.* New York: John Wiley & Sons, 1994.

Hamilton, John. *The Attorney General Through Janet Reno.* Edina, Minn.: Abdo and Daughters, 1993.

Meachum, Virginia. *Janet Reno: United States Attorney General.* Springfield, N.J.: Enslow, 1995.

R. Baird Shuman

See also Clinton, Bill; Clinton, Hillary Rodham; Clinton's impeachment; Hate crimes; Illegal immigration; Lewinsky scandal; McVeigh, Timothy; Montana Freemen standoff; Oklahoma City bombing; *Shaw v. Reno*; Waco siege; Whitewater investigation.

■ *Rent*

Identification Broadway musical
Author Music and lyrics by Jonathan Larson (1960-1996)
Date Premiered on Broadway on April 29, 1996

This prize-winning rock opera took Broadway by storm. Focusing on the lives of young New Yorkers struggling with HIV/AIDS, poverty, homelessness, and sexual identity, the show's creator attempted to bring a new layer of relevancy to musical theater.

Jonathan Larson got his start studying theater and music at Adelphi University; during that time, he met Stephen Sondheim, who became his mentor. After moving to New York City, the aspiring musical writer attempted to break into Broadway. Two of his pieces, *Superbia* and *Tick, Tick . . . Boom!* were staged in small workshop-type settings; in 1988, he won a Richard Rodgers Studio Production Award for the former. The idea for *Rent* came in collaboration with Billy Aronson, a young playwright, and was to be a modern retelling of Giacomo Puccini's opera *La Bohème* (pr. 1896). Puccini's is the story of struggling artists and philosophers living in the 1830's Parisian

Left Bank; *Rent* tells the story of young bohemian artists and musicians in 1990's New York lower East Side. Larson ultimately took the idea on his own and penned the music and book. Aronson is credited as "Original Concept/Additional Lyrics."

After repeated attempts and multiple revisions, Larson received a $45,000 Richard Rodgers Award in January, 1994, to stage a workshop version of the show the following October. After a well-received two-week run, plans were made for a full-scale workshop production at New York Theatre Workshop (NYTW). *Rent* was set to open on January 25, 1996. The night before, after the final dress rehearsal, Larson collapsed from an aortic aneurysm; the creator of *Rent* was dead at thirty-five. The official NYTW opening was delayed, but when the musical opened, it received critical acclaim. The first month of the workshop's performances sold out in a matter of days. Its run was extended by one month to the end of March and sold out within one week. *Rent* opened on Broadway on April 29, 1996, at the Nederlander Theatre. The U.S. national tour began in Boston in November, 1996, with other scheduled tours in Los Angeles, Toronto, and London for the following year.

Recognition *Rent* received multiple awards and international acclaim. In 1996, it received ten Tony Award nominations. It won for Best Musical, Best Book of a Musical (Larson), Best Original Score (Larson), and Best Featured Actor in a Musical (Wilson Jermaine Heredia). *Rent* tied with *Bring in 'da Noise, Bring in 'da Funk* and *The King and I* for four Tonys. Larson posthumously received the 1996 Pulitzer Prize in drama.

The New York Drama Critics' Circle awarded *Rent* Best Musical. *Rent* also received Drama Desk Awards for Outstanding Musical, Outstanding Music (Larson), Outstanding Featured Actor in a Musical (Heredia), and Outstanding Orchestrations (Steve Skinner), and the Drama League Award for Best Musical. The Theatre World Award for Outstanding New Talent went to two *Rent* cast members, Adam Pascal and Daphne Rubin-Vega. The *Village Voice*'s

The cast of Rent *at New York's Nederlander Theatre in 1996.* (AP/Wide World Photos)

Obie Awards for Outstanding Book, Music, and Lyrics (Larson), Outstanding Direction (Michael Greif), and Outstanding Ensemble Performance also speak to *Rent*'s success.

Impact Jonathan Larson set out to write a *Hair* (pr. 1967) for the 1990's. His rock opera was intended to be a response to the HIV/AIDS crisis and a celebration of the lives of those lost at a young age. He wanted to "reclaim Broadway from stagnation and empty spectacle . . . to bring musical theater to the MTV generation." By all critical accounts he succeeded, offering a generational anthem of sorts and bringing a new energy to the Great White Way. Many credit *Rent* with revitalizing musical theater as an art form. *New York Times* theater writer Peter Marks remarked that Larson "rekindled faith in the American musical when many in the theater business, particularly younger people, believed it had reached an artistic dead end."

Rent also brought to the public eye issues of sexuality, poverty, and homelessness and heightened awareness of the AIDS crisis. Critics argue that Larson gave warmth and emotion to difficult and controversial personae, particularly with a little-known disease and non-normative sexual identities.

Subsequent Events *Rent*'s enormous popularity resulted in a cult following. Fans of the rock opera camped outside the Nederlander Theatre for the chance to win one of the thirty-four seats in the first two rows. Seats were offered for $20, as *Rent*'s producers wanted to ensure that the musical was affordable for all. Fans who camped out multiple times were dubbed "Rent Heads," some seeing the show dozens of times.

Shortly after *Rent*'s Broadway debut, novelist Sarah Schulman threatened a plagiarism suit against the Larson estate, claiming that Larson had lifted entire portions of her book *People in Trouble* (1990). Schulman also did not appreciate what she viewed as the commodification of the gay culture portrayed in the musical, as well as the placement of straight allies as saviors in the homosexual cause. However, no claim was filed and no legal action taken.

Rent has enjoyed numerous tours across the United States and Canada, as well as several international tours, including Australia, the United Kingdom, Ireland, Italy, the Netherlands, Brazil, Spain, Japan, and South Korea. In 2005, *Rent* became a major motion picture from Revolution Studios and Columbia Pictures, starring many members of the original Broadway cast.

Further Reading

Larson, Jonathan. *Rent.* New York: Rob Weisbach Books/William Morrow, 1997. Compendium of photographs, stories, and libretto. Follows Larson's and *Rent*'s journey through the stories of those who knew Larson and those involved in the musical's production, including cast and family members.

Rapp, Anthony. *Without You: A Memoir of Love, Loss, and the Musical "Rent."* New York: Simon & Schuster, 2006. A fascinating backstage account of the production of *Rent* from an original cast member.

Schulman, Sarah. *Stagestruck: Theater, AIDS, and the Marketing of Gay America.* Durham, N.C.: Duke University Press, 1998. Schulman's provocative take on *Rent* and her argument for Larson's taking her plot and characters. Also offers a different perspective on the musical and its impact.

Meredith Holladay

See also AIDS epidemic; Alternative rock; Art movements; Broadway musicals; Homosexuality and gay rights; Music; Race relations; Religion and spirituality in the United States; Shepard, Matthew; Theater in the United States; Transgender community.

■ Republican Revolution

Definition A shift that gave Republicans control of both the House and Senate for the first time since 1952

Date November, 1994

The "Republican Revolution" was significant for many reasons, not the least of which was the fact that it was first time since Ronald Reagan left office that political candidates ran on pure conservatism. The event was inadvertently significant for President Bill Clinton, in that his reelection in 1996 signaled the demise of the revolution and resulted in the Senate refusing to remove him from office after his impeachment in 1998.

In the weeks leading up to the elections of November, 1994, polls showed that political change was imminent in the legislature of the United States. Yet, while it was obvious that change was coming, not many predicted a political shift of the magnitude that would take place.

The 1994 Republican Revolution was an event of near unprecedented political force. It took the reins of both houses of Congress from the Democrats, who had unflinchingly held them for decades, and gave them wholly to the American right. This seismic shift is best understood by viewing it through two key figures, President Bill Clinton and Speaker of the House Newt Gingrich, for it was as much a testimony to the failures of Clinton as to the ideals of Gingrich.

After Clinton's victory in the 1992 presidential race, the Democrats held not only both houses of Congress but the White House as well. Though the future seemed bright, Clinton's election was hard for his fellow Democrats, who were constantly asked to explain allegations tied to his governorship in Little Rock, Arkansas. Once in office, Clinton went back and forth on matters that his party held as paramount, and First Lady Hillary Rodham Clinton led an effort to overhaul the nation's health care system. Taken together, the allegations, Clinton's "waffling" on key Democratic issues, and outrage at the attempt to universalize health care were too much. The ambience of a honeymoon that normally surrounds the surge in political power that the Democrats managed in 1992 was gone a year and half later, as members of Congress in Clinton's own party distanced themselves from him. Subsequently, the American people were weary of both Clinton and the Democratic Congress. Public approval ratings for Congress fell to 18 percent in polls conducted in the spring of 1994.

The Republican Response While Clinton and Congress were losing favor with the American people, a group of congressional Republican candidates promising to give the government back to the people was garnering support. Led by men such as Dick Armey of Texas and Gingrich of Georgia, these Republicans outlined their agenda for change in the form of Gingrich's Contract with America. This contract contained ten parts, each of which was no less than a political promise to the American people. Among them were the Taking Back Our Streets Act, directed toward greater crime control; the American Dream Restoration Act, focusing on tax code reform; and the Personal Responsibility Act, designed to bring about welfare reform.

On November 8, 1994, the Republicans took control of both houses of Congress, with Gingrich becoming the first Republican Speaker of the House in four decades. They had accomplished this feat both by promoting the Contract with America as a solution to the big government policies of the Democrats and by campaigning nationally instead of through district-specific campaigns, although the norm in politics at that time was summed up in the popular maxim "All politics is local." On the other side of the aisle, Clinton and the Democratic leadership were stymied but not surprised. Shortly after the elections, Clinton held press conferences in which he said that the American people had sent a message that they did not want government to be as intrusive as it had been in the recent past.

The First Hundred Days After taking their places in Congress in January, 1995, the Republicans sought to emulate Franklin D. Roosevelt's first hundred days in office. By mid-April, the House of Representatives had passed most of the legislative items tied to the Contract with America, but they faced a tougher fight in the Senate.

Many of the freshmen Republicans who had run as conservatives, however, began to compartmentalize their conservatism and to describe themselves as either fiscal or social conservatives rather than purely conservative. This meant that among the newly elected Republican majority were true conservatives who opposed abortion and gun control and supported tax cuts, fiscal conservatives who supported tax cuts and business deregulation but who were not very concerned about stopping abortion or curtailing gun control, and social conservatives who opposed abortion and gun control but were not avidly opposed to the level of taxation then in place. Gingrich's coalition appeared less and less unified with time.

The election of 1996 brought an end to the Republican Revolution when Clinton defeated Republican presidential candidate Bob Dole for his second term. The Republicans had been given a chance and squandered it through a lack of party cohesion. Clinton, who had seen his chances of reelection drifting away in 1994, had found a way back into favor with his fellow Democrats.

Impact Ironically, the impact of the Republican Revolution remained strong until George W. Bush, a Republican, became president in 2001. The early months of the revolution had put so much pressure on Clinton that he signed welfare reform and other vital aspects of the Contract with America into law. Once Clinton left office and Bush was elected as a Republican who was not necessarily a conservative, enduring qualities of the revolution were undermined. Limited government, a staple of the revolution, was lost in the shuffle as Bush agreed to new entitlements and government expansion.

Further Reading

Garrett, Major. *The Enduring Revolution: How the Contract with America Continues to Shape the Nation.* New York: Crown Forum, 2005. Attempts to trace the enduring qualities or aspects of the Republican Revolution. It provides a brief overview of how the ideas of small government as espoused by Gingrich in 1994 was neither dead nor dying in some parts of the country ten years later.

Gimpel, James G. *Fulfilling the Contract: The First One Hundred Days.* Boston: Allyn & Bacon, 1996. Provides a statistical overview of the breakdown of the electorate and the Republican approach to the 1994 elections.

Gingrich, Newt. *Winning the Future: A Twenty-first Century Contract with America.* Washington, D.C.: Regnery, 2005. Gingrich tries to show the way to a continued Republican Revolution and thus smaller government, lower crime rates, and improved border security, among other things. A worthy read for anyone seeking to understand the philosophical underpinnings of the 1994 revolution.

AWR Hawkins III

See also Armey, Dick; Christian Coalition; Clinton, Bill; Conservatism in U.S. politics; Contract with America; Elections in the United States, midterm; Gingrich, Newt; Line Item Veto Act of 1996; Term limits.

■ Reséndiz, Ángel Maturino

Identification Serial murderer
Born August 1, 1959; Matamoros, Mexico
Died June 27, 2006; Huntsville, Texas

Reséndiz crisscrossed international borders to commit murder in several regions, demonstrating the difficulty of investigating murder by stranger and the porousness of U.S. borders.

Between 1997 and 1999, a series of murders occurred in the United States and Mexico that were connected by the crimes' proximity to railroad tracks. For instance, two University of Kentucky students walking beside some railroad tracks were assaulted, one murdered; in Texas, a neurologist who lived near a railroad was sexually assaulted and murdered; in Illinois, an eighty-year-old man was murdered less than a quarter mile from railroad tracks. The murderer in each case was a drifter named Ángel Maturino Reséndiz, dubbed the "Railway Killer."

For almost two years, Reséndiz rode the rails looking for victims. Like other serial murderers, Reséndiz was able to avoid detection by committing crimes in various jurisdictions, stowing away on freight trains and committing crimes wherever the train stopped. After choosing a likely victim and bludgeoning him or her with whatever object was at hand, Reséndiz rode the rails back to his wife in Mexico. Sometimes he stole from his victims, but more often Reséndiz left valuables behind, suggesting that murder itself was his goal.

Reséndiz often left evidence behind, including fingerprints. Eventually, investigators were able to identify him and convince his relatives to cooperate in order to prevent unnecessary bloodshed. He was arrested in July, 1999, and was later linked to at least fifteen murders around the United States. After being convicted and sentenced to death, Reséndiz confessed to murders in five states.

Impact Like most criminals of his ilk, Reséndiz has little personal significance. He was a sloppy, impulsive, brutal murderer. In the late 1990's, he found much more significance as a symbol of the threat posed by easily penetrated international borders and slack security. More tragically, Reséndiz's case demonstrates the difficulty of investigating murders committed by strangers with seemingly unfathomable motives. Had he not been so sloppy and left so much forensic evidence behind, Reséndiz might have been able to commit far more crimes before being caught.

Further Reading

Booth, Daniel. "Federalism on Ice: State and Local Enforcement of Federal Immigration Law." *Harvard Journal of Law and Public Policy* 29, no. 3 (2006): 1063-1083.

Clarkson, Wensley. *The Railway Killer.* London: John Blake, 2007.

Malkin, Michelle. *Invasion: How America Still Welcomes Terrorists, Criminals, and Other Foreign Menaces to Our Shores.* Washington, D.C.: Regnery, 2002.

Michael R. Meyers

See also Crime; Dahmer, Jeffrey; Ferguson, Colin; Illegal immigration; Latinos; Mexico and the United States.

■ Rice, Anne

Identification American novelist
Born October 4, 1941; New Orleans, Louisiana

Author of numerous horror fiction novels during the 1990's, Rice wrote stories about the supernatural that earned her a cultlike following of loyal fans.

Unbeknownst to Anne Rice at the time, the 1976 publication of her first horror novel, *Interview with the Vampire,* set the stage for the aspiring author to become one of the most-read authors of contemporary horror fiction during the 1990's. The critically acclaimed novel, which was written in the first person, explored the lives of the vampires Louis and Lestat. Her fluid storytelling, attention to detail, and sympathetic treatment of the characters redefined for readers the stereotypical image of vampires. In response to the book's success, Rice wrote *The Vampire Lestat* in 1985 and *The Queen of the Damned* in 1988. Both of these vampire stories were based on characters that were first introduced in her original vampire novel.

By the 1990's, Rice's vampire books became collectively known as The Vampire Chronicles, and her popularity soared. In 1994, Warner Bros. released the motion picture version of the book, *Interview with the Vampire: The Vampire Chronicles.* The film, which was a success at the box office, starred Tom Cruise as Lestat, Brad Pitt as Louis, Antonio Banderas as Armand, Christian Slater as the interviewer, and Kirsten Dunst as Claudia.

Anne Rice poses in 1992. (Hulton Archive/Getty Images)

As Rice became increasingly popular with her fans, their devotion to the author became cultlike. In response, Rice published four more books in the vampire series. These included *The Tale of the Body Thief* (1992), *Memnoch the Devil* (1995), *The Vampire Armand* (1998), and *Merrick* (2000). It was also in the 1990's that she expanded the vampire stories by creating another series known as New Tales of the Vampires. The first book in the series, *Pandora: New Tales of the Vampires,* was published in 1998. She published the second book in the series, *Vittorio the Vampire,* the following year. Amazingly enough, in addition to writing six vampire novels during the 1990's, Rice also entertained readers with the Lives of the Mayfair Witches trilogy. The three novels, *The Witching Hour* (1990), *Lasher* (1993), and *Taltos* (1994), told the story of the Mayfair Witches of New Orleans, Louisiana. Other novels that Rice completed during the decade included the gothic romance, *Violin* (1997), and *Servant of the Bones* (1996).

Impact Anne Rice achieved enormous success as a horror fiction novelist during the 1990's. Her novels introduced readers to a complex world in which vampires and witches lived. By humanizing her characters and making them almost romantic in nature, Rice helped to change the way people viewed the supernatural. Rice also earned the status of being one of the most talented and best-selling authors in contemporary times.

Further Reading

Ramsland, Katherine. *Prism of the Night: A Biography of Anne Rice.* Rev. ed. New York: Plume Books, 1994.
Riley, Michael. *Conversations with Anne Rice: An Intimate, Enlightening Portrait of Her Life and Work.* New York: Ballantine, 1996.

Bernadette Zbicki Heiney

See also Cruise, Tom; Film in the United States; Literature in the United States; Pitt, Brad.

■ Right-wing conspiracy

Definition An alleged conspiracy by right-wing opponents of U.S. president Bill Clinton intended to falsely implicate him in scandals

By asserting that President Clinton was the target of a right-wing conspiracy determined to damage him politically, Clinton's defenders sought to turn the tables against his opponents and convince the public that the numerous charges directed at him were unfounded.

Following the apparent suicide of deputy White House counsel Vince Foster in July, 1993, conspiracy theories began to circulate that his death might have been a murder orchestrated by President Bill Clinton. Allegations from Arkansas state troopers were

A Vast Right-Wing Conspiracy

On January 27, 1998, in an interview with Matt Lauer on NBC's Today Show, *First Lady Hillary Rodham Clinton defended her husband against allegations of sexual impropriety:*

CLINTON: Bill and I have been accused of everything, including murder, by some of the very same people who are behind these allegations. So from my perspective, this is part of the continuing political campaign against my husband. . . .

LAUER: Did [Kenneth Starr] go outside of his rights, in your opinion, to expand this investigation? After all, he got permission to expand the investigation from a three-judge panel.

CLINTON: The same three-judge panel that removed Robert Fiske and appointed [Starr]. The same three-judge panel that is headed by someone who is appointed by Jesse Helms and Lauch Faircloth. . . . It's just a very unfortunate turn of events that we are using the criminal justice system to try to achieve political ends in this country. . . .

LAUER: There have been reports that you've taken charge at the White House and decided to be the chief defender of your husband, of the president, and deflect these charges. How much of a role are you taking in this and do you think you should take?

CLINTON: Well, I certainly am going to defend my husband. And I'm certainly going to offer advice. But I am by no means running any kind of strategy or being his chief defender. He's got very capable lawyers and very capable people inside the White House, and a lot of very good friends outside the White House. . . .

LAUER: James Carville . . . has said that this is war between the president and Kenneth Starr. You have said, I understand, to some close friends that this is the last great battle and that one side or the other is going down here.

CLINTON: Well, I don't know if I've been that dramatic. That would sound like a good line from a movie. But I do believe that this is a battle. I mean, look at the very people who are involved in this. They have popped up in other settings. This is—the great story here for anybody willing to find it and write about it and explain it is this vast right-wing conspiracy that has been conspiring against my husband since the day he announced for president. A few journalists have kind of caught on to it and explained it. But it has not yet been fully revealed to the American public. And actually, you know, in a bizarre sort of way, this may do it.

published in 1994 claiming that Clinton had engaged in sexual improprieties while governor of Arkansas, which ultimately led to Paula Jones coming forward to sue the president for sexual harassment. Also in 1994, Kenneth Starr was appointed independent counsel to investigate the Whitewater land development project that was linked to the president and his wife, Hillary Rodham Clinton, an investigation that was later broadened to the Paula Jones and Monica Lewinsky matters. This combination of scandalous allegations continued to plague the Clinton White House and provide fodder for a continuous stream of news stories.

In 1995, the White House compiled a 331-page document that charged that a "media food chain" was passing conspiracy theories and innuendo from conservative newsletters and newspapers to Internet Web sites, which in turn passed them to the British tabloid press and to the right-wing American news media, the whole process allegedly backed by wealthy conservative foundations. On January 27, 1998, ten days after the Web site Drudge Report broke the news of the Lewinsky scandal, Hillary Clinton stated on national television that the real story to be told was how a "vast right-wing conspiracy" had conspired against her husband since he announced for president.

Impact Hillary Clinton's right-wing conspiracy charge attracted considerable press attention but was widely dismissed as an exaggeration, although it was generally conceded that her husband had been the target of persistent attacks on both a personal and political level from his conservative opponents. Public opinion polls showed that only a minority of Americans agreed that such a right-wing conspiracy existed. At the same time, President Clinton's approval ratings benefited from widespread satisfaction with the economy, and he continued to retain support from the Democrats in Congress that forestalled his removal from office after he was impeached in 1999. The emergence of proof that he had engaged in an affair with former White House intern Monica Lewinsky and lied under oath during the Jones civil case served to make him appear less an innocent victim of false charges, however, and while running for the Senate in 2000, Hillary Clinton maintained that she did not know the truth when she made her famous charge of a right-wing conspiracy.

Further Reading

Brock, David. *Blinded by the Right: The Conscience of an Ex-Conservative.* New York: Crown Publishers, 2002.

Toobin, Jeffrey. *A Vast Conspiracy: The Real Story of the Sex Scandal That Nearly Brought Down a President.* New York: Random House, 1999.

Larry Haapanen

See also Clinton, Bill; Clinton, Hillary Rodham; Clinton's impeachment; Clinton's scandals; Drudge, Matt; Journalism; Lewinsky scandal; Starr Report; Troopergate; Whitewater investigation.

■ Ripken, Cal, Jr.

Identification American baseball player
Born August 24, 1960; Havre de Grace, Maryland

Ripken, an all-star shortstop and third baseman for the Baltimore Orioles during the 1990's, broke Lou Gehrig's record for consecutive games played on September 6, 1995.

Cal Ripken, Jr., known as baseball's "Iron Man," was a Major League Baseball player from 1981 until 2001. He played shortstop and third base and spent his entire major-league career with the Baltimore Orioles. A nineteen-time all-star, Ripken played in all of the all-star games in the 1990's and was the Most Valuable Player (MVP) in the American League in 1991. Ripken was named MVP in the 1991 All-Star Game and won Golden Gloves in 1991 and 1992 for his outstanding fielding at shortstop. He won numerous other sporting awards and in 1999 was named to the prestigious Major League Baseball All-Century Team.

Ripken's most significant achievement during the 1990's was his breaking of Lou Gehrig's consecutive-games streak of 2,130 games. With a packed stadium at Baltimore and millions at home, the nation watched as he tied Gehrig's record on September 5, 1995, marking the event with a home run. Incredibly, on the following night he also hit a home run in the game that broke Gehrig's record. The stadium erupted after the home run, and a humble Ripken was pushed out of the dugout by his teammates to receive the praise of his fans. These two games are the most historic for Major League Baseball in the 1990's, as many credit Ripken for saving the game after the disastrous baseball strike of 1994. Ripken's consecu-

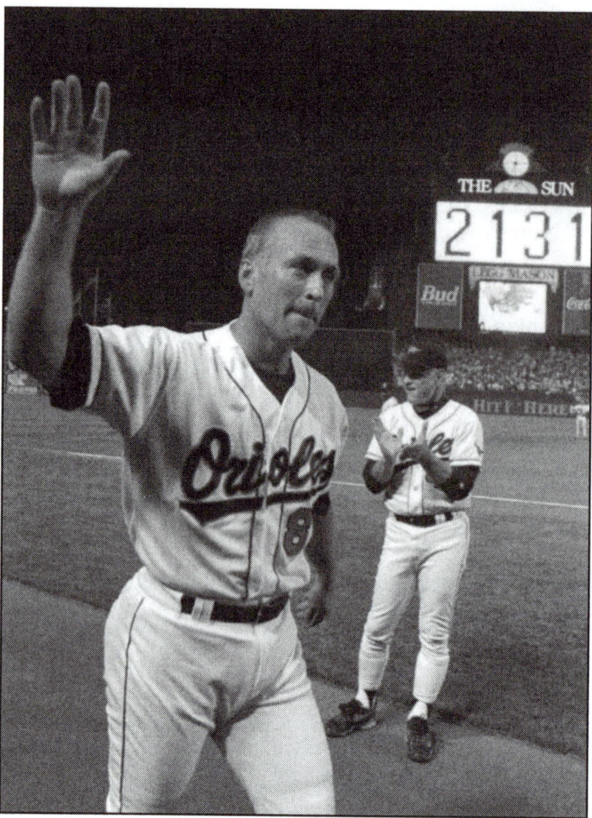

Cal Ripken, Jr., waves to fans after breaking Lou Gehrig's record of 2,130 consecutive games on September 6, 1995. (AP/Wide World Photos)

tive-game streak ended at 2,632 games on September 20, 1998, when he voluntarily missed a game.

Impact Ripken's significance extended far beyond his achievements on the field. In 1992, he was presented the Roberto Clemente Award for his character and outstanding contributions to his community. Standing at six feet, four inches, Ripken broke new ground at the shortstop position. In the past, players at this position had been small, quick, and generally not power hitters. With Ripken's success at shortstop, he paved the way for other larger shortstops that followed, such as Derek Jeter and Alex Rodriguez.

Subsequent Events Cal Ripken, Jr., retired from baseball in 2001 after he was again named the Most Valuable Player in the All-Star Game. Ripken was elected to the Baseball Hall of Fame in 2007 with the third-highest percentage of votes in history and the highest ever for a position player. He has continued his charitable works and has used his celebrity to advance youth baseball in the twenty-first century.

Further Reading

Beckett, James. *Nine Innings with Cal Ripken, Jr.* Dallas: Beckett, 1998.

Ripken, Cal, Jr. *Ripken: Cal on Cal.* Arlington, Tex.: Summit, 1995.

Ripken, Cal, Jr., and Mike Bryan. *The Only Way I Know.* New York: Penguin Books, 1997.

Douglas A. Phillips

See also Baseball; Baseball realignment; Baseball strike of 1994; Griffey, Ken, Jr.; Home run race; McGwire, Mark; Sosa, Sammy; Sports.

■ Roberts, Julia

Identification American actor
Born October 28, 1967; Smyrna, Georgia

One of the highest-paid actors of the 1990's, Roberts won moviegoers' hearts with her charm and varied roles.

Raised in a theater environment in which their parents hosted workshops for children, Julia Roberts and her brother, Eric (also an actor), showed an early interest in performance. She survived a difficult childhood to perform in four minor films and win a significant supporting role as a feisty waitress in *Mystic Pizza* (1988). The part sparked her casting, with Sally Field, as a fatally diabetic young mother-to-be in *Steel Magnolias* (1989), which culminated in an Oscar nomination and Golden Globe Award.

Roberts's career was launched after she starred in director Garry Marshall's romantic comedy *Pretty Woman* (1990), costarring Richard Gere, in which she played a good-hearted prostitute redeemed by a millionaire client. The role established her comedic star-quality appeal and won her an Oscar nomination and Golden Globe Award for Best Actress. A romantic-comedy favorite with both sexes, Roberts also proved popular with the critics, who applauded her acting in *My Best Friend's Wedding* (1997) and *Notting Hill* (1999). Her reunion with Gere in *Runaway Bride* (1999) capitalized on *Pretty Woman*'s success. Furthermore, Roberts's appeal and salary strengthened and steadily rose when she undertook serious roles in somewhat less successful films, including *Flatliners* (1990), *The Pelican Brief* (1993; based on John Grisham's novel), *Michael Collins* (1996), *Everyone Says I Love You* (1996; with director Woody Allen), and *Conspiracy Theory* (1997).

Along with her screen career, Roberts's lively love life endeared her to the tabloids. Boyfriends included Liam Neeson, Kiefer Sutherland, Daniel Day-Lewis, singer Lyle Lovett (a short-lived marriage ensued), Benjamin Bratt, and cameraman Daniel Moder (whom she married in 2002). Additionally, Roberts made television appearances on *Friends* and *Murphy Brown* and made goodwill tours for the United Nations Children's Fund (UNICEF). By the end of the 1990's, Roberts, one of the highest-grossing actors of the decade and one of America's favorite movie stars, had completed more than twenty-five films.

Roberts reached her greatest success in 2000 with her Academy Award-winning performance in the title role of director Steven Soderbergh's *Erin Brockovich,* based on the true story of a single mother who against all odds wins a hard battle against a California power giant that has contaminated the water supply. Without legal training, she worms into a job with a law firm and proceeds to unearth evidence that the corporate violator has denied liability while many people's health has been ruined. Similar to the real-life person, Roberts's character portrayed a pertinacious individual who dresses inappropriately (short skirts, low-cut tops) but connects effectively with the victims, enabling her firm to win a huge settlement. Critics and audiences praised Roberts's performance, which earned her $20 million, an Oscar for Best Actress, and other awards.

Impact Performances from *Pretty Woman* to *Erin Brockovich* made Julia Roberts the decade's most popular actress. Her best roles represented a warm yet independent woman not intimidated by male or corporate power.

Further Reading

Sanello, Frank. *Julia Roberts.* Edinburgh: Mainstream, 2000.

Spada, James. *Julia: Her Life.* New York: St. Martin's Press, 2004.

Christian H. Moe

See also Academy Awards; Allen, Woody; Film in the United States; *Friends*; Grisham, John; *Murphy Brown*; Television.

■ Rock, Chris

Identification African American comedian and actor

Born February 7, 1966; Andrews, South Carolina

Rock's humor represented an evolution in African American and urban-oriented, stand-up comedy.

Chris Rock's clenched-teeth delivery and energetic onstage pacing as he explained aspects of cultural and political phenomena to urban audiences made him one of the most popular stand-up comedians of the 1990's. In a style that could be described as one part rap artist, one part urban intellectual, Rock put into perspective the issues that confronted African Americans as well as Americans in general, taking on sensitive subjects such as race relations and black poverty.

Rock's particular brand of comedy seemed to resonate with African Americans who had been born during or after the Civil Rights movement of the 1960's, and who therefore were familiar with the comedian's topical humor about integrated schools, rap music, the Rodney King beating, and the dating scene in the 1990's. Additionally, Rock's stand-up

Chris Rock accepts his award for entertainment host for HBO's The Chris Rock Show *at the 1997 CableACE Awards.* (AP/Wide World Photos)

performances included material about the African American community's relationship with television news media and that community's internal divisions.

By 1990, Rock had already appeared on national comedy shows and in films, such as Home Box Office's (HBO) *Uptown Comedy Express* and *Beverly Hills Cop II* (1987) with Eddie Murphy. In 1990, Rock had become a regular on *Saturday Night Live*, where he remained until 1993. Throughout the early 1990's, Rock appeared in a variety of films, most of which held a great deal of significance for the new generation of African American urban audiences, including *New Jack City* (1991), *Boomerang* (1992), and *CB4* (1993), which he also cowrote.

The early 1990's saw Rock returning to television. In 1993, Rock briefly joined the cast of the Fox network variety show *In Living Color.* By 1994, he was headlining HBO's *Comedy Half-Hour.* Throughout the late 1990's, Rock's urban wit would be showcased on several HBO shows, including the Emmy Award-winning *Chris Rock: Bring the Pain* (1996) and *Chris Rock: Bigger and Blacker* (1999). In 1997, Rock was the host of HBO's *The Chris Rock Show.*

In the late 1990's, Rock appeared on a number of shows, including Bill Maher's *Politically Incorrect* on Comedy Central and the MTV Video Music Awards, which he hosted in 1997. In a return to film, Rock offered his trademark voice to a guinea pig character in Eddie Murphy's remake of *Dr. Dolittle* (1998) and starred as Rufus, the fictional thirteenth apostle, in Kevin Smith's *Dogma* (1999). Rock's relevance to the MTV generation was evidenced by his hosting the MTV Video Music Awards for a second time in 1999.

Impact Rock came into prominence at a time when African American comedians' routines were expected to contain a certain amount of vulgarity, following in the footsteps of previous decades' stars, such as Richard Pryor in the 1970's and Eddie Murphy in the 1980's. Rock's approach to comedy was traditional in that sense; his sharp insight demonstrated his cultural and political knowledge and illustrated the complexity of the postmodern, urban, African American experience, appealing to audiences who had yet to find a comedian who shared their voice.

Further Reading

Blue, Rose, and Corinne J. Naden. *Chris Rock, Comedian.* Philadelphia: Chelsea House, 2000.

Rock, Chris. *Rock This!* New York: Hyperion, 1997.

Zolten, J. Jerome. "Black Comedians: Forging an Ethnic Image." *Journal of American Culture* 16 (Summer, 1993): 65-76.

Dodie Marie Miller

See also African Americans; Cable television; Comedians; *In Living Color*; Late night television.

■ Rock and Roll Hall of Fame Museum

Identification Museum and archives dedicated to rock-and-roll music

Date Opened on September 2, 1995

Place Cleveland, Ohio

After years of planning, the Rock and Roll Hall of Fame Museum building was completed, providing a home for the Hall of Fame and a museum of memorabilia and interpretive experiences for visitors to enjoy.

In 1985, the officials of the Rock and Roll Hall of Fame Foundation decided to create a museum and archives dedicated to the heritage of rock-and-roll music. After an exhaustive search, world-renowned architect I. M. Pei was chosen to design the museum. In 1993, Pei's vision began to take shape as construction commenced on the building to house the Rock and Roll Hall of Fame Museum following a formal agreement with the city of Cleveland. Funding for the construction project came from a combination of public and private sources, and the project progressed rapidly as the Hall of Fame continued to induct rock-and-roll legends into its ranks while awaiting its permanent venue.

When completed in 1995, the Rock and Roll Hall of Fame Museum consisted of 150,000 square feet and carried an $84 million price tag. The building, which dominates the Lake Erie shoreline, is a dramatic representation of the raw power of rock-and-roll music. It uses daring geometric forms and cantilevered spaces anchored around a 162-foot tower to create exhibition areas. The tower, which emerges from the harbor, also anchors a large triangular-shaped tent made of glass that serves as one of the primary distinguishing features of the building. The building consists of spaces for exhibition and administrative functions as well as dedicated areas for library and archival functions.

Inductees into the Rock and Roll Hall of Fame, 1990-1999*

1990
Bobby Darin
Hank Ballard
Simon and Garfunkel
The Four Seasons
The Four Tops
The Kinks
The Platters
The Who
Charlie Christian
Louis Armstrong
Ma Rainey
Gerry Goffin and Carole King
Holland, Dozier and Holland

1991
Ike and Tina Turner
Jimmy Reed
John Lee Hooker
LaVern Baker
The Byrds
The Impressions
Wilson Pickett
Howlin' Wolf
Nesuhi Ertegun
Dave Bartholomew
Ralph Bass

1992
Bobby "Blue" Bland
Booker T. and the M.G.'s
Sam and Dave
The Isley Brothers
The Jimi Hendrix Experience
The Yardbirds
Elmore James
Professor Longhair
Bill Graham
Doc Pomus
Leo Fender

1993
Cream
Creedence Clearwater Revival
Etta James
Frankie Lymon and the Teenagers
Ruth Brown
Sly and the Family Stone
The Doors
Van Morrison
Dinah Washington
Dick Clark
Milt Gabler

1994
Bob Marley
Duane Eddy
Elton John
John Lennon
Rod Stewart
The Animals
The Band
The Grateful Dead
Willie Dixon
Johnny Otis

1995
Al Green
Frank Zappa
Janis Joplin
Led Zeppelin
Martha and the Vandellas
Neil Young
The Allman Brothers Band
The Orioles
Paul Ackerman

1996
David Bowie
Gladys Knight and the Pips
Jefferson Airplane
Little Willie John
Pink Floyd
The Shirelles
The Velvet Underground
Pete Seeger
Tom Donahue

1997
Buffalo Springfield
Crosby, Stills and Nash
Joni Mitchell
Parliament-Funkadelic
The (Young) Rascals
The Bee Gees
The Jackson Five
Bill Monroe
Mahalia Jackson
Syd Nathan

1998
Fleetwood Mac
Gene Vincent
Lloyd Price
Santana
The Eagles
The Mamas and the Papas
Jelly Roll Morton
Allen Toussaint

1999
Billy Joel
Bruce Springsteen
Curtis Mayfield
Del Shannon
Dusty Springfield
Paul McCartney
The Staple Singers
Bob Wills and His Texas Playboys
Charles Brown
George Martin

*Includes "Performers," "Early Influences," "Lifetime Achievement," and "Nonperformers" categories.

The official opening of the museum on September 2, 1995, kicked off a week of events celebrating rock-and-roll music that included a benefit concert with a stellar list of performances by rock-and-roll giants such as Chuck Berry, Johnny Cash, Jerry Lee Lewis, Bob Dylan, and Bruce Springsteen. At the museum's opening, its exhibits revolved around a large collection of John Lennon artifacts donated by Yoko Ono that included Lennon's guitar from the 1965 Beatles concert at Shea Stadium, written lyrics, and a pair of eyeglasses worn by Lennon while he lived in Hamburg.

Impact The Rock and Roll Hall of Fame Museum provided a centralized location for the preservation, commemoration, and promotion of rock-and-roll music. The museum uses its collections to tell the story of how and why this popular genre of music has had a tremendous impact on American culture. In this capacity, the Rock and Roll Hall of Fame serves as an important educational institution.

Further Reading

Juchartz, Larry, and Christy Rishoi. "Rock Collection: History and Ideology at the Rock and Roll Hall of Fame." *Review of Education, Pedagogy, Cultural Studies* 19, nos. 2/3 (May, 1997): 311-332.

Rock and Roll Hall of Fame. http://www.rockhall.com.

Talevski, Nick. *The Unofficial Encyclopedia of the Rock and Roll Hall of Fame.* Westport, Conn.: Greenwood Press, 1998.

Amanda Bahr-Evola

See also Architecture; Music.

■ Rock Bottom Remainders

Identification Rock band consisting of best-selling authors
Date Formed in 1992

In realizing the youthful dream of playing in a rock-and-roll band, a group of successful middle-aged professional writers spoke to the ascendancy of the culture of the baby-boom generation.

Taking its name from a publisher's term for heavily discounted books, the Rock Bottom Remainders is a group of well-known authors who gained a second celebrity through their participation in an enthusiastic amateur "garage band"-style rock group. The rock band was founded by literary publicist Kathi Kamen Goldmark in 1992 for a charity event at the American Booksellers Association convention. The group's sense of fun and its party-band performance style found an appreciative audience and attracted professional rock musicians such as Bruce Springsteen, Roger McGuinn, and Warren Zevon, who on occasion enjoyed sitting in with the band. Ever-shifting personnel included Dave Barry, Stephen King, Amy Tan, Barbara Kingsolver, Roy Blount, Jr., Robert Fulghum, Scott Turow, James McBride, and Matt Groening, with actual rock musician Al Kooper as musical director. Its repertoire consisted of classic blues and familiar rock standards, such as "Louie Louie," "Wild Thing," "Bye Bye Love," "Nadine," "Midnight Hour," and "Gloria."

Impact With a music video, an album, and performances for charity all over the country, the band enjoyed success throughout the 1990's and beyond. The band achieved legendary status when, in 1995, it was part of the famous celebration of the opening the Rock and Roll Hall of Fame in Cleveland, Ohio.

Further Reading

McGrath, Charles. "Rock On, but Hang On to Your Literary Gigs." *The New York Times,* June 4, 2007, p. E1.

Marsh, Dave, ed. *Mid-life Confidential: The Rock Bottom Remainders Tour America with Three Chords and an Attitude.* New York: Viking Press, 1994.

Margaret Boe Birns

See also Barry, Dave; King, Stephen; Kingsolver, Barbara; Literature in the United States; Music; Publishing; Rock and Roll Hall of Fame Museum.

■ Rock the Vote

Identification Political advocacy organization
Date Founded in 1990

Rock the Vote offered a nonpartisan voting drive for the under-thirty demographic, which had been notorious for abstaining from elections in the United States.

Rock the Vote is a nonprofit, nonpartisan organization devoted to engaging the youth of the United States in political discussion and participation. During the 1990's, Rock the Vote was lauded as responsible for stopping the twenty-year decline in youth voter turnout.

Early Years Jeff Ayeroff, a recording industry executive, in conjunction with other members of the recording industry, founded Rock the Vote in 1990 after perceived attacks on free speech. The first Rock the Vote campaign, "Censorship is UnAmerican," debuted that year, and celebrities like Iggy Pop, Red Hot Chili Peppers, and Woody Harrelson recorded public-service announcements for the organization.

In 1991, President George H. W. Bush vetoed the National Voter Registration Act (also known as the Motor Voter Act), a bill supported by Rock the Vote that would standardize voter registration through a variety of services like the Departments of Motor Vehicles, libraries, schools, and disability centers. The bill was later passed in 1993 and signed into law by President Bill Clinton. It came into effect in 1995.

1992, 1994, and 1996 Elections In 1992, more celebrities signed on to record public-service announcements, including R.E.M., Queen Latifah, and Aerosmith. Queen Latifah later hosted a special on the Fox network for Rock the Vote, which featured more celebrities such as Robin Williams, Michael Douglas, Madonna, Tom Cruise, and Chris Rock. The broadcast won a prestigious Peabody Award.

That year, more than 350,000 voters were registered by Rock the Vote. The organization is credited for the turnout of over two million new youth voters during that year's elections. Youth voter participation had been declining steadily over the previous twenty years but actually increased because of Rock the Vote's efforts. After signing the National Voter Registration Act into law in 1993, Clinton signed the National and Community Service Trust Act, which promoted volunteerism and was supported by Rock the Vote.

In 1994, Rock the Vote published its pamphlet "Rock the System: A Guide to Health Care for Young Americans" and distributed it free of charge. Rock the Vote also awarded R.E.M. the first annual Patrick Lippert Award, honoring former executive director Patrick Lippert, who had died in 1993 from complications related to AIDS. Queen Latifah and Pearl Jam were honored with the award in 1995. That year, Rock the Vote won a second Peabody Award for a series of short films focusing on health care.

In 1996, Rock the Vote expanded through a partnership with MTV's Choose or Lose campaign. The organization then debuted a program to register voters via phone and, in partnership with MCI, created the first Internet voter-registration program. Celebrities such as Drew Barrymore, Seal, L L Cool J, and Hootie and the Blowfish recorded public-service announcements, and the Ford Foundation gave Rock the Vote a grant to help fund its voter-registration campaign. Rock the Vote directly registered over half a million new voters for the 1996 elections.

As the decade wound down, Rock the Vote continued to record public-service announcements with celebrities. In 1998, the *Schoolhouse Rocks the Vote* album was produced and featured artists such as Isaac Hayes and Etta James. During the 1998 midterm election season, Rock the Vote registered over one-quarter of a million new voters. In 1999, First Lady Hillary Rodham Clinton was awarded the first Rock the Nation Award.

Impact Rock the Vote was directly responsible for the registration of over one million new voters during the 1990's and indirectly responsible for bringing even more of those voters to the polls. Through the use of new technology, celebrity and industry partnerships, and direct street contact, Rock the Vote has effectively brought the attention of the American youth to the political world.

Subsequent Events Rock the Vote has expanded beyond the United States since its inception in 1990, encouraging voters in other countries such as Ireland. The Rock the Vote movement expanded significantly during the 2000 and 2004 elections, became more aware of the growing number of Hispanic voters, and held a youth gathering after September 11, 2001, to discuss youth reactions and impact, later sending copies of the proceedings to Congress.

Further Reading

Connery, Michael. *Youth to Power: How Today's Young Voters Are Building Tomorrow's Progressive Majority.* Brooklyn, N.Y.: Ig Publishing, 2008. Connery examines how the current generation have become civically and technologically minded and are applying their skills to create a new progressive political atmosphere. Highlights some of the key figures responsible for the creation of this movement.

Eisner, Jane. *Taking Back the Vote: Getting American Youth Involved in Our Democracy.* Boston: Beacon Press, 2004. Discusses the lack of youth participation in voting since the 1970's, highlights reasons why youth choose not to vote, and suggests solutions to increase the youth voter turnout.

Rigby, Ben. *Mobilizing Generation 2.0: A Practical Guide to Using Web 2.0 Technologies to Recruit, Organize and Engage Youth.* San Francisco: Jossey-Bass, 2008. Demonstrates how to use the Internet to gather youth around nonprofit or political issues.

Rock the Vote. http://www.rockthevote.org. The site provides general information about the nonprofit, as well as links to register for voting and more information about political and social issues.

Emily Carroll Shearer

See also Bush, George H. W.; Clinton, Bill; Clinton, Hillary Rodham; Elections in the United States, midterm; Elections in the United States, 1992; Elections in the United States, 1996.

■ *Romer v. Evans*

Definition U.S. Supreme Court decision
Date Decided on May 20, 1996

This decision struck a Colorado state constitutional amendment prohibiting gay rights laws, aiding a later case that labeled laws forbidding consensual homosexual sodomy unconstitutional.

Colorado passed an anti-gay rights amendment to the state constitution in 1992 in the hopes of overturning existing gay rights laws. Amendment 2 prohibited people from claiming minority status based on sexual orientation and forbade the state and local government from protecting people because of their sexual orientation. An immediate lawsuit sought to keep the amendment from being enacted, claiming the change conflicted with the federal constitution.

The majority of the opposition stemmed from the federal Fourteenth Amendment, which requires the government to offer equal protection under the law to everyone. Additionally, those filing the suit argued that there was no logical government interest and that the amendment put an unreasonable burden on gay, lesbian, bisexual, and transgender (GLBT) victims to seek protection from discrimination.

The Colorado Supreme Court and District Court supported the opposition, in 1993, stating that Amendment 2 failed the strict scrutiny test, which requires laws to present a compelling state interest. The state of Colorado appealed to the federal Supreme Court in 1995. During oral arguments, the Supreme Court justices asked state counsel to justify the amendment's vague language and its preventing one group from being protected from prejudice unless by constitutional amendment.

The Supreme Court ruled 6 to 3 that the amendment was unconstitutional. However, whereas Colorado's Supreme Court and District Court focused on the law's failure to meet the strict scrutiny test, the federal Supreme Court declared that the law did not demonstrate a legitimate government interest. The Court determined that the law subjected homosexuals to unfair barriers to legal protection and forever prohibited its enactment.

Impact *Romer v. Evans* went against an earlier Supreme Court ruling, *Bowers v. Hardwick* (1986), upholding a Georgia law prohibiting consensual sodomy. Thus, *Romer* came into play in 2003, when *Lawrence v. Texas* reached the Supreme Court. That 2003 decision overturned the *Bowers* decision and prohibited the government from creating laws making homosexual sodomy illegal. Moreover, the language the Supreme Court used in the *Romer* ruling demonstrated that the real argument was about the morality of homosexuality. Even though the state claimed that Amendment 2 prevented gays and lesbians from having special rights, the Supreme Court felt strongly that, in reality, it would have singled out homosexuals for discrimination. Even the dissent showed this bias, suggesting that the amendment was acceptable because it protected heterosexual mores.

Further Reading

D'Emilio, John, William B. Turner, and Urvashi Vaid. *Creating Change: Sexuality, Public Policy, and Civil Rights.* New York: St. Martin's Press, 2000.

Gallagher, John, and Chris Bull. *Perfect Enemies: The Religious Right, the Gay Movement, and the Politics of the 1990's.* New York: Crown, 1996.

Walzer, Lee. *Gay Rights on Trial.* Santa Barbara, Calif.: ABC-Clio, 2002.

Jessie Bishop Powell

See also Homosexuality and gay rights; Supreme Court decisions; Transgender community.

■ Roth, Philip

Identification American author
Born March 19, 1933; Newark, New Jersey

During the 1990's, Roth produced five novels and one autobiographical volume about his relationship with his father. Two of the novels became part of his American trilogy, hailed as trenchant commentary on American life.

Philip Roth's output of books during the 1990's was great. Roth's first work of the decade, *Deception: A Novel* (1990), blurs the boundary between truth and fiction. As such, it fits in with many postmodernist works in which "truth" itself is regarded as a kind of fiction. His second, *Patrimony: A True Story* (1991), tells the story of his father's death. He wrote it, in part, to dispel the idea that Roth's relationship to his father was the same as that of Roth's frequent narrator, Nathan Zuckerman, who is estranged from his family as a result of the things he puts in his novels. The third, *Operation Shylock: A Confession* (1993), treats the idea of doubles, one of whom is a man in Israel who calls himself Philip Roth, claims to be the novelist, and works toward a plan that will send the Jews from Israel back to the European countries from which they came. This plan, the fictional Roth says, is the only way to save the lives of Israel's Jews. The next book, *Sabbath's Theater* (1995), treats Mickey Sabbath, whose literal theater involves hand puppets but whose metaphoric theater consists of himself and the people with whom he interacts. Sabbath is a lecherous character many readers find despicable.

The final two works of the decade, *American Pastoral* (1997) and *I Married a Communist* (1998), along with *The Human Stain* (2000), constitute Roth's American trilogy. In the first, he creates Seymour "Swede" Levov, a blond-haired, blue-eyed Jew from Newark, a former high school football hero, who marries an Irish Catholic who is a former Miss New Jersey. He moves to the country and tries to blend into the white Anglo-Saxon Protestant world that surrounds him, but his life falls apart when his daughter, Merry, protesting the war in Vietnam, sets off a bomb in the local post office. The explosion kills a man, and Merry goes underground.

I Married a Communist treats the era of Senator Joseph McCarthy, in which, as Roth depicts it, the idea of guilt by association replaced ideas of freedom and justice in America. Nathan Zuckerman, the narrator, sees his friend Ira Ringold, known to the radio audience as "Iron Rinn," destroyed by innuendo rather than any kind of judicial proceedings. Ringold loses his radio job and his influence because of the assertion—which is, incidentally, correct—that he is a communist.

Philip Roth. (©Nancy Crampton)

Impact Roth influenced a generation of Jewish American authors and Jewish Americans to reevaluate their positions in America and their ability to achieve the American Dream. He also showed that as a mature writer, he continued to write novels considered sensitive and powerful and involving fresh ideas.

Further Reading

Posnock, Ross. *Philip Roth's Rude Truth: The Art of Immaturity.* Princeton, N.J.: Princeton University Press, 2006.

Safer, Elaine B. *Mocking the Age: The Later Novels of Philip Roth.* Albany: State University of New York Press, 2006.

Richard Tuerk

See also Israel and the United States; Jewish Americans; Literature in the United States; Theater in the United States.

■ Ruby Ridge shoot-out

The Event Federal agents assault and besiege a family, resulting in deaths of a mother, child, and U.S. marshal

Date August 21-22, 1992

Place The remote mountains of northern Idaho

The Ruby Ridge incident led to a U.S. Senate investigation and increased mistrust of federal law enforcement.

Randy Weaver was a white separatist who lived with his family in a remote plywood cabin in northern Idaho. Their friend and neighbor was a young man named Kevin Harris. Attending the July, 1986, Aryan Nations World Congress, Weaver was befriended by a biker who called himself Gus Magisono but who was actually Kenneth Fadeley, an undercover informant for the federal Bureau of Alcohol, Tobacco, and Firearms (ATF). Three years later, Weaver sold him two sawed-off shotguns shorter than the legal limit. In 1990, the ATF threatened to prosecute Weaver unless he himself became an undercover informant; he refused and warned the Aryan Nations.

In December, 1990, Weaver was indicted for federal gun law violations. At the arraignment, Weaver was incorrectly told by the magistrate that if Weaver were convicted, his family might lose their home in order to pay for the court-appointed defense attorney. The trial was scheduled for February 20, 1991, but Weaver was incorrectly told that the trial date was March 20. Weaver had no intention of going to trial on any date and did not appear. Assistant U.S. attorney Ron Howen had Weaver indicted for failure to appear, and a warrant was issued for his arrest. The U.S. Marshals Service (USMS) was notified, and the agency deployed its paramilitary Special Operations Group (SOG). For sixteen months, the USMS surveilled Weaver's home.

The Marshals Attack and FBI Siege On August 21, 1992, six deputy marshals entered the Weaver property, and three of them threw rocks toward the cabin, alerting one of the Weavers' dogs. Weaver, Harris, and Weaver's fourteen-year-old son, Sammy, grabbed guns and went to investigate, thinking that the dog had detected game. The marshals shot the Weavers' dog. Marshal Larry Cooper fired his 9-millimeter machine pistol at Sammy, killing him with a shot in the back as he was running away. Marshal William F. Degan was fatally shot by Harris, who then fled with Randy Weaver to the cabin.

The Federal Bureau of Investigation (FBI) Hostage Rescue Team (HRT) was next brought in. Commander Richard Rogers created rules of engagement authorizing FBI snipers to shoot any adult male outside the cabin carrying a gun. The shoot-to-kill orders were approved by FBI supervisor Larry Potts, in violation of Idaho's homicide law.

At 6:00 P.M. on August 22, Weaver, Harris, and Weaver's teenage daughter Sara exited the cabin. FBI sniper Lon Horiuchi shot to kill Weaver but hit him in the shoulder. Standing in the cabin doorway, Weaver's wife, Vicki, holding her ten-month-old baby, Elisheba, shouted to the group to get inside. Horiuchi then fatally shot Vicki Weaver in the head, although he later claimed that he was aiming at her husband.

The siege ended after Vietnam War hero and right-wing commentator Bo Gritz volunteered to negotiate. Gritz talked Weaver into surrendering, in exchange for Weaver being allowed to meet with Gerry Spence, the famous criminal defense lawyer. Harris surrendered on August 30 and the Weavers on the following day.

Trial Spence took Weaver's case pro bono. At an April, 1993, trial, Weaver and Harris were acquitted of murder and all other charges, except for Weaver's failure to appear for the original trial. Judge Edward Lodge fined the FBI $1,920 for illegally withholding evidence and lying, and chastised their "callous disregard" for the rights of defendants and a "complete lack of respect" for the court. Weaver was sentenced to eighteen months, to be reduced by credit for the fourteen months he had already spent in custody.

Impact In 1995, a Senate subcommittee held hearings on Ruby Ridge. ATF director John Magaw promised to end immediately the agency's practice of paying informants on a contingency basis. (Fadeley had been paid this way.) The FBI decorated sniper Horiuchi for his work at Ruby Ridge. In 1995, Potts was appointed second in command of the FBI by Director Louis Freeh, but public outrage quickly forced him to resign. The USMS honored the six marshals as heroes. Coupled with the 1993 events at

Waco, Texas (where Potts, Rogers, and Horiuchi were prominently involved), Ruby Ridge prompted wide public concern that federal law-enforcement agencies were dishonest, out of control, and recklessly violent.

In 1995, the government paid $3.1 million to Weaver and his three surviving children in an out-of-court settlement. In 1997, after the federal government refused to prosecute any of its employees for their actions at Ruby Ridge, or for perjury, the Boundary County, Idaho, district attorney charged Horiuchi with the voluntary manslaughter of Vicki Weaver and charged Harris with the killing of Degan. The charges against Harris were dismissed that year. Horiuchi's lawyers had the case transferred from Idaho state court to federal district court. In 1998, the federal district court dismissed the charges on the grounds that Horiuchi, as a federal employee, was immune from prosecution for state law crimes.

Subsequent Events On June 5, 2001, an en banc panel of the U.S. Court of Appeals for the Ninth Circuit reversed the district court's decision. However, the prosecutor then had all the charges dismissed. In 2000, the federal government paid Harris $380,000 in compensation.

Further Reading

Bock, Alan W. *Ambush at Ruby Ridge: How Government Agents Set Randy Weaver Up and Took His Family Down.* Irvine, Calif.: Dickens Press, 1995. Fair and thoroughly researched history of the incident.

Spence, Gerry. *From Freedom to Slavery: The Rebirth of Tyranny in America.* New York: St. Martin's Press, 1993. The famed attorney who won Weaver's acquittal examines many issues, including the Weaver case.

U.S. Congress. Senate. Committee on the Judiciary. Subcommittee on Terrorism, Technology, and Government Information. *The Federal Raid on*

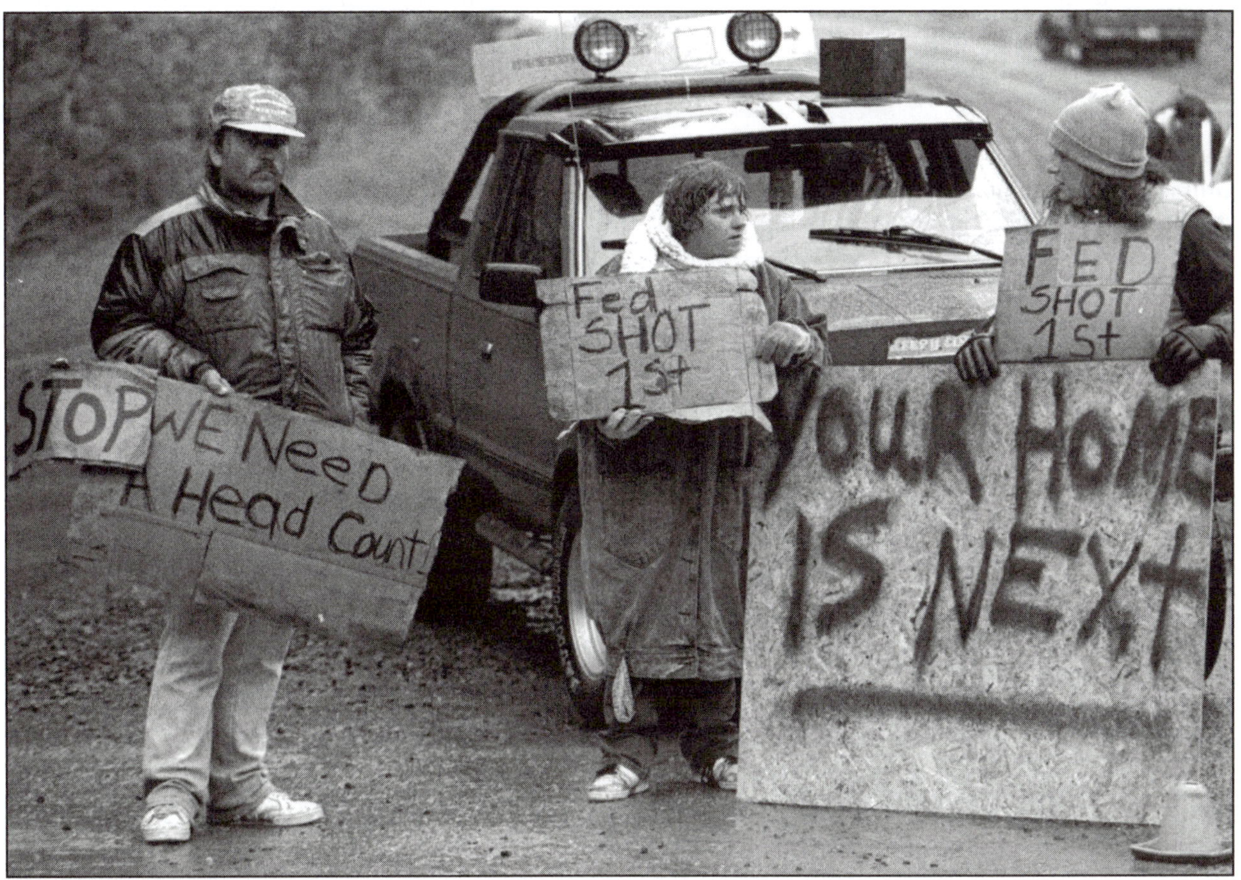

Supporters of Randy Weaver and his family in Ruby Ridge, Idaho, hold signs protesting the FBI's actions. (AP/Wide World Photos)

Ruby Ridge, ID. Washington, D.C.: Government Printing Office, 1997. Hearings before the subcommittee.

U.S. Department of Justice. *Department of Justice Report Regarding Internal Investigation of Shootings at Ruby Ridge, Idaho, During Arrest of Randy Weaver.* http://www.courttv.com/archive/legaldocs/government/rubyridge.html. New York: American Lawyer Media, 1994. The Department of Justice kept secret its internal investigation, but *Legal Times* obtained a copy.

Walter, Jess. *Ruby Ridge: The Truth and Tragedy of the Randy Weaver Family.* Rev. ed. New York: HarperPerennial, 2002. The author's coverage of the story for the Spokane *Spokesman-Review* earned him a Pulitzer Prize nomination.

Weaver, Randy, Sara Weaver, and Bill Henry. *The Federal Siege at Ruby Ridge: In Our Own Words.* Marion, Mont.: Ruby Ridge, 1998. The viewpoint of the father and his surviving daughter.

Whitcomb, Christopher. *Cold Zero: Inside the FBI Hostage Rescue Team.* Boston: Little, Brown, 2001. FBI sniper autobiography, with extensive material on Ruby Ridge.

David B. Kopel

See also Bush, George H. W.; Clinton, Bill; Crime; Gun control; Militia movement; Montana Freemen standoff; Oklahoma City bombing; Reno, Janet; Waco siege.

■ *Rules, The*

Identification Dating guidebook for heterosexual women

Authors Ellen Fein and Sherrie Schneider

Date Published in 1995

Full of advice the two authors heard from their grandmothers, this self-help book was intended to help the 1990's woman successfully attract a man who will propose marriage.

In February, 1995, two married women named Ellen Fein and Sherrie Schneider published a self-help book for women called *The Rules: Time-Tested Secrets for Capturing the Heart of Mr. Right,* which offers thirty-five pieces of advice to the 1990's American woman as she navigates the dating game. The book defines the kind of man that a "Rules Girl" should wed, a purpose illustrated on the front cover of the paperback edition with a picture of a large diamond engagement ring. The top five strategies to obtain this ring, and the promise of monogamy, are as follows: "Be a 'creature' unlike any other," "Don't talk to a man first (and don't ask him to dance)," "Don't stare at men or talk too much," "Don't meet him halfway or go Dutch on a date," and "Don't call him and rarely return his calls." Thirty more rules guide women through the entire dating process, including "Don't expect a man to change or try to change him" and "Don't discuss *The Rules* with your therapist," as well as sections encouraging young women to consider plastic surgery and to continue following the rules even against their parents' and friends' advice.

Impact After its publication, and with the help of the authors' appearances on such shows as *The Oprah Winfrey Show* and *20/20,* the dating and marriage guidebook quickly became a *New York Times* best seller. Simultaneously, groups of women worldwide began assembling themselves into self-help groups founded upon *The Rules,* and the authors offered personal consultations ranging from $50 to $250. The service became so popular that Fein and Schneider created a Web site for the book, where they market face-to-face, telephone, and e-mail consultations, as well as several spin-off publications, including *The Rules II: More Rules to Live and Love By* (1997). When Fein and Schneider announced the release of *The Rules III: Time-Tested Secrets for Making Your Marriage Work* in 2001, Fein also announced her divorce; the publicity unfavorably affected many women's faith in the book series. Nevertheless, *The Rules* has sold more than two million copies and has been published in twenty-seven languages.

Further Reading

Gerston, Jill. "So Many Rules, So Little Time." *The New York Times,* October 23, 1996, p. C1.

Leo, John. "Rule 36: Ignore rules 1 through 35." *U.S. News & World Report,* October 21, 1996, 38.

Walsh, Catherine. "The Rules Encourage Women to Take Responsibility for Their Lives and Not Be Victims in Romantic Relationships." *America* 175, no. 16 (November 23, 1996): 9.

Ami R. Blue

See also Fads; Marriage and divorce; *Men Are from Mars, Women Are from Venus*; Publishing.